Time Out

Chicago

timeout.com/chicago

Penguin Books

PENGUIN BOOKS

Published by the Penguin Group
Penguin Books Ltd, 80 Strand, London WC2R ORL, England
Penguin Books USA Inc., 375 Hudson Street, New York, New York 10014, USA
Penguin Books Australia Ltd, 250 Camberwell Road, Camberwell, Victoria 3124, Australia
Penguin Books Canada Ltd, 10 Alcorn Avenue, Toronto, Ontario, Canada M4V 3B2
Penguin Books (NZ) Ltd, cnr Rosedale and Airborne Roads, Albany, Auckland, New Zealand

Penguin Books Ltd, Registered Offices: Harmondsworth, Middlesex, England

First published 2000
Second edition 2002
10 9 8 7 6 5 4 3 2 1

Colour reprographics by Icon, Crowne House, 56-58 Southwark Street, London SE1 1UN
Printed and bound by Cayfosa-Quebecor, Ctra. de Caldes, Km 3 08 130 Sta, Perpètua de Mogoda, Barcelona, Spain

Edited and designed by
Time Out Guides Limited
Universal House
251 Tottenham Court Road
London W1T 7AB
Tel + 44 (0)20 7813 3000
Fax + 44 (0)20 7813 6001
Email guides@timeout.com
www.timeout.com

Editorial

Editor Will Fulford-Jones
Deputy Editor Ismay Atkins
Consultant Editor Mike Michaelson
Listings Editor Candace Dean
Proofreader Tamsin Shelton
Indexer Jackie Brind

Editorial Director Peter Fiennes
Series Editor Ruth Jarvis
Deputy Series Editor Jonathan Cox
Guides Co-ordinator Anna Norman

Design

Group Art Director John Oakey
Art Director Mandy Martin
Art Editor Scott Moore
Designers Benjamin de Lotz, Lucy Grant, Sarah Edwards
Scanning/Imaging Dan Conway
Ad Make-up Glen Impey
Picture Editor Kerri Littlefield
Deputy Picture Editor Kit Burnet
Picture Librarian Sarah Roberts

Advertising

Group Commercial Director Lesley Gill
Sales Director Mark Phillips
International Sales Co-ordinator Ross Canadé
Advertising Director, North American Guides Liz Howell
(1-808 732 4661/1-888 333 5776 US only)
Advertising in the US co-ordinated by *Time Out New York*
Alison Tocci (Publisher), Tom Oesau (Advertising Production
Manager), Maggie Puddu (Assistant to the Publisher)

Administration

Chairman Tony Elliott
Managing Director Mike Hardwick
Group Financial Director Kevin Ellis
Marketing Director Christine Cort
Marketing Manager Mandy Martinez
US Publicity & Marketing Associate Rosella Albanese
Group General Manager Nichola Coulthard
Production Manager Mark Lamond
Production Controller Samantha Furniss
Accountant Sarah Bostock

Features in this guide were written and researched by:
Introduction Will Fulford-Jones. **History** Victoria Cunha (*Killing time* Dave Chamberlain; *Meat the locals, Made in Chicago:*
Playboy Will Fulford-Jones). **Chicago Today** Dave Chamberlain. **Architecture** Will Fulford-Jones (*The basics* Emily Thomas;
A lovely view Victoria Cunha). **Fictional Chicago** Chris Jones (*Made in Chicago: Chris Ware* Dave Chamberlain). **The Blues**
Will Fulford-Jones. **Accommodation** Mike Michaelson (*See you at the bar* Will Fulford-Jones). **Sightseeing introduction,**
all sights and attractions reviews Will Fulford-Jones. **The Loop** Sara Burnett (*Walk on: Public art* Will Fulford-Jones; *Made in*
Chicago: Scott Turow Victoria Cunha). **Museum Campus & Near South Side** Sara Burnett. **Near North** Sara Burnett (*Walk on:*
Chicago churches; Where the streets have two names Will Fulford-Jones). **The Gold Coast** Sara Burnett (*Walk on: Astor Street*
Chris Barsanti). **Old Town** Sara Burnett. **Lincoln Park** Dave Chamberlain. **Lake View & Surrounds** Dave Chamberlain (*Made*
in Chicago: Wrigley Field Will Fulford-Jones). **Evanston & the North Shore Suburbs** Victoria Cunha. **The West Side** Chris Jones
(*Market down, Vision on* Gillian Darlow). **Wicker Park & Bucktown** Dave Chamberlain (*Worlds apart* Will Fulford-Jones).
Oak Park Victoria Cunha (*The Wright stuff* Chad Schlegel). **Hyde Park** Will Fulford-Jones. **Restaurants** Mike Michaelson (*Made*
in Chicago: Pizza Sam Jemielity; *Lining the stomach* Chris Barsanti). **Bars** Dave Chamberlain (*Hey, Mr DJ, take a record off,*
Walk on: Lincoln Avenue bars Will Fulford-Jones; *Made in Chicago: Goose Island* Emily Thomas). **Shops & Services** Emily
Thomas (*Mall talk* Isaac Davis). **Children** Cyndee Miller (*Hello dolly* Chris Jones). **Film** Chris
Barsanti. **Galleries** Victoria Cunha. **Gay & Lesbian** Matthew Michael Wright. **Music** Dave Chamberlain (*Now playing: Jazz*
Victoria Cunha). **Nightlife** John Dugan. **Sport & Fitness** Dave Chamberlain (*Go fish* Mike Michaelson). **Theatre, Dance &**
Comedy Chris Jones (Comedy classes, *Made in Chicago: Poetry slams* Emily Thomas). **Trips Out of Town: Illinois, Indiana,**
Michigan, Wisconsin Mike Michaelson (*Pump it up* Emily Thomas; *Your money or your life* Chris Jones). **Directory** Will
Fulford-Jones (*Made in Chicago: This American Life* Emily Thomas).

The Editor would like to thank:
Terry and Kristin Alexander, Liz Armstrong, Nyx Bradley, Jeff Fisher, Sarah Guy, Liam Hayes, Tricia Hosking, Sam Le Quesne,
Sara Ledoux at the Kimpton Group, Lesley McCave, Misha, Gerri Reardon, Glynis Steadman, Patricia Sullivan and
Derrek Hull at the Chicago Office of Tourism, Kelly Skrainy, Natalie Van Straaten at Chicago Gallery News, Paul Weldin, Ziggy,
and all contributors to the first edition, whose work formed the basis for parts of this book.

Maps by JS Graphics (john@jsgraphics.co.uk).
Public transportation maps used by kind permission of the Chicago Transit Authority.

Photography by Hannah Levy except: pages 7, 14, 17 and 202 AP Photo; pages 8, 10, 12 and 36 Hulton Archive; page 13
AKG; pages 15, 18, 19 and 38 Bettmann/Corbis; page 33 Channel 4; page 37 Touchstone Pictures; page 39 Redferns/
Cyrus Andrews; page 41 Redferns/Michael Ochs Archives; page 43 Peninsula Chicago Hotel; pages 108, 187, 253, 255
and 256 Illinois Department of Commerce and Community Affairs/Jeff Page; pages 175, 176 and 177 Paul Avis; page 191
AP/Golden Knights/Ken Kassens; page 198 Universal Pictures; page 257 Bob Rowan, Progressive Image/CORBIS; page
258 Layne Kennedy/Corbis.

The following images were supplied by the featured establishments or artist: pages 35, 56, 119, 213, 248, 254, 262,
264, 267, 268, 270, 273, 248, 274 and 275.

Contents

Introduction

It was forgotten for a while. New York took the East Coast tourist dollar, California nabbed the sun-seekers' cash and Florida surged in popularity as a family destination. Amid the hype, the Midwest in general and the Windy City in particular got left behind in the PR stakes. But with an admirable verve, it set about bettering itself, and people started showing up again. So much so, in fact, that in the early years of the new millennium, Chicago is again among the most visitable of all American cities.

It's an oft-stated opinion that Chicago is a big city with the heart of a small town. Close but no cigar: the truth is that it has the heart of many small towns. Every major city claims to be a city of neighbourhoods, but Chicago wears the description better than most. Countless communities and nationalities make their homes here, from lily-white yuppies in Lincoln Park to African-Americans on the South Side, via Mexican-dominated Pilsen, Little Warsaw, Little Italy, Ukrainian Village, Swedish-dominated Andersonville, Teutonic Lincoln Square and a host of others. The communities don't always co-exist in perfect harmony, but co-exist they do.

And there is a real sense of community here, an attitude that those from other big cities invariably envy. Even in the Loop, the frantic financial district, the bars – always a good judge of an area's character – are local hangouts: regulars and bartenders on first name terms, convivial to the last. Yet that's not to say that outsiders aren't welcome; they usually are. If you have a story to tell, a conversation to start, belly up to the bar and start talking. This might be a big city, but it's also the Midwest, and an almost freakish friendliness runs like a bloodline through the city.

A spectacular programme of improvements has meant the tourist industry has expanded apace in the last 15 years. New museums, increased visitor amenities and an ridiculous amount of hotel developments have all helped hugely; add in the thriving cultural scene and the palate-pleasing array of restaurants, and there can be little argument brooked with the statement that Chicago is a better place to visit than it's ever been.

Like every American city, Chicago is concerned about the impact September 11 will have on the city's tourism and convention industries. The economy here has grown more dependent on the dollars brought in by visitors: something has to pay for the myriad City Hall-instigated improvements, and innumerable jobs depend on the town at least holding its own as a destination. But Mayor Richard J Daley's attitude to tourism – essentially, if you build it they will come – looks set to continue, and understandably so. For when a city has as much to offer as this toddling town, as Sinatra sang, then come they surely will. Welcome to Chicago.

ABOUT THE TIME OUT CITY GUIDES

The *Time Out Chicago Guide* is one of an expanding series of Time Out City Guides, now numbering over 35, produced by the people behind London and New York's successful listings magazines. Our guides are all written and updated by resident experts who have striven to provide you with all the most up-to-date information you'll need to explore the city or read up on its background, whether you're a local or a first-time visitor.

THE LOWDOWN ON THE LISTINGS

Above all, we've tried to make this guide as useful as possible. Addresses, telephone numbers, websites, transport information, opening times, admission prices and credit card details are all included in our listings. And, as far, as possible, we've given details of facilities, services and events, all checked and correct as we went to press. However, owners and managers can change their arrangements at any time, and both opening times and admission prices may fluctuate. Before you go out of your way, we'd advise you whenever possible to phone and check opening times, ticket prices and other particulars.

While every effort has been made to ensure the accuracy of the information contained in this guide, the publishers cannot accept responsibility for any errors it may contain.

PRICES AND PAYMENT

Throughout this guide, we have noted where shops, restaurants, hotels, attractions and the like accept the following credit cards: American Express (AmEx), Diners Club (DC), Discover (Disc), MasterCard (MC) and Visa (V). Many businesses will also accept other cards, such as Carte Blanche, as well as travellers' cheques.

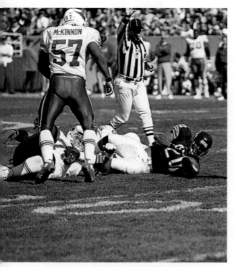

The prices we've supplied should be treated as guidelines, not gospel. If prices vary wildly from those we've quoted, please write and let us know. We aim to give the best and most complete advice, so we always want to know if you've been treated badly or overcharged.

THE LIE OF THE LAND

Chicago divides up fairly neatly into neighbourhoods. The financial centre downtown is called the Loop; just north of it is an area thick with consumer attractions known as Near North; nearby sits an upscale stretch of lakefront, the Gold Coast. Surrounding these hives of activity to the north, south and west are rings of residential neighbourhoods, among them Old Town, Lincoln Park, Lake View, Wicker Park, Bucktown and Pilsen. We have used these names – and others – throughout the guide; though the boundaries between them are often a little blurry, there's a map of Chicago's neighbourhoods on page 67.

The city's street layout, on a grid system, is fairly easy to follow. In this book, we've listed the nearest cross-street for each address.

TELEPHONE NUMBERS

The Chicago region boasts five telephone area codes. The majority of numbers listed in this guide fall into the 312 and 773 area codes, with area codes 847, 708 and 630 covering

the suburbs. When dialling from a number from within the same area code – for example, when dialling a 312 number from a number that also has a 312 prefix – there's no need to dial the code: simply dial the last seven digits of the phone number. When dialling from outside the area you're calling – for example, when phoning a 773 number from a 312 number – dial 1 first, then the ten-digit number as listed in the guide.

To reach numbers listed in this book from the UK, dial 00 (the international access code), 1 (the code for the US) and then the number as it appears in the book. For more on phone numbers, turn to page 289.

ESSENTIAL INFORMATION

For all the practical information you might need for visiting the area – including emergency numbers, websites, useful numbers for business travellers and conventioneers, and full details of the local transport system – turn to the Directory chapter at the back of this guide. It starts on page 278.

MAPS

At the back of this guide are a series of maps that detail much of central Chicago, as well as an overview map of the city, a map relating to the Trips Out of Town chapter and maps of the Chicago public transportation system. Many of the city's main attractions, from museums and architecturally renowned buildings to theatres and sporting stadia, have been marked on the map. Wherever possible, map references have been provided for the venues listed in this guide. The maps start on page 301. In addition to the maps at the back of the book, there's a map of the city's neighbourhoods on page 67 and a map of Milwaukee on page 271.

LET US KNOW WHAT YOU THINK

We hope you enjoy the *Time Out Chicago Guide*, and we'd like to know what you think of it. We welcome tips for places that you consider we should include in future editions and take note of your criticism of our choices. There's a reader's reply card at the back of this book for your feedback, or you can email us at chicagoguide@timeout.com.

BLUE MAN GROUP "SEE THIS SHOW!"
—E! Entertainment News

Blue Man Group's debut album, **AUDIO**, available everywhere.
BRIAR STREET THEATRE 3133 NORTH HALSTED CHICAGO
FOR SHOWTIMES OR TICKETS, CALL 773.348.4000 OR *ticketmaster* 312.902.1500

NEW YORK   BOSTON   CHICAGO   LAS VEGAS   **1.800.BLUEMAN / blueman.com**

In Context

History

Second city, but hardly second best.

IN THE BEGINNING

Missionary Father Jacques Marquette and cartographer Louis Jolliet were the first to explore the lower Lake Michigan region. In 1673, the pair attempted to follow the Mississippi and its tributaries as far as possible to the north-east. Chartered and funded by the governor of New France (now Quebec), Marquette and Jolliet's party travelled to the native village of Kaskaskia (near what is now Utica, Illinois) on the Illinois River before proceeding north-east on the Des Plaines River.

After reaching what the Native Americans who lived in the area called 'Checagou' (believed to translate as 'wild onion', which grew in the area), the explorers floated on down the Chicago River to Lake Michigan before heading north to Green Bay in the fall of 1673. After that successful trip, Marquette returned to the area in 1674 and spent the winter as a temporary resident of what would later become known as Chicago before returning to Kaskaskia in the spring. He died the same year; Jolliet never returned to the area again.

The first permanent non-native resident of Chicago, Jean Baptiste Point du Sable, came to the area almost exactly a century later. The son of a French father and white mother, the black du Sable married a Potawatomie native named Catherine, and established a fur trading post at the mouth of the Chicago River as early as 1772. During the Revolutionary War, Du Sable was suspected of being an enemy sympathiser and was imprisoned at a military outpost, but returned to the Chicago River area in 1779. A year later, he sold his property to a fur trapper, who in turn sold it to John Kinzie, a trader eventually nicknamed the 'Father of Chicago'.

THEY FORT THE LAW

Fearful of further trouble after the war, the government decided a military presence was necessary in the area, and so Fort Dearborn was built in 1803 at what is now the south end of the Michigan Avenue Bridge. Then the major western US Army garrison in the country, it occupied a strategic point near the southern end of Lake Michigan on the south side of the Chicago River across from Du Sable's cabin.

Sure enough, the US was soon at war with the British, and by the summer of 1812, tensions between soldiers and natives (who were bought off by the British) were at an all-time high. Despite efforts to appease the Potawatomie native leaders, it was clear to Captain Nathaniel Heald, in charge of Fort Dearborn, that safety concerns were so great that the fort should be evacuated. Accompanied by an escort of friendly Miami natives from Indiana led by Captain William Wells, the garrison began its journey along the lake, but was ambushed by natives. Heald and his wife were taken prisoner, but almost all the others who were attempting to leave the fort were executed; in all, 53 settlers and natives died. The Potawatomies returned three days later and burnt the fort.

Soon, though, things returned to normal, and the area started trading again. John Kinzie, who had established his base in Chicago by 1804 and fled the city during the massacre, returned in 1816 and resumed trading. His descendants continued to make themselves known through their various civic and industrial ventures in the remaining years of the 19th century, and today's Kinzie Street, which lies north of the Chicago River, is testimony to his influence.

Another early settler, Gurdon S Hubbard, arrived from Montreal in 1818, the same year Illinois joined the union as a state, and quickly established a fur trade route from Danville, Illinois to Chicago nicknamed 'Hubbard's Trail'. Later, Hubbard bought an American Fur Company franchise and made a mint. Established in 1808 by German immigrant John Jacob Astor, the American Fur Company grew to rival established Canadian fur and dry goods trading companies that did business with the Native Americans and other settlers.

By the time Chicago was incorporated as a town in 1833, Hubbard had settled permanently, and went about diversifying his interests into meatpacking, shipping, insurance and real estate. Despite several setbacks, Hubbard persevered, and his own prosperity mirrored that of his adopted hometown. When he died in 1886, aged 87, Chicago's population numbered three-quarters of a million people, compared to just a couple of hundred at the time Hubbard had first settled in the city.

PIONEER CHECKPOINT

When the Erie Canal opened in 1825, it linked the Hudson River – and, thus, the East Coast – with Buffalo, New York (on Lake Erie). The canal opened travel and commerce into Illinois, a development that favoured Chicago's growth, especially with regard to pioneers coming from more populous areas in the east. A prime example was William Ogden, a transplanted

Yankee who came west in 1835 to sell a parcel of land for a family member, but who stayed and became mayor of Chicago two years later.

Famed meatpacking mogul Philip Armour also moved to Chicago from Milwaukee after the Civil War ended, and earned millions selling barrels of pork. Armour employed refrigerated train cars for shipping fresh meat, expanded the use of animal by-products, and diversified into other businesses to widen his empire. Yet another entrepreneur, Cyrus McCormick – after whom McCormick Place is named – found Chicago to be hospitable to his Virginia-bred sensibilities. McCormick, who went on to invent the grain reaper, even borrowed money from Ogden to build his factory. During his time here, McCormick became active in Democratic politics, and ran unsuccessfully for Congress in 1864.

Another person from Yankee stock who shaped Chicago was Long John Wentworth, twice Republican mayor, six-term Democratic US Congressman, editor of the city's first newspaper (the *Chicago Democrat*, which merged with the *Tribune* when the Civil War broke out in 1861), egotist and bon vivant. He stood six foot six inches (1.98 metres) tall, weighed over 300 pounds (136 kilogrammes) and had a reputation for grand living.

Wentworth was an early antagonist of vice, and it was he, along with Scottish-born detective Allan Pinkerton, who tried to put a lid on the town's lawlessness. Police raids commissioned by Wentworth on the city's red-light districts were unsuccessful, though, and he spent the rest of his post-political life quietly on a farm in suburban Summit. However, Pinkerton was appointed a deputy sheriff in 1852, and eventually expanded his agency's influence into government by providing assistance to the Union Army at President Lincoln's request.

TRAINS AND BOATS AND PLAINS

An economic depression that swept the country in 1837, known as the Panic, threatened to put a lid on Chicago's growth. However, the Panic also coincided with Chicago achieving official city status, and in the following years things picked up again. Eleven years later, two projects were completed that were to signal the beginnings of immense growth in the city: the first telegraph line reached the city, radically improving communications, and, crucially, the Illinois-Michigan Canal was finally completed, almost two decades after work on it had begun.

The canal created a connection with vessels sailing to and from the Atlantic Ocean via the Great Lakes. The previous year, the River and Harbor Convention held in Chicago had

Allan Pinkerton, scourge of crims. *See p7.*

promoted waterway trade to thousands of attendees, many of whom hailed from the east. The event simultaneously began Chicago's long tenure as a host city for national and international conferences and meetings.

Furthermore, the same savvy investors soon became aware of the city's potential as a railway hub. Because of its central location and existing trade connections, Chicago indeed became a crucial checkpoint for railway commerce in the US. Soon livestock, lumber, grain and other goods were speedily transported through Chicago in previously unheard of quantities. As a consequence, more and more industries established their headquarters on the south-western shores of Lake Michigan rather than at rival St Louis, Missouri, 300 miles (483 kilometres) away. Chicago had become the largest railroad centre in the country by 1856.

Coming at the juncture of such rapid technological development, the Civil War also spurred Chicago's population growth, as the more northerly city surpassed St Louis. Indeed, St Louis's port on the Mississippi was blockaded by Navy vessels for the duration of the conflict, constricting trade movement, and Chicago benefited hugely: its population had topped 300,000 by 1870.

Another industry that reaped great rewards from the burgeoning railway network was that of steel manufacturing. South Chicago – situated along the banks of Lake Michigan at the mouth of the Calumet River – became home to a number of blast furnaces, which set the stage for further growth. By the turn of the century, steel production in the area fully accounted for 50 per cent of the entire domestic output. Employment of immigrant, unskilled labour in the mills was also a major factor in the growth and development of Chicago's extreme south-east neighbourhoods.

> **'Without the fire, Chicago would not have had the opportunity or incentive to rebuild itself in such dramatic fashion.'**

In fact, more than half Chicago's population in 1870 was foreign-born, with Germans, Irish, Bohemians and Scandinavians representing a majority of the immigrant groups. The rapid population growth in the city led to the construction of cheap, wooden buildings: lumber was easy to come by at the time, and also cheap. By the fall of 1871, a number of fires had taken their toll in and around the city, but no one would have guessed that a conflagration of such fury and force was imminent.

FIRING THE IMAGINATION
On 8 October 1871, a fire broke out adjacent to an immigrant neighbourhood that bordered the central business district. Spreading to the north-east, the blaze gained momentum and was not slowed even upon reaching the south branch of the Chicago River. A dry summer, a massive amount of wooden constructions (including roadways) and convection whirls called 'Fire Devils' that enabled the blazes to leap over rivers once they'd started all contributed to the horrific inferno.

Over the good part of two nights and one day, Chicago's citizenry fled with only their most essential possessions, with few buildings surviving. By the time the fire finally burned itself out in Lincoln Park, several miles to the north, it had left an unprecedented level of destruction in its wake: over an area stretching from Taylor Street north to Fullerton and from the Chicago River east to Lake Michigan, 17,000 buildings were destroyed, 98,000 people were left homeless and 300 lives were lost.

However, Chicago retained much of its human and business resources, and relief efforts soon gave way to rebuilding ventures.

The downtown business district merchants, bloodied but unbowed, wasted no time in obtaining loans and hiring rebuilding crews to construct new, fireproof buildings. A mere 12 months after the fire, 300 new structures had been erected; and after a few years, taller, fireproof buildings stood proudly in the downtown sector, beckoning architects to develop the already-existing elevator buildings into what were later termed 'skyscrapers'. In fact, without the fire, Chicago would probably not have had either the opportunity or incentive to rebuild itself in such a dramatic fashion: today, the city boasts perhaps the finest collection of architecture in the US.

WATER, WATER EVERYWHERE

Another elemental problem, that of water, also needed to be addressed by the city planners following the fire. Despite the seemingly unlimited supply of freshwater provided by Lake Michigan, the polluting matter being dumped into the Chicago River in vast quantities was in danger of permanently befouling the city's water supplies. By 1879, the heavy rains that swept the filth further into the lake prompted such severe outbreaks of cholera and dysentery that state leaders formed the Chicago Board of Sewerage Commissioners.

The eventual solution to the problem affected not only city residents but also those from downstate, since the plan involved forcing the river to flow not towards but away from the lake. Therefore, the sewage that had previously flowed unchecked into the clear waters of Lake Michigan would be redirected to the Mississippi River by means of a channel built to extend to a tributary in Lockport, Illinois. This channel, later known as the Sanitary and Ship Canal, was commissioned in 1889, and opened the following year against legal protests on behalf of the city of St Louis. The suit was dropped when the water was deemed safe as it reached its new destination in the south.

WORKERS' PLAYTIME

However, it wasn't all plain sailing, for the workers were getting restless. A nationwide railroad strike in the 1870s affected Chicago more than most, pitting out-of-work rioters against state militia units. During the strike, crowds assembled by the thousands to hear speeches espousing workers' rights. The mayor issued warnings to those not affected by the walkout, especially women and children, to stay at home away from the out-of-control mobs. A number of protesters and civilians died in the violence in Chicago, which mirrored the national climate as workers everywhere struggled to gain rights and power.

Killing time

Chicago gained infamy in the Roaring '20s thanks to Al Capone. Corrupt politicians have tried to disprove the old maxim that all publicity is good publicity. But the Windy City's dark side is far blacker than mere gangster wars and vote-rigging. Three of America's most hideous killers did their dirty work here, bookending a history of murder in Chicago that spans 100 years.

That history starts in the 19th century in what is now a vacant lot at 701 W 63rd Street in Englewood. In 1884, the lot was purchased by **Herman Webster Mudgett** (aka HH Holmes), ostensibly to build a hotel. Instead, though, he constructed a castle of horrors that was, the *Tribune* wrote, 'From cellar to garret... designed for the commission of crime'. In his labyrinth of chambers, staircases and traps, he murdered countless people (so well did he destroy the bodies that the number was never pinned down), asphyxiating them in an airtight room or poisoning them. He was caught in Philadelphia for another murder, and hanged in 1896.

Three generations later, a drifter from Dallas, **Richard Speck**, arrived in Chicago. On the night of 13 July 1966, Speck forced his way into the South Chicago Community Hospital on the 2300 block of E 100th Street, bound and gagged eight student nurses and proceeded to strangle them. It was labelled the crime of the century, and Speck was apprehended three days later in a skid row flophouse (since demolished to make room for the Presidential Towers). He was sentenced to 1,200 years in jail, but died of a massive heart attack at Joliet's State Penitentiary in 1991.

The worst was yet to come. Between 1975 and 1978, **John Wayne Gacy** killed 33 boys and buried them at his house at 8213 W Summerdale Avenue near O'Hare Airport. Gacy, who worked as a clown at children's parties, lured teenagers into a game involving handcuffs, a game that eventually led to death by strangulation or bludgeoning. For three years, Gacy buried the bodies in the 19-inch crawl space under his home. If it wasn't for his last victim, 15-year-old Bobby Piest, telling his mother he was going to Gacy's house to ask about a job, Gacy may have been killing even now. He was executed on 9 May 1994.

Meat the locals

The meatpacking industry became established in Chicago some years prior to the Chicago Fire of 1871. The expansion of the railroads and the opening of the Illinois–Michigan Canal helped to make the city the Midwest's capital of industry. As farmers realised it made greater economic sense to send their hogs to Chicago for slaughter and then distribution rather than to kill them at home, the city's meatpacking industry grew. In 1864, as some local wag pointed out, the hogs killed in Chicago would have stretched to New York City if laid end to end. Happily, they weren't, as this would have stunk out half the country. Instead, the overpowering smell of dead pig was confined to Chicago, and in particular to a square mile on the South Side that opened as the Union Stockyards in 1865.

From here, the industry boomed, as railroad convenience begat entrepreneurial genius. The hog-killing was lucrative enough, but meat baron Gustavus Swift was determined to find a way to work cattle into the business. The problem was that although he could kill cattle meant for East Coast cities in Chicago – indeed, all the cattle passed through the city for auction before being shipped live by railroad – they lost their freshness by the time they reached the East Coast (pork was salted or smoked in Chicago, which preserved it).

Rubbing his hands at the thought of the bounty that awaited him, a frustrated Swift set to work on a solution. After several false starts, his engineer Andrew Chase came up with the refrigerated railcar. It revolutionised

the business, allowing Swift to kill cattle in the city and distribute the goods safely to the East Coast. Soon, Swift was controlling all the stages of meat production, from the sale of the steer to its slaughter to its eventual distribution. By the turn of the century, Swift (who once boasted that he used 'everything but the squeal'), his rival Philip Armour and the other local yards were slaughtering over ten million animals a year in Chicago, employing 40,000 locals in the process.

Although working conditions were unsafe, unhealthy and unpleasant in the stockyards – they didn't improve even after a federal investigation reached the same conclusions as Upton Sinclair's brutal exposé, *The Jungle* – Chicago remained the US meatpacking capital for several generations, its prosperity shaping the lives of thousands. But in the 1960s, a change as radical as that wrought by Swift a century earlier occurred. Entrepreneurs with their eye on a fortune set up Iowa Beef Packers, a chain of slaughterhouses that massively undercut the Chicago businesses and moved trade away from the South Side.

Within a decade, the Chicago stockyards were gone, the city no longer Hog Butcher for the world. Its industrial legacy is huge, but in Chicago, it's just left a neighbourhood that's never quite recovered from its loss. A mass of deprived housing projects and shabby warehouses ring the area, though some swear that if you listen carefully, you can hear the howls of a dying cow drift by on the wind, a ghostly reminder of the area's past.

Another workers' revolt, the Haymarket Square riot of 1886, was a watershed in the struggle between self-described 'anarchist' workers and their bosses. On the night of 4 May, a public gathering to protest against the treatment of workers at the McCormick Harvesting plant turned violent when a bomb was thrown into the crowd. Several people, including one police officer, were killed, and ten defendants were indicted. Of the eight that stood trial, four were executed and three were pardoned, largely thanks to attorney John Peter Altgeld. The 'Haymarket martyrs', as they came to be known, inspired the socialist celebrations of workers in May that continue to this day.

SEATS OF LEARNING

The year 1892 was an important one in the educational life of the city, as William Rainey Harper became the first president of the University of Chicago. The holder of a PhD from Yale, Harper had hoped to found an institution of higher learning in the Midwest, where he was born. But by convincing local philanthropists such as Marshall Field of the importance of a university to the life of Chicago, Harper was able to realise his dream on a parcel of land at 57th Street and Ellis Avenue.

Harper was something of a progressive for his time, and envisioned his university offering an equal education for both men and women students, a university press that stood ready to disseminate its teachings throughout the country, and the use of a quarter system to allow for greater flexibility among the schedules of faculty and staff. Although Harper's premature 1906 death from cancer at the age of 49 came prior to the establishment of a medical school at the campus, it's partly thanks to his quest for excellence that today's University of Chicago Hospitals, as well as its other schools and divisions, are counted among the very best in their field. The university eventually played a key role in the development of nuclear energy when, in 1942, a team led by Enrico Fermi built the first ever nuclear reactor, an event that led to the Manhattan Project and the first atomic bomb.

SOCIAL EXPERIMENTS

By the early post-Civil War years, George Pullman's sleeping and dining train cars were the standard for the industry. However, Pullman was searching for a way to reduce the unrest among his workers, and in so doing hit upon the idea of a planned community, an idea that had been tried in England. His vision for a self-contained industrial city was realised over 3,000 acres (1,215 hectares), which he purchased in Lake Calumet to the south of Chicago.

At Pullman City, designed by Solon S Beman, employees were ensconced within a residential system that was expected to generate a profit, just as did the Pullman factory. Despite the decent amenities – a park, a church, a hotel, a theatre, churches and shops – workers were asked higher rents for their living quarters than those outside the district. They also had to walk to the edge of Pullman City for a drink at a tavern: the whole of the 'town' was dry.

The employees grew disgruntled and, in 1894, staged a strike that dragged on as their boss refused to compromise. The American Railway Union's president, Eugene V Debs, eventually intervened on behalf of the workers, instigating a boycott of Pullman cars across the nation. Rioting ensued, before President Grover Cleveland threatened to send in federal troops to replace the police militia that had been involved in keeping the peace up until that point. Eventually, in July, the strike was broken and the Pullman plant reopened in August with a substantial percentage of new workers.

'The Levee district took corruption and decadence to a new level in Chicago.'

Even when criticised by members of his own family for his behaviour towards employees, Pullman never conceded to the opposition. When he died three years later, he was buried under tons of asphalt to stop resentful workers desecrating his body. The town was annexed to Chicago in 1899, and was designated a national landmark 72 years later.

Not far from Pullman City, a different kind of social experiment was brought to fruition in 1889, when Jane Addams founded America's first settlement centre at 800 S Halsted Street. Inspired by a visit to Toynbee Hall in London, Addams decided to start her own version of its scheme: Hull-House provided day-care facilities and assorted social services to an embattled and deprived local community made up mostly of immigrants and living in abject squalour.

Unafraid of controversy, Addams constantly wrestled with the city's political entities, which she viewed as inadequate in their response to the needs of the neighbourhoods, particularly with respect to sanitation and health. More often than not, she won the argument. With co-founder Ellen Gates Starr, Addams – the 1931 recipient of the Nobel Peace Prize for her humanitarian, feminist and internationalist work – contributed one of the most enduring and comprehensive human rights organisations to a city that, at the turn of the century, had a population of over one and a half million.

Midway Plaisance during the successful **World's Columbian Exposition**.

FAIR'S FARE

Held just 22 years after the Chicago Fire of
1871, the World's Columbian Exposition was
a prime opportunity for Chicago to showcase
its growth. A team of planners and designers
led by Daniel Burnham and Frederick Law
Olmsted created a gasp-inducing series of
grand attractions in a 'White City' that thrilled
over 25 million attendees. Some 46 nations
provided 250,000 displays in its various halls.
The first ever Ferris wheel, standing 250 feet
(76 metres) tall and featuring 36 cars that each
could hold up to 60 people, was built for the
fair, though the most financially successful
attraction was the 'Streets in Cairo' section that
featured an exotic dancer named Little Egypt.

This exposition kicked off a renaissance of
popular culture in Chicago that extended into
the next century, and which expanded the
leisure activities of residents and visitors
to encompass dance halls, movie palaces,
nightclubs, amusement parks and vaudeville
shows. All these forms of entertainment
became popular and accessible both in the
city's downtown and in its neighbourhoods.

SODOM AND TOMORROW

At the end of the 19th century, the Levee
district took corruption and decadence to a
new level in the history of Chicago. Located in
the First Ward, the inhabitants of the Levee
included gamblers, johns, drunks, prostitutes
and penny-ante criminals. However, its
denizens took second place to the colourful
brothels themselves: the Everleigh Club (run by
sisters Minna and Ada), Freiberg's dance hall,
the Library, the House of All Nations and the
Opium Den, among others. For such activity to

flourish, favours had to be granted and eyes
had to look the other way more often than not.

On the legislative front, 'machine' politics
and ward 'bosses' were becoming the standard
among the various districts. In more prosperous
neighbourhoods, fancy balls were held as
political party fundraisers, made popular in
the First Ward by Chicago aldermen Michael
'Hinky Dink' Kenna and John 'Bathhouse'
Coughlin. These two unscrupulous politicians
had a knack for entertaining others while lining
their own pockets with illicit lucre from
businesses grateful for their favours.

Eventually, the moral adversaries of the
goings-on in the Levee were prompted to put
an end to the lawlessness. A Vice Commission
appointed by the mayor enabled enforcers to
shut down brothels based on the lost taxable
income to the city. After the Everleigh closed its
doors, the rest of the Levee's institutions were
systematically raided until both patrons and
proprietors wearied of the law's interference.

One of the beneficiaries of Kenna's and
Coughlin's largesse was Charles Tyson Yerkes.
A Philadelphian by birth and a broker by trade,
he settled in Chicago in the 1880s and began
to buy favours from the aldermen in a bid to
gain control of the city's streetcar lines. Using
stockholders' money to pay himself first while
investors went without, he systematically
expanded his activities into ownership of trolley
cars and elevated train car lines.

But finally, the 'traction king', as Yerkes
was by then known, stepped too far over the
line, when he inspired his political cohorts to
introduce a bill that would extend his transit
franchise for another 50 years without any
compensation to the city. Although the bill was
passed in 1895, it was repealed after two years

of public protest. Yerkes soon tired of the fray and moved to London; some 42 years after his 1905 death, the Chicago Transit Authority was created as a municipal agency to oversee the city's various mass transportation entities.

INSULLATION

Another man who left an impression on the city through his business dealings and philanthropy was utilities magnate Samuel Insull. After emigrating from Britain to the US in 1881 as Thomas Edison's assistant, Insull proved his worth by increasing Edison's domestic business fourfold, and became president of the Chicago Edison Company in 1892. Insull also left his mark on the city by his role as one of the forces behind the railroads that connect Chicago to its suburbs, now known as the Metra.

Insull's passion after hours was for the opera; so much so that he proposed to build a new opera house for the town that would be financially supported by offices within the building (much like Adler and Sullivan's Auditorium Building, completed in 1889). Insull soon had the support of the major arts patrons, but he insisted on looking after the entire project, hiring the firm of Graham, Anderson, Probst and White to design the structure.

> **'Eliot Ness and his cohorts were termed "the Untouchables" for their resistance to Mob bribery.'**

The Civic Opera House was completed in 1929, shortly after the stock market crash. The irony, of course, was that Insull's empire began to fall apart even as his magnificent new structure welcomed its first patrons through its doors. After losing all of his companies, he travelled to Europe for a brief respite, before returning to the States to withstand court proceedings regarding fraud and embezzlement, among other charges. After being acquitted, he died of a heart attack in a Paris subway in 1938 with less than a dollar's worth of change in his pocket. With the Civic Opera House, Insull left a fond legacy to the citizens of his adopted city, but one that was all the more bittersweet for his meteoric rise and subsequent downfall.

PAYING THE BILL

On the political front, the father-and-son mayoral legacies of Carter Harrison I and II dating back to the 1870s left large shoes to fill. The 24th mayor of Chicago, Harrison senior (a five-term mayor) was the presiding official during rebuilding after the Chicago Fire of 1871, as well as during the World's Columbian

Exposition. Later, Harrison junior, the 30th mayor of Chicago but the first to be born in the city, showed himself to be even more reform-minded than his father. Also winning five terms in office, he was known for his fair dealings with immigrant and minority groups, and was successful in closing down the prostitution houses of the Levee district during his tenure.

But there were some personalities up to the task of filling the Harrisons' shoes, one of which was William Hale 'Big Bill' Thompson, three-time mayor. Thompson was an athlete, a scion of a real estate business family and a powerful friend to the likes of Al Capone. Furthermore, he was a popular if none-too-bright politician, and came to power as the Republican candidate for mayor in 1915, but lost his second campaign, for US Representative, three years later.

Thompson was re-elected mayor of Chicago in 1919, but though he was an enthusiastic recipient of many minority votes, his passivity during the Chicago Race Riots that same year may have hurt his chances for re-election. In the summer of 1919, an isolated incident on one of Chicago's beaches set off five days of rioting between whites and blacks, leaving over 35 people dead and hundreds more injured. Things escalated further with the death of black

The Depression hit Chicago hard. *See p14.*

teenager Eugene Williams, who drowned at the segregated 29th Street beach on 27 July 1919 after a reputed confrontation between blacks and whites prevented him from coming ashore.

Williams's death was the spark that set alight a series of violent racial confrontations in the city. When word got out about it, the story soon changed, claiming that he had been stoned to death and prompting fury among blacks. After several attempts to quell the violence without force, Mayor Thompson asked the governor of Illinois for the assistance of state troops. Too late, 5,000 men were summoned to keep the peace. When coupled with Thompson's pro-German stance during World War I, the reasons for his fall from grace become obvious.

After an unsuccessful mayoral campaign against William E Dever, Thompson won the city election again in 1927, but during his reign, the city lost control of the town to criminals, the most infamous of whom was Al Capone. There were 62 bombings in the city in 1928 attributed to the Mob, mostly directed against reform leaders. Thompson's building campaigns, including beautification of streets and bridges, were the best thing about his administrations. However, his refusal to give up politics even after two more defeats in the mayoral campaigns and one way-out attempt to gain the governorship of the state in 1936 by forming a party of his own was typical of the careerist politician and limelight addict he had become.

PROHIBITION AND DEPRESSION

The Prohibition Era in the United States began when, on 16 January 1920, Congress ratified the 18th Amendment banning the manufacture and sale of alcohol. Chicago's involvement in the days prior to the amendment came chiefly through Evanston resident Frances Willard. Willard had founded the Women's

The great migration

In the years leading up to the Race Riots of 1919, the African-American population of Chicago increased rapidly. In what became known as the Great Migration, huge numbers of African-American residents of states such as Alabama, Arkansas, Louisiana, Mississippi, Tennessee and Texas moved north in the years between 1890 and World War I. New York, Chicago and Philadelphia were home to a quarter of northern black residents by 1910.

Many reasons for the movement of so many black families and individuals from the south have been cited: the problems of low crop prices, racial discrimination and hatred in the south, the temptation of higher wages, better education and the chance for a new beginning in the north without the shadow of slavery. In time, migration clubs, church networks and other agencies were formed to specifically assist those making the transition. The migration also brought other pressing issues, such as abusive working conditions, inadequate housing, discrimination and poverty, to the forefront of the Chicago social agenda.

Indeed, the social, political and popular effects of the migration were evident. Ida B Wells, a noted black writer and civil rights advocate, created the Negro Fellowship League in 1908, providing lodgings, assistance in finding employment, and a reading room with periodicals from both northern and southern cities. In politics, Mayor William Thompson successfully cultivated black constituents by having black politicians speak to them on his behalf. And in the near-South Side locale known as Bronzeville, many black artists, writers, businessmen and entrepreneurs made their presence known, much as in New York's Harlem. Louis Armstrong (*pictured*), Nat 'King' Cole, Scott Joplin and publishing magnate John H Johnson were just a few of Bronzeville's more famous residents.

Not your average lovers' gift: the aftermath of the **St Valentine's Day Massacre**.

Christian Temperance Union in 1874, whose membership – which eventually peaked at 175,000 – advocated the prohibition of liquor as a means to protect the family against the harmful effects of alcohol. The temperance movement gained momentum in the post-World War I years, culminating in its followers obtaining signed pledge cards from untold numbers. The pledge of temperance was a factor in the political climate that fuelled the need for alcohol restrictions, first at the community and state levels, then at the federal level.

However, the ideals of the 18th Amendment caused unbearable hypocrisy within American society, corruption at all levels of government, and an astounding death toll linked to the alarming crime rate. Chicago was in the thick of the action, with Al Capone's empire leading the bootleggers and ensuring the local police looked the other way through some handsome payoffs.

Capone's nemesis, US marshal and special Prohibition task force agent Eliot Ness, and his cohorts were later termed 'the Untouchables' for their resistance to Mob bribery. From a tiny office on Wabash Street, Ness and his fellow agents gathered evidence against gangsters with booze-running rings, such as Capone, Dion O'Banion and others. However, they weren't able to prevent Capone's most notorious killing: seven members of the Bugs Moran gang were gunned down by four counterfeit cops, later discovered to be Capone's henchmen, in what

became known as the St Valentine's Day Massacre of 1929. Capone had ordered the hit, and while the feds couldn't pin the killings on him, he was convicted of tax evasion two years later and sent to Alcatraz.

In the later 1920s and early 1930s, or so some historians have theorised, the Depression itself acted as a force for the repeal of the 18th Amendment. This was because of the changes it produced in American society, and the accompanying political and economic shifts that it brought about in the social structure. When, in 1933, almost three-quarters of convention delegates voted to pass the 21st Amendment repealing Prohibition, it was clear the individual states would again gain control of the regulation and taxation of alcohol, and that the public sale of 'demon rum' would be legal across the nation once more.

During the Depression, more changes in the city's immigrant population base, and subsequently in Chicago politics, occurred. Anton 'Tony' Cermak, a Czech coal miner's son and street vendor, became mayor in 1931 by the largest margin in the history of city elections. Cermak tried to balance the budget by reducing the swollen payrolls left by his predecessor and applying for federal relief, but due to the poor economy, the existing fiscal problems were immense. Worse was to follow when, in 1933, Cermak was struck by an assassin's bullet intended for President Franklin D Roosevelt; Cermak was in Miami to parley with the

Made in Chicago Playboy

Depending on your politics, you can either blame or thank the penny-pinching accountants at *Esquire* magazine. The publication decided to move from Chicago to New York in 1951, taking with it most of its staff. Among them was a 25-year-old copywriter who, while valuing his career, also didn't want to leave the town in which he had been born and raised. He asked for a meagre raise of $5 a week; the accountants said no. So when *Esquire* upped and went to the Big Apple, Hugh Hefner stayed behind, borrowed eight grand from friends and family, and decided to start his own magazine.

The first edition of *Playboy*, put together by Hefner on the kitchen table of his apartment at 6052 S Harper Avenue in the suburb of Hyde Park, emerged blinking in December 1953. The magazine featured a piece on jazz musicians Tommy and Jimmy Dorsey and a Sherlock Holmes story by Arthur Conan Doyle. But even back then, claims that you were buying *Playboy* for the articles rang rather hollow: the centre pages of the publication contained a naked photograph of Marilyn Monroe.

Fifty years on, it's hard to convey the impact *Playboy* had on American sexual mores. This was not only a decade and a half before the sexual revolution of the 1960s, it was also several years before even rock 'n' roll. As late as 1957, TV producers shot Elvis Presley from the waist up for fear that his pelvic manoeuvrings would turn innocent young girls into insatiable sexual animals.

Prior to the magazine's first issue, no mainstream publication had dared publish shots of naked women: the US Post Office wouldn't ship them and newsstands wouldn't sell them. (The shots of Monroe that Hefner used had been in circulation for years, but no one had dared to publish.) But when money talks, business listens, and *Playboy* was soon making a lot of people a lot of money. The first issue sold an astonishing 55,000 copies at 50¢ each, and Hefner was in business.

And how. Before long, *Playboy* was the talk of America. Hefner quickly realised that selling magazines to men is all about creating tangible and appealing aspirations for them, and playing on them for all they were worth. Hence, the models were pinned, with a transparently fake intimacy, as Playmates, while the editorial content tended towards surprisingly highbrow topics (Jack Kerouac, Woody Allen and Isaac Asimov all wrote for the magazine) and tips on how to attain lifestyle cool. The magazine was sold as an accessory that no wannabe sophisticated man-about-town should be without. And the wannabes bought it in their millions.

Hefner was quick to capitalise. *Playboy* went global, tapping into the libidos of sexually repressed gentlemen across the globe. Then, in 1960, a Playboy Club opened at 116 E Walton, becoming the first in a chain that spread as far as London, Nassau, Osaka and Des Moines. But Hefner left time for pleasure: now divorced from his wife, he was living the life of Riley at the Playboy Mansion at 1340 N State Street. Or he would have been, except he was getting laid far more often that Riley did, and making far more money.

The magazine's rise was inexorable through the 1960s and early 1970s; the November 1972 edition sold a staggering 7.16 million copies. Not that there weren't hiccups along the way, mind. Feminist groups have long

president about federal assistance to Chicago under the 'New Deal'. Though Cermak lingered for over two weeks, the wound proved fatal.

Cermak didn't even live long enough to see Chicago's second World's Fair. Entitled the 'Century of Progress', it was held 40 years after the Columbian Exposition – in a neat nod to the earlier wing-ding, Daniel Burnham's two sons Hubert and Daniel were appointed as architect and secretary respectively to the board of trustees – and stayed open for two summers (1933 and 1934). While not as striking as its predecessor, it was popular and profitable: the money raised aided the arts organisations

involved in preserving the fair's exhibits, including the Museum of Science and Industry (built for the earlier Columbian Exposition), the Adler Planetarium and the South Park Corporation (later taken over by the Chicago Park District).

After World War II, Chicago benefited from a huge economic boom. Still growing, its population topped 3.6 million in 1950, and affluence was everywhere, as people began to move from the city to the suburbs. Five years later, the city was to reach a turning point in its history with the election of one of the most famous American city mayors of the century.

Larry Flynt's *Hustler* pushed the pornographic envelope further than *Playboy* had ever shoved it. Hefner's airbrushed cheesecake spreads were superseded on shelves by spreads of a very different kind, as gynaecological porn became the norm and *Playboy* began to seem outmoded. The 1980s saw the magazine's stock fall further, as it struggled to adapt to the world's ever-changing attitudes. Still, it's a sign of just how far ahead of the pack *Playboy* was that even after the 1980s, a decade even Hefner admits was poor for the company, it remained the best-selling men's magazine in the US.

The last decade or so has at least seen an increase in the profile of *Playboy*, as the company has attempted to turn its fortunes around from its offices at 660 Lake Shore Drive. Hefner is more visible than ever, his four identikit blonde girlfriends always at his side, while in that circuitous way that fashion has of repeating itself, the magazine has picked up some vestiges of retro cool.

However, it's not all good news. Sales of the magazine are less than half what they were at its peak. Guys after a sneaky glimpse at a pretty model are now getting their wank matter from increasingly lascivious bottom-shelf men's mags such as *Maxim*; those after something harder have found plenty of options on the top shelf and online that make *Playboy*'s pictorials look like kids' stuff. The misery has been compounded by huge losses accrued at playboy.com. All in all, the future looks uncertain. *Playboy* turns 50 in 2003, but few analysts are daring to predict that it'll be a happy birthday for a publication that kickstarted a revolution from a South Side apartment.

singled out the magazine for criticism and abuse, and a damning article by Gloria Steinem on her experiences as a bunny girl in New York made the writer's name and sullied *Playboy*'s.

The magazine survived these attacks with ease, but the 1970s threw up challenges that proved harder to shrug off. Empowered by the permissiveness of the 1960s, Bob Guccione's *Penthouse* and, more notoriously,

DEUS EX MACHINE
In 1955 Richard J Daley won the first of six straight terms as mayor. Skilled in the machine politics tradition through his chairmanship of the Cook County Democratic party, Daley was an Irish-Catholic Democrat who gained the favour of minority and working class voters by his straight talk and get-the-job-done attitude. His mettle, though, would be tested by the city's challenges during the next two decades: corrupt police, spiralling crime and racial tensions, the latter epitomised by the civil unrest triggered by the assassination of activist and civil rights leader Dr Martin Luther King, Jr.

King had come to Chicago several times during the mid 1960s, and with each visit he had pointed up more of the problems faced by the urban minority community. Inadequate housing, job discrimination, poverty and illiteracy were just a few of the issues that King hoped to bring to the fore. However, he was met with scorn by whites, even after several meetings with Daley in a bid to set up a Citizens Advisory Committee to address racial tensions.

When King announced his intention to take up residence in a slum building in the Lawndale neighbourhood, the owners of the structure took him to court. Various rallies and marches led by King in white neighbourhoods led to police intervention, which in turn set the stage for the widespread burning and looting of white-owned businesses that occurred mainly in black neighbourhoods on the West Side immediately following King's death in April 1968. To mitigate the chaos, Daley called in the National Guard, but it was only the beginning of a turbulent year, which culminated in a national PR disaster for Daley and his administration.

RIOT POLICE

The Democratic National Convention of 1968, held in Chicago, was to be another test for Daley and his tough reputation in the face of forces beyond his control. Anti-war protesters had come to the city in their hundreds to celebrate the 'Festival of Life' sponsored by a group of counter-cultural mischief-makers known as the Yippies, and threatened to create mayhem. However, it wasn't the demonstrators who proved to be violent; rather, it was Daley's Chicago Police who caused much of the trouble. During the convention, national TV broadcast the melées between the 'pigs' and the 'flower children', at the expense of the city's reputation. Daley stuck with his hard line, though, which only grew increasingly indefensible.

Trouble on the **West Side**.

The subsequent scapegoating of several protesters from the demonstrations became a famous 1969 federal court case later termed the 'Chicago Eight' trial. Indicted for conspiring to cause riots, the recalcitrant defendants – including Abbie Hoffman, Tom Haydn and Bobby Seale – found themselves at the centre of the controversy, and made the most of it by hiring brash New Yorker William M Kunstler as their attorney. A seasoned though embattled judge, Julius J Hoffman, presided over the chaotic but enormously entertaining 100-day trial, which ended with the jubilant defendants being acquitted on the charge of inciting riots. A parade of well-known witnesses, frequent outbursts against the court and the colourful personalities of those on trial made for lively coverage in the press. It was established three years later that the FBI, with the complicity of Hoffman, had bugged the offices of the defendants' attorneys.

'Racial problems continued and many white residents left for the suburbs.'

Another confrontation between police and radicals occurred in 1969, when the Weathermen's 'Days of Rage' were fashioned after ambushes by the Black Panther party. The Weathermen were an offshoot radical subgroup of the Students for a Democratic Society (SDS) who advocated armed overthrow of US governmental entities to atone for the country's exploitation of foreign nations and its military action in Vietnam. Members of the group vandalised property and attacked police in the Loop and the Gold Coast; skirmishes between civilians and uniformed cops occurred mostly on the North Side and in the Civic Center.

By the time the violence had ceased, dozens of police and demonstrators had been injured. Unfortunately, the constructive gains of these bloody protests were few, and it may have been symbolic that the leader of the Chicago chapter of the Black Panther party, Fred Hampton, died in a police raid that December. Racial problems in the city continued into the following decade and, for better or worse, many white residents chose to leave for the suburbs in a phenomenon termed 'white flight'.

THE CULTURE CLUB

The arts took off in Chicago after the turbulent 1960s. Along Lincoln Avenue and in other North Side locations, the now legendary Organic, Wisdom Bridge, Victory Gardens and St Nicholas theatres, in addition to the more established Goodman and Second City,

The Yippies received a cooler welcome at the **Democratic Convention of 1968**. *See p18.*

produced such important contributors to the medium as playwright David Mamet, actors Joe Mantegna and Dennis Franz, and director Robert Falls. Later, the Steppenwolf Theatre added to the Chicagoan star roster with the likes of John Malkovich, Joan Allen and Gary Sinise.

Meanwhile, to avoid the high costs of filming in New York, film producers started to turn to Chicago as a place to make movies while at the same time cutting expenses by utilising the local union and non-union talent base. *The Blues Brothers* kickstarted the trend, which resulted in the setting up of the Chicago Film Office.

THE DALEY DOUBLE

City politics were far from dormant after Daley's death in 1976. Three years later, Democrat Jane Byrne, a protégé of Daley's, ran against incumbent mayor Michael Bilandic and won by 17,000 votes. Her effort was helped by Chicago's largest ever snowfall that season – 82 inches (over two metres) in all – with which Bilandic was spectacularly ill-equipped to deal. Byrne proved to be up to the task of surface gestures such as festivals, but her tactics behind closed doors were strident and often inconsistent.

The next mayoral primary saw Byrne, Richard M Daley (son of Richard J) and a black candidate named Harold Washington in a three-way heat for the Democratic nomination. After winning the 1983 primary, Washington went on to become Chicago's first black mayor, and over

the next four years battled long and hard with the city council. Washington's death in office of a heart attack in 1987 marked another political milestone for Chicago in that his replacement, former alderman Eugene Sawyer, was also black. Sawyer ran for mayor in 1989, but was defeated by Richard M Daley in the first of his three (so far) consecutive terms.

Chicago's status as an industrial city may be gone, but it's regaining the prosperity that illuminated its early history. The transformation of the Loop in the 1970s into a financial capital helped, as has the burgeoning convention industry responsible for thousands of jobs in the service industry. The recent era has seen city beautification, notable public works, huge private investment in new commercial buildings and residential space, and the emergence of Chicago as a world-class city.

But the mainstay of Chicago's prosperity and growth has been its 'I Will' spirit. By balancing its natural, cultural and civic resources and celebrating its diversity, locals take pride in the motto 'Urbs in Horto' ('city in a garden'). And just like real gardens, sometimes seeming disasters only make the plants grow stronger.

▶ For more on **local theatres**, *see p240.*
▶ For more on the **University of Chicago**, *see p124.*
▶ For more on **Hull-House**, *see p111.*

Key events

1673 Father Jacques Marquette and Louis Jolliet discover what later becomes Chicago.
1779 Jean Baptiste Point du Sable becomes the first permanent resident of the area.
1812 53 settlers are killed by natives in the Fort Dearborn Massacre.
1818 Illinois receives statehood.
1837 Chicago incorporates as a city; William Ogden is elected its first mayor.
1847 The Chicago River and Harbor Convention promotes waterway commerce.
1848 The Illinois-Michigan Canal is built; the Chicago Board of Trade is established.
1850 Northwestern University opens.
1860 Abraham Lincoln is nominated as Republican presidential candidate in Chicago.
1871 The Chicago Fire destroys $200-million worth of property and claims over 250 lives.
1872 The first mail-order catalogue business is begun by Aaron Montgomery Ward.
1879 The Chicago Academy of Fine Arts (later the Art Institute of Chicago) is incorporated.
1886 The Haymarket labour riot takes place, with eight policemen and four civilians killed.
1889 Social reformer Jane Addams opens Hull-House; architect Frank Lloyd Wright builds his own residence in Oak Park.
1891 The Chicago Orchestra, later the Chicago Symphony Orchestra, is established.
1892 The first elevated train service is offered to commuters in the central district.
1893 The World's Columbian Exposition.
1894 Pullman train employees strike for improved working conditions.
1900 Chicago River is made to run backwards towards the Mississippi for sanitary purposes.
1903 A fire at the Iroquois Theatre kills 600, prompting national laws for public buildings.
1909 Daniel Burnham, city visionary, unveils his park-filled Plan of Chicago.
1915 The Eastland pleasure vessel capsizes in the Chicago River, killing 812.
1919 Race riots rage in July: 38 die.
1920 Eight Chicago White Sox players, among them 'Shoeless' Joe Jackson, are banned from baseball after fixing the 1919 World Series.
1921 The Field Museum opens.
1924 Leopold and Loeb are sentenced to life in prison for murder.
1926 National radio broadcasts of *Amos 'n' Andy*, *Fibber McGee and Molly* and other popular shows start to originate from Chicago.
1929 Seven bootleggers are executed in the St Valentine's Day Massacre.

1933 The Century of Progress World's Fair opens, as does the Museum of Science and Industry; Mayor Anton Cermak is killed by a gunman intending to shoot President-elect Franklin D Roosevelt in Miami.
1934 John Dillinger is shot and killed at the Biograph movie theatre in Lincoln Park.
1942 Physicist Enrico Fermi conducts successful nuclear chain reaction experiments at the University of Chicago.
1953 Hugh Hefner publishes the inaugural monthly issue of *Playboy* in December.
1955 Richard J Daley is elected mayor; O'Hare International Airport opens in October; the first McDonald's is opened by Ray Kroc in suburban Des Plaines.
1958 A fire at Our Lady of the Angels school kills three nuns and 87 children.
1959 The first ever Second City cabaret show takes place; Chicago becomes an ocean port with the opening of the St Lawrence Seaway.
1967 A blizzard in January closes down the city with 22 inches of snow; Riverview, a North Side amusement park for 63 years, closes.
1968 Riots take place after the murder of Martin Luther King, Jr; the Democratic National Convention is marred by violence.
1969 The Chicago Seven trial takes place; two radicals die in a Black Panther raid.
1971 The Union Stockyards close after 105 years of continuous livestock trading.
1973 The Sears Tower opens in May.
1976 Mayor Richard J Daley dies in office.
1979 *The Blues Brothers* is filmed in the city; an American Airlines DC-10 crashes near O'Hare Airport, claiming 273 lives.
1986 The Chicago Bears rout the New England Patriots 46-10 to win their first Super Bowl.
1987 Mayor Harold Washington dies in office.
1988 Floodlights are installed at Wrigley Field.
1989 Richard M Daley, son of Richard J Daley, is elected mayor of Chicago.
1992 The Chicago River floods underground tunnels, causing $1 billion of damage.
1994 The United Center opens.
1995 Temperatures top 100 degrees for five straight days in July, killing 550 people.
1996 Michael Jordan and the Chicago Bulls win their sixth NBA championship.
1999 Over 200 statues are displayed as part of the 'Cows on Parade' outdoor exhibition; Richard M Daley is re-elected for a third term.
2002 The 16-acre Millennium Park, designed by Frank Gehry, nears completion.

Chicago Today

Give us this day our Daley bread.

When tourists think of the United States, three cities usually come to mind. New York, the brightest city in the world; Los Angeles, home to Hollywood; and Chicago, the focal point of the Midwest, and, much to the scorn of current mayor Richard M Daley, the one-time nexus of Prohibition-era gangsterland.

History has turned the Chicago of the Roaring '20s and Depression-era 1930s into a larger than life myth, with images of Al Capone in combat with Eliot Ness, gun battles in the streets and a speakeasy on every block. Legend versus history is often disappointing, but it was a violent time, and no matter how much Chicago tries to shed the image, it just won't shift.

Although crime remains an ongoing issue for residents, as it does in many major US cities, 21st-century Chicago doesn't live up to its gangster reputation. With constant gentrification of the outlying neighbourhoods and the ever-expanding bubble of downtown high-rises and condo developments, the face of Chicago changes almost on a monthly basis. Areas that were once ghettos are now hipster

neighbourhoods, housing projects have been turned into parks, and industrial corridors have morphed into artist communities.

But the real action doesn't take place in an underground speakeasy or inside a construction development, but instead inside City Hall. Though outside Chicago, it's assumed that the city's nickname of the Windy City comes from the legendary gusts that blow in off the lake, the true impetus behind the name is politics, with 'windy' referring to the politicians' ability to spin a story to the people. Mayor Richard M Daley – son of the late Richard J Daley, who was mayor from 1955 to 1976 – is *the man*, ruling the city with an iron, albeit clumsy, fist. The Democratic machine lives, but with Daley at the helm, it's a kinder, gentler creation.

CRIME AND THE CITY SOLUTION

When discussion begins of any big American city, the list of topics is usually headed by crime. Chicago is no exception, though it's arguable that its past – Capone and the Mob, Dillinger, Speck and Gacy – only spurs on the conversation apace.

That said, crime was, for the majority of the 1980s and 1990s, on the decline here. Violent crime in the city has dropped by a little more than one per cent every year for a decade. In 2001, however, city officials were embarrassed when Chicago again gathered the distinction of America's murder capital. Chicagoans were quick to note that the events of September 11 were not counted in New York City's murder statistics, but that's still scant consolation.

By and large, the higher murder numbers are a result of increased gang activity: drive-by shootings in the name of neighbourhood solidarity or drug-selling turf wars. Though the Mafia has all but faded away, youth gangs have more than picked up its mantle. However, this kind of urban violence is largely out of sight and – city fathers hope – out of mind for visitors. As are the parlous states the neighbourhoods themselves are in, but more of that later.

Mayor Daley is not without solutions, though they're occasionally somewhat misguided. His attempt at establishing anti-loitering laws was declared unconstitutional, but he's successfully lobbied for harsher penalties against criminals who use firearms and supported making hate crimes a federal offence. Though his attempts at creating harsher gun legislation have often been met with dissent by downstate – primarily Republican – lawmakers, his commitment to reducing crime in Chicago appears genuine.

THE BLUSTERY WIND

As Illinois's major population centre, Chicago and Mayor Daley exert an extraordinary influence on the state's politics. But it's a large state, and despite the fact that the infamous Democratic Machine – a term that predates even the reign of Richard J Daley – rolls on in Chicago, downstate lawmakers and voters tend to remain conservative and Republican. It goes without saying that there is resentment on both sides, with Chicago receiving much of the federal funds and the lawmakers in Springfield constantly trying to undo Mayor Daley's legislation.

State issues aside, Chicago politics are tainted by the blood of corruption. Though Mayor Daley, like any good politician, keeps himself squeaky clean, scandals have come close to his office. Nothing in the last few years has matched Operation Silver Shovel, a huge scandal exposed by the FBI that uncovered – among other things – illegal waste dumping throughout the city; little, too, has equalled the late 1990s news that more than a million dollars were owed to the state by state employees, dubbed 'scofflaws'. But recently, Cicero township president Betty Loren-Maltese has been accused of everything from rebuilding the Mafia to skimming town funds to not living in

Cicero but Las Vegas. As long as there are city halls in Chicagoland, it seems, there'll be corruption. Yet Chicagoans have learned to take their politicians' shortcomings in their stride, with a sense of roll-the-eyes humour.

WINNERS...

Whatever criticisms locals level at Mayor Daley, forgetting the city's tourist industry is not one of them. Daley has seemed almost obsessed at times with drawing new visitors to town, throwing money at schemes he hopes will induce more outsiders to show up here. And show up they have. There's no doubt that Chicago is a lot more visitor-friendly than it was even a decade ago, and Daley can claim plenty of credit for that state of affairs.

> 'The contrast between the gleaming Loop skyscape and the morass of housing projects couldn't be greater.'

Some of the projects have been vast undertakings. The development of the area around the Field Museum, Adler Planetarium and the Shedd Aquarium from a fume-choked, freeway-dominated muddle into the green and inviting Museum Campus cost $60 million and has been an unqualified success. The renovation of Navy Pier in the early 1990s delighted visiting families, though the results largely are bland and generic. The overhaul of Wacker Drive was long overdue. And McCormick Place, the largest convention centre in the US, draws millions of conventioneers a year, who crank up the economy by billions with their expense-account spending.

More of these big projects are on the way. The construction of Millennium Park might have become a local joke, so delayed has it been for innumerable reasons (witness the name; it hadn't opened by 2002), but when it's complete, it'll make the Loop's lakefront even more appealing. Even the venerable Soldier Field, home of the Chicago Bears and Chicago Fire, is undergoing a $365-million rebuild that will displace both the Bears and Fire throughout 2002 and into 2003.

But the money and effort put into smaller projects has proved to be just as well spent. Downtown is simply a lot cleaner and prettier than it's ever been; a small measure in financial terms, but one that has helped imbue many locals with civic pride. Chicago's calendar is now blocked out with festivals of every shape and size; almost too many, in fact. And the introduction of the Chicago Greeter programme in April 2002, in which local volunteers escort small groups around their neighbourhoods in what are usually highly personal guided tours, adds an appealingly unshowy element to a tour schedule already overrun with options.

... AND LOSERS

Like any gentrification process, however, the making over of Chicago has not been without its victims. And the city's victims, perhaps predictably, are the city's poor. In an effort to put a happy face on the city, government officials have put a virtual stranglehold on those with the least amount of power. And when they haven't put a stranglehold on them, they've merely ignored them.

In the Near North area stands the Cabrini-Green housing development. Never the most appealing of areas, it was for years riddled with crime and poverty, an eyesore on an improving cityscape. Something needed to be done. But Cabrini is now an island surrounded by million-dollar condominiums and upscale housing developments. And to go along with this gentrification, the council has tried to force the residents out through a housing voucher plan (Section 8) that scatters housing project residents throughout the city and suburbs. As of 2002, less than 15 per cent of Cabrini was occupied; though a few urban activists keep fighting, it's a battle that's been all but lost.

It's a similar story elsewhere. In Wicker Park, the influx of yuppie money and the subsequent increase in housing costs have forced the neighbourhood's traditional population, mainly Puerto Ricans and African-Americans, further west. A little south, between Little Italy and Pilsen, lie scenes of appalling, almost primitive urban deprivation. Entire housing blocks lie junked, their windows shattered; a hopeless, desperate sight. It's a similar story further south and west. Take a journey to Oak Park on the Green line or by bus to Hyde Park and you'll see, en route, the Chicago that the Office of Tourism goes out of its way not to promote. The contrast between the gleaming Loop skyscape and the desolate morass of ugly, crime-ridden housing projects couldn't be greater.

POST SEPTEMBER 11

Of course, the steel-and-glass skyscraper of a tourist and convention industry that Daley has built over the last decade or two could yet topple like a house of cards. But in mid-2002, Chicago is by no means the only city worrying about the impact on tourism of September 11. When the planes hit the World Trade Center, the town panicked. Chicago, with its arrogant, skyscraper-dominated financial district, seemed an obvious target. The Sears Tower was closed to visitors for several weeks; security alerts were frequent.

Renovation work on **Wacker Drive**.

Things had calmed down six months later, as they had throughout much of the US. But economically, the city is still worried about when – even if – things will pick up again. Immediately post-September 11, when most of the world was at first unable and then unwilling to fly, Chicago was an eerily quiet place. Conventions were cancelled, vacations too. A city that should have been in the middle of its busiest visitor season was all but deserted.

Chicago will surely be aided in its economic recovery by the fact it relies on two separate sectors: the leisure travellers and the conventioneers. Its facilities for the latter remain unparalleled, and as long as people feel the need to stage conventions, Chicago will reap the financial rewards. But this is still an uncertain time for a city that's staked so much on its ability to draw the out-of-state dollar.

Yet despite the realities of September 11, and its image in some quarters as a gun-toting capital of gangsters, Chicago is one of the fastest growing cities in the country: beautification everywhere, tourist dollars higher than ever and some of the best nightlife in the world. Granted, it isn't perfect. But the City that Works is doing just that to ensure it keeps getting better, and its spot as jewel of the Midwest seems secure for decades to come.

Architecture

If you build it, they will come.

Other metropolises lay claim to having more buildings per square mile, perhaps rightly. Of late, others have boasted that they have the tallest skyscrapers. Chicago, though, can claim the most dynamic, architecturally significant collection of edifices in the world. Here, it's quality, not quantity, though the latter was obviously not far from some architects' minds.

Though boat tours offer a fine perspective on the city's architecture, Chicago's dramatic skyline is, perhaps, best viewed from the window of a plane circling overhead, where one can clearly observe the point at which the still blue waters of Lake Michigan suddenly give way to glittering spikes of steel jabbing skyward. You could say that the skyline is a metaphor for the city itself: a jarring spectacle of industry and ingenuity rising from middle America, albeit one that's taken on a new poignancy since September 11.

BRIGHT SPARKS
The story of Chicago's ascent from ramshackle Midwestern berg to world-class architectural showcase began in 1871, with what seemed like

the end for those who lived in the city at the time. On the night of 8 October, a fire broke out in the barn behind the home of Patrick and Catherine O'Leary on the city's Near West Side and raced north and east. When it finally burned itself out two days later, much of the city was reduced to smouldering ruins.

While many theories exist about what caused the fire – from Mrs O'Leary's much-maligned cow to a fiery meteorite – most will agree that poor urban planning was ultimately to blame. At the time, the city was a veritable tinderbox: two-thirds of the city's 60,000 buildings were made of wood, while of the city's 60-odd miles of paved streets, most were covered with wooden planks. Add to that the city's crowded conditions and lack of fire codes, and, with hindsight, disaster was all but inevitable. The blaze, though, was the spur for the city to rebuild itself with dramatic immediacy.

THE CHICAGO SCHOOL
Refusing to be beaten by the tragedy, the city fathers were determined to rebuild their city to greater glory. Once the rubble was cleared

away, scores of architects converged on the city, drawn by the idea of a clean slate, a city without an established, confining architectural heritage.

Among them was Louis Sullivan. Born and educated in Boston, Sullivan arrived in Chicago in 1873 and went to work for Dankmar Adler, a German émigré with a firmly established architectural firm. Despite – or, more likely, because of – their differences in personality, the two worked well together, Sullivan's erratic moods and artistic hauteur tempered by Adler's sober professionalism. Sullivan, along with a handful of noteworthy contemporaries including William LeBaron Jenney and Daniel H Burnham, would help define what eventually came to be known as the Chicago School style.

The Chicago School's biggest innovation was the use of an interior steel structure to distribute the weight of a building. Previously, constructing taller buildings meant thickening the load-bearing exterior masonry walls to support the weight of upper floors. The result was frequently a squat, fortress-like structure, such as the **Auditorium Building** (50 E Congress Parkway, at S Wabash Avenue): designed by Adler and Sullivan and completed in 1889, it combined a 4,200-seat auditorium with offices and a hotel. Owned by Roosevelt University since 1946, the Auditorium Theatre remains one of the city's premier theatre and music venues. Catch a Broadway-style show to get a view of the spectacular interior, with its dramatic arches, gilded plater reliefs and rows of sparkling electric lights.

The **Fine Arts Building** (410 S Michigan Avenue, at E Van Buren Street), constructed by Solon Spencer Beman in 1885 as a showroom for Studebaker carriages, is another classic example of load-bearing masonry construction. As, too, is the **Monadnock Building** (53 W Jackson Street, at S Dearborn Street). Designed by Burnham and John Welborn Root in 1891, the hulking Monadnock was the last skyscraper to be built from solid masonry construction.

Most experts agree that the first official 'skyscraper' to use a steel skeletal frame was the Home Insurance Building, constructed seven years earlier by Jenney at LaSalle and Adams streets. Don't bother looking for it, though, as it was demolished in 1931. Do, though, bother looking for the striking **Marquette Building** (140 S Dearborn Street), perhaps the most attractive of the pioneering steel-framed constructions, and the triptych of other early skyscrapers nearby on Dearborn: Burnham's 1897 **Fisher Building** (343 S Dearborn Street), Holabird and Roche's 1894 **Old Colony Building** (407 S Dearborn Street) and William LeBaron Jenney's 1891 **Manhattan Building** (431 S Dearborn Street).

Chicago School buildings are tall and rectangular with flat roofs, and often made up of three distinct elements: base, rise and capital. Their grid-like steel structure is often recognisable on the structure's outer surfaces. With the steel frame taking care of the heavy lifting, exterior walls are opened up for windows and other non-load-bearing materials, most often light-coloured terracotta. Buildings constructed in the Chicago School style avoid unnecessary ornamentation in favour of utilitarian simplicity: it was, after all, Chicago School heavy-hitter Sullivan who declared that 'form follows function'.

'It took an outsider to kick off the most striking period in Chicago's architectural history.'

The **Reliance Building**, at the intersection of State Street and Congress Parkway, is a classic example of Chicago School innovations. Built in 1894 by Burnham along with Root and Charles Atwood, the soaring Reliance makes use of a Chicago School mainstay, the oriel window: a protruding bay window that runs the length of the building, underscoring its soaring

An early skyscraper in the Loop.

The basics

Scanning the city's towering buildings does make for dazzling eye candy; a trip up the Hancock will convince even seen-it-all cynics of that. But there's nothing like a museum when it comes to really getting a lofty education.

The **Chicago Architecture Center**, down in the Loop at 224 S Michigan Avenue (312 922 3432/www.architecture.org), is the newest cultural institution to pay homage to those that literally shaped the city. Its 2001 opening finally provided a home worthy of the name for the Chicago Architecture Foundation, which for years was forced to sell merchandise and book its excellent tours (for which, *see p66*) from an underwhelming storefront.

Centre-stage here is the CitySpace gallery, which features architects' models, videotaped interviews with designers, an illustrated timeline of buildings and an understandably popular model of downtown Chicago designed by Skidmore, Owings & Merrill. Head to this space first, as the background it provides will make the temporary exhibits in the Lecture Hall and Atrium galleries that much more interesting.

Architecture 101 duly passed, you're free to head to the shop to book your tour, clear the shelves of reading matter and pick up a Frank Lloyd Wright umbrella. On your way out, be sure to check the searchable database of noteworthy buildings. After a visual rifle through this treasure trove of arches, arcades and atriums, you'll know exactly where to set your sights when you come back out on to Michigan Avenue.

---

verticality. With its abundance of large plate glass windows, the Reliance presaged the future of the modern-day skyscraper; in recent years, it's undergone effective renovations and is now the Burnham Hotel.

Other Loop buildings are just as typical of the style. Take Burnham's **Santa Fe Building** (née the Railway Exchange Building; 224 S Michigan Avenue): Burnham was so proud of it he moved his offices in there, and it now aptly provides a home for the Chicago Architecture Foundation (*see p26* **The basics**). Don't miss Burnham's majestic **Rookery** (209 S Lasalle Street, at W Adams Street), named for the birds that once inhabited it and boasting a Lloyd Wright atrium; or Sullivan's **Carson Pirie Scott Building**

(1 S State Street, at Madison Street), which makes use of another common design element, the Chicago Window, one large pane of glass flanked by two smaller opening windows.

THE BEAUX ARTS

When the World's Columbian Exposition (aka the World's Fair) came to Chicago in 1893, Burnham was tapped to oversee the construction of the buildings in which the exhibits were to be housed. However, the popularity of his gleaming white Beaux Arts classical constructions changed the course of architecture in the early 20th century, effectively – and ironically – outmoding the reigning Chicago School in the process.

Burnham's 'White City' was levelled when the Columbian Exposition ended, and the area was paved over to create Meigs Field, a small airstrip. However, its influence remains in three classic Chicago landmarks: 1893's **Art Institute** (111 S Michigan Avenue, at W Adams Street), the ostentatious 1897 **Chicago Cultural Center** (78 E Washington Boulevard, at N Michigan Avenue), designed by the New England firm of Shepley, Rutan and Coolidge, and Rapp and Rapp's restored **Chicago Theater** (175 N State Street, at E Lake Street).

Burnham is now best remembered for a contribution that lasted a little longer: the 1909 Chicago Plan, which mapped out the city's development. In addition to traffic-relieving bi-level thoroughfares around the downtown area (such as Wacker Drive, which hugs the south bank of the Chicago River), Burnham's plan minimised lakefront development, a shrewd move that resulted in the expansive lakefront parks that stretch from the South Side to the northern suburbs.

Other designers remained unimpressed by the Beaux Arts aesthetic, with one Wisconsin-born architect making a particular impact. **Frank Lloyd Wright** began his professional career at the office of Adler and Sullivan, but after being fired for moonlighting, he set up his own practice in Oak Park. It was here that he formulated what would become known as the Prairie Style of architecture, and a walk around the neighbourhood in which he built 25 homes remains an enlightening experience. For more on his Oak Park work, including details of tours, *see p120* **The Wright stuff**; for more on his **Robie House** in Hyde Park, one of the greatest buildings of the last century, *see p123*.

TOWARDS MODERNISM

Chicago School had become old hat by the 1920s, and architects began looking elsewhere for inspiration. The result was a 20-year period when Chicagoans concentrated not on one style,

Day and night: the **Wrigley Building** (*left*) and the **Tribune Tower**. *See p29.*

The **Sears Tower**.
See p31.

but toyed with many. Take, for example, the **Tribune Tower** (435 N Michigan Avenue, at E Hubbard Street). The design for the offices of the city's largest newspaper, the *Tribune*, was chosen after a 1922 contest. The winning entry was the New York duo of Howell and Hood's limestone-clad 456-foot (139-metre) Gothic tower, complete with flying buttresses at its ornate crown. Embedded in the walls around the entrance are artefacts from significant structures around the world, from the Great Pyramids at Cheops to Notre-Dame Cathedral.

Just across the street is the **Wrigley Building** (400 N Michigan Avenue, at E Kinzie Street), a massive wall of a building completed in 1924 that rises majestically over the Chicago River. The white terracotta that covers the building starts off cream-coloured at street level, but gets lighter towards the top of the structure. At night, when the façade is illuminated by giant floodlights, the *trompe l'oeil* gives the building a glorious, glowing aspect.

Although it never really took off in Chicago, art deco did get a look in here. And there's no finer example of it than Holabird and Root's **Chicago Board of Trade Building** (141 W Jackson Boulevard), over 70 years old but still striking. Approach it down Lasalle for the full, dramatic effect, and look 45 storeys up for the crowning statue of Ceres. Other admirable deco buildings include the **Carbide and Carbon Building** (230 N Michigan Avenue, at E Lake Street), the former **Playboy Building** (919 N Michigan Avenue, at E Walton Street), and the onetime **Chicago Daily News Building** (400 W Madison Street, at N Canal Street).

The enormous **Merchandise Mart**, situated by the river at N Wells Street, was the largest building in the world when it was completed in 1931. The building's dramatic waterfall-style limestone façade rises 25 storeys above the Chicago River, with sculptures of the busts of some of America's leading merchants, including Marshall Field, A Montgomery Ward and Frank W Woolworth, lining the riverfront esplanade. The building was commissioned by Marshall Field to house the department store's wholesale operation, along with those of other furniture and interior design shops. It was sold to the Kennedy family in the years following the Depression, though a 1991 renovation created a public mall on the first two floors.

THE INTERNATIONAL STYLE

Despite all the local innovation, it took an outsider to kick off arguably the most striking period in Chicago's architectural history. Ludwig Mies van der Rohe arrived in the city in 1938, bringing with him the International Style. This new movement was founded in Germany

A lovely view

A little way beyond the left-field bleachers at Wrigley Field lies a curious little thoroughfare that, uneasily but proudly, recalls the horse-and-buggy days of pre-Edwardian London. If you stroll this shady Wrigleyville lane, don't be surprised if you imagine looking in a window to see Professor Henry Higgins admonishing flower girl Eliza Doolittle to once and for all, 'Stop dropping those aitches!'

An exaggeration, perhaps, but only barely, especially in comparison to the streets that surround Alta Vista Terrace. This narrow, one-block street, hemmed in by Sheridan to the north, Kenmore to the east, Grace to the south and Seminary to the west, is incongruous in the extreme, but has with it an absolute charm. The story goes that after a vacation in London, Chicagoan real estate developer Samuel Eberly Gross was inspired to create a slice of merrie olde England right in his own backyard, and acted on the impulse late in his successful career.

With the exception of the occasional lick of paint, Alta Vista Terrace has remained all but unchanged since its completion in 1904. The houses – and they are still all houses; none has yet been converted into apartments – are row homes, although this bland description doesn't begin to capture their attractions. The properties on the 'Street of 40 Doors', as it's nicknamed, are handsome, but the real joy is in the detailing: on the actual buildings, of course, but also in the way the street is made into more than the sum of its parts. Each side of the street echoes the other: the design of each individual dwelling matches that diagonally across from it, promoting what a plaque from the Chicago Historical and Architecture Landmarks Commission accurately calls a 'unity and harmony rarely found elsewhere in the city'. As architectural follies go, it's considerably more worthwhile than most.

but borrowed heavily from the strident simplicity of the Chicago School, ultimately carrying it to new extremes. Buildings in the International Style feature cubic shapes, long horizontal bands of glass called 'ribbon windows', low, flat roofs, and open floorplans divided by movable screen walls. Often coloured white, these buildings, usually constructed

Don't look down

Chicago's ten tallest buildings.

Sears Tower

233 S Wacker Drive, the Loop.
Completed 1974. **Height** 1,450ft/442m.
The tallest building in the US. The observation deck at the Sears, the world's tallest building from 1974 to 1996, is one of the city's most popular tourist attractions.
See p32 and p70.

Aon Center

200 E Randolph Street, the Loop.
Completed 1973. **Height** 1,136ft/346m.
Chicago's tallest building for only a year, and The Skyscraper Formerly Known As The Amoco Building. The exterior was completely repanelled when the marble that once graced it started to fall off a decade after completion.

John Hancock Center

875 N Michigan Avenue, Near North.
Completed 1970. **Height** 1,127ft/344m.
Chicago's tallest building from 1969 to 1973, the Hancock (*pictured*) is now part office building, part tourist attraction: its Skydeck offers better views than the Sears.
See p32 and p91.

AT&T Center

227 W Monroe Street, the Loop.
Completed 1989. **Height** 1,007ft/307m.
This grand office building was designed by Skidmore, Owings & Merrill, who also dreamed up the Sears and the Hancock.

2 Prudential Plaza

180 N Stetson Avenue, the Loop.
Completed 1990. **Height** 995ft/303m.
The tallest reinforced concrete building in town. Its elder (b.1955) and smaller (601ft/183m) sibling, 1 Prudential Plaza, is at 130 E Randolph Street.

311 S Wacker Drive

311 S Wacker Drive, the Loop.
Completed 1990. **Height** 961ft/293m.
In the shadow – literally – of the Sears Tower, this reinforced concrete building almost appears turreted at its top.

900 N Michigan Avenue

900 N Michigan Avenue, Near North.
Completed 1989. **Height** 871ft/265m.
Home to the Four Seasons hotel, a mall, a cinema, offices, apartments and a massive parking garage.

Water Tower Place

845 N Michigan Avenue, Near North.
Completed 1976. **Height** 859ft/262m.
It's another mixed-use building (apartments, shops, offices), but Water Tower Place looks dreary next to its neighbour, the Hancock.

Bank One Plaza

2 S Dearborn Street, the Loop.
Completed 1969. **Height** 850ft/259m.
Also known as the First National Bank Building, this Loop landmark is distinguished by its curving form and its Chagall sculpture outside.

Park Tower

800 N Michigan Avenue, the Loop.
Completed 2000. **Height** 844ft/257m.
One of the most recent cloudbursting additions to the Chicago skyline was built to house a new Park Hyatt hotel, after the previous Hyatt was knocked down in 1998.

Water Tower Place

from glass, steel and concrete, are devoid of ornamentation and regional characteristics. The emphasis is on the horizontal plane, even – perhaps perversely – in skyscrapers.

After serving as director of the Bauhaus from 1930 to 1933, Mies van der Rohe came to the US aged 52, where he became a professor at the Armour Institute (later renamed the Illinois Institute of Technology) in 1938. A year later, he redesigned the campus, creating a handful of striking buildings that demonstrated his affection for steel-framed glass and cubic abstraction, not to mention a willingness to make his buildings adaptable to suit the changing needs of the occupants. While they may lack frills, Mies van der Rohe's buildings are of unquestionable versatility and functionality. 'I don't want to be interesting,' he once commented. 'I want to be good.'

> ### 'Not everyone took to Mies van der Rohe, something apparent from the "corncob" towers of Marina City.'

Chicago offers several other opportunities to admire Mies van der Rohe at the peak of his powers. Upon their completion in 1951, the stunning **Lake Shore Drive Apartments** (860-80 N Lake Shore Drive, at E Chestnut Street) were light years ahead of their time. A classic example of the International Style, the state-of-the-art 26-storey twin towers were an instant commercial and critical success. The **Federal Center**, meanwhile, is the unofficial name of a grouping of buildings constructed between 1964 and 1975 at 200 S Dearborn Street (at W Adams Street). You'll immediately recognise Mies van der Rohe's signature curtain wall of glass, supported by steel black I-beams that support individual panes, emphasising the building's internal skeletal structure; indeed, almost turning it inside out in the process. The grey granite used to pave the plaza continues uninterrupted into the lobby, creating a feeling of openness and flow.

The 52-storey **IBM Building** (300 N Wabash Avenue, at E Wacker Drive) was begun in 1969 and completed after Mies van der Rohe's death in 1969 by one of the architect's associates. The architect, who told students that 'God is in the detail', lavished careful attention on every aspect of his creations, even going so far as to design the furniture for them. The building's voluminous glass-walled lobby – a Mies van der Rohe staple – is decorated with his chrome and leather Barcelona chairs, designed for an exposition in 1929.

BEYOND MIES VAN DER ROHE

Not everyone took to Mies van der Rohe's aesthetic, though, something immediately apparent from the two vast, 61-storey 'corncob' towers of the **Marina City** apartment complex (west of the Wrigley Building on the north bank of the river). Constructed of reinforced concrete, the individual floors of each tower are cantilevered out from the main core, which houses elevator shafts and garbage chutes. A theatre venue constructed between the two towers in 1966 is now occupied by the House of Blues.

Donald Trump's plans to build the world's tallest building on the banks of the Chicago River were shelved after September 11, so the tallest building in town will remain the **Sears Tower** (233 S Wacker Drive, at W Adams Street), undoubtedly the most famous

Smurfit-Stone Building. *See p73.*

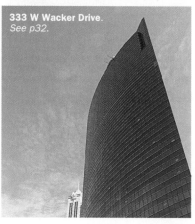

333 W Wacker Drive. *See p32.*

Look up when walking the Loop, or you'll miss details like these, on buildings everywhere.

skyscraper in Chicago. Formerly the world's tallest structure – it was unseated by the Petronas Towers in Kuala Lumpur, Malaysia, in 1996 – the 1,454-foot (443-metre) black aluminium and amber glass tower clearly owes a debt to the International Style with its chunky, cubist proportions.

At 1,127 feet (344 metres), the **John Hancock Center** (875 N Michigan Avenue, at E Chestnut Street) is second only to the Sears on the Chicago skyline. Vaguely pyramid-shaped, the building gradually tapers from street level to its top floor. The building's distinctive, visible X-shaped structural supports evenly distribute the enormous weight of the building and help it resist the tremendous forces of wind at its higher elevations. One of the world's tallest multipurpose buildings, the Hancock is occupied by retail outlets and restaurants on its lower floors, and office space and condominiums on the upper floors, while the building even boasts its own post office and supermarket. The top floor is occupied by an upscale (but of *course*) bar/restaurant and a slightly less exclusive observatory.

While the International Style Federal Center pushed the boundaries of what a government building should look like, Helmut Jahn's dome-shaped **James R Thompson Center** (formerly the State of Illinois Centre; 100 W Randolph Street, at N Clark Street) blew critics away when it was completed in 1985. Despite its stridently modern appearance, the building pays subtle homage to traditional government buildings, with its abstract suggestion of the classic cupola. The main attraction, though, is the wonderful 230-foot (70-metre) atrium created by the rotunda; ample lighting, exposed elevator shafts and mechanics, and reflective surfaces create a vibrant sense of movement.

Another attention-grabbingly curvaceous modern building sits a few blocks west on the banks of the Chicago River. William E

Pedersen's **333 W Wacker Drive** was built on the bend of the river, and its curved frontage echoes the shape of the waterway in spectacular fashion. Look at it from the opposite bank of the river, or – better still – from a moving boat, from where the subtly stunning ways the light and reflections play on the rounded frontage are best appreciated.

And now, as they say, for something completely different… If you have access to a car or don't mind a short train ride, take a day trip to the **Bahá'í House of Worship** (*see p108*), north of the city in Wilmette, Illinois, near Northwestern University. Completed in 1953, the Bahá'í House was the first temple of the Bahá'í faith built in the western hemisphere. Surrounded by quiet gardens, the breathtaking, gleaming white dome-like structure is covered with rich lacy ornamentation and inscribed with verses from the Bahá'í Writings. A visitors' centre offers additional information and maps. To get there, take the Red line north to Howard, then get the Purple line north to Linden and walk three blocks east. Arriving by car from the south, take Lake Shore Drive north to the Sheridan Road exit, then continue north on Sheridan to Linden Street.

The buildings discussed in these pages, along with many others, are highlighted by a variety of architectural walking, boat, bus and bike tours offered by the **Chicago Architecture Foundation** (*see p26* **The basics**; 312 922 8687/www.architecture.org). If you want to get the stories behind the architecture in the city, told with a rare panache and enthusiasm, head here first.

▶ For more on the architecture of **Astor Street**, *see p96*.
▶ For more on the **Sears Tower**, *see p70*.
▶ For more on the **Prairie Avenue Historic District**, *see p85*.

Fictional Chicago

Read all about it. Or watch it instead.

LITERARY CHICAGO

Carl Sandburg stared at the bloody stockyards of his home city in 1914 and saw a 'Hog Butcher for the World' (*Chicago Poems*, 1916). Sure, the restaurants are hip now, the buildings scrape the sky, yuppies rule the yacht-infested lakefront and condos are pushing out the meatpackers. But when it comes to the fictional image of Chicago, Sandburg set in place an all-purpose metaphor of blue-collar brawn and grit that neither seismic historical change nor a city perpetually concerned with bolstering its public image can ever entirely banish.

Born in Galesburg, Illinois and a leader of the so-called 'Chicago Renaissance' of arts and letters, Sandburg wrote about a city where the workers' shoulders were outsized. He told of women with painted faces who lured farm boys, of a hardbitten town where tools were made, where wheat was stacked, where the railroads seemed to handle all of America's freight, both actual and metaphorical. Sandburg's Chicago may have been strong, proud and alive but it was coarse. This was a city where you could read hunger on a man's face.

Sandburg was not the only brave soul who committed the stench of the stockyards to paper. The Baltimore-born **Upton Sinclair**'s 1906 masterpiece *The Jungle* told of spoiled meats, acrid acids and dangerous vats of lard in the stockyards. If there's one image that has pervaded Chicago's place in 20th-century literary history, it's the city's identity as a worker's town. In the 1930s and '40s, **Nelson Algren** – *The Man With the Golden Arm*, *Walk on the Wild Side* – set about achieving a youthful ambition: to become the closest thing to Gorky that America had produced. And it wasn't too hard to persuade readers and publishers that he was living in the right spot.

Algren's Chicago had achieved more industrial prowess and political might than Sandburg could ever have thought possible. And thanks to the wealth of the industrials and their status-hungry wives, culture was winning over carcasses. But Algren still saw a 'city on the make', and positioned himself as a scribe of the impoverished. So when Simone de Beauvoir began an affair with this self-styled poet of the addict, prostitute, murderer and prisoner, the

Made in Chicago Chris Ware

While it's not really a hotbed of illustrative activity, Chicago is home to a pair of globally known comic-book artists. However, the space between the two is night and day. At one end of the spectrum is Frank Miller, DC Comics artist and originator of the *Dark Knight* Batman series. At the other, the south to Miller's north, is Chris Ware.

Chicagoans were first made aware of Ware, who originally hails from Nebraska, when *Newcity* began running his work in the 1990s. A measure of fame came with Ware's comic-book series, *Acme Novelty Library* (which, by mid 2002, had reached volume 15). But his profile soared in 2000 when he published his first full-length graphic novel, *Jimmy Corrigan: The Smartest Kid on Earth*. The depressing story of a boy who one day receives a letter from a father he doesn't know, the book and its author were hailed as 'Genius' by the likes of *Time* magazine and the *New York Times*; in the UK, *Jimmy* went

on to win the *Guardian*'s prestigious First Book Award in 2001. With his adroitly intricate drawing, awe-inspiring use of colour and storylines that often end in tears, Ware has helped not only to redefine the comic-book genre, but also to legitimise it.

It's perhaps unsurprising to learn that Ware himself is almost as painfully introverted as his two main characters, Jimmy Corrigan and Rusty Brown (about whom Ware is currently working on a full-length book): you're unlikely to see him signing copies of his books or comic strips. **Quimby's Store** in Wicker Park (1854 W North Avenue; 773 342 0910) was the first place to sell Ware's work, and is still one of the finest and most unusual bookstores in the city. Quimby's has a large selection of Ware's work, although it doesn't yet have the *Rusty Brown* comic novel: Ware admits the work process is slow and expects it only to be 'done by the time the last of my hair falls out'.

Parisian sophisticate was slumming it. And when Algren brought Ms de B to Chicago to live in his one-room apartment in the Polish section of town, the feminist found herself hanging out around police line-ups and strip joints rather than drawing rooms and cafés.

'Chicagoans have never placed much separation between labour and art.'

The sex, say de Beauvoir's letters, was great. But in the end, Sartre and the South Bank won out over Polish sausage. Algren – and, by extension, his Chicago – felt betrayed. He'd surely forgotten his own published words of advice: 'Never sleep with someone whose problems are greater than your own.' A steak-sized chip on the shoulder is a vital part of the literary consciousness of the Second City, so the pain probably did Algren some good.

The literature of hard graft can be found in the works of **Studs Terkel**, the living poet laureate of Chicago grit and paradox, and an author best known for his five books of oral history that include *Working* and *The Good War*. He may have been born in New York, but Terkel is adored in an adopted hometown he once described as a 'city of hands', as distinct from all those other pretentious cities of paper. In fact, the only kind of paper Chicago respects

is newsprint. From **Ben Hecht** and **Charles MacArthur**'s 1928 Broadway pageant, *The Front Page*, to the mythology surrounding late *Tribune* columnist **Mike Royko**, broadsheet wordsmiths have always commanded a special respect. After all, it's writing in the form of honest daily labour. Or perhaps it's just because the ink comes off on your hands.

Chicagoans have never placed much separation between labour and art, and the divide between writer and the regular Joe or Jane is less pronounced than elsewhere. No one has much time for literary awards, writer's circles, aesthetic movements or other fanciness. And writers have usually had to leave town before they started making real money.

This house style – call it a city style – has resulted in native literary types that don't fit. You'll find the real **Ernest Hemingway** in Key West, not the Chicago suburb of Oak Park in which he was born: he never had it in his soul. Uncharitable souls said the same of Canadian-born **Saul Bellow**, a long-time Chicago-based author, professor and winner of the 1976 Nobel Prize for Literature, when he moved to Boston in the late 1990s. The town's most noted playwright lives in Boston, too, but his Chicago identity is far more secure.

When he was writing his early dramas and living on the North Side, **David Mamet** spent his days driving a cab. His singularly clipped and profanity-laden style of dialogue may have

reflected the new urban vibe of the 1970s and 1980s, but Mamet's Chicago was still a town of workers, even if the collars had turned white from fear. Adrift and in agony, the lost souls in *Sexual Perversity in Chicago* copulate more from desperation than abandon. If Sandburg's Hog Butchers had a 1980s equivalent, it was the hapless losers pedalling swampland from their Chicago office in *Glengarry Glen Ross*. Sales represented the rump of the American dream and Chicago was the place to make the cut.

Mamet's crowd, of course, rarely ventured south of downtown. Chicago's large African-American population and segregated urban divide have made the city a popular flashpoint for America's long series of agonised literary wails over the horrors of racism. In the historically pivotal 1959 drama *A Raisin in the Sun*, Chicagoan **Lorraine Hansberry** depicted heaven for Mama, Walter Lee and the other hard-working Youngers as a new house on Clybourn Avenue on the white side of town.

And when **Richard Wright** came here from Mississippi in the 1930s and imagined an innocent black man (Bigger Thomas) charged with the murder of a white woman in *Native Son*, he fictionalised a scenario that would be played out for real countless times in his adopted city. **Gwendolyn Brooks**, resident of Chicago since the age of one month, would have understood Bigger Thomas's agonies. 'Swing low swing low sweet sweet chariot,'

Brooks wrote in her poem *Of DeWitt Williams on His Way to Lincoln Cemetery*, 'He was nothing but a plain black boy'.

When poetry slam pioneer **Marc Smith** looks out at post-Sandburg, postmodern Chicago, he sees traders with suntans, players with railroads and a City of Big Business Ventures. In their leisure time, such folks likely read the artful bestsellers of **Scott Turow**, a Chicago author-lawyer who writes on the train on his way into work, or maybe **Bill Granger**, a *Tribune* journo turned mystery writer. So did the glorification of the worker go west with the information age?

Actually, fictional Chicago has always been shot through with paradox. **Hugh Hefner** published the seemingly Californian *Playboy* magazine here in the prosaic Midwest; and, in the 1910s, **Harriet Monroe**'s *Poetry* magazine specialised in TS Eliot and Ezra Pound, spawning its own literary movement. Chicago never could be reduced to hogs and social anguish, though two other early works, **Theodore Dreiser**'s *Sister Carrie* (1900) and **James T Farrell**'s *Studs Lonigan* trilogy (1932-35), come with plenty of the latter.

There is, however, nothing ambiguous about the literary influence of **Oprah Winfrey**. Once the publishing industry saw that a book-jacket sticker announcing 'Oprah's Book Club' sent sales through the roof, all new releases began to fight for the endorsement of the most famous

Upton Sinclair, king of the jungle. *See p33.*

Chicagoan. Predictably, there was a backlash. But when the snobby **Jonathan Franzen**, author of *The Corrections*, dared to suggest in late 2001 that an Oprah seal was a trashy moniker – several weeks after his book had been just so fêted, its sales boosted through the ceiling – he was promptly disinvited from the Chicago-based talk show and made to look like a petulant child. In the great Chicago literary tradition, Dame Oprah knows all about revenge.

CHICAGO ON FILM

A bulldog took a mouthful out of the leading man's arse during the filming of **The Tramp and the Dog** (1896), the first movie shot here. In the following years, 'Colonel' William Selig produced a slew of silent westerns, romances and animal adventures. As Selig's career flourished, so did those of his local competitors. L Frank Baum's Oz Films produced the first screen version of his **The Wizard of Oz** (1925), which featured Oliver Hardy making another fine mess as the Tin Man.

Several African-American film companies, including Foster Photoplay and Birth of a Race Photoplay, tried to redress racial stereotypes prevalent in mainstream film production. Director Oscar Micheaux, whose posthumous fan club includes Spike Lee and Julie Dash, is now lauded for his Chicago-borne creations, including a three-hour epic entitled **The Homesteader** (1919); **Within Our Gates** (1920), an initially censored attack on mob lynchings; and **Body and Soul**, which marked the 1924 film debut of Paul Robeson.

At the top of Chicago's huge silent film industry, however, was the Essanay Film Manufacturing Company. Founded by George Spoor and former Selig western star Gilbert

'Bronco Billy' Anderson, Essanay introduced such talents as gorgeous Gloria Swanson, heart-throb Francis X Bushman, cross-eyed vaudevillian Ben Turpin and Wallace Beery, perhaps film's first cross-dresser.

The most famous of Essanay's actors, though, was Charlie Chaplin, who commanded the highest weekly salary known to the 1914 film industry: a whopping $1,250. His **New Job**, starring Chaplin and Swanson, was shot entirely in Chicago and released in 1915, just shortly before a perpetually pissed-off Chaplin returned to California. The Essanay studios still stand, though remodelled, at 1333-45 Argyle Street. But the lousy weather and lure of Hollywood ultimately put an end to the Chicago film studios, and by the beginning of World War II, it was little more than a location shoot; or, when budgets were tight, a city to be recreated on sunny California sound stages.

While most actors and directors worked on their tans for the next 30-plus years, some movie greats managed to get shot in the Windy City. Based on an unsolved murder, **Call Northside 777** brought Jimmy Stewart to 1947 Chicago as a reporter struggling to help a wrongly accused man. With similar persistence, Cary Grant survived his narrow escape from a mercenary crop duster only to confront a suspicious Eva Marie Saint at the Ambassador East Hotel in Alfred Hitchcock's **North by Northwest** (1959). The film version of **Native Son**, in which author Richard Wright himself played Bigger Thomas, juxtaposed downtown glitter with life on the South Side.

Though **The Front Page** (1931) and its 1940 remake **His Girl Friday** created a fake Chicago in California, a young Sidney Poitier actually showed up here in 1961 to star in **A Raisin in the Sun**. Chicago also had its share of twisted cult hits, including **Mickey One** (1965), in which Warren Beatty played a comic pursued by mobsters and his own imagination (hard to know which is scarier), and **The Gore-Gore Girls** (1972), made by Herschell Gordon Lewis, the 'Godfather of Gore'.

Filming slowed further during the mayoral term of Richard J Daley, after he was angered by footage used by director Haxell Wexler in **Medium Cool**, which blended fact with fiction in its tale of a television cameraman's coverage of the 1968 Democratic National Convention and the ensuing riots. To punctuate the drama, the activist director sent his actors and camera crew deep into the fray in Grant Park to film several brutal scenes. The movie led to an unofficial ban on co-operation with filmmakers. Even for ready cash, permits were suddenly tough to snag.

On location

● The urban expanse known as **Daley Plaza** (50 W Washington Boulevard, the Loop) has hosted befuddled Neanderthals (*The Naked Ape*), Elizabeth Shue (*Adventures in Babysitting*), and National Guardsmen, tanks and 500 extras on the lookout for John Belushi and Dan Aykroyd in *The Blues Brothers*.

● For a holier Blues Brothers moment, check out the **Pilgrim Baptist Church** (3235 E 91st Street, South Side), scene of soul-stirring celluloid preaching by James Brown.

● **The Drake Hotel** (140 E Walton Place, Gold Coast) attracts a cosmopolitan crowd: Cary Grant and Eva Marie Saint graced the lobby during Hitchcock's *North by Northwest*; Julia Roberts plotted against Cameron Diaz in *My Best Friend's Wedding*; and Tom Cruise awaited *Risky Business* girl-for-hire Rebecca DeMornay in the hotel's Palm Court.

● Another hotel, the **Hilton Chicago** (720 S Michigan Avenue, South Loop) dates back to 1927 and has provided settings for *The Package*, *My Best Friend's Wedding*, *Home Alone II: Lost in New York* and *US Marshals*. However, it's best known for *The Fugitive*, where its Grand Ballroom, laundry room and towering rooftop provided the backdrop for Harrison Ford's athletic escapade.

● Remember the baby carriage that careened down a marble staircase during the shoot-out between Eliot Ness (Kevin Costner) and Al Capone's lackeys in *The Untouchables*? Well, the location where it was shot, **Union Station** (210 S Canal Street, West Town), was also the final destination of the Silver Streak, which crashed through a model of the terminus in the 1976 movie of the same name.

● Beware dark **Lower Wacker Drive**, replete with murderers (*Henry: Portrait of a Serial Killer*) and car chases (*Primal Fear* and *Thief*).

● Similarly, **Lake Shore Drive** has been the site of many high-speed escapades, including the Porsche-driving, pimp-eluding scene in *Risky Business*, the demolition derby finale of *The Blues Brothers*, and illicit Ferrari cruising in *Ferris Bueller's Day Off*.

● The prosthetics lab of **Cook County Hospital** (1835 W Harrison Street, West Town) helped Harrison Ford begin his search for the one-armed wife-killer in *The Fugitive*. Exterior shots of it show up regularly on **ER**.

● Robert DeNiro and David Caruso propped up the bar at **Club Lago** (331 W Superior Street, Near North) in *Mad Dog and Glory*.

Cusack turns it up in **High Fidelity**.

● *Backdraft* incinerated the former **Cuneo Press Building** (455 W Cermak Street, West Town), rousing Kurt Russell from his headquarters at the **Chinatown Fire Station** (4195 S Archer Avenue, South Side).

● The **Maxwell Street District Police Station** (943 W Maxwell Street, West Town) provided the exterior for the *Hill Street Blues* cop shop in the show's opening credits.

● Meg Ryan hooked up with one of the Baldwin brothers while bartending at the **Green Mill** (4802 N Broadway, Uptown) in *Prelude to a Kiss*.

● Nick Hornby may have set the book in London, but when John Cusack decided to move *High Fidelity* to Chicago for his movie version, he made the most of the location: among the real-life spots in which he shot are the **Music Box Theatre** (3733 N Southport Avenue, Lake View: Wrigleyville), the **Double Door** (1572 N Milwaukee Avenue, Wicker Park) and the **Silver Cloud Bar & Grill** (1700 N Damen Avenue, Wicker Park).

● In *About Last Night*, Rob Lowe and Demi Moore completed their sexual preliminaries at **Mother's** (26 W Division Street, Gold Coast). Non-fictional one-night stands remain a speciality of the bar.

● And finally, Paul Newman taught Tom Cruise the tricks of the trade at pool halls in *The Color of Money*. To trace their potting adventures, visit **Chicago's Finest Billiards** (6414 S Cottage Grove, South Side), the **Ginger Man** (3740 N Clark Street, Lake View: Wrigleyville) and **Chris's Billiards** (4637 N Milwaukee Avenue, Ravenswood).

Jake, Elwood and Mayor Jane Byrne changed all that. A cornball story that sent two besuited siblings careening through Chicago in an effort to save their childhood orphanage, **The Blues Brothers** was filmed in the city in 1979 and released the following year. Though it died at the box office, it proved a watershed for movie-making in Chicago: ever since, the city has been courting Hollywood with all the charm it can muster, drawing films including **Ordinary People** (1980), **The Color of Money** (1986), **The Untouchables** (1987), **Wayne's World** (1992), **My Best Friend's Wedding** (1997) and **Never Been Kissed** (1999).

Chicago's museums and housing projects have provided ample fodder for horror. A brain-sucking monster lurked in the basement of the Field Museum in **The Relic** (1996); **Candyman** (1992) munched at Cabrini-Green; and parts of **Damien: Omen II** (1978) and **Flatliners** (1990) were set in the Museum of Science and Industry. Elsewhere, **Risky Business** (1983), the getting-laid-thanks-to-a-friendly-call-girl story that gave the world Tom Cruise, is memorable for a midnight El ride with Rebecca DeMornay.

'They've always got snow machines running full blast in LA when they film *ER* – don't they know it's occasionally summer here?'

It gets worse, though. For among many other sins, Chicagoan John Hughes inflicted the so-called Brat Pack on an unsuspecting world. The careers of such barely pubescent actors as Molly Ringwald, Ally Sheedy, Judd Nelson and Matthew Broderick were launched by the acne-riddled Hughes films **Sixteen Candles** (1984), **The Breakfast Club** (1984), **Weird Science** (1985) and **Ferris Bueller's Day Off** (1986), while future child litigant Macauley Culkin was **Home Alone** (1990) in Chicago's poshest 'burbs. Ugly kid: who could blame the parents?

Hughes chooses to make his films here because he's from here. And as the city's actors, writers and directors have gained Hollywood clout, more folks have been bringing the cameras home. A product of the South Side, Andrew Davis has shot all his films in Chicago, including **The Package** (1989), starring Gene Hackman; **The Fugitive** (1993) with wrongly accused Harrison Ford; and **Chain Reaction** (1996), featuring the unlikely Keanu Reeves – who also starred in 2001's Chicago-set Little League flick **Hardball** – as a scientist. Many Chicago-trained actors also come back to develop new films, such as happened with

City chronicler **Studs Terkel**. *See p34.*

John Cusack's recent vehicle **High Fidelity** (2000). Other recent star-studded pics from Chicago include **Ali** (2001), complete with a bulked-up Will Smith, and Steven Soderbergh's Sammy-less remake of **Ocean's Eleven** (2001).

Sometimes, even clout-free local movies have broken out of the pack, especially if critics Roger Ebert and the late Gene Siskel lent their weight. Such was the case with acclaimed documentary **Hoop Dreams**. Filmed over four years by Steve James and released in 1994, it followed the lives of two African-American boys, aspirant basketball players both. A similar surprise success was the chilling **Henry: Portrait of a Serial Killer** (1986), which launched the career of director John McNaughton.

TV shows such as **Married with Children**, **The Bob Newhart Show** and **Good Times** hinted at Chicago locales, but never left the sun. They've always got snow machines running full blast in LA when they film **ER** – don't they know it's occasionally summer here? – but at least the show films its bloodcurdling crash scenes in Chicago: look for cars shattering plate glass windows and the like.

Television in Chicago, though, has all but dried up. In fact, MTV's **The Real World** was one of only two primetime shows that shot a full season here in 2001. Of course, one-time Cincinnati mayor Jerry Springer continues to broadcast the woes of America's lowlifes from his Streeterville base. But this dumb endeavour is no threat to the Queen of Chicago Media. From her Harpo Studios on the West Side, **Oprah Winfrey** – her again – dictates tastes, makes careers and has more significance in Hollywood than all of the Chicago silent movie pioneers put together.

▶ For more on **Hemingway**, *see p118.*
▶ For more on **Scott Turow**, *see p79.*
▶ For more on **The Real World**, *see p117.*

Little Walter.

The Blues

It's Muddy, it's Buddy, it's Jake and Elwood… It's Chicago.

Many styles of music are closely associated with one city. New Orleans and jazz, Memphis and rock 'n' roll, and Nashville and country, to name but three. Yet few cities are so wedded to a style that a subgenre takes its name from the town. This is one of the exceptions. Chicago and blues go together like ham and eggs, like bass and drums, like one bourbon, one scotch and one beer.

IN THE BEGINNING

Blues has its musical origins in the Deep South at the turn of the last century, and finds a direct musical antecedent in the call-and-response songs and improvised, often mournful field hollers sung by black slaves as they worked in the fields and on the plantations. However, with the development of the blues as a performing art, echoes of ragtime, minstrelsy and even church music can be heard in the music.

Though in the early 20th century, there was no real repertoire of standard songs, the forms that the songs took were themselves beginning to become standardised. The most resonant of

them took as its lyrical skeleton two repeated lines followed by a different but rhyming third line that acts as a pay-off: an AAB structure. It's this format that has held firm for a century as the hook on which a 12-bar blues is hung.

However, more fundamental to the genesis of the music was the use of microtonally flattened notes that fell outside the realms of the normal 12-note chromatic scale as played on a piano, and that hadn't been heard in American or European music before. Specifically, the lazy, pained flattening of the third meant that the music was essentially in neither a major nor minor key. These notes are known as 'blue notes', and lend their name to the blues.

It wasn't until Memphis composer WC Handy published *Memphis Blues* in 1912 that the word and the style became widely known. Handy was nicknamed the Father of the Blues, a misleading term: he merely popularised the style, and his music has little in common with latter-day blues. But Handy's success brought blues if not into the mainstream, then certainly some way towards it.

From here, the blues took a myriad of turnings. On one hand were the garrulous, almost vaudevillian female blues belters of the 1920s, such as Bessie Smith and Ma Rainey (most famous for her take on *See See Rider*). On the other were the likes of Robert Johnson and Charlie Patton, downbeat Mississippi Delta bluesmen who accompanied themselves on fingerpicked acoustic guitars. The songs were still mostly built around the AAB structure, but they were being interpreted in wildly different ways, from Texas to Georgia and various points en route. But not, yet, in Chicago, still a largely white town at the turn of the 20th century.

MELROSE PLACE

The history of blues in Chicago starts some two decades after WC Handy, with an ambitious local music publisher. Lester Melrose was strictly a small-time industry figure when, in the early 1930s, he approached two national record labels, Columbia and Victor, with a pitch to supply them with what were then called 'race records' – jazz and blues sides made mostly by African-Americans and tilted squarely at a black audience – with which to stock newly popular jukeboxes. The labels bought the proposal; all Melrose needed now were the musicians.

He was in the right place to find them. Hundreds of thousands of black Americans had moved to Chicago in the two decades leading up to World War I in search of prosperity in what was known as the Great Migration, and so the town had a deep and varied pool of black musical talent from which to draw. Someone had to draw on it, and Melrose got there quicker and with greater ruthlessness than anyone else.

Melrose's production business flourished; without him, it's likely that many Chicagoan musicians of the 1930s would have gone unrecorded. Among those he captured on tape and sold to Victor, which then released them on its Bluebird imprint, were Big Bill Broonzy, raised in Arkansas but resident in Chicago since 1920; pianist Memphis Slim, who arrived 17 years later; and Sonny Boy Williamson, known to his mother as John Lee Williamson in his hometown of Jackson, Tennessee. These three, though, were just the tip of a very large iceberg. Post-Depression, optimism was high and business was good. Melrose supplied the cuts, and Victor paid him. So he supplied it with more.

The advent of World War II put a stop to Bluebird. Shellac rationing meant fewer records could be cut; then, powerful musicians' union head JC Petrillo ordered a ban on recording in 1942 after a dispute over royalties due to musicians from jukebox broadcasts. However, the impact had been made. Melrose's work had established Chicago as a thriving blues capital

of sorts, even if many of his musicians were not native to the city and the blues they were playing – often with a full band, yet mostly acoustic and strangely polite in comparison to what came only a decade later – could hardly be pinned as uniquely Chicagoan.

Melrose is best remembered for two things. The first is that he was one of the first record producers to employ a house band to back up his artists, an idea later adopted by countless labels from Motown to PWL. Broonzy, 'Blind' John Davis and Washboard Sam were among the regulars Melrose used as sidemen.

> **'Chess was no labour of love: it was purely business. The brothers saw a gap in the market and worked flat out to fill it.'**

Yet Melrose also found fame for his tight-fistedness, a characteristic most apparent from the story of Arthur 'Big Boy' Crudup, a Mississippian singer who moved to Chicago in the late 1930s. When he arrived, he was so poor that his home was a cardboard box under the now-demolished 39th Street CTA station. But Crudup was spotted by Melrose playing at a party, and was signed to Bluebird almost immediately. Several minor hits followed.

The relationship turned sour when, in 1947, Crudup became aware that Melrose had not paid him royalties he was owed. Crudup left Bluebird and, with it, the spotlight. But when Elvis Presley's 1954 recording of Crudup's *That's All Right, Mama* hit pay dirt, Crudup was again denied his financial due. Despite taking Melrose to court, he still hadn't seen a penny of it when he died in 1974. It wouldn't be the first time a white executive was accused of exploiting black musicians in Chicago.

CHECKMATES

The irony of the black, urban, working class Chicago blues that emerged in the 1940s is that it took two Jewish, urbane, middle class Polish immigrants to bring it to a wide audience. Leonard and Phil Chess had arrived in Chicago from Poland as children in 1928, Leonard aged 11 and Phil four years his junior. By the early 1940s, the pair were in the nightlife industry, running bars in black neighbourhoods on the South Side of Chicago. Live music was essential to the success of their business, with the Macomba Lounge at 3905 S Cottage Grove Avenue doing a particularly brisk trade. It was the success of the Macomba, coupled with the brothers' realisation that many of the musicians

Label boss **Leonard Chess**.

they were hiring had no means to record or release their music, that led them to buy into a jazz-dominated local label called Aristocrat.

By the late 1940s, the blues had morphed wildly from its southern roots, as much out of necessity as anything. The relatively quiet fingerpicking and all-acoustic set-up just wouldn't do here: the bars in which the musicians played were too noisy, and the music got drowned out by boozy chatter. So in order to make themselves heard, musicians began to turn to electric guitars and other amplification. The blues, once plaintive and rustic, was now urban, aggressive and lasciviously sexual.

One of the first records the Chess brothers cut for their new label was *Johnson Machine Gun*, recorded by local pianist Sunnyland Slim. It was a notable release in that it didn't fit in with Aristocrat's jazz-leaning catalogue. But it was also important in that it brought the brothers' attention to Slim's guitarist, a 33-year-old gentleman whose legal name was McKinley Morganfield, but who was better known to local audiences as Muddy Waters. Waters was soon cutting his own records for Chess, and by 1950, when the brothers bought Aristocrat outright, changed its name to Chess Records and made it their business to concentrate solely on blues, he had become the label's anchor.

And it was the 1950s that made Chess and, with it, what became known as the Chicago blues. Waters was the linchpin of the scene and the local hero, enjoying success with tunes such as *Mannish Boy*, *Rollin' Stone* (from which a certain 1960s British band took their name) and *I Just Want to Make Love to You*. But soon, the American public was becoming acquainted with other bluesmen from the city. Harmonica wizard

Little Walter, bottleneck guitarist Elmore James and feisty singer Sonny Boy Williamson (no relation to the Melrose protégé, who was murdered in 1948 by muggers on the South Side) all had R&B hits in the wake of Waters' success.

Others had less commercial success but a considerable cultural impact. Howlin' Wolf's furied take on the electric blues, for example, was only really appreciated in later years. And multitasking producer/bassist/fixer Willie Dixon stayed largely in the background during the blues golden age, though his name appears on the writing credits for such staples as *Hoochie Coochie Man*, *Wang Dang Doodle* and *Little Red Rooster*.

It's hard to overestimate the impact the newly electrified Chicago blues had on popular culture. The music and its makers were still, of course, largely ghettoised. But change was on its way, albeit slowly. Jackie Robinson's appearance on a Major League Baseball field in 1951, the first African-American to play in the majors, was a signal event in the history of black America, but it found parallels in the quietly growing acceptance of black culture among white audiences. It would be many more years before significant progress was made, but this was a start.

SHOW ME THE MONEY

Having found success with Chicago blues, the Chess brothers branched out beyond the city, and beyond the blues, to greater financial rewards. Doo-wop acts such as the Moonglows and the Flamingos signed with Chess, but the real success came in 1955, when the brothers signed St Louis, Missouri's Chuck Berry to the label in 1955 and hit pay dirt with *Maybelline*. Bo Diddley, too, was attracting attention with his chugging rock 'n' roll on Checker Records, a Chess subsidiary. Still, the tale of Chess and rock 'n' roll would make a chapter by itself, one there's not room to write here.

The success of Chess spawned several imitators in Chicago, though none had the same level of success. Vee-Jay issued early records by John Lee Hooker, Jimmie Reed and – bizarrely – poet Langston Hughes in the years after its founding in 1953, while Cobra's most notable artist was Otis Rush. But by the time the 1960s rolled around, the popularity of Chicago urban blues was on the wane, a fact illustrated by the decision of Phil and Leonard Chess to let go of many of their blues artists. Junior Wells, Koko Taylor and Buddy Guy, Chicagoans all, emerged during the 1960s, but otherwise, pickings were slim. And while the blues had a positive influence on the music of Jimi Hendrix and Led Zeppelin (to name but two), the more generic tributes paid to it in the work of white musicians such as the Rolling Stones and overbearing local guitarist Paul Butterfield were well meant but ultimately unconvincing and more rooted in rock 'n' roll than the blues.

Like Melrose, the Chess brothers have often been accused of exploiting black musicians on their books. And like Melrose, there's some truth in this. In 1964 the Stones visited Chess to find Muddy Waters employed not as a musician, but as a painter in the studio where they were about to record. Bo Diddley, meanwhile, was not alone in griping about his lack of royalty payments from the pair.

Certainly, neither brother was a particular fan of the blues. The running of Chess Records was by no means a labour of love: it was purely business. Like all good entrepreneurs, the Chess brothers saw a gap in the market and worked flat out to fill it; the proof of this is apparent in the haste with which they cut back on their blues releases when rock 'n' roll hit big.

Yet the musicians, too, wanted and needed an outlet for their music, and Chess was more beneficial to them than competitors might have been. There was a respect between the two camps that there often hadn't been between Melrose and his musicians; both sides, perhaps, realised that the relationship was mutually beneficial. As Nadine Cohodas puts it in her marvellous history of Chess Records, *Spinning Blues into Gold*, the Chess brothers earned their spurs with the musicians because they made their living within the black community, not merely from it. It helped, too, that some blacks saw the Chess brothers as outsiders due to their Jewishness, an outsider status.

21ST CENTURY BLUES

The last few decades have seen the blues settle into an easy predictability, not just in Chicago but across the world. Yet, while popular, its most famous protagonists have fallen short of the mark. The music of Stevie Ray Vaughan was all bluff and bluster, poor man's Hendrix personified; for all his passionate live shows, the similarly heralded Robert Cray has failed to catch fire on record; and Eric Clapton's attempts have proven entirely worthy but entirely dull. All lack the raw power and energy of those 1950s recordings, which still jump from speakers with an ear-catching verve and vitality some half a century after they first emerged. But more than that, the contemporary blues tend to lack the era-defining, genre-defying originality.

The blues still carries on in Chicago, though, but now drags along with it a respectability it took 40 years to earn. The old Chess studio at 2120 S Michigan is now a museum, the Blues Heaven Foundation, while the Harold Washington Library holds a substantial blues

archive of documents, records and interviews. Conversely, though, the Maxwell Street Market, where many blues legends used to set up and perform for tips, has been bulldozed to make way for the University of Chicago. Progress, eh?

The blues has also become quite a draw downtown. At Blue Chicago, a wide-eyed, lily-white audience of conventioneers and tourists rack up extravagant bar tabs on their Gold Cards to the musical accompaniment of *Sweet Home, Chicago*. A half-mile away, the only real blues you'll get in the extravagant House of Blues hotel emerge when you see the bill at the end of your stay. Going only to either of these establishments and expecting to experience the Chicago blues is like showing up in the city with an urge to sample Chicago-style pizza and then eating only at Pizza Hut.

That said, of course, authenticity is notoriously elusive. The atmosphere at the South Side's Checkerboard Lounge, arguably the city's most fabled blues joint and long pinned as one of its grittiest and most real, today occasionally verges on tourist attraction status. Meanwhile, Rosa's, which opened in the 1980s about as far on the South Side as it's possible to get, draws its fair share of tourists and has managed to become the consensus pick as the town's best blues club among aficionados, purists and musicians.

In other words, authenticity doesn't guarantee quality, and vice versa. You want a down and dirty Chicagoan blues experience? Take a cab to the South Side, still every bit as inaccessible, black-dominated and dangerous as it was 50 years ago, and check out what's going on at neighbourhood hangouts such as Lee's Unleaded Blues or the Celebrity Lounge. But you want to hear decent blues? You're just as likely to find it uptown as down south.

For blues is mainstream now, a long way removed from its oppressed roots in the Deep South. And Chicago blues, at least for most visitors and locals, is miles away – in geography and spirit – from its South Side origins. Whether you approach it via a Disneyfied juke joint downtown or an unheralded corner bar away from the tourist drag – or any number of places in between – is up to you. But before you do, listen to some of the classic old cuts from the late 1940s and early 1950s. And you'll understand why, over 50 years after its inception, Chicago blues is still remembered with such fondness, enthusiasm and reverence.

▶ For more on **blues clubs**, *see p222*.
▶ For more on the **Blues Heaven Foundation**, *see p85*.
▶ For more on **Chicago music**, *see p293*.

Accommodation

Accommodation   44

Accommodation

Some 30,000 rooms… And you still may not get one if you don't book ahead.

It's feast or famine when it comes to Chicago hotels. When a major convention is in town – such as the annual houseware and hardware shows or the restaurant show that draws in excess of 100,000 delegates – those 'no vacancy' signs are likely to pop up just as quickly as the prices. Annually, Chicago hosts myriad conventions, trade shows and other meetings that attract more than 4.4 million attendees.

Hotel pricing in Chicago is basically a case of what the market will bear. That room you're eyeing up just off the Magnificent Mile with the rack rate of $225 a night may be had for a mere $75 during a lean weekend in February. Then, just one week later, when a big convention is due to hit town, the price may balloon to $315.

Locals are amazed at the alacrity with which new hotels are springing up in Chicago. Even a sluggish economy hasn't put a dampener on the hotel-building activity (though the aftermath of 9/11 saw the hotels empty in a hurry and many hoteliers bite their nails nervously). The city has no shortage of rooms at the high end, aimed squarely at business travellers. Chicago's central business district now offers close to 30,000 hotel rooms. Recent openings have included superstars such as the **Peninsula Chicago** and the **Sofitel Chicago Water Tower**; more, such as a 1,594-room **Adams Mark**, are on the drawing boards.

Where Chicago disappoints is in the lack of rooms at moderate and budget rates. In summer and at peak convention times, this can be a prohibitively expensive city to visit from the accommodation point of view. However, when calling to book, always ask about special offers and deals: the discounts offered can be huge.

The rates listed below are meant as a guide, with the highest figure in each category the amount you can expect to pay in peak season. These prices exclude the crippling hotel tax, which runs to 14.9 per cent on rooms and hotel services. We've only listed those hotels within reasonable distance of downtown, though other chain hotels can be found further out of town (at O'Hare Airport, for example). For a list of 1-800 numbers and websites for the main hotel chains, *see p51* **The chain gang**.

BOOKING AGENCIES AND B&B

The **Illinois Reservations Service** (1-800 356 6302) provides a free room-hunting service for hotels within Chicago. If you cancel, you may be charged a booking fee depending on the hotel's policy. **Hot Rooms** (1-800 468 3500/ 773 468 7666/www.hotrooms.com) provides a similar service, though if you cancel, you will automatically be billed $25.

Bed and breakfast is also available in Chicago. If you'd rather avoid the big downtown properties, then B&B can be arranged in local properties through **Bed & Breakfast Chicago** (1-800 375 7084/773 394 2000/www.chicago-bed-breakfast.com).

The Loop

Deluxe

Fairmont Chicago

200 N Columbus Drive, at E Lake Street, IL 60601 (1-800 526 2008/312 565 8000/fax 312 856 1032/ www.fairmont.com). CTA Lake (Red) or State (Brown, Green, Orange, Purple). Rates $149-$349 single; $174-$374 double; $249-$449 suite. **Credit** AmEx, DC, Disc, MC, V. **Map** p305 J11.
Not only are these digs exceedingly comfortable – oversized bathrooms, separate dressing rooms, fluffy towelling robes, in-room spa services complete with chocolate-covered strawberries and champagne – but they're easy to get to without trudging down long corridors: none of the Fairmont's 692 rooms and suites is more than four doors away from a lift. This is the ultimate hotel for 'cocooning', given the ultra-comfortable guestrooms and in-house attractions. Tea is served in the art-filled sunken lobby and the art deco Metropole lounge attracts top jazz performers. Facelifts during 2002 closed Primavera Ristorante and gave a new look to sophisticated Entre Nous, adding a warm colour scheme. **Hotel services** *Babysitting. Bars (3). Business services. Disabled: adapted rooms. Gym. Laundry (valet). Limousine service. No-smoking floors. Parking ($33). Restaurants (2). TV lounge.* **Room services** *Dataport. Minibar. Room service (24hrs). TV: cable/pay movies/VCR ($62/day).*

Hotel 71

71 E Wacker Drive, at N Wabash Avenue, IL 60601 (1-800 252 7466/312 346 7100/fax 312 346 1721). CTA Lake (Red) or State (Brown, Green, Orange, Purple). Rates $129-$369 single; $149-$389 double; $550-$1,000 suite. **Credit** AmEx, DC, Disc, MC, V. **Map** p305 H11.
The former Clarion Executive Plaza, made over for autumn 2002, sports a new name, a new look, and a new milieu in a plaza created by the $300-million

Wacker Drive reconstruction. This 1970s high-rise takes on a funky appearance with fibre optics and video art in the lobby and 'ghost' mirrors in the elevator corridor. A major part of a $20-million renovation included remodelling guestrooms (claimed to be the largest in the city, a legacy from the building's intended function as an apartment block).
Hotel services *Bar. Business services. Concierge. Disabled: adapted rooms. Gym. Limousine services. No-smoking floors. Parking ($28). Restaurant.* **Room services** *Dataport. Minibar. Room service (6.30am-10pm). TV: cable/pay movies/satellite/VCR/web TV.*

Hyatt on Printers Row

500 S Dearborn Street, at E Congress Parkway, IL 60605 (1-800 233 1234/312 986 1234/fax 312 939 2468/www.hyatt.com). CTA Harrison (Red), LaSalle (Blue) or Library (Brown, Orange, Purple). **Rates** $159-$325 single/double; $550-$800 suite. **Credit** AmEx, DC, Disc, MC, V. **Map** p305 H13.
Hotels are relatively scarce in the South Loop, but this is a gem: historic, modern, comfortable and within walking distance of Grant Park, the Harold

The best Hotels

For staying in with the in-crowd
W Hotels. *See p45 and p57.*

For downtown lodgings at uptown prices
Essex Inn. *See p51.*

For new-school luxury
Peninsula Chicago. *See p53.*

For old-school luxury
The Drake. *See p60.*

For uptown comfort
Willows. *See p64.*

For deafening decor
House of Blues or **Hotel Monaco**. *See p55 and p47.*

For the views
The Swissôtel. *See p45.*

For a home suite home
Embassy Suites Hotel Chicago Downtown–Lakefront. *See p55.*

For affordable Gold Coast lodgings
The Claridge. *See p62.*

For star value
The Omni Ambassador East. *See p63 and p60* **Star gazing**.

Washington Library Center, the Loop theatre district and State Street's shops. The stylish 161-room hotel occupies the shell of two historic buildings, one of which was a printing plant; the design and decor are influenced by Frank Lloyd Wright. The rooms, all of which were renovated in 2001, are sleek and equipped with high-tech electronics for work and play, while off the lobby is Prairie, known for its creative adaptations of heartland cooking (*see p126*).
The other main Hyatt in downtown Chicago, the **Hyatt Regency** (151 E Wacker Drive, the Loop; 1-800 233 1234/312 565 1234), has less character and is aimed squarely at the convention market. That said, with two huge towers holding over 2,000 rooms, it does hold the crown for the biggest Hyatt in the world.
Hotel services *Babysitting. Bar. Business services. Concierge. Disabled: adapted rooms. Gym. Laundry (valet). Limousine service. No-smoking floors. Parking ($31). Restaurant. Lounge.* **Room services** *Dataport. Minibar. Room service (6am-10pm). Turndown (on request). TV: cable/pay movies.*

Swissôtel

323 E Wacker Drive, at N Columbus Drive, IL 60601 (1-800 654 7263/312 565 0565/fax 312 565 9930/ www.swissotel.com). CTA Lake (Red) or State (Brown, Green, Orange, Purple). **Rates** $269-$449 single/double; $595-$2,500 suite. **Credit** AmEx, DC, Disc, MC, V. **Map** p305 J11.
In another key move on the chessboard of hotel ownership, the Raffles group of Singapore acquired this property in 2001. Occupying a triangular glass highrise, it's high-tech, from ergonomically designed furniture to a 42nd-floor state-of-the-art fitness spa offering amazing views of Lake Michigan. In fact, every room is designed to provide a lake or river view. Carnivores will find prime beef at Palm, while the new owners introduce a clutch of restaurants.
Hotel services *Bars (2). Business services. Concierge. Disabled: adapted rooms. Gym. Laundry. Limousine service. No-smoking floors. Parking ($33). Restaurants (4). Swimming pool (indoor).* **Room services** *Dataport. Minibar. Room service (24hrs). Turndown (on request). TV: cable/pay movies/satellite/VCR/web TV.*

W Chicago City Center

172 W Adams Street, at N LaSalle Street, IL 60603 (1-877 946 8357/312 332 1200/fax 312 917 5771/www.whotels.com). CTA Quincy (Brown, Orange, Purple). **Rates** $155-$429 single/double; $350-$1,000 suite. **Credit** AmEx, DC, Disc, MC, V. **Map** p305 H12.
Since it began life in 1929 as a private men's club, this stunning Beaux Arts building has undergone major changes. The most recent was a full-scale renovation that converted it in 2001 to one of Starwood's globally hip W Hotels. Thankfully, the mahogany and marble two-storey lobby featuring vaulted arches and a gold-leaf ceiling was left intact. Most evenings, the lobby is abuzz with the spill-out from the We restaurant and bar, which a young, hip crowd of locals has made its own. With high-tech

As the girls fought desperately for the attention of the
Parisian known only as Jacque, a complimentary plate of
brie was being delivered to their room courtesy of the
concierge who thought it was he, the girls had fancied.

Born of modern style and historic
passion, the Hotel Burnham is truly
a luxurious and unique Chicago
experience. From the turn of the
century wrought iron and glass

facades in the lobby to the seductively
extravagant rooms, Hotel Burnham is
the ideal place to bring your highest
expectations. Join us this weekend for
a getaway you won't soon forget.

The Atwood Café at the **Hotel Burnham**.

extras such as high-speed dataport connectivity, the property offers 390 guestrooms, 11 suites and 38 loft-style rooms.
Hotel services: *Babysitting. Bars (3). Business services. Concierge. Disabled: adapted rooms. Gym. Laundry (valet). Limousine service. No-smoking floors. Parking ($32). Restaurant.* **Room services**: *Dataport. Minibar. Room service (6am-11pm). Turndown (on request). TV: cable/pay movies.*

Expensive

Hotel Burnham

1 W Washington Street, at N State Street, IL 60602 (1-877 294 9712/312 782 1111/fax 312 782 0899/www.burnhamhotel.com). CTA Washington (Blue, Red). **Rates** $139-$295 single/double; $189-$395 suite. **Credit** AmEx, DC, Disc, MC, V. **Map** p305 H12.
One of Chicago's newest hotels is also one of its oldest: the Reliance Building, right in the thick of things on State Street, was developed in 1894 by gifted architects Burnham and Root, and was beautifully restored a century later after a period of disrepair (*see p25*). It's now a National Historic Landmark. There are 103 guestrooms and 19 suites, with rooms bearing the Kimpton Group's colourful trademark decor: here, it's indigo blue and gold fabrics mixed with mischievous cherubs and musical figures. Staff are convivial, and the atmosphere is one of easy, unenforced jollity. The Atwood Café is a good spot for dinner and an even better place for lunch.

Hotel services *Bar. Business services. Concierge. Disabled: adapted rooms. Gym. Limousine service. No-smoking floors. Parking ($29). Restaurant.* **Room services** *Dataport. Minibar. Room service (24hrs). Turndown. TV: cable/pay movies.*

Hotel Monaco

225 N Wabash Avenue, at E Wacker Drive, IL 60601 (1-800 397 7661/312 960 8500/fax 312 960 8538/www.monaco-chicago.com). CTA Lake (Red) or State (Brown, Green, Orange, Purple). **Rates** $139-$299 single/double; $239-$425 suite. **Credit** AmEx, DC, Disc, MC, V. **Map** p305 H11.
Designer Cheryl Rowley had a blast decorating the outrageous, colourful lobby of this boutique, and it works. Indeed, the lobby is a popular evening gathering place where complimentary wine is served around a limestone fireplace, while the 192 rooms pick up the colourful theme with bright red quilted headboards and warm greens and yellows; amenities include robes and mahogany writing desks. Off the lobby is Mossant, which serves what some claim are Chicago's best pommes frites (*see p127*). Nice gimmicks include offering each guest a pet for the duration of their stay and 'meditation stations' – climb-in, cushioned window nooks.
Hotel services *Babysitting. Bar. Business services. Concierge. Disabled: adapted rooms. Gym. Laundry (valet). No-smoking floors. Parking ($28). Restaurant.* **Room services** *Dataport. Minibar. Room service (24hrs). Turndown (on request). TV: cable/pay movies.*

Accommodation

Palmer House Hilton

*17 E Monroe Street, at S State Street, IL 60603
(1-800 445 8667/312 726 7500/fax 312 917 1707/
www.chicagohilton.com). CTA Monroe (Blue, Red).*
Rates $129-$349 single/double; $400-$1,100 suite.
Credit AmEx, DC, Disc, MC, V. **Map** p305 H11.
On 26 September 1871, the first Palmer House opened
to the public. Just 13 days later, it burned to the
ground in the Chicago Fire. Undaunted, Potter
Palmer raised the money to rebuild and the hotel was
back in business by July 1873. Although it has the
distinction of being the longest continuously operat-
ing hotel in America, it constantly updates guest
amenities. Its opulent lobby is a showpiece, with
Victorian and Florentine gilt and frescoes and a spectacular ceiling with 26 individual oil paintings by
noted 19th-century muralist Louis Pierre Rigal. Find
exotic cocktails at Trader Vic's and bountiful buffets
at the French Quarter.
Hotel services *Babysitting. Bars (3). Beauty salon
(unisex). Business services. Concierge. Cooking
facilities (some suites). Disabled: adapted rooms.
Gym. Laundry valet. Limousine service. No-smoking
rooms. Parking ($23-$31). Restaurants (3).
Swimming pool (indoor). TV lounge.* **Room
services** *Kitchenette. Minibar. Room service
(6am-2am). Turndown (Executive Level only). TV:
cable/pay movies/satellite. VCR (chargeable service).*

Renaissance Chicago Hotel

*1 W Wacker Drive, at N State Street, IL 60601
(1-800 468 3571/312 372 7200/fax 312 372 0093/
www.renaissancehotel.com). CTA Lake (Red) or State
(Brown, Green, Orange, Purple).* **Rates** $199-$279
single; $199-$279 double; $339-$539 suite.
Credit AmEx, DC, Disc, MC, V. **Map** p305 H11.
This comfortable hotel is ideal for the kind of person
who likes to cover all bases. It's large but not too large,
with 27 storeys and 553 rooms, and is well located for
the Loop, the Mag Mile and the downtown financial
enclaves. For those who prefer to eat in, the Great
Street Restaurant features a contemporary American
menu and Cuisines Café is a French bistro with pastries, light luncheon fare and Starbucks coffee. All
guestrooms have bay windows, with views of the
skyline, the river and (a distant) Lake Michigan.
Hotel services *Babysitting. Bars (2). Beauty salon.
Business services. Concierge. Disabled: adapted
rooms. Gym. Laundry. Limousine service. No-smoking
rooms. Parking (valet: $32). Restaurants (2).
Swimming pool (indoor).* **Room services** *Dataport.
Minibar. Room service (24hrs). Turndown. TV:
cable/pay movies/web TV.*

Sheraton Chicago Hotel & Towers

*301 E North Water Street, at N Columbus Drive, IL
60611 (1-800 233 4100/312 464 1000/fax 312 329
6929/www.sheratonchicago.com). CTA Grand (Red).*
Rates $99-$299 single/double; $350-$3,500 suite.
Credit AmEx, DC, Disc, MC, V. **Map** p306 J11.
This 1.2 million sq ft (111,600sq m) Near North behe-
moth catches the rhythms of the river it overlooks.
A massive lobby with imported marble and rich
wood accents has huge picture windows, while at
Waves lobby piano bar, ceiling mirrors reflect the

river and create a wave-like effect. Spectators is an
upscale sports bar with comfortable green leather
couches and views of the Centennial Fountain that,
in warm weather months, periodically arcs a jet of
water across the river. At each end of the lobby are
quiet, perpetual waterfalls in black granite, while the
glass entrance doors mimic Frank Lloyd Wright.
Hotel services *Bars (3). Business services.
Concierge. Disabled: adapted rooms. Gym. Laundry
(valet). No-smoking rooms. Parking ($23-$32).
Restaurants (4). Swimming pool (indoor).* **Room
services** *Dataport. Minibar. Room service (24hrs).
Turndown (on request). TV: cable/pay movies.*

Silversmith

*10 S Wabash Drive, at E Madison Street, IL 60603
(1-800 227 6963/312 372 7696/fax 312 372 7320/
www.crowneplaza.com/chi-silversmith). CTA Madison
(Brown, Green, Orange, Purple) or Monroe (Blue,
Red).* **Rates** $149-$259 single/double; $169-$299 suite.
Credit AmEx, DC, Disc, MC, V. **Map** p305 H12.
Tucked away under the El, this boutique hotel has
a deliberate Frank Lloyd Wright flavour, including
a wrought-iron accent piece in each room. Listed on
the National Register of Historic Landmarks, the
1897 building is handsomely clad in dark green,
highly glazed terracotta, and was built to house
silversmiths (hence the name) and jewellers. The
lobby takes on a companionable air 5-9pm with a
cash bar, and from Monday to Thursday at 9pm,
complimentary evening dessert is served: coffee, tea,
gourmet cheesecake and freshly-baked cookies.
Hotel services *Babysitting. Bar. Business services.
Concierge. Disabled: adapted rooms. Gym. Laundry
(valet). Limousine service. No-smoking floors.
Parking ($25). Restaurant.* **Room services**
*Dataport. Minibar. Room service (6am-midnight).
Turndown. TV: cable/pay movies/web TV.*

Moderate

Congress Plaza

*520 S Michigan Avenue, at E Congress Parkway, IL
60605 (1-800 635 1666/312 427 3800/fax 312 427
7264/www.congressplazahotel.com). CTA Harrison
(Red) or Library (Brown, Orange, Purple).* **Rates**
$109-$185 single; $129-$210 double; $250-$700 suite.
Credit AmEx, DC, Disc, MC, V. **Map** p305 J10.
Although faded around the edges, this dowager is
alive and well and humming with activity. History
has been made in this hotel, built in 1893 for the
World's Columbian Exposition. Roosevelt accepted
the 1921 Democratic presidential nomination in the
Gold Room: peek inside to admire its intricate gold-
leaf filigree and four oil paintings on the ceiling. The
lobby has original mosaics and a White House chair
said to have been a favourite of several presidents.
If you request an east-facing guestroom, you'll enjoy
stunning views of Lake Michigan.
Hotel services *Bar (1). Business services. Concierge.
Disabled: adapted rooms. Gym. Limousine service. No-
smoking floors. Parking ($28). Restaurant (1).* **Room
services** *Dataport. Minibar. Room service (6.30am-
10pm). Turndown. TV: cable/pay movies/VCR.*

The **Hotel Allegro**. They don't do sedate.

Hotel Allegro

*171 W Randolph Street, at N LaSalle Street, IL
60601 (1-800 643 1500/312 236 0123/fax 312 236
0917/www.allegrochicago.com). CTA Clark (Blue,
Brown, Green, Orange, Purple).* **Rates** $159-$279
single; $159-$279 double; $225-$395 suite. **Credit**
AmEx, DC, Disc, MC, V. **Map** p305 H12.

The whimsical Kimpton Group transformed the old
Bismarck Hotel into a funky, colourful 483-room art
deco beauty that's pretty to look at and fun to visit.
The Allegro sports a showbiz theme: rooms are decorated in vibrant colours, while the theatrically
themed suites include one decorated like the set of
Rent. As at the other Kimpton hotels (the Burnham
and the Monaco), guests enjoy a daily complimentary wine hour. The adjoining 312 is operated by
celeb chef Dean Zanella and features creative Italian-
American specialities (*see p127*), while the Encore
Lunch Club and Liquid Lounge are more happening
hangouts. All rooms have fax machines, CD players
and complimentary coffee.
Hotel services: *Babysitting. Bar. Beauty salon.
Business services. Concierge. Disabled: adapted rooms.
Gym. Laundry (valet). Limousine service. No-smoking
floors. Parking ($20-$28). Restaurants (2).* **Room
services**: *Dataport. Minibar. Room service (6.30-
1am). Turndown (on request). TV: cable/pay movies.*

South Loop

Deluxe

Hilton Chicago

*720 S Michigan Avenue, at E Balbo Drive, IL 60605
(1-800 445 8667/312 922 4400/fax 312 922 5240/
www.chicagohilton.com). CTA Harrison (Red).*
Rates $139-$339 single; $164-$364 double; $550-
$10,000 suite. **Credit** AmEx, DC, Disc, MC, V.
Map p305 J13.

Back in 1927, when this property opened as the
Stevens Hotel, it was the largest hotel in the world
with some 3,000 rooms. Although it's gone through
countless changes since then, it remains something
of a beast – virtually a city within a city – with 1,544
rooms. The vast, always-crowded public spaces are
decorated with fine art, flower arrangements and
plush carpets. A concierge level in the tower has its
own check-in and levels of pampering consistent
with the premium prices. Kitty O'Shea's is an Irish-
ish pub where the brogues are real (thanks to an
exchange programme with Ireland), while
Buckingham's fine-dining restaurant offers prime
beef and single malt Scotch.

Hotel services *Babysitting. Bars (3). Beauty salon. Business services. Concierge. Disabled: adapted rooms. Gym. Laundry. Limousine service. No-smoking floors. Parking ($23-$28). Restaurants (3). Swimming pool (indoor).* **Room services** *Dataport. Minibar. Room services (24hrs). Turndown (on request). TV: cable/pay movies/web TV.*

Budget

Essex Inn

800 S Michigan Avenue, at E 8th Street, IL 60605 (1-800 621 6909/312 939 2800/fax 312 939 0526). CTA Harrison (Red). **Rates** $79-$169 single; $89-$179 double; $169-$475 suite. **Credit** AmEx, DC, Disc, MC, V. **Map** p306 J14.

This 1970s-style hotel has been made over, with the addition in 2002 of a rooftop indoor pool and fitness centre. As a result, you can get a comfortable suite with a million-dollar view of the lake, Museum Campus and Soldier Field for next to nothing. Parking, too, is a bargain at $20 with in-and-out privileges. All 254 rooms now include dataports, voicemail, cable TV and fluffy towels seven times the thickness of those they replaced. The Savoy Bar and Grill has also been renovated and offers a full-service menu. Located alongside Hilton's flagship hotel, this is in the 'best buy' category.

Hotel services *Bar (1). Business services. Concierge. Disabled: adapted rooms. Garden (rooftop). Gym. Laundry. Limousine service. No-smoking floors. Parking ($20). Restaurant (1). Swimming pool (indoor).* **Room services** *Dataport. Room service (5.30-11am, 5-8.30pm). TV: cable.*

Near North

Deluxe

Chicago Marriott

540 N Michigan Avenue, at E Ohio Street, IL 60611 (1-800 228 9290/312 836 0100/fax 312 836 6938/www.marriott.com). CTA Grand (Red). **Rates** $189-$339 single/double; $595-$795 suite. **Credit** AmEx, DC, Disc, MC, V. **Map** p306 J10.

As the century turned, the jackhammers stopped and this Magnificent Mile branch of the worldwide Marriott chain emerged from a cocoon of scaffolding sporting an elegant silver-grey sheaf of polished granite. This 46-storey, 1,192-room monster has acquired new neighbours since its makeover, including upmarket mall the Shops at North Bridge (*see p169* **Mall talk**). As it is, though, the hotel is quite self-sufficient with a pair of full-service restaurants, two lounges, a branch of Kinko's and a health club/sports centre that includes an indoor pool and an outdoor sports deck with basketball courts.

Hotel services *Babysitting. Bars (2). Beauty salon. Business services. Concierge. Disabled: adapted rooms. Gym. Laundry (valet). Limousine service. No-smoking floors. Parking ($32). Restaurant.* **Room services** *Dataport. Minibar. Room service (5am-1am). Turndown. TV: cable/pay movies.*

Hotel Inter-Continental

505 N Michigan Avenue, at E Grand Avenue, IL 60611 (1-800 628 2112/312 944 4100/fax 312 944 1320/http://hotels.chicago.interconti.com). CTA Grand (Red). **Rates** $189-$409 single; $209-$429 double; $375-$3,500 suite. **Credit** AmEx, DC, Disc, MC, V. **Map** p306 J10.

Architecture buffs love this 807-room hotel, built in 1929 as the Medinah Athletic Club. Get a tape deck from the concierge for a self-guided tour of eight floors that are an unusual textbook of styles: French Renaissance to Byzantine. Visit Tarzan's swimming pool: an opulent Venetian-style pool with stained glass and Majolica tiles where Olympic gold medallist and movie Tarzan Johnny Weissmuller trained. Guestrooms are also lavish, with rare woods, thick carpets and bedspreads that replicate a 19th-century French design. Although it hangs on to its history, this property is constantly upgrading itself, spending a quarter of a billion dollars since the late 1980s.

The chain gang

'So, you're not with the convention? Sorry, sir, we're fully booked.' Looks like you're staying out of the city centre. And possibly, if you're really unlucky, near the airport. Try these chains for details of all their Chicagoland locations.

Deluxe/Expensive

Hilton 1-800 445 8667/www.hilton.com.
Sheraton 1-800 233 1234/www.sheraton.com.

Moderate

Holiday Inn 1-800 465 4329/www.basshotels.com/holiday-inn.
Howard Johnson 1-800 654 2000/www.hojo.com.
Marriott 1-800 228 9290/www.marriott.com.
Radisson 1-800 333 3333/www.radisson.com.

Budget

Best Western 1-800 528 1234/www.bestwestern.com.
Comfort Inn 1-800 228 5150/www.comfortinn.com.
Days Inn 1-800 325 2525/www.daysinn.com.
Motel 6 1-800 466 8356/www.motel6.com.
Super 8 1-800 800 8000/www.super8.com.
Travelodge 1-800 578 7878/www.travelodge.com.

Hotel services *Babysitting. Bars (2). Business services. Concierge. Disabled: adapted rooms. Gym. Laundry (valet). Limousine service. No-smoking floors. Parking ($34). Restaurant. Swimming pool (indoor). TV lounge.* Room services *Dataport. Kitchenette. Minibar. Room service (24hrs). Turndown. TV: cable/pay movies.*

Le Meridien Chicago

520 N Michigan Avenue, at E Grand Avenue, IL 60611 (1-800 543 4300/312 645 1500/fax 312 645 1550/www.lemeridien-chicago.com). CTA Grand (Red). **Rates** $139-$350 single/double; $500-$1,500 suite. **Credit** AmEx, DC, Disc, MC, V. **Map** p306 J10.
You may feel inclined to don a jaunty beret for a stay at this 311-room addition to the French luxury chain. French is spoken at the check-in counter, whimsical French art decorates the lobby, and classic steak frites are served at a sophisticated bistro finished with mahogany and ruby tones. There's history here too. Enclosing the new hotel is the reconstructed limestone façade of the landmark McGraw Hill Building. Amenities include rich down duvets and bathrooms with a deep-soaking tub, separate shower and granite dressing table. The hotel sits atop the Shops at North Bridge (*see p169* **Mall talk**).
Hotel services *Babysitting. Bar. Business services. Concierge. Disabled: adpated rooms. Garden. Gym. Laundry (valet). Limousine service. No-smoking floors. Parking ($33). Restaurant.* Room services *Dataport. Minibar. Room service (24hrs). Turndown. TV: cable/pay movies/Sony playstation.*

Park Hyatt Chicago

800 N Michigan Avenue, at W Chicago Avenue, IL 60611 (1-800 633 7313/312 335 1234/fax 312 239 4000/http://parkchicago.hyatt.com). CTA Chicago (Red). **Rates** $365-$475 single/double; $695-$1,200 suite. **Credit** AmEx, DC, Disc, MC, V. **Map** p306 J10.
As the century turned, one of Chicago's luxury hotels disappeared, then arose phoenix-like as a 203-room superstar housed in a slender 67-storey residential tower, one of only 17 Hyatt hotels and resorts worldwide to bear the elite Park Hyatt name. High-tech to the core, rooms have DVD players and flat-screen LCD televisions. The stunning art collection includes pieces by Isamu Noguchi and Dale Chihuly and has as its centrepiece Gerhard Richter's rendition of Milan's Piazza del Duomo, purchased at Sotheby's in London for $3.6 million. Its restaurant, NoMI, has panoramic views, a terrace and French-inspired cuisine.
Hotel services *Babysitting. Bar. Beauty salon. Business services. Concierge. Disabled: adapted rooms. Garden. Gym. Laundry (valet). Limousine service. No-smoking floors. Parking ($15). Restaurant. Swimming pool (indoor). TV lounge.* Room services *Dataport. Minibar. Room service (24hrs). Turndown. TV: cable/pay movies.*

Peninsula Chicago

108 E Superior Street, at N Michigan Avenue, IL 60611 (1-866 288 8889/312 337 2888/fax 312 751 2888/http://fasttrack.chicago.peninsula.com).
CTA Chicago (Red). **Rates** $445-$455 single/double; $500-$4,500 suite. **Credit** AmEx, DC, Disc, MC, V. **Map** p306 J10.
This ultra-swanky icon, opened in 2001, spells luxury all the way, from a window-wrapped spa occupying the top two floors of a 20-storey tower to a distinguished art collection throughout. Bliss may be soaking in a marble tub as you look down on Michigan Avenue. Even high-tech bedside control panels are user-friendly. Find a piano tinkling in the minstrel gallery during afternoon tea, and a pally bar with live entertainment. Shanghai Terrace is a contemporary version of a 1930s Shanghai cocktail and supper club, with French doors opening on to a terrace for alfresco dining (try the dim sum).
Hotel services *Babysitting. Bar. Business services. Concierge. Disabled: adapted rooms. Garden. Gym. Laundry (valet). Limousine service. No-smoking floors. Parking ($35). Restaurants (5). Swimming pool (indoor).* Room services *Dataport. Minibar. Room service (24hrs). Turndown. TV: cable/pay movies/web TV.*

Expensive

See also p63 **Omni Chicago**, *and p62* **Westin River North**.

Allerton Crowne Plaza

701 N Michigan Avenue, at E Huron Street, IL 60611 (1-800 621 8311/312 440 1500/fax 312 440 1819/www.allertonchi.crowneplaza.com). CTA Chicago (Red). **Rates** $129-$209 single/double; $159-$259 suite. **Credit** AmEx, DC, Disc, MC, V. **Map** p306 J10.
It's a case of déjà vu at this 443-room historic hotel, which reopened in the late 1990s after a $50-million restoration: vintage photographs and blueprints were used to restore the brickwork and carved stone details of the northern Italian Renaissance exterior. The Allerton was built in 1924 as a men's 'club hotel' and was Michigan Avenue's first high-rise. Since designated as a historic landmark, it was widely known for the Tip Top Tap (a sign still glows from atop the hotel), a popular 1940s and '50s lounge. Taps on Two specialises in heartland cuisine.
Hotel services *Babysitting. Bar. Business services. Concierge. Disabled: adapted rooms. Gym. Laundry (valet). Limousine service. No-smoking floors. Parking ($32). Restaurant.* Room services *Dataport. Minibar. Room service (24hrs). Turndown. TV: cable/pay movies.*

Doubletree Guest Suites

198 E Delaware Place, at N Mies van der Rohe Way, IL 60611 (1-800 424 2900/312 664 1100/fax 312 664 9881/www.doubletreehotels.com). CTA Chicago (Red). **Rates** $129-$349 suite. **Credit** AmEx, DC, Disc, MC, V. **Map** p306 J9.
Climb out of the indoor pool on the 30th floor, and huge windows reveal a larger body of water – Lake Michigan – stretching toward the horizon. Located in the shadow of the Hancock Center, this all-suites hotel is anchored by two excellent restaurants. Mrs Park's Tavern is full-service and upscale, while the

well-regarded Park Avenue Café is more formal and open only for dinner and a superb Sunday dim sum brunch. Comfortable suites feature a bedroom with separate parlour and convertible sofa, while a $7-million lobby refurbishment has created a spacious, pleasant area.
Hotel services *Babysitting. Bars (3). Business services. Concierge. Disabled: adpated rooms. Gym. Laundry (valet). Limousine service. No-smoking floors. Parking ($32). Restaurants (2). Swimming pool (indoor).* **Room services** *Dataport. Minibar. Room service (24hrs). TV: cable/pay movies/web TV.*

Embassy Suites Hotel Chicago Downtown–Lakefront
511 N Columbus Drive, at E Ohio Street, IL 60611 (1-866 866 8098/312 836 5900/fax 312 836 5901/ www.chicagoembassy.com/1.html). CTA Grand (Red). **Rates** $139-$349 suite. **Credit** AmEx, DC, Disc, MC, V. **Map** p306 H10.
This all-suites hotel opened in 2001 and is destined to become a Streeterville hotspot, as it adds to the facility list a 21-screen movie complex, health spa, two restaurants and shops. Built with the chain's signature atrium (15 storeys high), the hotel has an attractive lobby with waterfall and reflective pool. Room rates include cooked-to-order breakfasts and two-hour cocktail parties with free premium booze. Stretch your budget further by taking advantage of the suite's galley kitchen. On weekdays, this property is popular with business travellers (and those who approve their expense accounts); on weekends, economy-minded families take over.
The **Embassy Suites Chicago Downtown** (600 N State Street, Near North; 1-800 362 1779/312 943 3800) is not quite as smart, but it still offers fine accommodation at similar prices and contains an indoor pool and fitness centre.
Hotel services *Babysitting. Bar. Business services. Concierge. Disabled: adapted rooms. Gym. Laundry (valet). Limousine service. No-smoking floors. Parking ($25-$31). Restaurant. Swimming pool (indoor).* **Room services** *Dataport. Kitchenette. Room service (11am-11pm). Turndown. TV: cable/pay movies.*

Fitzpatrick Chicago Hotel
166 E Superior Street, at N Michigan Avenue, IL 60611 (312 787 6000/fax 312 787 6133/ www.fitzpatrickhotels.com). CTA Chicago (Red). **Rates** $129-$309 single/double; $159-$419 suites. **Credit** AmEx, DC, Disc, MC, V. **Map** p306 J10.
Dublin-based ownership of this property has brought all things Irish to Streeterville, from the name on the marquee and pictures of GBS and Brendan Behan in the pub, to beef and Guinness pie on the menu and a concierge with the brogue of County Clare. A complete makeover has brightened up the rooms while keeping one of its finest assets, the rooftop pool. Off the lobby is Benihana, the popular Japanese steak-house; downstairs, Fitzers is decorated with solid wood furniture and offers Guinness on tap, plus fish and chips, Irish stew, corned beef and cabbage (all preciously listed as main 'fayre').

Hotel services *Babysitting. Bar. Beauty salon. Business services. Concierge. Disabled: adapted rooms. Gym. Laundry (valet). Limousine service. No-smoking floors. Parking ($33). Restaurant (breakfast only). Swimming pool (indoor).* **Room services** *Dataport. Minibar. Room service (24hrs). Turndown. TV: cable/pay movies.*

Hilton Garden Inn
10 E Grand Avenue, at N State Street, IL 60611 (1-800 445 8667/312 595 0000/fax 312 595 0955/ www.chicagodowntownnorth.gardeninn.com). CTA Grand (Red). **Rates** $99-$309 single/double; $350-$425 suite. **Credit** AmEx, DC, Disc, MC, V. **Map** p306 H10.
This spin-off may be small compared to Hilton's Chicago flagship (for which, *see p50*), but it is North America's largest Garden Inn. The hotel has free fitness and business centres, but none of those added extras that you won't use but will end up paying for. As a result, this pleasant property is an attractive option, offering sleek rooms at trimmed prices. Guestrooms also have refrigerators and microwave ovens and a 24-hour pantry in the lobby stocks microwaveable cuisine. Opened in 2002, Weber Grill prepares food on big Weber grills, just as suburbanites do at backyard cookouts. Complimentary access is offered to Gorilla Sports, a Bally-operated fitness centre.
Hotel services *Babysitting. Bar. Business services. Concierge. Cooking facilities (microwave). Disabled: adapted rooms. Gym. Laundry (valet). Limousine service. No-smoking floors. Parking ($20-$30). Restaurant. Swimming pool (indoor).* **Room services** *Dataport. Kitchenette (microwave, fridge). Room service (6am-11pm). Turndown (VIPs). TV: cable/pay movies/web TV.*

House of Blues
333 N Dearborn Street, at the Chicago River, IL 60610 (1-800 235 6397/312 245 0333/fax 312 245 0504/www.loewshotels.com/houseofblueshome.html). CTA Grand (Red) or Merchandise Mart (Brown, Purple). **Rates** $119-$349 single/double; $350-$2,500 suite. **Credit** AmEx, DC, Disc, MC, V. **Map** p306 H11.
Guests get plenty of exposure to music at this spunky hotel in the shadow of Marina City, right by the Chicago River. There's the complimentary CD that comes at check-in, plus Sunday gospel brunch and a wide range of performers at the adjoining House of Blues club. The outlandish design, both in guestrooms and public spaces, makes it a fun place to stay. The decor looks like a 1940s movie set for an Arabian Nights-type production, including a huge gold Buddha guarding the entrance and vibrant, colourful folk art throughout. The complex houses the popular Bin 36, combining a cutting-edge restaurant, bar and wine shop.
Hotel services *Babysitting. Bars (2). Business services. Concierge. Disabled: adpated rooms. Gym. Laundry (valet). No-smoking floors. Parking ($28). Restaurant.* **Room services** *Dataport. Minibar. Room service (24hrs). Turndown (on request). TV: cable/pay movies/web TV.*

Peninsula Chicago. *See p53.*

See you at the bar

You could stay in your room and empty the minibar, of course. But that's not really much fun at all, especially not in a town so well stocked with real bars in its hotels. So, where to head for a sip or six among Chicago's hotel lounges?

You want upscale? You want the **Coq d'Or** at the Drake (*see p60*) or the **Pump Room** at the Omni Ambassador East (*see p63*), local legends both, or the classy **Metropole Lounge** at the Fairmont Chicago (*see p44*).

You want fashionable? You want any one of the bars at either of the **W Hotels** (*see p45 and p57*) in town, which are usually packed to bursting with black-clad hipsters with bursting wallets and swollen egos. That said, the less

ostentatious bar (and clientele) at **Peninsula Chicago** (*see p53*) ought to imbue you with enough kudos to get you through your stay.

And you just want a drink? You probably want **Kitty O'Shea's**, whose Irish theme comes with all the corporate transparency you'd expect of a Hilton bar (*see p50*), but which can at least be counted upon to pour a decent pint of Guinness. The Palmer House Hilton's branch of Hawaiian-themed **Trader Vic's** (*see p49*) is every bit as silly as the others. But for garish cocktails served in glasses the size of fishbowls, it's the only option. And if you don't go expecting the blues, then the **Kaz Bar** at the House of Blues (*see p55*) is usually a fun place to get loaded.

W Chicago Lakeshore

644 N Lake Shore Drive, at E Ohio Street, IL 60611 (1-877 946 8357/312 943 9200/fax 312 255 4411/ www.whotels.com). CTA Chicago (Red)/29, 65, 66 bus. **Rates** $239-$475 single/double; $675-$1,200 suite. **Credit** AmEx, DC, Disc, MC, V. **Map** p306 K10. Although suffering from an acute case of the Ws (Wave restaurant, Whiskey Sky nightclub, a 'whatever, whenever' button on the phone for 24-hour services), Chicago's second W Hotel is fun. Made over from a 1960s Days Inn, its Asian-influenced look has the stylish young urban professional crowd swarming to its lobby bar. Guestrooms, featuring teak furniture and dark red accents, look out on to Lake Michigan and the buzz of Navy Pier. Amenities include plush bathrobes, high-tech electronics and whimsical in-room touches (such as copies of the *Guinness Book of Records*).
Hotel services *Babysitting. Bars (2). Business services. Concierge. Disabled: adapted rooms. Gym. Laundry (valet). Limousine service. No-smoking floors. Parking ($33). Restaurant. Swimming pool.* **Room services**: *Dataport. Minibar. Room service (24hrs). Turndown. TV: cable/pay movies/web TV.*

Wyndham Chicago

633 N St Clair Street, at E Erie Street, IL 60611 (312 573 0300/fax 312 274 0164/ www.wyndham.com). CTA Chicago (Red). **Rates** $149-$349 single/double; $299-$499 suite. **Credit** AmEx, DC, Disc, MC, V. **Map** p306 J10. When Wyndham selected the Streeterville neighbourhood to establish its presence in downtown Chicago, it added another top-notch hotel/restaurant combination to Chicago's upper echelons. This full-service flagship occupies the lion's share of a 28-storey multi-use tower just a block east of Michigan Avenue. Its casual yet classy restaurant, Caliterra (*see p131*), quickly made the top ten lists of dining critics and has an attractive bar offering soft music

and a light supper menu. The generously sized guestrooms have nine-foot ceilings and offer high-speed internet access.
Hotel services *Babysitting. Bar. Business services. Concierge. Disabled: adpated rooms. Gym. Laundry (valet). Limousine service. No-smoking floors. Parking ($34). Restaurant. Swimming pool (indoor).* **Room services** *Dataport. Minibar. Room service (24hrs). Turndown. TV: cable/pay movies/web TV.*

Moderate

Best Western Inn of Chicago

162 E Ohio Street, at N Michigan Avenue, IL 60611 (1-800 557 2378/312 787 3100/fax 312 573 3180/ www.bestwestern.com). CTA Grand (Red). **Rates** $79-$189 single; $89-$189 double; $130-$375 suite. **Credit** AmEx, DC, Disc, MC, V. **Map** p306 J10. This modestly priced 354-room hotel provides a million-dollar location just a block east of Michigan Avenue. The standard rooms offer all the amenities that you'd expect from this chain, but you also get the opportunity to live it up in a penthouse suite for an incredibly low price. Upping the ante will buy a suite with access to a rooftop patio. Back down to earth, you'll find cheap eats at the Newsmaker Café, a basic coffee shop with an interesting and unusual theme: more than 200 photos and artefacts chronicling the history of journalism in Chicago.

Of the other Best Westerns in Chicago, the **Best Western River North** (125 W Ohio Street; 312 467 0800) offers similarly excellent value for money (not least because it has a rooftop sundeck, an indoor heated pool and free parking); the new-ish **Best Western Hawthorne Terrace** in Lake View (3434 N Broadway; 1-888 675 2378/773 244 3434) is a small but splendid gem; and the **Best Western Grant Park** (1100 S Michigan Avenue; 1-800 472 6875/312 922 2900) in the South Loop is slightly cheaper and slightly less appealing than its siblings.

Hotel services *Babysitting. Bar (1). Business services. Concierge. Disabled: adapted rooms. Gym. Laundry. Limousine service. No-smoking floors. Parking ($22-$24). Restaurant (1).* **Room services** *Dataport.Room service (6am-10pm). Turndown. TV: cable/pay movies.*

Courtyard By Marriott

30 E Hubbard Street, at N State Street, IL 60611 (1-800 321 2211/312 329 2500/fax 312 329 0293/ www.marriott.com). CTA Grand (Red). **Rates** $109-$400 single/double; $149-$440 suite. **Credit** AmEx, DC, Disc, MC, V. **Map** p306 H11.

Comfortable lodgings, competitive prices (a double in summer is usually under $200), superb location. Just two blocks north of the river, it's handy for the Loop's financial and theatre districts, yet is only a few minutes' walk from the Mag Mile. Business travellers can take advantage of a spacious desk and two-line phones with voicemail. If you simply want to relax, head for the gym, pool and sundeck. A café serves breakfast and lunch, while a bistro serves up casual dinners. A 2001 renovation spruced up the lobby and the 354 guestrooms and added high-speed internet access.

Hotel services *Babysitting. Bar. Business services. Disabled: adapted rooms. Gym. Laundry (valet). Limousine service. No-smoking floors. Parking ($19-$29). Restaurant. Swimming pool (indoor). TV lounge.* **Room services** *Dataport. Room service (4.30-11pm). TV: cable/pay movies.*

Hampton Inn & Suites

33 W Illinois Street, at N Dearborn Street, IL 60610 (1-800 426 7866/312 832 0330/fax 312 832 0333/ www.hamptoninn.com). CTA Grand (Red). **Rates** $89-$189 single/double; $129-$229 suite. **Credit** AmEx, DC, Disc, MC, V. **Map** p306 H11.

Most Chicago hotels of recent vintage are makeovers. This 230-room property opened in 1998 as the first newly constructed hotel in Chicago in five years (kicking off a surge of new hotel construction). It is, however, mindful of Chicago's architectural heritage: guests are treated to an exhibition of archaic photographs and artefacts from historic buildings, such as a stair stringer from Adler and Sullivan's Chicago Stock Exchange building. Rooms range from standard guestrooms to apartment-style suites.

Hotel services *Babysitting. Bar (2). Business services. Concierge. Disabled: adapted rooms. Gym. Laundry. Limousine service. No-smoking floors. Parking ($33). Restaurant (2). Swimming pool (indoor).* **Room services** *Dataport. Kitchenette (selected rooms). Minibar. Room service (6.30am-11pm). Turndown. TV: cable/pay movies/web TV.*

Lenox Suites

616 N Rush Street, at E Ontario Street, IL 60611 (1-800 445 3669/312 337 1000/fax 312 337 7217/www.lenoxsuites.com). CTA Grand (Red). **Rates** $199-$244 suite. **Credit** AmEx, DC, Disc, MC, V. **Map** p306 J10.

Long before Chicago became a major travel destination, this was a modest residential hotel. Lately, the neighbourhood has become a hot tourist draw,

making this hotel (with 324 studios and suites) a good buy. Regardless of blue-blood neighbours, you can save cash eating in: rooms include full kitchens (with stove, fridge and microwave), with dishes and utensils available on request. Guests receive a daily basket of baked goods and there's both an inexpensive diner and a branch of Houston's (great soups and salads) on the premises. Accommodation ranges from studios to one-bedroom suites.

Hotel services *Babysitting. Bars (2). Business services. Concierge. Cooking facilities. Disabled: adapted rooms. Gym. Laundry. Limousine service. No-smoking floors. Parking ($32). Restaurant (2).* **Room services** *Dataport. Minibar. Room service (6.30am-11pm). Turndown. TV: cable/pay movies.*

Marriott Fairfield Inn & Suites

216 E Ontario Street, at N St Clair Street, IL 60611 (1-800 228 2800/312 787 3777/fax 312 787 8714/ www.fairfieldinn.com). CTA Grand (Red). **Rates** $99-$199 single/double; $129-$249 suite. **Credit** AmEx, DC, Disc, MC, V. **Map** p306 J10.

Although its rooms have a formulaic similarity to those of other mid-range chains, this new property, completed in 2001, offers a great location-price ratio just a few blocks east of Mag Mile. Complimentary breakfast is served in a bright common room where fresh fruit, coffee and tea are available 24/7. There's also a small exercise room, free local calls and complimentary newspapers. In addition to 159 rooms (which, though plain, are comfortable enough), it offers 26 suites (containing 32in TVs and CD sound systems). Suites are a good buy if you snag one at the low end.

Hotel services *Business services. Disabled: adapted rooms. Gym. Laundry (valet). Limousine service. No-smoking floors. Parking ($33). TV lounge.* **Room services** *Dataport. Minibar. TV: cable/pay movies/web TV.*

Radisson Hotel & Suites

160 E Huron Street, at N Michigan Avenue, IL 60611 (1-800 333 3333/312 787 2900/fax 312 787 5158/www.radissonchicago.com). CTA Chicago (Red). **Rates** $129-$279 single/double; $159-$309 suite. **Credit** AmEx, DC, Disc, MC, V. **Map** p306 J10.

A rare and treasured asset of this mid-range, mid-size (350-room) hotel is its outdoor rooftop pool: it's a favourite spot among sunseekers, who occupy chaise longues sheltered by a glass windbreak and enjoy great views. The Radisson's location adjacent to the Mag Mile makes it popular with both tourists and business travellers. Guestrooms, which include 96 suites, are cosy and well equipped (including high-speed internet access), reflecting a 2001 renovation. Off the lobby is Becco D'Oro, specialising in excellent – if pricey – regional Italian fare.

Hotel services *Babysitting. Bar (1). Business services. Concierge. Disabled: adapted rooms. Gym. Laundry. Limousine service. No-smoking rooms. Parking ($32). Restaurant (1). Swimming pool (outdoor).* **Room services** *Dataport. Kitchenette. Minibar. Room services (24hrs). TV: cable/pay movies/web TV.*

The **Howard Johnson Inn** may not be much to look at, but the location's great.

Raphael

201 E Delaware Place, at N Mies van der Rohe Way, IL 60611 (1-800 983 7870/312 943 5000/ fax 312 943 5480/www.raphaelchicago.com). CTA Chicago (Red). **Rates** $99-$159 single/double; $199-$259 suite. **Credit** AmEx, DC, Disc, MC, V. **Map** p306 J9.

Spruced up for the 21st century with new tuck-pointing, the Raphael is one of a bounty of hotels east of the Mag Mile. Twinned with the Tremont (*see p62*), it's a perfectly pleasant place to stay for those seeking quasi-European lodgings in a central location. Opened as a hotel in 1978, the Raphael bills itself as 'Chicago's elegant "little" hotel'. Design-wise, there's something of a medieval vibe going on in the lobby, though the comfortable rooms and suites are done out in more of a 19th-century fashion. Staff are able to assist in most business-related tasks.
Hotel services *Concierge. Disabled: adapted rooms. Laundry (valet). Limousine service. No-smoking floors. Parking ($32). TV lounge.* **Room services** *Dataport. Minibar. TV: cable/pay movies/web TV.*

Budget

Howard Johnson Inn

720 N LaSalle Street, at W Superior Street, IL 60610 (1-800 446 4656/312 664 8100/fax 312 664 2365/www.igohojo.com). CTA Chicago (Brown, Purple, Red). **Rates** $79-$135 single/double; $149 suite. **Credit** AmEx, DC, Disc, MC, V. **Map** p306 H10.

There's no pretence about this old-style, two-storey motor court. An anachronism in the heart of trendy River North, its central courtyard provides free parking – a cost-saver in a city where hotels charge upwards of $20 a day to stash your motor. (However, it is first-come, first-served, with about 30 parking spots to divvy up among 71 rooms.) There's no need

to fret about a $20 breakfast from room service: the hotel doesn't offer either. But attached to the hotel is a cheerful diner where cooked breakfasts are $3.45.
Hotel services *Concierge. Disabled: adpated rooms. Gym. No-smoking floors. Parking (free, but call to check availability). Restaurant.* **Room services** *Dataport. TV: cable.*

Ohio House

600 N LaSalle Street, at W Ontario Street, IL 60610 (312 943 6000/fax 312 943 6063). CTA Grand (Red). **Rates** $77-$100 single; $104-$119 double; $126-$140 suite. **Credit** AmEx, DC, Disc, MC, V. **Map** p306 H10.

This timeworn motel offers rooms at budget rates in a desirable River North location. The free parking is another big budget-stretcher, as is the coffeeshop that offers mammoth breakfasts (two each of eggs, pancakes, bacon, and sausages) for $3.80 and Friday-night fish and chips for $5.95. A large room above the office – management calls it a 'suite' – includes refrigerator, microwave and sleeper sofa and could conceivably hold a family of five or six (it goes for $140).
Hotel services: *No-smoking rooms. Parking (free). Restaurant.* **Room services**: *Dataport. Telephone. TV: cable.*

Red Roof Inn

162 E Ontario Street, at N St Clair Street, IL 60611 (1-800 466 8356/312 787 3580/fax 312 787 1299/ www.motel6.com). CTA Grand (Red). **Rates** $80-$130 single; $97-$160 double; $113-$170 suite. **Credit** AmEx, DC, Disc, MC, V. **Map** p306 J10.

Usually, you'll look for this no-frills lodging chain along the nation's highways or in the far-flung suburbs. However, here's one in the heart of the city, just a block east of Michigan Avenue, occupying the building of a French-owned boutique hotel that went bust. Though the chandeliers have gone, the hotel

completed a renovation in 2001 and the rooms, though predictable, are clean, comfy and cheap. Adjoining the hotel is Coco Pazzo Café, a well-regarded Italian eaterie with a delightful sidewalk café (*see p133*).
Room services *Business services. Disabled: adapted rooms. Limousine service. No-smoking floors. Parking ($22-$30). Restaurant.* **Room services** *Dataport. Kitchenette (suites only). TV: cable/pay movies.*

Gold Coast

Deluxe

The Drake

140 E Walton Street, at N Michigan Avenue, IL 60611 (1-800 553 7253/312 787 2200/fax 312 787 1431/www.thedrakehotel.com). CTA Chicago (Red). **Rates** $355-$460 single/double; $465-$2,500 suite. **Credit** AmEx, DC, Disc, MC, V. **Map** p306 J9.
London has its Dorchester, New York its Plaza. Chicago, though, has the Drake. As icon hotels will, it attracts royalty (Princess Diana) and Hollywood (Julia Roberts in *My Best Friend's Wedding*). But mostly, this is a trad 'old money' hotel favoured by Chicago socialites. Built in 1920, the Drake exudes style, with velvet seats on elevators, bowls of fresh

fruit on each floor and rooms with graceful high ceilings and a full range of modern amenities. Superb seafood is served in the Cape Cod Room (*see p137*) and harp music is performed in the classic Palm Court. One of Chicago's best piano bars is the Coq d'Or (*see p154* **Hey Mr DJ…**), where Craig Lanigan plays piano and Arlene Bardelle belts out show tunes.
Hotel services *Babysitting. Bars (2). Beauty salon. Business services. Concierge. Disabled: adapted rooms. Garden. Gym. Laundry (valet). Limousine service. No-smoking floors. Parking ($31). Restaurants (2).* **Room services** *Dataport. Minibar. Room service (24hrs). Turndown. TV: cable/pay movies.*

Four Seasons

120 E Delaware Place, at N Michigan Avenue, IL 60611 (1-800 332 3442/312 280 8800/fax 312 280 9184/www.fourseasons.com). CTA Chicago (Red). **Rates** $425-$475 single; $435-$515 double; $450-$585 suite.* **Credit** AmEx, DC, Disc, MC, V. **Map** p306 J9.
You'll get an idea of the Four Seasons' decorous comfort as you explore public spaces decorated with Italian marble, glittering crystal and exquisite woodwork. There's twice-daily maid service and a carafe of water delivered at turndown. Those in search of edibles and potables will find the acclaimed Seasons restaurant, a clubby cigar bar, and a lounge with a companionable fireplace, a waterfall and lovely

Star gazing

Mob-movie mavens who remember volatile Joe Pesci in *Goodfellas* might be surprised to find him in person and in good voice at Coq d'Or, the piano bar at the **Drake** hotel (*see above*). They shouldn't. Pesci was discovered as a singing waiter in the Bronx, and when he visits Chicago, the Drake is one of his favourite hangouts. Liza Minnelli, too, has been known to stop by and belt out a number or two at the bar of this legendary hotel, one of a handful in Chicago that has become a star in its own right through the patronage of other celebs.

Most hotels go to great lengths to protect the privacy of famous guests and won't disclose their presence. The Drake tries, but its frequent appearances in movies (*My Best Friend's Wedding* and *Hoffa*, to name but a couple) only add to its mythology. And sometimes, if the celeb is big enough, it's impossible not to draw a crowd: such as when Princess Di stayed here in 1996. Other past Hollywood guests included Bing Crosby, Gloria Swanson, Mary Pickford, Walt Disney, Sophia Loren, Dan Aykroyd, Andy Garcia and Penny Marshall. The list of world leaders who've roomed at the Drake is similarly lengthy: Herbert Hoover, Madame Chiang

Kai-shek, Queen Elizabeth II, Norway's King Olaf V, Prince Charles, Nancy Reagan, Margaret Thatcher, Bill Clinton…

One hotel that is happy to rent you quarters used by stars is the **Omni Ambassador East** (*see p63*). Indeed, the Omni has gone so far as to name more than a dozen of its suites after celebs who've stayed here. Ask for the Frank Sinatra Suite, where Frank slept in 1994 after an evening that saw him and a group of friends celebrate long into the night in the hotel's Pump Room. Other former occupants include Richard Gere (while filming *Primal Fear*), Gary Cooper, Kevin Bacon, Robert Redford and Elizabeth Shue.

Musicians, of course, need somewhere to stay when they hit town, and the **Hotel Monaco** (*see p47*) has attempted to corner the market with a suite built for musicians. Britney Spears (OK, we were using the word 'musician' in its broadest possible sense) and James Taylor are among those who've stayed in a room that holds a display of eight gold records, a fully loaded digital jukebox and a television set that appears to have been thrown through a window (courtesy of the Steppenwolf Theatre prop shop).

Talbott Hotel. *See p62.*

views of the Magnificent Mile. Completing this array of pampering services is a full-service spa that debuted in 2001, with a swimming pool covered by a skylight and surrounded by Roman columns.
Hotel services *Babysitting. Bar. Business services. Concierge. Disabled: adpated rooms. Gym. Laundry (valet). Limousine service. No-smoking floors. Parking ($20-$29).* **Room services** *Dataport. Minibar. Room service (24hrs). Turndown. TV: cable/pay movies.*

Ritz-Carlton Chicago

160 E Pearson Street, at N Michigan Avenue, IL 60611 (1-800 621 6906/312 266 1000/fax 312 266 1194/www.fourseasons.com). CTA Chicago (Red).
Rates $295-$490 single/double; $450-$1,625 suite.
Credit AmEx, DC, Disc, MC, V. **Map** p306 J9.
The lavish lobby of the Ritz-Carlton is a soothing, restful place, with a massive skylight and bubbling fountain that provides a soft background for the many activities held in lobby bars and restaurants. Under the guidance of Sarah Steger, the Dining Room is one of the finest restaurants in town. Spacious guestrooms feature 9ft (3m) ceilings, attractive green and red colour schemes, cherrywood furnishings and marble bathrooms. Premier rooms on the 30th floor guarantee spectacular views of the city. Opened for 2002, the Spa at the Carlton Club features more than 25 treatments.
Hotel services *Babysitting. Bars (2). Business services. Concierge. Cooking facilities (suites only). Disabled: adapted rooms. Gym. Laundry (valet). Limousine service. No-smoking floors. Parking ($34). Restaurants (3). Swimming pool (indoor).* **Room services** *Dataport. Kitchenette (suites only). Minibar. Room service (24hrs). Turndown. TV: cable/pay movies/web TV.*

Sofitel Chicago Water Tower

20 E Chestnut Street, at N Wabash Avenue, IL 60611 (1-877 813 7700/312 324 4000/fax 312 324 4026/www.sofitel.com). CTA Chicago (Red).
Rates $299-$469 single/double; $499-$1,500 suite.
Credit AmEx, DC, Disc, MC, V. **Map** p306 H9.
This European import, which opened in a plum Gold Coast location in 2002, is a striking addition and attractive addition to the Chicago skyline. Paris-based architect Jean-Paul Viguier used a stunning prism-shaped design for this 32-storey, 415-room luxury property. As French as the croissants baked daily on the premises, this hotel offers contemporary French cuisine at Café des Architectes and Med-influenced dishes at Cigale. All rooms and suites have spacious marble bathrooms with separate tub and glass-enclosed shower and are stocked with Roger & Gallet toiletries. High-tech conveniences include a laptop-sized safe and fax-printers provided on request.
Hotel services *Babysitting. Bar (1). Business services. Concierge. Disabled: adapted rooms. Gym. Laundry. Limousine service. No-smoking floors. Parking ($33). Restaurants (2).* **Room services** *Dataport. Minibar. Room service (24hrs). Turndown. TV: cable/pay movies/web TV.*

Expensive

Sutton Place

21 E Bellevue Street, at N Rush Street, IL 60611 (1-800 606 8188/312 266 2100/fax 312 266 2141/ www.suttonplace.com). CTA Clark/Division (Red).
Rates $305-$335 single; $330-$360 double; $395-$1,500 suite. **Credit** AmEx, DC, Disc, MC, V.
Map p309 H9.

The 246-room Sutton Place is unabashedly modern. A series of floral Mapplethorpe photographs decorate lobby and rooms, which should give some idea as to the modish nature of the place. Rooms are all of uniform size, so you know what you're getting when you pick from spacious kings, double doubles, junior suites (one room, with a large living area) and penthouse suites (six). All boast modern, slightly hip decor, wonderfully deep baths with separate showers, and stereo systems.
Hotel services *Babysitting. Business services. Concierge. Disabled: adapted rooms. Gym. Laundry (valet). Limousine service. No-smoking floors. Parking ($32). TV lounge.* **Room services** *Dataport. Minibar. Room service (24hrs). Turndown. TV: cable/pay movies/web TV.*

Talbott Hotel

20 E Delaware Place, at N Rush Street, IL 60611 (1-800 621 8506/312 944 4970/fax 312 944 7241/ www.talbotthotel.com). CTA Chicago (Red). **Rates** $149-$329 single/double; $319-$469 suite. **Credit** AmEx, DC, Disc, MC, V. **Map** p306 H9.
If this boutique hotel in a 1920s building is reminiscent of a small, upmarket European hotel, it's for good reason. During a trip to Europe, owner Basil Kromelow was captivated by elegant, family-owned hotels; duly inspired, he opened the Talbott in 1987. Guestrooms were treated to an $8-million renovation completed in 2002, providing new carpeting, wireless internet access and marble bathrooms with dual-sink granite dressing tables. The showpiece at Basil's, a 45-seat lounge with a light menu, is a 19th-century walnut bar imported from Italy.
Hotel services *Babysitting. Bar. Business services. Concierge. Disabled: adapted rooms. Gym. Laundry (valet). Limousine service. No-smoking floors. Parking ($22). Restaurant.* **Room services** *Dataport. Minibar. Room service (7am-11pm). Turndown. TV: cable/pay movies.*

Tremont Hotel

100 E Chestnut Street, at N Michigan Avenue, IL 60611 (1-800 621 8133/312 751 1900/fax 312 751 8641/www.tremontchicago.com). CTA Chicago (Red). **Rates** $139-$279 single/double; $189-$399 suite. **Credit** AmEx, DC, Disc, MC, V. **Map** p306 J9.
Tucked away on Chestnut Street, the Tremont Hotel is twinned with the nearby Raphael (*see p59*). Both are small, European in flavour, nicely decorated – check out the architecturally themed pictures – and centrally located. A renovation has smartened the lobby with new hardwood floors and oversized leather chairs. Adjoining Mike Ditka's Restaurant (*see p129*), part-owned by the former Bears coach, provides room service, while Tremont House, on the other side of the hotel, contains 12 suites and is geared towards those staying in town for a while.
Hotel services *Babysitting. Bars (2). Business services. Disabled: adapted rooms. Gym. Laundry. Limousine service. No-smoking floors. Parking ($32). Restaurant (1).* **Room services** *Dataport. Kitchenette. Minibar. Room service (6am-11pm). TV: cable/pay movies.*

Westin Hotel

909 N Michigan Avenue, at E Delaware Place, IL 60611 (1-800 228 3000/312 943 7200/fax 312 943 9347/www.westinmichiganave.com). CTA Chicago (Red). **Rates** $119-$299 single/double; $500-$2,500 suites. **Credit** AmEx, DC, Disc, MC, V. **Map** p306 J9.
Mostly, hotels are in the business of selling sleep. Acknowledging this, Westin equips its rooms with the 'Heavenly Bed', designed to promote zzzs. It features pillowtop mattress set, cosy down blanket, three sheets, a comforter, duvet and five fluffy pillows. A massive refurb spruced up guestrooms (done in rich gold, forest green and cranberry) and public spaces, and added the 300-seat Grill on the Alley, operated by a Beverly Hills-based chain.
The other Westin in Chicago, the **Westin River North** (320 N Dearborn Street, Near North; 1-800 937 8461/312 744 1900), offers fine business services and well-appointed if pricey rooms, perfectly suited to the expense-account traveller. Rates are similar.
Hotel services *Babysitting. Bar. Beauty salon. Business services. Concierge. Disabled: adapted rooms. Gym. Limousine service. No-smoking floors. Parking ($32). Restaurant.* **Room services** *Dataport. Minibar. Room service (24hrs). Turndown. TV: cable/pay movies.*

Whitehall Hotel

105 E Delaware Place, at N Michigan Avenue, IL 60611 (1-800 948 4255/312 944 6300/fax 312 944 8522/www.thewhitehallhotel.com). CTA Chicago (Red). **Rates** $119-$299 single/double; $500-$2,500 suite. **Credit** AmEx, DC, Disc, MC, V. **Map** p306 J9.
Anyone who visited Chicago in the 1970s may recall the cachet attached to this small luxury hotel and dining club. After being shuttered for several years, the Whitehall is receiving guests in refurbished European-style rooms featuring mahogany armoires and Chippendale desks. The 221-room boutique hotel occupies a landmark building, developed in 1928 to house luxury apartments. The panelled lobby retains its English club look, while a stylish American bistro, Molive, has supplanted the private dining club. Its sidewalk atrium is great for people-watching (and offers 40-plus wines by the glass).
Hotel services *Bar. Business services. Concierge. Gym. Laundry (valet). Limousine service. No-smoking floors. Parking ($30.50). Restaurant.* **Room services** *Dataport. Minibar. Room service (24hrs). Turndown. TV: cable/pay movies/web TV.*

Moderate

Claridge

1244 N Dearborn Street, at W Goethe Street, IL 60610 (1-800 245 1258/312 787 4980/fax 312 266 0978/www.claridgehotel.com). CTA Clark/Division (Red). **Rates** $149-$180 single; $169-$205 double; $350-$450 suite. **Credit** AmEx, DC, Disc, MC, V. **Map** p307 H8.
The Claridge blends almost seamlessly into the tree-lined surroundings of Dearborn Street, offering serene classiness at decent prices. The rooms vary considerably in size, but all are clean, comfortable

and unfussily decorated. A degree of sophistication comes from art lining the hotel's corridors (originals by noted Chicago illustrator Bill Olendorf are also found in the bedrooms) and the eclectic global cuisine of Foreign Affairs. A new day spa offers massages, manicures, facials and aromatherapy.
Hotel services *Bar. Business services. Disabled: adapted rooms. Gym. Laundry (valet). Limousine service. No-smoking floors. Restaurant. TV lounge.* **Room services** *Dataport. Minibar. Room service (6-10am, 3pm-midnight). TV: cable/pay movies.*

Omni Ambassador East

1301 N State Street, at E Goethe Street, IL 60610 (1-800 843 6664/312 787 7200/fax 312 787 4760/www.omnihotels.com). CTA Clark/Division (Red). **Rates** $199-$239 single/double; $319-$469 suite. **Credit** AmEx, DC, Disc, MC, V. **Map** p306 H8.
A $22-million renovation programme has restored this landmark hotel, opened in October 1926, to its former glory. Offering 285 guestrooms, the hotel takes credit for pioneering the concierge concept in American hotels, first offering this amenity in 1957. The hotel, which added the 'Omni' to its name in 1986, retains a genteel air with many original features, from Italian marble in the lobby to crystal

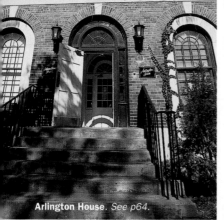

Arlington House. *See p64.*

chandeliers. Popular with celebs (some of the well-appointed suites bear the names of Hollywood stars), it also houses the infamous Pump Room, which still attracts show-biz elite.

The **Omni Chicago** (676 N Michigan Avenue, Near North; 1-800 843 6664/312 944 6664), meanwhile, is an all-suites property boasting an excellent Michigan Avenue location.
Hotel services *Babysitting. Bar. Beauty salon. Business services. Concierge. Cooking facilities (suites only). Disabled: adapted rooms. Gym. Limousine service. No-smoking floors. Parking ($34). Restaurant. TV lounge.* **Room services** *Dataport. Minibar. Room service (24hrs). Turndown. TV: cable/pay movies.*

Seneca

200 E Chestnut Street, at N Mies van der Rohe Way, IL 60611 (1-800 800 6261/312 787 8900/fax 312 988 4438/www.senecahotel.com). CTA Chicago (Red). **Rates** $89-$209 single/double; $109-$289 suite. **Credit** AmEx, DC, Disc, MC, V. **Map** p306 J9.
The staff at the Seneca like to refer to the hotel as one of the city's best-kept secrets. Situated just off Michigan Avenue, it's a pleasingly grand hotel offering luxury at prices that put many of its competitors to shame. The deluxe one-bedroom suites are just that, boasting spacious lounges and kitchens. These arguably represent the best value of the hotel's 66 guestrooms (all with kitchenette) and 57 suites. Its three independently operated restaurants are Chalfin's Delicatessen, the Saloon steakhouse (*see p136*) and Cantare, which serves good northern Italian fare.
Hotel services *Bars (2). Beauty salon. Business services. Concierge. Cooking facilities. Disabled: adpated rooms. Gym. Laundry (valet). Limousine service. No-smoking floors. Parking ($30). Restaurants (3).* **Room services** *Dataport. Room service (7.30am-11pm). TV: cable.*

Lincoln Park

Budget

Comfort Inn Lincoln Park

601 W Diversey Parkway, at N Clark Street, IL 60614 (1-800 228 5150/773 348 2810/fax 773 348 1912/www.comfortinn.com). CTA Diversey (Brown, Purple). **Rates** $95-$159 single/double; $225 suite. **Credit** AmEx, DC, Disc, MC, V. **Map** p308 G4.
Located in the heart of lively Lincoln Park, this budget hotel is housed in an attractive four-storey brick building accented with colourfully striped awnings. The cookie-cutter rooms are basic but clean, and the continental breakfast served in the French provincial-style lounge and off-street courtyard parking are added bonuses. For less than the price of a downtown room, you can upgrade to a suite with a jacuzzi.
Hotel services *Business services. Disabled: adapted rooms. Gym. No-smoking floors. Parking ($10).* **Room services** *Cooking facilities (suites only). Dataport. TV: cable.*

Days Inn Lincoln Park North

644 W Diversey Parkway, at N Clark Street, IL 60614 (1-888 576 3297/773 525 7010/fax 773 525 6998/www.lpndaysinn.com). CTA Diversey (Brown, Purple). **Rates** *$101-$160 single; $131-$190 double; $215-$290 suites.* **Credit** *AmEx, DC, Disc, MC, V.* **Map** p308 F4.

Located at the busy intersection of Broadway, Clark and Diversey, this decent option – the highest-rated Days Inn in Illinois, no less – offers basic rooms decorated in fresh, light colours. A complimentary continental breakfast is served in a comfortable sitting area off a lobby decorated with a showcase of collector plates, and there are complimentary passes available for the Bally's health club next door. Also in Chicago is the **Days Inn Gold Coast** (1816 N Clark Street, Lincoln Park; 1-800 325 2525/312 664 3030), which offers a similar range of amenities.
Hotel services *Business services. Disabled: adapted rooms. Gym. Laundry (valet). No-smoking floor. Parking ($8.75-$20).* **Room services** *Dataport. TV: cable.*

Willows

555 W Surf Street, at N Broadway, IL 60657 (1-800 787 3108/773 528 8400/fax 773 528 8483/ www.lakeviewchicago.homestead.com/willows.html). CTA Diversey (Brown, Purple). **Rates** *$99-$199 single/double/suite.* **Credit** *AmEx, DC, Disc, MC, V.* **Map** p309 F3.

A French Renaissance feel dominates at this cosy hotel up near the busy Clark/Diversey intersection. The entire hotel has been refurbished and renovated and looks much better for it: the TVs even have the full 100-plus gamut of cable stations. Fans of minor hotel curiosities (and of vintage private-eye movies) will enjoy riding in the original 1920s Otis elevator, creaks 'n' all. Room rates include continental breakfast and the location is within walking distance of Lincoln Park Zoo (*see p103*) and the Peggy Notebaert Nature Museum (*see p101*).
Hotel services *Concierge. Gym. Limousine service. No-smoking floors. Parking ($18-$25).* **Room services** *Dataport. TV: cable.*

Lake View

Moderate

See also p57 **Best Western Hawthorne Terrace**.

Budget

City Suites

933 W Belmont Avenue, at N Sheffield Avenue, IL 60657 (1-800 248 9108/773 404 3400/fax 773 404 3405/www.cityinns.com). CTA Belmont (Red). **Rates** *$99-$199 single/double/suite.* **Credit** *AmEx, DC, Disc, MC, V.* **Map** p309 E3.

This 45-room boutique hotel is next to the Belmont El station, a hub that will get you downtown inside of 15 minutes. If you're a baseball fan – as many

guests here are – the location is ideal, just four blocks from Wrigley Field. The neighbourhood offers a lively mix of gentrified, bohemian and gay and lesbian lifestyles. The hotel has an art deco feel and spotless suites include sleeper sofa, armchair, refrigerator, and spacious workstation with dataport. A continental breakfast is included in the price.
Hotel services *Concierge. Gym. Limousine service. No-smoking floors. Parking ($18-$25).* **Room services** *Dataport. TV: cable.*

Majestic

528 W Brompton Avenue, at N Lake Shore Drive, IL 60657 (1-800 727 5108/773 404 3499/fax 773 404 3495/www.cityinns.com). CTA Addison (Red). **Rates** *$99-$199 single/double/suite.* **Credit** *AmEx, DC, Disc, MC, V.* **Map** p309 G1.

As with its sister properties City Suites and the Willows, this inn says good morning to guests with complimentary breakfast and sends them off to explore the neighbourhood. Set on a quiet, tree-lined residential street within walking distance of the Lincoln Park Zoo and less than five blocks from Wrigley, it's housed in a building dating from the 1920s and offers 31 rooms and 22 suites. Buses along Lake Shore Drive, half a block to the east, get you to the Magnificent Mile in about 15 minutes.
Hotel services *Concierge. Cooking facilities (microwave, fridge). Gym. Limousine service. No-smoking floors. Parking ($18-$25).* **Room services** *Dataport. Iron (some rooms). Kitchenette. TV: cable.*

Hostels

Arlington International House

616 W Arlington Place, at N Geneva Terrace, Lincoln Park, IL 60614 (1-800 467 8355/773 929 5380/fax 773 665 5485/www.arlingtonhouse.com). CTA Fullerton (Brown, Purple, Red). **Rates** *$22-$65.* **Credit** *MC, V.*

Chicago International Hostel

6318 N Winthrop Avenue, at W Rosemont Avenue, North Side, IL 60660 (773 262 1011/fax 773 262 3673/chicagohostel@hotmail.com). CTA Loyola (Red). **Rates** *$15-$40.* **No credit cards.**

Garden Home Hostel

2822 W 38th Place, at S California Avenue, South Side, IL 60632 (773 254 0836/ www.hostels.com/fatjohnnies). Bus 94, 95. **Rates** *$12.* **No credit cards.**

HI-Chicago

24 E Congress Parkway, at S State Street, the Loop, IL 60605 (312 360 0300/fax 312 360 0313/ www.hichicago.org). CTA Harrison (Red) or LaSalle (Blue, Brown, Orange, Purple). **Rates** *$28-$34.* **Credit** *MC, V.* **Map** p305 H13.

International House of Chicago

1414 E 59th Street, at S Dorchester Avenue, Hyde Park, IL 60637 (773 753 2270/fax 773 753 1227/ http://ihouse.uchicago.edu). Metra 59th Street. **Rates** *$50.* **Credit** *MC, V.* **Map** p311 Y17.

Sightseeing

Features

Maps

Introduction

Welcome to Chicago.

Your first dilemma? Where to start. Your next dilemma? How to fit it all in.

You won't be stuck for things to do in Chicago. Even leaving aside all the shopping, dining and after-hours cultural options, the town has attractions and museums galore; more than that, though, many of the various neighbourhoods in which they're located are worth a wander in their own right. Don't just stay downtown around the Loop or Michigan Avenue: attractive though these areas are, you won't find the real Chicago until you head to more residential parts of town.

Speaking of wandering, Chicago rewards the pedestrian. The city's grid layout is easy to figure out (*see p281*), and the land is fairly flat. Pray the weather holds, and then take to the streets. The public transportation here is good, too: the El serves most corners of the city, with buses and the Metra rail section picking up the rest of the slack and the city's own free trolley service ferrying tourists around downtown, especially to and from Navy Pier.

If you plan to visit a number of attractions, the **Citypass** is a good idea. For $39 ($29 children), it entitles you to entry at the Art Institute, the Shedd Aquarium, the Adler Planetarium, the Field Museum, the Museum of Science and Industry and the John Hancock Observatory, at a saving of almost 50 per cent on regular admission prices. You can buy a Citypass at any of the six attractions to which it offers entry; no advance booking is necessary. For more, see www.citypass.com.

Tours

Chicago Architecture Foundation
Chicago Architecture Foundation, Santa Fe Building, 224 S Michigan Avenue, at E Jackson Boulevard, the Loop (312 922 8687/3432/www.architecture.org). **Tickets** prices vary. **Credit** AmEx, DC, Disc, MC, V. **Map** p305 J12.

The CAF offers a variety of terrific tours throughout the year. The popular River Cruise offers a survey of the city's architecture, and is the best of the city's myriad water tours. Yet the range of tours available is staggering, from bus tours around the Loop and Oak Park, to bike tours up the lakefront, via walks through many of the city's neighbourhoods. Booking is recommended (especially for the River Cruise), either from CAF HQ, its branch in the John Hancock Center or Ticketmaster (312 902 1500).

The best Things to do

Chicago Historical Society
A great museum for a great city. *See p100.*

Lincoln Park Zoo
Walk with the animals. *See p103.*

Wrigley Field
Take me out to the ballgame... *See p104.*

Oak Street Beach
A wonderful anachronism. *See p98.*

Museum Campus
Three great museums side by side. *See p81.*

Art Institute
A world-class collection. *See p79.*

Chicago Architecture Foundation River Cruise
The lowdown on the high buildings. *See p66.*

Grant Park
In summer, when the music festivals move in. Millennium Park promises much too. *See p78.*

Mexican Fine Arts Center Museum
The town's top community museum. *See p113.*

Oak Park
See why Lloyd Wright settled here, and why Hemingway left. *See p118.*

John Hancock Observatory
Its views aren't bettered anywhere. *See p91.*

Wicker Park nightlife
MTV's *Real World* didn't kill it... Yet. *See p162.*

Sculpture in the Loop
America's most magnificent collection of public art? *See p74* **Walk on.**

Sightseeing

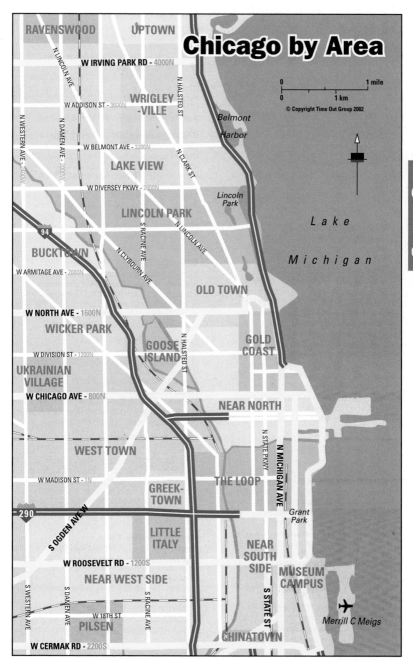

Chicago by Area

RAVENSWOOD
UPTOWN

W IRVING PARK RD - 4000N

WRIGLEY
-VILLE

W ADDISON ST - 3600N

W BELMONT AVE - 3200N

LAKE VIEW

W DIVERSEY PKWY - 2800N

LINCOLN PARK

BUCKTOWN

W ARMITAGE AVE - 2000N

OLD TOWN

W NORTH AVE - 1600N

WICKER PARK

GOOSE
ISLAND

GOLD
COAST

W DIVISION ST - 1200N

UKRAINIAN
VILLAGE

W CHICAGO AVE - 800N

NEAR NORTH

WEST TOWN

W MADISON ST - 1N

GREEK-
TOWN

THE LOOP

LITTLE
ITALY

W ROOSEVELT RD - 1200S

NEAR WEST SIDE

NEAR
SOUTH
SIDE
MUSEUM
CAMPUS

W 18TH ST

PILSEN

Merrill C Meigs

W CERMAK RD - 2200S

CHINATOWN

N LINCOLN AVE

N HALSTED ST

N WESTERN AVE - 2400W

N DAMEN AVE - 2000W

N CLARK ST

N RACINE AVE

N LINCOLN AVE

N CLYBOURN AVE

N HALSTED ST

N STATE PKWY

N MICHIGAN AVE

S OGDEN AVE W

S WESTERN AVE

S DAMEN AVE

S RACINE AVE

S STATE ST

94

290

Belmont
Harbor

Lincoln
Park

Lake

Michigan

Grant
Park

0   1 mile

0   1 km

© Copyright Time Out Group 2002

Neighbourhood watch

THE LOOP The financial centre of Chicago, the Loop stretches south from the Chicago River to Congress Parkway, and covers the area west to Union Station.

NEAR SOUTH SIDE Dropping down from Polk Street to around Cermak, the Near South Side takes in the attraction-dominated **Museum Campus**, on the edge of Burnham Park and Lake Michigan, and Chicago's **Chinatown**.

NEAR NORTH The Near North area covers a wedge north from the Chicago River. Here you'll find the shopping of the **Magnificent Mile**, some posh hotels and hundreds of eateries. The blocks west of Clark Street are known as **River North**, home to galleries and nightlife venues. East of Michigan is **Streeterville**, where you'll find Navy Pier.

GOLD COAST Swanky in the extreme, the Gold Coast sits between Oak Street and North Avenue to the east of Clark Street. This is where you'll find the most expensive real estate in the city, but also, in an ironic twist, its nastiest bars, near the junction of State and Division.

OLD TOWN A historic, mostly residential area just north of the Gold Coast that contains the Chicago Historical Society.

LINCOLN PARK Taking in part of the huge park from which it takes its name, the smart, yuppie-dominated area named after the vast, lakefront park also includes DePaul University.

LAKE VIEW Stretching north from Diversey to around Irving Park Road, Lake View is an increasingly lively neighbourhood that encompasses **Boystown**, Chicago's main gay and lesbian drag, and **Wrigleyville**, the area around Wrigley Field. Slightly further north are largely residential neighbourhoods such as **Uptown**, **Ravenswood** and **Andersonville**.

WEST SIDE West of the Loop sits West Town, a once shabby area that's slowly coming up the property ladder as scruffy old warehouses get converted into loft apartments. In this area you'll also find the ethnic neighbourhoods of **Greektown**, **Little Italy** and **Pilsen**.

HYDE PARK While dominated by the University of Chicago, this South Side neighbourhood is also home to the rather lovely Washington Park.

Chicago Greeter
Chicago Cultural Center, 77 E Randolph Street, at N Michigan Avenue, the Loop (312 744 8000/ www.chicagogreeter.com). CTA Randolph (Brown, Green, Orange, Purple). **Tickets** free. **Map** p305 J12.
Modelled on New York's Big Apple Greeter, Chicago Greeter, which started in April 2002, offers visitors the chance to be taken around neighbourhoods by local volunteers with their own highly personal stories to tell. A unique way to see the city, and a potentially great one. Try to book a week or more ahead.

Chicago Neighbourhood Tours
Chicago Cultural Center, 77 E Randolph Street, at N Michigan Avenue, the Loop (312 742 1190/ www.chgocitytours.com). CTA Randolph (Brown, Green, Orange, Purple). **Tours** 9.30am/10am Sat. **Tickets** $25-$50; $20-$45 concessions. **Credit** AmEx, MC, V. **Map** p305 J12.
The Chicago Office of Tourism offers these informative bus tours, which focus on a different neighbourhood each week, with visits to historical sites, museums and attractions. Special themed tours, such as the Roots of Chicago Blues, are also available.

Chicago Trolley Company
312 663 0260/www.chicagotrolley.com. **Tours** 9am-5pm daily. **Tickets** $20; $10-$17 concessions. *2-day pass* $25. **Credit** AmEx, DC, Disc, MC, V
A hop-on/hop-off service that trawls the major sights. Guides indicate points of interest along the way. Tickets are only available on board.

Loop Tour Train
Chicago Cultural Center, 77 E Randolph Street, at N Michigan Avenue, the Loop (312 744 2400). CTA Randolph (Brown, Green, Orange, Purple). **Tours** May-Sept 11.35am, 12.15pm, 12.55pm, 1.35pm Sat. **Tickets** free. **Map** p305 J12.
Travel the El from Randolph station, while guides from the Chicago Architecture Foundation fill you in on local history.

Lake & river cruises
Countless operators offer cruises on Lake Michigan from Navy Pier, including **Seadog** (312 822 7200), **Shoreline** (312 222 9328), **Spirit of Chicago** (312 836 7899) and **Ugly Duck Cruises** (630 916 9007). For tours of the Chicago River, try **Mercury** (312 332 1353) or **Wendella Boats** (312 337 1446). And to sail in the stunning 148ft (45m), four-masted tall schooner **Windy**, call 312 595 5555.

Untouchables Tour
605 N Clark Street, at W Ohio Street, Near North (773 881 1195/www.gangstertour.com). CTA Grand (Red). **Tours** 10am Mon-Wed; 10am, 1pm Thur; 10am, 1pm, 7.30pm Fri; 10am, 1pm, 5pm Sat; 11am, 2pm Sun. **Tickets** $22; $16 children. **Credit** MC, V. **Map** p306 H10.
The Untouchables Tour kicks off from the Rock 'n' Roll McDonald's, visiting the actual sites of some of the city's biggest gangster shoot-'em-ups, including the Dillinger murder and the St Valentine's Day Massacre. Costumed guides provide the gory details.

The Loop

In Chicago's financial district, the stakes are high. But the buildings are higher.

Chicago's elevated train system loops the Loop, rattling overhead day and night.

If the streets and buildings of the Loop could talk, their stories would be among the city's most compelling. In this square mile, political dynasties have wielded enormous power, architectural jewels have formed neck-craning streetscapes, fortunes have been made and lost. If you want to get up close and personal with power in Chicago, start here in the area contained by the Chicago River to the north, Grant Park to the east, Congress Parkway to the south and Clinton Street to the west.

The Loop gets its name from the cable cars that circled it during the area's first heyday in the 1880s. Today, the elevated train tracks that circle the area provide an echo back to the past; literally, for their rattle and hum is a Loop constant. After staggering a bit in the 1940s – when many entertainment venues folded and businesses fled to the suburbs – the Loop today is experiencing a rebirth. Business has returned, the theatres have been renovated and people are even moving back into the area.

The Loop is at its busiest from 7am to 7pm Monday to Friday, when office workers and politicians flood its stately buildings. Outside these hours, the place can seem downright deserted: at night, the main signs of life are locals leaving the theatre and tourists returning to their hotels, though there are several noteworthy restaurants in the area.

West Loop

More than any other landmark, the **Sears Tower** (*see p70*) symbolises Chicago. Built in 1974, it was the world's tallest building until Malaysia upped the ante in 1996. At 1,454 feet (443 metres) – 110 storeys, plus protruding antennae – it's still America's largest.

Nine steel tubes of varying heights form the frame of the black aluminium- and glass-covered building, designed by the Chicago firm of Skidmore, Owings & Merrill. Only two of the tubes continue to the top, giving the structure a multi-tiered look. Tickets for the observatory can be bought in the atrium off Wacker Drive, where you'll also find *Universe*, a large sculpture by Alexander Calder representing the sun, a pendulum and three flowers. Just south of the Sears Tower is **311 S Wacker Drive** (at W Jackson Boulevard), the tallest reinforced concrete building in the world. It has an exterior of glass and pink granite surrounded by a neatly landscaped yard: at night, the crown of the 65-storey structure is lit up like a Christmas tree.

Head back north up Wacker and you'll find one of the Loop's most compelling sights. On two trading floors at the **Chicago Mercantile Exchange** (30 S Wacker Drive, at W Madison Street; 312 930 8249/www.cme.com), men and

But could Sosa homer with it? Claes Oldenburg's **Batcolumn**.

women jump up and down, hollering and waving as they negotiate the futures and options on foreign currencies, gold and pork bellies. The visitors' galleries are located above each floor, and are open for tours 8am-3.15pm, Monday to Friday.

A block north is the **Civic Opera House** (20 N Wacker Drive, at E Madison Street; *see p225*). Home to the Lyric Opera since 1950, the Civic is centred around a lavish art deco auditorium adorned in red and orange with gold leaf accents; with a capacity of over 3,500, it's the second-largest opera house in the country. Renovated in 1996, the 1929 building still has the terracotta and bronze forms of a trumpet, lyre and the masks of tragedy and comedy on its interior and exterior walls. For the river-facing **333 W Wacker Drive** building – just north of here – *see p32*.

The Loop extends west over the Chicago River to encompass the **Citicorp Center**, home to the Richard B Ogilvie Transportation Center (aka Northwestern Station; 500 W Madison Street, at N Canal Street) and the former Northwestern Atrium Center. Further south, **Union Station** (210 S Canal Street, at W Adams Street; 312 655 2385) lays easy claim to the title of Chicago's most famous train station. A baby carriage was caught in a shoot-out on the stairway from Canal Street to the waiting area in *The Untouchables*, though in real life, it's a less outrageous place.

Thousands of riders pass through here daily; sunlight streams through skylights ten storeys high and on to the statues inside the station, built in 1925 and restored in 1992.

The West Loop soon morphs into Greektown and a deeply hip loft-dominated locale variously named River West or West Loop Gate (*see p109*), but before it does, you'll run into the most extraordinary of all Chicago's sculptures: Claes Oldenburg's *Batcolumn*, a 100-foot (31-metre) baseball bat outside the Social Security Administration Building at 600 W Madison.

Sears Tower

233 S Wacker Drive, at W Jackson Boulevard (312 875 9696/www.theskydeck.com). CTA Quincy (Brown, Orange, Purple). **Open** *May-Sept* 10am-10pm daily. *Oct-Apr* 10am-8pm daily. **Admission** $9.50; $7.75 over-65s; $6.75 3-11s; free under-3s. **Credit** AmEx, Disc, MC, V. **Map** p305 G12.

It's impossible to know whether the Sears Tower – at 1,454ft (443m), the tallest building in the US – will ever regain the aura of glamour it held prior to 11 September 2001. Before then, it was an American landmark, to Chicago what the World Trade Center was to New York. Now, of course, New York has no World Trade Center, and the Sears Tower has lost its gloss. Evacuated several times in the hours, days and weeks after September 11, it remained closed to visitors for some time after the attacks on New York and Washington, DC (yet, a little oddly, it was still open to the office workers who occupy most of the building's 110 storeys five days a week).

Ironically, then, there's never been a better time to visit the Skydeck, which offers predictably spectacular views – up to 50 miles (80km) on a clear day – from its perch 1,353ft (412m) up. A $4 million refurbishment has resulted in a number of improvements to the observation deck, from the purely cosmetic and gimmicky (the blast-off videos that play in the elevators as they launch skywards) to the genuinely useful (better telescopes). The slightly smaller John Hancock Observatory (*see p91*) still affords better views and the luxury of a bar at the top, but if it's a tell-your-friends, been-there-done-that conversation piece you're after, the Sears is the one to climb.

Inner Loop

LaSalle Street

East of Wacker Drive sits LaSalle Street, the financial district of the Midwest. This tag has its roots as far back as 1848, when a group of merchants founded the **Chicago Board of Trade** (141 W Jackson Boulevard, at S LaSalle Street; 312 435 3590) to regulate the grain futures market. On the building's exterior, sculptures of men holding wheat and corn loom over an entrance, while a 30-foot (nine-metre) statue of Ceres, the Roman goddess of agriculture, sits atop the roof. Deals are still made for corn, wheat, soybeans, government bonds, gold and silver in the art deco building, erected in 1930. Traders can be seen from a fifth-floor visitors' centre overlooking the pits; free tours of the action are offered every half-hour from 9am to 1.30pm, Monday to Friday.

An addition to the Board of Trade was built in 1980, connecting the building via a pedestrian bridge to the **Chicago Board Options Exchange** (400 S LaSalle Street, at W Van Buren Street; 312 786 5600/www.cboe.com) and creating the largest contiguous trading floor space in the United States. Groups of ten or more can tour the facility for free between 8.30am and 3.15pm from Monday to Friday, with a fourth-floor viewing room available for individuals or groups of any size. Just a few blocks away you'll find other financial giants in South Loop, for which *see p80*.

Back in the 19th century, birds nested in the rundown temporary City Hall at 209 S LaSalle Street, at W Adams Street. When the current structure was built in 1888, the birds were remembered in the new name of the building, the **Rookery**. Two rooks at the LaSalle Street entrance still serve as reminders, though a 1991 renovation ensured there is nothing dilapidated about the Rookery today. A spiral staircase climbs to the top floor of the building, and the lobby walls, redesigned by Frank Lloyd Wright in 1905, are lined with marble.

Randolph Street & around

Chicago's politics – and that of much of the state – play out in the buildings along a stretch of Randolph Street between LaSalle and Dearborn. Indeed, the enormous building on Randolph between LaSalle and Clark bears the name of a former governor of Illinois, and houses hundreds of city workers. The **James R Thompson Center** (312 814 6667) is named after the former governor who commissioned it, and does little to blend in with its surroundings.

Thompson called it 'a building for the 21st century' when it was dedicated in 1985. Ho hum. Still, the interior does have some redeeming features. Offices circle an indoor atrium, skylights flood the granite floor and glass elevators shoot visitors to the top of the 17-storey building. Shops and a food court occupy the lower levels, while state offices line the other floors. Still, unless you're in need of a local driver's licence, there's little reason to stop here.

City Hall and the **County Building** (Cook County, that is) sit opposite the Thompson Center, on the block bounded by Randolph, Washington, Clark and LaSalle. The fifth floor is home to the city's mayor and city council; on good days, a meeting of the council can be the best show in town. Meetings are held every two weeks and are open to the public: call 312 744 3081 for details.

Across the street from City Hall – on Randolph between Clark and Dearborn – stands the **Daley Center**, named after Chicago's long-time mayor (and father to the current mayor) Richard J Daley. Cook County's court system also has its headquarters in this rust-coloured high-rise, but it's best known for the sculpture by Picasso that graces its plaza (*see p74* **Walk on**). The building was erected in 1965, and the sculpture followed in 1967, much to the dismay of mayor Daley, who wasn't much of a Picasso fan. A Christmas tree is put up each year in the Daley Plaza, which also plays host to concerts every weekday of the year, farmers' markets and the occasional protest. An eternal flame burns in memory of war dead.

Rising 400 feet (122 metres) above ground from its base a block south of City Hall on Washington, the **Chicago Temple** (77 W Washington Street, at N Clark Street; 312 236 4548/www.chicagotemple.org) is known as the 'Chapel in the Sky'. The headquarters of the First United Methodist Church of Chicago has an eight-storey spire visible only from a distance, a sanctuary and office space. On an exterior first level wall, a series of stained-glass windows depict the church's history in Chicago. Take a tour at 2pm Monday to Saturday, or after the 8.30am and 11am services on Sunday.

Sightseeing

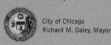

Museum of Broadcast Communications, in the Chicago Cultural Center. *See p78.*

State Street

… Or 'State Street, that great street', the stuff songs are made of. Closed to traffic in 1979 to form a pedestrian mall, the stretch of which Sinatra sung was reopened to vehicles in 1996. A $25-million facelift widened the streets, added landscaping, and helped restore life to the road.

Top on the list of landmarks on State is **Marshall Field's** (111 N State Street, at E Randolph Street; *see p168*), which has occupied its current site since 1868 despite being twice destroyed by fire (once in the Chicago Fire of 1871, again in 1887). The store's selection of goods follows Field's philosophy of 'Give the lady what she wants', and today offers 75 acres of merchandise in more than 400 departments.

A $115-million renovation gave new life to the building in 1992. A Tiffany mosaic dome (c907) still stands high above one atrium, and the clock at State and Randolph, the inspiration for a Norman Rockwell painting that graced the cover of the *Saturday Evening Post* on 3 November 1945, still keeps perfect time; indeed, the original Rockwell hangs inside the store, near the seventh-floor visitors' centre. During holidays, crowds line up to take in the store's animated window displays.

North on State is the **Chicago Theatre** (175 N State Street, at W Randolph Street; *see p241* **As good as new**). You can't miss the red vertical marquee of this former movie house, which opened in 1928 and which today plays host to a variety of shows. Opposite is the splendid new **Gene Siskel Film Center** (164 N State Street, at W Randolph Street; *see p203*).

Look south on State, meanwhile, and you'll be face to face with one of Chicago's greatest restoration projects, the **Reliance Building** (1 W Washington Street, at N State Street). Built in 1895, the Reliance was once one of the more elegant early Chicago skyscrapers, but years of neglect left it in disrepair. The city bought the building in 1996, before the Kimpton Group moved in and converted it into a hotel three years later. The **Hotel Burnham** is named after famed architect Daniel Burnham, whose firm designed the building.

Carson Pirie Scott (1 S State Street, at E Madison Street; *see p168*), another of Chicago's largest department stores, sits to the south of Marshall Field's. Designed by Louis Sullivan in 1899, it was one of the architect's last Chicago commissions. Just off State Street at Monroe to the west is the **Shubert Theatre** (22 W Monroe Street, at S State Street; *see p241* **As good as new**), built in 1904 and home to some of the biggest Broadway shows to visit Chicago, while east is the **Palmer House Hilton** (17 E Monroe Street, at S State Street), whose elegant lobby is worth a peek even if you can't afford to stay (it's one of the Loop's dearest hotels).

A block further south on Adams is another holdover from days of yore: the **Berghoff** (17 W Adams Street, at S State Street; *see p150*). Built in 1872, it served as an outdoor beer garden for the World's Columbian Exposition, and today is one of only two buildings with cast-iron fronts still left in the city (the other is the **Page Brothers Building**; 177 N State Street, at E Lake Street).

East Loop

Michigan Avenue & around

A grand, open street, Michigan Avenue is packed with buildings and sights of cultural interest. The Michigan Avenue bridge – with its spectacular views of the Loop – is a good place to start. Heading southwards, look out for the **Carbide & Carbon Building** (230 N Michigan Avenue, at E South Water Street), boasting a green terracotta tower trimmed in gold leaf and an awe-inspiring lobby of marble with glass ornamentation, and the **Smurfit-Stone Building** (150 N Michigan Avenue, at E Randolph Street), built in 1983

Sightseeing

Walk on Public art

Your neck will be cricked. The prevalence of skyscraping buildings in the Loop means it's hard not to walk around with eyes to the sky, head in the same clouds that the structures all but touch. But if you can bear to snap your head to eye level, you'll notice some striking sculptures; not quite one on every corner, but still plenty. Many are huge, though given the imposing surroundings, the artists had to think big in order to be noticed.

There are countless examples of public art around the Loop. For this, thank the council, which passed a groundbreaking ordinance 25 years ago that forced those in charge of municipal building projects to commission art for them. Private companies followed suit, and the result has been an array of sculptures that complement the excellence of the architecture. Here's a baker's dozen of the finest pieces, strung together into a walk that ought to take a leisurely 90 minutes or so.

Start at Madison Plaza, on the north-west corner of Madison and Wells.

Louise Nevelson's *Dawn Shadows* (1983) is purported to have been influenced by the design of the El. Don't worry, though: Chicago's rail system is more reliable than this monstrous black form might suggest it to be.

Head east along Madison for a block, then take a left and walk along LaSalle for two blocks.

Freeform, which sits on the façade of the Illinois State Office Building at 160 N LaSalle Street, is one of several Loop works by local artists. Indeed, **Richard Hunt** has many works on display in the city, though this eye-catching abstract piece is perhaps his most prominent.

Walk back down LaSalle and take a left along Randolph to the front of the James R Thompson Center.

Located on Thompson Center's plaza, **Jean Dubuffet**'s fibreglass *Monument With Standing Beast* can't help but catch the eye. Dubuffet always had time for the city after it greeted a 1951 lecture he gave at the Arts Club of Chicago with a rapturous reception. He termed his sculpture 'Drawing that extends into space'; there are many similarities between this work and the primitivism of his drawings.

Carry on east along Randolph for a block, to the corner with Dearborn.

Hardly your average dentist, **Herbert Ferber** filled the hours not spent drilling holes inside people's mouths by sculpting works such as this 30-year-old untitled piece.

From here, cross Randolph and head south down Dearborn for half a block to the plaza outside the Daley Center.

It's known locally only as *The Picasso*. However, given that **Pablo Picasso** didn't give it a title himself when he donated it to the city in 1967 – a city, incidentally, that he never visited – this is unsurprising. It's every bit as odd and striking as you might expect, though it's believed to be based on the head of a woman.

Continue down Dearborn to the next junction. Cross the road, then turn right into Washington.

and home to Yaacov Agam's aluminium sculpture, *Communication X9*. Also within spitting distance is the **Hellenic Museum & Cultural Center** (*see p77*).

Two nearby architectural sights worth a short detour from Michigan proper are the **Aon Center** (200 E Randolph Street, at N Columbus Drive), formerly known as the Amoco Building, and, slightly to the west, **1 Prudential Plaza** (130 E Randolph Street,

at N Stetson Avenue), which displays a form of the Rock of Gibraltar, the company's trademark. However, if you're pressed for time, your first port of call should really be the **Chicago Cultural Center** (*see p77*), Michigan's pièce de résistance. An architectural gem, tourist resource, gallery, concert venue and office block in one, it is also home to the unheralded but terrific **Museum of Broadcast Communications** (*see p78*).

Sightseeing

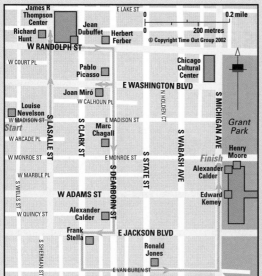

Outside the Brunswick Building at 69 W Washington sits *Miró's Chicago*. Created by **Joan Miró** in collaboration with ceramics expert Joan Artigas, it was eventually completed in 1981.

Double back up Washington, then take a right at the junction with Dearborn and continue south.

In the rest of the world, he's better known for his paintings. However, Chicagoans know **Marc Chagall** more as a sculptor, thanks to his vibrant, 70-foot (21-metre) mosaic *The Four Seasons* (*pictured left*), now under a glass cover at Bank One Plaza.

Continue south down Dearborn for two blocks to Federal Center Plaza.

Alexander Calder was once asked why he had called his vast, hooped sculpture *Flamingo*. The questioner doubtless expected an answer swamped in rhetoric, explanatory

of method and meaning. Calder, though, replied, 'It was sort of pink and has a long neck.' He got that right.

Carry on south. At the next junction, cross the road and turn right into Jackson.

Between 1986 and 1997, **Frank Stella** created 266 works of art based on or influenced by *Moby-Dick*. Few are more striking than *The Town-Ho's Story*, a jarring, 18-foot (5.5-metre) high collection of mangled metal that dominates the lobby of the Ralph H Metcalfe Federal Building.

Continue east to the junction with Clark, then take a left; then take the next left along Van Buren to the junction with State Street.

Pritzker Park, designed by **Ronald Jones** and completed in 1991, is less sculpture and more landscape garden. However, its highlight, an interpretation of Magritte's *The Banquet*, is reason enough to take the detour this way on your walk.

Continue down Van Buren to Michigan Avenue and turn left.

Edward Kemey's *Lions* is the most famous sculpture in Chicago. These two local landmarks sit, fierce and fearsome, guarding the entrance of the Art Institute, and have done for almost a century.

Just north of the main entrance, in the Institute's McCormick Memorial Court, sit two more works by notable sculptors: *Flying Dragon*, another vast piece by **Alexander Calder**, and *Large Interior Form*, whose three holes distinguish it immediately as a work by British sculptor **Henry Moore**.

Further south is **Symphony Center** (*see p226*), home to the Chicago Symphony. Made up of three wings connected by a central rotunda, the facility encompasses the 1904 Orchestra Hall, host for 200 concerts a year, a park, a store and an education and administration wing. There's also ECHO, a rather clunky acronym for the Eloise W Martin Center of the Chicago Symphony Orchestra, a hands-on learning centre for children and

adults. Down the block from the Symphony Center is the **Santa Fe Building** (224 S Michigan Avenue, at E Jackson Boulevard), designed in 1904 by Daniel Burnham. And now firmly ensconced inside the building is the marvellous **Chicago Architecture Foundation**, which offers lectures and more than 50 tours on foot, boat, bike and even bus, covering vast swathes of Chicago (*see p26* **The basics**).

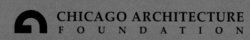

Chicago Cultural Center.

Continuing south, the **Fine Arts Building** at 410 S Michigan Avenue once housed the showrooms of the Studebaker Company, which in 1895 was showing carriages rather than cars. Soon after, it was converted into a theatre on the first floor and studios on the upper floors, and the words 'All Passes – Art Alone Endures' were carved inside the entrance. Frank Lloyd Wright had a studio here at one time, as did L Frank Baum, author of *The Wizard of Oz*.

The **Auditorium Building** (430 S Michigan Avenue, at E Congress Parkway; 312 922 4046), a stone's toss from the Fine Arts Building, is sometimes billed as the building that put Chicago on the cultural map. Conceived as the city was gearing up for the World's Columbian Exposition, its theatre was dedicated in 1889 by President Benjamin Harrison as the first home of the Chicago Opera. During World War II, it was converted into a servicemen's centre, and the stage was used as a bowling alley. In 1960 the Auditorium Theater Council was formed and raised $3 million for restoration work; it reopened in 1967. It's now on the National Register of Historic Places, and open again as a theatre. Tours can be arranged on 312 431 2354.

Chicago Cultural Center

78 E Washington Boulevard, at N Michigan Avenue (312 346 3278/312 744 6630/ www.cityofchicago.com). CTA Randolph (Brown, Green, Orange, Purple) or Washington (Blue, Red). **Open** 10am-7pm Mon-Wed; 10am-9pm Thur; 10am-6pm Fri; 10am-5pm Sat; 11am-5pm Sun. **Admission** free. **Map** p305 J12.

This block-long building was built in 1897 and offers a great deal for the architectural and design connoisseur: two Tiffany domes, a grand marble staircase, several glass mosaics and. Exhibitions, lectures and concerts are held here regularly, and it's an invaluable resource for cultural information. The **Museum of Broadcast Communications** (*see p78*) is on the ground floor.

Hellenic Museum & Cultural Center

4th Floor, Atlantic Bank Building, 168 N Michigan Avenue, at E Randolph Street (312 726 1234/ hellenicmuseum.org). CTA Lake (Red) or State (Brown, Green, Orange, Purple). **Open** 10am-4pm Mon-Fri. **Admission** *Suggested donation* $4. **Credit** MC, V. **Map** p305 J11.

Dedicated to the preservation of Greek culture, Chicago's Hellenic Museum derives many of its pieces from the collections of local Greek families, but it's by no means only of interest to those with Greek connections. Impressively instructive in relating the history of Greeks in America and in Chicago in particular, the museum offers a rota of temporary exhibitions – recent displays have included the history of Chicago's Greektown and a photographic review of Crete's changing culture – alongside a programme of lectures, discussions and performances.

Sightseeing

Need to cool off? Head for the **Buckingham Fountain** in Grant Park.

Museum of Broadcast Communications

Chicago Cultural Center, 78 E Washington Boulevard, at N Michigan Avenue (312 629 6000/www.museum.tv). CTA Randolph (Brown, Green, Orange, Purple) or Washington (Blue, Red). **Open** 10am-4.30pm Mon-Sat; noon-5pm Sun. **Admission** free. **Map** p305 J12.

The fact the Museum of Broadcast Communications doesn't have its own building – it's tucked shyly away in the Chicago Cultural Center – may contribute to its low profile. But try not to miss out: the MBC, which turned 15 in June 2002, is a little gem. The pick of the permanent exhibits is the Radio Hall of Fame, a series of imaginative displays devoted to innovative broadcasters such as Jack Benny and Don McNeill. Cubs fan can enjoy a permanent exhibition, installed in 2001, that commemorates the career of legendary broadcaster Jack Brickhouse.

The temporary shows on a variety of topics are usually winning, while the second-floor archive – open to the public – holds 13,000 TV shows, 4,000 radio programmes, 11,000 commercials and 5,000 newscasts. But the real kicks here are interactive: budding sportscasters can attempt to call a half-inning of baseball, but even that pales next to the TV studio where, by booking ahead and forking out $20, visitors can record their own TV newscast and walk away with a tape of their efforts. Terrific fun.

Grant Park

East of the Loop along Lake Michigan is Grant Park, which stretches from Randolph south to Roosevelt roughly between Michigan Avenue and the lake. Built on landfill in the 1920s, the park's 220 acres (89 hectares) are home to the **Petrillo Music Shell** (*see p225* **Chicago calendar**), festivals such as the **Taste of Chicago** (*see p190*) and two rose gardens. It's also nationally known as the site of riots during the 1968 Democratic National Convention.

A new park, costing over $230 million, is scheduled to be completed in Grant Park's north-west corner by 2003. That said, the park's proposed name – **Millennium Park** – should indicate just how badly construction has been held up. When – and if – the project is finally finished, it will include newly commissioned sculptures and a vast band shell designed by Frank Gehry, the architect behind the Guggenheim Museum in Bilbao, Spain.

Today, Grant Park's most recognisable feature is **Buckingham Fountain** (in operation from 1 May until mid October), a gift to the city in 1927 from the family of Clarence Buckingham, a trustee and benefactor of the Art Institute. Modelled after the fountain in Versailles, only to twice its size, the fountain uses more than a million gallons of water. It symbolises Lake Michigan and is surrounded by a pool edged by four bronze sea horses representing Michigan, Illinois, Minnesota and Wisconsin, the four states that border the lake. Framed by more than 5,000 rose bushes, the pink marble fountain is lit in the evening, making it a popular attraction. And on the Michigan Avenue edge of Grant Park, two lions guard the entrance to the **Art Institute of Chicago**, one of Chicago's most magnificent edifices and one of the world's great museums.

Sightseeing

Made in Chicago Scott Turow

'I was now up to the intersection of Duhaney and Shields, one of these grand city neighborhoods, the league of nations, four blocks with eleven languages, all of them displayed on the garish signs flogging bargains that are pasted in the store windows'
(from *Pleading Guilty*)

Before anyone had ever heard of John Grisham, a native Chicagoan wrote a novel that set the standard for the (post)modern American legal thriller. *Presumed Innocent*, Scott Turow's first novel, emerged fairly quietly in 1987. However, the book took off dramatically, acclaimed by critics and adored by the public, and was made into a very successful movie starring Harrison Ford just three years later. Not bad for a novel written by a lawyer as he rode on the train to work.

The Burden of Proof, Pleading Guilty, The Laws of Our Fathers and *Personal Injuries*, all of them crime-themed pageturners set in Kindle County, followed *Presumed Innocent* on to bookstore shelves and to the top of the bestseller lists. Kindle is fictional, but if parts of it seem to find echoes in Chicago, there's a good reason. As Turow admits, 'Kindle County is surely inspired by Cook County, but is not a clone. There are places like Lower Wacker Drive that show up as Lower River Drive and other locales that are entirely imaginary, or drawn from other cities.'

That's as maybe. But Chicago, with its mix of Midwestern mores and bustling urbanity, is as integral to Turow's books as any human character. If you were to swing by the Criminal Courts at 26th and California on the South-west Side, you'd likely recognise them from Turow's books. Scenes set in the halls of power are also fairly faithful to their Chicago originals: the City Hall/Cook County Building

in the Loop, for example, bounded by LaSalle, Randolph, Washington and Clark. There are others, too.

'These days, Lower River, as this area was known, was eerie with the garish yellow glow of sulfur lamps... the air sang with the racing pitch of tires on the roads above and the windy commotion of that traffic... the flow of hot merchandise across the trucking piers, by rumor, was still steady'
(from *The Burden of Proof*)

Turow's success hasn't caused him to give up his day job. He's still a partner at law firm Sonnenschein, Nath & Rosenthal, spending his time on white-collar criminal litigation from offices in the Sears Tower. But between this work, raising three kids and playing the occasional gig with terrifying all-authors rock band the Rock Bottom Remainders (alongside the unlikely likes of Stephen King, Dave Barry and Greil Marcus), Turow still finds time to pen a novel every three years or so, with his sixth, *Reversible Errors*, out in late 2002.

Turow often cites Nobel Prize-winning fellow Chicagoan Saul Bellow as one of his two major influences (the other is Dickens). He's not quite that good, of course. But his books are far from the trashy potboilers of popular misconception. Even if their city doesn't always come away spotless from his portrayals, Chicagoans can feel proud.

'Kindle County, Seth thinks. Always something dirty doin. Always amazing him. Will he ever escape this place? No... This is where his dreams are set. In the air of childhood, tinted with the oily-smelling smoke and ash of burnt coal. No escaping'
(from *The Laws of Our Fathers*)

Art Institute of Chicago

111 S Michigan Avenue, at W Adams Street (312 443 3600/www.artic.edu). CTA Adams (Brown, Green, Orange, Purple) or Jackson (Blue, Red). **Open** 10.30am-4.30pm Mon, Wed-Fri; 10.30am-8pm Tue; 10am-5pm Sat, Sun. **Admission** *Suggested donation* $10; $6 5-16s, over-55s, students; free under-5s. Free to all Tue. **Credit** AmEx, DC, Disc, MC, V. **Map** p305 J12.

Opened in 1879 as a school and museum, the Art Institute grew into a world-famous museum known for its collections of Impressionist and post-Impressionist paintings. Among the most famous

pieces are Picasso's *The Old Guitarist*, Seurat's *A Sunday on La Grande Jette – 1884* (which Ferris Bueller ogled at on his day off), Edward Hopper's *Nighthawks* and Grant Wood's *American Gothic*, though the museum also holds numerous Van Goghs, Magrittes, Matisses, Whistlers, Homers, Monets and Renoirs. Less celebrated but equally worthy are the Asian, medieval, modern and Renaissance art collections, while other diversions include a faithfully rebuilt model of the old Chicago Stock Exchange, a sculpture garden, a paperweight collection, and Kraft's Education Center, which has dozens of games to keep children interested during

Look up when you're walking in the Loop, or you'll miss details like this, on Madison.

what could well be a whole day's visit; especially when you bear in mind the splendid temporary exhibitions that keep things fresh for the locals and provide tourists with one more reason to visit this exceptional institution.

South Loop

The **One Financial Place** building (440 S LaSalle Street, at W Congress Parkway) stands above the Eisenhower Expressway. If you're in a car, you can't miss it: traffic heading in or out of the Loop drives under the building, through arches that serve as stilts. Built in 1985 by the same architects who drew the **Sears Tower** (*see p70*), it's home to the top-rated **Everest** restaurant (*see p127*) and the **Midwest Stock Exchange**, the second-largest in the US.

When the 16-storey **Monadnock** Building was erected in 1891 at 53 W Jackson Boulevard (at S Dearborn Street), it was the tallest and heaviest load-bearing structure in the world. Today, it's still the world's tallest all-masonry building, and in order to support the weight, the building's walls are six feet (two metres) thick at the base and thin out as the building rises.

The top 16 floors of the **Metropolitan Correctional Center**, a triangular building at 71 W Van Buren Street (at S Federal Street), house federal prisoners and suspects awaiting trial. Windows on those floors can be only five inches wide, the maximum size allowed by the Federal Department of Corrections – so small that no bars are required – and a total of 44 prisoners can be held here at one time. Offices occupy the bottom 11 floors, so don't worry if the windows there look a little large.

Welcome respite comes courtesy of the **Harold Washington Library Center** (400 S State Street, at W Congress Parkway; 312 747 4999/www.chipublib.org), named after the city's first African-American mayor and located at the southern tip of the Loop on State Street. Built in 1991 of granite and brick with a terracotta exterior, the building blends in with its long-standing neighbours, borrowing details from some of Chicago's most famous structures. Inside is a 400-seat auditorium theatre, the Chicago Blues Archives, the Jazz, Blues and Gospel Hall of Fame, and some two million volumes to pore over (including a small sale area, Second Hand Prose, which sells books retired from circulation for 25 cents and up). South and east of the library is the **Spertus Museum** (*see below*).

On S Dearborn Street between Congress and Polk is a strip known as **Printer's Row**, which takes its name from the printers that dominated the area in the late 19th century. The printers have long since gone, though, and the area – along with the neighbourhood known as **Dearborn Park** just south of it – is now dominated by yuppie-owned lofts and condos. Still, there are a fair few decent cafés and restaurants around here – the pick of them being **Prairie** (*see p126*) – and a stroll around here during the day makes a pleasant contrast from the frequently chaotic Loop.

Spertus Museum

Spertus Institute of Jewish Studies, 618 S Michigan Avenue, at E Harrison Street (312 322 1747/ www.spertus.edu). CTA Harrison (Red).
Open 10am-5pm Mon-Thur; 10am-3pm Sun. Free to all Fri. **Admission** $5; $3 children, seniors, students. **Credit** MC V. **Map** p305 J13.
Created to reflect the rich diversity of Jewish culture, the sizeable Spertus Museum on Michigan Avenue offers an impressive collection of artefacts from all over the world: a staggering 10,000 in total, including ancient Torah scrolls. However, the permanent displays here – which also include the Zell Holocaust Memorial, and a lively facility for kids in the basement, the Rosenbaum Artifact Center – tend to take second billing to the temporary shows and lectures, many with a historical slant. The Asher Library holds some 100,000 books alongside periodicals, sound recordings and videos, and is open to everyone.

Museum Campus & Near South Side

Before the South Side's urban sprawl come three world-class tourist attractions.

Museum Campus

No prizes for guessing what the dominant attractions are around these parts. The area in question, a small pocket of culture south of the Loop near Soldier Field, was only christened in the late 1990s, after Lake Shore Drive was shunted away from the lake. The three attractions – the Adler Planetarium, the Shedd Aquarium and the Field Museum – that had long called the area home finally became more accessible to pedestrians, who can now skip merrily between the three without risking being turned into roadkill by the passing traffic. For years, the adventures detailed in the Field Museum were chicken feed compared to the expedition pedestrians had to endure even to reach it.

Any comprehensive tour of Chicago's attractions really ought to start at this large, grassy quad. Museum Campus is roughly equivalent to a mid-sized city park in area and holds the nation's oldest planetarium (indeed, the oldest in the western hemisphere), its largest aquarium and one of the world's finest anthropological resource centres. Get off the El at Harrison and take a slight detour through Grant Park via the Buckingham Fountain (*see p78*); you'll be left with a 20-minute walk to the museums along the lake path, which on a sunny day is among the loveliest strolls in the city.

Adler Planetarium

1300 S Lake Shore Drive, at E Solidarity Drive (312 322 0590/www.adlerplanetarium.org). CTA Roosevelt/State (Red) or Roosevelt/Wabash (Green, Orange). **Open** 9.30am-4.30pm daily. **Admission** *Museum & one show* $13; $12 over-65s; $11 4-17s. Additional show $3. *Mon & Tue, Sept-Feb* free museum; $6 one show; $3 additional show. **Credit** AmEx, Disc, MC, V. **Map** p305 J14.

The name of this facility on the banks of Lake Michigan is only semi-appropriate: this excellent enterprise is a lot more than just a planetarium. For a start, there are actually two planetariums here: the high-tech StarRider Theater, added as part of a $40-million facelift in the late 1990s, and the Sky Theater, an old-school affair. Between them, they offer four shows that run in rotation throughout the day; try *Images of the Infinite*, a fascinating survey of snaps taken from the Hubble Telescope.

However, allow some time to wander around the Astronomy Museum here, underplayed on the promotional literature and in other guidebooks but actually just as appealing, if not more so, than the planetariums themselves. Reached via a disorienting walkway, the opening exhibit offers assorted titbits – if the earth is a baseball, then the moon is a ping-pong ball eight feet away – that set the tone for the remainder of the museum: it's interactive, interesting and kid-friendly without being dumbed-down. Look out, in particular, for the vast Dearborn telescope (part of the museum's enviable collection of historically significant scientific instruments) and the fun 3-D Milky Way Galaxy.

Adler Planetarium.

311 S Wacker Drive
See p30 & p69

Sears Tower
See p30 & p70

AT&T Center
See p30

Bank One Plaza
See p30

55 E Monroe Building

Leo Burnett Building

RR Donnelley Building

The view from outside the Adler Planetarium.

The building that holds the Planetarium, built in 1930, is a 12-sided architectural marvel, each side representing a sign of the zodiac. And even if you don't plan on going inside, it's worth strolling down to it: the grass verge outside offers one of the best and most complete land-locked, ground-level views of Chicago's skyline.

Field Museum of Natural History

1400 S Lake Shore Drive, at E Roosevelt Road (312 922 9410/www.fieldmuseum.org). CTA Roosevelt/ State (Red) or Roosevelt/Wabash (Green, Orange). **Open** *late May-early Sept 9am-5pm daily. Early Sept-late May* 10am-5pm Mon-Fri; 9am-5pm Sat, Sun. **Admission** $8; $4 3-11s, seniors, students; free under-3s. Free to all Mon & Tue, Sept-Feb. **Credit** AmEx, Disc, MC, V. **Map** p305 J14.

The Field Museum opened as part of the World's Columbian Exposition in 1893 as the Columbia Museum of Chicago, but was renamed after philanthropist and department store magnate Marshall Field in the early 20th century, and moved to its jaw-dropping location soon after. A must-see for anyone visiting Chicago, the museum is one of the most impressive natural science centres in the world, with a wealth of biological and anthropological exhibits and world-class on-site research facilities.

The big draw here is Sue, the world's largest Tyrannosaurus rex. Since she made her debut here in the late 1990s, Sue has become a mini-industry all by itself (its sex is actually unknown; it's named after Susan Hendrickson, who unearthed the skeleton in North Dakota in 1990). Kids come here just to

Smurfit-Stone Building
See p73

IBM Building
See p31

1 Prudential Plaza
See p30 & p74

2 Prudential Plaza
See p30 & p74

Aon Center
See p30

Blue Cross-Blue Shield Tower

400 E Randolph Building

John Hancock Center
See p30 & p89

Park Shore Apartments

see her standing proudly near the north entrance of the museum, while parents rue the amount and variety of Sue merchandise available at the well-stocked museum shops. Sue even gets a store all to herself on the Upper Level, though this is little wonder when you learn that the dinosaur cost the museum a cool $8.36 million at auction.

Popular though Sue is, she's by no means the whole story. The Field is too big to comfortably get around in a day, but pick up a map and plan your visit carefully, and you'll be rewarded. Among the standout exhibits are the display on the North American Indian, the World of Birds corner ('Hear the kookaburra laugh!'), the large section on Africa (which includes an instructive section on slavery), the educative, push-button What is an Animal?, and

the famed (and stuffed) lions of Tsavo. Egyptology remains one of the major thrusts of the museum; Inside Ancient Egypt, where visitors explore a burial chamber and visit a village by a stream, remains one of its most popular attractions.

All these exhibits are on the Ground Level. The displays on the Upper Level are slightly more adult-oriented (with the exception of the McDonald's Fossil Preparation Lab), while the Lower Level is largely set aside for temporary exhibits – on topics from chocolate to Freud – and the much-trailed but frankly disappointing disappointing Underground Adventure. If you still can't decide what to see, time your visit to coincide with one of the fine free tours of the museum's highlights, which take place at 11am and 2pm during the week.

The **Field Museum**. *See p82.*

Shedd Aquarium

1200 S Lake Shore Drive, at E McFetridge Drive (312 939 2438/www.sheddaquarium.org). CTA Roosevelt/ State (Red) or Roosevelt/Wabash (Green, Orange). **Open** *Sept-May* 9am-5pm Mon-Fri; 9am-6pm Sat, Sun. *June-Aug* 9am-6pm daily. **Admission** *Aquarium* $8; $6 3-11s, over-65s; free under-3s. *Aquarium & oceanarium* $15; $11 3-11s, over-65s; free under-3s. *Mon & Tue, Sept-Feb* Aquarium free; oceanarium $7; $5 3-11s, over-65s; free under-3s. **Credit** AmEx, Disc, MC, V. **Map** p305 K14.

The Shedd Aquarium is housed in a beautiful, circular 1920s building on the lake, and holds every conceivable kind of fish and water mammal. Enter through the main lobby and you'll be greeted by a large Caribbean coral reef exhibit, spectacularly plonked in the middle of a large domed hall. From this central root protrude a number of branches – corridor-like exhibition spaces devoted to themes from the exotic (African tropical fish) to the everyday (trout native to the lakes and rivers of Illinois). The displays are clearly labelled and the layout of the exhibits – you can approach them in any order – means that even when the museum's busy, there are always displays less crammed than others.

The aquarium doubled in size in 1991 with the addition of its spectacular $45-million Oceanarium. It's an extraordinary place, dominated by a vast tank in which whales and dolphins swim and perform shows several times daily for enthusiastic crowds. Out of showtimes, it looks strangely empty, until you discover the downstairs viewing galleries that offer a window into underwater. Elsewhere, there are exhibits on sea lions and penguins (more graceful in water than out of it). However, though the Oceanarium's raison d'être is to recreate the conditions of the Pacific Northwest, it's never lived down the controversy generated when it was announced it would be home to five beluga whales, in the process removing them from their Arctic habitats. There have also been whisperings that the Oceanarium has not proven as popular as management has hoped, rumours given credence by the speed with which the aquarium laid off 15% of its staff after September 11. Still, face facts: if you have kids, you'll be joining the two million who come here annually whether you like it or not. And you probably will. Like it, that is.

Near South Side

As is the way in so many major US cities, population overspill and entrepreneurial savvy have meant that previously rundown areas in Chicago are rapidly being converted into bijou locales for urbanites with the facility to drop several hundred thousand dollars. Wicker Park and Bucktown, once dilapidated but now very much up and coming, are the most obvious examples of such gentrification, with the area around Fulton Market on the West Side not far behind them, but parts of the Near South Side are rapidly being upgraded in a similar fashion.

The key word there is 'parts', however. The Near South Side – which can be loosely defined as stretching from Roosevelt Road in the north down to McCormick Place and the I-55 in the south, east of the Chicago River – is still a very bitty area. The character can change in a block or two: in the space of three-quarters of a mile, you can find suited conventioneers, a thriving Chinese community, a pocket of architectural history, derelict and soon-to-be-converted warehouses and down-at-heel housing projects. It's not, perhaps, as unsafe as it looks, but care should still be taken walking in some areas, while others – the housing project that falls halfway between Prairie Avenue and Chinatown – should be completely avoided.

If you're here on business and, specifically, for a convention, you're likely to find yourself at **McCormick Place** (E 23rd Street, at S Lake Shore Drive) for much of your stay. A gargantuan site that's home to about 500 zillion conventioneers each year, it doesn't bear detailing in any great depth. Still, a few points are worth making: first, it's vast, with over two million square feet (over 186,000 square metres) of meeting space and excellent facilities; second, the massive conventions held here are the reason why mere vacationers have trouble finding a hotel room in Chicago; and third, it's an absolute bugger to get back from at the end of the day. For more information, consult its website, www.mccormickplace.com, or call 312 791 7000.

Just north of McCormick Place is the **Prairie Avenue Historical District**, which is where you'll find some lovely examples of old Chicago architecture. During the late 1900s, before the city's shift in opulent living from the South Side to the North Side, this was the grandest part of town, home to many of the city's leading magnates and high-society types. Tours of **Clarke House** and **Glessner House** (*see p86*) are available, though while you're there, be sure to take a peek at the exteriors of the neighbouring houses, which include the **William B Kimball House**, the **Joseph G Coleman House** and the **Elbridge G Keith House**, all on S Prairie Avenue at No.1801, No.1811 and No.1900 respectively. Ask nicely, and your guide will be able to fill you in on the intriguing history of the area and these houses in particular. (Incidentally, and somewhat bizarrely, the Kimball and Coleman houses are now home to the US Soccer Federation.)

Back to the present, though, and a quick stroll around the surrounding streets will reveal real signs of gentrification. Old warehouses have been converted into lofts, and new apartment complexes have sprung up around the area. A nearby building holds the **National Vietnam Veterans' Art Museum** (*see p86*),

but by the time you've reached the **Blues Heaven Foundation** (*see below*), the feel of the locale has changed again.

It'll change again a half-mile further west in Chicago's Chinatown, located near the junction of W Cermak Road and S Wentworth Avenue (where you'll find the Red line's Cermak-Chinatown stop). Here, you'll find the majority of the Near South Side's nightlife, much of it in the shape of fantastic Chinese restaurants such as **Emperor's Choice** (*see p149*).

Blues Heaven Foundation

2120 S Michigan Avenue, at E 21st Street (312 808 1286/www.2120.com). CTA Cermak-Chinatown (Red). **Open** noon-2pm Mon, Wed-Fri; noon-3pm Sat. **Admission** $10; $8 high school students; $5 over-55s; $3.75 6-12s. **Credit** MC, V. **Map** p304 J16. Chicago is, among other things, home to more blues legends, clubs and stories than anywhere besides Clarksdale, Mississippi and maybe Memphis, Tennessee. The former headquarters of Chess Records – aka the home of Chicago blues – is now a non-profit museum, and is as good a place as any to learn about Chicago's rich blues history.

Tours of the Blues Heaven Foundation are comprehensive, erudite and, unlike a lot of museum tours, actually fun. Blues heroes like Willie Dixon (who set up the Blues Heaven Foundation to preserve the Chess legacy, and whose widow bought the building in which it sits), Koko Taylor (whose long-ago classic *Wang Dang Doodle* may as well be the Chicago anthem) and Muddy Waters (who surely needs no introduction) recorded here, and their presence is felt

Clarke House, a Prairie Avenue gem. *See p86.*

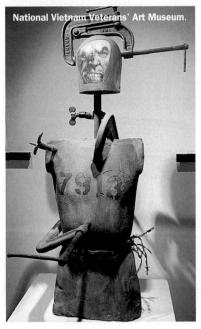

National Vietnam Veterans' Art Museum.

in every corner of the building. Incidentally, rock scholars may find the building's address already rings a bell: if so, it's probably because the Rolling Stones recorded a song entitled *2120 South Michigan Avenue* after a session here.

Glessner House & Clarke House Mansion

1800 S Prairie Avenue, at E 18th Street (312 326 1480/www.glessnerhouse.org). CTA Cermak-Chinatown (Red). **Open** *Glessner House tours* noon, 1pm, 2pm Wed-Sun. *Clarke House tours* 1pm, 2pm, 3pm Wed-Sun. **Admission** *1 house* $7; $6 over-55s, students. *Both houses* $11; $9 over-55s, students. Free to all Wed. **Credit** MC, V. **Map** p304 J16.

Although a walk around the Prairie Avenue Historic District is enjoyable, it'd be foolish not to take the opportunity to tour two of the area's finest buildings while you're there. The Clarke House, a breathtaking Greek revival built in 1836, is the oldest house in the city and an impressive monument to the area's past glories. It's also the grander of the two buildings, although arguably the lesser in terms of architectural importance. Remarkably, it's had to be moved twice to avoid demolition.

The Glessner House was built half a century after its near-neighbour by Henry Hobson Richardson, who died in the same year the building was completed (1886). It was a very radical building for its time – something that should be immediately apparent from the prepossessing granite exterior – and caused outrage among the Glessners' neighbours. Happily, the family stuck out the haranguing and the building survives to this day (despite a demolition threat in 1966). Fascinating tours of both houses are conducted by Chicago Architecture Foundation volunteers; meet up in the Glessner's coach house, whose entrance sits on 18th Street.

National Vietnam Veterans' Art Museum

1801 S Indiana Avenue, at E 18th Street (312 326 0270/www.nvvam.org). CTA Cermak-Chinatown (Red). **Open** 11am-6pm Tue-Fri; 10am-5pm Sat; noon-5pm Sun. **Admission** $5; $4 seniors, students. Free to all Wed. **Credit** MC, V. **Map** p304 J16.

The only museum of its type in the US, this spacious spot in the Prairie Avenue Historic District is devoted entirely to art produced by veterans of the conflict in Vietnam, the vast majority of it taking conflict as its subject matter. But as artist Michael Aschenbrenner points out in an introduction to the exhibits, the art here is not just about 'broken bones and bleeding soldiers': the art here clearly goes deeper than these surface images, and acted as a form of therapy for some of the artists on display. Among the standouts are Laszlo Kondor's combat photographs, Ca Ba Minh's eye-catching oils, and the truly hideous *Real Dead Dead* by Art Dockter. The most striking and iconic exhibit, though, hangs from the ceiling: *Above and Beyond* features 58,226 silver dogtags, one for each American who died or went missing in action during the war.

Near North

Shops, galleries, restaurants, clubs… Welcome to downtown Chicago.

You'll know you're in the **River North** district when you suddenly find yourself blinded by bars and restaurants that have been marked by garish landmarks such as those that adorn the Rainforest Café (a big green frog) and the Hard Rock Café (an oversized guitar). Move beyond the gaudy eateries, however, and you'll be delighted by the galleries that are increasingly taking over as River North's claim to fame.

River North, which runs south of Chicago Avenue and west of Rush Street to the Chicago River, is dominated by its cosy commercial galleries and neon-lit nightlife. The stretch of Michigan Avenue known as the **Magnificent Mile** is all about shopping, shopping, shopping. East of Michigan Avenue is **Streeterville**, home to Navy Pier, the excellent Museum of Contemporary Art (*see p94*) and an array of hotels. Together, these three neighbourhoods make up the area broadly known as Near North, the hub of Chicago consumerism.

River North & surrounds

Settled by Irish immigrants in the 1840s, River North was a largely industrial area until the end of World War I, when many factories began to fail. The area hit bottom in the 1950s, when its stately homes were converted into low-rent apartments. Two decades later, however, abandoned buildings morphed into artists' studios and dance clubs, and entertainment venues opened at a furious rate. At night, the area – not least around Clark Street – is a magnet for out-of-towners looking to pay too much for a drink.

Welcome contrast can be found in the area bounded by Chicago (north), Wells (east), Erie (south) and Orleans (west) during the day: known as the River North Gallery District, these streets contain 70 galleries, all of which welcome casual visitors (*see p205*). However, the area's popularity with young artists is nothing new: lawyer and philanthropist Lambert Tree built **Tree Studios** (4 E Ohio Street, at N State Street) as an affordable home for Chicago artists in 1894. Most of the city's best-known artists have lived or worked here. The city fathers saved the buildings from the wrecking ball in 2001; now, artists share the space with the Medinah Temple Association, whose main building is where Tree's home stood. The faces of Lambert and his wife Ann can be seen in carvings near the Ohio Street entrance.

The **Magnificent Mile**.

Walk on Chicago churches

Much of downtown Chicago revels in the spiky modernity of its architecture. But hidden between the skyscraping offices, malls and hotels are several churches, providing solace from the hectic streetlife and a little calm amid the steel and glass. None is especially old – the Chicago Fire of 1871 saw to that – but in this context, they look and feel a great deal more ancient than they actually are.

This 1.5-mile (2.5-kilometre) walk takes in seven houses of worship, though forward planning is required if you want to see inside all seven on one jaunt: service times vary and not every church is open to the public every day. Call to check.

Start at the corner of Wabash and Huron, near Chicago station on the Red line. Erected in 1857 and rebuilt after the Chicago Fire, the Episcopalian **St James Cathedral** (*pictured*; 65 E Huron Street; 312 787 7360/ www.saintjamescathedral.org; tours after 11am Eucharist first Sun of month, or by request) is a handsome building. The unusual interior walls are decorated with stencil patterns in more than 20 colours; you'd never guess it from the traditionally Gothic exterior.

St Andrew's Chapel details the odd tale that surrounds the founding of the Brotherhood of St Andrew in 1893. As the story goes, a bible class was interrupted by a drunk looking for solace. The students were unable to help, but he inspired them to found an evangelical society. The Brotherhood is now a worldwide group with thousands of members. The whereabouts of the drunk are not recorded.

Head west down Huron, then take the first right up State and walk north for two blocks. **Holy Name Cathedral** (735 N State Street; 312 787 8040/www.holynamecathedral.org; tours by request) has served as the cathedral of the Catholic Archdiocese of Chicago for more than a century. Built in 1875, more than 5,000 people attended the Victorian Gothic cathedral's dedication and parade. Note the crucifix above the main altar, designed by

Italian artist Ivo Demetz, and the monumental gallery organ, installed in 1989.

From here, walk up State for two blocks, then turn right into Chestnut and continue two blocks to the junction with Rush. The **Quigley Seminary** (103 E Chestnut Street; 312 787 9343/www.quigley.org; tours noon-2pm Tue, Thur-Sat) is named after Archbishop James Quigley, who established a school in 1905 to prepare boys for the priesthood. The Gothic buildings and courtyard were modelled after the Sainte-Chapelle in Paris. The highlight is the St James Chapel (312 787 8625/www.windows.org), whose choice of URL only hints at the beauty of its 14 stained-glass windows. Smart visitors time a visit to coincide with a concert here.

Continue along Chestnut for a block, to the junction with Michigan Avenue. The impact of the **Fourth Presbyterian Church** (126 E Chestnut Street; 312 787 4570/www.fourthchurch.org; tours after 11am service Sun) has been diminished by the Hancock Center opposite. However, the church still impresses. Check out the fountain

Tree Studios sits in the heart of one of Near North's main entertainment districts. The local authorities here tried to christen the streets bordered by Michigan, Hubbard, State and Ontario with the name North Bridge, but the tag has never caught on with either visitors or locals. Neither, it must be said, has the area, an unprepossessing collection of retail outlets and pricey eating and entertainment options, such

as the sports-themed **ESPN Zone** (*see p153*). However, the 2001 closure of DisneyQuest doesn't bode well for the future of North Bridge: if Disney can't make it here, who can?

Several blocks south-east of Tree Studios stands the former nemesis of Chicago's criminal contingent. **Courthouse Place** (54 W Hubbard Street, at N Dearborn Street), the former Cook County Court building, was built in 1892 as the in the ivy-trimmed courtyard, a retreat from the maddening strip. The church moved here in 1914, when it outgrew its previous site at Rush and Superior. This one replaced its first home, destroyed by the Chicago Fire on the night it was dedicated.

Continue north up Michigan and follow it as it turns into Lake Shore Drive. Six blocks north, you'll reach Division; here, turn left. After a visit to St James Chapel, the stained glass at the **Lake Shore Drive Synagogue** (70 E Elm Street; 312 337 6811; tours by request) might initially seem lame. However, only a wearied scholar will fail to be taken in by its exuberance and colour. The synagogue was built at the tail-end of the 19th century; its opening hours can be erratic, so call ahead to check before showing up.

Carry on east up Division and turn right into Dearborn; walk north for 400 metres. The Gold Coast is a quiet locale. However, that changes when the late 19th-century **St Chrysostom's Episcopal Church** (1424 N Dearborn Parkway; 312 944 1083/ www.saintc.org; tours by request) decides to remind the locals of its looming Gothic presence. The church lets rip its monster 43-bell Crane Memorial Carillon; as aural torture goes, this ding-dong racket is up there with anything in the city.

Carry on to the junction with North Avenue, and turn left. Follow the road around and up Clark, past the Chicago Historical Society. Named after 19th-century evangelist Dwight L Moody and completed in 1925, the huge **Moody Church** (1630 N Clark Street; 312 943 0466/www.moodychurch.org; tours by request) stands as grand witness to a more God-fearing age than ours. Built in 1925, it holds some 3,800 worshippers; among the building's more notable features are the chandelier-lit balcony and the vast proscenium arch beneath which the choir sits.

second county courts facility. It's now an office building, but over the years it has been the site of some great legal stories: chief among them, the 1924 performance of attorney Clarence Darrow that saved convicted murderers Leopold and Loeb from a certain death sentence. Courthouse Place was also formerly used for hangings, and is purported to be haunted.

The remaining attractions in River North are architectural, none more special than **Marina City** (300 N State Street, at the Chicago River). Two buildings house trapezoid apartments on the top 40 floors, with the lower 20 used for parking. The towers, nicknamed the Corncobs for reasons that will become obvious the moment you see them, are best admired from the south bank of the River, especially at night.

Further west is a monument to consumerism that rivals any on the Mag Mile. Originally built in 1931 as showrooms and a wholesale office for Marshall Field, the **Merchandise Mart** (between Wells and Orleans , on the Chicago River; 312 644 4664) is second in size only to the Pentagon, with 4.2 million square feet (390,000 square metres) of floor space. Field sold the building to Joseph P Kennedy when the Mart hit hard times in the 1930s, and it was Kennedy who installed the freakish Merchandise Mart Hall of Fame in 1953, honouring captains of industry with busts. Today, tours of the 600 showrooms are given at noon on weekdays, though the lower two levels have been open to the public as a retail shopping mall since 1991.

The Magnificent Mile

A couple of years after World War II, real estate developer Arthur Rubloff launched a promotional campaign aimed at revitalising Michigan Avenue by renovating old buildings and erecting new ones. As part of his schtick, he fancifully pinned the strip as the 'Magnificent Mile'. And the schtick worked. Within years, the area had been regenerated, and Rubloff had made a mint. The later addition of buildings such as the John Hancock Center and the level of civic pride exhibited by the city – check out the beautiful lights that line the street at Christmas, for example – have made the mile a genuinely magnificent one.

Michigan Avenue is best approached from its south side, where a wander north over the Chicago River will afford some revealing views of the waterside architecture and the sweep of the river. Opened at the south end of Michigan Avenue in 1920, the **Michigan Avenue Bridge** was a boon to the area north of the Chicago River, making access to the Loop that much easier for residents and businessmen. A plaque at the south-eastern end of the bridge commemorates Fort Dearborn, the military outpost from which the city developed, while four sculptures on pylons along the bridge represent major Chicago events: the arrival of Jolliet and Marquette, trader Jean Baptiste Point du Sable's settlement, the Fort Dearborn Massacre and the rebuilding following the Chicago Fire of 1871.

However, stand on the bridge as the sun sets on a summer's day and it's unlikely you'll notice any of them, such are the stunning views from the bridge itself. Not even the **Chicago Sun-Times Building**, west of Michigan along the river and designed to resemble a steel barge, can ruin the vista. Donald Trump has proposed a plan to demolish the building and replace it with a multipurpose skyscraper that would become Chicago's fourth tallest building.

The home of the city's other main daily paper is far more handsome. The design for **Tribune Tower** (435 N Michigan Avenue, at E Illinois Street) was selected in 1922 by then-publisher Colonel Robert McCormick from a field of international entries. The Gothic tower houses the daily newspaper, the *Trib*-owned WGN radio station – the letters stand for World's Greatest Newspaper – and CLTV, Chicago's local television news station. Scattered about the first-floor exterior of the building are stones purportedly pirated from landmarks around the world by *Tribune* hacks, among them chunks from the Alamo, St Peter's Basilica, the Berlin Wall and the Parthenon. Tours of the tower are available, but only by booking on 312 222 2116.

The headquarters of the Wrigley chewing gum company are located across the street from Tribune Tower in the **Wrigley Building** (400 N Michigan Avenue). A white terracotta building designed by the same architects who created Union Station (*see p70*) and the Merchandise Mart (*see above*), the building has stood at the base of Michigan Avenue since 1922. The clock tower was based on a similar tower on the cathedral in Seville, Spain.

While Michigan Avenue has its share of breathtaking architecture, the main reason most people flock here is to shop. The endless rows of retail outlets don't disappoint: from the five-storey Crate & Barrel to Burberry's, Tiffany to Niketown, the streets are lined with temples to consumerism. It's easy to miss the **Terra Museum of American Art** (*see p92*).

The are several malls between Oak Street and the river. Among them are **The Shops at North Bridge** at No.520; **Chicago Place** at No.700; **Water Tower Place** at No.835; and **900 N Michigan Avenue**, where you'll find Bloomingdale's. (For more on them all, *see p169* **Mall talk**). Intersecting Michigan is Oak Street, Chicago's equivalent of Rodeo Drive, complete with upscale designer boutiques including Versace, Betsey Johnson and Barney's.

The **Water Tower** and **Chicago Water Works** (163 E Pearson Street, at N Michigan Avenue; 312 744 2400) were two of the few structures to survive the Chicago Fire of 1871. When Oscar Wilde visited the city in 1882, he described the tower as 'a castellated monstrosity with pepper boxes stuck all over it'. That doesn't stop people from gathering in the small plaza around the building, a favourite spot for amateur musicians and artists looking for a little spare change. The Water Tower is home to an art gallery, while the Water Works houses a visitors' centre, a deli, a gift shop and an

Looking north from the **John Hancock Observatory**. Don't forget your camera.

animated 'Honest' Abe Lincoln. It's here, too, that visitors line up to nab a (desperately uncool but kinda fun) ride on a horse-drawn carriage.

Standing near the tip of N Michigan Avenue, around the point where the already posh Near North melds into the even posher Gold Coast, is the **John Hancock Center** (*see below*), a little – well, smaller – brother to the Sears Tower but the reigning king of the Mag Mile. The criss-cross braces that form the outer frame of the 1,107-foot (337-metre) tall building were designed to keep the structure from swaying in the wind. High-speed elevators whisk visitors to the 94th floor, which affords predictably stunning views of the city. Much of the building is residential, while lower levels and the sunken plaza house assorted gift and clothing stores and the Cheesecake Factory, a restaurant.

Across the street from 'Big John' is the **Fourth Presbyterian Church**, built in 1914 (*see p88* **Walk on**). And a block north is the **Drake Hotel**, which has played host to the rich and famous since its opening in 1920. The hotel was designed to resemble a Renaissance palace: a gorgeous second-floor lobby welcomes guests to over 500 plush rooms, while the first floor is lined with small retail shops. Located inside are the Cape Cod Room and Coq d'Or, a dark lounge known for knock-'em-dead Martinis (*see p154* **Hey, Mr DJ...**).

John Hancock Observatory

875 N Michigan Avenue, E Delaware Place (Hancock Center 1-888 875 8439/www.hancock-observatory.com). CTA Chicago (Red). **Open** 9am-11pm daily. **Admission** $9.50; $7.50 over-62s; $6 5-12s; free under-4s. **Credit** Disc, MC, V. **Map** p306 J9.
The Hancock is only the second highest observation point in Chicago, but such arguments are all relative: when you're this high – the 94th-floor Skydeck is 1,000ft (305m) above the streets – it hardly matters that another building across town is a tad taller. In any case, the views afforded from atop the Hancock are superior to those visible from the top of the Sears. For one thing, because it's right in the Loop, the Sears lacks the perspective on the skyscraping architecture of Chicago's financial district that the Hancock's location, just over a mile north, allows. And for another, while the Sears observation deck is indoors, the Hancock boasts an open-air skywalk. Other attractions include a History Wall, outlining significant moments in Chicago's past; a surprisingly decent 95th-floor restaurant called the Signature Room (bookings essential; call 312 787 9596), where the waiters consider it a slow night if nobody proposes marriage to their dining partner; and a relatively relaxed bar, the Signature Lounge, on the floor above (open until 12.30am nightly except Friday and Saturday, when it serves an hour longer). But it's the views you're really here for, of course, and – if you pick a clear day – the views you'll get.

Where the streets have two names

Trust us: it's not as confusing as it first appears. Contrary to what you might think from the signage, roads in Chicago don't have two names. However, many of them do have supplementary monikers designed to celebrate the citizens of the city. That said, cartographers pay no notice: this dual-naming process is purely honorary, with the streets keeping and still using their original names. But the programme does offer an intriguing window into the history of the city, while also rewarding those who've made a contribution to it.

The decision to tag small stretches of road – a block or two is typical – with the name of a person is taken in the communities themselves: by community groups made up entirely of local residents, or by chambers of commerce. Once a name's been chosen, the groups then approach their local alderman, who takes the suggestion to the city council for approval (or not). This procedure has been repeated over 900 times since the scheme began in the 1970s, and has honoured a staggering range of people, from local do-gooders to world-famous entertainers.

This being Chicago, musicians are very well represented. Gospel act **Albertina Walker and the Caravans** (3500-3700 S Cottage Grove Avenue), blues legend **Muddy Waters** (900-1000 E 43rd Street) and soul singer **Lou Rawls** (4700-5100 S Wentworth Avenue) are paid tribute on the South Side, while **Curtis Mayfield** (800-1000 N Hudson Avenue) and the group **Chicago** (originally Chicago Transit Authority, until the CTA intervened; 140-200 W Chicago Avenue) are honoured in the Near North area. All are known across the planet; all made their home in Chicago.

Some musical honorees are cult heroes in the city: venerable blues busker **Maxwell Street Jimmy Davis** (1600-1700 W Madison Street), say, or folk singer **Steve Goodman** (4500-4600 N Lincoln Avenue), who had a hit with *A Dying Cub Fan's Last Request* three years before succumbing to leukemia in 1984. Others' associations with the city are more tenuous: **Sir Georg Solti** (50-100 E Adams Street, right by Symphony Center), former director of the Chicago Symphony Orchestra, and **Frank Sinatra** (0-65 E Bellevue Place, Near North), who made the definitive recordings of city anthems *Chicago* and *My Kind of Town*.

Sports personalities, too, are represented on street signs. **Jack Brickhouse Way** (400-430 N Michigan Avenue) and **Harry Caray Drive** (0-50 W Kinzie Street) are named for broadcasters; **George Halas Drive** (100 S-600 N Lake Shore Drive) and **Mike Ditka Way** (65-100 E Chestnut Street) both honour coaches of the Chicago Bears, while **Bill Veeck Drive** (3100-3500 S Shields Drive) is named for the baseball impresario who planted the ivy on the walls at Wrigley Field. Pioneering athlete **Jesse Owens** (0-100 W 125th Street), who moved to the city in 1949, gets a street way down south, while **Harlem Globetrotters Way** sits right by the Bulls' home at the United Center (1800-1900 W Madison Street) and quietly commemorates the team's founding in Chicago in the 1920s.

Culture vultures may wish to grab their cameras and head to **Ken Nordine Lane** (6100-6200 N Kenmore Avenue), **Nelson Algren Avenue** (1800-2200 W Evergreen Avenue) or either of the two **Bob Fosse Way**s (0-20 N Monroe Street, and 4400-4500 N

Terra Museum of American Art

664 N Michigan Avenue, at E Erie Street (312 664 3939/www.terramuseum.org). CTA Grand (Red). **Open** 10am-8pm Tue; 10am-6pm Wed-Sat; noon-5pm Sun. **Admission** $7; $3.50 seniors; free under-14s, students, teachers, veterans. Free to all Tue, Thur, 1st Sun of mth. **Credit** AmEx, MC, V. **Map** p306 J10.
Founded by Daniel Terra, a businessman with a passion for art and the money to back it up, the Terra Museum opened in the suburb of Evanston in 1980. Seven years later, it moved to its present location on the Magnificent Mile, where it sits quietly but incongruously, a cultural oasis on a commerce-dominated strip. Selections from the 700-work permanent collection, which includes works from Max Weber, Edward Hopper and Theodore Robinson, make up

some of the displays, but the main attraction is the roster of temporary shows, which have run the gamut in recent years from a retrospective of Jasper Johns prints to 2001's fine exhibition of Latino art from the last two centuries.

Streeterville

Like River North, Streeterville has climbed to its affluent status from humble beginnings. It became a trash dump more than a century ago thanks to a thug from Milwaukee named Captain George Wellington Streeter, who grounded his boat and began collecting money from contractors who wanted to leave their

Paulina Street). Choreographer Fosse was responsible for *Cabaret*; Algren wrote books such as *The Man with the Golden Arm*; and Nordine is a poet, voiceover artist and all-round cult hero. From Chicago's journalism industry, the **Irv Kupcinet Bridge** (crossing the river at Wabash Avenue, near the *Sun-Times* offices) and **Mike Royko Place** (500 N Michigan Avenue, by the *Tribune* building) represent two of the town's most famous columnists, while **Louis 'Studs' Terkel Bridge Parkway** (800-900 W Division Street) pays tribute to the oral historian and author of *Division Street*.

However, while celebrities such as these catch the eye, the vast majority of people honoured are famous only in their own communities. There's **Sophie Madej**, celebrated at 1532-1800 N Damen Avenue after a campaign by regulars at the Busy Bee restaurant in Wicker Park she's run for over 30 years. There's **Ralph Newman**, a leading authority on Abraham Lincoln until his death in 1998 and now honoured at 0-65 E Walton Place. And there's **Harry and Gunther Kempf Plaza**, which sits outside the Chicago Brauhaus at 4732 N Lincoln Avenue: the pair own the bar, much revered by the local German community.

Other streets are named for even more unsung heroes. **Florence Stoller Way** (3800 W Eastwood Street) is named for a local lady who's spent her life voluntarily trying to improve the neighbourhood in which she lives, Albany Park. **Phil Coronado Drive** (1800-1890 S Wood Street) serves a similar purpose in Pilsen. Some are silly: **Abe 'Fluky' Drexler Way** (6800-6900 N Western Avenue) is named for the inventor of the Chicago-style

hot dog. Others are rather more serious: **Clarence S Darrow Way** (0-100 W Hubbard Street) gives props to the legendary lawyer, defender of Leopold and Loeb and harsh critic of the death penalty. A few are simply sad: **Frankie Kajari Way** (5000-5270 N Las Casas Avenue) takes its name from the son of two police officers who died of leukemia aged ten.

Of the 920-odd streets, slightly more than a quarter have been christened in honour of religious figures or places. From the last Bishop of Chicago (**His Eminence Joseph Cardinal Bernardin Way**, at 732-800 N State Street) to an Indian monk who gave a presentation on Hinduism at the World's Columbian Exposition of 1893 (**Swami Vivekananda Way**, 100-200 S Michigan Avenue) via the half-dozen or more streets named for churches, it seems Chicago is a more God-fearing town than is immediately apparent.

But, of course, who to honour next? Well, we'd humbly suggest Cubs fan **Ronnie 'Woo-Woo' Wickers** (sit in the bleachers at any game at Wrigley and you'll spot him right away); *Wizard of Oz* author **L Frank Baum**; kids TV presenter **Frazier Thomas**; rock groupie **Cynthia Plastercaster**; **Catherine O'Leary**, the woman whose cow is purported to have started the Chicago Fire of 1871; legendarily large **William 'The Refrigerator' Perry**, defensive tackle for the Super Bowl-winning 1985 Bears; street troubadour **Wesley Willis**; **Jake and Elwood Blues**; *This American Life* host **Ira Glass**; **Frederick Rueckheim**, who invented Cracker Jack here in the late 1800s; outsider artist **Mr Imagination**… Hell, the only worry is finding enough streets.

waste. However, in 1918, the courts ordered Streeter's removal, and wealthy settlers who made the Near North area their home in the 19th century laid claim to the area. Streeterville is now home to some of the city's most expensive real estate. **Navy Pier** and the **Museum of Contemporary Art** (for both, *see p94*) aside, actual sights are few and far between, but the presence of a handful of fine restaurants and some elegant hotels mean that many visitors find themselves here anyway.

When compared to its all-conquering near-neighbour Navy Pier, the nearby **North Pier** (435 E Illinois Street, at N Lake Shore Drive; 312 836 4300) appears on a far more human scale:

it's as much residential neighbourhood as tourist trap. That said, what it lacks in whizz-bang attractions, it makes up for with peace and quiet. Wander to the eastern end of the pier to find the Centennial Fountain and Arc, commemorating the city's Water Reclamation District. An arc of water shoots out of the fountain and into the river – and sometimes on to passing boaters – every hour on the hour for ten minutes between 10am and 2pm, and 5pm and midnight from 1 May until 1 October.

Close by at Columbus and Illinois is the **NBC Tower**, built in 1989 but designed to blend in with the 1920s and '30s art deco skyscrapers that surround it. Two of the nation's trashiest

and a great shop). If not everything succeeds – 2001's chaotic multimedia show *The Short Century*, focusing on 50 years of politics, art and social history in Africa, didn't quite work – it's not for want of trying. And when the shows do hit the mark, as with a recent and long-overdue retrospective of HC Westermann and a survey of Ludwig Mies van der Rohe's American work, they're must-sees.

Navy Pier

Navy Pier hasn't always been the glittering tourist façade it is today. Built as a commercial shipping pier in 1916, it became more or less deserted when most commercial ships were re-routed to a South Side pier instead. The US Navy occupied the pier during World War II, and the 50-acre site also served as the first campus for the University of Illinois at Chicago.

However, in 1995, the city completed a massive four-year renovation of the pier, which today is home to a 15-storey Ferris wheel ($4), an IMAX cinema (*see p203*), a six-storey glass atrium with a botanical garden, a hand-painted musical carousel ($3, or $2.50 for under-12s and seniors), mini-golf ($6/$5), over a dozen restaurants, and the Skyline Stage (312 595 7437), where outdoor concerts are held in summer. Shops, a festival hall and a grand ballroom are located inside. Culture buffs head here at night for shows at the eye-catching **Chicago Shakespeare Theater** (*see p241*), and during the day for a glance through the enjoyable **Smith Museum of Stained Glass Windows** (312 595 7437; admission free).

Time your visit carefully, and you'll be seduced by the calm and the fresh breeze whipping in at the end of the pier. If you're feeling more energetic, take a ride on one of the boats that dock along the south side of the pier: most offer trips throughout the day and evening. Navy Pier is also, first and foremost, a family attraction: there's plenty for young 'uns to do, but the **Chicago Children's Museum** (*see p194*) is the highlight by some way.

Just outside Navy Pier to the north, off Lake Shore Drive, is **Olive Park**, a quiet green space with room for picnicking. The small Ohio Street Beach is located to the immediate west, and offers great views of the skyline. A sculpture garden honouring Jane Addams is located here.

Museum of Contemporary Art.

talk shows – those hosted by Jerry Springer and Jenny Jones – are taped here, while the **NBC Store** at N Columbus Drive does a brisk trade in merchandise marked with the same peacock design that tops the building's spire. Alongside the NBC Tower, between the river and the Tribune Tower, is **Pioneer Court**, a plaza lined with trees and fountains.

Museum of Contemporary Art

220 E Chicago Avenue, at N Mies van der Rohe Way (312 280 2660/www.mcachicago.org). CTA Chicago (Red). **Open** 10am-8pm Tue; 10am-5pm Wed-Sun. **Admission** $10; $6 seniors, students; free under-12s. Free to all Tue. **Credit** AmEx, DC, Disc, MC, V. **Map** p306 J9.

While the Art Institute has a pair of lions to guard it, the MCA needs no such deterrents: the $46-million building, designed by Berlin architect Josef Paul Kleihues and opened to coincide with the MCA's 30th birthday in 1997, is imposing enough from the outside. However, while its exterior is daunting and not universally admired, it's a different story inside: since it opened, its vast exhibition spaces – totalling 220,000sq ft (20,460sq m) – have proved supremely adaptable.

While there is a strong permanent collection here, the emphasis is on the temporary shows. The MCA's scattershot approach to programming is admirable and pays plenty of dividends, both with its exhibitions and the performances that take place within its walls (including theatre, dance, performance art and chamber music; there's also a library, a lecture hall, a sculpture garden, a café, a theatre carrying the imprimatur of the ubiquitous Wolfgang Puck,

Navy Pier

600 E Grand Avenue, at Lake Michigan (312 595 7437/www.navypier.com). CTA Grand (Red)/29, 65, 66 bus. **Open** *Nov-May* 10am-8pm Mon-Thur; 10am-10pm Fri, Sat; 10am-7pm Sun. *Late May-early Sept* 10am-10pm Mon-Thur, Sun; 10am-midnight Fri, Sat. *Early Sept-Oct* 10am-9pm Mon-Thur; 10am-11pm Fri, Sat; 10am-7pm Sun. **Admission** free. **Credit** varies with shop, attraction, restaurant. **Map** p306 K10.

Sightseeing

The Gold Coast

Show me the money, honey…

One glance around the neighbourhood, and it's easy to see how it got its name. Bounded by Chicago and North Avenues, Clark Street and Lake Michigan, the Gold Coast is home to Chicago's most luxurious (and expensive) homes, its wealthiest residents, and its most stately buildings.

And it's been this way almost since the beginning. An entrepreneur named Potter Palmer built a $250,000 'mansion to end all mansions' here in 1882, making him the Gold Coast's first settler. Over the years, others followed suit; including the Roman Catholic church, whose Archbishop still calls the neighbourhood home, and Hugh Hefner, who chose the building at 1340 N State Street to house his Playboy Mansion. Gigantic homes and luxury high-rise apartment buildings with bird's-eye views of Lake Michigan remain prominent today, though Palmer's Castle, as it was dubbed, was torn down in 1950 to make room for one of those high-rises, still standing at 1350 N Lake Shore Drive.

In the middle of all the stately homes and high-rises is the junction of Rush and Division Streets. Since the 1920s, Rush has had more bars and restaurants per square foot than any other stretch in Chicago, and the concentration of nightlife reaches its apogee at Division. Though most natives wouldn't be seen dead within a mile of it, the block along Division between Rush/State and Dearborn is popular with conventioneers, suburbanites and sad-sack singles on the pull. Late at night, the streets flood with people and the scene can get a little out of hand: when the Chicago Bulls won the NBA title in 1996, for example, people celebrated here by trashing cars and starting fires. Rest assured, though: as the Bulls aren't in danger of winning anything in the foreseeable future, such an event is unlikely to occur any time soon.

Near Lincoln Park

Given the area's wealth, you'd expect there to be at least one stupendously posh school in the Gold Coast, and the **Latin School of Chicago** doesn't disappoint. With a high school student body of about 400, it is one of the city's most

Chicago's capital of sex: the **Playboy Mansion** on State Street.

Walk on Astor Street

There's a masochistic glee that comes with looking at houses that are grander than anything you might ever live in yourself. For that, and for a window into a time when Chicago's wealthiest citizens jostled for bragging rights by building more luxurious mansions than their neighbours, it's hard to beat a stroll down Astor Street. Springtime, of course, is best, as lake breezes ruffle the trees and sunlight dapples the sidewalks and façades, but this is a gorgeous pocket of the city at any time of year.

Astor Street rose to become the city's premier address after the Chicago Fire of 1871, when the city was forced to rebuild its downtown with a vengeance. That said, the short stretch of road didn't really come into its own until the turn of the century (it wasn't even entirely paved until 1905).

Unlike the barn-like palaces that languished on Prairie Avenue, previously the city's most desirable address, the mansions built here by the likes of Cyrus McCormick and the Goodmans were more like overgrown townhouses. Without much in the way of yards – except what space they found in interior courtyards – the houses run right up against each other and form a long chain of mostly similar but sometimes wildly varying styles. Most of the houses were built in one of three architectural styles: Queen Anne, Romanesque or Georgian Revival, though their gaudy coats of arms, turrets and balconies were later dubbed 'Stockyard Renaissance' by one wag.

From the late 19th century until World War II, the street was home to many of the richest men and women in the city (an old joke talked about the Astor Street dowager who was going to protest against the building of a nearby supermarket but first had to have her butler explain what one was). But after the war, the lure of the North Shore put the area on the skids: many of the buildings were knocked down in the 1960s to make room for the faceless high-rise apartment buildings that stud the Gold Coast.

Community protest got the area declared a Landmark District in 1975, the first such area in Chicago. Things have since improved dramatically: on your stroll down the road, which shouldn't take more than 45 minutes even at a leisurely pace, you'll notice that the homes are now in largely excellent shape, unsurprising given that 300 buildings in the area are now on the National Register of Historic Places.

Start on the south-west corner of N Astor Street and W North Avenue (almost opposite the strange 1918 monument to dentist GV Black in Lincoln Park, which glares down Astor).
Its postal address is 1555 N State Parkway, but the **Archbishop's Residence** stretches an entire block to Astor. The northern anchor of Astor Street, this 1885 Queen Anne mansion is built of red brick with sandstone trim and has 19 chimneys poking up to the sky. There's also a coach house and landscaped grounds here (it's the only property on Astor to have a proper lawn); Pope John Paul II stayed here during his historic 1979 visit.

Head south down Astor one block, to the north-west corner of Astor and Burton.
At 1500 N Astor Street is the imposing edifice of the palazzo that former mayor Joseph Medill built for his daughter, **Mrs Robert Patterson**, in 1893. It's in excellent shape, with the orange brick walls, terracotta trim and inviting courtyard all having aged well. Enlarged by Cyrus McCormick in the 1920s, it's now divided into frighteningly exclusive condominiums.

Cross to the opposite (south-eastern) corner of the Astor and Burton junction.

expensive and highest-rated private schools. Catch a glimpse of the privileged few in the large brick building at 59 W North Avenue on the edge of Lincoln Park. Nearby, the **International Museum of Surgical Science** (*see below*), two blocks east and one block south, depicts the history of surgery in dizzying – and sometimes nauseating – detail; a block west is historic **Astor Street**, packed wall to wall with beautiful architecture. *See above* **Walk on**.

International Museum of Surgical Science

1524 N Lake Shore Drive, at E North Avenue (312 642 6502/www.imss.org). CTA Clark/Division (Red)/72, 73, 151 bus. **Open** 10am-4pm Tue-Sat. **Admission** $6; $3 over-60s, students. **Credit** AmEx, MC, V. **Map** p307 H7.
Readers of a nervous disposition, turn the page now. Everyone else – particularly those with a yen for gruesome medical ephemera – should consider making a detour to this unique museum, which

The **John L Fortune House** at 1451 N Astor Street was built in the Jacobethan style in 1910 by Howard Van Doren Shaw. It has a clean country house look to it that is more akin to the houses in Wilmette.

Cross back to the other side of Astor and continue south.

A tall, skinny slice of art deco simplicity, the **Edward P Russell House** at 1444 N Astor Street faces the world with a sleek stone façade imported from France and carved decorative panels. The building was completed in 1929.

Carry on heading south.

David Adler designed 1406 N Astor Street in 1922 for steel magnate **Joseph T Ryerson**. Its look was patterned, mostly successfully, after Parisian hotels.

Cross the street again to the eastern side of Astor and continue south.

One of the real landmarks on this walk is the **James Charnley House** at 1365 N Astor Street. A simple but compact building that's now the headquarters of the Society of Architectural Historians, it was built in 1892 and designed by the great Frank Lloyd Wright while he was still working under the auspices of Louis Sullivan's firm (he was later fired for moonlighting). It's a mix of their styles, combining Lloyd Wright's sweeping horizontal lines and Sullivan's ornamentation.

Head on further south, but only as far as the house next door.

The Georgian mansion at **1355 N Astor Street** was designed by Howard Van Doren Shaw in 1914, and was once the residence of **William O Goodman** (who lends his name to the Goodman Theater downtown). The marble archway and spiked fence give it a hint of Versailles, as does the tantalising glimpse through a gate of a lost-in-time courtyard.

Head south, crossing the street at Goudy Square Park (named for lawyer William C Goudy), to the north-west corner of Astor and Goethe.

Unlike the other high-rises that dot Astor, the anomalous construction at 1300 N Astor Street has some character. Designed by one-time Astor resident **Bertrand Goldberg** (who also built the corncob towers of Marina City) and completed in 1963, it's a 28-storey tower that sits on a small glass box and some precariously slender columns.

Cross to the north-east corner of Astor and Goethe.

Wrap up your walk with a look at two early high-rises at 1301 N Astor Street and 1260 N Astor Street. Built in the early 1930s by **Philip B Maher**, they're almost identical examples (15 and 16 storeys, respectively) of art deco luxury, their clean lines and artful minimalism providing a bridge between the new and old Gold Coasts.

---

celebrated its 50th birthday in 2002. Although it aims to recount the history of surgery over its four floors and 32 rooms, most of the museum is ordered not chronologically but by subject; handy if you have a particular fetish for, say, terrifying *Marathon Man*-like dental equipment. In truth, the museum suffers a little from the blindness of academia: while many of the explanations and labels attached to the displays would be adequate for those with a background in the subject, they're not enough to really enlighten the medical novice. Still,

the items here are often so striking – a plastic surgery display, a delightful copy of Napoleon's death mask – that the museum succeeds regardless.

Oak Street Beach & surrounds

Founded by a group of society women that included the wife of meatpacking titan Ogden Armour, Jane Addams and Gwetholyn Jones, the **Three Arts Club** (1300 N Dearborn Street, at W Goethe Street; 312 944 6250/ www.threearts.org) was intended as a refuge for young women studying painting, drama or music in the 'wicked city'. Built by Holabird and Root in 1914 to resemble a Tuscan villa, the four-storey building is a Chicago landmark and the only club of its kind still in existence (in their day, similar spots could be found in Paris, New York and London). Today, the original three arts – literary, performance and visual – have expanded to include architecture, interior design, and fashion. Visitors, including men, are welcomed through the hallowed doors for exhibitions, concerts and even the occasional open house event.

Cut along Goethe Street – stopping, if you're thirsty, for a drink in the splendidly louche **Pump Room** (*see p155*) – and head across to the lake. Three blocks south you'll find the impressive **Lake Shore Drive Synagogue** (*see p88* **Walk on**); and a little further south from there – along Lake Michigan off Oak Street – is the **Oak Street Beach**, where Chicago's beautiful people go to sun, swim and be seen. Considered the Riviera of Chicago's shoreline, the strip attracts legions of scantily clad men and women, Rollerbladers, cyclists, runners and walkers. In summer, volleyball nets are put up and vendors sell food, drinks and the occasional souvenir. Pedestrian access is via underpasses located across from the Drake Hotel at Michigan Avenue and Oak Street.

Cut back along Walton Street for several blocks until you reach the green space bound by Delaware, Walton, Dearborn and Clark. This is **Washington Square**, Chicago's first public park. The square has been the location of

Astor Street. *See p96* **Walk on**.

numerous spirited protests over the years: a group of German beer hall owners held demonstrations here against the city's increased liquor-licence fees in the 1850s; 70 years later, it had become a soapbox spot for radical speakers on Sunday evenings. The park is calmer today.

Overlooking the square is the stunning **Newberry Library** (60 W Walton Street, at N Clark Street; 312 943 9090). Chicago's research library for the humanities was founded in 1887 at the request of Walter L Newberry, banker and land speculator who wanted a library to 'serve the city he loved and helped to build'. Its (non-circulating) collections are rich in history, literature, genealogy and cartography, though it also houses a collection of Jefferson's letters, acts as a home to the Chicago Genealogical Society and hosts seminars, lectures and concerts. Outside of the excellent book fair in summer, and Christmas's bazaar assembling 40 gift shops from museums, cultural centres and other non-profit organisations, non-scholars won't find much to do, but the building itself, designed by Henry Ives Cobb and completed in 1893, is worth a stop: free tours are conducted on Thursdays at 3pm and Saturdays at 10.30am.

Museum of Surgical Science. *See p96*.

Old Town

The Gold Coast's younger, more mischievous brother.

Before the Chicago Fire of 1871 pushed hundreds of German immigrants into the streets around W North Avenue, the stretch of land between North, Armitage, Larrabee and Clark was known as the 'cabbage patch', as it was little more than a patchwork of gardens and cow pastures. After the blaze, many of the neighbourhood's historic homes were built, and the influx of German shops and restaurants along North Avenue earned the thoroughfare the moniker 'German Broadway'. It wasn't until after World War II that the area took up its present name of Old Town.

The development of the Cabrini-Green housing project along Division Street in the late 1950s lowered rents in the surrounding area, changing the face of Old Town's south-west corner. Today, the high-rises are slowly being evacuated and boarded up – and the area around them, perhaps predictably, developed into pricey townhouses and condominiums – but the neighbourhood is still best avoided by tourists and others unfamiliar with the area.

Much to the delight of residents and business owners, the Old Town Triangle District, lined with 19th-century cottages, was designated a Chicago landmark in 1977, thanks to the efforts of artists and preservationists who called it home. Seven years later, the triangle was added to the National Register of Historic Places, and the area – which had long been rather raffish and down-at-heel – began to smarten up.

The designations helped raise property values and prompted a flood of renovations, new developments and commercial venues, especially along Wells Street and Armitage Avenue. Today, it's home to some of the city's most expensive housing, as well as some unique speciality shops and restaurants. But true to its history, the area still includes its share of cosy neighbourhood bars and comfortable homes.

Local tradition dictates that if you can hear the bells of the gargantuan **St Michael's Church** (1633 N Cleveland Avenue, at W North Avenue; 312 642 2498), you're in Old Town. Of the five bells in the tower, the smallest weighs 2,500 pounds (1,133 kilogrammes), while the largest tops out at an amazing 6,000 pounds (2,778 kilogrammes), so the noise they make is anything but quiet. Built in the centre of the neighbourhood in 1869 on land donated by early beer baron Michael Diversey, St Michael's was

partially gutted by the Chicago Fire two years later. The Germans rebuilt the Romanesque church in just a year, and in 1888 hired a New York artist to restore the interior and place a steeple at the top of the church tower. By 1892 it had become Chicago's largest German parish. Inside the brick building, which is open to the public, is a carved wooden altar and glorious stained-glass windows; outside are stone columns of varying heights and several roofs with intricate brickwork.

Nearby is another house of religion, albeit a very different one. The striking **Midwest Buddhist Temple** (435 W Menomonee Street, at N Hudson Avenue; 312 943 7801), nestled in among a neighbourhood of close brick homes, was built by one of many Japanese immigrants who settled in Old Town in the 1940s and '50s. The walls and pagoda-like roof of the temple stand atop a one-storey concrete base; a gold Buddha is one of the few objects inside the temple. The congregation, about 80 per cent Japanese, hosts a festival each year of Japanese culture, dance, music and food.

Midwest Buddhist Temple.

Culture of a different sort can be found around the junction of Wells and North. In the late 1960s and 1970s, this area was a busy mix of harmlessly high hippies and bright-eyed tourists, who headed here for folk music and other flower-child diversions. After a period of decline, it's now it is hopping again – albeit more sedately – with sophisticated restaurants, yuppie bars, stylish shops and ever-present, ever-popular **Second City** (*see p246*). Founded by Mike Nichols, Elaine May and friends in 1959, taking its name from a disparaging article about Chicago that appeared in the *New Yorker*, it's an Old Town staple and the home of improv. Its list of alumni is a who's who of American comedy: John Belushi, Ed Asner, Alan Arkin, Bill Murray and Shelley Long, to name a few. The cast follows the same format that set the theatre's wheels in motion in the 1960s: a mix of skits, sketches and improvisations.

Second City is located inside **Piper's Alley**, an enclosed mall that was home to the Piper family bakery in the late 1800s. Also included in the building is a movie theatre, several shops and a Starbucks; nearby are an assortment of other bars and eateries, with the **Old Town Ale House** (*see p155*) especially worth a diversion. Close by are a cluster of other Old Town landmarks: the enormous **Moody Church** (*see p88* **Walk on**); the **Chicago Historical Society** (*see below*); and the southern tip of **Lincoln Park** (*see p101*).

Chicago Historical Society

1601 N Clark Street, at W North Avenue (312 642 4600/www.chicagohistory.org). CTA Sedgwick (Brown, Purple). **Open** 9.30am-4.30pm Mon-Sat; noon-5pm Sun. **Admission** $5; $3 over-65s, students; $1 6-12s; free under-6s. Free to all Mon. **Credit** AmEx, DC, Disc, MC, V. **Map** p307 H7.

Founded in 1852 and dedicated to the preservation, dissemination and interpretation of the history of Chicago, the Chicago Historical Society might be the city's oldest cultural institution, but it's also still among its best. The permanent exhibits here detail many facets of the town's history, and include Chicago's first locomotive, the Illinois Pioneer Life Gallery – where costumed docents demonstrate early crafts – and the popular diorama room, where the exhibits make up a Chicago History 101. There are artefacts from the Chicago Fire of 1871 and the Civil War on display, as well as the nation's largest 19th-century women's costume collection, the table upon which Abraham Lincoln signed the Emancipation Proclamation, George Washington's inaugural suit and Al Capone's mugshot.

The temporary exhibits, though, are usually just as interesting and varied; recent shows have taken in the Roaring '20s and revered local photography firm Hedrich-Blessing. Modern extensions to the Society's 1932 brick Georgian building house a tastefully stocked gift shop – the selection of books, in particular, is impeccable – and the Big Shoulders Café, which does a fine Sunday brunch with live jazz. A programme of lectures, discussions and tours provides added interest.

Crilly Court

Crilly Court, one block west of Wells, bears the name of Daniel F Crilly, a South Sider who bought the block and then put in a street of his own. Between 1885 and 1893, Crilly built row houses on the west of the block and four-storey apartment buildings on the east, above the doors of which he carved the names of his four children, Edgar, Oliver, Isabelle and Erminnie. Edgar renovated the buildings some 50 years later, closing off the alleys to form a series of courtyards. The restoration was one of the first in the Old Town Triangle, and the younger Crilly is credited with leading the way in the historical preservation of the locale.

Several homes near Crilly Court have their own historic significance. The residence at 216 W Menomonee Street is believed to have been a 'fire relief cottage', built by the city following the Great Fire to provide shelter for homeless residents. Built at a cost of about $75, some of the homes were also used to serve food and distribute clothing.

The 1872 frame house at 1802 N Lincoln Park West is one of only a handful of wooden farmhouses left in the area. Further north are two other frame houses built in the early 1870s for the Frederick Wacker family, prominent German brewers. Frederick's son Charles, a member of Chicago's planning commission for 17 years and the namesake of Wacker Drive, lived in the carriage house at 1836 N Lincoln Park West, while his father lived at the Swiss chalet-style residence at 1838 N Lincoln Park West. Frame houses like these are uncommon in the area because of the restrictions on building materials the city imposed after the Chicago Fire of 1871.

Just down the street, the row houses at 1826-34 N Lincoln Park West were designed by Adler and Sullivan from 1884 to 1885: displaying Louis Sullivan's love of geometric ornamentation, they're rare examples of his early residential work. All of the homes are now private residences.

Lincoln Park

Animal magic in the largest park of its kind in America.

Fifty per cent larger than New York's Central Park, Lincoln Park is the largest metropolitan park in the United States, running along Lake Michigan from North Avenue (around the 1600 N block) up to Hollywood Avenue (5700 N). However, most head to the part of the park bordered by North Avenue in the south and Diversey to the north, a stretch that parallels the residential neighbourhood named after it (bordered to the east by Lake Michigan and the west by the Chicago River).

The park

Lincoln Park was established in the 1860s, after a sprawling cemetery that once stood here was cleared. The bodies went north to Graceland and Rosehill cemeteries, apart from that of hotelier Ira Couch, whose family notoriously went to court to prevent the city moving their beloved's grave. They succeeded and the **Couch Mausoleum** stands near the junction of LaSalle Drive and Clark Street, not far from the world's oldest statue of President Abraham Lincoln, after whom the park is named.

Couch aside, the park soon became a popular attraction among locals while, at the same time, the area to the west became more densely populated with European immigrants. It's remained popular, too, largely because of the **Lincoln Park Zoo** (*see p102*).

Just north of the zoo's main entrance is the **Shakespeare Garden**, which contains a variety of flowers and plants mentioned in the Bard's plays. The garden also houses a bronze bust of the playwright that dates back to 1894 – one of more than 20 sculptural monuments dating from the late 19th century, maintained with funds raised by an advocacy group in a monument 'adoption' – and the Bates Fountain, a popular cooling destination in summer. The broad lawn leads to a three-acre **Lincoln Park Conservatory**, a Victorian greenhouse erected in 1892. The tropical setting allows plants from all over the globe to flourish. Admission is free. Just across Fullerton Avenue is the **Peggy Notebaert Nature Museum** (*see below*).

The best way to enjoy Lincoln Park is to stroll its many paths, which offer excellent views of the city centre, the lake, the playing fields, the ponds, the chess tables and the park benches. Be warned, though: on sunny weekends, the zoo is a

Follow the yellow brick road to **Oz Park**. *See p103*.

Follow the yellow brick road to **Oz Park**. *See p103*.

maze of baby strollers and screaming tots. For those hoping to cover a little more ground, there are half a dozen bicycle shops along the park's edge that rent by the day or by the hour. Alternatively, paddleboats are for rent at a South Pond kiosk for $9 an hour (mid May to mid October); right next door is historic **Café Brauer** (2021 N Stockton Drive; 312 280 2724).

Chicago Academy of Sciences Peggy Notebaert Nature Museum

2430 N Cannon Drive, at W Fullerton Avenue (773 755 5100/www.naturemuseum.org). CTA Fullerton (Brown, Purple, Red). **Open** 9am-4.30pm Mon-Fri; 10am-5pm Sat, Sun. **Admission** $6; $4 over-65s; $3 3-17s; free under-3s. Free to all Tue. **Credit** AmEx, Disc, MC, V. **Map** p308 H5.

Its location, along Lincoln Park's North Pond, is ideal; its $31-million, 73,000sq ft (6,740sq m) building is grand; the fanfare that greeted its opening was enormous… So why does the Peggy Notebaert Nature Museum disappoint? The finger of blame should first be pointed at the permanent exhibits, none of which excites. Ameritech Environmental Central fails to

Central Park SummerStage

presented by

Heineken®

CATCH A WORLD OF PERFORMERS AMERICAN MUSIC WORLD MUSIC SPOKEN WORD MODERN DANCE INTERNATIONAL CABARET DJ'S ELECTRONIC MUSIC PERFORMANCE ART OPERA WORLD SHOPS KIDS ROCK N' ROLL AFRICAN MUSIC COUNTRY REGGAE HIP HOP POETRY BRAZILIAN FUNK CALYPSO GOSPEL CELTIC

NEW YORK CITY'S FAVORITE FREE PERFORMING ARTS FESTIVAL

TRADITIONAL DANCE TRIP-HOP R&B BHANGRA SOUL GYPSY MUSIC BLUEGRASS SALSA SOUL COMPAS MERENGUE SKA SAMBA BLUES LATIN ROCK AFRO-BEAT RAI JAZZ HOUSE MUSIC BEAT BOX SOCA ZYDECO QWAALI POPULAR MUSIC CLASSICAL MANGUE BEAT AND MUCH, MUCH MORE CONCERTS DANCE SPOKEN WORD OPERA FAMILY EVENTS MID JUNE - MID AUGUST *www.SummerStage.org*

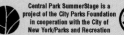

Central Park SummerStage is a project of the City Parks Foundation in cooperation with the City of New York/Parks and Recreation

All shows at Rumsey Playfield,
72nd Street, Mid Park
INFO/VOLUNTEER HOTLINE: 212.360.2777
Pick up a summer issue of *Time Out New York* Magazine
for a complete listing of Central Park SummerStage events.

engage audiences in a series of important issues, while the C Paul Johnson Family Water Lab counters its subject matter with dry presentation. City Science, a mocked-up bungalow that aims to educate kids in domestic science, is a little better, but the only thing that really pleases is the Judy Istock Butterfly Haven, a glass-topped space populated by over 50 species of butterfly. Indeed, the most attractive part of the museum is the outdoor pond and walkway that can be enjoyed for free, leaving the admission fee to be invested in a good lunch instead.

Lincoln Park Zoo

2150 N Cannon Drive, at W Webster Avenue (312 742 2000/www.lpzoo.com). CTA Fullerton (Brown, Purple, Red). **Open** *Zoo buildings Nov-Mar* 10am-4.30pm daily. *Apr, May, Sept, Oct* 10am-5pm daily. *June-Aug* 10am-5pm Mon-Fri; 10am-6.30pm Sat, Sun. *Zoo grounds Nov-Mar* 8am-5pm daily *Apr, May, Sept, Oct* 8am-6pm daily. *June-Aug* 8am-6pm Mon-Fri; 8am-7pm Sat, Sun. **Admission** free. **No credit cards. Map** p308 H5.

Compared to its competitors, it's small, and lacks the whizz-bang technology on which other attractions in the city rely to draw their crowds. That said, though, quintessentially Chicagoan activities don't get more enjoyable than strolling through Lincoln Park Zoo on a sunny weekday afternoon. The zoo opened in 1868 after the park was presented with two swans by New York's Central Park; 135 years later, and it's a 35-acre site holding 1,000 species, including the child-friendly Farm in the Zoo.

It isn't difficult to see everything in an afternoon. The biggest draws are the Kovler Lion House, the Lester E Fisher Great Ape House – the zoo is a world leader in gorilla breeding, with more than three dozen born here since 1970 – and the African elephants, though visitors to the latter exhibit should make it a point to be alert at all times. Signs posted along the fence warn spectators that elephants occasionally hurl objects from their pen. What the signs fail to mention is that the 'objects' in question are lumps of their own dung.

Flying shite aside, though, it's a hugely attractive place, and one of which the locals are rightly very proud. Their delight in the facility becomes more justifiable when you learn that since 1995, the zoo has been run not by the city but by the Lincoln Park Zoological Society, with two-thirds of its income coming from private sources. That being the case, it's remarkable that admission to the zoo is free.

The neighbourhood

Lincoln Park only began to take off as a residential neighbourhood in the 1970s, but it's now a sought-after address among the young and the restless. Tree-lined residential streets lead – if you're lucky – to attractive corner bars and appealing shops. Tourist attractions are few and far between, unless you're something of an amateur criminologist.

Peggy Notebaert Nature Museum. *See p101.*

West of the zoo lies the site of the infamous St Valentine's Day Massacre, where, on 14 February 1929, seven members of Bugs Moran's gang were executed against a garage wall by Al Capone's henchmen. Though Moran escaped (he'd overslept), the killings broke him and cemented Capone's position at the forefront of Chicago's lucrative organised crime world. The garage, at 2122 N Clark Street, has since been replaced by a lawn. But the incident still resonates: the **Chicago Pizza & Oven Grinder Company** opposite at No.2121 (773 248 2570) tells the tale on its menus.

Several blocks north-west is the sight of another fabled gangland killing: that of John Dillinger, a professional crim who had escaped from police custody in Crown Point, Indiana, where he was awaiting trial for the murder of a cop. He'd been pinned as Public Enemy Number One by the FBI, who tracked him down to the **Biograph Theatre** (2433 N Lincoln Avenue) on 22 July 1934. As he left a screening of *Manhattan Melodrama*, police surrounded him; when he tried to escape, he was shot dead. The crowd of bystanders who witnessed the killing dipped their skirts and handkerchiefs in his blood as gory souvenirs.

The Biograph stopped functioning as a first-run cinema a couple of years ago. However, it still opens for special events from time to time, while Dillinger himself is remembered on the anniversary of his death each year: 'fans' meet at the **Red Lion Pub** (*see p158*) across the street, then follow a bagpipe procession to the scene of the outlaw's grisly demise.

These days, Lincoln Park is far more sedate, though students at nearby DePaul University pump some unruly life into the bar-dominated stretches of Lincoln Avenue most evenings. On the off-chance that Lincoln Park itself didn't provide enough green pleasantness, then be sure to pop by **Oz Park** (2021 N Burling Street): guarded by a statue of the Tin Man, it takes its name from the seminal book and Judy Garland-starring movie, whose author L Frank Baum lived in Chicago.

Lake View & Surrounds

One baseball team, two movie theatres, countless nationalities.

Prior to 1889, Fullerton Parkway formed the city's northern boundary. Above Fullerton lay the rural Lake View Township, which stretched north to Devon and from the lake to Western Avenue. In 1889 it was annexed by the city. Today, only the southernmost portion of the township retains the name, the northern reaches having been carved into the neighbourhoods of Wrigleyville, Roscoe Village, Andersonville, Edgewater, Buena Park, North Center, St Ben's, Lincoln Square and Uptown. Lake View quickly developed as a residential and entertainment district, with high rents keeping factories away.

Lake View's most recent change of identity began in the '70s, when climbing property values in Lincoln Park resulted in the migration of young professionals. South Lake View began a slow gentrification that resulted in higher rents and the opening of upmarket boutiques and eateries. Today, it's a classy neighbourhood with just enough grit to keep things interesting. Of course, Lake View's most prized possession is its lakefront, which takes in the northern end of Lincoln Park. In summer, the park offers a multitude of activities (jogging paths, tennis courts) and inactivities (snooze the day away in the grassy fields).

The south-east portion of Lake View, known as **Boystown** for its large gay population (*see p210*), is its cultural and nightlife centre, not to mention its commercial heart. However, though you'll find a few chainstores here, the shopping opportunities up here are more unusual. Leave the Belmont El station and head north up Clark or Halsted, or south down Broadway. Among the picks: the **Unabridged Bookstore** (*see p166*); clothing store the **Alley** (*see p174*); and **Uncle Fun** (*see p186*), which offers a selection of bizarre knick-knacks, kitsch and gag gifts.

Also near the Belmont El station is the 1912 **Vic Theatre** (*see p200*), a former vaudeville house with marble staircases, ornate mouldings and excellent acoustics. It has found fame for its Brew & View movie nights, where the audience is encouraged to get tanked and shout at the screen. Fun, but if you're looking for a more highbrow experience, head up Southport Avenue to the **Music Box** (*see p105* and *p203*).

Made in Chicago Wrigley Field

When it was built by Zachary Taylor Davis in 1914, it was unique. Not in terms of design – it was patterned after the Polo Grounds, home of the New York Giants – but because it was the first baseball stadium in this part of town. The locals took to it, attracted by geographical novelty and the excitement of a new league. As it turned out, the park outlasted the team it was built to house.

Known as the North Side Ballpark, then Weeghman Park and then Whales Park, it was built for the Whales of the Federal League, set up by Charles Weeghman in 1914 to challenge the established American and National Leagues. Crowds were good, but the league was beset by financial problems brought on by legal action from the AL and NL.

When the league folded in late 1915, Weeghman bought the NL's Cubs and shipped them across town to his ballpark. But he didn't last much longer than his Whales: financial troubles in 1918 forced him to sell the team. The year 1920 saw the stadium renamed Cubs Park, but in 1926, its name was changed yet again to recognise its new owner. It's been Wrigley Field ever since.

William Wrigley, the chewing gum magnate who bought the team, appointed his son Philip president in 1925, and it was he who presided over many changes to the park. The grandstand was extended to two decks in 1925, while the bleachers were added in 1937 and built up to their current size soon after. Indeed, 1937 proved a crucial year for the ballpark: it was then that Wrigley's right-hand man, the iconoclastic Bill Veeck, built the gorgeous, enormous scoreboard and planted ivy in the outfield walls. The stadium's hardly changed since.

Yet while other old stadia have succumbed to the wrecking ball in recent years, Wrigley's reputation has grown, and it's now arguably the most treasured stadium on earth. Over the last four decades, it's weathered fashions

Wrigleyville

Lake View was changed forever in 1914 with the construction of **Wrigley Field**, the home of the Chicago Cubs and a genuine American landmark (*see p104* **Made in Chicago**). The Cubs dominate the area near the junction of Clark and Addison, so much so that the streets around it were given the name **Wrigleyville** by local real estate developers keen to give their turf a little extra kudos. The name has stuck.

However, not every bar around here is a sports bar: the **Metro** (*see p220*), one of the town's leading music venues, sits a few doors down from the **Ginger Man** (*see p161*), whose ambience is miles away from the likes of **Murphy's Bleachers** (*see p161*). And it's unlikely that too many of Wrigley Field's beer-guzzling denizens are regulars at the **Music Box** (*see p203*), west of the ballpark.

That said, the Music Box does have one thing in common with Wrigley: both are classics of a bygone era. Built in 1929 – with an orchestra pit, just in case the newfangled talkies flopped – it's an extraordinarily over-the-top Italian Renaissance-inspired construction whose survival was ensured by a renovation two decades ago. The main theatre, seating 750, uses *trompe l'oeil* paintings of garden walls to create the illusion of sitting in an outdoor courtyard, with a ceiling covered with twinkling stars and moving cloud formations.

Also in the area

West of Lake View, around the junction of Roscoe and Damen, is **Roscoe Village**, a once down-at-heel neighbourhood that has seen property prices spiral as Lake View itself gets overrun by people who can no longer afford to live in Lincoln Park. It's a quiet, homely 'hood, lacking the nightlife of Lake View; that's just how the locals would like to keep it.

North-east Lake View Township, known today as **Uptown**, was a playground for gangsters like Al Capone, who appreciated the anonymity afforded by hanging out in 'the sticks'. The **Green Mill** jazz club (*see p224*) was a popular haunt back in the day, and was even operated by Al Capone in the '20s.

The first Northern European immigrant to Lake View was a Swede named Conrad Sulzer who arrived in 1836, sparking an influx of Scandinavians and Germans whose influence remains to this day. The epicentre of Teutonic culture is still **Lincoln Square**, at the junction of Lincoln and Western and Lawrence Avenues. Shop there for home-made Bratwurst at **Meyer's**, an authentic Old World deli, or buy imported soaps, lotions and homeopathic remedies at the **Merz Apothecary** (*see p184* **Doctors' orders**). Lincoln Square – nicknamed Sauerkraut Boulevard by locals – is also the site of the annual German-American Festival, held in September (*see p191*).

Sightseeing

for artificial turf, for concrete, for the mallparks of the late 1980s (of which there's a perfectly ugly example on the South Side in the shape of Comiskey Park). It's even seen, in recent years, a trend for building ballparks that ape the stadia of old.

But there's nowhere like Wrigley. It begins with the ride in on the Red line to Addison and a wander around the homey neighbourhood in which the ballpark sits, thronging with people on gamedays. It ends, or ought to, with a drink in one of the numerous sports bars nearby. And somewhere in the middle, the Cubs will lose. But if you're going to watch your team lose, it might as well be in a lovely ballpark: intimate, comfortable, packed with delightful details and eccentricities (the hand-operated scoreboard, the 'W' and 'L' flags that fly to denote a Cubs win or loss, the numbers 14 and 26 on the foul poles celebrating ex-Cubs Ernie Banks and Billy Williams) and without a bad seat in the place.

Lake View's **Music Box Theatre**. *See p105.*

Chicago's Swedish-Americans, meanwhile, are now mostly in **Andersonville**, an endearingly scruffy neighbourhood centred around N Clark Street and W Foster Avenue that's also home to a large gay community (*see p210*).

Martin D'Arcy Museum of Art

Cudahy Library, Loyola University, 6525 N Sheridan Road, at W Arthur Avenue (773 508 2679/ http://darcy.luc.edu). CTA Loyola (Purple, Red). **Open** *Aug-May* noon-4pm Tue-Sat. *June, July* hours vary. **Admission** free. **No credit cards**.

It's quite a trek, but take a book for the lengthy ride north on the Red line and the journey ought to fly by. And when you get there, you'll be glad you made the effort to visit this fine museum devoted to medieval, Renaissance and baroque art. Founded by Father Donald Rowe in 1969 – and named after Rowe's mentor, an art-loving Jesuit priest who inspired Rowe when he studied with him in Oxford – its collection runs to over 500 pieces and includes paintings by Tintoretto and Guercino alongside an assortment of decorative arts, jewellery, sculpture and liturgical vessels. Lectures and concerts (often from Loyola students) punctuate proceedings.

Swedish American Museum Center

5211 N Clark Street, at W Foster Street (773 728 8111/www.samac.org). CTA Berwyn (Purple, Red). **Open** 10am-4pm Tue-Fri; 10am-3pm Sat, Sun. **Admission** *Suggested donation* $4; $3 children, over-65s, students; free under-1s. Free to all 2nd Tue of mth. **No credit cards**.

The Swedish American Museum Center enjoys healthy support in Andersonville, a neighbourhood that's long been heavily populated by Swedish immigrants. This support has meant the museum has been able to move forwards: alongside the permanent displays, recent years have seen the opening of an interactive Children's Museum of Immigration, while the museum is also trumpeting plans commemorating Swedish-American Buzz Aldrin's moon landing with a special exhibition. Classes (in everything from cooking to dancing via the Swedish language), concerts and movies round off the enterprise.

▶ ## Made in Chicago
Wrigley Field (continued)

A few tips, though. Book tickets in advance, as many games sell out (*see p234* for ticket information). Wrap up warm: the main stands, shaded from the sun, can get chilly when the wind whips in, as it often does. Whether you enjoy sitting out in the fabled bleachers – and while our favourite spot is down the fine-base line close to the field, everyone should sit in the bleachers at least once – depends on whether you view the self-described Bleacher Bums as garrulous, gregarious entertainers, or as drunk, loudmouthed bums. And if you've time, take a tour of the park, held on a dozen dates each season. Booking is essential.

All may seem sweetness and light so far, but there's a storm brewing behind the scenes. The Tribune Co, which bought the team in 1981, are in a dispute with locals over plans to expand the stadium. Owners contend they need to increase capacity to maximise revenue; fans argue that to mess

with perfection would be inexcusable. Change is viewed with deep suspicion around here: the stadium didn't add floodlights until 1988, becoming the last major-league ballpark to do so. Even now, the majority of games are played in daylight.

Whoever wins the argument, it seems unlikely that the Cubs will leave Wrigley for years; few would bet against them celebrating the park's centenary here in 2014. For one thing, Wrigley's a Chicago landmark; for another, it's still a great place to watch a game. But more than that, baseball values its history more than any other sport, which makes Wrigley its second most treasured asset (Fenway Park in Boston opened two years earlier). And at a time when the executives of Major League Baseball seem to be trying to put the public off their sport, Wrigley Field, conversely and effortlessly, makes it seem like the only game in the world.

Evanston & the North Shore Suburbs

Head north from Chicago, and you'll reach some charming, moneyed towns.

Evanston

A good-sized suburb just north of Chicago that signals the beginning of an affluent region referred to as the North Shore. The home base of Northwestern University, the only private school in the Big Ten. A hub of the Women's Christian Temperance Union movement that predated Prohibition early in the last century.

No matter how Chicagoans choose to pin it, Evanston is in the midst of a rejuvenation. Its attractive location (on Lake Michigan) and relatively easy accessibility to Chicago – take the Purple line express to and from Davis – has long made it a popular suburb with those who need to live near the city but don't like to live in it, with the presence of such an impressive college only adding to its affluence. However, a flurry of condominium construction in the late 1990s has begun to attract more twenty- and thirtysomethings to the town, complementing the existing mix of more established groups (students, families, the elderly).

It's a handsome place, if a little bland after the architectural assault that is Chicago. The streets are lined with old-growth maples, oaks and elms that thrive in the rich prairie soil; the public parks and beaches are cherished by long-time residents; and the streets are eerily spotless. The Temperance Union would love it, of course.

No one comes to Evanston for the nightlife. There are few decent bars and nightclubs to speak of. That said, there are coffeehouses galore; and more than a few decent places to eat. The casual, exclusively vegetarian **Blind Faith Café** (525 Dempster Street; 847 328 6875) serves made-to-order smoothies and blended juices alongside quesadillas and hearty macrobiotic plates. **Walker Bros Original Pancake House** (153 Green Bay Road; 847 251 6000) is tops for scrumptious pancakes, crêpes and omelettes, and boasts some striking stained-glass lamps and murals. **Hecky's** (*see p143*) smokes up some outstanding barbecue, while **Trio** (1625 Hinman Avenue; 847 733 8746) offers an upscale attitude and a spectacular, eclectic menu.

Northwestern University

Founded in 1851, this respected undergraduate institution has grown to encompass numerous graduate schools (including medical, law and business), and garner numerous awards for scholastic and research excellence. Student dormitories, classroom buildings and other structures take up approximately 240 acres at the park-like lakefront campus in north-east Evanston. Its journalism, speech and performance departments are consistently top ranked, and its combined library holdings are among the very finest among comparable US private universities.

The college, though, also garners a great deal of attention on its sporting programme, and most particularly on its football team, the Wildcats. However, the team's been feeble for several years now – running to a 2-6 record in 2001 and finishing last in the Big Ten – which means you should be able to get tickets for a game if you want. Call 847 491 2287 for details. (Speaking of sports, Evanston's Wells Field and James Park are unique among Chicago parks: during summer, both stage cricket matches.)

Opened in 1975, the **Pick-Staiger Concert Hall** (1977 S Campus Drive (on the Arts Circle); 847 491 5441/467 4000) is a combination classroom and performance facility for a variety of groups. Solo recitals, lectures, orchestra, jazz and chamber music concerts connected with the school, as well as outside artists such as the Chicago Chamber Musicians and the Evanston Symphony Orchestra, keep the space in use on a near-constant basis.

Mary & Leigh Block Museum of Art
Northwestern University, 1967 S Campus Drive (on the Arts Circle), Evanston (847 491 4000/ www.blockmuseum.northwestern.edu). CTA Foster (Purple). **Open** 10am-5pm Tue, Wed, Fri, Sat; 10am-8pm Thur; noon-5pm Sun. **Admission** free. **No credit cards**.
Visual arts are celebrated at this multifaceted university space, which encompasses four galleries and additional room for films, concerts and symposia. The museum's extensive collection of works

includes prints, photographs and drawings spanning almost 500 years. A sculpture garden features works by Miró, Hepworth and Arp.

Other North Shore suburbs

From Evanston, it only gets posher. The North Shore is made up of towns like it, only smarter and even more moneyed. Aside from their attractions – the **Bahá'í Temple** in **Wilmette**, Glencoe's **Chicago Botanic Garden** – these are places that offer little to the casual visitor. But a quick drive up and around the area is fascinating, if only to see how the other half lives.

Chicagoans head up this way for one of two reasons. The main one, usually at the behest of their kids, is **Gurnee Six Flags Great America** (I-94/I-294 from Chicago, exit at Route 132; 847 249 1776/www.sixflags.com). It is, of course, an amusement park, and an exhausting one. Exorbitant prices, retch-inducing thrill rides, carbohydrate-laden food and shops galore. Come away sunburned, foot-weary and broke. If you're lucky. For revenge, drag the young 'uns to the **Gurnee Mills** outlet mall (*see p169* **Mall talk**) afterwards, then bring 'em to **Mathon's** (6 E Clayton Street, Waukegan; 847 662 3610) so you can indulge in the terrific fried perch.

Far more cultural is the world-renowned **Ravinia Festival**, a summer-long music winging-ding with a wonderfully inclusive approach to programming: the Chicago Symphony one night, the Hubbard Street Dance Company the next, followed by Tony Bennett, Willie Nelson and the B-52s (not, thankfully, together). For more on Ravinia, *see p226.*

Bahá'í Temple House of Worship
112 Linden Avenue, Wilmette (847 853 2300/ www.us.bahai.org/how). CTA Howard (Red), then train to Wilmette. **Open** *May-Sept* 10am-10pm daily. *Oct-Apr* 10am-5pm daily. **Admission** free. **No credit cards**.
A North Shore landmark, this 50-year-old, 164ft (50m) domed house of worship resembles a blinding white spaceship, with lacy touches and an Eastern (as in Asian) feel. Photo opportunities abound in the surrounding gardens and reflecting ponds. An architectural marvel.

Chicago Botanic Garden
1000 Lake Cook Road, Glencoe (847 835 5440/ www.chicago-botanic.org). Metra Glencoe. **Open** 8am-sunset daily. **Admission** free. **No credit cards**.
Pleasant and serene, this sizeable Glencoe park is actually a series of outdoor environments focusing on different horticultural traditions (the English rose and Japanese tea, to name but a couple). Large lagoons and bike trails encourage visitors to plan a several hour or all-day stay.

Great Lakes Naval Museum
Naval Training Center, Camp Barry, Building 158, Buckley Road & North Sheridan, Waukegan (847 688 3154/www.ntcgl.navy.mil/museum.htm). No public transportation. **Open** 1-4pm Fri; 7am-3pm Sat, Sun. **Admission** free. **No credit cards**.
On the lakefront grounds of the Great Lakes Naval Training Center, this small but noteworthy establishment outlines the history and highlights of the US Navy's only 'boot camp' for new recruits and officer candidates. War memorabilia and vintage uniforms are here on display too.

The **Bahá'í Temple House of Worship**.

The West Side

From the down at heel to the up and coming, and everything in between.

From the late 1880s, German, Irish, Russian, Greek and Eastern European immigrants streamed into the industrial and residential area that now forms three distinct Chicago neighbourhoods: **Greektown**, **Little Italy** and **Pilsen**. Thanks to their working class heritage, there aren't exactly well-preserved historical sites on every corner. But for the adventurous modern visitor, the chance these areas offer to explore and experience kitsch-free Chicago communities should be seized.

North and east of Greektown is an area known loosely as **West Town**, although small warehouse-dominated pockets of it have been renamed as **River West** (north of around Kinzie and south of Chicago Avenue) and **West Loop Gate** (around Fulton Market) by real estate developers looking to add kudos. It's worked, too: Fulton Market, especially, is a highly desirable area among hip young things, even if the neighbourhood doesn't yet have the amenities to go with the ridiculous apartment prices.

While care should be exercised around here, especially after dark, the best way to explore these neighbourhoods is to set out on foot along their main streets. A decent place to start is by taking the Blue line out to UIC-Halsted, and walking north. After a block, you'll be greeted by some nasty pseudo-Grecian columns that sprang up in 1996 when Mayor Richard M Daley wanted to impress delegates to the Democratic Convention, and that signal the start of the first of the aforementioned West Side locales.

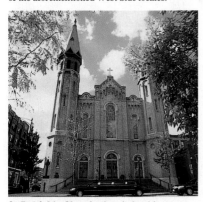

St Patrick's Church, the city's oldest.

Greektown

Actual Greek residents may be thin on the ground in Greektown – the University of Chicago shunted most of them to the suburbs – but the area along Halsted from Van Buren north to Monroe is still the Midwest's biggest Hellenic commercial area. Cheap and cheerful Greek restaurants abound here, and an eclectic array of treats can be found at the local bakery, jewellery shop and the bizarre **Athenian Candle Company** (300 S Halsted Street; 312 332 6988). There are plans to build a museum honouring the Greek-American experience on the site of the **N Turek & Sons** hardware store at 333 S Halsted Street.

One block from Halsted Street, on the other side of the freeway at Adams and Des Plaines, sits **Old St Patrick's Church** (700 W Adams Street; 312 648 1021), one of the first churches in America built to serve Irish immigrants. Built in 1856 and decorated with muted stained-glass windows, it's the oldest church in Chicago and among the few buildings that managed to survive the Chicago Fire of 1871. Inside is a fascinating mix of pagan and Christian symbols. It hosts the entertaining **World's Largest Block Party** (*see p190*) in July.

The West Loop & River West

The Greektown stretch of Halsted Street forms the eastern border of the West Loop. Once known for its warehouses and factories, this formerly industrial locale has become one of the hottest residential areas in town. From Halsted to Racine, Randolph Street is the epicentre of the loft and restaurant developments that have sprung up: trendy nightclubs and bars sit next to such old-line wholesale establishments as the Puckered Pickle Company and the Hot Potato.

However, on Fulton Market, two blocks north of Randolph – the best old market architecture lies between Halsted and Morgan Streets – there is a palpable tension between the working class meatpackers and the encroaching middle class population. The old meat and veg places are losing ground to the Fulton Market district's new hip identity: galleries (*see p208*) sit next to restaurants such as **Rushmore** (1023 W Lake Street; 312 421 8845), El trackside nightclubs like **Blonde** (820 W Lake Street; *see p231*) and a

Market down

So, you're looking to experience the birthplace of Chicago blues. You want to visit the exact spot where Little Walter, Bo Diddley and Muddy Waters held their historic open-air jam sessions, free to any lucky soul who happened to be passing. Well, then get yourself to Maxwell Street. And start your tour by standing smack-bang in the middle of the Dan Ryan Expressway.

The days when electric blues riffs flooded Maxwell Street are over. The construction of the Dan Ryan sparked a trend that, thanks to several decades of gentrification and the University of Illinois's land thirst, has gradually squeezed the street into oblivion.

Students and yuppies may be the new norm, but the memory of Maxwell Street lives on in the hearts of many old-timers who remember a thriving district that as recently as 2001 featured such holdouts as Reverend John Johnson's Heritage Blues school bus and Nate's Deli. Nate's, where Aretha Franklin famously sang *Think* for *The Blues Brothers*, is now a university parking lot.

Founded by Eastern European Jewish immigrants in the late 1880s (the name was made official in 1912), the junction of Maxwell and Halsted Streets long featured an open-air market where street merchants, tailors, junk pedlars and food vendors hawked their wares from pushcarts, stalls and storefronts. Haggling was customary, with the adage 'Cheat You Fair' emblazoned on at least one vendor's sign.

After World War I, when industrial Chicago beckoned wave after wave of Southern blacks with the promise of lucrative factory jobs, the tenor of Maxwell Street changed dramatically. African-American newcomers displaced the Jewish residents, who stayed on as shopkeepers, and the market became a Sunday affair. The Southern arrivals brought with them the Delta blues, which found new expression in the electric sound of the urban North. A tradition of outdoor entertainment quickly transformed Maxwell Street into a rousing Deep South juke joint, with blues greats and novices gathering on street corners and in back alleys.

But not everyone appreciated the festivities. The city changed the local zoning designation in 1994, and the Sunday market was moved to its current site on Canal Street. More recently, Original Jim's Red Hots, with its signature Chicago Polish

sausage, was shifted to a new location on Union Street. Even the UIC campus paper condemned Maxwell Street's remains as a 'smelly, rickety eyesore of a shit-house'. Despite advocates' best efforts – which ranged from an application for landmark status to a hunger strike by a 70-year-old – University Village, UIC's profitable expansion project that will ultimately sprout more than 900 luxury condos, levelled most of the old Maxwell Street buildings in 2001.

Once the construction frenzy fades, a few buildings and several façades will be restored, albeit as trendy decor for a parking garage. But now and forever, Maxwell Street enthusiasts will be singing the wrong kind of blues.

flurry of loft conversions. But still the old ways remain in a few pockets. For a vision of anti-yuppie, carnivorous hell, check out the **Peoria Packing Co** (1300 W Lake Street, where huge piles of bloody raw meat, pigs' feet and cows' hooves are heaped up for eager budget buyers.

Calmer West Loop options include the chance to kvetch with Chicago's most famous resident. At **Harpo Studios** (yes, it's her name spelled backwards; 1058 W Washington Boulevard; 312 591 9222/www.oprah.com), visitors can book free tickets to recordings of *Oprah* (call at least a month ahead). Nearby sits the **Museum of Holography** (*see below*); while just under a mile further west on Madison Street is the huge **United Center** (*see p234*), which houses the once-great, now-pathetic Chicago Bulls, the Blackhawks hockey team, numerous music acts and, every couple of years in a big top set up in the car park, Cirque du Soleil. Most sports fans see only the arena – and maybe a bar – before heading back to less interesting parts of town.

Museum of Holography
1134 W Washington Boulevard, at N Racine Avenue (312 226 1007/www.holographiccenter.com). CTA Ashland (Green) or Racine (Blue). **Open** 12.30-4.30pm Wed-Sun. **Admission** $4; free under-6s. **No credit cards**.
Holography is a noble profession when applied to medicine. It has proven to be a valuable tool for prac-titioners of ophthalmology, pathology and dentistry, and new uses for it continue to be discovered even now. However, it should also be pointed out that just as its usefulness in science can't be denied, so its ugliness as art is similarly indubitable. Hundreds of silvery heads and figures stare unnervingly out from the walls of this museum, many of them clad in the garish fashions of the 1980s (when holographic art had its 15 minutes of fame). Eyes open and close, smiles crease and fold, all in shimmering reds and greens and blues. If you like holograms, as the say-ing goes, you'll love this, but to the non-aficionado… Well, take a look at your credit card. There: that's a hologram. Jolly good. Now, haven't you got anything better to do?

Heading south

Stroll down Halsted south from Greektown, and you'll soon find yourself surrounded by the brutalist architecture of the **University of Illinois at Chicago** (UIC) campus, built in the 1960s as a sprawling interruption to the historic neighbourhoods that surround it. A casual eye may have difficulty discerning the university's laudable attempts to soften its concrete landscape by adding trees and grassy medians throughout the busy campus; for non-academics, the **Jane Addams Hull-House Museum** (*see below*) makes it worth the trek.

A couple of blocks further south of Hull-House lies the now-redeveloped area that gave birth to the Chicago blues. The **Maxwell Street Market**, formerly on Halsted Street between Roosevelt and 14th, was an unreconstructed city gem for years. Sadly, it's now been reconstructed: only a few of the original storefronts still stand at the old site; music, too, has moved elsewhere (*see p110* **Market down**). Still, the multi-ethnic market soldiers on half a mile east at Canal Street. The low-priced Sunday offerings remain wide and varied, with the array of toys, shoes, tools and thrift-store oddities – as well as roasted corn, *churros, carne asada*, candies and fresh fruit – creating a visual and sensual feast.

Jane Addams Hull-House Museum
University of Illinois at Chicago, 800 S Halsted Street, at W Polk Street (312 413 5353/www.uic.edu/jaddams/hull). CTA UIC-Halsted (Blue). **Open** 10am-4pm Mon-Fri; noon-5pm Sun. **Admission** free. **No credit cards.**
After an 1888 visit to Toynbee Hall in London, Jane Addams and Ellen Gates Starr returned to Chicago vowing to start something similar. A year later, Hull-House opened its doors. It began, like Toynbee Hall, as a settlement house, providing social services for the working class residents of a neighbourhood deprived of outside help and forced to live in hideous conditions. It soon expanded, though, stretching to include educational facilities, an unofficial centre for local social campaigners, and the city's first ever swimming pool, public kitchen and gymnasium. The fame of Addams and Hull-House grew, inspiring other socially conscious men and women around the US just as Addams herself had been inspired by Toynbee Hall. Addams became the first American woman to win the Nobel Peace Prize in 1931; she died four years later, aged 74.

Addams's work is continued elsewhere in the city, but of her 13-building complex, two structures remain: the original 1856 mansion donated by Charles Hull, and the dining hall. The former of these two buildings has been restored to how it was when Addams opened it, with exhibits, photographs and a 15-minute slide show providing an introduction to the American labour movement and the social prob-lems faced by immigrant populations that settled on Chicago's West Side, and how Hull went about solv-ing them. Enlightening and inspiring.

Little Italy

A stroll west from Halsted on Taylor Street along the south side of the UIC campus leads into Little Italy, a friendly neighbourhood where red sauce and meatballs fuel the local action. On hot summer nights, people drive from the suburbs just to stand in line for the flavoured ices and snowballs at **Mario's Italian Lemonade** stand.

In a bizarre bit of urban planning, a decayed public housing project sits smack in the middle of Little Italy's Taylor Street promenade of restaurants and shops and necessitates some night-time caution. (As part of a controversial gentrification plan, the city is slowly demolishing such buildings and relocating the low-income residents.) But just west of the projects, Little Italy has a maze of fascinating residential sidestreets that reward exploration. Head north on Loomis to view the classic Chicago three-flats and stoops that line the street, and turn east on Lexington to enjoy the beautiful old homes that overlook **Arrigo Park**, a peaceful green that stands out amid this brick, stone and stucco landscape.

Back at the **Scafuni Bakery** at 1337 W Taylor Street (312 733 8881), the wrinkled proprietresses serve up bread rolls, fresh-baked cookies and pastries. All things edible and Italian can be procured at the upscale **Conte di Savoia** grocery store at No.1438 (*see p179*), while down the street at prime people-watching spot the **Rosebud Café** (1500 W Taylor Street; 312 942 1117), the portions of home-made pasta are stomach-stretching, and photos of fedora-

Mexican Fine Arts Center Museum.
See p113.

sporting former regulars adorn the walls. Taylor is capped off by the **Pompei Bakery** at No.1455 (312 421 5179), which serves up a yummy culinary concoction called pizza strudel. The main attraction here, however, is the indoor mural celebrating the restaurant's founding family, who all eerily display exactly the same face on a series of different bodies.

The **National Italian American Sports Hall of Fame** is being erected directly across Taylor Street from the **Piazza DiMaggio**, an interesting plaza dedicated to every Italian-American's favourite son, who died in 1999. The Hall, a local joke due to huge construction delays, is scheduled to be completed some time during the next two years, and will feature such disparate treats as Mario Andretti's car and Cubs announcer Harry Caray's glasses.

Pilsen

First things first: the grim walk through the projects from Little Italy to Pilsen is avoidable at all hours, and especially so at night. You're best off catching a cab (if you can find one) or taking the Blue line one stop from Polk to 18th. But when you finally get there, you'll find an area that has far more to offer than just its flagship attraction, the impressive **Mexican Fine Arts Center Museum** (*see p113*).

The largest Mexican and Mexican-American community in the Midwest, Pilsen was settled in the 1800s by German, Czech and Polish immigrants drawn to work on the railroads. Industrialisation and the concomitant urban issues transformed the working class locale into a hub of labour activism by the late 19th century. As immigrant quotas began to restrict the influx of Southern and Eastern Europeans in the 1920s, Pilsen began to take on a Latino flavour. The murals on 18th Street, proclaiming 'Unidos Para El Progreso' and other ardent slogans, continue the area's activist tradition.

While a sizeable artistic community inhabits the blocks around the intersection of 18th and Halsted, the main commercial ebullience of Pilsen lies further west on 18th Street between Racine and Paulina, where street vendors and murals abound and salsa music pours out of passing vehicles. At the **Tortilleria Sabinas** factory at No.1509, watch through giant glass windows as the staff make tortillas in the back. If that makes you hungry, try the left-leaning **Café Jumping Bean** (1439 W 18th Street; 312 455 0019) or, better still, the long-established and homey **Restaurante Nuevo León** (1515 W 18th Street; 312 421 1517), which offers the best food in Pilsen. The entire front of this low-cost eaterie, composed of two buildings, is covered by a huge, colourful mural.

Vision on

When the *Wall of Respect* appeared on the side of a grocery and liquor store at 43rd and Langley on the South Side in 1967, Chicago's community mural movement was born. Bearing the subtitle 'Created to Honor Our Black Heroes and to Beautify Our Community', it featured 50 portraits of famous black Americans – among them Malcolm X, Marcus Garvey and Muhammad Ali – painted by over 20 African-American artists led by painter William Walker.

The mural sparked a people's art movement that spread through Chicago's minority communities. Neighbourhood agendas and political sentiments found expression on railroad underpasses, bridges, businesses and community centres. Rooted in the political movements of the 1960s, the cultural activism of the community mural movement championed social justice and local heritage.

The vast majority of the murals are clustered on the South and West Sides, and in Pilsen. To the south, the Donnelley Center Community Art Garden at 3947 S Michigan Avenue features both the jazzy *Another Time's Voice Remembers My Passion's Humanity* (1975) and the monumental *The Great Migration* (1995); and *Childhood is Without Prejudice* (1977) at E 56th Street and S Stony Island Avenue in Hyde Park envisions racial harmony through a series of overlapping and interlocking faces. The most notable work out west is perhaps the *History of the Packinghouse Worker* (1974) at 4859 W Wabash Avenue, which recalls Diego Rivera in both style and theme.

In Pilsen, *Galería del Barrio* stretches along W 16th Street from S Racine Street to S Blue Island Avenue and features contemporary cultural images of La Raza painted by local students and residents in the late 1970s and again in the 1990s. *Casa Aztlán* (1970-73), painted on the walls of the community centre at 1831 S Racine Avenue, depicts Mexican and Chicano struggles for justice.

Many of the murals date back several decades and are beginning to show the ravages of time and weather. Even *Wall of Respect* was destroyed in a 1971 fire. But fading masterpieces such as *Tilt: Together Protect the Community* (at the corner of Fullerton and Washtenaw, north-west of Bucktown), painted in 1976 by John Pitman Weber to show a mixed community fending off threats from gangs, and *Wall of Daydreaming/Man's Inhumanity to Man* (E 47th Street and S Calumet Avenue), Walker's 1975 South Side project depicting the vitality of the street, may yet be saved by community appeals and restoration efforts. Here's hoping.

Nearby on Ashland, **Rustico's Rancho Viejo** (1812 S Ashland Street; 312 733 9251) inhabits a building that encapsulates the 'hood's ethnic history. Once a *sokol* (school) for Czech and Polish immigrants and then later a dance hall, this artisans' store now sells a wide variety of Mexican crafts. Carved wooden furniture, Oaxacan figurines and vibrant paintings adorn the former stage, balcony and dancefloor.

Mexican Fine Arts Center Museum

1852 W 19th Street, at S Damen Avenue (312 738 1503/www.mfacmchicago.org). CTA 18th Street (Blue). **Open** 10am-5pm Tue-Sun. **Admission** free. **No credit cards.**
Having expanded in recent years, the Mexican Fine Arts Center Museum now seems firmly ensconced in Pilsen. And long may it remain so, too: this is

perhaps Chicago's most enjoyable community museum. Though several of its galleries are given over to temporary exhibits, the highlight for most visitors is the permanent display here. Entitled *Mexicanidad: Our Past is Present*, it offers a whistle-stop chronological tour of Mexican arts and culture, with the aid of music, art, religious artefacts and assorted ephemera. All the exhibits come with informative and engaging captions (in both English and Spanish), meaning you can happily spend an hour and a half just in this one exhibition without your attention wandering. Call ahead for details of music, dance and other performances – especially if you're here during the annual Day of the Dead festival, from September to early December – or for information on their Yollocalli programme, which aims to introduce young people to art in a variety of hands-on ways.

Wicker Park
& Bucktown

MTV loves it here. But the hip locals in this arty 'hood don't love MTV in return.

The Wicker Park/Bucktown/Ukrainian Village area is an extension of Chicago's Milwaukee Avenue corridor, a major diagonal thoroughfare that served as a pathway of urban expansion after the Chicago Fire of 1871. Originally a path made by local Native Americans in order to follow buffalo to the Chicago River prior to the settling of Chicago, Milwaukee Avenue became a plank-road thoroughfare that connected the north-west farming areas to the core of the city.

Though the Milwaukee corridor has historically been an artery of ethnic settlement, its recent hipness, with its extensive nightlife and artistic ambience, has attracted younger, whiter and more moneyed residents; or gentrification, as it's commonly known. As a result, the borders of Wicker Park, Bucktown and Ukrainian Village are far from rigid, more real estate names than neighbourhood titles. As a rule of thumb, beginning where Milwaukee Avenue meets the Kennedy Expressway, the Milwaukee Avenue corridor follows Chicago Avenue west to Western Avenue, and then follows Milwaukee north until around Armitage. The southern portion is **Ukrainian Village** or West Town, the central is **Wicker Park**, and the northern section – essentially, a little bit north of the buzzing Milwaukee/ North/Damen intersection – is **Bucktown**.

The development of the area is a microcosm of Chicago's ethnic settlement. Though Wicker Park and Bucktown predominantly house young professionals and those Hispanics who haven't yet been pushed further west by rising housing costs, the area was originally settled by Germans after the Chicago Fire. They built stately houses – many of which still exist – in the area around the plot of recreational land that is the actual Wicker Park. Ukrainian Village was settled primarily by Poles, Ukrainians and Russians, and remains one of the city's largest bubbles of East Slavic population, though one look at the Spanish-language billboards betrays Hispanic influence as well, specifically, Puerto Rican and Mexican.

Until a decade ago, Wicker Park was considered to be one of Chicago's most dangerous neighbourhoods. However, the

poshing-up has smoothed out some of the locale's rougher edges and made it destination number one for Chicago's adventurous young professionals and artistic types. Don't take that to mean the area is completely cleaned up; if you're not careful, trouble isn't hard to find, especially in the summer months.

Ukrainian Village & Lower Wicker Park

Any tour of Wicker Park and Ukrainian Village begins at the south-west corner of Milwaukee Avenue and Augusta Boulevard, where the **Polish Roman Catholic Union of America** stands. This is the home of the oldest Polish fraternal organisation in the US, founded, as the sign says, in 1873: one of the founders, Vincent Barzynski, was a vital figure in the development of Chicago's Polish community. It's also home to the **Polish Museum of America**: founded in 1961, it's the largest and oldest ethnic museum in America. *See p116.*

A block to the west and north stands the **Northwestern University Settlement House** (1400 W Augusta Boulevard, at N Noble Street), homebase of the organisation founded by sociologist Charles Zeublin. A lesser-known cousin of Jane Addams's **Hull-House** *(see p111)*, it played a critical role in the development of American social service. The building was designed by architect Irving K Pond, who earned a name as a developer of settlement houses, and the building still houses social service organisations.

Further north-west, the three-way intersection of Milwaukee, Division and Ashland marks the **Polonia Triangle**, known throughout the city's history as Polish Downtown and the one-time heart of Polish Chicago. The large white terracotta building that's now a bank was once the home of *Dziennik Zwiazkowy*, Chicago's largest Polish-language daily newspaper, as well as the Jan Smulski Bank Polski. Just to the east, at 1520 W Division Street, is a large grey building that once housed the Polish National Alliance, the largest fraternal Polish organisation in the country.

St Volodymyr's Orthodox Cathedral.

On the corner of Evergreen and Noble stands the gigantic **St Stanislaus Kostka** (1351 W Evergreen Avenue; 773 278 2470), completed in 1881 and home to Chicago's first Polish-Catholic congregation. Modelled after a church in Krakow, Poland, St Stanislaus boasted one of the United States' largest congregations – believed to be close to 5,000 families – at the turn of the 19th century. The church was dedicated and served by Vincent Barzynski until his death in 1899. Outside of service hours, it's open only by appointment.

One block north of the church is Blackhawk Street, which will take you back to Ashland. Though redevelopment has reared its ugly head

here, there are still a few pre-20th-century homes built during the height of the area's economic prosperity. The oldest homes are easily distinguished by the fact that they are built below sidewalk level, an oddity resulting from an 1850 decision by the city to raise sidewalks in order to facilitate better drainage.

The heart of the Ukrainian Village, though, is further west. At the south-west corner of Haddon and Leavitt stands the **Holy Trinity Orthodox Cathedral** (1121 N Leavitt Street, at W Haddon Street; 773 486 4545), the first Orthodox and Greek Rite church to drop anchor in the community. Founded in 1892 by Carpatho-Ukraine immigrants in 1892 as St Vladimir's Russian Orthodox Church, it was redesigned by Louis Sullivan to resemble a Slavic church. Tsar Nicholas II donated $4,000 towards the construction. The new church was consecrated in 1903 and was designated a place of worship and a cathedral by the Russian Orthodox Church in 1923. It was added to the National Register of Historic Places in 1976 and was assigned Chicago Landmark status three years later. It's open to visitors by prior appointment only.

A couple of blocks away, on the north-eastern corner of Oakley and Cortez, is **St Volodymyr's Ukrainian Orthodox Cathedral** (739 N Oakley Boulevard, at W Superior Street; 773 276 3990). Built in 1911, it marks the proper entrance to Ukrainian Village and was the first religious institution formed by local Ukrainians in the area. Call ahead if you'd like to look around.

Head south on Oakley until Rice, where you can't miss the huge, Byzantine-styled **St Nicholas Ukrainian Catholic Cathedral** (2238 W Rice Street, at N Oakley Boulevard; 773 276 4537), modelled after the cathedral in Kiev, Ukraine. Originally completed in 1915 and renovated in 1975, it was founded by Uniate Catholics, who hailed from Galicia and the Carpatho-Ukraine. St Nicholas was the community centre of Ukrainians until 1968, when a split in the parish over use of the Gregorian and Julian calendars divided the congregation and sent many to the SS Volodymyr & Olha church. The interior of St Nicholas is among Chicago's most elaborate, with ornate paintings and carpentry dominating the interior cupolas and imparting a distinctive Byzantine flavour. It's well worth stopping in for a look, but call ahead.

The rest of the splintered parish can now be found at **SS Volodymyr & Olha Church** (739 N Oakley Boulevard, at W Superior Street; 773 276 3990), a modern-Byzantine edifice with golden cupolas and a gigantic mosaic in front depicting the conversion of the Ukraine to

Christianity in 988 by St Volodymyr. The church is a piece of living history where the Eastern Rites are still practised and services are conducted in traditional Ukrainian. You can usually pop your head in between 9am and 4pm during the week.

A little north on Chicago Avenue, among authentic Ukrainian and Russian businesses, stands the diminutive **Ukrainian Institute of Modern Art** (*see below*).

Polish Roman Catholic Union of America & Polish Museum of America

984 N Milwaukee Avenue, at W Augusta Boulevard (773 384 3352/www.prcua.org/pma). CTA Chicago (Blue). **Open** 11am-4pm Mon-Wed, Fri-Sun. **Admission** *Suggested donation* $3; $1 concessions. **No credit cards.**

While it does a fine job at explaining the history of the city's Polish settlers, the Polish Museum of America has a colourful history of its own. Opened in 1937, its collection expanded dramatically when an array of exhibits the Polish government had sent to New York for display at the 1939 World's Fair became stuck in the US when Poland was invaded.

The museum purchased many of the artefacts for its archives, which then grew further when noted Polish pianist Ignacy Paderewski left many of his personal effects to the museum in 1941.

The museum now complements its permanent collection with temporary shows, classes and talks. Staff are only too keen to explain the history of Chicago's Polish community if asked; but if a taste of Polish culture inspires you to try a taste of Polish cuisine, they're also happy to recommend one of the many Polish restaurants in Little Warsaw, further up Milwaukee Avenue.

Ukrainian Institute of Modern Art

2320 W Chicago Avenue, at N Oakley Boulevard (773 227 5522/www.brama.com/uima). Bus 66. **Open** noon-4pm Wed, Thur, Sat, Sun. **Admission** free. **No credit cards.**

You might, from its name, expect this operation to be devoted to modern art from Ukrainian artists. And you'd be absolutely right. This non-profit organisation has a small permanent collection, which usually takes second billing to temporary shows on such topics as graphics and war art (the latter exhibition organised in association with the National Vietnam Veterans Art Museum, for which *see p86*). Lectures and screenings keep the locals interested.

Wicker Park & Bucktown

From the **Ukrainian Institute of Modern Art**, it's a walk east down Chicago and then north up Ashland to Milwaukee Avenue. Head north-west up Milwaukee and, once you pass Wood Street, you'll be on one of the city's hippest nightlife corridors.

At the bewildering three-way intersection of Milwaukee, North and Damen stands the **Northwest Tower**, a 12-storey art deco building completed just before the Depression in 1929 by the architectural firm Holabird & Root. The one-time centre of Wicker Park's business, the Northwest Tower – aka the Flatiron Building – was virtually empty by 1970, but a restoration plan in 1984 has again filled the building with offices and businesses. Many of the neighbourhood's numerous galleries are found near this intersection, as are a liver-boggling amount of nightclubs, bars and restaurants.

South of the intersection, just off Damen, is Pierce Street, lined with fine examples of the large homes built in the area by earlier German and Polish residents. At **2141 W Pierce** stands a house adorned with an Orthodox cross on top: built in the late 19th century, it was once the home of the archbishop of the Russian Orthodox Holy Virgin Protection Church. The **Gingerbread House** (2137 W Pierce, at N Leavitt Street) was built in 1888 by Herman

Northwest Tower, the heart of Wicker Park.

Worlds apart

It's just a television show. Just a silly television show on a silly television channel. It's not that big a deal.

But it was.

When word got out in July 2001 that MTV had arrived in Wicker Park to film a series of docusoap *The Real World*, a few locals were a little miffed. Fair enough: the idea of having a camera crew lurking around your home for four months wouldn't appeal to many.

But while that might have been an irritation, it wasn't what raised the locals' ire. Rather, it was fears that their beloved Wicker Park would become too gentrified and pricey, just another ordinary suburb, bled dry of all the things they loved about it when it was down at heel, a no-go area. *Notting Hill* syndrome, in other words.

In truth, though – and much like Notting Hill – the gentrification of the area had begun several years ago. The arrival of the loathsome MTV was merely the most tangible sign that the neighbourhood was not what it once was. It also, though, provided a focal point for the anger of long-time locals about the Starbucking of the area, the draining of its character, the ever-escalating rents. (Quietly, too, they were pissed off that now MTV had moved in, it could never be cool again.)

The protests started quietly. The occasional poster and placard, a few passers-by hollering at the door of the loft, at 1931 W North

Avenue. But they quickly escalated. It wasn't unusual to find a herd of protesters outside the loft: especially after chucking-out time in the local bars, when drinkers were at their most voluble. Indeed, protests were so intense that several people were arrested at the site. Red paint was flung over the door of the loft; later, one of its windows was broken.

With a couple of exceptions, the cast seemed to take all this in good grace. A few worked at the **Piece** (1927 W North Avenue; 773 772 4422), a brewpub across the road from their loft; on- and off-duty, they were spied in such local staples as **MOD** (*see p146*). But for the most part, they seemed to steer clear of Wicker Park's nightlife, something due only in part to the fact that many of the bars in the area refused to let them in. (One local bookstore even put a sign in the window banning both cast and crew.)

The MTV crew finished filming in November 2001 – the rumour is that they left several weeks early, tired of all the hassle – and celebrated the end of their shoot with a party. Pointedly, the venue they chose was about as far from Wicker Park as possible in style and geography: **Jilly's Bistro and Retro Club** on the Gold Coast (*see p154*). Since they left, work has begun on turning the North Avenue loft into a branch of Bally's Total Fitness gym.

Just a silly television show?

Weinhardt, a German merchant responsible for making Wicker Park a German enclave in the 1870s. Across the street at No.2138 stands the **Padrewski House**, built in 1886 and originally called the Runge-Smulski House, but renamed after the famous Polish pianist who reputedly entertained a crowd from the porch of the property.

Slightly south on Damen, you'll find the plot of land that gives the area its name: **Wicker Park**, originally donated to the city by German Protestants Charles and Joel Wicker in 1870. A word of warning: the northern border of Wicker Park (along Wicker Park Street) is occasionally lined with gang-affiliated drug dealers. Don't hassle them, and they won't hassle you.

And for the literary minded, walk one block south of the park to Evergreen Street, aka Nelson Algren Avenue (*see p92* **Where the streets have two names**). Algren, author of *The Man With the Golden Arm* and one of Chicago's most accomplished writers, lived at 1958 W Evergreen Street, in a third-floor

apartment, from 1959 to 1975. In front of the house is a small Chicago Tribute sign; a plaque commemorates his residency, next to the large window on the first floor. Further south on Damen (at Division), is the **Rainbo Club** (*see p163*), Algren's watering hole. Further across, on Claremont Street just north of North Avenue, is the **Pedro Albizu Campos Museum of Puerto Rican History and Culture** (*see below*).

Pedro Albizu Campos Museum of Puerto Rican History & Culture

1671 N Claremont Street, at W North Avenue (773 342 8023). CTA Western (Blue (NW)). Open noon-4pm Thur-Sun. **Admission** free. **Map** p310 A7.
Pedro Albizu Campos was a noted Puerto Rican liberation activist, but while the ten-year-old museum that bears his name does offer some political history among its exhibits – there's a permanent display on Puerto Ricans in the US – it's not devoted solely to such matters. A collection of art by Puerto Rican and Puerto Rican-American artists adds perspective, as do the rotating exhibits and lectures.

Oak Park

Welcome to the most storied of Chicago's outlying suburbs.

To begin to understand Oak Park, you ought to take the El train to get there. Hop on the Green line in the Loop, and it's a half-hour or so away. But before you arrive, you'll journey through some of the most squalid areas of Chicago. Glance out of the window, and you'll see some true urban deprivation, abandoned cars and burned-out housing projects dotting the landscape. These are desperately forgotten neighbourhoods, cash-poor and with little hope of improvement. But when you reach Oak Park, it becomes clear where all the money went.

Oak Park forms a perfect rectangle, bordered by Chicago (Austin and North Avenues) to the east and north, by River Forest and Forest Park to the west (Harlem Avenue) and Berwyn to the south (Roosevelt Road). Pretty as a picture, it's the archetypal American suburb (more on the houses in a moment). And in terms of location, it's perfect for its residents: the El offers easy access to Chicago's main business district, the public school system is progressive and the shopping is good (especially around the Harlem Avenue–Lake Street intersection). No wonder property values here have gone through the roof faster than Charlie in his glass elevator.

It's a conservative place, this. Always has been. There are churches on every corner, and barely a bar in sight. The streets are leafy, the traffic calm. The combination village hall/police station – the suburb is run under the manager/trustee model – on Madison Street characterises its commitment to political fairness and safety for its residents and visitors, of which there are a surprisingly large amount. This is a proud town.

Yet Oak Park is also characterised by the creativity and diversity of its citizenry. The cultural scene here is rich, if hardly cutting-edge. Among the treats is the Oak Park Festival Theatre, which runs from June through August in Austin Gardens and has featured the likes of David Mamet and William H Macy (708 524 2050/www.oprf.com/festival), and the locals treasure the Frank Lloyd Wright architecture that dominates a handful of streets (see p120 **The wright stuff**).

While it's thriving in the early 21st century, you can't help but sense that Oak Park would be happier back in the 1950s. It's a city that yearns for simpler times, and still, to some

extent, belongs in them. Times when the family all sat down for Sunday lunch together after going to the local church. Times when teenagers wouldn't try and sneak into the local bar, but would instead wander over to **Petersen's Ice Cream Parlor** (1100 Chicago Avenue; 708 386 6131) for a sundae or a float and be home by 10pm. Times before abandoned cars, burned-out housing projects. Walking through the town, you can understand why in 1976, America's bicentennial, Oak Park was officially tagged as an All-American City.

Ernest Hemingway Birthplace & Museum

Birthplace: 339 N Oak Park Avenue, at W Erie Street. Museum: 200 N Oak Park Avenue, at W Ontario Street (708 848 2222/www.hemingway.org). CTA Oak Park (Green). **Open** 1-5pm Thur, Fri, Sun; 10am-5pm Sat. **Admission** $6; $4.50 students, seniors; free under-5s. **No credit cards**.

Looked after by the Hemingway Foundation, the house at 339 N Oak Park Avenue where Ernie emerged has been open for tours for years. The displays at the home include photographs, furnishings and the like connected with Hemingway's childhood years. A museum two blocks away (200 N Oak Park Avenue) continues the theme, with videos, books, posters and other Ernestabilia. All very well and good, of course, but the fact that Hemingway himself despised Oak Park, leaving as soon as he could (aged 18, for Kansas City, Missouri and a job on a newspaper) and memorably referring to it as a place of 'wide lawns and narrow minds', is rather skimmed over. Hemingway may have been in Oak Park, but Oak Park wasn't in Hemingway.

Unity Temple

875 Lake Street, at N Kenilworth Avenue (708 383 8873/www.unitytemple-utrf.org). CTA Oak Park (Green). **Open** 10.30am-4pm Mon-Fri; 1-4pm Sat, Sun. **Admission** $6; $4 concessions. **Credit** AmEx, MC, V.

This functioning Unitarian Universalist church space, designed by Frank Lloyd Wright in 1905 and eventually completed in 1908, is notable for its striking first-floor sanctuary and community room. Also of interest are the physical expressions of Wright's notions of divinity and sacred space found throughout (such as light fixtures, leaded glass windows and furniture); his love of music still manifests itself in the regular concerts that are held here. During the week, you can take a self-guided tour; at weekends, it's guided tours only.

Hello tiger! **Brookfield Zoo.**

Oak Park Conservatory

*615 Garfield Street, at S East Avenue (708 386
4700/www.oprf.com/conservatory). CTA Oak Park
(Green).* **Open** 2-4pm Mon; 10am-4pm Tue-Sun.
Admission *Suggested donation* $1; 50¢ children.
No credit cards.
More than a greenhouse, this 73-year-old windowed
structure is easily visible from the main highway
and contains three large theme rooms (tropical, fern
and desert). A 5,000sq ft (465sq m) building, opened
in 2000, provides additional space for social and educational events. Rehn Park next door contains tennis courts and a swimming pool.

Pleasant Home/Historical Society of Oak Park & River Forest

*217 S Home Avenue, at Pleasant Street (708 383
2654/848 6755/www.oprf.com/oprfhist). CTA
Oak Park (Green).* **Open** *Tours Mar-Nov* 12.30pm,
1.30pm, 2.30pm Thur-Sun. *Dec-Feb* 12.30pm,
1.30pm Thur-Sun. **Admission** $5; $3 concessions.
No credit cards.
A 30-room residence designed in 1897 by Prairie
School architect George W Maher, Pleasant Home
and its surrounding park is used primarily for group
events such as association meetings and wedding
receptions. However, there's also a photograph and
document archive here, plus a charming little local
museum with exhibits relating to long-time local resident Edgar Rice Burroughs and the ubiquitous Mr
Hemingway. You can only visit the museum and
home as part of a tour.

Nearby

Brookfield Zoo

*3300 Golf Road, at 31st Street & 1st Avenue,
Brookfield (708 485 0263/www.brookfieldzoo.org).
Metra Hollywood (Zoo Stop).* **Open** *Memorial
Day (last Mon of May)-Labor Day (1st Mon in
Sept)* 9.30am-6pm daily. *Labor Day-Memorial Day*
10am-5pm daily. **Admission** $7; $3.50 seniors,
3-11s; free under-3s. **Credit** AmEx, DC, Disc,
MC, V.
Brookfield Zoo, a short ride away from Oak Park, is
a world away from its compatriot in Lincoln Park
(*see p103*), in terms of geography, tone and size.
Over 200 acres of land are dedicated to keeping more
than 400 species of wildlife, including thousands
of individual birds, mammals and fish. Cages are
largely eschewed in favour of a convincing attempt
at keeping it wild, with the animals roaming freely
(it's all relative, of course) to the delight of the kid-
heavy crowds. The dolphin shows in the Seven Seas
Panorama are predictably popular, with the newly
installed seals and walruses providing fine a support act of sorts. And, of course, absolutely everyone loves the inquisitive meerkats. The two areas
of the zoo specifically designed for kids allow adult
visitors a little more peace and quiet than might
otherwise be the case, but this is basically a family
attraction through and through. Parents should
come prepared for an expensive time in the well-
stocked gift shop afterwards.

The Wright stuff

Ask John Q Public who the world's greatest architect is or was, and chances are he'll reply 'Frank Lloyd Wright'. Even the most casual observer of popular culture is aware of the importance of Wright's contributions to modern architecture, even if they've never seen his work. Strange, considering the Chicago-based architect made his most lasting contributions to the art form not by designing grandiose public buildings or flashy skyscrapers, but rather by constructing isolated residences for rich suburbanites, shuttered from the prying eyes of the common man. The fact that the homes he built so greatly altered norms of residential construction is a testament to his genius; that his once-revolutionary design elements are now taken for granted bears witness to the prophetic prescience of his designs.

Raised in Wisconsin, Wright arrived in Chicago in the years following the Great Fire and went to work in the offices of Adler and Sullivan, where he was assigned to the firm's residential design department. Eschewing the Beaux Arts style popular at the time, Wright's residential designs had much in common stylistically with the International Style of architecture, which was taking hold in Europe around the end of the century.

In 1893, though, Wright was fired from Adler and Sullivan for moonlighting and set up his own practice at his home in suburban Oak Park, which he shared with his wife Catherine Tobin and six children. At his home studio, Wright spent the next decade defining what would come to be known as the Prairie Style. Among the results of his labours are the 25 homes the architect designed for his Oak Park neighbours, such as those at 1019, 1027 and 1031 W Chicago Avenue and at 210, 318 and 333 N Forest Avenue (*pictured above*). All can still be seen today, with both guided and self-guided tours available from the **Frank Lloyd Wright Home and Studio**.

Both of Wright's parents belonged to the Unitarian Church, which encourages followers to approach religion through nature, and science and art, disciplines that reveal the underlying principles of God's universe. Indeed, Wright's respect for natural elements and precise geometry is apparent in his designs. Prairie Style homes, most constructed of light-coloured brick and stucco, are low, ground-hugging, rectangular

structures with broad gabled roofs, sweeping horizontal lines and open, flowing floor plans. Most importantly, perhaps, they blend in with their surroundings, imitating the wide open, flat topography of the Midwest plains. Common features include enclosed porches, stout chimneys and overhanging eaves.

Wright left his home studio in 1909 and sold the property in 1925. Some 49 years later, the building had been so abused and altered by subsequent owners that it barely resembled the architect's original design. That same year, the Frank Lloyd Wright Home and Studio Foundation was formed to acquire the home and studio, oversee a $3-million restoration that returned the property to its 1909 appearance, and open it to the public as a museum and education centre.

One of the last designs to come out of Wright's Oak Park studio was the **Robie House** (*see p123*), located near the University of Chicago on the city's South Side. Wright began work on the home of Chicago industrialist Frederick C Robie in 1909, a project the architect would later proclaim 'the cornerstone of modern architecture'.

When asked what his best building was, the self-aggrandising Wright answered, 'My next one'. It seems that he was right. If not his best, at least one of his most famous buildings, New York City's Guggenheim Museum, was the last he designed before his death in 1959. Indeed, Wright designed notable buildings all over the world, but, luckily for visitors, the city where he got his start remains the best place to see the man's works at the peak of his career.

Frank Lloyd Wright Home & Studio

951 W Chicago Avenue, at N Forest Avenue (708 848 1976/1978/www.wrightplus.org). CTA Harlem/Lake. **Tours** 11am, 1pm, 3pm Mon-Fri; every 15mins 11am-3.30pm Sat, Sun. **Admission** $8; $6 concessions.

Hyde Park

Dominated by the university, this South Side campus holds much of interest.

Though the locale surrounding the Adler Planetarium, the Shedd Aquarium and the Field Museum has claimed the word 'Campus' as part of its name (*see p81*), it's fair to say that Hyde Park is far more deserving of such a moniker. For this implausibly pleasant little village – and village it near enough is – takes as its centrepiece the campus of the **University of Chicago**. As with most neighbourhoods whose dominant feature is a university, Hyde Park is at least partly defined by the students who call the area home for nine months of the year.

But while the students of DePaul University in Lincoln Park (*see p101*) are, by and large, young and lively – a fact apparent enough from an early-evening trawl around some of the local bars – Hyde Park boasts more graduates than undergraduates. As a result, the area is rather more sedate and relaxed than its collegiate compatriot to the north, though there are bustling areas of activity around 53rd and 57th streets. Not that it's all students around here: far from it, in fact. The areas to the south, north and west of the locale are shabby, to say the least, but Hyde Park itself is smart and decidedly middle class. It's also home to a number of fine museums and one truly great one in the not inconsiderable form of the **Museum of Science & Industry** (*see p123*).

After the MSI, Hyde Park's other museums have a tough job competing. But compete they do. Head east on 58th Street into the body of the university itself – passing Frank Lloyd Wright's **Robie House** (*see p123*) on the way – and you'll find the University of Chicago's world-class **Oriental Institute Museum** (*see p123*). Two blocks north and one block west is the small but perfectly formed **David & Alfred Smart Museum** (*see p121*). And west from there, in the sedate surroundings of Washington Park, is the **DuSable Museum of African American History** (*see p122*).

While you're here, of course, you may want to check out the university itself. It operates free tours every Saturday at 10am (information on 773 702 8374), though we've provided our own walking tour of the campus highlights, for which *see p124* **Walk on**.

David & Alfred Smart Museum

University of Chicago, 5550 S Greenwood Avenue, at E 55th Street (773 702 0200/ http://smartmuseum.uchicago.edu). Metra 55th Street. **Open** 10am-4pm Tue, Wed, Fri; 10am-9pm Thur; noon-6pm Sat, Sun. **Admission** free. **No credit cards. Map** p311 X17.
The main problem with the University of Chicago's Smart Museum – named for the two publishers of *Esquire* magazine, whose family foundation

The imposing **Museum of Science & Industry**. *See p123*.

provided the funds to open the facility – is its size. With a dizzyingly eclectic collection of 7,500 objects, from 21st-century works all the way back to others from 5,000 years ago, the museum could really do with a bigger space than the (admittedly well ordered) one in which it currently sits. Temporary exhibits complement the rotating displays. Small, then, but formed fairly perfectly.

DuSable Museum of African American History

740 E 56th Street, at S Cottage Grove Avenue (773 947 0600/www.dusablemuseum.org). CTA Garfield (Green). **Open** 10am-5pm Mon-Sat; noon-5pm Sun. **Admission** $3; $2 over-62s, students; $1 6-13s; free under-6s. Free to all Sun. **Credit** AmEx, Disc, MC, V. **Map** p311 X17.

Anthony Caro's *High Table* sits outside the **David & Alfred Smart Museum**. *See p121.*

With a mission to preserve and interpret the history and achievement of African-Americans, the DuSable Museum was founded in 1961 and named after Chicago's first permanent settler. It is the nation's oldest African-American history museum and holds over 1,300 artefacts, including a sweeping collection of slave and civil rights memorabilia and a fine collection of African-American art, selections of which are on display in rotation. Other permanent displays focus on blacks in aviation and Harold Washington, the city's first black mayor, though temporary exhibitions and a host of lectures, readings and education programmes keep staff busy.

Museum of Science & Industry

5700 S Lake Shore Drive, at E 57th Street (773 684 1414/www.msichicago.org). Metra 59th Street. **Open** 9.30am-4pm Mon-Fri; 9.30am-5.30pm Sat, Sun. **Admission** $9; $7.50 over-65s; $5 3-11s. Free to all Mon & Tue, Jan, Feb, first wk in June, mid Aug-mid Dec. **Credit** AmEx, Disc, MC, V. **Map** p311 Z17.

You thought the Art Institute was big? Well, this museum's no midget, either. Built in 1893 for the World's Columbian Exposition as the Palace of Fine Arts and converted to its present use in the 1920s, the MSI is truly gigantic. Good job, too, as it's one of the city's most popular attractions, despite the fact that it sits way out of the centre of town.

The challenge for every science museum, of course, is to try not just to represent advances in technology, but also to keep pace with it in its exhibits. And while a couple of the more whizz-bang aspects are good – notably the predictably oversubscribed Omnimax cinema and the surprisingly decent internet exhibit Networld – there are some real clunkers here, too: the F14 flight simulator (Main Floor East) is stupendously creaky, the Virtual Reality auditorium (Main Floor West) has dated about as well as *The Lawnmower Man*, and the simulated 727 take-off and landing (Balcony West) is underwhelming in the extreme.

Perhaps surprisingly, though, it's the low-tech attractions that are among the most popular. While the girls queue up to peer into Colleen Moore's Fairy Castle (Ground Floor, by the Yellow Stairs), an enormous, gaudy but intricate dolls' house, the boys stare agog at the huge John Deere machinery in The Farm (Ground Floor, by the Red Stairs). The long lines that form outside the re-creation of Coal Mine (Main Floor, by the Rotunda) hide an exhibit that kids enjoy far more than adults, who'd do better to check out the beautifully preserved Silver Streak train in the foyer.

These exhibits are just the tip of the iceberg, though: if you want to see everything here, it'll take you at least a day. Another problem with the size and shape of the museum is that it's very easy to get lost in it, or at least not find what you're looking for. The colour-coded zoning system used on the maps is extremely disorienting, but to be fair, it's hard to figure out how staff could have come up with anything much easier to negotiate. Well worth a visit, though.

Oriental Institute Museum

University of Chicago, 1155 E 58th Street, at S University Avenue (773 702 9507/ www-oi.uchicago.edu). Metra 59th Street. **Open** 10am-4pm Tue, Thur-Sat; 10am-8.30pm Wed; noon-4pm Sun. **Admission** free. **No credit cards. Map** p311 X17.

The University of Chicago's Oriental Institute Museum is a world-class showcase for the history, art and architecture of the ancient Near East (it got its misleading name before the phrase 'Middle Eastern' was coined). Or, at least, it will be when the extensive renovation works are finally completed. All five galleries have benefited from the project, scheduled for completion in 2003; only two of the five galleries had opened in mid-2002. Sure, the work is unlikely to have resulted in the kind of bells-and-whistles transformation popular with today's museums, but it will certainly end up providing a less shabby home for this outstanding collection of artefacts from Egypt, Mesopotamia, Persia, Assyria and beyond. While you're here, don't miss the museum store: the Suq, among whose stock is a charming range of imported jewellery.

Robie House

5757 S Woodlawn Avenue, at E 58th Street (708 848 1976/1978/www.wrightplus.org). Metra 59th Street. **Tours** 11am, 1pm, 3pm Mon-Fri; every 20mins 11am-3.30pm Sat, Sun. **Admission** $9; $7 6-18s, over-65s; free under-6s. **Credit** AmEx, Disc, MC, V. **Map** p311 Y17.

There's no danger of missing this one on your way down Woodlawn Avenue; and if you have even a basic knowledge of architecture, you'll guess who's behind this fantastically striking construction. Commissioned by Chicago industrialist Frederick C Robie and completed in 1910, the Robie House is Frank Lloyd Wright at his finest. A masterpiece of the Prairie Style, it features dramatic horizontal lines, emphasised by steel-reinforced beams that extend 20ft (6m) past the walls; daring cantilevered surfaces; expansive stretches of glass; and Wright's signature open floorplan. Wright used patterned glass doors and walls to eliminate the traditional 'room as a box' aesthetic and maximise flow and light. The property came to alter the course of American residential design, backing up Wright's self-aggrandising belief that it was 'the cornerstone of modern architecture'. It regularly features near the top of lists detailing the most important buildings of the 20th century.

The Robie House remained a private residence until 1926, when it was sold to the Chicago Theological Seminary. For the next 40 years, ownership changed hands repeatedly; it narrowly escaped demolition in 1957. Six years later, it was donated to the University of Chicago, which, in 1992, joined forces with the Home and Studio Foundation and the National Trust for Historic Preservation to restore the house and maintain it as a museum. Guided tours take place daily, though simply walking past and admiring its exterior costs nothing.

Sightseeing

Walk on Collegiate Hyde Park

Hyde Park is dominated by the University of Chicago; a visit here can't help but pass by its landmarks. Here are a dozen of the more interesting structures on campus.

Begin at the corner of 59th and Woodlawn.
It looks pretty big out front. But **Ida Noyes Hall** (1212 E 59th Street) is even bigger once inside. It was built in 1916 as a women's hall of residence; now, there's a cinema and a swimming pool tucked away inside it.

The **Rockefeller Memorial Chapel** (5850 S Woodlawn Avenue; 773 702 2100) is named for the man whose cash funded the building of the university. Built to the dauntingly Gothic designs of Bertram Goodhue in 1928, it's notable for some stained glass and a surfeit of statues that decorate the exterior. Avoid it on Sunday nights in summer, when the 72-bell carillon is brought to hellishly clanking life.

Walk a block west down Woodlawn, then take the next right up University.
The improvements programme at the university's **Oriental Institute Museum** (*see p123*) has been going on for years. However, two of the five galleries are now open, with the others hopefully not too far behind. Steps away from here sits the **Chicago Theological Seminary** (1164 E 58th Street; 773 752 5757): visit the quietly lovely Thorndike Hilton Memorial Chapel and the Seminary Cooperative Bookstore (*see p166*) downstairs.

Continue north up University Avenue to the south-west corner with E 57th Street.
If you're lucky, your visit to Hyde Park will coincide with a concert at **Mandel Hall** (1131 E 57th Street; 773 702 8069). Some top-notch classical ensembles play on at this beautifully maintained auditorium.

Walk north up University Avenue for a block, then turn left into E 56th Street.
The **David & Alfred Smart Museum** (*see p121*) is the second university museum en route. Stop to see which items from their expansive collection are on display in its cosy space.

Continue west down E 56th for a block, then turn left down Ellis Avenue.
A Henry Moore sculpture, **Nuclear Energy**, stands on the site of Stagg Field, the long-since demolished football field. Here, Enrico Fermi conducted the first successful nuclear experiment on 2 December 1942; exactly 25 years later, this statue was unveiled.

Stroll down Ellis and then turn left into E 57th Street.

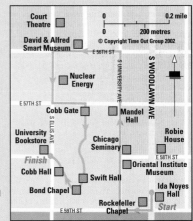

The gothic **Cobb Gate** makes for a grand entrance to the college, and made for a grand exit for Billy Crystal and Meg Ryan when they set off to drive to New York in *When Harry Met Sally*. Ask a student to explain the frivolous collegiate myth that has grown up around the figures on it: from the admissions secretary at ground level to the final-year students up top.

Walk through the Cobb Gate and continue south to the traffic circle.
The portentous **Swift Hall**, in the heart of the campus, is now home to the university's Divinity School. It figures, then, that right next to it should be the **Bond Chapel**, all dark woods and studied calm behind its imposing double doors. It's a popular venue for weddings among alumni.

Cobb Hall is the oldest building on campus, dating back to 1892, and takes its name from the architect who designed 18 of the college buildings, Henry Ives Cobb. Inside, the university's Renaissance Society mounts exhibitions of unapologetically modern art in the Bergman Gallery (773 702 8670/ www.renaissancesociety.org).

Cut through the passageway between Cobb Hall and the Administration building and head north up Ellis Avenue.
It's the least interesting of all the literary outlets in bookstore-dominated Hyde Park, but the Barnes & Noble-run **University Bookstore** (970 E 58th Street; 773 702 8729) does succeed in drawing a mix of students needing textbooks and tourists needing souvenirs.

Eat, Drink, Shop

Restaurants

Steak your claim on a pizza the action.

The meatpackers have been replaced on the West Side by arty loft-dwellers; downtown is more highfalutin than ever. But just when it seemed safe to assume Chicago had shaken its meat-and-potatoes image, the steakhouse returned. And how: in River North, they're everywhere. **Sullivan's Steakhouse** (*see p131*) sits opposite **Ruth's Chris Steakhouse** (*see p131*), with New York import **Smith & Wollensky** a mere moo away. **Keefer's** (*see p131*) has proved popular since opening, while beef reigns at heavy hitters such as the **Capital Grille** (*see p129*), the **Grillroom Chophouse** (*see below*), **Morton's**, the **Saloon** and **Gibsons Steakhouse** (for all, *see p136*).

However, though steak remains king of the table, it's not the be-all and end-all: stylish, cutting-edge restaurants are legion here. Book ahead if you want to sample the exemplary cooking of long-established chefs **Charlie Trotter** (*see p137*), Rick Tramonto and Gale Gand at **Tru** (*see p131*) and Rick and Deanne Bayless at **Frontera Grill/Topolobampo** (*see p133*); reservations might also be necessary for relative newcomers, such as Carrie Nahabedian at **Naha** (*see p129*), John Bubala at **Thyme** (*see p145*), Michael Taus of **Zealous** (*see p132*) and Bruce Sherman of **North Pond Café** (*see p139*).

Chicago's ethnic diversity is reflected in its restaurants, many easy on the wallet. Some neighbourhoods are dominated by one cuisine. The number of Germans in **Lincoln Square**, north of Lake View, is reflected in its many Teutonic eateries. It's a similar story in Swedish locale **Andersonville**, Indian-dominated **West Rogers Park** and **Little Warsaw** up on Milwaukee Avenue, where there are pierogi purveyors aplenty; to the west, **Greektown**, **Little Italy** and Mexican-American **Pilsen**; and, on the South Side, **Chinatown**. Elsewhere, try the lean pampas steaks of Argentina, crunchy Vietnamese spring rolls and Jamaican jerk chicken; Hawaiian butter basil mahi mahi, Cuban shredded beef and Hungarian goulash; Russian borscht, Armenian lamb kebabs, Italian beef sandwiches.

Setting off on such culinary adventures is fun, of course, and you won't be short of options. But you'd be remiss if you didn't at least sample Chicago's signature deep-dish pizza. Heart-stoppingly good, in every sense of the word.

The Loop

American

See also the above-par bar fod at the **Berghoff** (*p150*), **Cavanaugh's Bar & Restaurant** and **Miller's Pub** (for both, *see p151*).

Grillroom Chophouse & Wine Bar

33 W Monroe Street, at S Dearborn Street (312 960 0000). CTA Monroe (Blue). **Open** 11.30am-10.30pm Mon-Fri; 5.30-10.30pm Sat, Sun. **Main courses** $10-$32. **Credit** AmEx, DC, Disc, MC, V. **Map** p305 H12.
This clubby chophouse has a split personality. Brokers, lawyers and glad-handing pols show up for lunch; at night come crowds of theatre-goers. Prime steaks include flavourful bone-in versions of fillet and ribeye and a hefty 24-ounce porterhouse.

Prairie

Hyatt at Printers Row, 500 S Dearborn Street, at W Congress Parkway (312 663 1143). CTA LaSalle (Blue) or Library (Brown, Orange, Purple). **Open** 6.30-10am, 11.30am-2pm, 5-10pm daily. **Main courses** $22-$40. **Credit** AmEx, DC, Disc, MC, V. **Map** p305 H13.
Many of the recipes here are based on Midwest staples. But there is also a strong creative twist evident in such dishes as Iowa pork chop with barbecue butter, roasted buffalo with shallot sauce, and brandied duck and pheasant loaf. The decor is a take on Frank Lloyd Wright's Prairie School.

Quincy Grille on the River

200 S Wacker Drive, at W Adams Street (312 627 1800/www.quincygrille.com). CTA Quincy (Brown, Orange, Purple). **Open** 11.30am-2pm Mon-Fri. *Dinner* 5-7pm Sat and other opera nights (late Sept-late Mar.* **Main courses** $20-$24. **Credit** AmEx, DC, Disc, MC, V. **Map** p305 G12.
Should you witness a mass exodus from this pleasant riverside restaurant, it will not be because of the seafood-accented menu – good reason to linger – but because curtain-up is approaching at the nearby Lyric Opera. Go for the pre-theatre specials and enjoy the views of the river in a clubby atmosphere.

Rivers

30 S Wacker Drive, at W Monroe Street (312 559 1515/www.riversrestaurant.com). CTA Quincy (Brown, Orange, Purple). **Open** 8-10am, 11am-2.30pm, 5-9pm Mon-Fri; 5-9pm Sat. **Main courses** $15-$30. **Credit** AmEx, DC, Disc, MC, V. **Map** p305 G12.
On warm summer evenings, patrons at Rivers spill out on to the covered patio by the water; during the season, the opera crowd eats in the rather stylish

contemporary dining room. Rivers' high-quality signature dishes include pan-seared grouper, sautéd chicken with shrimp and spicy seafood stew.

French

Everest
440 S LaSalle Street, at One Financial Place (312 663 8920/www.leye.com). CTA LaSalle (Brown, Orange, Purple). **Open** 5.30-9pm Tue-Thur; 5.30-10pm Fri, Sat. **Main courses** $30-$45. **Credit** AmEx, DC, Disc, MC, V. **Map** p305 H13.
One of Chicago's top restaurants, figuratively and literally, sits on the 40th floor of the Stock Exchange. It's a romantic spot with sumptuous decor featuring leopard-print rugs, fresh flowers and candlelight. The contemporary menu reveals the Alsatian roots of chef Jean Joho; a dégustation menu is available.

Mossant
Hotel Monaco, 225 N Wabash Avenue, at E Wacker Drive (312 236 9300). CTA Lake (Red) or State (Brown, Green, Orange, Purple). **Open** 7-10am, 11.30am-2.30pm, 5-9pm Mon-Thur; 7-10am, 11.30am-2.30pm, 5-10pm Fri; 8am-noon, 5-11pm Sat. **Main courses** $15-$22. **Credit** AmEx, DC, Disc, MC, V. **Map** p305 H11.
Named after a Parisian milliner, Mossant tries hard to resemble a French bistro. Beef Burgundy (served en croute) is a menu staple, as are braised lamb shoulder and mussels steamed in white wine and fennel. Sink into a leather booth and admire the posters and artwork that play on the hat theme.

Italian

Italian Village Restaurants
71 W Monroe Street, at S Dearborn Street (312 332 7005/www.italianvillage-chicago.com). CTA Monroe (Blue, Red). **Open** 11am-1am Mon-Thur;

The best Restaurants

For the finest meal you'll ever eat
Charlie Trotter's. *See p137.*

For the fattiest meal you'll ever eat
Pizzeria Uno. *See p143* Made in Chicago.

For going the whole hog
Robinson's No.1 Rib. *See p128* Capital of 'cue.

For breakfast
Leo's Lunchroom. *See p149.*

For something simple
Penny's Noodle Shop. *See p141.*

11am-2am Fri, Sat; noon-midnight Sun. **Main courses** $11-$25. **Credit** AmEx, DC, Disc, MC, V. **Map** p305 H12.
Three restaurants under one roof offering distinct dining choices: upscale Vivere serves contemporary regional cuisine; the Village offers standards such as chicken Vesuvio; while folksy La Cantina focuses on seafood. Ideal for pre- or post-theatre dining.

Nick & Tony's
1 E Wacker Drive, at N State Street (312 467 9449). CTA Lake (Red) or State (Brown, Green, Orange, Purple). **Open** 11.30am-10pm Mon-Thur; 11.30am-11pm Fri; 5-11pm Sat; 5-10pm Sun. **Main courses** $10-$30. **Credit** AmEx, DC, Disc, MC, V. **Map** p305 H11.
This hard-working Loop eatery serves morning coffee, fresh baked goods and lunchtime sandwiches to office workers, moves on to pre-theatre menus, then welcomes its regular dinner crowd. Decorated as a take on a 1940s Italian chophouse, Nick & Tony's offers decent meat dishes and well-made pasta, including vegetarian options.

312
Hotel Allegro, 136 N LaSalle Street, at W Randolph Street (312 696 2420/www.allegrochicago.com). CTA Clark (Blue, Brown, Green, Orange, Purple). **Open** 7-10am, 11am-3pm, 5-10pm Mon-Thur; 7am-10am, 11am-3pm, 5-11pm Fri, Sat; 8am-11am, 11.30am-3pm, 5-10pm Sun. **Main courses** $13-$24. **Credit** AmEx, DC, Disc, MC, V. **Map** p305 H12.
It's named after a Chicago area code, but that's the only phoney thing about this Italian-American eaterie. The room blends earthy tones with sunny colours and features gilt mirrors, mica chandeliers, wall sconces, lots of fresh flowers and companionable booth seating. A popular pre-theatre spot.

Trattoria No.10
10 N Dearborn Street, at W Madison Street (312 984 1718). CTA Washington (Blue, Red). **Open** 11.30am-2pm, 5.30-9pm Mon-Thur; 11.30am-2pm, 5.30-10pm Fri; 5.30-10pm Sat. **Main courses** $15-$27. **Credit** AmEx, DC, Disc, MC, V. **Map** p305 H12.
This Loop favourite is in a basement, but what an elegant basement: with umber tones, terracotta floors, arched stucco walkways, murals and original art, it's as easy on the eye as the Italian food – fresh risotto and handmade ravioli – is on the palate.

Lunch stops, diners & delis

Encore
Hotel Allegro, 171 W Randolph Street, at N LaSalle Street (312 338 3788). CTA Clark (Blue, Brown, Green, Orange, Purple) or Washington (Brown, Orange, Purple). **Open** 11am-midnight Mon-Fri; 4pm-midnight Sat, Sun. **Main courses** $7-$8. **Credit** AmEx, DC, Disc, MC, V. **Map** p305 H12.
There's a Jekyll and Hyde personality to this eaterie in the Loop: lunch counter by day, hip lounge by night. For a casual lunch, try home-made soups and carved, slow-cooked beef brisket sandwiches with

Capital of 'cue

Forget Kansas City: Arthur Bryant's, touted by writer Calvin Trillin as 'the world's best restaurant', is touristy and overrated. And, anyway, Chicago has plenty of smoke and fire, plus its own controversy: which are best, South Side or North Side ribs?

On the North Side, **Hecky's** (*see p143*) makes no bones – so to speak – about the reason for its success: a sign screams, 'It's the sauce'. Aficionados go for meaty rib tips (the brisket end, cut off the bone). Hecky Powell is proud that his is the only Illinois restaurant cited by the Environmental Protection Agency... for smoke violation.

Another favourite is the **Fireplace Inn** (1448 N Wells Street, Old Town; 312 664 5264), where fall-off-the-bone baby back ribs arrive in hefty slabs, while Ol' Blue Eyes was a fan of the baby back ribs at **Twin Anchors, Inc** (*see p156*). Skip **Carson's: the Place for Ribs** (612 N Wells Street, Near North; 312 280 9200); instead, make the trek to the **Gale Street Inn** (4914 N Milwaukee Avenue; 773 725 1300), where the sauce is sweet and tangy.

South of the river, begin at **Miller's Pub** (*see p151*), where the ribs are plump and the sauce is sweet. Then take the trek to **Lem's Bar-B-Que House** (5914 S State Street, South Side; 773 684 5007), a takeout joint where the rib tips are tantalising. Another South Side hotspot is **Leon's Bar-B-Q** (8251 S Cottage Grove Avenue, South Side; 773 488 4556):

the spicy sauce is potent enough to dissolve your fillings. Note, though, that both Lem's and Leon's sit in neighbourhoods that are at best gritty, at worst downright dangerous. Take a cab and have it wait while you order.

But forget north or south: it turns out the 'cue king of Chicago is on the West Side. Back in 1982, Charlie Robinson, an ice-cream distributor, entered Chicago's first Royko Ribfest, a 400-competitor cook-off organised by columnist Mike Royko. Charlie's smoky ribs came out on top; the following year he opened a tiny eatery in Oak Park (940 W Madison Avenue; 708 383 8452).

The rest, as they say, is history. **Robinson's No.1 Rib** expanded to Lincoln Park (655 W Armitage Avenue; 312 337 1399), and now sells millions of bottles of the smoky, spicy sauce each year. Charlie also offers a version with some extra heat, and a sweet classic brown sugar sauce, plus five rub-in spices. He's learned that when it comes to barbecue and sauce, it's tough to get people to agree.

---

home-made barbecue sauce. After 3pm, Encore offers a light menu, accompanied by DJs and cocktails in an edgy lounge.

Mrs Levy's Delicatessen

Sears Tower, 233 S Wacker Drive, at W Jackson Boulevard (312 993 0530). CTA Quincy (Brown, Orange, Purple). **Open** 6.30am-3pm Mon-Fri. **Main courses** $1.99-$7. **Credit** AmEx, DC, Disc, MC, V. **Map** p305 G12.

Just because it isn't old doesn't mean it isn't a real deli. Sandwiches are piled high with lean pastrami and corned beef, and matzoh ball soup and other soups are made from scratch daily. Home-made meatloaf and chicken pot pies are popular, as are creamy milkshakes.

Regimental Grill

10 S Riverside Plaza, at E Monroe Drive (312 726 9347). CTA Madison (Brown, Green, Orange, Purple) or Monroe (Blue, Red). **Open** 6am-8pm Mon-Fri. **Main courses** $6-$14. **Credit** AmEx, MC, V. **Map** p305 K12.

Looking for an early breakfast? This is a comfy spot – warm maple furniture, emerald plaids – for bacon and pancakes, as well as fancier fare such as eggs Benedict and frittata. It's also a popular luncheon venue with office workers: the London broil and the crab cake sandwich are both good choices.

Russian

Russian Tea Time

77 E Adams Street, at S Michigan Avenue (312 360 0000/www.russianteatime.com). CTA Adams (Brown, Green, Orange, Purple). **Open** 11am-9pm Mon, Sun; 11am-11pm Tue-Thur; 11am-midnight Fri, Sat. **Main courses** $12-$26. **Credit** AmEx, DC, Disc, MC, V. **Map** p305 J12.

A shot of iced vodka at this old-world café comes complete with six-step instructions on how to down it with accompanying toasts, whistling sounds, and the smelling of black pumpernickel bread. It's all fun, and the hearty food is authentic: Ukrainian borscht, stuffed cabbage, sautéd chicken livers...

Seafood

Catch 35

35 W Wacker Drive, at N Dearborn Street (312 346 3500/www.catch35.com). CTA Lake (Red) or State (Brown, Green, Orange, Purple). **Open** 11.30am-2pm, 5-9.30pm Mon-Thur; 11.30am-2pm, 5-10pm Fri; 5-10pm Sat; 5-9pm Sun. **Main courses** $20-$50. **Credit** AmEx, DC, Disc, MC, V. **Map** p305 H11.
There's no catch to this good-looking spot for fresh-as-possible seafood, where Bangkok-born founding chef Eak Prukpitikul adds an Asian spin. Offerings include Szechwan scallops and stir-fried rock shrimp with Hunan pepper sauce. There's an urbane piano bar and a colourful bi-level dining room.

Near North

American

For **Carson's: the Place for Ribs**, *see p128* **Capital of 'cue.**

Blackhawk Lodge

41 E Superior Street, at N Wabash Avenue (312 280 4080). CTA Chicago (Red). **Open** 5-10pm Mon-Sat; 11am-3pm, 5-9pm Sun. **Main courses** $19-$27. **Credit** AmEx, DC, Disc, MC, V. **Map** p306 H10.
This faux Northwoods lodge interprets American cooking with the likes of smoked beef tenderloin flavoured with Jack Daniels and roast duck with black fig polenta. Meals begin auspiciously with sweetcorn and cheddar muffins and buttermilk biscuits.

Capital Grille

633 N St Clair Street, at E Ontario Street (312 337 9400/www.thecapitalgrille.com). CTA Grand (Red). **Open** 11.30am-2.30pm, 5-10pm Mon-Fri; 5-11pm Sat; 5-10pm Sun. **Main courses** $20-$30. **Credit** AmEx, DC, Disc, MC, V. **Map** p306 J10.
This high-end steakhouse sports a locker packed with dry-aged beef, an extensive wine cellar and a clubby ambience of polished leather and gilt-framed oil paintings. Tender steaks are hefty in size and price; the hamburger is one of the city's best.

Crofton on Wells

535 N Wells Street, at W Grand Street (312 755 1790/www.croftononwells.com). CTA Grand (Red). **Open** 11.30am-2.30pm, 5-10pm Mon-Thur; 11.30am-2.30pm, 5-11pm Fri; 5-11pm Sat. **Main courses** $15-$26. **Credit** DC, Disc, MC, V. **Map** p306 H10.
This minimalist, 70-seat storefront showcases the considerable talents of chef-owner Suzy Crofton, whose delicious seasonal American cuisine is prepared with French flair. Start with crab cakes; move on to pork loin with apple chutney.

Heaven on Seven on Rush

2nd floor, 600 N Rush Street, at E Ohio Street (312 280 7774/www.heavenon7.com). CTA Grand (Red). **Open** 11am-10pm Mon-Thur, Sun; 11am-11pm Fri, Sat. **Main courses** $10-$20. **Credit** AmEx, DC, Disc, MC, V. **Map** p306 J10.
Sassy Cajun cooking moved to the Mag Mile when a popular Loop lunch counter spawned this spin-off. Some complain it's too boisterous and full of tourists, but hey: that makes it just like the Big Easy, right? Specialities include gumbo, jambalaya, étouffée and po-boy sandwiches.
Nearby is another reputable N'Awleens-style café, **Club Creole** (226 W Kinzie Street; 312 222 0300/ www.clubcreole.com).
Branches: 111 N Wabash Avenue, the Loop (312 263 6444); 3478 N Clark Street, Lake View (773 477 7818).

Lawry's the Prime Rib

100 E Ontario Street, at N Michigan Avenue (312 787 5000/www.lawrysonline.com). CTA Grand (Red). **Open** 11.30am-2pm, 5-11pm Mon-Thur; 11.30am-2pm, 5pm-midnight Fri, Sat; 3-10pm Sun. **Main courses** $20-$30. **Credit** AmEx, DC, Disc, MC, V. **Map** p306 J10.
It's more American than British, but it does serve the best roast beef in town and the setting is reminiscent of an English carvery. Moreover, it accompanies its beef with light and fluffy Yorkshire pudding. Prime rib is served tableside with mashed or baked potato and whipped cream horseradish.

Mike Ditka's Restaurant

Tremont Hotel, 100 E Chestnut Street, at N Rush Street (312 587 8989/www.mikeditkaschicago). CTA Chicago (Red). **Open** 10am-11pm Mon-Thur; 10am-midnight Fri, Sat; 10am-10pm Sun. **Main courses** $17-$32. **Credit** AmEx, DC, Disc, MC, V. **Map** p306 H9.
Although 'Da Coach' has long since departed the Bears, Ditka remains popular in Chicago. American Bistro cooking is exemplified by Ditka's favourite food: double-cut pork chops, accompanied by grilled pancetta and a honey and green peppercorn sauce at this memorabilia-packed joint.

Naha

500 N Clark Street, at W Illinois Street (312 321 6242). CTA Grand (Red) or Merchandise Mart (Brown, Purple). **Open** 11.30am-2.15pm, 5.30-9.30pm Mon-Thur; 11.30am-2.15pm 5.30-10pm Fri; 5.30-10pm Sat. **Main courses** $27-$39. **Credit** AmEx, DC, Disc, MC, V. **Map** p306 H10.
For years, Gordon Sinclair brought class to a seedy stretch of River North. Now that he's retired, the Nahabedian cousins are carrying on his culinary traditions. Their makeover is clean and contemporary, with walnut floors and chairs and light, airy colours; the seasonal American cuisine has strong Mediterranean influences. Start with chilled white and green asparagus and move on to veal ribeye or roasted duck with braised turnips.

Redfish

400 N State Street, at W Kinzie Street (312 467 1600/www.redfishamerica.com). CTA Grand (Red). **Open** 11am-11pm Mon-Thur; 11am-2am Fri, Sat. **Main courses** $16-$28. **Credit** AmEx, DC, Disc, MC, V. **Map** p306 H11.

Eat, Drink, Shop

Chalk up another triumph for central casting. Here's another eaterie that looks as though it belongs on a Louisiana bayou, done out with Southern bric-a-brac and a Bayouz Grocery with a front stoop where good ol' boys entertain. The kitchen is deft with Cajun and Southern specialities, from po-boys to pulled pork.

Roy's

720 N State Street, at E Superior Street (312 787 7599). CTA Grand (Red). **Open** 5.30-9.30pm Mon-Thur; 5-11pm Fri, Sat; 5.30-9pm Sun. **Main courses** $18-$29. **Credit** AmEx, DC, Disc, MC, V. **Map** p306 H10.

There's plenty of eye candy at this Hawaiian import, including a high-decibel bar where Martinis are served in stainless steel 'glasses' that hold their chill. The kitchen struts its stuff with fusion cuisine full of exotic flavours and signature dishes such as lean, meaty honey-mustard beef short ribs, teriyaki grilled salmon, steamed snapper and blackened ahi.

Sullivan's Steakhouse

415 N Dearborn Street, at W Hubbard Street (312 527 3510). CTA Grand (Red). **Open** 5.30-11pm Mon-Sat; 5.30-10.30pm Sun. **Main courses** $15-$25. **Credit** AmEx, DC, Disc, MC, V. **Map** p306 H11.

This retro 1940s chophouse is decorated with prize-fight photos and a replica of John L Sullivan's championship belt. Prime beef is seared at high heat with a salt-and-pepper crust sealing in the juices. Sides, big enough to share, include creamed spinach, mushroom caps and horseradish mashed potatoes.

Steak reigns supreme around these parts. On the opposite corner is a branch of **Ruth's Chris Steak House** (431 N Dearborn Street; 312 321 2725); not far away is another top steak place, **Kinzie Chop House** (400 N Wells Street; 312 822 0191); near that is **Keefer's** (20 W Kinzie Street; 312 467 9525).

Tru

676 N St Clair Street, at E Huron Street (312 202 0001/www.trurestaurant.com). CTA Chicago (Red). **Open** 5.30-10pm Mon-Thur; 5.30-10.15pm Fri, Sat. **Set menus** $75-$125. **Credit** AmEx, DC, MC, V. **Map** p306 J10.

Multi-course tasting menus showcase the creativity of chef-owners Rick Tramonto and Gale Gand, in their crisply minimalist room. The menu offers an incredible range of flavours: try the 'caviar staircase' (an elaborate serving dish) or potato-crusted Scottish salmon with artichoke salad. Book weeks ahead.

Zinfandel

59 W Grand Avenue, at N Dearborn Street (312 527 1818/www.zinfandelrestaurant.com). CTA Grand (Red). **Open** 5-10pm Mon-Thur; 5-11pm Fri, Sat. **Main courses** $18-$25. **Credit** AmEx, DC, MC, V. **Map** p306 H10.

Regional cooking at its best. A month-by-month tour of the USA takes in the cuisines of Hawaii, Texas, the South Carolina low country and Pennsylvania Dutch country. Decor is funky rustic with folk art and batiks; try the braised pot roast, devilled cod cakes or pan-roasted Pacific salmon.

Asian & Pan-Asian

Bistro Pacific

680 N Lake Shore Drive, at E Erie Street (312 397 1800). CTA Chicago (Red). **Open** 11.30am-2.30pm, 5-10pm Mon-Thur; 11.30am-2.30pm, 5-11pm Fri; 5-11pm Sat. **Main courses** $9-$11. **Credit** AmEx, DC, Disc, MC, V. **Map** p306 K10.

Korean, Japanese, Chinese… you'll find a taste of each at this handsome eaterie. It's great for romance on a budget, with dark, secluded, candlelit booths and a menu that offers mains at great prices. Graze on steamed dumplings, or try the sushi or maki.

Vong's Thai Kitchen

6 W Hubbard Street, at N State Street (312 644 8664/www.leye.com). CTA Grand (Red). **Open** 11.30am-2pm, 5.30-9.30pm Mon-Thur; 11.30am-2pm, 5-11pm Fri, Sat; 5-9pm Sun. **Main courses** $14-$20. **Credit** AmEx, DC, Disc, MC, V. **Map** p306 H11.

Jean-Georges Vongerichten uses more than 150 herbs and spices to create his French-influenced Thai cuisine. After reinventing this stylish eaterie, he reopened it with a more casual atmosphere and scaled down prices. Try five-spiced onion-crusted beef – sort of a Thai beef stew – or flavourful grilled chicken over noodles with green peppercorns.

Chinese

Ben Pao

52 W Illinois Street, at N Dearborn Street (312 222 1888/www.leye.com). CTA Grand (Red). **Open** 11.30am-10pm Mon-Thur; 11.30am-11pm Fri; 5-11pm Sat; 5-10pm Sun. **Main courses** $9-$15. **Credit** AmEx, DC, Disc, MC, V. **Map** p307 H10.

With a sleek interior, dramatic pillars and running water, Lettuce Entertain You's first Chinese eaterie combines harmony and balance with appealing food. A satay bar offers grilled-to-order skewered meats with sauces, while house specialities include shrimp dumplings and black pepper scallops.

PF Chang's China Bistro

530 N Wabash Avenue, at E Grand Avenue (312 828 9977/www.pfchangs.com). CTA Grand (Red). **Open** 11am-11pm Mon-Thur; 11am-midnight Fri, Sat; 11am-10pm Sun. **Main courses** $8-$13. **Credit** AmEx, DC, Disc, MC, V. **Map** p306 H10.

Good food, a sleek, upmarket setting and decent theatre. There are dishes from Canton, Shanghai, Szechwan, Hunan and Mongolia, but the shrimp dumplings and orange peel beef stand out. Ever-popular are lettuce wraps that you eat like tacos.

Eclectic

Caliterra

Wyndham Chicago Hotel, 633 N St Clair Street, at E Erie Street (312 274 4444). CTA Chicago (Red). **Open** 6.30am-11pm daily. **Main courses** $21-$35. **Credit** AmEx, DC, Disc, MC, V. **Map** p306 J10.

Eat, Drink, Shop

This stylish hotel eaterie offers a nonpareil North California- and Tuscany-influenced menu. Specialities include veal chop with portobello fries and white bean relish, and five-spice seared duck breast. Every month John Coletta features one type of food, such as risotto, and soft-shelled crab.

Spago

520 N Dearborn Street, at W Grand Avenue (312 527 3700). CTA Grand (Red). **Open** 11.30am-2pm, 5.30-10pm Mon-Fri; 5-10pm Sat. **Main courses** $19-$32. **Credit** AmEx, DC, Disc, MC, V. **Map** p306 H10.

Hollywood celeb chef Wolfgang Puck imported his inventive Cal-Asian cuisine to Chicago via chef François Kwaku-Dongo. Attractive but noisy art-decorated dining rooms are the settings for sophisti-cated cooking that only occasionally slips. Try duck pot stickers with tamarind sauce or hearty goulash.

Zealous

419 W Superior Street, at N Hudson Avenue (312 475 9112). CTA Chicago (Brown, Purple). **Open** 11am-2pm, 5.30-10.30pm Tue-Fri; 5.30-10.30pm Sat. **Main courses** $15-$32. **Credit** AmEx, DC, MC, V. **Map** p306 G10.

Sunshine streams through the skylights of this con-verted loft: all earthy hues and mossy greens, a 15ft (4.5m) glass wine cellar and a chef's table concealed by tall bamboos the focal points. Mains include a Thai take on steak and eggs and pan-seared scal-lops with wide rice noodles.

French

Brasserie Jo

59 W Hubbard Street, at N Dearborn Street (312 595 0800/www.brasseriejo.com). CTA Grand (Red). **Open** 11.30am-4pm, 5-10.30pm Mon-Thur; 11.30am-4pm, 5-11.30pm Fri, Sat; 4-10pm Sun. **Main courses** $15-$30. **Credit** AmEx, DC, Disc, MC, V. **Map** p306 H11.

As faux brasseries go, this one has a good pedigree. Created by Alsatian chef Jean Joho – of Everest fame (*see p127*) – it's the best bet in town for a croque mon-sieur, but also features Alsatian specialities such as sausages with sauerkraut. In the bar, you'll find French beer in bottles, recorded accordion music, and free Alsace-style pizza on Tuesdays (5-7pm).

Dining Room at the Ritz-Carlton

160 E Pearson Street, at N Michigan Avenue (312 573 5223/www.fourseasons.com). CTA Chicago (Red). **Open** 6-10pm Mon-Thur; 6-11pm Fri, Sat; 10.30am-3pm Sun. **Main courses** $28-$40. **Credit** AmEx, DC, Disc, MC, V. **Map** p306 J9.

Oprah Winfrey, Mayor Daley and Christie Hefner are among the dealmakers who favour this stylish room. Chef Sarah Stegner's brand of contemporary French cuisine uses fresh regional ingredients and brings more than a few surprises. Five-course dégus-tation menus, one of them vegetarian, simplify ordering. Sunday brunch is the city's best, although note that booking is essential.

Topolobampo. *See p133.*

Les Nomades

222 E Ontario Street, at N St Clair Street (312 649 9010/www.lesnomades.net). CTA Grand (Red). **Open** 5-9pm Tue-Sat. **Set menu** $75. **Credit** AmEx, DC, Disc, MC, V. **Map** p306 J10.
Roland and Mary Beth Liccioni's take on classic French cuisine has a handsome setting. Menus incorporate fresh produce from their garden, such as the zucchini blossoms they stuff with lobster mousse, and verbena used to flavour ice-cream destined to accompany tasty fig tart.

NoMI

7th floor, Park Hyatt Chicago, 800 N Michigan Avenue, at W Chicago Avenue (312 335 1234/http:// parkchicago.hyatt.com/). CTA Chicago (Red). **Open** 6.30-10.30am, 11.30am-2pm, 6-10pm Mon-Fri; 7-11am, noon-3pm, 6-10pm Sat, Sun. **Main courses** $26-$39. **Credit** AmEx, Disc, DC, MC, V. **Map** p306 J10.
This glittering showcase for the considerable talents of Sandro Gamba overlooks the Mag Mile, Water Tower and distant Lake Michigan. Start with white bean soup or apple salad and move on to roasted rack of lamb, guinea fowl with onion jam, and chocolate fondant cake. This is a splurge spot, with a 3,500-bottle wine cellar to help you celebrate.

Indian

Klay Oven

414 N Orleans Street, at W Hubbard Street (312 527 3999). CTA Merchandise Mart (Brown, Purple). **Open** 11.30am-2.30pm, 5.30-10pm Mon-Fri; noon-3pm, 5.30-10pm Sat, Sun. **Main courses** $15-$18. **Credit** AmEx, DC, Disc, MC, V. **Map** p306 G11.
While Chicago can't compare with London in sheer number of good-quality Indian restaurants, it does have a sizeable Indian population and some good Indian eateries. This one is close to the Loop and specialises in tandoor oven cooking. The all-you-can-eat buffet lunch is a good buy at $8.95.

Italian

See also p143 **Made in Chicago: Pizza** for details of **Lou Malnati's Pizzeria**, **Original Gino's East** and **Pizzeria Uno**.

Coco Pazzo

300 W Hubbard Street, at N Franklin Street (312 836 0900). CTA Merchandise Mart (Brown, Purple). **Open** 11.30am-2.30pm 5.30-10.30pm Mon-Thur; 11.30am-2.30pm 5.30-10.30pm Fri; 5.30-11pm Sat; 5-10pm Sun. **Main courses** $13-$30. **Credit** AmEx, DC, MC, V. **Map** p306 G11.
This pricey Italian eaterie – the café is cheaper – offers the flavours of Tuscany in a pretty setting. Its warm, earthy decor is enhanced by exposed beams on the ceiling, blue velvet drapes and a potato theme. Try grilled meat, pasta and thin-crust pizzas from the blue-tiled ovens.
Branch: *Coco Pazzo Café* 636 N St Clair Street, Near North (312 664 2777).

Harry Caray's

33 W Kinzie Street, at N Dearborn Street (312 828 0966/www.harrycarays.com). CTA Grand (Red). **Open** 11.30am-2.30pm, 5-10.30pm Mon-Thur; 11.30am-2.30pm, 5-11pm Fri, Sat; 4-10pm Sun. **Main courses** $10-$30. **Credit** AmEx, DC, Disc, MC, V. **Map** p306 H11.
Named after the beloved Cubs broadcaster, this flamboyant restaurant offers a mix of standard Italian dishes and cuts of meat. Baseball fans enjoy the giant bat and 'Holy Cow!' sign outside and the uniforms, helmets and photographs inside. Stop by, if only for a beer and some home-made potato chips.

Latin, Mexican & Spanish

Frontera Grill/Topolobampo

445 N Clark Street, at W Illinois Street (312 661 1434/www.fronterakitchens.com). CTA Grand (Red) or Merchandise Mart (Brown, Purple). **Open** *Frontera Grill* 11.30am-2.30pm, 5-10pm Tue-Thur; 11.30am-2.30pm, 5-11pm Fri; 10.30am-2.30pm, 5-11pm Sat. *Topolobampo* 11.30am-2pm, 5.30-9.30pm Tue-Thur; 11.30am-2pm, 5.30-10.30pm Fri; 5.30-10.30pm Sat. **Main courses** *Frontera* $16-$22. *Topolobampo* $25. **Credit** AmEx, DC, Disc, MC, V. **Map** p306 H11.
These two adjoining restaurants serve authentic regional Mexican dishes – some say the best north of the border – created from recipes gathered by owners Rick and Deanne Bayless in Mexico. Upscale Topo accepts reservations, its sister restaurant does not (expect to wait at peak times); both are tremendous. The chef's tasting dinner offers five courses for $70, or $100 with wine.

Mambo Grill

412 N Clark Street, at W Hubbard Street (312 467 9797/www.mambogrill.com). CTA Grand (Red) or Merchandise Mart (Brown, Purple). **Open** 11am-10pm Mon-Thur; 11am-11pm Fri; 5-11pm Sat. **Main courses** $9-$23. **Credit** AmEx, DC, Disc, MC, V. **Map** p306 H11.
Vibrant colours, a dark postmodern interior and hot South and Central American specialities make this a River North favourite. Unexpected twists and unusual sauces set off traditional Latin dishes: Cuban sandwiches are a good bet, as are spicy pork tamales. A favourite on the Mambo's pan-Latin menu is tequila-marinated skirt steak.

Nacional 27

325 W Huron Street, at N Orleans Street (312 664 2727/www.leye.com). CTA Chicago (Brown, Purple). **Open** 5-9.30pm Mon-Thur; 5.30pm-midnight Fri, Sat. **Main courses** $13-$26. **Credit** AmEx, DC, Disc, MC, V. **Map** p306 G10.
An veritable encyclopaedia of Latin food, this: Nacional 27 serves cuisine from – you guessed it – 27 Central and South American nations. Included are lean, flavourful Argentinian Pampas steaks and ropa vieja, the classic Cuban stew. Be warned, though: the centre of the room morphs into a dancefloor.

Eat, Drink, Shop

Lunch stops, diners & delis

For **Boston Blackies**, *see p153*. For kid-friendly **Ed Debevic's** and **Rock 'n' Roll McDonald's**, *see p197*.

Club Lago

331 W Superior Street, at N Orleans Street (312 337 9444). CTA Chicago (Brown, Purple). **Open** 10.30am-8pm Mon-Fri; 11.30am-3pm Sat. **Main courses** $8-$12. **Credit** AmEx, DC, Disc, MC, V. **Map** p306 G10.

'Club' is a misleading description of this gritty saloon, a neighbourhood holdout in gentrified River North. Lago attracts a loyal lunch and early dinner crowd who go for the signature green noodles al forno, oven-baked with a blend of three cheeses. Family-owned for half a century, the place seldom misses a trick with its Italian-American standards.

Mr Beef on Orleans

666 N Orleans Street, at W Huron Street (312 337 8500). CTA Chicago (Brown, Purple). **Open** 7am-4.45pm Mon-Fri; 10.30am-2pm Sat. **Main courses** $3-$5. **Map** p306 G10.

Italian beef sandwiches are done to perfection at this hole in the wall. Thin slices of juicy beef are garnished with peppers; Italian sausage sandwiches are also good. For those who prefer not to have juice on their chin, subs are offered at a deli counter.

Mediterranean

Wave

644 N Lake Shore Drive, at E Ontario Street (312 255 4460/www.waverestaurant.com). CTA Grand (Red). **Open** 6.30-10.30am, 11am-2pm, 5pm-2am Mon-Thur, Sun; 6.30-10.30am, 11am-2pm, 5pm-2am Fri, Sat. **Main courses** $16-$25. **Credit** AmEx, DC, Disc, MC, V. **Map** p306 K10.

It may face Lake Michigan, but it's the Mediterranean that influences this stylish restaurant. Hip young patrons (black outfits, chunky boots) spill from hotel lobby to crowded bar to dining room, a sleek space featuring glass and stone, cool hues of blue, charcoal and slate grey and red accents. Look for risotto, Provençal mussels and bouillabaisse.

Seafood

Shaw's Crab House & Blue Crab Lounge

21 E Hubbard Street, at N State Street (312 527 2722/www.leye.com). CTA Grand (Red). **Open** 11.30am-10pm Mon-Thur; 11.30am-11pm Fri, Sat; 5-10pm Sun. **Main courses** $14-$25. **Credit** AmEx, DC, Disc, MC, V. **Map** p306 H11.

Head to the lounge for top-quality seafood, live jazz and blues and no cover charge. Patrons enjoy oysters on the half-shell, shrimp, clams, mussels, New England clam chowder and a variety of sandwiches, including pepper-crusted yellowfin tuna.

Taste first, health last: **Mr Beef**.

Thai

Erawan

729 N Clark Street, at W Superior Street (312 642 6888/www.erawangroup.com). CTA Chicago (Red). **Open** 5-10pm Mon-Thur; 5-10.30pm Fri, Sat; 5-9pm Sun. **Main courses** $18-$36. **Credit** AmEx, DC, Disc, MC, V. **Map** p306 H10.

You half expect a crouching tiger on the whimsical rooftops while sitting in this upmarket Thai eaterie. Authentic cuisine with creative western influences starts with dumplings and moves on to lobster, sea bass, and beef, lamb and duck curries. There's optional seating at floor-level tables (with wells to accommodate western limbs).

Star of Siam

11 E Illinois Street, at N State Street (312 670 0100). CTA Grand (Red). **Open** 11am-9.30pm Mon-Thur, Sun; 11am-10.30pm Fri, Sat. **Main courses** $5-$10. **Credit** AmEx, DC, Disc, MC, V. **Map** p306 H11.

Meatless masterpieces

Good vegetarian-specific eateries are few and far between in this meat-lovers' paradise. However, most restaurants at least pay lip service to veggies, while other restaurants do considerably better at catering for the non-carnivore.

Among them are **Caliterra** (*see p131*), which usually offers four to six vegetarian items, such as Yukon Gold potato gnocchi and ricotta tortellini. Even swankier are the **Dining Room at the Ritz-Carlton** (*see p132*) and **Ambria** (*see p139*), both of which offer special vegetarian dégustation menus. **Zealous** (*pictured; see p132*), too, specialises in five-course and seven-course vegetarian menus, and has four or five items available á la carte.

For those on a budget, Indian eatery **Klay Oven** (*see p133*) not only sprinkles vegetarian courses throughout its menu, but also offers a 14-item vegetarian section. **Mirai Sushi** (*see p147*) in Wicker Park offers numerous vegetarian menu items. In Hyde Park, head to **Mellow Yellow** (*see p149*) for great vegetarian chili and crêpes, and when in Lake View, try **Penny's Noodle Shop** (*see p141*)

Though the decor is considerably more appealing than the usual Thai storefront, prices are just as affordable. Its contemporary look features exposed bricks and beams, light woods and plum-and-orange accents. Spices range from mild to super-hot.

Gold Coast

American

The Saloon
200 E Chestnut Street, at N Mies van der Rohe Way (312 280 5454). CTA Chicago (Red). **Open** 11.30am-10pm Mon-Thur, Sun; 11.30am-11pm Fri, Sat. **Main courses** $12-$35. **Credit** AmEx, DC, Disc, MC, V. **Map** p306 J9.
The look and feel of a traditional New York steakhouse, but at Chicago prices. Select a marbled, aged cut of beef au naturel and have it prepared with a peppercorn crust, blackened or al forno (with garlic, parmesan and mushrooms), then settle back in the mahogany-panelled room and tuck in. Not far away is a branch of steak chain **Morton's** (1050 N State Street; 312 266 4820) and the hugely popular **Gibsons Steakhouse** (1028 N Rush Street; 312 266 8999).

Culinary schools

CHIC Café
361 W Chestnut Street, at N Orleans Street (312 944 0882). CTA Chicago (Brown, Purple). **Open** noon-1pm Mon-Fri, Sun; noon-1pm, 7-8pm Fri, Sat. **Set menus** $15-$25. **Credit** MC, V. **Map** p306 G9.
Find tomorrow's superstar chefs today in the dining room of this cookery school (the name is an acronym for Cooking & Hospitality Institute of Chicago). The cuisine will please your palate, while the prices will ease your pocket: bring wine and enjoy excellent three-course lunches or dinners.

French

Bistrot Zinc
1131 N State Street, at W Elm Street (312 337 1131). CTA Clark/Division (Red). **Open** 11.30am-3pm, 5-10pm Mon-Fri; 10am-3pm, 5-11pm Sat; 10am-3pm, 5-9pm Sun. **Main courses** $12-$20. **Credit** AmEx, DC, MC, V. **Map** p306 H9.
It's a stretch to compare Chicago's nightlife corridor with the boisterous Pigalle district of Paris. But you could almost get away with it at this neighbourhood café, with its rattan café seating and French-made zinc bar. Start with steamed mussels or onion tart and move on to bouillabaisse or Parisian-style roast chicken with smoked bacon, garlic and onions.

Twelve 12
1212 N State Street, at E Division Street (312 951 1212/www.twelve12.com). CTA Clark/Division (Red). **Open** 5.30-10pm Mon-Thur; 5.30-11pm Fri, Sat. **Main courses** $16-$28. **Credit** AmEx, DC, Disc, MC, V. **Map** p307 H8.

This subdued remake of the flashy, over-the-top State Room brings fine dining to Chicago's boisterous nightclub corridor. Talented chef David Shea may start you with fish soup or braised oxtail paired with grilled shrimp, followed by venison, pork loin, or grilled beef ribeye with potato soufflé.

Italian

Café Luciano
871 N Rush Street, at E Delaware Place (312 266 1414). CTA Chicago (Red). **Open** 11.30am-10.30pm Mon-Thur, Sun; 11.30am-11.30pm Fri, Sat. **Main courses** $11-$20. **Credit** AmEx, DC, Disc, MC, V. **Map** p307 H9.
A window table is a delightful spot for people-watching, but this trattoria also serves decent Tuscan fare. Try creamy country-style rigatoni flavoured with Italian bacon and sweet sausage. Or, for a simple, satisfying lunch, pair fennel-flavoured escarole soup with crusty bread and a salad.

Latin, Mexican & Spanish

Su Casa
49 E Ontario Street, at N Rush Street (312 943 4041). CTA Grand (Red). **Open** 11.30am-11pm Mon-Thur, Sun; 11.30am-midnight Fri, Sat. **Main courses** $10-$19. **Credit** AmEx, DC, Disc, MC, V. **Map** p306 J10.
Though you could find more creative and, frankly, better Mexican food around, if you hanker for a simple taco, burrito or combination platter, this is several comfortable cuts above a standard taco joint. Prices are friendly and the Margaritas potent.

Seafood

Cape Cod Room
Drake Hotel, 140 E Walton Street, at N Michigan Avenue (312 440 8414). CTA Chicago (Red). **Open** noon-11.30pm daily. **Main courses** $20-$40. **Credit** AmEx, DC, Disc, MC, V. **Map** p306 J9.
If that trim man with intense blue eyes and snowy white hair looks familiar, well, Paul Newman is an occasional guest here, and partial to a bit of Dover sole. A fixture at the Drake since 1933, the Cape Cod Room restaurant serves fresh – and expensive – seafood. The cosy room features nautical trappings.

McCormick & Schmick's
41 E Chestnut Street, at N Rush Street (312 397 9500). CTA Chicago (Red). **Open** 11.30am-11pm Mon-Thur, Sun; 11.30am-midnight Fri, Sat. **Main courses** $13-$40. **Credit** AmEx, DC, Disc, MC, V. **Map** p306 J9.
This Portland, Oregon chain has anchored along Chicago's Gold Coast with a handsome dining room accented with mahogany, stained glass and brass. Booths for up to seven ('snugs') can be curtained off with draperies. Fish is flown in daily, providing up to 35 fresh selections.

Vietnamese

Le Colonial
937 N Rush Street, at E Oak Street (312 255 0088). CTA Chicago (Red). **Open** noon-2.30pm, 5-11pm Mon-Fri; noon-2.30pm, 5pm-midnight Sat; 5-10pm Sun. **Main courses** $14-$25. **Credit** AmEx, DC, MC, V. **Map** p306 H9.
Revolving ceiling fans, louvred shutters, potted palms, sepia photos and lots of bamboo recall the French colonial era in Saigon during the 1920s. Recommended are the spicy beef salad, the gingered roast duck and the chi-chi upstairs bar. A pleasant alfresco terrace (enclosed during cooler months) overlooks Rush Street.

Old Town

American

For the **Fireplace Inn**, *see p128* **Capital of 'cue**. *See also* **Twin Anchors, Inc** (*p156*).

Charlie Trotter's
816 W Armitage Avenue, at N Halsted Street (773 248 6228/www.charlietrotters.com). CTA Armitage (Brown, Purple). **Open** from 6pm Tue-Sat. **Set menus** $100-$120. **Credit** AmEx, DC, Disc, MC, V. **Map** p307 F6.
Chicago's best-known chef never runs out of creative ideas. This 1880s townhouse is the nerve centre for an Epicurean empire that includes a TV show and cookbook series. The real thing's the food, though, and the inventive multi-course menus don't disappoint. Book for weekend dining up to three months ahead; the wait for weekdays is 'only' four weeks.

Fondue

Geja's Café
340 W Armitage Avenue, at N Lincoln Avenue (773 281 9101/www.gejascafe.com). CTA Armitage (Brown, Purple). **Open** 5-10.30pm Mon-Thur; 5pm-midnight Fri; 5pm-12.30am Sat; 4.30-10pm Sun. **Main courses** $20-$36. **Credit** AmEx, DC, Disc, MC, V. **Map** p307 G6.
Cheesy but romantic: sharing a pot of fondue in a candlelit setting with a flamenco guitarist playing in the background. A long-standing favourite left over from the fondue craze of the '60s, its survival isn't surprising given the excellent cheese, beef, poultry and chocolate fondues, and the superb wine list.

French

Bistrot Margot
1437 N Wells Street, at W North Avenue (312 587 3660/www.bistrotmargot.com). CTA Sedgwick (Brown, Purple). **Open** 5-9pm Mon, Sun; 5-10pm Tue-Thur; 5-11pm Fri, Sat. **Main courses** $12-$19. **Credit** AmEx, DC, Disc, MC, V. **Map** p307 H7.

With style, elegance and a sense of folly, this art nouveau eaterie is like a Toulouse-Lautrec painting. A bar and open kitchen anchor two dining rooms; warm-weather patrons spill on to a sidewalk café. Margot's beef Wellington may be the best you've tasted, but check first – it appears only about once a week.

Italian

Trattoria Dinotto

163 W North Avenue, at N Wells Street (312 787 3345). CTA Sedgwick (Brown, Purple). **Open** noon-10pm Mon-Thur; noon-11pm Fri, Sat. **Main courses** $10-$16. **Credit** AmEx, DC, Disc, MC, V. **Map** p307 H7.
A neighbourhood favourite that looks and feels like a trattoria you'd find tucked away on a backstreet in Rome. It's run by Dino Lubbat, with his father George tending the bar and mother Sue greeting guests. The pastas are well made, and you can't go wrong with veal marsala or scaloppine.
Branch: 215 W North Avenue, Old Town (312 202 0302).

Latin, Mexican & Spanish

¡Salpicon!

1252 N Wells Street, at N Division Street (312 988 7811/www.salpicon.com). CTA Clark/Division (Red). **Open** 5-10pm Mon-Thur; 5-11pm Fri, Sat; 11am-2.30pm, 5-10pm Sun. **Main courses** $16-$25. **Credit** AmEx, DC, Disc, MC, V. **Map** p307 H8.
This colourful storefront showcases the stylish Mexican regional cooking of Priscilla Satkoff, born in Mexico City and apprenticed at the Frontera Grill (*see p133*). Vivid colours and primitive folk art set the stage for artfully prepared and sophisticated dishes. Ceviche and charcoal-grilled fish are tops.

Lincoln Park

American

For **Robinson's No.1 Ribs**, *see p128* **Capital of 'cue**. *See also* the bar food at **John Barleycorn Memorial Pub** (*p157*) and the **Red Lion Pub** (*p158*).

Eclectic

North Pond Café

2610 N Cannon Drive, in Lincoln Park (773 477 5845/www.northpondrestaurant.com). Bus 29. **Open** *June-mid Oct* 11.30am-2pm, 5.30-10pm Tue-Fri; 11am-2pm, 5.30-10pm Sat, Sun. *Mid Oct-June* 5.30-10.30pm Tue-Sun. **Main courses** $24-$30. **Credit** AmEx, DC, Disc, MC, V. **Map** p308 G4.
This jewel of a café has added lustre since the 2002 addition of a glass-enclosed patio and stone fireplace. Formerly an ice skaters' warming house, it's decorated in an Arts and Crafts style and now serves delicious seasonal cuisine.

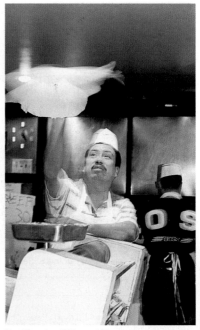

Healthy pizza? Yes, at **Bacino's**. *See p140.*

French

Ambria

2300 N Lincoln Park West, at W Belden Avenue (773 472 5959/www.leye.com). CTA Fullerton (Brown, Purple, Red)/29 bus. **Open** 6-9.30pm Mon-Fri; 5-10.30pm Sat. **Main courses** $33-$36. **Credit** AmEx, DC, Disc, MC, V. **Map** p308 G5.
Book ahead, dress up and then settle down to enjoy what many locals swear blind is Chicago's finest French restaurant. Chef Gabino Sotelino deserves all the plaudits he gets for his upscale take on French cuisine. But it's the attention to detail that really sets Ambria apart, from sommelier Bob Bansberg to the presence of a vegetarian dégustation menu alongside the regular option.

Aubriot

1962 N Halsted Street, at W Armitage Avenue (773 281 4211). CTA Armitage (Brown, Purple). **Open** 5.30-9pm Tue-Thur; 5-10pm Fri, Sat; 5-8.30pm Sun. **Main courses** $17-$31. **Credit** AmEx, DC, Disc, MC, V. **Map** p308 F6.
It seemed like an audacious move at the time, but young chef Eric Aubriot has proved his staying power four years after opening this stellar eaterie at the age of 26. The food is slyly inventive French, with fish (especially the sea bass) usually a perfect choice. It's worth booking ahead.

Eat, Drink, Shop

Curry favour at the **Viceroy of India**. *See p144.*

Italian

Bacino's

2204 N Lincoln Avenue, at W Webster Avenue (773 472 7400). CTA Fullerton (Brown, Purple, Red).
Open 11am-10.30pm Mon-Thur, Sun; 11am-midnight Fri, Sat. **Main courses** $10-$17. **Credit** AmEx, DC, Disc, MC, V. **Map** p308 F5.
A notable entry in the Chicago deep-dish pizza field, this mini-chain offers what may seem like an oxymoron: heart-healthy pizza, which blends low-fat cheeses, spinach, fresh mushrooms, herbs and spices. Still more amazing than the concept itself is that it actually tastes good.
Branches: 118 S Clinton Street, West Town (312 876 1686).

Jewish & Kosher

Shallots

2324 N Clark Street, at W Fullerton Avenue (773 755 5205/www.shallots-chicago.com). CTA Fullerton (Brown, Purple, Red). **Open** 11.30am-1.30pm, 5.30-9.30pm Mon-Thur; 1hr after dusk-midnight Sat (late Oct-late Mar only); 5.30-10pm Sun. **Main courses** $17-$45. **Credit** MC, V. **Map** p308 F5.
As this upmarket restaurant proves in glorious fashion, there's more to Kosher cooking than chicken livers. Chefs Laura Frankel and Dennis Wasko prepare superb Mediterranean-based food that also happens to be glatt (pure) Kosher. It almost defies belief that dazzling desserts, such as baked Alaska and chocolate mousse cake, contain no dairy. The burgundy decor and tile mosaics are pretty, the food impeccable.

Latin, Mexican & Spanish

Café Ba-Ba-Reeba!

2024 N Halsted Street, at W Armitage Avenue (773 935 5000/www.cafebabareeba.com). CTA Armitage (Brown, Purple). **Open** noon-10pm Mon-Fri, Sun; noon-midnight Fri, Sat. **Tapas** $4-$8. **Credit** AmEx, DC, Disc, MC, V. **Map** p308 F6.
Cosy neighbourhood, cosy restaurant. Of course, the conviviality of an evening at this labyrinthine gem is helped along by the fact that everyone shares the scran: it's a tapas place, and a fine one at that. It's popular, too; prepare for a wait on weekends.

Chipotle Grill

2256 N Orchard Avenue, at N Belden Avenue (773 935 6744). CTA Armitage (Brown, Purple). **Open** 11am-10pm daily. **Main courses** $4-$6. **Credit** MC, V. **Map** p308 F5.
Haute cuisine it ain't, but the stomach-lining Mexican nosh served up in seconds at this enticing chain – with a branch on Broadway in Lake View – is several cuts above the likes of Taco Bell. A vast burrito is perfect preparation for a night of beery excess. **Branches**: throughout the city.

Lunch stops, diners & delis

Clarke's

2441 N Lincoln Avenue, at W Montana Street (773 472 3505). CTA Fullerton (Brown, Purple, Red). **Open** 24hrs daily. **Main courses** $3-$7. **Credit** AmEx, Disc, DC, MC, V. **Map** p308 F5.
It's a diner, Clarke's, but it's a very Lincoln Park diner: more modish food than your average Golden Pancake-type spot, higher prices, and with a more

collegiate/yuppie-ish clientele. Still, if you can cope with the sometimes slack service (20 minutes for a milkshake? C'mon), this is a nice late-night standby.

Four Farthings Tavern

2060 N Cleveland Avenue, at W Dickens Avenue (773 935 2060/www.fourfarthings.com). CTA Armitage (Brown, Purple). **Open** 11.30am-10.30pm Mon-Fri; 11.30am-11pm Sat; 10am-10pm Sun. **Main courses** $9-$26. **Credit** AmEx, DC, Disc, MC, V. **Map** p308 G6.

One side of this 1890s saloon is a lively bar where a young crowd shoot pool, watch sports and enjoy superior pub grub; the bottled beer of the month is $2 a pop. An adjoining dining room, with warm wood panelling and deep booths, serves remarkably good food, including roast beef and fresh seafood.

Toast

746 W Webster Avenue, at N Halsted Street (773 935 5600). CTA Fullerton (Brown, Purple, Red). **Open** 7am-3pm Mon-Fri; 8am-4pm Sat, Sun. **Main courses** $7-$13. **Credit** AmEx, DC, Disc, MC, V. **Map** p308 F5.

There's a lot more to this joint than just browned bread, but the best thing at this fine breakfast/lunch joint is the coronary-inducing French toast. Two caveats, though: it's busy at weekends, and while parents with children are welcome, the presence of squealing kids may not be to everyone's taste.

Mediterranean

Clark Street Bistro

2600 N Clark Street, at W Wrightwood Avenue (773 525 9992). CTA Fullerton (Brown, Purple, Red). **Open** 4.30-10pm Mon-Thur; 11.30am-11pm Fri, Sat; 10am-10pm Sun. **Main courses** $7-$19. **Credit** AmEx, DC, Disc, MC, V. **Map** p308 E4.

In an area where eating options lurch wildly from stolid bar grub to high-end dining, the Clark Street Bistro offers a fine mid-range alternative. The food is Mediterranean and the atmosphere quaint; tuck into either steak or chicken.

Lake View & Wrigleyville

American

For **Deville**, *see p212. See also* the bar food at the **Duke of Perth** (*p159*), the **Harmony Grill** (*p221*) and **Resi's Bierstube** (*p162*).

Deleece

4004 N Southport Avenue, at W Irving Park Road (773 325 1710/www.deleece.com). CTA Sheridan (Purple, Red). **Open** 5.30-10pm Mon, Tue; 11.30-2.30pm, 5.30-10pm Wed, Thur; 11.30am-2.30pm, 5.30-11pm Fri, Sat; 10.30am-2.30pm, 5-9pm Sun. **Main courses** $10-$25. **Credit** AmEx, DC, Disc, MC, V.

Downtown food at midtown prices with an uptown attitude. The meals here might be classy and

contemporary – you can't go wrong with something fishy – but the atmosphere is never uptight, and while it's no budget café, the prices are certainly right. Sunday brunch is a delight.

Erwin

2925 N Halsted Street, at W Oakdale Avenue (773 528 7200/www.erwincafe.com). CTA Wellington (Brown, Purple). **Open** 5.30-10pm Mon-Thur; 5.30-11pm Fri, Sat; 5-9pm Sun. **Main courses** $12-$21. **Credit** AmEx, DC, Disc, MC, V. **Map** p309 F3.

There's not much that's really fancy about this Lake View restaurant, but it's not scruffy, either. In that regard, the decor's like the food: smart, simple and appealing. Chef Erwin Drechsler serves hearty American fare for a crowd that's largely local. Save room for dessert.

Asian & Pan-Asian

Hi-Ricky

3730 N Southport Avenue, at W Waveland Avenue (773 388 0000). CTA Addison (Red). **Open** 11.30am-10pm Mon-Thur; noon-11pm Fri, Sat; noon-10pm Sun. **Main courses** $7-$11. **Credit** AmEx, Disc, MC, V. **Map** p309 D1.

Know you fancy Asian food but can't make up your mind from exactly which country it should hail? Hi-Ricky is the perfect compromise: the menu offers assorted dishes from Vietnam, China, Thailand and Indonesia. The satay is ridiculously good.

Penny's Noodle Shop

3400 N Sheffield Avenue, at W Roscoe Street (773 281 8222). CTA Addison (Red). **Open** 11am-10pm Tue-Thur; 11am-10pm Fri, Sat; 11am-10pm Sun. **Main courses** $4-$6. **No credit cards**. **Map** p309 E2.

The clue's in the name: this is a straight-ahead, frill-free noodle joint, albeit one of the best in an area not short on similar options. The locals know it, too, which is why you'll more than likely have to wait for somewhere to sit. But it'll probably be worth it. **Branch**: 950 W Diversey Parkway, Lake View (773 281 8448).

Yoshi's Café

3257 N Halsted Street, at W Melrose Street (773 248 6160). CTA Belmont (Red). **Open** 5-10pm Tue-Thur; 5-11pm Fri, Sat; 11am-2.30pm, 5-9.30pm Sun. **Main courses** $13-$27. **Credit** AmEx, DC, MC, V. **Map** p309 F2.

The Yoshi is Yoshi Katsumura, owner and chef of the restaurant that bears his name. The café is a casual spot on a Boystown strip. And the food? A palate-boggling melange of Japanese and French cuisine that's far more pleasing than you'd think from the idea of it. Settle in with some seafood.

Eclectic

For the **Kit Kat Lounge & Supper Club**, *see p212.*

Blink and you'll miss the service at **Nine**. *See p145.*

Italian

Buca di Beppo

*2941 N Clark Street, at W Wellington Avenue (773
348 7673/www.bucadibeppo.com). CTA Belmont
(Red).* **Open** 5-10pm Mon-Thur; 5-11pm Fri; noon-
11pm Sat; noon-10pm Sun. **Main courses** $20-$25.
Credit AmEx, DC, Disc, MC, V. **Map** p309 F3.
Buca di Beppo is pure fun, from the sultry Sophia
Loren photos to the irreverent displays relating to
the papacy. Prices are reasonable and sharing essential for huge platters of immigrant Southern Italian
food: almost everyone leaves with a brown carrier
bag of extras. Good for groups.

Jewish & Kosher

Bagel Restaurant & Deli

*3107 N Broadway, at W Barry Avenue (773 477
0300/www.bagelrestaurant.com). CTA Belmont
(Red).* **Open** 8am-10pm Mon-Thur, Sun; 8am-11pm
Fri, Sat. **Main courses** $4-$16. **Credit** AmEx,
MC, V. **Map** p309 F3.
OK, Katz's Lower East Side it ain't. But it has been
around for 50-plus years and uses recipes that
arrived with the owners' grandparents. Salamis
hang in the entrance, pickles are delivered to tables.
You can order egg creams, boiled beef tongue, hefty
pastrami sandwiches, and potato knishes. And you
won't kvetch about the great soup, either.

Latin, Mexican & Spanish

Café 28

*1800 W Irving Park Road, at N Ravenswood Avenue
(773 528 2883). CTA Irving Park (Brown).* **Open**
5.30-9pm Mon; 11.30am-2.30pm, 5.30-10pm Tue-
Thur; 11.30am-2.30pm, 5.30-10.30pm Fri; 10am-2pm,
5.30-10.30pm Sat; 9am-2pm, 5.30-9pm Sun. **Main
courses** $9-$20. **Credit** AmEx, DC, Disc, MC, V.

With black bean soup thick enough to spread and
Cuban-style sandwiches featuring shredded beef
with onions and roasted pork in garlic, this is a good
lunch spot. For dinner, it is cosy and romantic, serving Cuban-style ribeye, chipotle grilled chicken, and
honey and jalapeño pork chops.

Lunch stops, diners & delis

For **Melrose** and **Nookies Tree**, *see p212.*

Bar Louie

*3545 N Clark Street, at W Addison Street (773 296
2500). CTA Addison (Red).* **Open** 11am-2am daily.
Main courses $7-$10. **Credit** AmEx, DC, Disc, MC,
V. **Map** p306 H10.
These neighbourhood eating and drinking spots are
catching on faster than you can say 'Martini'.
Though the formula is similar, each bar is a little different: some have outdoor seating, while some serve
breakfast or brunch. The Italian-American assortment of appetisers, salads, sandwiches, pizzas and
pasta is ideal for late-night dining.
Branches: throughout the city.

Swedish

For **Ann Sather**, *see p211.*

Turkish

A La Turka

*3134 N Lincoln Avenue, at N Ashland Avenue
(773 935 6101). CTA Southport (Brown).*
Open 11am-10pm Mon-Thur, Sun; 11am-11pm
Fri, Sat. **Main courses** $11-$20. **Credit** AmEx, DC,
Disc, MC, V. **Map** p309 D3.
Purportedly the first Turkish restaurant in Chicago;
and, as far as we can tell, its best. You can usually
tell the quality of a Turkish restaurant from its meze,
and on that count, A La Turka delivers. The mains

are just as good: try some succulent lamb. Avoid weekends if you'd rather not be disturbed by the in-house entertainment: a belly dancer.

Further North

American

Hecky's Barbecue
1902 Green Bay Road, Evanston (847 492 1182). CTA Foster (Purple). **Open** 11am-9pm Mon-Thur; 11am-10pm Fri, Sat; 2-8pm Sun. **Main courses** $12-$18. **Credit** AmEx, Disc, MC, V.

If you believe Chicago's only good ribs originate on the South Side, check out this Evanston storefront (*see p128* **Capital of 'cue**. Hecky's does a huge takeaway and delivery business, even to rib-hungry travellers stuck in queues at O'Hare.

German

Chicago Brauhaus
4732 N Lincoln Avenue, at W Lawrence Avenue (773 784 4444/www.chicagobrauhaus.com). CTA Western (Brown). **Open** 11am-2am Mon, Wed-Sun. **Main courses** $8-$18. **Credit** AmEx, DC, Disc, MC, V.

Made in Chicago Pizza

It's a great invention: all the classic ingredients of pizza, only more so. More cheese than a *Brady Bunch* retrospective. A crust so thick it makes French baguettes look like toothpicks. Artery-clogging amounts of meat. But Chicago-style pizza veterans, like tequila aficionados, all have a horror story: the story of the day they had 'one too many' slices with disastrous results. The result is that they didn't fancy pizza again for a very long time.

Don't miss out on this Chicago institution, but please wait until you're so hungry that you can barely stand. Then go shopping at Marshall Field's, or visit every room in the Art Institute, or run the Lakefront Trail... anything, really, but do it until your eyes are crossing from hunger pangs. Then hang around for another hour. Only now will you be ready to appreciate Chicago-style pizza. And don't be stupid about finishing every slice: listen to your stomach and your various heart valves. This is the Everest of pizza, and the old climber's saying applies: the mountain doesn't care about your well-being.

The man responsible is Ike Sewell, who invented this manhole-cover of a meal in the 1940s. It was during World War II that Sewell, a native Texan and all-American football player at the University of Texas, opened **Pizzeria Uno** with a partner. The story goes that Sewell wanted to run a Mexican joint, but his partner hated Mexican food so they chose pizza instead. Sewell, though, baulked at the wimpy size of standard 'za, and opted instead to load up cheese in a deep dish inside a ridiculously thick crust. Chicago-style pizza was born. The deep-dish business was booming enough by 1955 for Sewell to open **Pizzeria Due**, while he also served as a 'za mentor of sorts: one of his

early partners, Rudy Malnati, along with his son Lou, eventually broke away to open **Lou Malnati's Pizzeria**.

Sewell eventually licensed the name, and the Pizzeria Uno logo can now be spied in towns across the globe. The original, however, still serves the best in town. To sample the true Sewell lineage, you'll have to go to either Pizzeria Uno or Due. But Lou Malnati's serves an impressive version that was learned at the feet of the master, while the **Original Gino's East** is up there with the pair of them. Just don't make plans for breakfast the next day. Or lunch.

Lou Malnati's Pizzeria
439 N Wells Street, at W Hubbard Street (312 828 9800/www.loumalnatis.com). CTA Merchandise Mart (Brown, Purple). **Open** 11am-11pm Mon-Thur; 11am-midnight Fri, Sat; noon-10pm Sun. **Main courses** $10-$20. **Credit** AmEx, DC, Disc, MC, V. **Map** p306 H11.
Branches: throughout the city.

Original Gino's East
633 N Wells Street, at W Ontario Street (312 943 1124/www.ginoseast.com). CTA Chicago (Brown, Purple). **Open** 11am-11pm Mon-Thur, Sun; 11am-midnight Fri, Sat. **Main courses** $9-$22. **Credit** AmEx, DC, Disc, MC, V. **Map** p306 H10.
Branches: throughout the city.

Pizzeria Uno
29 E Ohio Street, at N Wabash Avenue (312 321 1000). CTA Grand (Red). **Open** 11.30am-1am Mon-Fri; 11.30am-2am Sat; 11.30am-11.30pm Sun. **Main courses** $6-$20. **Credit** AmEx, DC, Disc, MC, V. **Map** p306 H10.
Branch: *Pizzeria Due* 619 N Wabash Avenue, Near North (312 943 2400).

Eat, Drink, Shop

Blackbird. *See p146.*

You'll hear German spoken on streetcorners and in shops around the Lincoln Square neighbourhood, and you'll likely hear it at this eatery. The Brauhaus resembles a Munich beer hall, and attracts many German patrons. Try schnitzel, smoked pork loin, Koenigsberger Klopse (meatballs in caper sauce) or other German specialities.

Indian

Viceroy of India
2520 W Devon Avenue, at N Maplewood Avenue (773 743 4100). Bus 155. **Open** noon-3.30pm, 5-10pm Mon-Thur, Sun; noon-3.30pm, 5-10.30pm Fri, Sat. **Main courses** $9-$16. **Credit** AmEx, DC, Disc, MC, V.
Chicago's Little Bombay is centred along half a dozen blocks of W Devon Avenue. This atmospheric restaurant, with sitar music and Mughal-style carvings, specialises in North Indian cuisine but also offers some dishes from the south. The chicken tandoori and tender lamb shish kebab usually satisfy most western tastes.

Polish

Lutnia
5532 W Belmont Avenue, at N Central Avenue (773 282 5335). Bus 77, 85. **Open** noon-11pm Tue-Fri; 1-11pm Sat, Sun. **Main courses** $10-$25. **Credit** MC, V.
In a city second only to Warsaw in Polish population, you must try some Polish cooking. Lutnia is 'posh Polish': not much of a culture shock and far removed from the numerous storefronts on Milwaukee Avenue (such as longtime favourite **Red Apple** at No.3121; 773 588 5781). Inside you'll find a pianist, candelabra, white napery, fresh roses and tableside cooking. But you'll also find a pierogi or two among the stroganoff.

Seafood

Don's Fishmarket & Tavern
9335 Skokie Boulevard, Skokie (847 677 3424). Metra Morton Grove. **Open** 11.30am-11pm Mon-Thur; 11am-midnight Fri, Sat; 4-10pm Sun. **Main courses** *Tavern* $6-$10. *Dining room* $18-$21. **Credit** AmEx, DC, Disc, MC, V.
It's worth the trip to Skokie just for this eaterie. Don't be put off by the faux nautical decor: Don's is the place for perfectly prepared lobster, crab claws or simply grilled fresh fish. The wine list is easy on both the wallet and palate. Time a visit to Skokie to coincide with the various local celebrations, especially the annual Lobsterfest.

Swedish

Svea
5236 N Clark Street, at W Foster Avenue, Andersonville (773 275 7738). CTA Berwyn (Red). **Open** 7am-4pm daily. **Main courses** $3-$8. **No credit cards.**
A favourite Sunday morning Andersonville destination, Svea specialises in the 'Viking breakfast'. It's substantial enough to keep you going all day, and, anyway, don't all self-respecting pillagers start the day with a plateful of eggs, sausage, fried potatoes, pancakes and toast? You'll also find such staples as pea soup, meatballs and pickled herring.

Thai

Arun's
4156 N Kedzie Avenue, at W Berteau Avenue (773 539 1909/www.arunsthai.com). CTA 80 bus. **Open** 5-10pm Tue-Sun. **Main courses** *Dégustation* $85. **Credit** AmEx, DC, Disc, MC, V.
The antithesis of the low prices and basic decor of storefront Thai restaurants, and both one of Chicago's top eateries and one of its prettiest. It offers only a dégustation menu. But for 12 exquisitely prepared and presented courses (plus a duo of desserts), it's well worth a splurge.

Vietnamese

Pasteur
*5525 N Broadway, at W Bryn Mawr Avenue
(773 878 1061). CTA Bryn Mawr (Red).*
Open 5-10pm Mon-Wed; noon-10pm Fri, Sat,
Sun. **Main courses** $15-$27. **Credit** AmEx, DC,
Disc, MC, V.
Named after the Saigon street where the owners had
their family home, stylish Pasteur has a tropical,
colonial look, with high ceilings, churning fans and
potted palms. Large-scale paintings illustrate temples and the Vietnamese countryside. Try bouillabaisse, curried chicken, or salmon fillets baked in
a traditional clay pot.

West Town

American
For Oak Park's **Robinson's No.1 Ribs**,
see p128 **Capital of 'cue**.

Nine
*440 W Randolph Street, at N Canal Street (312 575
9900). CTA Clinton (Green).* **Open** 11.30am-10pm
Mon-Wed; 11.30am-11pm Thur; 11.30am-midnight
Fri; 5pm-midnight Sat. **Main courses** $15-$35.
Credit AmEx, DC, MC, V. **Map** p305 G11.
This super-slick hotspot attracts a sprightly crowd
of traders and professionals. Nine is dressed up with
mosaic glass pillars bathed in lavender light and a

granite champagne-and-caviar bar beneath a domed
silver-leaf ceiling. Starters include tiered shellfish
platters and tiny flavourful steamed mussels; follow
with aged prime steak or veal porterhouse.

One Sixtyblue
*160 N Loomis Street, at W Randolph Street (312
850 0303/www.onesixtyblue.com). CTA Ashland
(Green).* **Open** 5.30-10pm Mon-Thur; 5.30-11pm
Fri, Sat. **Main courses** $20-$27. **Credit** AmEx,
DC, MC, V.
Michael Jordan is a co-owner of this stylish restaurant. In fact, two of his favourite dishes are menu
staples: 'peekytoe crab' (layered potato and crab)
and Delmonico steak. The name incorporates the
street number and colour of the gaudy blue exterior
of the building, a former pickle factory.

Eclectic

Thyme
*464 N Halsted Street, at W Grand Avenue (312 226
4300/www.thymechicago.com). CTA Clinton (Green).*
Open 5.30-10.30pm Tue-Thur; 5.30-11pm Fri, Sat;
5-9pm Sun. **Main courses** $18-$27. **Credit** AmEx,
DC, MC, V. **Map** p306 F10.
Inside, chandeliers fashioned from stainless steel
and cobalt water bottles accent the eclectic decor and
flames leap from a wood grill in an open kitchen,
where John Bubala prepares French-American cuisine with fresh products raised on small farms.
Outside is the city's best restaurant garden.

Pegasus. Winged horse is conspicuous by its absence from the menu. *See p146.*

French

Blackbird
619 W Randolph Street, at N Jefferson Street (312 715 0708/www.blackbirdrestaurant.com). CTA Clinton (Green). **Open** 11.30am-2pm, 5-10.30pm Mon-Thur; 11.30am-2pm, 5-11.30pm Fri; 5-11.30pm Sat. **Main courses** $16-$29. **Map** p305 F11.
The first restaurant in West Loop's Restaurant Row to leap eastward across the Expressway is gathering a toque full of honours. Tables at first seem uncomfortably close, but the atmosphere is so congenial, the cooking so sublime, that it doesn't really matter. (The name has nothing to do with the food: it's French slang for a plump Merlot grape).

Greek

Costa's
340 S Halsted Street, at W Van Buren Street (312 263 9700). CTA UIC-Halsted (Blue). **Open** 11am-11pm Mon-Thur; 11am-midnight Fri, Sat; noon-11.30pm Sun. **Main courses** $10-$29. **Credit** AmEx, DC, Disc, MC, V.
You'll find all the old favourites at this rather handsome Greektown eaterie, along with some unexpected and innovative twists. Start with taramasalata on crusty Greek bread, then look to moussaka, red snapper or lamb chops, kebabs and other excellent grilled meats.

Pegasus
130 S Halsted Street, at W Adams Street (312 226 3377/www.pegasuschicago.com). CTA UIC-Halsted (Blue). **Open** 11am-midnight Mon-Thur; 11am-1am Fri; noon-1am Sat; noon-midnight Sun. **Main courses** $5-$25. **Credit** AmEx, DC, Disc, MC, V.
This Greektown restaurant proves there's more to Greek food than just bog-standard gyros. Start with grilled octopus and move on to a delicious pasta dish made with morsels of beef or lamb braised with plum tomatoes, olive oil, wine, herbs and garlic. A rooftop deck provides one of Chicago's finest alfresco dining spots and offers an unobstructed view of the city's skyline.

Italian

Misto
1118 W Grand Avenue, at N Aberdeen Street (312 226 5989). CTA Grand (Blue). **Open** 11.30-2.30am, 5.30-10pm Mon-Thur; 11.30am-2.30pm, 5.30-11pm Fri; 5.30-11pm Sat. **Main courses** $14-$24. **Credit** AmEx, MC, V.
Head for this neighbourhood Italian eaterie on Saturday nights: marvellously named owner Donny Greco is as talented at the mic as he is at the stove, performing standards with style and ease. The food is good, too: seared sea scallops, roasted pork loin, and well-prepared pasta served in a casual, candlelit dining room.

Latin, Mexican & Spanish

Mas
1670 W Division Street, at N Paulina Street (773 276 8700/www.masrestaurant.com). CTA Division (Blue). **Open** 5.30-10pm Mon-Thur, Sun; 5.30-11.30pm Fri, Sat. **Main courses** $17-$27. **Credit** AmEx, DC, MC, V. **Map** p310 C8.
This trendy 'Nuevo Latino' restaurant has earned such a loyal following that it has spawned a sibling. Don't miss the black bean soup or tender smoked beef short rib with garlic mash and mustard greens. Brazil's national cocktail, the caipirinha, is a potent mix of fresh limes, sugar and cachaca.
Branch: Otra Mas 3651 N Southport Avenue, Lake View (773 348 3200).

Lunch stops, diners & delis

Lou Mitchell's
565 W Jackson Boulevard, at S Jefferson Street (312 939 3111). CTA Clinton (Blue). **Open** 5.30am-3pm Mon-Sat; 7am-3pm Sun. **Main courses** $6-$8. **No credit cards.**
There's often a long wait at this breakfast favourite but bonuses include Milk Duds for waiting female patrons. Hearty breakfasts, served sizzling in iron skillets, come with double-yoke eggs and doorstep-sized Greek toast with home-made marmalade. Pancakes, waffles and omelettes are good too.

Seafood

Bluepoint Oyster Bar
741 W Randolph Street, at N Halsted Street (312 207 1222). CTA Clinton (Green). **Open** 11.30am-10.30pm Mon-Thur; 11.30am-11pm Fri; 5-11pm Sat; 5-10.30pm Sun. **Main courses** $18-$27. **Credit** AmEx, DC, Disc, MC, V.
This Randolph seafood house has established itself as one of Chicago's best. Fresh fish and shellfish are flown in daily and the tiled raw bar offers an incredible selection of oysters. The 'retro-cool' design – the place resembles an art deco/1940s fish house – includes bold terrazzo floors, potted palms, piscatorial prints, exposed ductwork and huge portholes.

Wicker Park & Bucktown

American

MOD
1520 N Damen Avenue, at W Pierce Avenue (773 252 1500/www.modrestaurant.com). CTA Damen (Blue). **Open** 5.30-10pm Mon-Thur, Sun; 5.30-11.30pm Fri, Sat. **Main courses** $16-$28. **Credit** AmEx, MC, V. **Map** p310 B7.
If any restaurant is indicative of the changes that have hit Wicker Park in recent years, it's MOD, a sleek and swanky eaterie done out with slightly sneery design flourishes (including what are the

Eat, Drink, Shop

Perpetually busy **Soul Kitchen**, in a rare quiet moment.

most uncomfortable chairs in America) and packed nightly with the beautiful people. Good job Kelly Courtney's inventive cuisine rises above it all.

Soul Kitchen

1576 N Milwaukee Avenue, at N Damen Avenue (773 342 9742). CTA Damen (Blue). **Open** 5-10.30pm Mon-Thur; 5-11.30pm Fri; 10am-2pm, 5-11.30pm Sat; 10am-2pm, 5-10.30pm Sun. **Main courses** $15-$25. **Credit** AmEx, MC, V. **Map** p310 B7.

It's about location, location, location, preach real estate dealers, and there's no doubt the proprietors of Soul Kitchen were listening. Situated right in the thick of the action, it draws plenty of passing trade and bustles nightly with activity. Hardly a place for a romantic meal, but lovers of hearty Caribbean- and Latin-influenced food should make the effort.

Asian & Pan-Asian

Mirai Sushi

2020 W Division Street, at N Damen Avenue (773 862 8500). CTA Damen (Blue). **Open** 5.30-10.30pm Mon-Thur, Sun; 5.30-11.30pm Fri, Sat. **Main courses** $9-$16. **Credit** AmEx, DC, Disc, MC, V. **Map** p310 B8.

This hip Wicker Park eatery, with an imposing two-storey glass façade, offers fashionable sushi and saké. Six chefs work the sushi bar creating a flurry of sights and sounds. Upstairs, the lounge heats up later, with a DJ weaving a mix of lively beats.

Eclectic

Spring

2039 W North Avenue, at N Milwaukee Avenue (773 395 7100). CTA Damen (Blue). **Open** 5.30-10pm Tue-Thur; 5.30-11pm Fri, Sat; 5.30-9pm Sun. **Main courses** $12-$25. **Credit** AmEx, DC, MC, V. **Map** p310 B7.

Formerly Chicago's most storied bathhouses, 2039 W North is now an award-winning restaurant with cutting-edge cuisine and a soothing Zen garden. New American dishes focus on seafood with Japanese influences in a setting that features white-glazed brick from the building's historic past. Try halibut, grilled sea scallops or roasted duck.

French

Sinibar

1540 N Milwaukee Avenue, at W North Avenue (773 278 7797/www.soundsofsinibar.com). CTA Damen (Blue). **Open** 8pm-2am Mon-Fri, Sun; 8pm-3am Sat. **Main courses** $5-$12. **Credit** AmEx, DC, Disc, MC, V. **Map** p310 B7.

For late-night eats, head for the casbah – in nearby Wicker Park – and eat both well and cheaply. Noted chef John Bubala (of Thyme; *see p145*) is the man behind this place, where the decor is spunky Moroccan (Berber carpets, tasselled pouffes) and the clientele are cool.

Lining the stomach

Contrary to what you might think, it's not all the beer that makes many Chicagoans so heavy-set: it's the greasy food they mow through at the end of a night-long tour of the city's groggeries. While most of the city's restaurants close at a decent hour, there are a good number that stay open late primarily to service those with a serious need to put something besides Goose Island in their belly.

The heart of the city's bar scene is the Rush/Division corridor. If you're near Division before 5am, step into the long line at the hole-in-the-wall **Five Faces** (10 W Division Street, Near North; 312 642 7837) for burgers, gyros and the best fries you'll think you've ever tasted. Just south of Rush is the more civilised **Tempo** (6 E Chestnut Street, Near North; 312 943 4373), where the suitably surly Slavic staff serve up sizzling omelettes 24 hours a day.

If you've just gotten an earful of blues at **Kingston Mines** (*see p223*) or any other Halsted nightspot, you could try **La Bamba** (2557 N Halsted Street, Lincoln Park; 773 477 7491). The burritos are only decent, but you can get them until 5am on weekends, and, as the place advertises, they are 'as big as your head'.

For those looking for something a touch more refined – entrées after martinis rather than hot dogs after beers – try **Iggy's** (700 N Milwaukee Avenue, West Town; 312 829 4449), which has great pastas and a popular outdoor patio in the summer, or the chic French-Italian cuisine at **Pasha's** (642 N Clark Street, Near North; 312 397 0100), served until 3am.

Some don't see the need to leave the bar to get their grub. The **Twisted Spoke** (501 N Ogden Street, West Town; 312 666 1500) is a double whammy: a biker bar that also prepares a wicked barbecue feast. Weekend brunch is great, but on Saturdays at midnight, it's Smut 'n' Eggs, breakfast served to the accompaniment of hardcore pornography on a big screen. Bless.

Italian

A Tavola

2148 W Chicago Avenue, at N Hoyne Avenue (773 276 7567/www.atavola-restaurant.com). CTA Damen (Blue). **Open** 5.30-10.30pm Mon-Sat. **Tickets** $16-$24. **Credit** AmEx, DC, Disc, MC, V. **Map** p310 B7.

Though it's been here for over six years now, rehabbers haven't yet clawed a solid foothold around this tiny restaurant in Ukranian Village: a real charmer with hardwood floors, grey walls decorated with tasteful black and white nudes and crisp white napery set with fresh flowers. Regional Italian food features hearty white bean soup, fried zucchini blossoms, risotto and well-made pastas.

Fortunato

2005 W Division Street, at N Damen Avenue (773 645 7200). CTA Damen (Blue). **Open** 5.30-10pm Mon-Thur, Sun; 10am-2pm, 5.30-11pm Fri, Sat. **Main courses** $13-$18. **Credit** AmEx, Disc, DC, MC, V. **Map** p310 B7.

This casual room with a glass-enclosed kitchen and wood-burning stove appeared in 2002, using local and organic produce and hand-making its pastas daily. Simple dishes such as grilled T-bone steak on

Eat, Drink, Shop

a bed of arugula with balsamic vinegar share the spotlight with creations including polenta with roasted duck, figs, and honey sauce.

Lunch stops, diners & delis

Leo's Lunchroom
1809 W Division Street, at N Wood Street (773 276 6509). CTA Damen (Blue). **Open** 8am-10pm Tue-Sun. **Main courses** $9-$14. **No credit cards.** **Map** p310 C8.
Despite the scruffy storefront, Leo's has good food to go. For breakfast, try corned beef hash, veggie omelettes and breakfast burritos overstuffed with eggs, potatoes, jalapeños and onions. Some patrons are in suits, others wear jeans with wallets on chains.

South Side

American

For **Lem's Bar-B-Que House** and **Leon's Bar-B-Q**, *see p128* **Capital of 'cue.**

Mellow Yellow
1508 E 53rd Street, at S Harper Avenue (773 667 2000). Metra 53rd Street. **Open** 7.30am-10.30pm Mon-Thur, Sun; 7.30am-11.30pm Fri, Sat. **Main courses** $3-$10. **Credit** AmEx, DC, Disc, MC, V. **Map** p311 Y6.
University of Chicago students and faculty head to this long-time, homely Hyde Park favourite for potent chili (including a vegetarian version). Quiche, crepes, and hamburgers also are reliable choices, with rotisserie chicken a specialty. Breakfasts include omelettes and Swedish pancakes with lingonberries.

Chinese

Emperor's Choice
2238 S Wentworth Avenue, at W Cermak Road (312 225 8800). CTA Cermak/Chinatown (Red). **Open** 11.30-1am Mon-Sat; 11.30am-midnight Sun. **Main courses** $7-$40. **Credit** AmEx, Disc, MC, V.
Unlike some of its cavernous tourist-trap neighbours, this Chinatown joint is a small, intimate storefront with soft lighting, fine art and delicate china. It offers some of the city's best Cantonese and other Chinese cooking, especially seafood: try Peking lobster, spicy Hunan shrimp or steamed oysters.

Three Happiness
2130 S Wentworth Street, at W Cermak Road (312 791 1228). CTA Cermak/Chinatown (Red). **Open** 10am-11pm Mon-Sat; 10am-10pm Sun. **Main courses** $8-$9. **Credit** AmEx, MC, V.
One of the more popular restaurants in Chinatown, this huge eaterie is famous for its dim sum. Choose from a staggering spread of more than 60 items: 20-plus varieties of steamed dumplings, plus deep-fried pastries, wrapped shrimp, spare ribs with black bean sauce and (too) much more.

Get full of the joys of **Spring**. *See p147.*

Bars

Whether you prefer Singapore slings or Schlitz, Chicago will quench your thirst.

In a city of neighbourhoods, every corner has its own tavern that acts as an embassy of goodwill and good spirit for the area. And we mean every corner – even the Loop has a healthy handful of good, old-fashioned drinking establishments complete with spirited characters behind and in front of the bar. Whether you're looking to re-live your college days, watch the game or get dressed up to the nines and whittle away time with Chicago's beautiful people, the city offers a smorgasbord of watering holes.

Generally speaking, bars are microcosms of their respective neighbourhoods' demographics. Downtown bars are frequented by businessmen and tourists, Lincoln Park by yuppie-friendly sports fans, Lake View by the post-collegiate crowd and Wicker Park by the hipsters. And no matter where you go, once you're inside it's worth looking up: the city's oldest bars are denoted by unique tin ceilings.

With the exception of the Loop, Chicago's bars close around 2am, with a handful shutting down at 4am; most establishments stay open one hour later on Saturday. But strict alcohol regulations in the city mean that the bars must be closed by said hour, so you're likely to get last call about 45 minutes earlier. About once

every six months the city engages in sting operations to catch bars serving to under-age drinkers, so taverns are understandably paranoid: unless you look 50, you'll be asked for a photo ID (a drivers' licence or passport; anything with your date of birth on it) and you won't get in without one. Don't take it personally: staff are simply protecting their jobs.

For the best hotel bars in town, *see p57*.

The Loop

Nightlife comes to a halt in the Loop sooner than in the rest of the city. Most Loop bars are frequented by the post-work crowd and tourists; on weekends, drinkers tend to stay away, so don't be surprised if night-time resembles a cemetery. As a rule of thumb, stick to the South Loop, as bars tend to be a little seedier; and, hence, more populated by locals.

Alcock's Inn
411 S Wells Street, at W Van Buren Street (312 922 1778). CTA LaSalle (Blue, Brown, Orange, Purple). **Open** 10am-late Mon-Fri; 10.30am-late Sat. **Credit** AmEx, MC, V. **Map** p305 H13.
This sports bar fills after the market closes and attracts crowds before, during and after Bears games. The place can get rowdy, especially on the Olympic-themed deck after the traders get off work.

Berghoff
17 W Adams Street, at S State Street (312 427 3170). CTA Adams (Brown, Green, Orange, Purple) or Jackson (Blue, Red). **Open** 11am-9pm Mon-Thur; 11am-9.30pm Fri; 11am-10pm Sat. **Credit** AmEx, MC, V. **Map** p305 H12.
Founded as an outdoor beer garden in 1893, the Berghoff holds City Liquor Licence No.1 and has been serving Berghoff beer since the end of Prohibition. It also serves food, but for a less formal bite, try the Berghoff Café, a stand-up bar dishing up German food on the eastern end of the main floor.

Cactus
404 S Wells Street, at W Van Buren Street (312 922 3830/www.dontdrinkandtrade.com). CTA LaSalle (Blue, Brown, Orange, Purple). **Open** 11am-midnight Mon-Fri. **Credit** AmEx, DC, Disc, MC, V. **Map** p305 H13.
Another popular watering hole among the local traders, this Tex-Mex-inspired joint serves a wide selection of beers (including many Mexican choices) and tequilas. Games and TVs give the place a sporty frat bar feel; nachos and burgers are on the menu.

The best Bars

For the dedicated boozer
Tuman's Alcohol Abuse Center. *See p163.*

For feeling board
Blue Frog. *See p153.*

For baby back ribs
Twin Anchors, Inc. *See p156.*

For shooting stick
Ginger Man. *See p161.*

For house calls
Danny's Lounge. *See p162.*

For singing along
Zebra Lounge. *See p155.*

For watching the game
Gamekeepers. *See p157.*

Cardozo's Pub

*170 W Washington Street, at N LaSalle Street
(312 236 1573). CTA Washington (Brown,
Orange, Purple).* **Open** 10.30am-9pm Mon-Fri.
Credit AmEx, DC, Disc, MC, V. **Map** p305 H12.
There's something of an everybody-knows-your-
name-and-they're-all-glad-you-came atmosphere at
this Loop bar. A mix of traders and locals huddle
around the bar in the early evenings, shooting the
shit and losing track of time in the cosy basement.

Cavanaugh's Bar & Restaurant

*Monadnock Building, 53 W Jackson Boulevard, at
S Dearborn Street (312 939 3125). CTA Jackson
(Blue, Red) or Library (Brown, Orange, Purple).*
Open 11am-9.30pm Mon-Fri. **Credit** AmEx, DC,
MC, V. **Map** p305 H13.
Grab a booth at this unassuming tavern inside the
Monadnock's six-feet-thick walls and chat about the
building's unusual architecture, but don't get there
too late: the place closes at 10pm sharp. Pastas and
sandwiches make up the menu.

Govnor's Pub

*207 N State Street, at E Lake Street (312 236 3696).
CTA Lake (Red) or State (Brown, Green, Orange,
Purple).* **Open** 11am-2am Mon-Fri; 11am-midnight
Sat; 11.30am-8pm Sun. **Credit** AmEx, Disc, MC, V.
Map p305 H11.
This comfy English-style pub is popular before
shows, as well as with the typical lunch and after-
work crowd. In the summer months, limited outdoor
seating is available.

Metropole

*Fairmont Hotel, 200 N Columbus Drive, at
E Lake Street (312 565 7444). CTA Lake (Red)
or State (Brown, Green, Orange, Purple).*
Open 11am-11.30pm Mon-Thur; 11am-1am Fri, Sat.
Credit AmEx, DC, Disc, MC, V. **Map** p305 J11.
The dancefloor in front of the stage fills up quickly,
as hotel guests and older music connoisseurs enjoy
small-time jazz, blues and swing acts in this hotel
bar. Something of a joke among the youngsters.

Miller's Pub

*134 S Wabash Avenue, at E Adams Street (312 645
5377). CTA Adams (Brown, Green, Orange, Purple)
or Monroe (Blue, Red).* **Open** 11am-3.30am daily.
Credit AmEx, DC, MC, V. **Map** p305 H12.
The walls of this boozer, founded in 1935, are covered with signed photos of Regis Philbin types who
have visited over the years. Though, in fairness, it
was also a favourite of the genuinely legendary Bill
Veeck. There's decent chophouse-style food, but
most people come for the drinks and ambience.

Monk's

*203 W Lake Street, at N Wells Street (312 357
6665/368 0958). CTA Clark (Blue, Brown,
Green, Orange, Purple).* **Open** 10am-2am Mon-Fri.
Credit AmEx, MC, V. **Map** p305 H11.
This Irish-ish pub is a real spit-and-sawdust place:
the floor is covered in peanut shells, and the lighting is dim. Loud (no exaggeration here) music

The **Berghoff**. *See p150.*

cranks from the well-stocked jukebox, as the bartenders serve frosted mugs and pints. One of only a
few late-night bars in the Loop, and a seedy treat.

South Loop Club

*701 S State Street, at E Balbo Drive (312 427 2787).
CTA Harrison (Red).* **Open** 11am-4am Mon-Fri,
Sun; 11am-5am Sat. **Credit** AmEx, DC, Disc, MC, V.
Map p305 H13.
It bills itself as a neighbourhood bar, but it's not in
any sort of a neighbourhood, and it's slanted to the
sports crowd. Still, the South Loop Club is a matey
place that's often busy, in part due to the lack of
other bars nearby and its proximity to Columbia
College. Good news: it's open very late.

Near North

For every early-closing post-work hangout in
the Loop, there are two late-opening weekend
hangouts across the River. Although tourists
flock to the likes of the Hard Rock Café and
the Rainforest Café, head east and you'll find
yourself among a more upscale and less
garish crowd.

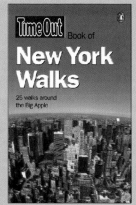

Billy Goat Tavern

Lower level, 430 N Michigan Avenue, at E
Hubbard Street (312 222 1525). CTA Grand (Red).
Open 7am-2am Mon-Fri; 10am-3am Sat; 11am-2am
Sun. **No credit cards. Map** p306 J11.
The journo bar made famous by *Saturday Night
Live* is what you'd expect: Schlitz on tap, cuttings
on the wall, cooks hollering 'cheezborger'. If you're
lucky, you'll see owner Sam Sianis, whose ances-
tor put a curse on the Cubs decades ago when his
goat wasn't allowed into Wrigley Field.

Blue Frog

*676 N LaSalle Street, at W Erie Street (312 943
8900). CTA Chicago (Brown, Purple, Red).*
Open 11.30am-midnight Mon-Thur; 11.30am-2am Fri;
6pm-3am Sat. **Credit** AmEx, MC, V. **Map** p306 H10.
A vast range of beers, some decent food... And
every board game you can name, from Monopoly
and Truth or Consequences to Ker-Plunk and 'most
everything in between. Mindless fun.

Boss Bar

*420 N Clark Street, at W Hubbard Street (312 527
1203). CTA Grand (Red) or Merchandise Mart
(Brown, Purple).* **Open** 10.30am-4am Mon-Fri,
Sun; 10.30am-5am Sat. **Credit** AmEx, DC, MC, V.
Map p306 H11.
The Boss is named after the late Mayor Richard J
Daley, a huge mural of whom hangs inside the store-
front bar. A jukebox blasts classic rock; when the
weather's nice, the garage door front is pulled open.

Boston Blackie's

*164 E Grand Avenue, at N St Clair Street (312
938 8700). CTA Grand (Red).* **Open** 11am-11pm
Mon-Sat; noon-10pm Sun. **Credit** AmEx, DC, Disc,
MC, V. **Map** p306 J10.
A comfortable bar serving Chicago's best burgers.
The two-fisted juicy half-pounders are good with blue
cheese or olives and a side of not-overly-greasy steak
fries is big enough to share.

Brehon Pub

*731 N Wells Street, at W Superior Street (312
642 1071). CTA Chicago (Brown, Purple).*
Open 11am-2am Mon-Fri; noon-3am Sat; noon-2am
Sun. **Credit** AmEx, DC, MC, V. **Map** p306 H10.
This homey Irish saloon – a better Emerald option
than the themey Fadó on the corner of Clark and
Grand – found notoriety during the Mirage Scandal
of 1978, when a hidden camera caught politicians on
the take. It's now less eventful but no less charming.

ESPN Zone

*43 E Ohio Street, at N Dearborn Street (312 644
3776/www.espnzone.com). CTA Grand (Red).*
Open 11.30am-midnight Mon-Thur; 11.30am-1am
Fri; 11am-1am Sat; 11am-midnight Sun.
Credit AmEx, Disc, MC, V. **Map** p306 H10.
The sports network's huge dining and entertainment complex opened in 1999, and is now a fixture
for the city's sports nuts and overgrown kids, who
tackle the climbing wall and virtual reality games
with glee. On game days, get there early.

Green Door Tavern

*678 N Orleans Street, at W Huron Street (312
664 5496). CTA Chicago (Brown, Purple).*
Open 11.30am-10pm Mon, Tue; 11.30am-midnight
Wed, Thur; 11.30am-2am Fri, Sat; noon-9pm Sun.
Credit AmEx, Disc, MC, V. **Map** p306 G10.
Antiques and memorabilia hang from the ceiling of
this building, one of the first to be built after the 1871
fire. It's been a bar since 1921 and still sports some
of its original fixtures. A decent selection of beers
(including monthly-changing microbrews) and food
draws a suit-and-tie crowd, especially for lunch.

Harry's Velvet Room

*56 W Illinois Street, at N Dearborn Street (312 527
5600). CTA Grand (Red).* **Open** 6pm-2am Mon, Tue;
6pm-4am Wed; 5pm-4am Thur, Fri; 8pm-5am Sat.
Credit AmEx, DC, Disc, MC, V. **Map** p306 H11.
Sink into one of the couches or lounge chairs in this
dimly lit basement lounge, and enjoy a cigar and a
Martini with everyone else while listening to everything from tiki music to soul. The bar is stocked with
top-shelf liquor, wines and champagnes.

Lizzie McNeil's

*400 N McClurg Street, at E North Water Street
(312 467 1992). Bus 29, 56, 65, 66.* **Open** 1pm-1am
Mon-Fri; 11.30am-1am Sat, Sun. **Credit** AmEx, MC,
V. **Map** p306 J11.
A small Irish pub facing the river. The fine selection
of beer on tap and the jukebox with everything from
big band to Elvis to top 40 hits all appeal, but better still, it rarely gets as packed as its neighbours.

O'Neill's Bar & Grill

*152 E Ontario Street, at N Michigan Avenue (312
787 5269). CTA Grand (Red).* **Open** 11am-2am
Mon-Fri, Sun; 11am-3am Sat. **Credit** AmEx, Disc,
MC, V. **Map** p306 J10.
A dark and narrow tavern off Michigan Avenue,
with nicely priced burgers and beers. Walk through
to the back to enjoy the rear patio, a kind of secret
garden in the middle of the madness of downtown.

Pippin's

*806 N Rush Street, at W Chicago Avenue (312 787
5435/www.rushanddivision.com). CTA Chicago
(Red).* **Open** 11am-4am Mon-Fri, Sun; 11am-5am Sat.
Credit AmEx, DC, MC, V. **Map** p306 J10.
This small pub owns the oldest liquor licence on
Rush Street. Rarely busy, it's a good place to sit
dropping peanut shells on the floor and plugging the
jukebox with change.

Redhead Piano Bar

*16 W Ontario Street, at N State Street (312 640
1000/www.redheadpianobar.com). CTA Grand
(Red).* **Open** 7pm-4am Mon-Fri, Sun; 7pm-5am Sat.
Credit AmEx, DC, MC, V. **Map** p306 H10.
A piano bar that manages to be swanky without
being sniffy, the Redhead fills up quickly with an
ageing but still-hip clientele. who enjoy live piano-
accompanied crooning nightly. Look a little smart
or you won't get past the splendid sign outside.

Eat, Drink, Shop

Gold Coast

You've got two types of bar in the Gold Coast. Division Street between Dearborn and State is dominated by terrifyingly loud collegiate bars frequented exclusively by tourists and a loutish post-frat shack suburban sports crowd. In the nooks and crannies, however, taverns become dens of swank where the retro-cool go out to be seen. Either way, you'll pay through the nose.

Blue Agave
1050 N State Street, at W Maple Street (312 335 8900). CTA Clark/Division (Red). **Open** 11.30am-12.30am Mon-Thur; 11.30am-2am Fri-Sun. **Credit** AmEx, MC, V. **Map** p306 H9.
Stuffed burros, sombreros, serapes hanging from the ceiling, cacti everywhere, assorted margaritas; yes, it's a Mexican bar, with a dozen or so Mexican beers to vouch for it. Food can be had upstairs.

Dublins
1030 N State Street, at W Maple Street (312 266 6340). CTA Clark/Division (Red). **Open** 11am-4am Mon-Fri, Sun; 11am-5am Sat. **Credit** AmEx, DC, Disc, MC, V. **Map** p306 H9.
This little green pub nestled among the bustling Rush Street scene attracts a healthy after-work crowd, though weekend evenings are to be avoided.

That said, in the summer, the outdoor patio is a nice enough place to people-watch while enjoying a well-poured glass of Guinness.

Hotsie Totsie Yacht Club & Bait Shop
8 E Division Street, at N State Street (312 337 9128). CTA Clark/Division (Red). **Open** noon-4am Mon-Fri, Sun; 5pm-5am Sat. **No credit cards**. **Map** p307 H8.
A rowboat hangs outside this bar, a nautical motif continued inside, but the real charms of this place are the regulars and the fact it's rarely crowded. Harry Caray, Frankie Avalon and Sammy Davis Jr have all sipped here at one time or another.

Jilly's Bistro & Jilly's Retro Club
1007 N Rush Street, at W Oak Street (312 664 1001). CTA Chicago (Red). **Open** 3pm-2am Mon-Fri; 1pm-3am Sat; 5pm-2am Sun. **Credit** AmEx, DC, Disc, MC, V. **Map** p306 H9.
This is where the fat cats hang, so expect to be on your best behaviour – and maybe to shell out some cash – to get a seat inside. The club is for dancing, while the bistro is more casual.

PJ Clarkes
1204 N State Street, at W Division Street (312 664 1650). CTA Clark/Division (Red). **Open** 11.30am-2am Mon-Sat; 10am-2am Sun. **Credit** AmEx, DC, Disc, MC, V. **Map** p307 H8.

Hey, Mr DJ, take a record off

Happily, Chicago's not all about the blues: just imagine what a miserable town it'd be if it was. For a town that's had a clutch of terrific showtunes penned about it, it's unsurprising that the toddlin' town still has pockets of sophistication in the shape of some belting piano bars. Admission's free and – for the first two on the list, at least – it's best to look smart. Other than that, the only rule is that you really shouldn't ask for *My Kind of Town* or *Chicago*...

Legendary crooner Buddy Charles retired from his regular gig a few years back. But while Charles is irreplaceable, the Drake Hotel's **Coq d'Or** (140 E Walton Street, Gold Coast; 312 787 2200) has kept on with the music at its swanky bar, with chanteuse Arlene Bardelle a regular fixture. Expect smoke, showtunes and a bar tab big enough to swear you off booze for life. In a word? Classy.

The **Redhead Piano Bar** (*see p153*) can be classy some nights, too: midweek, it's nicely chilled. But come the weekend, the surprisingly capacious hangout fills to bursting with a good-time crowd on the make, belting

out *Tiny Dancer* and *Sweet Caroline* until they choke on the cigar smoke. Don't get too dolled up, but don't show up in a T-shirt, cut-offs or sneakers either.

Gay piano bar **Gentry** (*see p215*) is usually a mellower affair. Its location on the shabbiest part of State Street is decidedly insalubrious, but through the tinted windows, things get smarter in the surprisingly airy room. The acts here are usually grand, although quality at the open-mic night on Sunday is predictably patchy.

Its location in Wicker Park, an area not noted for its loucheness until recently, could have been the death of **Davenport's** (1383 N Milwaukee Avenue; 773 278 1830). However, contrary to expectations, the lounge has flourished. The backroom hosts jazz and cabaret stars, but more fun is to be had in the garish piano bar out front. Take the mic if you dare.

Singing along is actively encouraged over at the **Zebra Lounge** (*see p155*) on State Street, meanwhile, where a crowd of lushes, luvvies and funseekers belt out the tunes ever more

A casual, old-fashioned tavern, this is Chicago's take on the New York club of the same name. The clientele has earned the place the title of 'the divorce bar'.

Pump Room

Omni Ambassador East, 1301 N State Street, at E Goethe Street (312 266 0360/www.pumproom.com). CTA Clark/Division (Red). **Open** 3.30pm-1am Mon-Thur; noon-1am Fri, Sat; noon-10.30pm Sun. **Credit** AmEx, Disc, MC, V. **Map** p307 H8.
If you can get in – there's a dress code – this Chicago legend and celeb fave is a bunch of swanky fun. Settle back with a cocktail and feel like a million dollars. Service is atrocious, but that's hardly the point.

Underground Wonder Bar

10 E Walton Street, at N State Street (312 266 7761). CTA Chicago (Red). **Open** 4pm-4am Mon-Fri; 4pm-5am Sat; 8pm-4am Sun. **Credit** AmEx, DC, MC, V. **Map** p306 H9.
A favourite celebrity haunt, the long narrow bar features live jazz every day of the year. Located in the lower level (as alluded to in the name), the place can be easy to miss. But an eclectic, funky and friendly crowd manages to find it, and so should you.

Zebra Lounge

1220 N State Street, at W Division Street (312 642 5140). CTA Clark/Division (Red). **Open** 4.30pm-2am Mon-Fri, Sun; 4.30pm-3am Sat. **Credit** AmEx, MC, V. **Map** p307 H8.

raucously as the night goes on. Stick a buck or two in the pot on the bar if you have a request, and don't go playing wallflower: the only way you'll be embarrassed here is by not joining in.

Practically everything is zebra-striped inside this landmark, open inside the Canterbury Court apartment block since 1933. There's piano music and singalongs, but mainly it's the crowd that's worth checking out: casts from musicals join in and sometimes lead the impromptu performances. A treat.

Old Town

Old Town's bars are laid-back and tame: perfect for an over-25 crowd. The action's concentrated around North and Wells, though there are a few places off the beaten path that are worth finding. The later it gets and the closer you are to the Pipers Alley complex (home to Second City), the more likely you are to encounter a post-theatre crowd, both audiences and cast.

Burton Place

1447 N Wells Street, at W Burton Place (312 664 4699). CTA Sedgwick (Brown, Purple). **Open** 11am-4am Mon-Fri, Sun; 11am-5am Sat. **Credit** AmEx, Disc, MC, V. **Map** p307 H8.
The quintessential corner tavern. Young regulars fill the seats at the bar early and, in the winter months, it's a battle for a spot beside the roaring fireplace. There's a party room upstairs that serves as an escape when the place gets too crowded.

Marge's Pub

1758 N Sedgwick Street, at W Menomonee Street (312 787 3900). CTA Sedgwick (Brown, Purple). **Open** noon-2am Mon-Fri, Sun; noon-3am Sat. **Credit** MC, V. **Map** p307 G7.
Once a speakeasy, Marge's has stood the test of time as the rest of Old Town grew around it. Tucked on the corner of a residential block, it's now a favourite neighbourhood watering hole. Over the bar hang pictures of legendary Chicagoans, including the late Mayor Daley and Mike Ditka. The beer selection is weak, but you're coming here to drink Bud anyway.

Old Town Ale House

219 W North Avenue, at N Wieland Street (312 944 7020). CTA Sedgwick (Brown, Purple). **Open** noon-4am Mon-Fri, Sun; noon-5am Sat. **No credit cards**. **Map** p307 G7.
An Old Town staple, where Second City cast members mingle with bums, yuppies and everyone in between. Inside, murals offer a glimpse at the characters who've hung here, while the jukebox has been voted the city's best. Don't miss the signed picture of America's most famous drinker, George Wendt.

Roadhouse

1653 N Wells Street, at W North Avenue (312 440 0535). CTA Sedgwick (Brown, Purple). **Open** 4pm-4am Mon-Fri; noon-5am Sat; noon-4am Sun. **Credit** AmEx, MC, V. **Map** p307 H7.
The Roadhouse is one of the few places along this strip that gets downright crazy. Dirt-cheap drinks specials doubtless help, as do the DJs who spin house, techno and disco on the weekends. A cheese-fest, but better than its competitors.

Eat, Drink, Shop

Regulars past and present prop up the wall at the **Old Town Ale House**. *See p155.*

Twin Anchors, Inc

*1655 N Sedgwick Street, at W North Avenue
(312 266 1616). CTA Sedgwick (Brown, Purple).*
Open 5-11pm Mon-Thur; 5pm-midnight Fri; noon-
midnight Sat; noon-10.30pm Sun. **Credit** AmEx, DC,
Disc, MC, V. **Map** p307 G7.
For over 60 years, people have been flocking to Twin
Anchors for its baby back ribs, and the wood-panelled front bar. Stop in for a beer, but beware the
temptations of the barbecue and the fine jukebox.

Lincoln Park

Lincoln Park is loaded with an insane number
of clubs and bars aimed at entertaining the
disposable-income crew. Though bars along
Halsted and Lincoln attract the largest crowds,
a stroll up the sidestreets – all perfectly safe –
will yield a boozer before long. Great for
barhopping, especially if you like sport and
23-year-old girls. *See also p158* **Walk on**.

Beaumont

*2020 N Halsted Street, at W Armitage Avenue
(773 281 0177). CTA Armitage (Brown, Purple).*
Open 5pm-4am Mon-Fri; 3pm-5am Sat; 10am-4am
Sun. **Credit** AmEx, DC, Disc, MC, V. **Map** p308 F6.
Dance central for the strip of bars and restaurants
that line Halsted from North Avenue up to Fullerton.
The crowd is a mix of DePaul students and fun-
minded Lincoln Park types finishing a night of
drinking and hoping not to go home alone.

Burwood Tap

*724 W Wrightwood Avenue, at N Burling Street
(773 525 2593). CTA Fullerton (Brown, Purple,
Red)/8 bus.* **Open** 11am-2am Mon-Fri, Sun; 11am-
3am Sat. **No credit cards. Map** p308 F4.
The unassuming purple awning masks the bustling
vibe of this capacious neighbourhood favourite that
was established in 1933. The pool table and the TVs
add to the attraction of the twin bars for the crowd
of young professionals and college types.

Charlie's Ale House

*1224 W Webster Avenue, at N Racine Avenue (773
871 1440). CTA Fullerton (Brown, Purple, Red).*
Open 5pm-2am Mon-Fri; 11am-2am Sun; 11am-3am
Sat. **Credit** AmEx, DC, Disc, MC, V. **Map** p308 E5.
Most come to Charlie's for the selection of beers, and
spend the evening discussing their retirement plans.
Offensively yuppie-ish, it's redeemed by its beauti-
ful 80-year-old bar and large, ivy-lined beer garden.
Closing is flexible: one night midnight, the next 2am.

Delilah's

*2771 N Lincoln Avenue, at W Diversey Parkway,
Lincoln Park (773 472 2771). CTA Diversey (Brown,
Purple).* **Open** 4pm-2am Mon-Fri, Sun; 4pm-3am Sat.
Map p308 E4.
A full-on rock 'n' roll bar, with a great atmosphere,
a gloriously hip crowd and DJs from Sunday to
Thursday: Monday is punk night, with Wednesdays
devoted to insurgent country. Delilah's boasts the
largest selection of whiskies in the Midwest, and its
imported beer selection is unparalleled. Ace.

Eat, Drink, Shop

Gamekeepers
*345 W Armitage Avenue, at N Lincoln Avenue
(773 549 0400). CTA Armitage (Brown, Purple)/
11, 22, 36 bus.* **Open** 5pm-4am Mon-Fri; 10am-5am
Sat; 10am-4am Sun. **Credit** AmEx, Disc, MC, V.
Map p308 G6.
If Kincade's (*see below*) is the sports bar of choice out
west in Lincoln Park, then Gamekeepers is its east-
side match. Though located just a block from the
park, drinkers here prefer to enjoy their sports either
sat on a barstool or sat in the bleachers (always with
beer in hand). Not the place for quiet conversation
or cocktails, needless to say.

John Barleycorn Memorial Pub
*658 W Belden Avenue, at N Lincoln Avenue (773
348 8899/www.johnbarleycorn.com). CTA Fullerton
(Brown, Purple, Red).* **Open** 3pm-2am Mon-Fri;
9am-3am Sat; 9am-2am Sun. **Credit** AmEx, MC, V.
Map p308 F5.
A neighbourhood favourite, this comfortable and
roomy tavern was forced into a stint as a Chinese
laundry during Prohibition, but never stopped serving liquor (it also served as a speakeasy). The hard-
drinking spirit remains firmly intact here, though
it's classier than the sports bars nearby. Try a
Bloody Mary and Guinness with Sunday brunch.

Kincade's
*950 W Armitage Avenue, at N Sheffield Avenue
(773 348 0010). CTA Armitage (Brown, Purple).*
Open 11am-2am Mon-Fri, Sun; 11am-3am Sat.
Credit AmEx, DC, Disc, MC, V. **Map** p308 E6.
The area's reigning sports bar and pick-up joint. The
38 TVs and ample beer selection attract hordes of
frat brothers decked out in the regalia of their alma
mater. On Saturdays during college football season,
Kincade's can have the feel (and smell) of college
bleachers during a big game.

Local Option
*1102 W Webster Avenue, at N Seminary Avenue
(773 348 2008). CTA Fullerton (Brown, Purple,
Red).* **Open** 5pm-2am Mon-Fri; 3pm-3am Sat; noon-
2am Sun. **Credit** AmEx, MC, V. **Map** p308 E5.
Local Option is an unpretentious neighbourhood
hangout for DePaul students and other locals tired
of the yuppie theme that predominates the area.
A pool table and several TVs offer diversion, cheap
pitchers provide the beer, everything from acid jazz
to country music can be heard.

Lucky Strike
*2747 N Lincoln Avenue, at W Diversey Parkway
(773 549 2695). CTA Diversey (Brown, Purple).*
Open 5pm-2am Mon-Fri; noon-3am Sat; noon-2am
Sun. **Credit** AmEx, DC, Disc, MC, V. **Map** p308 E4.
This bar does everything it can to keep you
busy, with a pool hall and bowling lanes supple-
menting the good beer and whiskey choices. It's
art deco in theme and staffed by a friendly bunch,
with a crowd that tends to be just-out-of-college aged
and unable to hold their liquor. Nonetheless, it's a
good time all the same.

Bras and balls: **Weed's**. *See p159.*

McGee's

950 W Webster Avenue, at N Sheffield Avenue (773 549 8200/www.bar1events.com). CTA Fullerton (Brown, Purple, Red). **Open** 11am-2am Mon-Fri, Sun; 10am-3am Sat. **Credit** AmEx, DC, Disc, MC, V. **Map** p308 E5.

An attractive neighbourhood sports bar, McGee's is more low-key than Kincade's and lacks the locker-room smell of Gamekeepers. On weekends, DePaul students and young Lincoln Park professionals pack in for burgers and football.

Red Lion Pub

2446 N Lincoln Avenue, at W Fullerton Avenue (773 348 2695/www.redlionpub.com). CTA Fullerton. **Open** 1.30pm-2am daily. **Credit** AmEx, DC, MC, V. **Map** p308 F5.

Authentic (ish), British and rumoured to be haunted, the Red Lion is full of character, dark wood and heavy food. The downstairs bar and restaurant have low ceilings and an excellent beer selection (plus great fish and chips), while the cosier upstairs bar has a backroom and a sizeable rooftop beer garden.

Walk on Lincoln Avenue bars

Its reputation is well earned. Lincoln Park really does have an extraordinary concentration of bars and a liver-defying number of drinkers to fill them. But with such a reputation come pitfalls for the visitor. The streets might be lined with boozers, but where are the good ones?

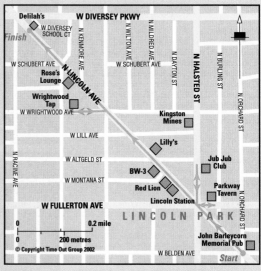

Certainly, there are plenty of horrible hangouts here. Noisy sports bars rub shoulders with sweaty singles spots, populated in the main by moneyed graduates from the Division Street University of Boorishness. Among the most avoidable are the cluster of bars near the **Alumni Club** (2251 N Lincoln Avenue) and **Deja Vu** (2624 N Lincoln Avenue). However, in among the crap are some gems, which, with a little planning, can be strung together into an appetising pub crawl. There are countless possible routes around the area, but this one – focused on Lincoln Avenue – is about as good and as varied as they come.

Start at the north-east corner of W Belden Avenue and N Lincoln Avenue, a ten-minute stroll from Fullerton El station or accessible by bus on the 8 (Halsted Street) or 11 (Lincoln Avenue) routes.

The atmosphere at the **John Barleycorn Memorial Pub** (*see p157*) is less foreboding than its surprisingly grand frontage may suggest. Inside, it's a good, old-fashioned neighbourhood hangout, popular among shit-shooting affluentials. A nice place to start.

*Continue north up Lincoln to the junction with Halsted and Fullerton. If there's a game on, turn into Fullerton to the **Parkway Tavern** (748½ W Fullerton Avenue; 773 327 8164) for a beer; if not, stroll up Halsted.*

The **Jub Jub Club** (2447 N Halsted Street; 773 665 7557) attempts the unattemptable: serving classy cocktails to a locale awash with Bud buddies. It does pretty well, too, primarily by pitching itself as much as neighbourhood hangout as swanky lounge. Try a Martini.

*Double back down Halsted, and take the first right up Lincoln. On your left is **Lincoln Station** (2432 N Lincoln Avenue; 773 472 8100), a sports bar that also serves decent, stomach-lining food. On your right is the Biograph Theater, where John Dillinger was shot. And opposite it is...*

The Store

2002 N Halsted Street, at W Armitage Avenue (773 327 7766). CTA Armitage (Brown, Purple). **Open** 3pm-4am Mon-Fri; 11am-5am Sat; 11am-4am Sun. **Credit** AmEx, Disc, MC, V. **Map** p308 F6.
Though the multiple TVs and pool table could pin it as a sports bar, the Store's principal attraction is its 4am closing time. The bar is long and narrow, and seating consists mainly of bar stools. A good last-call bar if you're not willing to face the noise at the considerably more hectic Beaumont up the road.

Like most American pubs that purport to be authentically British, the **Red Lion Pub** (*see p158*) is nothing of the sort. However, despite its theminess (there's a red phone box *inside* the pub) the boozer delivers with a friendly atmosphere and fine beer garden.
Continue up Lincoln, stopping at **BW-3** *(2464 N Lincoln Avenue; 773 868 9453) for buffalo wings or* **Lilly's** *(see p223) for some blues. At Wrightwood, turn left.*
Lincoln Park doesn't want for cosy corner bars. However, you could do worse than the **Wrightwood Tap** (1059 W Wrightwood Avenue; 773 549 4949), an unpretentious spot that hooks locals who'd rather chill to kitschy 1980s hits than dry-hump to techno or holler at a televised sports game.
Double back up Wrightwood and turn left up Lincoln Avenue.
On a strip dominated by frat shacks and singles bars, **Rose's Lounge** (2656 N Lincoln Avenue; 773 327 4000) stands out a mile. A shabby entrance leads into a dingy, divey room, presided over by Rose herself. Cosy up to the bar and quietly suck back a couple of cheap drafts, revelling in the lack of lairy jocks.
Continue north up Lincoln for about a block, crossing the road.
Shelf after shelf of whiskies indicate that **Delilah's** (*see p156*) is a place for serious drinkers; and if you've made it this far, count yourselves among them. Though it may initially seem wildly different from the bar where the crawl started – just as the Barleycorn is smart and sporty, Delilah's is scruffy and dark, a real rock 'n' roll hangout – closer examination reveals that both are friendly bars frequented by regulars. If you can hack the often-loud, often-punkish music, it's the perfect place for a nightcap, not least because outside, you're sure to find a cab to take you home.

Webster's Wine Bar

1480 W Webster Avenue, at N Clybourn Street (773 868 0608/www.websterwinebar.com). Bus 73. **Open** 5pm-2am Mon-Fri; 4pm-3am Sat; 5pm-2am Sun. **Credit** AmEx, DC, Disc, MC, V. **Map** p308 D5.
This quiet wine bar is tucked away at the far west end of Lincoln Park on the edge of the Chicago River's northern branch. The knowledgeable staff offer an impressive choice of wines, complemented by a menu of appetisers and regular live jazz.

Weed's

1555 N Dayton Street, at W Weed Street (312 943 7815). CTA North/Clybourn (Red). **Open** 3pm-1.30am Mon-Sat. **Credit** AmEx, MC, V. **Map** p307 F7.
A peculiar spot in the middle of nowhere – west of Old Town, south of Lincoln Park – but worth seeking out. The bras hanging from the ceiling bear witness to the power of the lubrication served by the sunglassed bartender (a strangely lifelike bust of whom graces the bar) and the lubricity of the clientele. The later it gets, the stranger it gets.

Lake View

Lake View is a little yuppie-ish, but on a lesser scale and with a more eclectic flavour than Lincoln Park. Lake View proper is huge, taking in Wrigleyville to the north, Roscoe Village to the west and Boystown, Chicago's largest concentration of gay and lesbian citizens, along the lakefront (for gay bars, *see p212*).

Duke of Perth

2913 N Clark Street, at W Oakdale Avenue (773 477 1741). CTA Wellington (Brown, Purple). **Open** 5pm-2am Mon; 11.30am-2am Tue-Fri; 11.30am-3am Sat; noon-2am Sun. **Credit** AmEx, DC, MC, V. **Map** p309 F3.
Chicago goes Scottish at this Lake View staple. The food is fish 'n' chips, the drinks are whiskies (75 varieties, no less) and the garden is a delight during summer. Homesick Scots may not, however, have their pangs for auld tradition entirely sated.

Elbo Room

2871 N Lincoln Avenue, at W George Street (773 549 5549/www.elboroomchicago.com). CTA Diversey (Brown, Purple). **Open** 7pm-2am Mon-Fri; 7pm-3am Sat; 8pm-2am Sun. **Credit** AmEx, Disc, MC, V. **Map** p309 D3.
This bar and live music venue has a funky, upscale retro atmosphere without trying too hard, unlike many latecomers to the '60s kitsch scene. Have a drink in the smallish bar among the hip patrons, or pay the cover and head downstairs to the claustrophobic, cavelike underground music venue.

Schubas Tavern

3159 N Southport Avenue, at W Belmont Avenue (773 525 2508/www.schubas.com). CTA Southport (Brown). **Open** 11am-2am Mon-Fri; 8am-3am Sat; 9am-2am Sun. **Credit** AmEx, DC, Disc, MC, V. **Map** p309 D3.

Eat, Drink, Shop

Made in Chicago Goose Island

It's a beer, we'll give you that. But it is to Budweiser what Marshall Field is to Kmart, what a hand-rolled Cuban cigar is to a Marlboro Light. You want a thinking person's beer? While it's being crafted, the brewers listen to National Public Radio. Goose Island beers, which have been made on Chicago's West Side since the late 1980s, really are intended for a smarter bunch of drinkers.

Company founder John Hall didn't have visions of mass distribution or commercial slots during the Super Bowl when he founded the company in the mid 1980s. His masterplan was to fill a niche for a local craft beer: something that would satisfy discriminating taste buds and teach people a thing or two about hops and barley in the process. The first variety, Honker's Ale, was introduced in 1988 and sold solely from Hall's Goose Island brewpub on Clybourn Avenue, named for a small island in the nearby Chicago River (the island is so-called because Chicago's Irish community used to raise domestic geese there long ago). And that, it seemed, was that.

However, Goose Island has grown, and grown, and grown. The 1990s saw Hall open a second brewpub in Wrigleyville and a new brewery and bottling plant on Fulton Street – where the brewmaster is Greg Hall, John's son – just to keep up with demand. For Goose Island is no longer sold only in Chicago: it's now exported all over the Midwest. Today, the company creates around a dozen brews at any one time, from an aromatic oatmeal stout to the fruity India Pale Ale, which are now shipped across the Midwest.

However, following the when-in-Rome principle, since you're in Chicago, you might as well go directly to the fountain. At the two brewpubs, you'll find varieties made especially for every season – the German-style Summertime Kölsch is a must-taste – along with a few staples that are always on tap. With a pint in your hand, you'll be joining the ranks of beer aficionados that are far happier contemplating and consuming their brew than merely being sold it during the half-time commercial break.

Goose Island

Lincoln Park *1800 N Clybourn Avenue, at W Willow Street (312 915 0071). CTA North/Clybourn (Red).* **Open** 11am-1am Mon-Thur, Sun; 11am-2pm Fri, Sat. *Tours* 3pm Sun ($3). **Credit** AmEx, DC, Disc, MC, V. **Wrigleyville** *3535 N Clark Street, at W Eddy Street (773 832 9040). CTA Addison (Red).* **Open** *Oct-Mar* 4-11pm Mon-Wed; 4pm-midnight Thur; 4pm-2am Fri; 11am-2am Sat; 11am-11pm Sun. *Apr-Sept* 11am-midnight Mon-Thur; 11am-2am Fri; 10am-2am Sat; 10am-midnight Sun. **Credit** AmEx, DC, Disc, MC, V. **Map** p309 E1.

Eat, Drink, Shop

Housed in a 90-year-old building, Schubas is a typical vintage pub, with a 30ft (10m) mahogany bar and tin ceilings. But it's the busy backroom that puts it on the map: there's music most nights, with a lean towards indie-rock bands and singer-songwriters.

Southport Lanes & Billiards
3325 N Southport Avenue, at W Aldine Avenue (773 472 6600/www.southportlanes.com). CTA Southport (Brown). **Open** 4pm-2am Mon-Fri; noon-3am Sat; noon-2am Sun. **Credit** AmEx, DC, Disc, MC, V. **Map** p309 D2.
When the conversation runs dry, you'll have plenty of distractions here: seven billiard tables ($9-$12/hr) and four bowling lanes ($14/hr). However, the attraction is not so much the games as the well-scrubbed clientele that comes to play.

Star Bar/Pops for Champagne
2934 N Sheffield Avenue, at W Oakdale Avenue (773 472 7272/1000/www.popschampagne.com). CTA Wellington (Brown, Purple). **Open** 5pm-2am Mon-Fri, Sun; 5pm-3am Sat. **Credit** AmEx, Disc, MC, V. **Map** p309 E3.
Because it's in Lake View and not the Gold Coast where it belongs, this pair goes out of its way to lord its upscale pretensions over the great unwashed. It's actually one bar with two themed rooms: the quiet, cosy and formal Star Bar, and the opulent wine bar Pops (which has live jazz; *see p224*). Dress up.

Will's Northwoods Inn
3030 N Racine Avenue, at W Nelson Street (773 528 4400). CTA Wellington (Brown, Purple). **Open** 11.30am-2am Mon-Fri, Sun; 11.30am-3am Sat. **Credit** AmEx, MC, V. **Map** p309 E3.
Decorated with stuffed pike and moose heads, Will's is a mecca for homesick cheeseheads who come to watch Packers games and quaff a Leinenkugel. The Musky Fest in September features a free buffet, a Wisconsin trivia contest and the (tongue-in-cheek) election of the Musky Queen.

Wrigleyville

Cubby Bear
1059 W Addison Street, at N Clark Street (773 327 1662/www.cubbybear.com). CTA Addison (Red). **Open** 4pm-2am Mon-Fri; 11am-3am Sat; 11am-2am Sun. **Credit** AmEx, DC, Disc, MC, V. **Map** p309 E1.
Located across from the Friendly Confines, this perpetually expanding bar is packed with sports fans on game days. In the off-season, the emphasis is on undemanding live music and dancing, and Sunday is highlighted by brunch.

Ginger Man
3740 N Clark Street, at N Racine Avenue (773 549 2050). CTA Addison (Red). **Open** 3pm-2am Mon-Fri; noon-3am Sat; noon-2am Sun. **Credit** AmEx, Disc, MC, V. **Map** p309 E1.
This edgy Wrigleyville institution has been known to blare classical music to keep Wrigley's gameday crowds at bay, preferring to cater to theatre-goers

heading to a nearby show or of-age hipsters looking for a drink after a gig at the Metro. There's a good selection of beers, and movie nuts may recognise the pool room from 1986's *The Color of Money*.

Irish Oak
3511 N Clark Street, at W Addison Street (773 935 6669/www.irishoak.com). CTA Addison (Red). **Open** 11am-2am Mon-Fri, Sun; 11am-3am Sat. **Credit** AmEx, DC, Disc, MC, V. **Map** p309 E1.
Chicago is full of Irish-themed bars, but this one strikes the best balance between authenticity and tedious old-country kitsch. The usual Irish fare comes with a modern twist, including the prettiest, if not the tastiest, fish and chips for miles. There's live music on Wednesdays and weekends.

Murphy's Bleachers
3655 N Sheffield Avenue, at W Waveland Avenue (no phone). CTA Addison (Red). **Open** 9am-2am Mon-Fri, Sun; 9am-3am Sat. **No credit cards.** **Map** p309 E1.
Located behind Wrigley, Murphy's affords sports fans the rare opportunity to pay $4.50 for a can of Old Style. Most patrons amass on the sidewalk before or after Cubs games to bask in the sun, people-watch and booze it up. A gameday tradition.

Sheffield's Wine & Beer Garden
3258 N Sheffield Avenue, at W Aldine Avenue (773 281 4989). CTA Belmont (Brown, Purple, Red). **Open** 3pm-2am Mon-Fri; noon-3am Sat; noon-2am Sun. **Credit** AmEx, DC, Disc, MC, V. **Map** p309 E2.
Far enough away from Wrigley Field to elude most fans, Sheffield's is a great pre- or post-game hangout. There's the all-important beer garden, but the best seat is on an elevated bench just inside the front door to the right: perched over the bouncer's shoulder, you can check out all the folks who come in.

Sluggers World Class Sports Bar
3540 N Clark Street, at W Addison Street (773 248 0055). CTA Addison (Red). **Open** 3pm-2am Mon-Fri; 11am-3am Sat; 11am-2am Sun. *Cubs home games* open from 10am. **Credit** AmEx, DC, Disc, MC, V. **Map** p309 E1.
This Wrigleyville landmark has been voted the best sports bar in Chicago and the third best in the country. Downstairs, there's the typical array of pool tables; upstairs are pitching machines, basketball hoops, video games and Hi-Ball, a game that resembles two-on-two basketball on a tiny trampoline.

Smart Bar
3730 N Clark Street, at N Racine Avenue (773 549 4140). CTA Addison (Red). **Open** 10pm-4am Mon-Fri, Sun; 10pm-5am Sat. **Credit** AmEx, MC, V. **Map** p309 E1.
Once the epicentre of Chicago's punk scene, the Metro's downstairs nightclub still attracts a punky crowd, with DJs spinning house, techno and the like. If dancing isn't your thing, then shoot some pool or grab a spot in the booths that surround the dancefloor and check out the goths.

Eat, Drink, Shop

Rainbo Club. *See p163.*

Roscoe Village

Beat Kitchen

2100 W Belmont Avenue, at N Hoyne Avenue (773 281 4444/www.beatkitchen.com). Bus 50, 77. **Open** 11am-2am Mon-Fri, Sun; 11am-3am Sat. **Credit** AmEx, Disc, MC, V.

Recently remodelled, the Beat Kitchen has become garage-rock central in the back, while the front offers a long, cosy bar. The menu features a selection of quietly inventive bar food.

Resi's Bierstube

2034 W Irving Park Road, at N Damen Avenue (773 472 1749). CTA Irving Park (Brown). **Open** 3pm-2am Mon-Fri, Sun; 3pm-3am Sat. **Credit** AmEx, DC, Disc, MC, V.

This German bar/restaurant offers lots of imports on tap, served inside or in one of the city's best beer gardens. The menu offers traditional schnitzels and from 5pm (Mon-Thur), cantankerous barmatron Edith makes delectable potato pancakes.

Village Tap

2055 W Roscoe Street, at N Hoyne Avenue (773 883 0817/www.jakstap.com). CTA Paulina (Brown)/50 bus. **Open** 5pm-2am Mon-Thur; 3pm-2am Fri; noon-3am Sat, Sun. **Credit** AmEx, DC, Disc, MC, V.

This neighbourhood pub has filled up as affluent twentysomethings have moved further and further westward. The $3.50 microbrew pints and $11 pitchers appeal, as does the dressed-up pub grub and spacious garden (heated in winter).

Wicker Park & Bucktown

The bars of Wicker Park and Bucktown are wildly diverse and generally racially balanced, with any given crowd to be found on any given night. If the bar you're in isn't your thing, just walk north or south on Damen and you're guaranteed to encounter something to your liking. Note, however, that the further south you go, the seedier the neighbourhood becomes.

Betty's Blue Star Lounge

1600 W Grand Street, at N Ashland Street (312 243 8778). CTA Grand (Blue). **Open** 11.30am-4am Mon-Fri, Sun; 11.30am-5am Sat. **No credit cards.**

What was once a seedy bar in a seedy locale has turned into a late-night hipster bar in a seedy locale. The patron base comprises jungleheads, hip hop kids, garage rockers and rockabillies; its eclectic flavour makes it *the* West Side destination after other bars have closed. DJs spin nightly, throwing down lounge to the Wu-Tangs.

Club Foot

1824 W Augusta Street, at N Wood Street (773 489 0379). CTA Division (Blue). **Open** 8pm-2am Mon-Fri, Sun; 8pm-3am Sat. **No credit cards. Map** p310 C9.

Ukrainian Village's version of Delilah's (*see p156*), Club Foot serves a gentler crowd than its abrasive North Side brother. DJs spin a decent mix, but Club Foot sets itself apart by the decor: wall-mounted cases are filled with everything from a signed Devo jumpsuit to a complete set of *Star Wars* figures.

Danny's Lounge

1951 W Dickens Avenue, at N Damen Avenue (773 489 6457). CTA Damen (Blue)/50, 73 bus. **Open** 7pm-2am Mon-Fri, Sun; 7pm-3am Sat. **No credit cards. Map** p310 C6.

Danny's used to be a house. And at first glance, it still is: the structural alterations in its transition to boozer have been minimal, and the ambience is still more house party than bar. Beneath dim and forgiving lights, self-aware hipsters sup beers while a DJ plays a soundtrack of downtempo tunes. Nice.

Estelle's

2013 W North Avenue, at N Damen Avenue (773 782 0450). CTA Damen (Blue). **Open** 7pm-4am Mon-Fri, Sun; 7pm-5am Sat. **Credit** AmEx, MC, V. **Map** p310 B7.

Though the decor at Estelle's has improved – and the times have changed – it still pulls in a rock 'n' roll crowd, though the jukebox offers everything from Elvis to Peter Tosh. Lines often form in front after the other bars have closed, so get there by 1am.

Gold Star Lounge

1735 W Division Street, at N Wood Street (773 227 8700). CTA Division (Blue). **Open** 4pm-2am Mon-Fri; 3pm-3am Sat; 3pm-2am Sun. **No credit cards**. **Map** p310 C8.

Though it looks like a dump from the street, the Gold Star has become a Mecca for Chicago's indie-rock crowd, though the earlier it is, the more likely you are to encounter some of the area's pre-gentrification denizens. Think of it as a Rainbo (*see below*) for a less pretentious crowd.

Lava Lounge

859 N Damen Avenue, at W Chicago Avenue (773 772 3355). Bus 50, 66. **Open** 5pm-2am Mon-Fri; 7pm-3am Sat; 6pm-2am Sun. **Credit** MC, V.

The cosy Lava attracts a mix of locals during the week and North Siders at weekends. The three-room bar seems small, but the backrooms are full of nooks for small parties and booths for larger groups. The draft microbrews change monthly.

Lemmings

1850 N Damen Avenue, at W Moffat Street (773 862 1688). CTA Damen (Blue). **Open** 4pm-2am Mon-Fri; noon-3am Sat; noon-2am Sun. **Credit** AmEx, MC, V. **Map** p310 B6.

A quiet neighbourhood bar frequented by locals and often a getaway from the thumping bar scene up the street, Lemmings is a friendly Schlitz with no pretension. The crowd of regulars is a little older and quieter than is the norm around here.

Marie's Rip Tide Lounge

1745 W Armitage Avenue, at N Wood Street (773 278 7317). CTA Damen (Blue)/50, 73 bus. **Open** 8pm-4am Mon-Fri, Sun; 8pm-5am Sat. **No credit cards**. **Map** p310 C6.

Old school in all but clientele, this hangout draws the kind of young hipsters who still appreciate their elders and betters. And for elder and better, read Marie, who's presided over this room since before many of her regulars were born. It's a frill-free joint, but that's really the point. And the music is fab.

Matchbox

770 N Milwaukee Avenue, at W Chicago Avenue (312 666 9292). CTA Chicago (Blue). **Open** 4pm-2am Mon-Fri; 2pm-3am Sat; 2pm-2am Sun. **Credit** AmEx, MC, V.

The tiniest bar you'll ever drink in, the Matchbox is on the southernmost region of Wicker Park, and is something of a local legend. The bartenders know

their liquor, so if you want a Sidecar or Harvey Wallbanger made correctly, come here. Be prepared to wait for a seat along the bar, as it fills up fast.

Pontiac Café & Bar

1531 N Damen Avenue, at N Wicker Park Avenue (773 252 7767). CTA Damen (Blue). **Open** noon-2am Mon-Fri, Sun; noon-3am Sat. **Credit** MC, V. **Map** p310 B7.

With a full menu of sandwiches, Italian snacks and panini, the Pontiac is one of Wicker Park's most visited bars, especially in summer when the sidewalk beer garden explodes with beautiful people and bitter hipsters. The full bar is stocked with both the very expensive and very cheap.

Rainbo Club

1150 N Damen Avenue, at W Division Street (773 489 5999). Bus 50, 70. **Open** 4pm-2am Mon-Fri, Sun; 4pm-3am Sat. **No credit cards**. **Map** p310 B8.

Once a haunt of Nelson Algren, the Rainbo is a favourite with locals, artists, musos and writers. You'll catch some attitude if you're not one of the above, and the bartenders work as if their legs are made of lead. All the same, there's a genuinely artsy atmosphere here: you may spot any number of semi-famous locals, plus more soon-to-bes and wannabes.

Silver Cloud Bar & Grill

1700 N Damen Avenue, at W Wabansia Avenue (773 489 6212). CTA Damen (Blue). **Open** 11.30am-2am Tue-Fri; 10am-3am Sat; 10am-midnight Sun. **Credit** AmEx, DC, Disc, MC, V. **Map** p310 B7.

A midscale bar and restaurant that serves some of the city's best bar food, the Silver Cloud has become a local favourite. There's a long bar for the drinkers, booths and tables for diners (try the incredible grilled cheese) and a rotating choice of microbrews.

Tuman's Alcohol Abuse Center

2201 W Chicago Avenue, at N Leavitt Street (no phone). Bus 66. **Open** 2pm-2am Mon-Fri, Sun; 2pm-3am Sat. **No credit cards**.

A bar for the pure-bred drinker. The crowd at this gem is one of the most diverse in the city: bikers, businessmen, punks and hip hoppers all co-exist in harmony thanks to Tuman's ultra-cheap booze. Prices tend to vary round by round, but it's cheaper than any other bar you'll find in the city.

South Side

Woodlawn Tap

1172 E 55th Street, at S Woodlawn Avenue (773 643 5516). Metra 55th-56th-57th Street. **Open** 10.30am-2am Mon-Fri, Sun; 10.30am-3am Sat. **No credit cards**. **Map** p311 X17.

Legendary owner Jimmy Wilson died in 1999, but – after a period of closure – the Woodlawn Tap is still pouring beers for the predictably thirsty students at the University of Chicago. The decor ain't much – hell, there ain't much decor – but the matey atmosphere is cherishable. There's jazz on Sundays.

Eat, Drink, Shop

Shops & Services

The Magnificent Mile is just the beginning of Chicago's shopping circuit.

Woodn't it be nice: smarten up your house at **Jay Robert's**. *See p165.*

When it comes to combing the streets for haute styles and too-cool sales, Chicago's shopping scene is unmatched. Call it Paris on the Lake. The Milan of the Midwest. Whichever way, this is one city with a downtown that's big on dress-up. Check out the bag-toters on **Michigan Avenue**: the Champs-Elysées of the Windy City, where major chains and department stores bring the buying pace to fever pitch. Those on the hunt for Beverly Hills will find their treasures – luxury linens, kicky footwear, designer gowns – along **Oak Street**. The Loop's **State Street** is another shopping district and if you're not ready to splurge, then eyeing up the handsome window displays of the strip's department stores should keep you happy.

A shopping expedition beyond downtown turns up more. You'll get in the gift-buying state of mind along quaint Armitage Avenue in **Lincoln Park**, where independent businesses cater to an upwardly mobile crowd. The gentrifying locales of **Wicker Park** and **Bucktown** are turning into bona fide retail districts, and the goods found in these 'hoods are all about high design: edgy European furniture, funky home decor, understatedly cool clothing. That's not to mention all those stores that have stood the test of time, like the age-old booksellers found in **Hyde Park**, or the antiques shops on Belmont and Lincoln Avenues. The options are unlimited. So warm up your wallet and get on out there.

Antiques

Chicago's antiques district, found on Belmont between Ashland and Western, is a mecca for period pieces. Today, it's rivalled by a strip of Lincoln Avenue between Diversey and Addison, where you'll find an assortment of ragtag antiques boutiques.

Eat, Drink, Shop

Broadway Antiques Market
6130 N Broadway, at W Hood Avenue, Rogers Park (773 743 5444/www.bamchicago.com). CTA Granville (Purple, Red). **Open** 11am-7pm Mon-Sat; noon-6pm Sun. **Credit** AmEx, Disc, MC, V.
This two-level antiques mall is used by 75 dealers as a showcase for everything from Victoriana to '70s collectibles. There's an emphasis on art deco, Arts and Crafts and modern movements.

Jay Robert's Antique Warehouse
149 W Kinzie Street, at N LaSalle Street, Near North (312 222 0167/www.jayroberts.com). CTA Merchandise Mart (Brown, Purple). **Open** 10am-5pm Mon-Sat. **Credit** AmEx, MC, V. **Map** p307 H11.
This River North outpost is highly regarded for its huge range of furniture: check out the period pieces, from country pine to Chippendale. There are also decent selections of antique clocks and stained glass.

Modern Times
1538 N Milwaukee Avenue, at W North Avenue, Wicker Park (773 772 8871/www.moderntimeschicago.com). CTA Damen (Blue). **Open** 1-6pm Wed-Fri; noon-6pm Sat, Sun. **Credit** AmEx, MC, V. **Map** p310 C7.
This groovy antiques store specialises in the '40s, '50s and '60s. Look for furniture, jewellery and vintage wear, then rummage in the basement for downmarket bargains.

Pagoda Red
1714 N Damen Avenue, at W Armitage Avenue, Wicker Park (773 235 1188/www.pagodared.com). CTA Damen (Blue) or Western (Blue). **Open** 10am-6pm Mon-Sat; by appointment Sun. **Credit** AmEx, MC, V. **Map** p310 B6.
A surprising find on the second floor of a Bucktown loft, this antiques store specialises in Asian imports. Spacious and easy to navigate, Pagoda Red features wares – Nepalese rugs, sculptures, Zen-inspired paintings and more – fit for royalty.

Salvage One
1840 W Hubbard Street, at W 16th Street, West Town (312 733 0098). CTA Halsted (Orange). **Open** 10am-5pm Mon-Sat; 11am-4pm Sun. **Credit** AmEx, Disc, MC, V.
Love the thrill of the dig? Check out this massive four-floor warehouse that's filled to the rafters with beautiful and unusual furniture – fireplace mantels, claw-footed bathtubs, oak doors, bathroom fixtures and other architectural artefacts.

Arts & crafts

Paper Source
232 W Chicago Avenue, at N Franklin Street, Near North (312 337 0798/www.paper-source.com). CTA Chicago (Brown, Purple). **Open** 10am-7pm Mon-Fri; 10am-5pm Sat; noon-5pm Sun. **Credit** AmEx, Disc, MC, V. **Map** p306 G10.

A long-time favourite among do-it-yourself-invite types, this store has a huge variety of papers for writing, wrapping and binding, plus rubber stamps, wedding supplies and other creative gift items.

Pearl Art & Craft Supplies
225 W Chicago Avenue, at N Franklin Street, Near North (312 915 0200). CTA Chicago (Brown, Purple). **Open** 9am-7pm Mon-Sat; noon-5pm Sun. **Credit** AmEx, Disc, MC, V. **Map** p306 G10.
What began as an industrial paint store in New York City is now a national chain. The cluttered Chicago location is crammed with arts and crafts supplies to satisfy both suburban hobbyist and serious artist.

Books

General

Barbara's Bookstore
1350 N Wells Street, at W Schiller Street, Old Town (312 642 5044). CTA Clark/Division (Red). **Open** 9am-10pm Mon-Sat; 10am-9pm Sun. **Credit** AmEx, Disc, MC, V. **Map** p307 H8.
Barbara's is a cosy hangout with all the bustle of a superstore but none of the bureaucracy. The local chain has strong politics and current affairs sections, as well as a great array of art books.
Branches: throughout the city.

Barnes & Noble
1130 N State Street, at W Cedar Street, Gold Coast (312 280 8155/www.bn.com). CTA Clark/Division (Red). **Open** 9am-11pm Mon-Sat; 10am-10pm Sun. **Credit** AmEx, DC, Disc, MC, V. **Map** p306 H9.
In a gratifying break from the norm, the on-the-ball staffers at this wood-panelled store make a genuine effort to find you the book you're looking for. The magazine section is dense and varied.
Branches: 659 W Diversey Parkway, Lake View (773 871 9004); 1441 W Webster Avenue, Lincoln Park (773 871 3610).

The best Shops

For getting the blues
Jazz Record Mart. *See p183.*

For the sweet-toothed
Vosges Haut-Chocolat. *See p179.*

For John Wayne wannabes
Alcala's Western Wear. *See p174.*

For Sarah Jessica Parker wannabes
Barney's New York. *See p168.*

For saying it with flowers
Green. *See p178.*

Talk of the devil: the
Occult Bookstore. *See p167.*

Borders Books & Music

830 N Michigan Avenue, at N Pearson Street, Near North (312 573 0564/www.borders.com). CTA Chicago (Red). **Open** 8am-11pm Mon-Sat; 9am-9pm Sun. **Credit** AmEx, DC, Disc, MC, V. **Map** p306 J9.
The Mag Mile's megalithic, four-storey Borders has laid-back staff who are willing to help… if you can find any among the huge crowds, that is. There's more hustle and bustle here than in your average bookstore, due in part to the frequent live performances in the café.
Branches: 2817 N Clark Street, Lake View (773 935 3909); 150 N State Street, the Loop (312 606 0750).

Seminary Cooperative Bookstore

5757 S University Avenue, at E 58th Street, Hyde Park (773 752 4381/www.semcoop.com). Metra 59th Street. **Open** 8.30am-9pm Mon-Fri; 10am-6pm Sat; noon-6pm Sun. **Credit** AmEx, Disc, MC, V. **Map** p311 X12.
Right in the hub of Hyde Park's 'bookstore row', this shop is revered by local academics. There are obscure texts galore, leaving even the most intrepid bookworm happy. The 57th Street location offers tomes of a more general nature.
Branches: 1301 E 57th Street, Hyde Park (773 684 1300); Newberry Library Bookstore, 60 W Walton Street, Near North (312 255 3520).

Unabridged Bookstore

3251 N Broadway, at W Belmont Avenue, Lake View (773 883 9119). CTA Belmont (Brown, Purple, Red). **Open** 10am-10pm Mon-Fri; 10am-8pm Sat, Sun. **Credit** AmEx, Disc, MC, V. **Map** p309 F2.
This bookstore largely reflects the neighbourhood folk who shop there: it has a huge gay and lesbian selection, as well as photocentric magazines for the same crowd. There are also sizeable children's and travel sections.

Specialist

Abraham Lincoln Book Shop

357 W Chicago Avenue, at N Orleans Street, Near North (312 944 3085/www.alincolnbookshop.com). CTA Chicago (Brown, Purple). **Open** 9am-5pm Mon-Sat. **Credit** MC, V. **Map** p306 G10.
This pleasingly central 60-year-old shop devoted to Abraham Lincoln and Civil War lore is also the founding site of the Civil War Round Table, a discussion group that keeps stories of the blue and the grey alive.

Act 1 Bookstore

2540 N Lincoln Avenue, at W Wrightwood Avenue, Lincoln Park (773 348 6757/www.act1books.com). **Open** 10am-8pm Mon-Wed; 10am-6pm Thur-Sun. **Credit** AmEx, Disc, MC, V. **Map** p308 E4.
Aspiring actors are the target market for this thespy shop dealing in industry rags, screenplays and acting tomes galore. However, many people stop in just to get the dish on the newest courses and audition notices.

Read about your pet subjects at the three branches of **Powells**.

Children in Paradise Bookstore

*909 N Rush Street, at E Chestnut Street, Gold Coast
(312 951 5437/www.childreninparadise.com). CTA
Chicago (Red).* **Open** 10am-7pm Mon-Thur; 10am-
8pm Fri, Sat; noon-5pm Sun. **Credit** AmEx, MC, V.
Map p306 H9.

Literature for littl'uns is the focus at this Gold Coast
spot. Sit in on one of its story hours and see young
ones squirm in their Prada-clad mothers' laps.

Occult Bookstore

*3rd floor, 1579 N Milwaukee Avenue, at N
Damen Avenue, Wicker Park (773 292 0995/
www.occultbookstore.com). CTA Damen (Blue).*
Open noon-7pm Mon-Sat; noon-6pm Sun.
Credit MC, V. **Map** p310 B7.

Stargazers find terra firma at this store specialising in astrology, yoga, UFOs and psychic phe-
nomena. Other wares include computerised
horoscopes, incense, tarot cards and essential oils.

Prairie Avenue Bookshop

*418 S Wabash Avenue, at E Van Buren Street,
the Loop (312 922 8311/www.pabook.com). CTA
Jackson (Red).* **Open** 10am-6pm Mon-Fri; 10am-4pm
Sat. **Credit** AmEx, Disc, MC, V. **Map** p305 H13.

One of the Midwest's most impressive architectural
bookstores, with 15,000 titles on architecture, interiors, city planning and graphic design. Get cosy in
the sit-around furniture by Frank Lloyd Wright,
Mies van der Rohe and Le Corbusier.

Quimby's Bookstore

*1854 W North Avenue, at N Milwaukee Avenue,
Wicker Park (773 342 0910/www.quimbys.com).
CTA Damen (Blue).* **Open** noon-10pm Mon-Fri;
11am-10pm Sat; noon-6pm Sun. **Credit** AmEx, MC,
V. **Map** p310 B7.

Find the newest in underground self-published pro-
paganda or check out the comic and book selections
(McSweeney's aplenty) at this Bucktown joint.

The Savvy Traveller

*310 S Michigan Avenue, at E Jackson Boulevard, the
Loop (312 913 9800/www.thesavvytraveller.com).
CTA Adams (Brown, Green, Orange, Purple) or
Jackson (Red).* **Open** 10am-7.30pm Mon-Sat; noon-
5pm. **Credit** Disc, MC, V. **Map** p305 J13.

The best travel bookstore in Chicago by a mile, the
Savvy Traveller has a phenomenally wide range of
tomes on all corners of the globe, and comes with
the bonus of personable and knowledgeable staff.

Used & antiquarian

Afterwords New & Used Books

*23 E Illinois Street, at N State Street, Near North
(312 464 1110). CTA Grand (Red).* **Open** 9am-9pm
Mon-Thur; 9am-11pm Fri; 10am-11pm Sat; noon-7pm
Sun. **Credit** AmEx, MC, V. **Map** p306 H11.

Afterwords specialises in obscure and out-of-print
books. Customers can access the internet from store
computers and order customised stationery.

Powells

*1501 E 57th Street, at S Harper Avenue, Hyde Park
(773 955 7780/www.powellschicago.com). Bus 6.*
Open 9am-11pm daily. **Credit** MC, V. **Map** p311 Y17.

Powells processes hundreds of remainders a day.
The South Side stores have strong academic sections, while the North Side branch has a large art
and photography selection and a rare book room.
Branches: 828 S Wabash Avenue, South Loop (312
341 0748); 2850 N Lincoln Avenue, Lake View (773
248 1444).

Department stores

Barney's New York
25 E Oak Street, at N Rush Street, Gold Coast (312 587 1700/www.barneys.com). CTA Clark/Division (Red). **Open** 10am-7pm Mon-Sat; noon-6pm Sun. **Credit** AmEx, Disc, MC, V. **Map** p306 H9.
This sleek urban store is where no-nonsense professionals and socialites come to shop. Barney's has transferred its NYC sophistication to Chicago lock, stock and barrel: attitude included.

Bloomingdale's
900 N Michigan Avenue, at E Walton Street, Near North (312 440 4460/www.bloomingdales.com). CTA Chicago (Red). **Open** 10am-8pm Mon-Sat; noon-7pm Sun. **Credit** AmEx, MC, V. **Map** p309 J9.
On a Mag Mile awash in staid tradition, Bloomies is about having fun. A must for the younger shopper, its six levels are packed with fashions for the free-spirited: don't miss the terrific shoe department.

Carson Pirie Scott
1 S State Street, at E Madison Street, the Loop (312 641 7000/www.carsons.com). CTA Madison (Brown, Green, Orange, Purple). **Open** 9.45am-7pm Mon-Wed, Fri; 9.45am-8pm Thur; 9.45am-6pm Sat; 11am-6pm Sun. **Credit** AmEx, Disc, MC, V. **Map** p305 H12.
In existence for some 140 years, Carson's is a conservative mainstay. It's known for its practical (and practically priced) goods, not to mention its fabulous landmark Louis Sullivan design: you can't miss the iron embellishments on the north-west door.

Clocking on at **Marshall Field's**.

Lord & Taylor
Water Tower Place, 835 N Michigan Avenue, at E Chestnut Street, Near North (312 787 7400/www.lordandtaylor.com). CTA Chicago (Red). **Open** 10am-9pm Mon-Fri; 10am-8pm Sat; 11am-7pm Sun. **Credit** AmEx, Disc, MC, V. **Map** p306 J9.
One of the more conservative of the Mile's upscale shops, Lord & Taylor gets a nod for staying on the classic end of things. Knockout sales are frequent.

Marshall Field's
111 N State Street, at E Randolph Street, the Loop (312 781 1000/www.fields.com). CTA Randolph (Red). **Open** 10am-8pm Mon-Sat; 11am-5pm Sun. **Credit** AmEx, DC, Disc, MC, V. **Map** p305 H12.
As Chicago as it gets, Marshall Field's is where the city's sons and daughters have congregated for generations, whether lunching under the Christmas tree in the Walnut Room, sampling its famous chocolate Frango mints or buying essentials on one of the store's nine levels. Adding to the nostalgia is its architectural grandeur, most notably its mosaic-topped, domed atrium.
Branches: throughout the city.

Neiman Marcus
737 N Michigan Avenue, at E Chicago Avenue, Near North (312 642 5900/www.neimanmarcus.com). CTA Chicago (Red). **Open** 10am-7pm Mon-Sat; noon-6pm Sun. **Credit** AmEx, DC. **Map** p306 J10.
This store woos shoppers with its airy interior, haute fashions (from establishment names such as Chanel to up-and-comers), accessories and food. It's just a shame that everything's sickeningly overpriced.

Nordstrom
520 N Michigan Avenue, at Grand Avenue, Near North (312 464 1515/www.nordstrom.com). CTA Grand (Red). **Open** 10am-8pm Mon-Sat; 11am-6pm Sun. **Credit** AmEx, DC, Disc, MC, V. **Map** p306 J10.
Technically not a department store (there are no home furnishings to be found here), Nordstrom is known mostly for its fab fashions, especially in its shoe department. An on-the-ball concierge service is at your command, and the in-store café is perfect for shoppers looking to wind down at lunch (but get there by 12.30pm to snag a booth).

Saks Fifth Avenue
Chicago Place Mall, 700 N Michigan Avenue, at E Superior Street, Near North (312 944 6500/www.saks.com). CTA Chicago (Red). **Open** 10am-7pm Mon-Sat; noon-6pm Sun. **Credit** AmEx, DC, Disc, MC, V. **Map** p306 J10.
The upper crust have been at home at Saks since 1929, where traditional fashions take precedence over wild trends. Keep your eye on the great children's department and retooled menswear department across the street.

Sears
2 N State Street, at W Washington Street, the Loop (312 373 6040/www.sears.com). CTA Washington (Blue, Red). **Open** 9am-9pm Mon-Fri. **Credit** AmEx, Disc, MC, V. **Map** p305 H12.

Mall talk

Century Shopping Center

*2828 N Clark Street, at W Diversey Parkway,
Lake View (773 929 8100). CTA Diversey
(Brown, Purple).* **Open** 10.30am-9pm
Mon-Fri; 10.30am-6pm Sat; noon-6pm
Sun. **Map** p308 F4.
A small mall highlighted by a cinema (*see
p203*) and a **Bally's Total Fitness** (773 929
6900), plus branches of **Aveda** (773 289
1560), **Structure** (773 665 2192) and
Victoria's Secret (773 549 7405).

Chicago Place

*700 N Michigan Avenue, at E Superior Street,
Near North (312 642 4811/www.chicago-
place.com). CTA Chicago (Red).* **Open** 10am-
7pm Mon-Fri; 10am-6pm Sat; noon-5pm Sun.
Map p306 J10.
Head here for **Saks Fifth Avenue** (*see p168*),
cookstore **Williams-Sonoma** (312 787 8991),
festive shop **Christmas on the Avenue** (312
751 0506) and blarney-dominated gift shop
Joy of Ireland (312 664 7290).

Gurnee Mills

*6170 W Grand Avenue, off I-94/I-294 (exit
at Route 132, W Grand Avenue), Gurnee
(847 263 7500/www.gurneemills.com).*
Open 10am-9pm Mon-Fri; 10am-9.30pm Sat;
11am-6pm Sun.
A **JC Penney Outlet** (847 855 0470) and a **TJ
Maxx** (847 855 0146) draw bargain-hunters;
an **Abercrombie & Fitch Outlet** (847 855
2819), a **Banana Republic Factory Store**
(847 855 1198) and a **Gap Outlet** (847
855 9311) keep them there.

900 N Michigan

*900 N Michigan Avenue, at E Walton
Street, Near North (312 915 3916/
www.shop900.com). CTA Chicago (Red).*
Open 10am-7pm Mon-Sat; 10am-6pm Sun.
Map p306 J9.
Approachably upscale, 900 N Michigan offers
the city's only **Bloomingdale's** (*see p168*)
alongside branches of **Gucci** (*see p172*) and
Benetton (312 649 5873), a **Garber Furs**
store (312 642 6600) and a **Truefitt & Hill**
boutique (*see p182*).

Northbrook Court

*2171 Northbrook Court, off Route 41
(via I-94), Northbrook (847 498 1770/
www.shopnorthbrookcourt.com).* **Open** 10am-
9pm Mon-Fri; 10am-7pm Sat; 11am-6pm Sun.

As malls go, this one's fairly upmarket and
more pleasing than most, with the branches
of **DKNY** (847 664 7900) and **Aveda** (847
509 9354) only brought briefly down to earth
by the **Sam Goody** (847 480 0430).

Oakbrook Center

*Off I-88 (Cermax Road exit), Oak Brook (630
573 0700/www.oakbrookcenter.com).* **Open**
10am-9pm Mon-Sat; 11am-6pm Sun.
Neiman Marcus (630 572 1500) and **Saks
Fifth Avenue** (630 574 7000) are the
poshest of the six department stores here.
Otherwise, it's largely run of the mill stuff
from **Gap** (630 573 5145) to **Guess?** (630
954 2838), though the **Discovery Channel
Store** 630 571 1813) is a nice diversion.

Shops at North Bridge

*520 N Michigan Avenue, at E Grand
Avenue, Near North (312 327 2300/
www.northbridgechicago.com). CTA
Grand (Red).* **Open** 10am-7pm Mon-Sat;
noon-6pm Sun.
Nordstrom (*see p168*) is the flagship at this
new development, but **Hugo Boss** (312 660
0056) and **Oilily** (312 822 9616) and an
entire floor of kid-friendly stores (among them
a vast **LEGO Store** (312 327 2300) also
appeal to the largely non-native shoppers.

Water Tower Place

*835 N Michigan Avenue, at E Chestnut
Street, Near North (312 440 3166/
www.shopwatertower.com). CTA Chicago
(Red).* **Open** 10am-7pm Mon-Sat; noon-6pm
Sun. **Map** p306 J9.
Lord & Taylor and **Marshall Field's** (for both,
see p168) dominate, along with clothes
shops such as **Banana Republic** (312 642
7667), **French Connection** (312 932 9460)
and **Abercrombie & Fitch** (312 787 8825).

Woodfield Shopping Center

*Off Route 53 S (Woodfield Road exit),
via I-90, Schaumburg (847 330 1537/
www.shopwoodfield.com).* **Open** 10am-9pm
Mon-Sat; 11am-6pm Sun.
Five department stores, including a **Sears**
(847 330 2356) and a **Nordstrom** (847 605
2121), are joined by a **Crate & Barrel** (847
619 4200), a scarily popular **Thomas
Kinkade Gallery** (847 605 8311), tons of
middle American clothes chains (**Gap,
American Eagle, Eddie Bauer**) and – hurrah! –
a Mac-packed **Apple Store** (847 240 6280).

Eat, Drink, Shop

Tender Buttons.

Sears is back downtown for the first time in almost 20 years, though its clothing ranges don't appear to have changed since it was last here. Expect to find... well, exactly what you'd expect to find.
Branches: throughout the city.

Electronics

United Audio Centers
900 N Michigan Mall, 900 N Michigan Avenue, at E Walton Street, Near North (312 664 3100). CTA Chicago (Red). **Open** 10am-7pm Mon-Thur; 10am-8pm Fri; 10am-6pm Sat; noon-6pm Sun. **Credit** AmEx, Disc, MC, V. **Map** p306 J9.
Budding DJs will take a shine to this audio and video store with a wide selection of brands and prices.
Branch: Century Mall, 2828 N Clark Street, Lake View (773 525 7005).

Fabrics & trimmings

Fishman's Fabrics
1101 S Desplaines Street, at W Roosevelt Street, Near South Side (312 922 7250/www.fishmansfabrics.com). CTA Clinton (Blue). **Open** 9am-5.30pm Mon-Wed, Fri, Sat; 9am-8pm Thur. **Credit** AmEx, Disc, MC, V. **Map** p304 F14.
Three floors of cottons, wools, linens and laces grace the racks at this longtime Chicago fabric merchant, located on the near South Side.

Tender Buttons
946 N Rush Street, at E Oak Street, Gold Coast (312 337 7033). CTA Chicago (Red). **Open** 10am-6pm Mon-Fri; 10am-5.30pm Sat. **Credit** MC, V. **Map** p306 H9.
This Gold Coast treasure is a tiny museum-like boutique, featuring hundreds of buttons from antique to modern, plus cufflinks and studs.

Vogue Fabrics
Water Tower Place, 835 N Michigan Avenue, at E Chestnut Street, Near North (312 787 2521/ www.voguefabrics.com). CTA Chicago (Red).

Open 10am-7pm Mon-Sat; noon-6pm Sun.
Credit AmEx, Disc, MC, V. **Map** p306 J9.
A great variety of sewing materials is available at this local chain. Grab anything from pricey, hand-beaded bridal fabrics to simple knits on the cheap.

Fashion

Children

There's a branch of cheap, kid-friendly **Old Navy** at 35 N State Street in the Loop (312 551 0523), and two **Gap Kids** on N Michigan Avenue: one at No.555 (312 494 8580), and one in Water Tower Place at No.835 (312 944 3053).

Active Kids
1967 N Fremont Street, at W Armitage Avenue, Lincoln Park (773 281 2002/ www.activeendeavors.com). CTA Armitage (Brown, Purple). **Open** 10am-6pm Mon-Sat; noon-5pm Sun. **Credit** AmEx, MC, V. **Map** p308 F6.
Outdoor apparel, shoes and accessories for the little camper are found at this slip of a store. For parent store Active Endeavors, *see p185*.

Madison & Friends
940 N Rush Street, at E Oak Street, Gold Coast (312 642 6403/www.madisonandfriends.com). CTA Clark/Division (Red). **Open** 10am-6pm Mon-Wed, Fri, Sat; 10am-7pm Thur; noon-5pm Sun. **Credit** AmEx, MC, V. **Map** p306 H9.
The owners of this boutique strive to put some hipness into kids' clothes, though – of course – it's the parents who are more worried about the fashions.

Cleaning & repairs

Gibson Couture Cleaners
3432 N Southport Avenue, at W Roscoe Street, Lake View: Wrigleyville (773 248 0937). CTA Addison (Red). **Open** 7am-7pm Mon-Fri; 7am-5.30pm Sat. **Credit** AmEx, Disc, MC, V. **Map** p309 D2.

Eat, Drink, Shop

'Well, sir, I ain't a for-real cowboy...' **Alcala's Western Wear**. *See p174.*

Gibson specialises in special garment care at prices a bit steeper than a standard corner cleaner. Your goods are in trusted hands, though.

Harry's Gold Coast Shoe Repair

1 W Chestnut Street, at N State Street, Gold Coast (312 337 3742). CTA Chicago (Red). **Open** 8am-6.30pm Mon-Fri; 8am-5pm Sat. **Credit** AmEx. **Map** p306 H9.
Centrally located, Harry's is recommended for super-speedy shoe doctoring.

Designer

A stroll down E Oak Street turns up a roll-call some big names, including **Prada** (No.30; 312 951 1113) and **Ultimo** (No.114; 312 787 1171). Many are ensconced in converted townhouses, including **Jil Sander** and **Sonia Rykiel**.
The north end of N Michigan Avenue also yields plenty of high-end stores. The branch of **Ralph Lauren** (No.750; 312 280 1655) is the world's largest; **Giorgio Armani** (No.800; 312 751 5504) and **Chanel** (No.935; 312 787 5500) all offer wallet-emptying opportunities.

Bibabis

732 N Wells Street, at W Superior Street, Near North (312 988 9560). CTA Chicago (Brown, Purple). **Open** 11am-7pm Mon-Sat (*June-Aug* 1.30-6pm Sun). **Credit** AmEx, Disc, MC, V. **Map** p306 H10.

Designer Debra Ward works up the neat ensembles here. The look is playful, with cocktail dresses and ruffled blouses gracing the racks. Knitwear by Italian designer Sarah Pacini also features.

Cynthia Rowley

808 W Armitage Avenue, at N Halsted Street, Lincoln Park (773 528 6160). CTA Armitage (Brown, Purple). **Open** 11am-7pm Mon-Fri; 10am-6pm Sat; noon-5pm Sun. **Credit** AmEx, MC, V. **Map** p308 F6.
A hometown girl made good, Rowley sells her own affordable line of cutesy women's clothing and make-up from this Lincoln Park store.

Fitigues

939 N Rush Street, at E Walton Place, Gold Coast (312 943 8676/www.fitigues.com). CTA Chicago (Red). **Open** 10am-6pm Mon-Sat; noon-5pm Sun. **Credit** AmEx, MC, V. **Map** p306 H9.
The upscale everyday wear from this husband and wife team comes with an emphasis on comfy custom-made fabrics for women, men and children.
Branches: 2130 N Halsted Street, Lincoln Park (773 404 9696); 1535 N Dayton Street, Lincoln Park (312 255 0095).

Robin Richman

2108 N Damen Avenue, at W Webster Avenue, Bucktown (773 278 6150). CTA Western (Blue). **Open** 11am-6pm Tue, Wed, Fri, Sat; 11am-7pm Thur; noon-5pm Sun. **Credit** AmEx, Disc, MC, V. **Map** p310 B5.

This Bucktown staple offers a kind of 'peasant chic' look: flouncy fabrics of all kinds are intertwined with thick yarn created by Richman's own team. Antique-looking items (handsome bags, semi-precious jewellery and the like) make the atmosphere both rustic and ravishing.

Softcore

1420 N Milwaukee Avenue, at Wood Street, Wicker Park (773 276 7616). CTA Damen (Blue). **Open** *Apr-Dec 11am-8pm daily. Jan-Mar 11am-7pm daily.* **Credit** AmEx, Disc, MC, V. **Map** p310 C8.

Softcore deals in cutting-edge club gear and urban fashions. Find co-owners Suenman Lam and Obi Nwazota's signature line Octopussy here, along with skimpy frocks from New York labels. Accessories can be picked up on the cheap.

Su-Zen Boutique

2241 N Clybourn Avenue, at W Webster Street, Lincoln Park (773 477 9919/www.su-zen.com). Bus 73, 74. **Open** *11am-6pm Tue-Sat; noon-5pm Sun.* **Credit** AmEx, MC, V. **Map** p308 D5.

Designer Susan Hahn works up rich designs from handcrafted yarns and a bevy of interesting fabrics. While these finds are hardly priced to go, the versatility of the fashions promise a long, fashionable existence.

Erotic & fetish

Male Hide Leathers

2816 N Lincoln Avenue, at W Diversey Parkway, Lake View (773 929 0069/www.malehide.com). CTA Diversey (Brown, Purple). **Open** *noon-8pm Mon-Sat; noon-5pm Sun.* **Credit** AmEx, Disc, MC, V. **Map** p308 E4.

Nondescript from the exterior, inside Male Hide features leatherwear with a decidedly gay twist, including jackets, pants, boots and more.

Pleasure Chest

3155 N Broadway Street, at W Belmont Avenue, Lake View (773 525 7151/www.apleasurechest.com). CTA Belmont (Brown, Purple, Red). **Open** *10am-midnight daily.* **Credit** AmEx, Disc, MC, V. **Map** p309 F2.

If the ever-racey window displays don't catch your eye, then this store's selection of body gear will. A fun stop for bachelorette party gifts, Pleasure Chest also appeals to hardcore experimenters.

Lingerie

There are branches of **Victoria's Secret** in **Water Tower** Place and the **Century Mall** (for both, *see p169* **Mall talk**).

Isabella Fine Lingerie

1101 W Webster Avenue, at N Seminary Avenue, Lincoln Park (773 281 2352/ www.isabellafinelingerie.com). CTA Fullerton (Brown, Purple, Red). **Open** *11am-7pm Tue-Fri; 11am-6pm Sat; noon-5pm Sun.* **Credit** MC, V. **Map** p308 E5.

Designs from Cosabella, Dolce & Gabbana and others are found in this glamorous boutique. The items are gracefully displayed in small drawers, glass cabinets and a vintage pharmacy unit.

Trousseau

711 W Armitage Avenue, at N Halsted Street, Lincoln Park (312 751 1450). CTA Armitage (Brown, Purple). **Open** *11am-7pm Mon-Fri; 10am-6pm Sat; noon-5pm Sun.* **Credit** AmEx, MC, V. **Map** p308 F6.

This fun treasure chest offers skivvies ranging from flirty and inexpensive to ultra-lacey and sumptuous. Popular with Lincoln Park-area brides, the boutique is a great place for wedding-night lingerie.

Menswear

Bad Boys

3352 N Halsted Street, at W Roscoe Street, Lake View (773 549 7701/www.badboyschicago.com). CTA Belmont (Brown, Purple, Red). **Open** *noon-9pm Mon-Fri; 11am-9pm Sat; noon-5pm Sun.* **Credit** AmEx, DC, Disc, MC, V. **Map** p309 F2.

Popular with Boystown locals, this shop is big on underwear for tight-bellied guys. Fun clothing, some of it sporty, is also found here.

Davis for Men

824 W North Avenue, at N Clybourn Avenue, Lincoln Park (312 266 9599). CTA North/Clybourn (Red). **Open** *10.30am-7pm Mon-Fri; 10.30am-6pm Sat; 11.30am-5pm Sun.* **Credit** AmEx, DC, Disc, MC, V. **Map** p307 F7.

Designer looks at decent prices are the staples of this store, just north of downtown. With a welcoming atmosphere and a floor that's never too congested, Davis is a good place for shoe or suit shopping.

Kenneth Cole

540 N Michigan Avenue, at E Grand Avenue, Near North (312 644 1163/www.kennethcole.com). CTA Grand (Red). **Open** *10am-8pm Mon-Sat; noon-6pm Sun.* **Credit** AmEx, MC, V. **Map** p306 J10.

This emporium for urban uniform predominantly features Cole's shoes, but also offers shirts, fragrances, accessories and more. Leather merchandise is a big focus.

Shoes

Nordstrom and **Bloomingdale's** (for both, *see p168*) are both famed for their selections of women's shoes. For **Kenneth Cole**, *see above*.

Donald J Pliner

106 E Oak Street, at N Michigan Avenue, Near North (312 202 9600/www.donaldplinerchicago.com). CTA Chicago (Red). **Open** *10am-6pm Mon-Sat; noon-5pm Sun.* **Credit** AmEx, MC, V. **Map** p306 J9.

It's not hard to cosy up to this store, with its plush sofas and chairs scattered throughout. Those who dig the Pliner label keep their eyes on the boots, slingbacks and sexy stilettos.

Eat, Drink, Shop

G'bani

*949 N State Street, at E Walton Place, Gold Coast
(312 440 1718/www.gbani.com). CTA Chicago (Red).*
Open 10am-7pm Mon-Sat; noon-5pm Sun. **Credit**
AmEx, DC, MC, V. **Map** p306 H9.
The focus is on fresh, minimalist design at this
fashion-forward Gold Coast boutique, with stylish
selections from France and Italy. A newly added
clothing room is worth a look.

John Fluevog

*1539-41 N Milwaukee Avenue, at N Damen Avenue,
Wicker Park (773 772 1983/www.fluevog.com). CTA
Damen (Blue).* **Open** 11am-7pm Mon-Sat; noon-5pm
Sun. **Credit** AmEx, Disc, MC, V. **Map** p310 C7.
The trendy Canadian cobbler sells a wide selection
of kicks. There's not much variance between styles,
but what the shop does – wearable urban footwear,
basically – it does rather well.

Lori's Designer Shoes

*824 W Armitage Avenue, at N Dayton Street, Lincoln
Park (773 281 5655/www.lorisdesignershoes.com).
CTA Armitage (Brown, Purple).* **Open** 11am-7pm
Mon-Thur; 11am-6pm Fri; 10am-6pm Sat; noon-5pm
Sun. **Credit** AmEx, Disc, MC, V. **Map** p308 F6.
A fave with shoe-crazed Chicago women, this insti-
tution has one of the largest selections of American
and European designer shoes in the city, selling at
10-30% less than department store prices.

Speciality stores

Alcala's Western Wear

*1733 W Chicago Avenue, at N Ashland Avenue, West
Town (312 226 0152/www.alcalas.com). Bus 66.* **Open**
10am-8pm Mon, Thur, Fri; 10am-7pm Tue, Wed, Sat;
10am-5pm Sun. **Credit** AmEx, DC, Disc, MC, V.
Wanna rodeo? Slip on the Stetson to wallow in this
shop's selections of jeans, hats and cowboy boots
(some 10,000 pairs).

Rochester Big & Tall Men's Clothing

*840 N Michigan Avenue, at E Chestnut Street,
Near North (312 337 8877). CTA Chicago (Red).*
Open 9.30am-6.30pm Mon-Wed, Fri; 9.30am-7pm
Thur; 9.30am-6pm Sat; noon-5pm Sun. **Credit**
AmEx, DC, Disc, MC, V. **Map** p306 J9.
With a big guy spokesperson like John Madden, you
can only expect to find a huge range of clothing,
from fine tailored suits to sportswear and shoes for
sizes ranging from large to mammoth.

Tall Girl

*Chicago Place Mall, 700 N Michigan Avenue, at
E Superior Street, Near North (312 649 1303/
www.tallgirlshop.com). CTA Chicago (Red).*
Open 10am-7pm Mon-Fri; 10am-6pm Sat; noon-5pm
Sun. **Credit** Disc, MC, V. **Map** p306 J10.
As this retailer's name implies, Tall Girl features
styles for women in sizes up to 22. Both casual and
contemporary chic, the designs are in step with
up-to-the-minute trends.

Street

The Alley

*858 W Belmont Avenue, at N Clark Street, Lake
View (773 525 3180/www.etwisted.com). CTA
Belmont (Brown, Purple, Red).* **Open** 10am-10pm
Mon-Thur; 10am-midnight Fri, Sat; noon-8pm Sun.
Credit MC, V. **Map** p309 F2.
This emporium of alternative gear in Lake View –
look for its hearse in the neighbouring Dunkin'
Donuts lot – has everything a goth or punker needs.

Diesel

*923 N Rush Street, at E Walton Street, Gold Coast
(312 255 0157/www.diesel.com). CTA Chicago (Red).*
Open 10am-8pm Mon-Sat; 11am-6pm Sun.
Credit AmEx, Disc, MC, V. **Map** p306 H9.
A prime stomping ground for club cats with cash to
throw around. Its wide selection of jeans and other
body-conscious duds are ready-made for a fast
crowd, as dance music sets the buying pace.

Flashy Trash

*3524 N Halsted Street, at W Addison Street,
Lake View: Wrigleyville (773 327 6900/
www.flashytrash.com). CTA Addison (Red).*
Open 11am-8pm Mon-Sat; noon-6pm Sun.
Credit AmEx, Disc, MC, V. **Map** p309 F1.
Go glam! Vintage gear and designer goods are displayed with aplomb at this funky shop. There's plenty on the tightly packed racks, including bowling
shirts, cocktail dresses and kimonos.

Untitled

*2705 N Clark Street, at W Schubert Avenue, Lincoln
Park (773 404 0650/www.untitledchicago.com). CTA
Diversey (Brown).* **Open** 11am-8pm Mon-Thur;
11am-8.30pm Fri, Sat; noon-6pm Sun. **Credit** AmEx,
Disc, MC, V. **Map** p308 F4.
Stocking loose-fitting clothes and shoes for the
skater set (both men and women), Untitled also manages to attract a more well-heeled club crowd with
its sleek partywear.

Urban Outfitters

*935 N Rush Street, at E Walton Street, Gold Coast
(312 640 1919/www.urbn.com). CTA Chicago (Red).*
Open 10am-9pm Mon-Sat; noon-7pm. **Credit** AmEx,
Disc, MC, V. **Map** p306 H9.
Kind of a department store for hip young things,
Urban Outfitters offers furniture and accessories
alongside its substanstial stash of street fashions for
both sexes.
Branch: 2352 N Clark Street, Lincoln Park (773
549 1711).

Vintage & second-hand

Beatnix

*3400 N Halsted Street, at W Roscoe Street, Lake
View: Wrigleyville (773 281 6933). CTA Belmont
(Brown, Purple, Red).* **Open** noon-9pm Mon-Wed,
Fri; noon-10pm Thur; noon-midnight Fri, Sat; 11am-
10pm Sun. **Credit** MC, V. **Map** p309 F2.

Hat's the way to do it: **Strange Cargo.**

This colourful, multi-room shop has outfits and accessories, both new and used, to keep club kids, drag queens and muscle boys looking their best. A corner of the store is newly devoted to wigs.

Daisy Shop
6th floor, 67 E Oak Street, at N Michigan Avenue, Near North (312 943 8880/www.daisyshop.com). CTA Chicago (Red). **Open** 11am-6pm Mon-Sat; noon-5pm Sun. **Credit** AmEx, Disc, MC, V. **Map** p306 J9.
A discreet sixth-floor location offers cover to rich Gold Coast doyennes. One of several resale shops for women's couture, it offers swanky cast-offs at 50-80% off the regular steep prices.

Hollywood Mirror
812 W Belmont Avenue, at N Halsted Street, Lake View (773 404 2044). CTA Belmont (Brown, Purple, Red). **Open** 11am-7.30pm Mon-Thur; 11am-8.30pm Fri, Sat; 11am-6.30pm Sun. **Credit** AmEx, Disc, MC, V. **Map** p309 F2.
This retro shop has a huge selection of weathered jeans, bowling shirts and jackets. Not to mention the old-school furniture found on the lower level and the wide array of nostalgic items up for grabs upstairs (ever thought you'd be back into the Smurfs?).

Strange Cargo
3448 N Clark Street, at N Sheffield Avenue, Lake View: Wrigleyville (773 327 8090). CTA Addison (Red). **Open** 11.30am-6.45pm Mon-Sat; noon-5.30pm Sun. **Credit** MC, V. **Map** p309 E2.
This Wrigleyville favourite is a fun, prototypical thrift shop, with dresses, jeans, shirts, hats, coats,

shoes and assorted kitschy toys. Strange Cargo will also buy used duds if you've overpacked and can't get everything back home.

Wisteria
3715 N Southport Avenue, at W Grace Street, Lake View: Wrigleyville (773 880 5868). CTA Southport (Brown). **Open** 4-9pm Thur, Fri; noon-9pm Sat; noon-5pm Sun. **Credit** MC, V. **Map** p309 D1.
A visit to this vintage salon turns up wonderful heirlooms and period clothing for men and women (mostly '40s and '50s), plus an assortment of old suitcases, vintage ashtrays and kitchenware.

Womenswear

Anthropologie
1120 N State Street, at E Elm Street, Gold Coast (312 255 1848/www.anthropologie.com). CTA Clark/Division (Red). **Open** 10am-8pm Mon-Sat; 11am-6pm Sun. **Credit** AmEx, Disc, MC, V. **Map** p306 H9.
Clothes with romantic undertones, as well as bold, geometric patterns, are hawked at this boutique. The prices are steep considering these are pretty casual duds, but regular killer sales make it all worthwhile.

Betsey Johnson
72 E Oak Street, at N Michigan Avenue, Near North (312 664 5901). CTA Chicago (Red). **Open** 10am-6pm Mon-Sat; noon-5pm Sun. **Credit** AmEx. MC, V. **Map** p306 J9.
Splashy colours and fruity, flowery designs are the strongholds of wild child Betsey Johnson. The racks are packed with youthful, feminine clothing.

Flashy Trash. Blending in ain't an option. *See p174.*

Etre

1361 N Wells Street, at W Burton Place, Old Town (312 266 8101). CTA Sedgwick (Brown, Purple). **Open** 11am-7pm Mon-Fri; 11am-6pm Sat; noon-5pm Sun. **Credit** AmEx, Disc, MC, V. **Map** p307 H8.

Hard-to-come-by lines from Europe are found at this expansive boutique. Plaid seems to be the rage here, extending even to the kicks found in its shoe department (a huge back-of-the-house selection).

Jolie Joli

2131 N Southport Avenue, at N Clybourn Avenue, Lincoln Park (773 327 4917/www.joliejoli.com). CTA Armitage (Brown, Purple). **Open** 11am-7pm Tue-Thur; 11am-6pm Fri, Sat; noon-5pm Sun. **Credit** AmEx, MC, V. **Map** p308 D6.

This boutique works to include designers not otherwise represented in the Chicago area. Comfort is stressed here, as the space was arranged according to the advice of a feng shui specialist.

June Blaker

200 W Superior Street, at N Wells Street, Near North (312 751 9220). CTA Chicago (Brown, Purple). **Open** 10am-6pm Mon-Sat. **Credit** AmEx, DC, Disc, MC, V. **Map** p306 G10.

Fashionistas peruse this boutique for the latest from edgy Euro and Japanese designers, such as Comme des Garçons and Yohji Yamamoto. There is also a selection of jewellery and accessories.

Noir

1226 W Division Street, at Wood Street, Wicker Park (773 489 1957). CTA Damen (Blue). **Open** 11am-8pm Mon-Sat; noon-6pm Sun. **Credit** AmEx, Disc, MC, V. **Map** p310 B7.

While this boutique doesn't house particularly recognisable labels, the finds are fun and extremely affordable. Nightclub wear consumes most of the floor – think sequins, fur and faux leather.

P.45

1643 N Damen Avenue, at W North Avenue, Wicker Park (773 862 4523). CTA Damen (Blue). **Open** 11am-8pm Mon-Sat; noon-6pm Sun. **Credit** AmEx, Disc, MC, V. **Map** p310 B7.

This super-hip shop, featuring a sweeping interior designed by Suhail, is a piece of Soho in Chicago. The young proprietresses of the industrial-chic space have got exclusives on both local and New York up-and-comers – and they come at a price.

Sofie

1343 N Wells Street, at W Schiller Street, Gold Coast (312 255 1343/www.sofie-chicago.com). CTA Clark/Division (Red). **Open** *Jan-Feb* 11am-6pm Tue-Sat; noon-5pm Sun. *Mar-Dec* noon-7pm Mon; 11am-7pm Tue-Fri; 11am-6pm Sat; noon-5pm Sun. **Credit** AmEx, MC, V. **Map** p308 H8.

This new boutique is in step with the latest trends from New York and abroad. Tastefully arranged clothes are neither too racy nor too conservative for the style-conscious city slicker.

Tribeca

2480½ N Lincoln Avenue, at W Altgeld Street, Lincoln Park (773 528 5958). CTA Fullerton (Brown, Purple, Red). **Open** 11am-7pm Mon-Fri; 10am-6pm Sat; noon-6pm Sun. **Credit** AmEx, MC, V. **Map** p308 F5.

Party girls grab cute Custo tops here before making tracks to one of the sports bars in the area. Ever-feminine, Tribeca's designs are culled from the New York runways and are displayed in this tiny space.

Fashion accessories

Hats Plus

4706 W Irving Park Road, at N Milwaukee Avenue, Irving Park (773 286 5577). CTA Irving Park (Blue). **Open** 10am-6pm Mon-Wed, Fri, Sat; 10am-8pm Thur; 11am-5pm Sun. **Credit** AmEx, Disc, MC, V.

It's a big ol' hike here, but men who take their headgear seriously will want to make the effort for the city's largest choice of fur, felt, wool, straw and more.

Kate Spade

101 E Oak Street, at N Michigan Avenue, Gold Coast (312 654 8853/www.katespade.com). CTA Chicago (Red). **Open** *10am-6pm Mon-Sat; noon-5pm Sun.* **Credit** AmEx, MC, V. **Map** p306 J9.
Spade's power handbags are snapped up by discriminating fashionistas. At her Chicago boutique, grab a bag or get your mitts on another coveted Spade accessory: gloves, hats and so on. Hubby Jack Spade displays his menswear here.

Linda Campisano Millinery

900 N Michigan Mall, 900 N Michigan Avenue, at E Walton Street, Near North (312 337 1004). CTA Chicago (Red). **Open** *10am-7pm Mon-Sat; noon-6pm Sun.* **Credit** AmEx, Disc, MC, V. **Map** p306 J9.

Located on the sixth floor of the Bloomingdale's building, Campisano uses centuries-old wooden hat blocks to create original hats for both men and women, plus bridal veils and headpieces.

Silver Room

1410 N Milwaukee Avenue, at N Wood Street, Wicker Park (773 278 7130/www.thesilverroom.com). CTA Damen (Blue). **Open** *noon-8pm Mon; 11am-8pm Tue-Sat; 11am-6pm Sun.* **Credit** AmEx, Disc, MC, V. **Map** p310 C8.
The DJ indicates that this is one style-conscious store. Specialising in semi-precious jewellery, it also sells hats and a selection of super-fly sunglasses.

Spare Parts

2947 N Broadway Street, at W Wellington Avenue, Lake View (773 525 4242). CTA Wellington (Brown, Purple). **Open** *11am-8pm Tue-Sat; 11am-6pm Sun.* **Credit** AmEx, MC, V. **Map** p309 F3.

Doctors' orders

So, you head to the chain drugstore, chuck down your prescription and play the waiting game in the Hallmark aisle while it's being prepared. So far, so unmemorable; a scene you've doubtless played out a hundred times before. Well, it doesn't have to be this way...

Enter Merz Apothecary, an anomalous North Side spot that's been dealing in herbal and homeopathic medicines for over a century. Originally a place for the North Side's largely European immigrant population to get their remedies, Merz now attracts a diverse crowd with its mix of mind- and body-friendly products.

The store, though, barely survived to reach its 100th birthday. Founded in 1875 by local chemist Peter Merz, it nearly closed in 1972 when Merz's grandson Ralph, ready to retire,

couldn't find anyone to take it on. Salvation arrived in the shape of Abdul Quiyam, who bought the shop from Merz mere weeks before it was scheduled to shut.

Ten years later, Quiyam moved the store to larger premises in Lincoln Square. However, he made an admirable attempt to preserve the original's feel in the transition, furnishing his new shop with all manner of glorious, European-style trimmings: leaded glass windows, parquet floors, tin ceilings and solid oak cabinets. The original antique pharmacy jars even found their way here, and are now placed prominently on the shelves.

While the ambience is a throwback to the days when people took things easy and service was king (Quiyam himself still works the counter), the range of goods on offer is forward-thinking: organic toothpastes, aromatherapy kits, essential tree oils, all-natural soaps and plenty more. Vitamins are available in every formula and size, masses of ancient cold remedies sit on shelves, and many cures are made to order, both on site and via the non-traditional Merz website. Such innovations, and the loyal customer base that the apothecary commands, means it's a fool who'll bet against it racking up another century on the North Side of Chicago.

Merz Apothecary

4716 N Lincoln Avenue, at W Lawrence Avenue, Lincoln Square (773 989 0900/ www.smallflower.com). CTA Western (Brown). **Open** *9am-6pm Mon-Sat.* **Credit** AmEx, Disc, MC, V.

Eat, Drink, Shop

Garrett Popcorn Shop. *See p179.*

More or less any accessory can be found at this Boystown fave. The belts, handbags, wallets and sunglasses are versatile, lending themselves to just about any area of the fashion spectrum. Jewellery çomes from Patricia Locke, bags from Paris Focus.

Jewellery

For a salt-of-the-earth shop, hit **Jeweler's Row** in the Loop, a strip of jewellery stores on Wabash between Washington and Jackson. In particular, the **Jeweler's Center** at 5 S Wabash (312 853 2057/www.jewelerscenter.com) is home to some 150 jewellers, who between them take care of most shoppers' needs.

Ani Afshar
2009 N Sheffield Avenue, at W Armitage Avenue, Lincoln Park (773 477 6650). CTA Armitage (Brown, Purple). **Open** noon-8pm Mon-Fri; 10am-8pm Sat; 11am-5pm Sun. **Credit** MC, V. **Map** p308 E6.
Owner-designer Ani Afshar's boutique features her original designs. It's easy to take a shine to her pieces, which all feature semi-precious stones.

Tiffany & Co
730 N Michigan Avenue, at E Superior Street, Near North (312 944 7500/www.tiffany.com). CTA Chicago (Red). **Open** 10am-6pm Mon-Wed, Fri, Sat; 10am-7pm Thur; noon-5pm Sun. **Credit** AmEx, DC, Disc, MC, V. **Map** p306 J10.
Not as grand as the original on New York's Fifth Avenue, the Chicago Tiffany store still emits magnificence. If you can't afford any of the sparkling baubles here, think of it as a free museum.

Taköhl Design
110 N Peoria Street, at W Washington Boulevard, West Town (312 421 6222/www.treasurering.com). CTA Clinton (Green). **Open** 10am-6pm Mon-Fri by appointment. **Credit** AmEx, Disc, MC, V.
This gallery-style boutique features designer Tammy Kohl originals, and also doubles as her own work space. Check out the Takohl Treasure Ring, a locket-style piece with fun gems inside.

Flowers & garden supplies

Flower Bucket Shop
159 N Wells Street, at W Randolph Street, the Loop (312 759 5700). CTA Washington (Brown, Orange, Purple). **Open** 8am-6pm Mon-Fri. **Credit** AmEx, Disc, MC, V. **Map** p305 H12.
The Flower Bucket keeps all its blooms at wholesale prices and has made its reputation by selling roses at incredibly low prices; a dozen red ones, cash and carry, can be had for a mere ten bucks.
Branches: 1100 W Belmont Avenue, Lake View (773 935 9773); 1164 N LaSalle Street, Gold Coast (312 943 9773); 1375 E 53rd Street, Hyde Park (773 955 5700).

Green
1718 N Wells Street, at W St Paul Avenue, Old Town (312 266 2806). CTA Sedgwick (Brown, Purple). **Open** 9am-7pm Mon-Sat; 11am-6pm Sun. **Credit** MC, V. **Map** p307 H7.
This Old Town oasis doesn't just sell orchids, tropical plants and other flowering fronds: it's also a source of antique Chinese porcelain and ethnographic art from Africa, Asia and South America.

Urban Gardener
1006 W Armitage Avenue, at N Sheffield Avenue, Lincoln Park (773 477 2070/ www.urbangardenerchicago.com). CTA Armitage (Brown, Purple). **Open** 10am-6pm Mon-Sat; noon-5pm Sun. **Credit** Disc, MC, V. **Map** p308 E6.
Garden Design once selected this store, specialising in furniture, plant containers and other decorations, as one of the ten best shops in America. You'll lose yourself in its whimsical vintage walk-up layout.

Food & drink

Bread, cakes & pastries

Lutz Continental Café & Pastry Shop
2458 W Montrose Avenue, at N Western Avenue, Lincoln Square (773 478 7785). CTA Montrose (Brown). **Open** *Shop* 7am-8pm Tue-Thur, Sun; 7am-10pm Fri, Sat. *Café* 11am-8pm Tue-Thur, Sun; 11am-10pm Fri, Sat. **Credit** MC, V.
A sophisticated 54-year-old pâtisserie, Lutz is most famous for its German delicacies such as Black Forest gâteau, strawberry whipped cream and marzipan. If you feel like something stronger, there are also a number of rum- and liqueur-soaked cakes.

Paris Pastries
1822 W Montrose Street, at N Ravenswood Street, Ravenswood (773 784 2253). CTA Montrose (Brown). **Open** 7.30am-7pm Mon-Fri; 8am-6pm Sat; 9am-1pm Sun. **Credit** MC, V.
This hidden gem is as *français* as it gets. French pastry chef Jean-Yves concocts delectable croissants, apple tarts and mille feuilles. For lunch, drop in for a reasonably priced sandwich and kick back in the Provençal-style dining area.

Swedish Bakery
5348 N Clark Street, at W Summerdale Avenue, Andersonville (773 561 8919). CTA Berwyn (Purple, Red). **Open** 6.30am-6.30pm Mon-Thur; 6.30am-8pm Fri; 6.30am-5pm Sat. **Credit** AmEx, DC, Disc, MC, V.
This 70-year-old classic is incredibly popular. You'll always have to fight a throng to get to the tantalising array of cookies, breads and pastries, which is why there's always free coffee on tap while you wait.

Coffee & tea

Coffee & Tea Exchange
3311 N Broadway Street, at W Aldine Street, Lake View (773 528 2241/www.coffeeandtea.com). CTA Belmont (Brown, Purple, Red). **Open** 8am-8pm Mon-Thur; 8am-7pm Fri; 9am-7pm Sat; 10am-6pm Sun. **Credit** AmEx, Disc, MC, V. **Map** p309 F2.
With barrels of coffee beans consuming most of the floor space, this Lake View retailer draws a loyal java-happy crowd. A small selection of teapots, syrups and spices adds to the product mix.

Ten Ren Tea & Ginseng Company
2247 S Wentworth Avenue, at W 22nd Street, Chinatown (312 842 1171/www.tenren.com). CTA Cermak-Chinatown (Red). **Open** 9.30am-7pm daily. **Credit** AmEx, MC, V.
This expertly arranged Chinatown store sells Asian teas, from jasmine to Chinese black and green teas to a rare (and pricey) Mountain Green oolong tea.

Chocolate & confectionery

Blommer's Chocolate Factory
600 W Kinzie Street, at N Desplaines Street, West Town (312 492 1336). CTA Grand (Blue). **Open** 9am-5pm Mon-Fri; 9am-1pm Sat. **Credit** Disc, MC, V. **Map** p306 F11.
The factory provides cocoa powder, chocolate and cocoa butter to candy manufacturers, and sells it in its store. Check out the World's Largest Chocolate Bar, which weighs in at 10lb (4.5kg).

Garrett Popcorn Shop
670 N Michigan Avenue, at E Erie Street, Near North (312 944 2630/www.garrettpopcorn.com). CTA Grand (Red). **Open** 10am-8pm Mon-Sat; 10am-7.30pm Sun. **Credit** AmEx, MC, V. **Map** p306 J10.
At almost any time of the day, customers craving Garrett's caramel corn form a line outside its small storefronts, lured by the sugary aroma that wafts down the block.
Branches: 2 W Jackson Boulevard, the Loop (312 360 1108); 26 E Randolph Street, the Loop (312 630 0127); 4 E Madison Street, the Loop (312 263 8466).

Vosges Haut-Chocolat
Shops at North Bridge, 520 N Michigan Avenue, at E Grand Avenue, Near North (312 644 9450/www.vosgeschocolate.com). CTA Grand (Red). **Open** 10am-8pm Mon-Sat; noon-6pm Sun. **Credit** AmEx, Disc, MC, V. **Map** p306 H10.

Two childhood friends run this gourmet chocolatier, which specialises in truffles but also turns out chocs accented with rare spices and flowers.
Branch: Peninsula Hotel, 108 E Superior Street, Near North (312 337 2888).

Fruit & vegetables

Stanley's Fruits & Vegetables
1558 N Elston Avenue, at W North Avenue, Old Town (773 276 8050). CTA North/Clybourn (Red). **Open** *Oct-Mar* 6am-9pm Mon-Sat; 6am-8pm Sun. *Apr-Sept* 6am-10pm Mon-Sat; 6am-9pm Sun. **Credit** MC, V.
Home chefs are devoted to the high-quality and inexpensive produce at Stanley's, which is worth an extra stop on your shopping jaunt.

Health food

Whole Foods Market
3300 N Ashland Avenue, at W Henderson Street, Lake View (773 244 4200/www.wholefoodsmarket.com). CTA Paulina (Brown). **Open** 8am-10pm daily. **Credit** AmEx, Disc, MC, V. **Map** p309 D2.
Wildly popular and sometimes wildly expensive, this crunchy, full-service supermarket specialises in organic produce: there's honey on tap, vegetarian sushi and home-made salad dressings.
Branches: 50 W Huron Street, Near North (312 932 9600); 1000 W North Avenue, Lincoln Park (312 587 0648).

Speciality stores

L'Appetito
30 E Huron Street, at N State Street, Near North (312 787 9881). CTA Grand (Red). **Open** 10am-6.30pm Mon-Sat. **Credit** MC, V. **Map** p306 H10.
A great Italian grocery store, with imported meats and cheeses, plus the best submarine sandwiches in the city bar none.
Branch: John Hancock Center, 875 N Michigan Avenue, Near North (312 337 0691).

Conte di Savoia
1438 W Taylor Street, at N Ashland Avenue, West Town (312 666 3471). CTA Polk (Blue). **Open** 9am-7pm Mon-Fri; 9am-6pm Sat; 9am-4pm Sun. **Credit** AmEx, DC, Disc, MC, V.
Italian delicacies, from rare olive oils to spicy cuts of meat to rich cheeses. Don't leave without sampling the store's home-made pasta toppers, particularly the creamy, tomato-based Romano sauce.

Fox & Obel
401 E Illinois Street, at N Fairbanks Court, Near North (312 410 7301/www.fox-obel.com). CTA Grand (Red). **Open** 9am-9pm Mon-Sat; 9am-8pm Sun. **Credit** AmEx, Disc, MC, V. **Map** p306 J11.
Just what Chicago needed: a gourmet food emporium (cheeses, just-baked goods, fresh fish, etc), with an in-store café. Moochers fill up on free samples.

To market, to market

Shopping and dining are almost religious experiences here. It's no surprise, then, that the city hosts a slew of farmers' markets that get foodies jubilantly filling their bags in summer with a dizzying array of vegetables, fruits, breads and spices.

If you're a real cordon bleu, though, you'll want to check out where top local chefs go to gather prime produce: the **Chicago Green City Market**. Set on the lush garden lawn just north of the Chicago Historical Society at 1601 N Clark Street in Old Town, and held every Wednesday in summer (call 847 835 2240 for more details) the four-year-old market specialises in organic and naturally raised products, everything from Wisconsin farm-grown cheeses to fresh greens from rural Indiana.

The market highlights the resurgence in environmentally friendly cooking in the city and in the US as a whole. Many local chefs support Green City and mount ingredients-hunting expeditions there: famed cuisiniers known to give the market a tip of the toque include Rick Bayless of Topolobampo and the Frontera Grill (*see p133*), Kelly Courtney of MOD (*see p146*), and Priscila Satkoff of ¡Salpicon! (*see p139*).

Sarah Stegner, executive chef at the Dining Room at the Ritz-Carlton (*see p132*), is another huge supporter, visiting the market for organic produce and making a point of developing personal relationships with the farmers. You might spot her here on the lookout for cheeses: unsurprising, as the Dining Room has by far and away the best cheese cart in the city.

Come here with an inquisitive palate: you'll likely have a chance to sample some of the various products and ingredients. And with so many foodies on hand, you might just go home with a tip or two on how best to prepare them.

Supermarkets

Dominick's Finer Foods
1340 S Canal Street, at W Maxwell Street, West Town (312 850 3915). CTA Clinton (Blue). **Open** 24hrs daily. **Credit** AmEx, Disc, MC, V. **Map** p304 G15.
A Chicago favourite, Dominick's prides itself on freshness. Some locations, such as the one near the Fullerton El stop, pair a posh deli with a serviceable supermarket. Not all branches are open 24 hours.
Branches: throughout the city.

Jewel Food Stores
1210 N Clark Street, at W Division Street, Gold Coast (312 944 6950). CTA Clark/Division (Red). **Open** 24hrs Tue-Sun; 6am-midnight Mon. **Credit** AmEx, Disc, MC, V. **Map** p307 H8.
Almost as ubiquitous as Starbucks, Jewel is a pleasant, sprawling workhorse of a supermarket. It's sometimes paired with Osco Drug (*see p184*).
Branches: throughout the city.

Treasure Island
75 W Elm Street, at N Clark Street, Gold Coast (312 440 1144). CTA Clark/Division (Red). **Open** 7am-10pm Mon-Fri; 7am-8pm Sat; 7am-8pm Sun. **Credit** Disc, MC, V. **Map** p307 H8.
Billed as a European supermarket, Treasure Island sells exotic foodstuffs and dainties next to laundry detergents and potato chips. It's *the* destination for those hard-to-find, unusual cooking ingredients.
Branches: throughout the city.

Wine, beer & spirits

House of Glunz
1206 N Wells Street, at W Division Street, Gold Coast (312 642 3000). CTA Clark/Division (Red). **Open** 9am-7pm Mon-Fri; 10am-7pm Sat; 2-5pm Sun. **Credit** AmEx, MC, V. **Map** p307 H8.
The city's oldest wine shop harbours some of the world's oldest wines; its 25,000-bottle collection includes several that date back to the early 1800s.

Sam's Wine & Spirits
1720 N Marcey Street, at W Willow Street, Old Town (312 664 4394/www.samswine.com). CTA North/Clybourn (Red). **Open** 8am-9pm Mon-Sat; 11am-6pm Sun. **Credit** AmEx, Disc, MC, V.
A must for oenophiles, Sam's stocks Chicago's largest selection of imported wines. That's not to mention other alcohols, none of which seems too rare for the staff to get their hands on.

Furniture & home accessories

Dragonfly Collection
3221 N Clark Street, at W Belmont Avenue, Lake View (773 871 2139). CTA Belmont (Brown, Purple, Red). **Open** 11am-6pm Tue-Fri; 11am-5pm Sat; noon-5pm Sun. **Credit** Disc, MC, V. **Map** p309 F2.

City of Chicago Store

This sweeping two-level boutique deals in new and antique imports from Asia. Find vintage bowls, kitchen accessories, weathered tables and other home furnishings. Don't miss the Thai silk scarves.

ID

3341 N Clark Street, at W Roscoe Street, Lake View (773 755 4343). CTA Berlin (Brown, Purple, Red). **Open** noon-8pm Tue-Fri; 11am-7pm Sat; noon-5pm Sun. **Credit** AmEx, Disc, MC, V. **Map** p309 E2.
This über-minimalist home accessories store features expertly selected gadgets, Swedish furniture, bath products and garments by Richard Dayhoff.

Lille

1923 W North Avenue, at N Damen Avenue, Wicker Park (773 342 0563). CTA Damen (Blue). **Open** 11am-7pm Tue-Fri; 11am-6pm Sat; noon-5pm Sun. **Credit** AmEx, Disc, MC, V. **Map** p310 B7.
Lille's gallery-like setting makes you feel as if you're buying a work of art. Find high-tech gadgets for the home, as well as tasteful decorative accessories, such as tablecloths and vases.

Orange Skin

1429 N Milwaukee Avenue, at N Damen Avenue, Wicker Park (773 394 4500/www.orangeskin.com). CTA Damen (Blue). **Open** 11am-7pm daily. **Credit** AmEx, Disc, MC, V. **Map** p310 B7.
Local designer Obi Nwazota's latest endeavour deals in highly contemporary furniture culled from the hippest houses in Europe.

Gifts & souvenirs

For the **Illinois Artisans' Shop**, *see p204.*

Ancient Echoes

1003 W Armitage Avenue, at N Sheffield Avenue, Lincoln Park (773 880 1003/www.ancientechoes.com). CTA Armitage (Brown, Purple). **Open** 11am-7pm Mon-Fri; 10am-6pm Sat; noon-5pm Sun. **Credit** AmEx, MC, V. **Map** p308 E6.

Artisan jewellery is the big draw at this Armitage mainstay. During the holidays, you'll find elaborate ornaments, while fun, pick-me-up items (designer boxes, frames, etc) are found here year round.

Art Institute Museum Shop

111 S Michigan Avenue, at W Adams Street, the Loop (312 443 3583). CTA Adams (Brown, Green, Orange, Purple) or Jackson (Red). **Open** 10.30am-4.30pm Mon, Wed-Fri; 10.30am-7.30pm Tue; 10am-5pm Sat, Sun. **Credit** AmEx, Disc, MC, V. **Map** p305 J12.
Books, postcards, jewellery, stationery… It always requires a little discipline to avoid sneaking into this huge gift shop before a proper visit to the galleries.

Chicago Architecture Foundation Shop & Tour Center

224 S Michigan Avenue, at E Jackson Boulevard, the Loop (312 922 3432 x240/www.architecture.org). CTA Adams (Brown, Green, Orange, Purple). **Open** 9am-7pm Mon-Sat; 9.30am-6pm Sun. **Credit** AmEx, Disc, MC, V. **Map** p305 J12.
A fine selection of architectural books and other printed matter, jewellery, toys and objects inspired by Frank Lloyd Wright (Prairie-style shower curtains, anyone?) and other architectural masters. **Branch:** John Hancock Center, 875 N Michigan Avenue, Near North (312 751 1380).

City of Chicago Store

163 E Pearson Street, at N Michigan Avenue, Near North (312 742 8811/www.chicagostore.com). CTA Chicago (Red). **Open** 9am-5pm Mon-Sat; 10am-5pm Sun. **Credit** AmEx, MC, V. **Map** p306 J9.
Want to take a piece of Chicago back home with you? Out-of-service Chicago street signs and parking meters are among the city's cast-offs sold at this unique gift shop. More conventional souvenirs include ceramics, books, posters, T-shirts and CDs.

Gallery 37 Store

66 E Randolph Street, at N Wabash Avenue, the Loop (312 744 7274/www.gallery37.org). CTA Randolph (Brown, Green, Orange, Purple). **Open** 10am-6pm Mon-Sat. **Credit** Disc, MC, V. **Map** p305 H12.
One-of-a-kind paintings, sculptures, ceramics and other art objects created by apprentice artists. All proceeds go to non-profitmaking organisations. *See also p206* **Painting by numbers**.

Kool Thing

3821 N Lincoln Avenue, at W Grace Street, Ravenswood (773 327 2738). CTA Irving Park (Brown). **Open** 1-7pm Tue-Fri; noon-6pm Sat. **Credit** MC, V.
African finger pianos, hanging wooden bats, Virgin of Guadelupe shrines, Frida Kahlo bamboo curtains, Elvis earrings made from vintage bottlecaps. Oh, and a Haitian voodoo bottle with a doll's head inside.

Museum of Contemporary Art Store

220 E Chicago Avenue, at N Mies van der Rohe Way, Near North (312 397 4000). CTA Chicago (Red). **Open** 10am-8pm Tue; 10am-6pm Wed-Sun. **Credit** AmEx, DC, Disc, MC, V. **Map** p306 J9.

Eat, Drink, Shop

The MCA's store sells books, high-design home furnishings and jewellery in the same spirit as its galleries and packed with forward-looking art.

Paper Boy
1351 W Belmont Avenue, at N Southport Avenue, Lake View (773 388 8811). CTA Southport (Brown). **Open** noon-7pm Mon-Sat; 11am-5pm Sun. **Credit** MC, V. **Map** p309 D3.
The best selection of cards in town, plus stationery, wedding invites and other funky impulse items. Owned by the man behind Uncle Fun (*see p186*).

Sports World
3555 N Clark Street, at W Addison Street, Lake View: Wrigleyville (773 472 7701/www.cubworld.com). CTA Addison (Red). **Open** 9am-6pm daily; later on Cubs night games. **Credit** AmEx, DC, Disc, MC, V. **Map** p309 E1.
This shop does most of its trade on the 81 days each year the Cubs play: it's right by Wrigley Field. Come here for baseball shirts, caps, sweats and more.

Symphony Store
220 S Michigan Avenue, at E Adams Street, the Loop (312 294 3345). CTA Adams (Brown, Green, Orange, Purple). **Open** 10am-6.30pm Mon-Sat; 11am-6pm Sun; later on concert nights. **Credit** AmEx, DC, Disc, MC, V. **Map** p305 J12.
Impress the folks back home with some high-culture souvenirs from the world-renowned CSO, including a full range of recordings, posters, books and gifts.

Waxman Candles
3044 N Lincoln Avenue, at W Belmont Avenue, Lake View (773 929 3000/www.waxmancandles.com). CTA Southport (Brown). **Open** 11am-7pm Mon-Wed, Fri-Sun; 11am-8pm Thur. **Credit** AmEx, Disc, MC, V. **Map** p309 D2.
This shop sells candles of all shapes, colours and sizes: you can see them being made out back.

Health & beauty

Beauty products

Bravco Beauty Shop
43 E Oak Street, at N State Street, Gold Coast (312 943 4305). CTA Chicago (Red). **Open** 9am-6.30pm Mon-Wed, Fri, Sat; 9am-8pm Thur; 10am-5pm Sun. **No credit cards. Map** p306 H9.
A phenomenal amount of beauty goods are sold in this combination beauty shop and pharmacy, many at discounted prices. A girl's dream.

Endo-Exo Apothecary
2034 N Halsted Street, at W Armitage Avenue, Lincoln Park (773 525 0500/www.endoexo.com). CTA Armitage (Brown, Purple). **Open** 11am-7pm Mon-Thur; 11am-8pm Fri; 10am-6pm Sat; 11am-5pm Sun. **Credit** AmEx, Disc, MC, V. **Map** p308 F6.
Grab new skincare products and cosmetics (look for the Sundari and Poole lines), get your make-up done by a pro, and check out the vintage compacts.

Sasabee
1849 W North Avenue, at N Damen Avenue, Wicker Park/Bucktown (773 862 7740/www.sasabee.com). CTA Damen (Blue). **Open** noon-7pm Mon, Wed-Fri; 10am-7pm Sat; noon-5pm Sun. **Credit** AmEx, MC, V. **Map** p310 B7.
Girly-girl beauty products from abroad displayed in industrial environs. Prices are phenomenally steep.

Beauty services & spas

Kiva
196 E Pearson Street, at N Mies van der Rohe Way, Near North (312 840 8120/www.kivakiva.com). CTA Chicago (Red). **Open** 10am-5pm Mon, Sun; 10am-8pm Tue, Wed; 9am-9pm Thur; 9am-8pm Fri; 9am-6pm Sat. **Credit** Disc, MC, V. **Map** p306 J9.
One of the most luxurious spas in the city, Kiva's offerings include the Milk Paraffin Cocoon, an hour-long, head-to-toe heat and moisture treatment; and heavenly Ayurvedic treatments.

Salon & Spa Blue
2915 N Sheffield Avenue, at W George Street, Lake View (773 525 2583/www.salonblue.com). CTA Diversey (Brown, Purple). **Open** *Salon* 9am-7.30pm Tue, Wed; noon-7pm Thur; 10am-5pm Fri; 9am-6pm Sat; noon-6pm Sun. *Spa* call for details. **Credit** MC, V. **Map** p309 E3.
Hipsters, celebrities and edgy socialites go to Salon Blue. In addition to haircuts, the spa offers feelgood packages, including scalp treatments, rejuvenation massages, and hand and foot wraps.

Spa & Fitness Center at the Four Seasons
120 E Delaware Place, at N Michigan Avenue, Near North (312 280 8800/www.fourseasons.com/chicagofs). CTA Chicago (Red). **Open** 8am-8pm daily. **Credit** AmEx, DC, Disc, MC, V. **Map** p306 J9.
This pamper palace claims to indulge the five senses by providing massage, aromatherapy, nourishing elixirs and soothing music. There's a fitness club with weight training, steam rooms and a pool.

Urban Oasis
12 W Maple Street, at N State Street, Gold Coast (312 587 3500/www.urban-oasis.com). CTA Clark/Division (Red). **Open** noon-8pm Mon; 10am-8pm Tue-Thur; 9am-7pm Fri; 9am-5pm Sat; noon-5pm Sun. **Credit** AmEx, Disc, MC, V. **Map** p306 H9.
Every massage on the map is offered at Urban Oasis, including reflexology, deep tissue, sport, incense, hot stone and pregnancy massages. The Oasis salon also offers aromatherapy wraps and yoga classes.

Hairdressers

Studio 110
110 E Delaware Place, at N Michigan Avenue, Near North (312 337 6411/www.studio-110.com). CTA Chicago (Red). **Open** 10am-7pm Mon; 9am-8pm Tue-Sat; 10am-7pm Sun. **Credit**, MC, V. **Map** p306 J9.

This all-purpose salon tries hard to up the hip quotient with Warhol prints on the wall and a mirror ball on the ceiling. The cuts are good, too, starting around $50.

Truefitt & Hill
900 N Michigan Mall, 900 N Michigan Avenue, at E Walton Street, Near North (312 337 2525). CTA Chicago (Red). **Open** 7.30am-7pm Mon-Sat; 7.30am-6pm Sun. **Credit** AmEx, DC, Disc, MC, V. **Map** p306 J9.
A Brit classic, Truefitt offers cuts and shaves, as well as manicures, pedicures, beard trims, steam facials and shoe shines. Only the prices are modern.

Visionaries
357 W Chicago Avenue, at N Orleans Street, Near North (312 337 4700/www.visionarieschicago.com). CTA Chicago (Brown, Purple). **Open** 10am-7pm Wed-Fri; 9am-5pm Sat, Sun. **Credit** AmEx, MC, V. **Map** p306 G10.
A downtown mecca for African-American clients, Visionaries does it all, from natural styles, braids and locks, to relaxed 'dos or spiral cuts.

Malls
See p169 **Mall talk**.

Markets

Antiques & flea markets
On the third or fourth Sunday of the month, head to **Sandwich** (773 227 4464), about 60 miles (97 kilometres) west of Chicago. From May to October, it attracts about 600 dealers and hundreds of collectors. Less prestigious but still fun is the indoor **Kane County Flea Market** (630 377 2252), held on the first weekend of the month in the town of St Charles. For the **Maxwell Street Market**, *see p110*.

Farmers' markets
About two dozen farmers' markets are held in parks and parking lots from June to September. Downtown, try **Federal Plaza** (Tuesday) and **Daley Plaza** (Thursday). For the largely organic **Chicago Green City Market**, held in the park just north of the Chicago Historical Society, *see p180* **To market, to market**.

Music
The pick of the chains in town are the **Virgin Megastore** (540 N Michigan Avenue, Near North; 312 645 9300) and **Tower Records** (214 S Wabash Avenue, the Loop; 312 663 0660; 2301 N Clark Street, Lincoln Park; 773 477 5994). In the **Chicago Music Mart** (333 S State Street, the Loop), you can browse a dozen stores selling pianos, drums, sheet music and other goods.

Dr Wax
2523 N Clark Street, at W Wrightwood Avenue, Lincoln Park (773 784 3333/www.drwax.com). CTA Fullerton (Brown, Purple, Red)/22 bus. **Open** 11am-7pm Mon-Sat; 11am-6pm Sun. **Credit** AmEx, Disc, MC, V. **Map** p307 H8.
A selection of alternative, jazz, soul and imports on CD and vinyl, both new and used.
Branches: throughout the city.

Evil Clown
3418 N Halsted Street, at W Roscoe Street, Lake View: Wrigleyville (773 472 4761/www.evilclowncd.com). CTA Addison (Red). **Open** noon-10pm Mon-Fri; 11am-9pm Sat; noon-7pm Sun. **Credit** AmEx, MC, V. **Map** p309 F2.
Listen on headphones before you buy at this tidy little indie rock shop in Lake View. It stocks CDs only, both new and second-hand.

Gramophone Records
2663 N Clark Street, at W Drummond Place, Lincoln Park (773 472 3683/www.gramophonerecords.com). CTA Diversey (Brown, Purple). **Open** 11am-9pm Mon-Fri; 10.30am-8.30pm Sat; noon-6pm Sun. **Credit** AmEx, Disc, MC, V. **Map** p308 F4.
Club DJs shop at this legendary Lincoln Park store, on vinyl mix cassettes and some CDs. Those not au fait with the scene might feel a bit out of their depth.

Hear Music
932 N Rush Street, at E Walton Place, Gold Coast (312 951 0242). CTA Chicago (Red). **Open** 10am-10pm daily. **Credit** AmEx, DC, MC, V. **Map** p306 H9.
The selection at this Starbucks-owned shop covers a sweep of genres, all of which can be previewed before you buy. The store's 'Artist Choice' selections allow customers to survey musicians' picks.

Jazz Record Mart
444 N Wabash Street, at E Illinois Street, Near North (312 222 1467/www.jazzmart.com). CTA Grand (Red). **Open** 10am-8pm Mon-Sat; noon-5pm Sun. **Credit** AmEx, Disc, MC, V. **Map** p306 H10.
Knowledgeable staff lead shoppers through what is claimed to be the world's largest inventory of jazz and blues records. There's also gospel, R&B and world music, from the latest issues on Delmark Records (owned by the store's proprietor) to old 78s.

Reckless Records
1532 N Milwaukee Avenue, at N Damen Avenue, Wicker Park (773 235 3727/www.reckless.com). CTA Damen (Blue). **Open** 10am-10pm Mon-Sat; 10am-8pm Sun. **Credit** AmEx, Disc, MC, V. **Map** p310 B9.
Knowledgeable staff tend to stay behind the long counter at this indie haven. Helpful when asked, employees let you listen to CDs before you buy.
Branch: 3157 N Broadway Street, Lake View (773 404 5080).

Opticians
Both **Marshall Field's** and **Carson Pirie Scott** (for both, *see p168*) have optical counters.

Shops by area

The Loop

Art Institute Museum Shop (Gifts & souvenirs, *p181*); **Carson Pirie Scott** (Department stores, *p168*); **Chicago Architecture Foundation Shop & Tour Center** (Gifts & souvenirs, *p181*); **Flower Bucket Shop** (Flowers & garden supplies, *p178*); **Gallery 37 Store** (Gifts & souvenirs, *p181*); **Marshall Field's** (Department stores, *p168*); **Prairie Avenue Bookshop** (Books, *p167*); **The Savvy Traveller** (Books; *p167*); **Sears** (Department stores, *p168*); **Symphony Store** (Gifts & souvenirs, *p182*); **Toys R Us** (Toys, *p186*).

Near North

Abraham Lincoln Book Shop (Books, *p166*); **Afterwords New & Used Books** (Books, *p167*); **American Girl Place** (Toys, *p186*); **L'Appetito** (Food & drink; *p179*); **Betsey Johnson** (Fashion, *p175*); **Bibabis** (Fashion, *p172*); **Bloomingdale's** (Department stores, *p168*); **Borders Books & Music** (Books, *p166*); **Chicago Place** (*Box* Mall talk, *p169*); **City of Chicago Store** (Gifts & souvenirs, *p181*); **Daisy Shop** (Fashion, *p175*); **Donald J Pliner** (Fashion, *p173*); **FAO Schwarz** (Toys, *p186*); **Fox & Obel** (Food & drink, *p179*); **Garrett Popcorn Shop** (Food & drink, *p179*); **Jay Robert's Antique Warehouse** (Antiques, *p165*); **Jazz Record Mart** (Music, *p183*); **June Blaker** (Fashion, *p176*); **Kenneth Cole** (Fashion, *p173*); **Kiva** (Health & beauty, *p182*); **Linda Campisano Millinery** (Fashion accessories, *p177*); **Lord & Taylor** (Department stores, *p168*); **Museum of Contemporary Art Store** (Gifts & souvenirs, *p181*); **Neiman Marcus** (Department stores, *p168*); **Niketown** (Sport, *p186*); **900 N Michigan Avenue** (*Box* Mall talk, *p169*);

Nordstrom (Department stores, *p168*); **Paper Source** (Art supplies, *p165*); **Pearl Art & Craft Supplies** (Art supplies, *p165*); **Push Skateboarding** (Sport, *p186*); **Rochester Big & Tall Men's Clothing** (Fashion, *p174*); **Saks Fifth Avenue** (Department stores, *p168*); **Shops at North Bridge** (*Box* Mall Talk; *p169*); **Spa & Fitness Center at the Four Seasons** (Health & beauty, *p182*); **Sportmart** (Sport, *p186*); **Studio 110** (Health & beauty, *p182*); **Tall Girl** (Fashion, *p174*); **Tiffany & Co** (Fashion accessories *p178*); **Truefitt & Hill** (Health & beauty, *p183*); **United Audio Centers** (Electronics, *p171*); **Visionaries** (Health & beauty, *p183*); **Vogue Fabrics** (Fabrics & trimmings; *see p171*); **Vosges Haut-Chocolat** (Food & drink, *p179*); **Walgreens** (Pharmacies, *p185*); **Water Tower Place** (*Box* Mall talk, *p169*).

Gold Coast

Anthropologie (Fashion, *p175*); **Barnes & Noble** (Books, *p165*); **Barney's New York** (Department stores, *p168*); **Bravco Beauty Shop** (Health & beauty; *p182*); **Childen in Paradise Bookstore** (Books, *p167*); **Diesel** (Fashion, *p174*); **Fitigues** (Fashion, *p172*); **G'bani** (Fashion, *p174*); **Harry's Gold Coast Shoe Repair** (Fashion, *p172*); **Hear Music** (Music, *p183*); **House of Glunz** (Food & drink, *p180*); **Jewel Food Stores** (Food & drink, *p180*); **Kate Spade** (Fashion accessories, *p177*); **Madison & Friends** (Fashion, *p171*); **Sofie** (Fashion, *p176*); **Solomon-Cooper Drugs** (Pharmacies, *p185*); **Sun King Optical** (Opticians, *p184*); **Tender Buttons** (Fabrics & trimmings, *p171*); **Treasure Island** (Food & drink, *p180*); **Urban Oasis** (Health & beauty, *p182*); **Urban Outfitters** (Fashion; *p174*).

Eye Want

1543 N Milwaukee Avenue, at N Damen Avenue, Wicker Park (773 782 1744). CTA Damen (Blue). Open noon-7pm Mon-Sat. **Credit** AmEx, Disc, MC, V. **Map** p310 B7.

The styles at this laid-back store are made for fashionistas. There's an optometrist on site.

Sun King Optical

44 E Chicago Avenue, at N Wabash Avenue, Near North (312 649 9110/www.sunkingoptical.com). CTA Chicago (Red). Open 11am-7pm Mon, Tue, Thur; 11am-6pm Fri; 10am-6pm Sat; noon-5pm Sun. **Credit** AmEx, MC, V. **Map** p306 H10.

Prescription glasses, sunglasses, contacts and eye examinations are all available at this central store.

For **Merz Apothecary**, *see p177* **Doctors' orders**.

Osco Drug

3101 N Clark Street, at W Barry Avenue, Lake View (1-888 443 5701/773 477 1967/ www.jewelosco.com). CTA (Brown, Purple, Red). Open 7am-midnight daily. **Credit** AmEx, Disc, MC, V. **Map** p309 F3.

Like **Walgreens** (*see p185*), Osco Drug is more or less everywhere, including in **Jewel** grocery stores (*see p179*). The other vaguely central 24-hour branch is at 2940 N Ashland Avenue in Lake View (773 348 4156).

Eat, Drink, Shop

Old Town

Barbara's Bookstore (Books, *p165*); **Etre** (Fashion, *p176*); **Green** (Flowers & garden supplies, *p181*); **Sam's Wine & Spirits** (Food & drink, *p180*); **Stanley's Fruits & Vegetables** (Food & drink, *p179*).

Lincoln Park

Act 1 Bookstore (Books, *p166*); **Active Endeavors** (Sport, *p185*); **Active Kids** (Fashion, *p171*); **Ancient Echoes** (Gifts & souvenirs, *p181*); **Ani Afshar** (Fashion accessories, *p178*); **Cynthia Rowley** (Fashion, *p172*); **Davis For Men** (Fashion, *p173*); **Dr Wax** (Music, *p183*); **Endo-Exo Apothecary** (Health & beauty, *p182*); **Gramophone Records** (Music, *p183*); **Isabella Fine Lingerie** (Fashion, *p173*); **Jolie Joli** (Fashion, *p176*); **Lori's Designer Shoes** (Fashion, *p174*); **Su-Zen Boutique** (Fashion, *p173*); **Tribeca** (Fashion, *p176*); **Trousseau** (Fashion, *p173*); **Untitled** (Fashion, *p174*).

Lake View & Wrigleyville

The Alley (Fashion, *p175*); **Bad Boys** (Fashion, *p173*); **Beatnix** (Fashion, *p174*); **Century Shopping Center** (*Box* Mall talk, *p169*); **Coffee & Tea Exchange** (Food & drink, *p179*); **Evil Clown** (Music, *p183*); **Flashy Trash** (Fashion, *p174*); **Gibson Couture Cleaners** (Fashion, *p171*); **Hollywood Mirror** (Fashion, *p175*); **ID** (Furniture & home accessories, *p181*); **Male Hide Leathers** (Fashion, *p173*); **Osco Drug** (Pharmacies, *p184*); **Pleasure Chest** (Fashion, *p173*); **Salon & Spa Blue** (Health & beauty, *p182*); **Spare Parts** (Fashion accessories, *p177*); **Sports World** (Gifts & souvenirs, *p182*); **Paper Boy** (Gifts & souvenirs, *p182*); **Strange Cargo** (Fashion, *p175*); **Unabridged**

Bookstore (Books, *p166*); **Uncle Fun** (Toys, *p186*); **Waxman Candles** (Gifts & souvenirs, *p182*); **Whole Foods Market** (Food & drink, *p179*); **Wisteria** (Fashion, *p175*).

Further North

Broadway Antiques Market (Antiques, *p165*); **Hats Plus** (Fashion accessories, *p176*); **Lutz Continental Café** (Food & drink, *p178*); **Merz Apothecary** (Health & beauty; *p177*); **Paris Pastries** (Food & drink, *p178*); **Quake** (Toys, *p186*); **Swedish Bakery** (Food & drink, *p179*).

West Town & Far West Side

Alcala's Western Wear (Fashion, *p174*); **Blommer's Chocolate Factory** (Food & drink, *p179*); **Conte di Savoia** (Food & drink, *p179*); **Dominick's Finer Foods** (Food & drink, *p180*); **Salvage One** (Antiques, *p165*); **Taköhl Design** (Fashion accessories, *p178*).

Wicker Park & Bucktown

Eye Want (Opticians, *p184*); **John Fluevog** (Fashion; *p174*); **Lille** (Furniture & home accessories, *p181*); **Modern Times** (Antiques, *p165*); **Noir** (Fashion, *p176*); **Occult Bookstore** (Books, *p167*); **Orange Skin** (Furniture & home accessories, *p181*); **P.45** (Fashion, *p176*); **Pagoda Red** (Antiques, *p165*); **Quimby's Bookstore** (Books, *p167*); **Reckless Records** (Music, *p183*); **Robin Richman** (Fashion, *p172*); **Sasabee** (Health & beauty, *p182*); **Silver Room** (Fashion accessories, *p177*); **Softcore** (Fashion, *p173*).

South Side & Hyde Park

Fishman's Fabrics (Fabrics & trimmings, *p171*); **Powells** (Books, *p167*); **Seminary Cooperative Bookstore** (Books, *p166*); **Ten Ren Tea & Ginseng Co** (Food & drink, *p179*).

Eat, Drink, Shop

Solomon-Cooper Drugs
1051 N Rush Street, at E Cedar Street, Gold Coast (312 944 3577/www.solomoncooper.com). CTA Clark/Division (Red). **Open** 8am-8pm Mon-Fri; 9am-6pm Sat; 9am-3pm Sun. **Credit** AmEx, Disc, MC, V. **Map** p306 H9.
An independent pharmacy. Expect to pay a bit more, but you'll get great service in return.

Walgreens
757 N Michigan Avenue, at E Chicago Avenue, Near North (1-800 925 4733/312 664 8686). CTA Chicago (Red). **Open** 24hrs daily. **Credit** AmEx, Disc, MC, V. **Map** p304 J10.
Dozens of Chicago locations. There's another 24-hour store at 641 N Clark Street (312 587 1416).

Sport

See also p233.

Active Endeavors
935 W Armitage Avenue, at N Sheffield Avenue, Lincoln Park (773 281 8100/ www.activeendeavors.com). CTA Armitage (Brown, Purple). **Open** 10am-6pm Mon-Fri; 10am-5pm Sat; noon-5pm Sun. **Credit** AmEx, Disc, MC, V. **Map** p308 E6.
Find outdoor apparel from Patagonia, North Face, Moonstone and others, including tents, climbing gear, travel books, plus canoes and kayaks. **Branch**: Shops at North Bridge, 520 N Michigan Avenue, Near North (312 822 0600).

For wildly expensive but still-fashionable sneakers, head to **Niketown**.

Niketown

669 N Michigan Avenue, at E Huron Street, Near North (312 642 6363/www.nike.com). CTA Chicago (Red). **Open** 10am-7pm Mon-Fri; 9.30am-6pm Sat; 11am-6pm Sun. **Credit** AmEx, DC, MC, V. **Map** p306 J10.
Besides all the shoes and clothes, this multistoreyed temple to the swoosh has a basketball half-court, an aquarium and a video theatre showing commercials featuring His Airness and other Nike pitch people.

Push Skateboarding

40 E Chicago Avenue, at N Wabash Avenue, Near North (312 573 9996). CTA Chicago (Red). **Open** noon-7pm Tue-Sat; noon-5pm Sun. **Credit** AmEx, DC, MC, V. **Map** p306 H10.
Sure to please those tweenaged skate rats, this subterranean store stocks boards, T-shirts and has, like, some totally cool stickers.

Sportmart

620 N LaSalle Street, at W Ontario Street, Near North (312 337 6151/www.sportmart.com). CTA Grand (Red). **Open** 9.30am-9.30pm Mon-Fri; 9am-9pm Sat; 10am-7pm Sun. **Credit** AmEx, Disc, MC, V. **Map** p306 H10.
This eight-storey flagship store has entire floors given over to every possible athletic pursuit (except fishing). Busloads of tourists create a frenzy for the pro sports memorabilia.
Branch: 3134 N Clark Street, Lake View (773 871 8501).

Toys

See also p169 **Mall talk** for the **Lego Shop**.

American Girl Place

111 E Chicago Avenue, at N Michigan Avenue, Near North (887 247 5223/www.americangirl.com). CTA Chicago (Red). **Open** 10am-7pm Mon-Wed, Sun; 10am-9pm Thur, Fri; 9.30am-9pm Sat; 9.30am-7pm Sun. **Credit** AmEx, Disc, MC, V. **Map** p306 J10.

A one-stop source for all things American Girl: outfits, books, accessories and furniture for the dolls. Horribly disturbing or positively enchanting? You decide. *See p196* **Hello dolly**.

FAO Schwarz

840 N Michigan Avenue, at E Pearson Street, Near North (312 587 5000). CTA Chicago (Red). **Open** 10am-7pm Mon-Thur; 10am-8pm Fri, Sat; 11am-7pm Sun. **Credit** AmEx, DC, MC, V.
A magnificent, wildly tempting (for adults as well as kids) array of juvenilia that's almost a tourist attraction in its own right. Bring a credit card.

Quake

4628 N Lincoln Avenue, at W Eastwood Avenue, Uptown (773 878 4288). CTA Lawrence (Red). **Open** 1-6pm Wed, Thur; 1-9pm Fri; noon-9pm Sat; noon-5pm Sun. **Credit** MC, V.
The place to find that elusive Mystery Date game or that *Nightmare Before Christmas* figurine, along with retro lunchboxes, *Star Wars* swag and board games from the 1960s and '70s.

Toys R Us

10 S State Street, at W Madison Street, the Loop (312 857 0667/www.toysrus.com). CTA Madison (Brown, Green, Orange, Purple) or Monroe (Blue, Red). **Open** 9.30am-7pm Mon-Wed, Fri-Sun; 9.30am-7pm Thur. **Credit** AmEx, DC, Disc, MC, V. **Map** p305 H12.
A good bet on a rainy day. As well as toys (natch), it also has a Kids R Us clothing shop on the lower level.

Uncle Fun

1338 W Belmont Avenue, at N Southport Avenue, Lake View (773 477 8223/www.unclefunchicago.com). CTA Belmont (Brown, Purple, Red). **Open** noon-7pm Wed-Fri; 11am-7pm Sat; 11am-5pm Sun. **Credit** AmEx, MC, V. **Map** p309 D2.
Kids will love digging through drawers jammed full of plastic squirt cameras, fake barf and the like, all at quite reasonable prices.

Arts & Entertainment

By Season

Flower shows, food festivals, block parties and days of the dead: bring a diary and keep it handy to make sure you don't miss out.

Chicago is frequently described as a city of neighbourhoods. That might sound daft – what city isn't? – but it's abnormally true here, and nowhere more obvious than in the giddy procession of festivals and fairs that clog the city's social calendar. Some summer weekends it's hard to go three blocks without running into a knot of banners, booths and volunteers asking ten bucks for a wristband. But that doesn't mean that Chicago takes the rest of the year off from celebrating everything worth celebrating.

Not even the winters here – once hideous, recently mild – can stop the locals. In fact, the city seems to have taken winter as a challenge to come up with something – anything! – to do, as a smattering of cold-weather film festivals (see p200) lead into pre-holiday shopping calls to arms. Once the snow melts, however, things get serious, with the St Patrick's Day Parade kicking off the town's six-month season of outdoor gatherings organised around the basic principle of drinking beer from plastic cups.

In summer, the Mayor's Office of Special Events proves its worth. Grant Park gets trodden into dirt by the well-attended music festivals (see p225) and the **Taste of Chicago** (see p190). Street festivals focus on beers and bands, with book and art fairs appeasing culture vultures. Autumn cools things off with the **Chicago International Film Festival** (see p200) and the **Day of the Dead** (see p192). But drinkers need not quail at the falling leaves: there's still **Oktoberfest** (see p191)…

INFORMATION

Be sure to contact the hosting organisation, the **Mayor's Office of Special Events** (312 744 3315/www.cityofchicago.org/specialevents) or the **Chicago Office of Tourism** (312 744 2400/www.cityofchicago.org/tourism) for information: some existing festivities may change and many new ones are sure to appear through the year. The Chicago Office of Tourism's quarterly guide to seasonal events and celebrations, available from its branches at the **Chicago Water Works** and the **Chicago Cultural Center** (for both, see p290), may prove invaluable, with the Friday editions of the *Chicago Tribune* and the *Chicago Sun-Times* plugging gaps with pull-out events guides.

Spring

Other events include two March events on Navy Pier: the **Chicago Garden & Flower Show** (312 321 0077/www.chicagoflower.com), and **Spring Fling**, a family-oriented fun weekend (312 595 7437/www.navypier.com).

Spring & Easter Flower Show

Garfield Park Conservatory, 300 N Central Park Boulevard, at N Lake Street, West Side (312 746 5100). CTA Kedzie (Green) or Kedzie-Holman (Blue). **Date** Feb-June. **Map** p308 G5.
Lincoln Park Conservatory and the Garfield Park Conservatory boast a collage of the first blooms to escape the icy hold of winter. The opening reception is held at Garfield Park, and refreshments, children's activities and music are provided throughout the multi-month run (which actually starts in February, making its 'Spring' tag somewhat disingenuous).

St Patrick's Day

Downtown: Columbus Drive, from E Balbo Drive to E Monroe Street, the Loop (312 744 3315). CTA Adams (Brown, Green, Orange, Purple) or Jackson (Red). **Date** Sat near 17 Mar. **Map** p305 H11-13.
At the Downtown Parade, balloons are ushered through town by verdant floats, the Chicago River is dyed green, and festive Irish (plus many more Irish-ish) locals get trashed. Inevitably, any pub with Guinness duly proclaims itself the spiritual home of the party.

The best Events

For happy holidays
Magnificent Mile Lights Festival. *See p192.*

For getting drunk in public
St Patrick's Day Parade. *See p188.*

For the very, very fit
Chicago Marathon. *See p191.*

For a date
Ravinia Festival. *See p226.*

For taking to the air
Mayor Daley's Kids & Kites Festival. *See p189.*

That's one wacky optometrist's prescription. **Hallowe'en Celebrations**; *see p190.*

A more authentically emerald celebration can be enjoyed on the South Side, with a rougher, tougher parade down S Western Avenue from 103rd to 115th. The parties are stronger here, too. The South Side Parade takes place on the Sunday on or before 17 March; call 773 239 7755 for information.

Mayor Daley's Kids & Kites Festival

Montrose Harbor, North Side; Museum of Science & Industry, Hyde Park (312 744 3315/ www.cityofchicago/specialevents). **Date** Apr (Montrose Harbor) & Sept (MSI).
Kitefest offers classes on designing, constructing and (of course) flying kites. Skilled flyers perform displays of aerial acrobatics on the lawn, while young 'uns howl as they get their strings tangled up.

Summer

Neighborhood Summer Festivals

Various locations (312 744 3315). **Date** May-Oct.
Chicago's neighbourhoods take it in turns to celebrate during summer. Streets are blocked off for the weekend and vendors provide meals of the deep-fried or between-the-bun variety. Musicians of varying talent – alt-rock hero Bob Mould to sad-ass Grateful Dead cover bands – provide entertainment. Entry is sometimes steep, but many neighbourhoods turn cash over to charity or invest it in the community, so quit grumbling. A schedule can be obtained from the Mayor's Office of Special Events.

Printer's Row Book Fair

S Dearborn Street, between W Congress Parkway & W Polk Street, South Loop (312 987 9896/ www.printersrowbookfair.org). CTA Harrison (Red) or LaSalle (Blue). **Date** 1st wknd in June. **Map** p304 H13.

Printer's Row, once the wellspring of the city's publishing prosperity, rekindles its heritage once a year by offering a myriad of new and used books over a weekend in the South Loop. Over 170 of the nation's most diverse booksellers are represented. Authors give readings and signing.

Puppetropolis

Various locations (312 744 3315). **Date** June.
A fairly new and surprisingly high-profile 11-day festival of creepy but fun marionettes getting their strings pulled by avant-theatre types at a number of Chicago locations. The inaugural 2001 fest started with a big Julie Taymor show at the Field Museum.

Natsu Matsuri

Buddhist Temple of Chicago, 1151 W Leland Avenue, at N Broadway, North Side (773 334 4661/ www.budtempchi.org/natsumatsuri.html). CTA Lawrence (Purple, Red). **Date** last wknd in June.
This celebration features a variety of Japanese food, music, dance, arts and crafts. Among crowd favourites are a martial arts exhibition, a traditional tea ceremony and a haiku contest. Due to temple renovations, a smaller than usual festival was planned for summer 2002, with things due to return to normal for 2003.

Andersonville Midsommerfest

N Clark Street, between W Foster Avenue & W Berwyn Street, North Side (773 665 4682/773 728 2995/www.starevents.com). CTA Berwyn (Purple, Red). **Date** June.
Once the home of Chicago's prominent Swedish community, the business district of Clark in Andersonville is sequestered by maypole dancers, Swedes in colourful costumes and general revelry, including lots of music, during this fun festival.

Taste of Chicago

*Grant Park, the Loop (312 744 3315/
www.cityofchicago.org). CTA Adams (Brown, Green,
Orange, Purple) or Monroe (Red).* **Date** late June-
early July. **Map** p304-5 J11-14.

Chicago is home to about 5,000 restaurants, the cream
of which are represented at this ten-day, three million-
visitor food fair. Entry is free; instead, pay for tickets
to the various booths. Go early, as weekend and
evening crowds mean finding a seat is tricky.

Independence Day Fireworks

*Grant Park, the Loop (312 744 3315). CTA Adams
(Brown, Green, Orange, Purple) or Monroe (Red).*
Date 3 July. **Map** p304-5 J11-14.

Huge crowds turn out the day before Independence
Day to sway to live bands, then turn their eyes to
the sky for a spectacular fireworks display that manages to diminish the reach of the skyline. The display is best viewed from the environs of Grant Park
and along the lakefront. There are more festivities
and fireworks the next day and night at Navy Pier.

Race to Mackinac

*Monroe Harbor, Lake Michigan, 400 E Monroe,
the Loop (Chicago Yacht Club 312 861 7777/
www.chicagoyachtclub.org). CTA Adams (Brown,
Green, Orange, Purple).* **Date** late July. **Map** p305 K12.

The world's largest freshwater yacht race begins at
Monroe Harbor and ends 333 miles (536km) later at
Mackinac Island, Michigan. The party the preced-
ing night, open to the public, sees sailors spout their
lore and reverence for the regatta.

Sheffield Garden Walk

*N Sheffield Avenue, at W Webster Avenue, Lincoln
Park (773 929 9255/www.sheffieldfestivals.org).
CTA Armitage (Brown, Purple).* **Date** July. **Map**
p308 E5.

Lincoln Park's genteel homes open their gates to
admirers, on what is a charming way to spend a
summer's day. Garden curators linger, primed with
advice and pride. A peaceful retreat from the block
party's more boisterous elements.

World's Largest Block Party

*S Des Plaines Street from W Madison Street to W
Adams Street, W Monroe Street from N Jefferson
Street to I-94, West Side (312 648 1590/
www.worldslargestblockparty.com). CTA Clinton
(Green), Quincy (Brown, Orange, Purple) or
Washington (Brown, Orange, Purple).* **Date** late July.

A big drunken fundraiser for Old St Patrick's
Church, this is 48 hours of pricey over-21 revelry in
the streets around it. Those on the hunt should note
that in almost two decades of operation, the party
has been the meeting place for over 60 couples who
later married. Tickets are expensive, but the food is
great and the bluesy street fair rockers above par.

Venetian Night

*Lake Michigan, from the Adler Planetarium,
Museum Campus to Monroe Harbor, the Loop
(312 744 3315). CTA Adams (Brown, Green,*

The **Chicago Marathon**. *See p191.*

*Orange, Purple), Harrison (Red), Jackson (Red),
Madison (Brown, Green, Orange, Purple), Monroe
(Red), Roosevelt/State (Red), Roosevelt/Wabash
(Green, Orange).* **Date** late July. **Map** p304-5 K12-14.

Boat owners celebrate their water-borne community
by adorning their crafts with lights and parading
them along a waterfront packed with onlookers at
twilight. A brilliant fireworks display concludes it.

Bud Billiken Day Parade & Picnic

*From 39th Street, at S King Drive, to Washington
Park, at E 51st Street, Hyde Park (312 744 3315).
CTA 51st Street (Green) or Indiana (Green).* **Date**
2nd Sat in Aug. **Map** p311 X16.

This African-American parade is the third largest in
the nation. The patron, Bud Billiken, is associated
with an ancient Chinese guardian angel of children.
The parade begins on 39th Street and King Drive and
proceeds south to Washington Park, where a barbecue concludes the event.

Chicago Carifete

*Around Hyde Park, centred around E 59th Street
(773 509 5079). CTA Garfield (Green)/Metra 59th
Street.* **Date** late Aug. **Map** p311.

This celebration of Caribbean culture includes a
lively masquerade procession through the streets of
Hyde Park. Costumed bands with steel drummers
keep the parade in stride, while Caribbean cuisine
and stalls offering cultural wares are also on hand.

Autumn

Look out, too, for the three-week **Hallowe'en
Celebrations**, organised by the City of
Chicago and fronted by the suitably scary
Mayor Daley (www.ci.chi.il.us/SpecialEvents).

Top guns

Ever since the halcyon days of biplanes and Lucky Lindbergh, the American attitude to planes has been something along the lines of: why bother having them if you can't watch them rip by a couple of feet over your head at the speed of sound? Air shows have been a summertime staple in the US for as long as there have been planes: any self-respecting state fair or Fourth of July celebration has one in its repertoire. Often these shows consist of repainted cropdusters performing desultory tricks, or the Confederate Air Force flying painstakingly rebuilt World War II military planes at torpidly slow speeds.

However, the US military also likes to show off on the home front and is willing to lend out its arsenal of high-tech planes and top-notch pilots for the **Chicago Air and Water Show** (312 744 3315), the oldest and largest free air show in the country. Over a Saturday and Sunday in mid August, the lakefront around the North Avenue Beach, from Oak Street up to Diversey Parkway, is overwhelmed by two million people who come to gawp at planes doing amazing things at ridiculous speeds. A lucky few score places on the rooftops of nearby high-rises or in the Hancock Observatory deck; many more fill the 15,000 boats that crowd the lake itself. Everyone else contents themselves with folding chairs on the beach.

Whether or not you're discomfited by such a brash, balls-out display of military might, it's one hell of a sight. Genuine enthusiasts and whooping patriots thrill to the Navy and

Air Force's displays of multi-million-dollar weapons (from the slim and graceful F-18 Hornets to bulky killing machines such as the A-10 'Warthog'), while sporting types marvel at the water-ski enthusiasts, who dance with a watery death out on the waves. But the highlight of the show is the Air Force's Thunderbirds, a team of pilots who deal in death-defying acts of precision manoeuvring that never fail to send most people's hearts into their throats. A few civilian air teams also take to the skies to show off their skills.

In case all the festivities don't make it resemble a spectator sport, WBBM 780 radio provides play-by-play analysis from former pilot and official 'Voice of the Chicago Air and Water Show' Herb Hunter. But really, this is one event that's best seen and not heard.

German-American Festival
4700 N Lincoln Avenue, at W Leland Avenue, Far North (630 653 3018). CTA Western (Blue (N)). **Date** Sept.
Kind of a Diet Oktoberfest: it features all the ingredients of its Bavarian counterpart, with the notable exception of the stewed masses. The festival coincides with the Von Steuben Day Parade, which takes place in the Loop.

Berghoff's Oktoberfest
Berghoff, 17 W Adams Street, at S State Street, the Loop (312 427 3170/www.berghoff.com). CTA Adams (Brown, Green, Orange, Purple) or Monroe (Blue, Red). **Map** p305 H12.
A raucous but consistently popular street festival held in front of the restaurant of the same name in the Loop. This three-day beer fest comes complete with imported German bands, lots of men in those funny little shorts and Bratwursts galore within

stumbling distance. Just make sure you don't have to do anything important early the next morning.

Columbus Day Parade
Columbus Drive, from E Balbo Drive to E Monroe Street, the Loop (312 744 3315). CTA Adams (Brown, Green, Orange, Purple), Harrison (Red) or Jackson (Red). **Date** 2nd Mon in Oct. **Map** p305 H11-13.
A massive parade ensues on this national holiday, as locals celebrate in very jolly – and often alcohol-fuelled – fashion.

Chicago Marathon
Starts and finishes Grant Park, the Loop (312 904 9800/888 243 3344/www.chicagomarathon.com). **Date** Oct. **Credit** MC, V.
One of the flattest and, therefore, fastest marathons in the world, Chicago's annual 26-miler sees thousands of spectators take to the streets to cheer on the human river that circulates downtown.

Arts & Entertainment

The culture club

Aside from the events in this chapter, Chicago also stages a huge number of other cultural events, from music festivals to art fairs. We've listed these events in the relevant chapters under the heading **Chicago calendar**. So, for Chicago's art festivals, *see p209*; for local film festivals, *see p200*; for children's events, *see p195*; for gay and lesbian events, *see p215*; for music festivals, *see p225*; and for comedy festivals, *see p245*.

Day of the Dead

Mexican Fine Arts Center Museum, 1852 W 19th Street, at S Damen Avenue, Pilsen (312 738 1503/ www.mfacmchicago.org). CTA 18th Street (Blue). **Date** 1 Nov.

This celebration honours the gone-but-not-forgotten with exhibits at the Mexican Fine Arts Center Museum, in the heart of the largest Mexican community in the Midwest. Macabre but joyous art and other accoutrements are showcased. A procession kicks off at St Precopious School (1625 S Alport, at W 16th Street, Pilsen) and ends at the museum.

Christmas Around the World

Museum of Science & Industry, 5700 S Lake Shore Drive, at E 57th Street, Hyde Park (773 684 1414/ www.msichicago.org). Metra 59th Street. **Date** mid Nov-early Jan. **Map** p311 Z17.

A survey of the ways different communities celebrate the winter fills up the MSI over the festive season. Diwali, Hanukkah, Kwanzaa and Chinese New Year are among the festivals spotlighted, with local kids supplying decorations for Christmas trees. Theatre, dance and music shows jolly things along.

Magnificent Mile Lights Festival

N Michigan Avenue, from the Chicago River to E Oak Street, Near North (312 744 3315). CTA Chicago (Red) or Grand (Red). **Date** late Nov. **Map** p306 J9-11.

Millions of twinkling lights are laced along buildings and trees on Michigan Avenue, from Oak Street to the Chicago River. The lighting ceremony is followed by fireworks, with stage performances, a petting zoo and ice sculptures also on show. The crowds are dense, but the visual effect is sublime.

Holiday Tree Lighting Ceremony

Daley Plaza, W Washington Boulevard & N Dearborn Street, the Loop (312 744 3315). CTA Washington (Blue, Red). **Date** late Nov. **Map** p305 H12.

A giant 80ft (25m) tree constructed of numerous smaller evergreens is illuminated at Daley Plaza the night after Thanksgiving, usually around 4pm. Four giant toy sentries tower over onlookers and an enormous toy train roams the plaza's corner, adding to the skewed proportions of the whole event.

Two big trade fairs hit McCormick Place in winter: January's **Chicago Boat, RV & Outdoors Show** (1-888 322 9922) and February's **Chicago Auto Show** (630 495 2282/www.chicagoautoshow.com).

Christkindlmarket

Daley Plaza, W Washington Boulevard & N Dearborn Street, the Loop (312 644 2662/ www.christkindlmarket.com). CTA Washington (Blue, Red). **Date** late Nov-late Dec. **Map** p305 H12.

The German-American Chamber of Commerce converts Daley Plaza into a German-style market, with German food and art on offer.

Caroling to the Animals

2200 N Cannon Drive, at W Webster Avenue, Lincoln Park (312 742 2000/www.lpzoo.org). CTA Fullerton (Brown, Purple, Red). **Date** 1st Sun in Dec. **Map** p308 H5.

Hordes of visitors roam Lincoln Park Zoo singing carols to the bewildered inmates in what is, on the face of it, the strangest idea ever. Also around Christmas, the zoo runs **Zoolights**, a fabulously festive set of illuminations in the zoo's grounds.

Pre-Kwanzaa Celebration

South Shore Cultural Center, 7059 S Shore Drive, at E 71st Street, South Side (773 509 8080/312 747 2536). Metra South Shore. **Date** mid Dec.

Kwanzaa is an East African word meaning 'first fruits of the harvest' and is a time for celebration in traditional African society. The palatial South Shore Cultural Center marks the event with music, dance and a series of Afro-centric lectures and workshops.

Do-it-Yourself Messiah

Civic Opera House, 20 N Wacker Drive, at W Washington Boulevard, the Loop (312 294 3000). CTA Adams (Brown, Green, Orange, Purple). **Date** mid-late Dec. **Map** p305 J12.

A Chicago tradition, in which local have-a-go types join the Chicago Symphony Orchestra in a rousing rendition of Handel's classic. Hallelujah!

Black History Month

Various venues (312 642 4600). **Date** Feb.

Exhibitions on African-American heritage are rotated between Navy Pier, the Chicago Cultural Center and the Field Museum. The Chicago Historical Society also organises concerts, film screenings, theatrical productions, art shows, dance performances and lectures to complement the exhibitions.

Chinatown New Year Parade

Along S Wentworth Avenue, Chinatown (312 326 5320/www.chicagochinatown.org). CTA Cermak-Chinatown (Red). **Date** 1st Sun after Chinese New Year (early Feb).

Chinese New Year is celebrated with an array of festivities in Chinatown, such as parades, banquets, dances, music and a steady fanfare of firecrackers.

Children

Fast 'n' fatty food, glammy toy shops, whizz-bang attractions: take your pick...

No more virtual rollercoaster rides over at DisneyQuest. No more mac 'n' cheese at Michael Jordan's restaurant. Just what the heck is a kid supposed to do in this town? Worry not. Two kid-centric institutions may have shut up shop in the last couple of years, but Chicago still offers plenty of action for *les petits*.

If your kids are pre-teens, then start with the downtown area and bring a credit card. Near North is chock-a-block with shops selling all sorts of things kids will simply die if they don't get, themed restaurants with the bad food that kids amazingly find delicious and museums full of stuff they'll actually want to see (no matter that much of it is in the gift shop). And once you've done the rounds downtown, hit the 'hoods. Chicago's locales pride themselves on their cultural and ethnic diversity, so whether they're checking out the dragons at the South Side's Chinese New Year parade or taking in a polka on the North Side, children can get a dose of culture from every corner of the world.

Of course, Chicago's schizoid weather can be a factor in deciding what to do with the little darlings. During the summer, head for the lake front where they can build sandcastles, take a dip in the lake or pedal down the bike path. The city boasts more than 500 parks, so kids should find some sort of tot lot to their liking. But for a few months every year, temperatures plummet and it can be a challenge keeping the kids amused. Try one of the host of playhouses and dance companies that provide stellar

entertainment designed for children, or just wrap them (and yourself) up warm and go skating or tobogganing.

Teens, of course, are more unpredictable and often less easy to please. But shops are usually a safe bet, so bring out the plastic and head over to the downtown branches of **Urban Outfitters** (935 N Rush Street; 312 640 1919) and **Diesel** (*see p174*). Skate rats will dig **Push Skateboarding** (*see p186*), a subterranean skate shop with boards, T-shirts and some way-cool stickers. And every fashion-conscious high-schooler will enjoy the stores around Clark and Belmont, reached by taking the Red line to Belmont. Once a mecca for disenfranchised punkers, the area is now popular with teens looking for Emily T-shirts and Doc Martens shoes. Things can get a touch sketchy after dark but it usually makes for a lovely afternoon outing – and you don't have to tag along as they try on piles of sneakers in search of that elusive pair that doesn't, like, totally suck.

Babysitting & childcare

American Childcare Services

312 644 7300/www.americanchildcare.com.
Credit AmEx, MC, V.
A large staff of sitters provides childcare services to hotel guests looking for time away from the kiddies. Expect to pay around $15.50 per hour, though there's a four-hour minimum and a transportation fee of $5-$10. Clients should book 24 hours ahead. The agency also provides group childcare for conventioneers.

North Shore Nannies

847 864 2424/www.northshorenannies.com.
Credit MC, V (agency fee only; nanny to be paid by cash/cheque).
If Mary Poppins is booked out, this agency offers a nanny service for $10 per hour (there's a four-hour minimum) or $120 for overnight service, plus an additional agency fee of $18 for up to six hours, $30 for seven to 12 hours and $40 for 12 to 24 hours. Book ahead, especially at weekends.

Attractions & museums

Almost all of the city's museums include a little something for the kids; for details of them, *see chapter* **Sightseeing**. However, four attractions stand out from the pack in terms of their kid-friendliness.

The best Kids' stuff

For cooling off in summer
The walk-in fountain at **Navy Pier**. See p94.

For warming up in winter
The **toboggan slides**. See p197.

For the girliest of girls
American Girl Place. See p196 **Hello dolly**.

For the anstiest of teens
Shops near **Clark and Belmont**. See p193.

For eats with attitude
Ed Debevic's. See p197.

Arts & Entertainment

Let's go round again: the **Chicago Children's Museum**.

The fact that the **Field Museum of Natural History** (*see p82*) is the home of Sue, the world's largest T-rex, means it's perpetually packed with youngsters. If they tire of Sue, though, they'll go for the creepy-cool mummies and tombs in the Ancient Egyptian display. Check the temporary exhibits, too: the 2002 show on chocolate proved a predictable success.

While adults might think the massive walk-through heart at the **Museum of Science & Industry** (*see p123*) is kind of lame, children love it. The U505 submarine captured in battle during World War II is another fave, though the famous coal mine tends to have the longest queues. At the genetics exhibit, you can watch as chicks break out of their shells. Make time, too, for Colleen Moore's fairy castle and a collection of 500 fast food toys dating back to the practically prehistoric 1970s.

At the **John G Shedd Aquarium** (*see p83*) are whales, dolphins, sea otters and harbour seals. Plan it right and the kids can catch a pool-side feeding session, though the daily hand-feeding of fish by divers is just as popular. In the tide pool, kids can touch sea stars, crabs and other cool little things.

Finally, the **Art Institute** (*see p79*) offers an excellent programme of activities. Go for a treasure hunt there, where kids are encouraged to seek out a work of art from a series of clues. But do make sure they know that if and when they find it, they don't get to take it home.

Chicago Children's Museum

700 E Grand Avenue, at Navy Pier, Near North (312 527 1000/www.chichildrensmuseum.org). CTA Grand (Red)/29, 65, 66 bus. **Open** 10am-5pm Tue, Wed, Fri-Sun; 10am-8pm Thur. *School holidays* also 10am-5pm Mon. **Admission** $6.50; $5.50 over-65s; free under-1s. Free families 5-8pm Thur. **Credit** AmEx, Disc, MC, V. **Map** p306 K10.

Not only will kids have a blast here: they might even learn something. Aspiring archaeologists can dig for dino bones in a replica excavation pit, and those with a jones for 15 minutes of fame can host a mock TV show. Wee ones will probably opt for the play area with a bakery, a gas station, a bus and a construction zone. A new Play It Safe exhibit lets kids practise responses to common emergencies. Be warned, though: the exit leads into a well-stocked gift shop.

The Kids on the Fly branch (312 527 1000), on the departure level of Terminal 2 at O'Hare Airport, is not as extensive as the Navy Pier operation, but if you're stuck at the airport, there's only so long that kids will be content watching the planes take off and land. That's when you head here.

Children's Museum of Immigrant History

6500 S Pulaski Street, at W 65th Street, South Side (773 582 6500). CTA Pulaski (Orange). **Open** 10am-4pm daily. **Admission** $4; $3 over-65s, students; $1 3-12s. Free to all Mon. **Credit** AmEx, MC, V.

Designed to teach kids about cultural diversity, the museum features exhibits, workshops, live demonstrations and performances highlighting the arts, history and culture introduced to the US by various immigrant groups. It's part of the Balzekas Museum of Lithuanian Culture, and the kids section includes an exhibition where they can try out ancient Lithuanian folk instruments or dress up in traditional costumes.

Parks & gardens

In addition to the parks below, there's **Lincoln Park** (for full details, *see p101*), the city's premier outdoor attraction. The Children's Zoo offers an up-close-and-personal view of animals and throws in a crash course on conservation, while the Farm in the Zoo, a working replica of a Midwestern farm complete with red barns housing cows, sheep and horses, is getting smartened up. Best of all, admission's free.

Garfield Park

100 N Central Park Avenue, West Side (312 746 5092/www.chicagoparkdistrict.com). CTA Pulaski (Green). **Open** 9am-10pm Mon-Fri; 9am-5pm Sat, Sun. **Admission** free.

If the rugrats have some left-over energy you'd like them to expend, try this 185-acre park with a play-ground, baseball diamonds, soccer fields, basketball and tennis courts, a pool, a lagoon, a bike path and two sandpits. The conservatory, one of the US's largest, is a delightful spot when it's icky outside.

Oz Park

2021 N Burling Street, at W Webster Avenue, Lincoln Park (312 742 7898/www.chicagoparkdistrict.com). CTA Fullerton (Brown, Purple, Red). **Open** *Park* dawn-dusk daily. *Field house* 5-10pm Mon-Fri. **Admission** free. **Map** p308 F6.

Look for the silver statue of the Tin Man from *The Wizard of Oz*, whose author, L Frank Baum, lived in Chicago. Sports include basketball, volleyball, tennis and 16-inch softball (*see p235* **Play big**). There's a Dorothy's Playlot for the tots and – of course – a yellow brick road.

Entertainment

The glammed-up **Navy Pier** (for more, *see p94*) offers plenty for the young 'uns, including an IMAX cinema, a futuristic McDonald's with a laser-light show, a 150-foot (46-metre) Ferris wheel and, in winter, an ice rink.

Dave & Buster's

1030 N Clark Street, at W Oak Street, Gold Coast (312 943 5151/www.daveandbusters.com). CTA Clark/Division (Red). **Open** 11.30am-midnight Mon, Sun; 11.30am-1am Tue-Sat. **Admission** $5 from 10pm Fri, Sat. **Credit** AmEx, DC, MC, V. **Map** p306 H9.

Though the focus here is on arcade games, Dave & Buster's offers everything from shuffleboard to high-tech virtual reality kit. Frazzled adults can take the edge off with a cocktail.

Different Strummer

4544 N Lincoln Avenue, at W Wilson Avenue, Ravenswood (773 751 3398/www.oldtownschool.org). CTA Western (Brown). **Open** 10am-9pm Mon-Thur; 10am-5pm Fri-Sun. **Credit** AmEx, Disc, MC, V.

Part of the Old Town School of Folk Music Children's Center, Different Strummer's two branches offer plenty for the budding muso: CDs, videos and toy instruments, as well as real ones made especially for younger players.

Branch: 909 W Armitage Avenue, Old Town (773 751 3410).

EAA Young Eagles Program

Information 1-877 806 8902/reservations 312 409 5621/www.youngeagles.com.

Kids aged eight to 17 can hit the friendly skies and soar over Wrigley Field, the United Center, the Sears Tower and other Chicago landmarks in planes for free, thanks to volunteer pilots from the Chicago chapter of the Tuskegee Airmen. All participants get an official Young Eagle certificate.

Chicago calendar Children

In addition to boasting a mess of movie theatres, the city plays host to the **Chicago International Children's Film Festival**. Held at Facets Multimedia (*see p201*) each autumn, the event features a mix of indie flicks from around the world, along with appearances from some of the filmmakers. Just think of it as a sort of Sundance for the schoolyard set.

Scope out the next Picasso or Cartier-Bresson when Gallery 312 (312 942 2500; *see p207* **Painting by numbers**) offers **Young at Art**, an annual springtime exhibition where kids aged from eight to 12 display

their photos, paintings, prints and sculptures. And for a truly unusual urban experience, check out the Spectacle productions presented year-round by **Redmoon Theater** (www.redmoon.org). The All Hallows' Eve Ritual Celebration, held annually in Logan Square, features a dazzling array of stilt-walkers, fire-breathers and puppets of all shapes and sizes.

Finally, don't forget the numerous **neighbourhood festivals** that take place during summer (*see p189*). On any given weekend, there's some sort of street fair that usually has something for the kiddies.

Hello dolly

Regardless of whether your touring party contains any girls, American or otherwise, the eye-popping retail, food and entertainment emporium known as **American Girl Place** (for listings, *see p186*) is absolutely worth the short detour from the main Michigan Avenue drag. Daughters will love it, sons will sneer, but parents are frequently astonished by what is one of the slickest, most advanced retailing concepts in the world.

Visit Chicago during a school holiday and you'll encounter plenty of those who worship at its shrines. Just look around town for a girl about ten years old carrying a red bag with a really expensive-looking doll peeping out over the top. Her trip to American Girl was probably the reason why her family came to the city in the first place, because Chicago has the only American Girl in the country. Everyone else is stuck with the catalogue.

Founded on the proven notion that niche marketing pays off, the multi-floor American Girl is a store, restaurant and theatre devoted to fulfilling every desire of nice middle class girls aged between nine and 13 years old. Initially a series of books based on seven fictional characters who hail from various provocative periods in American history, the literature brand has now been (over-)extended to dolls, clothes, tea parties and, remarkably, full-blown musicals, created entirely in-house. The first *American Girl Revue* played to some 190,000 people; a sequel has followed.

It's easy to be cynical about a place where the staff look like models, dolls are given their own place setting at tables, and parents are slyly press-ganged into spending three-figure sums on multiple outfits for their little darlings' multiple dolls. And many people think that the American Girl shows are little more than extended infomercials.

But American Girl is a class act. Its target customers are treated like the dignified important adults their parents would like them to become, and the whole operation comes with a progressive message of the importance of female empowerment and education (Spice Girls? Who they?) that usually wins over even doubting anti-capitalists. If you do have a girl in tow, the terrific little show in the basement is like a pint-sized Broadway attraction, unique to Chicago. It'll teach your kid all the right stuff. But, like everything else here, it'll cost you.

Dress Like Your Doll

Toboggan slides

Information 1-800 870 3666. **Admission** $1.
Sled rental $3/hr. **Open** 10am-10pm daily, weather permitting. **No credit cards**.
Bundle the kids up good and they'll have a real blast whipping down the ice-covered slides at five Chicagoland locations: **Bemis Woods**, in Western Springs (708 246 8366); **Deer Grove 5** in Palatine (847 381 7868); **Jensen Slides**, west of Lincolnwood (773 631 7657); **Swallow Cliff** down in Palos Park, which hosted Olympic ski jump hopefuls in the 1920s and '30s (708 448 4417); and the **Dan Ryan Woods**, by Evergreen Park (773 233 3766). Before you get the kids all psyched, call ahead to check the weather conditions suit the slides; and bear in mind that none of the venues is easily accessible by the El.

WhirlyBall

1880 W Fullerton Avenue, at N Elston Avenue, Wicker Park (773 486 7777/www.whirlyball.com).
Bus 50, 74. **Open** noon-2am Mon-Fri; noon-3am Sat; noon-2am Sun. **Admission** $10/person per 30mins. Over-21s only after 5pm. **Credit** AmEx, DC, Disc, MC, V. **Map** p310 B5.
Think polo in bumper cars: two teams spin around a 4,000sq ft (372sq m) court, attempting to scoop up a ball and whip it at a backboard. Kids must be over 12 and measure 54in (137cm). Book ahead.

Theatre

In addition to those listed below, the **Puppet Parlor** (1922 W Montrose Avenue, at N Damen Avenue, Ravenswood; 773 774 2919) stages splendid marionette entertainments.

Chicago Playworks for Families & Young Audiences

DePaul's Merle Reskin Theatre, 60 E Balbo Drive, at S Wabash Avenue, South Loop (box office 312 922 1999/http://theatreschool.depaul.edu/perform).
CTA Harrison (Red). **Tickets** $8; $2 under-18mths. **Credit** Disc, MC, V. **Map** p305 H13.
Founded as the Goodman Children's Theater in 1925, Chicago Playworks, run by the Theater School at DePaul University, is one of the oldest continuously running children's companies. The playhouse presents three productions each season and offers post-show discussions and ice-cream socials with the cast and backstage tours.

Children's Theatre Fantasy Orchard

Mercury Theatre, 3745 N Southport Avenue, at W Waveland Avenue, Lake View: Wrigleyville (773 539 4200/325 1700/www.kidtheatre.com). CTA Addison (Red). **Tickets** $10. **No credit cards**. **Map** p309 D1.
Once upon a time, there was a theatre company that put on magical performances based on fairy and folk tales from around the world. People came from all around to see the company's annual presentation of *African Cinderella*. This was so successful, it spawned Asian and Spanish versions as well. And they all lived happily ever after.

Emerald City Theatre

Apollo Theater, 2540 N Lincoln Avenue, at W Wrightwood Avenue, Lincoln Park (Emerald City Theatre 773 529 2690/box office 773 935 6100/www.emeraldcitytheatre.com). CTA Fullerton (Brown, Purple, Red). **Tickets** $10; $8 children. **Credit** MC, V. **Map** p308 E6.
Jolly kids' fare, such as a *Winnie-the-Pooh* musical and a theatrical take on Tarzan, is offered by this fine establishment in its new digs at the Apollo Theater up in Lincoln Park.

Restaurants

Although Chicago is packed with places for children to eat, some are especially suitable for their discriminating taste buds.

Caesarland

7300 W Foster Avenue, at N Harlem Avenue, Harwood Heights (773 774 7330). CTA Harlem (Blue). **Open** 11am-9pm Mon-Thur, Sun; 11am-10pm Fri; 10.30am-10pm Sat. **Main courses** $10-$15. **Credit** AmEx, MC, V.
Part of the ubiquitous Little Caesar's chain, this outlet adds games to the recipe. In between scarfing down the mediocre pizza, kids can get their hands on a choice of play equipment, video games and rides. Admission is free; some games require tokens.

Ed Debevic's

640 N Wells Street, at E Erie Street, Near North (312 664 1707/www.eddebevics.com). CTA Chicago (Red). **Open** 11am-10pm Mon-Thur; 11am-11pm Fri, Sat. **Main courses** $5-$12. **Credit** AmEx, DC, MC, V. **Map** p306 H10.
The burgers are pretty dang tasty in this ersatz '50s diner. But the real attraction is the gum-snapping, beehive-wearing, insult-dispersing waitresses. The all-singing, all-dancing staff have also been known to jump up on the counters and shake it a little.

Margie's

1960 N Western Avenue, at W Armitage Avenue, Bucktown (773 384 1035). CTA Western (Blue (NW)). **Open** 9am-midnight Mon-Thur, Sun; 9am-1am Fri, Sat. **Main courses** $4-$8. **Credit** AmEx, Disc, MC, V. **Map** p310 A6.
This 80-year-old family business out west serves up a regular lunch menu. But whatever you do, leave enough room for the amazing desserts: home-made ice-cream, candies, chocolates, bon-bons and what's billed as the'world's largest sundae'.

Rock 'n' Roll McDonald's

600 N Clark Street, at E Huron Street, Near North (312 664 7940). CTA Grand (Red). **Open** 24hrs daily. **Main courses** $2-$4. **Credit** AmEx, Disc, MC, V. **Map** p306 H10.
Hardly your average Golden Arches, this McD's pays homage to rock 'n' roll with cut-outs of the Supremes and the Doors gracing the outside. Inside there are platinum Elvis records, life-size replicas of the Beatles and a candy-apple red '59 Corvette.

Arts & Entertainment

Film

The perfect date? For dinner, turn to page 126. For a movie, read on.

Still the most famous of all fictional Chicagoans: **Jake and Elwood**, the brothers Blues.

It's hard to imagine today, but the Loop used to be a veritable Shangri-La for movie-goers. With all the exuberance and hubris you'd expect of a boomtown, exhibitors erected a phalanx of mammoth palaces to feed the local appetite for moving pictures. Local theatre chains such as Balaban and Katz operated many of these cinemas, each of which seated thousands of patrons in fine, upholstered chairs under soaring arches festooned with gaudy faux-Moorish ornamentation; many offered jazz and vaudeville to boost attendance. While neighbourhood houses such as Uptown's Riviera and the Tivoli on the South Side (where the smartly dressed ushers were famously drilled to military standards) were no fleapits, there were still enough people willing to come downtown nightly in the 1910s, '20s and '30s to justify the existence of over a dozen theatres in the Loop alone.

As the Depression wore on, however, even the relatively cheap thrill of movie-going proved too expensive and the Loop theatres began to close.

Those that stayed open, such as the **Chicago Theatre** on State and the **Oriental Theatre** on Randolph (for both, *see p241* **As good as new**), relied increasingly on cheaper exploitation fare or live programming, while others were split into small, dim chambers, their façades only hinting at their former grandeur. And then, in the 1980s, Chicago was subject, like the rest of America, to an insidious invasion of cookie-cutter multiplexes with paper-thin walls and small screens.

These days, things are looking up. In the last few years, miserable holes such as the Water Tower and the Fine Arts have closed, while some gorgeous new spots – notably Evanston's **Century 12** – opened. If all goes well, too, a 21-screen behemoth will be opening in late 2002 near Navy Pier. With the relocation of the **Gene Siskel Film Center** and the opening of a **Landmark** arthouse in Lake View (for both, *see p203*, locals now have a fine selection of cinemas from which to choose. This chapter lists the best of them.

TICKETS AND INFORMATION

The best way to find out about what's playing when is in the local papers; the *Chicago Tribune*, the *Chicago Sun-Times*, the *Chicago Reader* and *Newcity* all run thorough movie listings. With the addition of so many screens in the last few years, sellouts are rarer, but they do still happen, especially at the handful of theatres that often get exclusive runs of new films (**Loews Cineplex Pipers Alley**, for example).

Buying tickets in advance is not as easy as merely calling the numbers listed in this chapter for each cinema: these mostly offer only information on screenings, and will not allow you to book in advance. For this, you'll need to visit in person, or call one of several phone and online agencies: both **Fandango** (1-800 555 8355/www.fandango.com) and the long-established **Moviefone** (312 444 3456/www.moviefone.com) offer tickets for the majority of first-run cinemas in the city, and accept American Express, Discover, Mastercard and Visa for phone and online bookings.

Parents should note that while kids are welcome during the day, many theatres won't admit children under six years old after 6pm.

Mainstream & first-run

Burnham Plaza
826 S Wabash Avenue, at E 9th Street, South Loop (312 554 9102/www.villagetheatres.com). CTA Harrison (Red), Roosevelt/State (Red) or Roosevelt/Wabash (Green, Orange). **Admission** $7.50; $4.75 concessions. *Before 6pm Mon-Fri* $4.75. **Credit** AmEx, MC, V. **Map** p304 H14.
A spacious multiplex in the South Loop, offering tickets for about a dollar less than average for new releases over five large screens with DTS sound.

Century 12 Evanston & CinéArts 6
1715 Maple Avenue, at Church Street, Evanston (847 492 0123/www.centurytheaters.com). CTA Davis (Purple). **Admission** $8.75; $5-$6.50 concessions. *Before 6pm Mon-Fri, before 2pm Sat, Sun* $5.50. **Credit** AmEx, Disc, MC, V.
The variety at this theatre – which boasts 12 screens for mainstream releases and six for artier fare – may make it worth the hike from downtown. The bistro serves particularly enjoyable martinis.

Loews Cineplex Esquire
58 E Oak Street, at N Michigan Avenue, Gold Coast (312 280 0101/www.loewscineplex.com). CTA Chicago (Red). **Admission** $8.75; $5.50 concessions. *Before 6pm Mon, Fri, 1st show Sat, Sun* $5.75. **Credit** AmEx, Disc, MC, V. **Map** p306 J9.
Once an art deco landmark, this three-storey cinema is now chopped up into five smaller screens, all a bit tatty and low-rent. Movies are a mix of arthouse fare and serious first-run Hollywood films.

Loews Cineplex McClurg Court 3
330 E Ohio Street, at N McClurg Court, Near North (312 642 0723/www.loewscineplex.com). CTA Grand (Red). **Admission** $8.75; $5.75 concessions. *Before 6pm Mon-Fri, 1st show Sat, Sun* $5.75. **Credit** AmEx, Disc, MC, V. **Map** p306 J10.
This three-piece cinema has become a hotspot for technically dazzling blockbusters, since its screens boast sophisticated sound systems. The gargantuan downstairs theatre is the most impressive.

Loews Cineplex 900 N Michigan
900 N Michigan Avenue, at E Delaware Street, Gold Coast (312 787 1988). CTA Chicago (Red). **Admission** $8.75; $5.50 concessions. *Before 6pm Mon-Fri, 1st show Sat, Sun* $5.50. **Credit** AmEx, Disc, MC, V. **Map** p306 J9.
The two screens of this cinema are located on the lower level of the upmarket mall. Busy on weekends, it's often nearly empty during the week.

Loews Cineplex Pipers Alley
1608 N Wells Street, at W North Avenue, Old Town (312 642 7500/www.loewscineplex.com). CTA Sedgwick (Brown). **Admission** $8.75; $5.25-$5.75 concessions. *Before 6pm Mon-Fri, 1st show Sat, Sun* $5.75. **Credit** AmEx, Disc, MC, V. **Map** p307 H7.
A generic four-screen miniplex in the same building as comedy legends Second City that shows mainstream arthouse films for locals who like their movies different but not *too* different. Book ahead: sellouts are common.

Loews Cineplex 600 N Michigan
600 N Michigan Avenue, entrance at N Rush Street & E Ohio Street, Near North (312 255 9340/www.loewscineplex.com). CTA Chicago (Red). **Admission** $8.75; $5.50 concessions. *Before 6pm Mon, Fri, 1st show Sat, Sun* $5.75. **Credit** AmEx, Disc, MC, V. **Map** p306 J9.
This three-tiered facility showcases first-run films on nine decent screens. A high proportion of films here are of the kiddie-friendly variety.

Loews Cineplex Webster Place 8
1471 W Webster Avenue, at N Clybourn Avenue, Lincoln Park (773 327 3100/www.loewscineplex.com). CTA Fullerton (Brown, Purple, Red). **Admission** $9; $5.50-$5.75 concessions. **Credit** AmEx, Disc, MC, V. **Map** p308 D5.

The best Cinemas

For the best intentions
The Gene Siskel Film Center. *See p203.*

For shouting at the screen
Brew & View at the Vic. *See p200.*

For quiet audiences
Landmark Century Center. *See p203.*

Chicago calendar Film

Chicago's film community is as diverse as the city's cultural composition. Among the dozen or more festivals each year are events devoted to Latino, Polish and Iranian movies, the nation's largest underground film festival, its second oldest lesbian and gay film festival and the continent's oldest competitive film festival.

Long before John Woo had met Tom Cruise, films from Hong Kong were being screened by the Art Institute's Film Center. Chow Yun-Fat is now a household name, but the cinema – now relocated and renamed in honour of Gene Siskel (see p203) – still packs out in March with its **Hong Kong Film Festival**. Expect the best and weirdest films from Asia's Hollywood, plus appearances by various directors and stars. For more, call 312 846 2800.

Award-winning feature-length and short films from Spain, Portugal, the US and Latin America are celebrated during the two-week **Chicago Latino Film Festival** at Facets Multimedia (see p201). Directors and actors attend to exhibit their works and moderate post-screening discussions; call 312 431 1330 or log on to its website, www.latinoculturalcenter.org, for details.

The **Chicago Lesbian & Gay International Film Festival** was first organised by Chicago Filmmakers (see p201) in 1981, and now spreads a blend of features, documentaries and shorts across 14 days each summer at the Music Box Theatre (see p203) and the Village Theatre (see p200). Various gay bars and clubs host opening night, post-screening and closing-night parties to jolly it all along. More information is available at 773 293 1447 or from www.chicagofilmmakers.org.

In just eight years, the **Chicago Underground Film Festival** (773 327 3456/ www.cuff.org) has evolved from a chaotic season of local works held in hotel conference rooms into the largest festival of its type in the country, showcasing new movies and fêting cult directors. Styles range from sober documentary to Dadaist experimentalism and the quality is varied, but outside this week in August, where else are you going to see this stuff?

Distinguished and fledgling directors offer up their latest works for scrutiny in early October at the two-week **Chicago International Film Festival**, the oldest competitive festival in North America. Screenings are scheduled throughout the city's arthouses – call 312 425 9400 or see www.chicagofilmfestival.com for schedules – with parties, tributes and other special events. Directors and stars are generally on hand to introduce the films, and critics such as Roger Ebert regularly hold special Q&A sessions with visiting luminaries. Book early or miss out.

For ten days in late October, hundreds of films for kids compete at Facets' world-class **Chicago International Children's Film Festival**. Animated and live-action shorts are chosen by a small jury of children and grown-ups, with filmmakers, animators and actors participating in workshops. Call 773 281 9075 or visit www.cicff.org for more.

This mall complex up on the fringes of Lincoln Park features a fairly predictable selection first-run Hollywood movies, with concurrent screenings for the top box-office grossers. Arrive early or book in advance on opening weekends, as seats here tend to sell out fast.

Village Theatre

1548 N Clark Street, at W North Avenue, Old Town (312 642 2403/www.villagetheatres.com). CTA Sedgwick (Brown, Purple). **Admission** $6. *Before 6pm* $4. **Credit** MC, V. **Map** p307 H7.

Once a haven for quirky cult items, Old Town's Village Theatre has lately moved to a more predictable bill of fare: mainstream flicks spiked with occasional arty films. The cinema itself is cheaper than the nearby Pipers Alley, but it's also noticeably less comfortable.

Second-run & repertory

Brew & View at the Vic Theatre

3145 N Sheffield Avenue, at W Belmont Avenue, Lake View (312 618 8439/773 929 6713/ www.brewview.com). CTA Belmont (Brown, Purple, Red). **Admission** $5. **No credit cards**. **Map** p309 E3.

This once-opulent theatre was designed as a vaudeville house, but now hosts concerts and films. Bars stay open during the flicks, and the bursts of commentary from the post-college crowd who attend are often more entertaining than the celluloid fare.

LaSalle Bank Theatre

4901 W Irving Park Road, at N Lamon Avenue, Irving Park (312 904 9442). CTA Irving Park (Blue)/54, 56, 80 bus. **Admission** $5; $3 concessions. **No credit cards**. **Map** p308 F5.

Arts & Entertainment

Throughout October, the Siskel Center runs a festival celebrating the cinematic output of Iran, home to many of the last decade's most acclaimed directors (Abbas Kiarostami, for example). There's no particular focus at its **Festival of Films from Iran** (312 846 2800), though it is often controversial: recently, one director was unable to appear after she was arrested by easily offended Iranian officials.

Finally, in December, the **New French Cinema Festival** at Facets Multimedia is a sampler pack of the most interesting films from France. Eschewing the lightweight Gallic sex comedies and costumed fluff that generally get exported to the US, it makes for an interesting and unique week. For details, call 773 281 4114 or check online at www.facets.org.

This anomalous revival house in town is located in the back of an old bank. It screens classic films (often silent) every Saturday night at 8pm, usually as part of breathtakingly comprehensive retrospectives.

Arthouse & speciality

The **Chicago Cultural Center** offers an ongoing monthly film event, International Dinner and a Movie. It features a classic foreign film, an introduction by a critic, and a catered dinner in the cuisine of the featured country. Recent offerings have been Jean Cocteau's 1946 version of *Beauty and the Beast* and Bryan Forbes's 1964 British psychological thriller *Séance on a Wet Afternoon*. Tickets are $15, and booking is required: call 312 742 8497.

Chicago Filmmakers
5243 N Clark Street, at W Berwyn Avenue, Andersonville (773 293 1447/ www.chicagofilmmakers.org). CTA Berwyn (Purple, Red). **Admission** $7. **Credit** MC, V.
A crucial resource, this non-profit group offers equipment, classes and film rental. It appears here as it also shows experimental films a few times a month, here and at Columbia College's Ferguson Hall (600 S Michigan Avenue; 312 663 1600). It sponsors the Chicago Lesbian & Gay International Film Festival (*see p200* **Chicago calendar**).

Facets Multimedia Center
1517 W Fullerton Avenue, at N Ashland Avenue, Lincoln Park (773 281 4114/9075/www.facets.org). CTA Fullerton (Brown, Purple, Red). **Admission** $7. **Credit** MC, V (online only). **Map** p308 D5.

Arts & Entertainment

Made in Chicago Siskel & Ebert

Back in 1975, the film critics for Chicago's two papers, the *Tribune* and the *Sun-Times*, started presenting a movie show on television. So far, so what. The idea was desperately simple: the pair sat in a movie theatre, showing clips from the week's flicks and each giving the film a 'thumbs up' or 'thumbs down' rating. However, *Sneak Previews*, as it was then called, quickly became an underground favourite on Chicago public television and soon moved into national syndication, turning its stars – the *Trib*'s Gene Siskel (*pictured left*) and Roger Ebert of the *Sun-Times* – into household names. The show went on to earn five Emmy nominations and garnered them their own honorary street sign in 1995.

The rotund, owly Ebert quickly became the star of the show. A born newsman, he got his first newspaper job at 15, covering the sports beat for a downstate paper. Starting as film critic at the *Sun-Times* a decade later in 1967, he quickly made a name for himself with his omnivorous love of cinema and, in 1975, became the first film critic to receive a Pulitzer Prize. While his tastes skewed toward the fantastic and the popular – as did his short-lived career as a scriptwriter, penning three Russ Meyer films in the 1970s – he was never afraid to stick his thumb in the eye of a bloated piece of Hollywood crap or skewer a precious slab of Euro-twaddle.

A North Side native and Yale graduate, Siskel was a tweedy enthusiast who loved nothing more than championing an unheralded movie but who never aspired to lofty filmic pretensions. Critical faves such as *Crumb* and *Fargo* made his film of the year lists as often as idiosyncratic choices like *Babe: Pig in the City* and *Wayne's World*.

Between them, the pair shunted film criticism, long the province of the arts pages, into the mainstream. Their verdict could help make or break a movie, and their reviewing shorthand of 'two thumbs up' or 'two thumbs down' became a nationally known catchphrase.

In 1999, though, the 24th year of their partnership, Siskel died at the age of 53 from complications arising from a brain tumour. He was eulogised by many directors – a rare thing for a critic – and film lovers around the world, and the Art Institute even renamed its theatre in his honour shortly before its relocation to a new Loop complex (*see p203*).

After Siskel's death, Ebert decided to keep the show going. To begin with, a revolving door let in and out a series of guest co-critics, but after a few months, Ebert settled permanently on Richard Roeper, a lightweight, smiley *Sun-Times* columnist. It was a lamentable choice, Roeper having neither the ability nor inclination to spar with Ebert in the manner that made the show's previous pairing so stimulating. Two thumbs down, in other words, though the show continues on WLS-7 in Chicago at 10.35pm on Saturday. But Ebert's writing is still as lively and fresh as ever: check the *Sun-Times* each Friday (or look online at www.sun-times.com/ebert) to find out his verdicts on the week's releases.

Facets' two theatres are stark, but the quality and selection of art films offered are exquisite. The main theatre showcases vintage classics and works by contemporary filmmakers, while the second is dedicated to documentary and esoteric projects. The non-profit group hosts the Chicago International Children's Film Festival each October and the New French Cinema Festival each December (for both, *see p200* **Chicago calendar**), and stocks a legendarily exhaustive library of 40,000 videos and DVDs for sale and rent.

Gene Siskel Film Center

164 N State Street, at W Randolph, the Loop (312 846 2800/2600/www.artic.edu/webspaces/ siskelfilmcenter). CTA Washington (Red). **Admission** $8. **Credit** AmEx, MC, V. **Map** p305 H12.

The Film Center departed its dark Art Institute theatre in 2001 for this gorgeous new complex. Films play on two large screens, with the programme filled with everything from experimental student works to contemporary foreign flicks. At least one director-slanted retrospective is featured each month, when lectures accompany the films. *See also p202* **Made in Chicago.**

Landmark Century Center Cinema

2828 N Clark Street, at W Diversey Parkway, Lake View (773 248 7744/www.landmarktheatres.com). CTA Belmont (Brown, Purple, Red). **Admission** $9; $6 concessions. **Credit** AmEx, MC, V. **Map** p308 F4.

Perched atop a mall, the Landmark screens a mix of first-run indie and foreign films in seven mid-sized theatres. Things can get a bit too precious – who needs that many kinds of popcorn toppings? – but on the whole, this is a fine enterprise. One of the hosts of the Chicago International Film Festival (*see p200* **Chicago calendar**).

Music Box Theatre

3733 N Southport Avenue, at W Waveland Avenue, Wrigleyville (773 871 6604/6607/ www.musicboxtheatre.com). **Admission** $8.50. *1st show Sat, Sun* $6.50. **No credit cards. Map** p309 D1.

A cherished outlet for foreign, classic and cult films, not least because it's one of the few vintage relics that hasn't been split into tiny screens. Mechanical clouds drift across the ceiling, twinkling stars illuminate Moorish adornments, and a vintage organ is played during silent films. The midnight films, everything from animation to '70s skin flicks, are a treasure; a smaller 100-seat screen space shows more avant-garde films. The Music Box hosts the Chicago International Film Festival and the Chicago Lesbian & Gay International Film Festival (for both, *see p200* **Chicago calendar**).

Lowes Cineplex Navy Pier IMAX

600 E Grand Avenue, at Lake Michigan, Near North (312 595 0090/www.loewscineplex.com). CTA Grand (Red). **Admission** $11; $9-$10 concessions. **Credit** AmEx, Disc, MC, V. **Map** p306 K10.

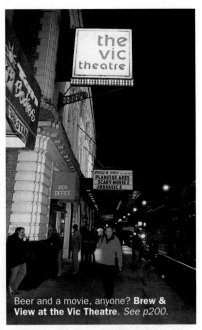

Beer and a movie, anyone? **Brew & View at the Vic Theatre.** *See p200.*

This hulk offers educational and scientific visual adventures, as well as 3-D movies that require the viewer to don a headset (arrive early to avoid being placed in the motion sickness seats at the sides). Popular 35mm films such as *The Matrix* are shown on weekends. For the Omnimax Cinema at the Museum of Science & Industry, which offers a similarly spectacular cinematic experience, *see p123.*

Three Penny Cinema

2424 N Lincoln Avenue, at W Fullerton Avenue, Lincoln Park (773 525 3514/3449/ www.3pennycinema.com). CTA Fullerton (Brown, Purple, Red). **Admission** $6.50; $4.50 concessions. **No credit cards. Map** p308 F5.

This skinny two-screen cinema is easy to miss, but the selection is sound – the Three Penny snatches arthouse movies from out-of-theatres, not-on-video limbo – and tickets are cheap.

University of Chicago Doc Films

Max Palevsky Cinema, Ida Noyes Hall, 1212 E 59th Street, at S Woodlawn Avenue, Hyde Park (773 702 8574/8575/www.docfilms.uchicago.edu). Metra 59th Street. **Admission** $4. **No credit cards. Map** p311 Y18.

The home of the longest-running student film society in the country screens 'socially relevant' movies daily throughout the academic year and four nights a week in summer in the 490-seat Max Palevsky Cinema. A typical week might offer *Rashomon*, *Total Recall*, *Bring It On* and some student flicks.

Galleries

It's not quite world class yet, but at street level Chicago has an 'art of gold.

Body art the **Ann Nathan** way. *See p205*.

It's not yet up there with the likes of London and New York. But after years of nurturing from committed locals, a vibrant art scene is flourishing in Chicago, and not just in the obvious places. Sure, art can of course be found in galleries, museums and at festivals. But you'll also spot it in unlikely places: corporate office buildings, restaurants, cafés, theatre lobbies, even – as with the assorted splendid sculptures in the Loop – on streetcorners.

The River North neighbourhood, particularly around the junction of Superior and Franklin Streets, is the most visible of Chicago's art-friendly areas, with over 70 galleries specialising in contemporary art in only a few blocks. However, a small segment of the West Side near Randolph Market has quickly filled with galleries and grown in popularity.

These two pockets of River North and the West Side are where you'll find the majority of Chicago's galleries, but there are others around the city. Around Michigan Avenue and the Gold Coast, the art is more traditional and the galleries more formal. Meanwhile, to some observers' delight and others' dismay, the once-thriving area around Wicker Park and Bucktown is steadily declining in artistic activity due to rent increases that both gallery owners and artists have found unmanageable.

Perhaps the most enjoyable parts of the art scene are the Friday night openings, especially in West Side and River North. People of all ages and backgrounds show up to see and be seen, snack on munchies and sup on wine. With so many distractions, be sure to take time to look at the art itself. Because most exhibitions run for four to six weeks, these major openings aren't weekly events, but you can expect at least one major wingding a month. Call ahead or check listings for details.

INFORMATION AND TOURS
For information about exhibitions, check the weekly *Chicago Reader* and the excellent *Chicago Gallery News*, published in January,

April and September and available free in many galleries. The Chicago/Midwest edition of Art Now's *Gallery Guide*, published monthly, is also a good starting point.

The Chicago Art Dealers Association hosts free tours of River North galleries most Saturdays at 10.30am, starting from Starbucks on the corner of Franklin and Chicago; they're a fine introduction to this hotbed of artistic activity. Call 312 649 0065 for more information.

Galleries

The Loop

You'll also find regular exhibitions over at multimedia venue the **HotHouse** (*see p220*).

Cassiopeia Fine Arts

330 S Dearborn Street, at W Jackson Boulevard (312 431 9000/www.cassiopeiafineart.com). CTA Jackson (Blue, Red) or Library (Brown, Orange, Purple). **Open** 10am-5pm Mon-Fri; also by appointment. **Credit** AmEx, Disc, MC, V. **Map** p305 H13.
Located in the historic Monadnock building, this gallery carries watercolours, prints and a fine collection of African art that includes wood carvings and decorative objects.

Fine Arts Building Gallery

Room 433, 410 S Michigan Avenue, at W Congress Parkway (312 913 0537/www.fabgallery.com). CTA Adams (Brown, Green, Orange, Purple) or Jackson (Red). **Open** noon-6pm Wed-Sat. **Credit** Disc, MC, V. **Map** p305 J13.

The best Galleries

Andrew Bae
Art that's equally at home in a condo or zendo. *See p205.*

Ann Nathan
The friendliest of all the River North galleries. *See p205.*

Fine Arts Building Gallery
Take a Loop lunchtime getaway to this handsome setting. *See p205.*

Peter Miller
For the best conceptual and technology-based shows in town. *See p209.*

RS Johnson
The gallery in Chicago that most resembles a museum. *See p207.*

This light and airy atrium courtyard features the work of artists who rent space in the landmark Fine Arts Building. Enjoy the elevator ride up in one of the Loop's few remaining human-operated cabs.

Illinois Art Gallery

Suite 2-100, 100 W Randolph Street, at N Dearborn Street (312 814 5322/www.museum.state.il.us). CTA Clark (Blue, Brown, Green, Orange, Purple). **Open** 9am-5pm Mon-Fri. **No credit cards. Map** p305 H12.
The varied installations at this newly renovated, government-sponsored space often focus on work by Illinois artists and/or art concerning issues of local interest. Recent shows have included exhibits on prairie wildlife and women in the Midwest. The Illinois Artisans' Shop, a unique arts and crafts store, is in the same building.

Poster Plus

200 S Michigan Avenue, at W Adams Street (312 461 9277/www.posterplus.com). CTA Adams (Brown, Green, Orange, Purple) or Monroe (Red). **Open** 10am-6pm Mon, Wed-Fri; 10am-8pm Tue; 9.30am-6pm Sat; 11am-6pm Sun. **Credit** AmEx, Disc, MC, V. **Map** p305 J12.
In addition to its ground-floor retail store, which sells calendars and other art-related items, Poster Plus's inviting second-floor showroom houses a collection of vintage posters.

Near North

River North

Aldo Castillo Gallery

233 W Huron Street, at N Franklin Street (312 337 2536/www.artaldo.com). CTA Chicago (Brown, Purple). **Open** 11am-6pm Tue-Sat. **Credit** AmEx, MC, V. **Map** p306 G10.
At the space he opened in 1993, Nicaraguan-born Castillo deals in Latin American art (primarily painting, sculpture, photography and works on paper), and occasionally offers educational programmes and live performances.

Andrew Bae Gallery

300 W Superior Street, at N Franklin Street (312 335 8601/www.andrewbaegallery.com). CTA Chicago (Brown, Purple). **Open** 10am-6pm Tue-Sat. **Credit** AmEx, MC, V. **Map** p306 G10.
Bae's focus is on artists, mainly Japanese and Korean, whose work has an Asian aesthetics will have 'contemporary universal appeal'. He also publishes monographs by individual artists such as Young June Lee and Kwang Jean Park.

Ann Nathan

218 W Superior Street, at N Franklin Street (312 664 6622/www.annnathangallery.com). CTA Chicago (Brown, Purple). **Open** 10am-5.30pm Tue-Fri; 11am-5pm Sat. **Credit** AmEx, MC, V. **Map** p306 G10.
Nathan's lovely gallery offers paintings and functional sculpture by well-known and emerging artists working in a multitude of media.

Arts & Entertainment

Byron Roche

Suite 105, 750 N Franklin Street, at W Chicago Avenue (312 654 0144/www.byronroche.com). CTA Chicago (Brown, Purple). **Open** 11am-6pm Tue-Sat. **Credit** Disc, MC, V. **Map** p306 G10.
Contemporary art in all media here, though the focus is on painting. Shows have included works by Margaret Evangeline, Jeremy Vajda and Ann Wiens.

Carrie Secrist Gallery

300 W Superior Street, at N Franklin Street (312 280 4500). CTA Chicago (Brown, Purple). **Open** 11am-6pm Tue-Fri; 11am-5pm Sat. **Credit** AmEx, MC, V. **Map** p306 G10.
Secrist exhibits a wide range of contemporary art made in all manner of media and by both new and established artists.

Galería Gaudí

708 N Wells Street, at W Superior Street (312 640 0517/www.galeriagaudi.com). CTA Chicago (Brown, Purple). **Open** 10am-6pm Tue-Sat. **Credit** AmEx, DC, Disc, MC, V. **Map** p306 G9.
This storefront, which is sister to a similarly named operation in Madrid, features classic and modern figurative art by contemporary Spanish artists such as Blanco Campos.

Gwenda Jay/Addington

704 N Wells Street, at W Superior Street (312 664 3406/www.gwendajay.com). CTA Chicago (Brown, Purple). **Open** 11am-6pm Tue-Sat. **Credit** AmEx, MC, V. **Map** p306 G9.
Modern art by artists who explore relationships between nature and culture, in both abstract and representational terms, using a range of media.

Habatat Galleries

222 W Superior Street, at N Franklin Street (312 440 0288/www.habatatchicago.com). CTA Chicago (Brown, Purple). **Open** 11am-5pm Tue-Sat; also by appointment. **Credit** AmEx, MC, V. **Map** p306 G10.

New kids on the Block

Its beginnings, as beginnings tend to be, were humble: an unsightly patch of downtown land spurned by local developers fearful of recession. When no buyer could be found for Block 37, which sat opposite Marshall Field's on State Street, Mayor Richard Daley decided to turn it over for use as a low-key arts training school for local youngsters. And what began as a low-budget experiment has spiralled into one of the city's success stories.

At the start, Gallery 37 aimed to train young Chicagoans in visual arts. Professional artists were hired to school 'apprentices' (who were paid for their work) for several months in summer, in the hope that these youngsters, many of whom came from deprived backgrounds, would then go on and use their skills to find work. In the first year, 260 apprentices passed through the scheme; a decade later, there were more than 15 times that number.

As the numbers grew, so did the scope of the project. Currently, Gallery 37 encompasses multiple training programmes for students over the age of 11 who are enrolled in Chicago's state school system (there are also some classes made available to the adult population through the city's colleges). Participants have access to diverse facilities including a theatre, a cooking school, multiple galleries and studios, a retail store and café, a computer lab, and impressive human and material resources that cover all the facets of the arts: painting,

sculpture, print-making, photography, ceramics, music, dance, theatre, audio-visual media, textiles and jewellery-making.

Of course, Gallery 37 didn't get to be a shining example of urban artistic inclusivity all by itself: it has powerful backers and has had plenty of help from the artistic and business worlds. The youth programme, a collaboration between the City of Chicago Department of Cultural Affairs and the Chicago Board of Education, only really took off when the Daleys – Mayor Richard and First Lady Maggie – gave it their full support. Maggie still chairs its board of directors.

These days, Gallery 37 is far from a humble operation. After a decade spent in tents, open only during summer, it has moved to a stunning 65,000 square feet (6,045 square metres) structure on Randolph in the newly revitalised Loop Theatre District. The lively vision of artists mentoring city youths continues to flourish in Chicago, but it's a concept that seems also to have travelled well: so far, more than two dozen cities in the US, the UK and Australia have developed programmes based on the Gallery 37 model. And all this because a few real estate firms briefly lost their bottle.

Gallery 37 Center for the Arts

66 E Randolph Street, at N Wabash Avenue, the Loop (312 744 8925/ www.gallery37.org). CTA Randolph (Brown, Green, Orange, Purple). **Open** 10am-6pm Mon-Sat. **Credit** Disc, MC, V. **Map** p305 H12.

Music and art make a cool combination at the **Hothouse**. *See p220.*

Blown and fabricated glass objects, both functional and decorative, from artists and artisans including Chihuly, Blank, Lipofsky, Rainey and Feldman.

Judy A Saslow

300 W Superior Street, at N Franklin Street (312 943 0530/www.jsaslowgallery.com). CTA Chicago (Brown, Purple). **Open** 10am-6pm Tue-Sat. **Credit** AmEx, MC, V. **Map** p306 G10.

Owner/curator Saslow, whose gallery is one of several in this building, is among Chicago's principal dealers in outsider art, promoting this developing fine art subculture through shows and other events. Nearby is **Carl Hammer** (740 N Wells Street; 312 266 8512), another leader in the field.

Robert Henry Adams Fine Art

715 N Franklin Street, at W Superior Street (312 642 8700/www.adamsfineart.com). CTA Chicago (Brown, Purple). **Open** 10am-5pm Tue-Fri; noon-5pm Sat. **Credit** MC, V. **Map** p306 G10.

Modern American paintings, drawings and sculptures from the early to mid 20th century by masters such as Avery, Carter and Man Ray. Exhibitions sometimes have a Chicago theme.

Stephen Daiter Gallery

Room 404, 311 W Superior Street, at N Franklin Street (312 787 3350). CTA Chicago (Brown, Purple). **Open** by appointment Tue-Thur; 11am-6pm Fri, Sat. **Credit** MC, V. **Map** p306 G10.

Daiter's walls are hung with vintage 20th-century documentary and experimental photography, including works by Andre Kertesz.

Magnificent Mile & Streeterville

Hilligoss Galleries

520 N Michigan Avenue, at E Grand Avenue (312 755 0300/www.hilligossgalleries.com). CTA Grand (Red). **Open** 10am-7pm Mon-Fri; 10am-6pm Sat; 11am-6pm Sun. **Credit** AmEx, Disc, MC, V. **Map** p306 J10.

A spacious two-storey showroom that carries work by a variety of international artists and modern masters such as Alexander Calder.

Peter Bartlow

44 E Superior Street, at N Michigan Avenue (312 337 1782/www.bartlowgallery.com). CTA Chicago (Red). **Open** by appointment Mon; 9.30am-5.30pm Tue-Fri; 10.30am-5pm Sat. **Credit** AmEx, MC, V. **Map** p306 J10.

Works in all media by emerging and established international artists, with Dufy and Miró among the more notable.

Richard Gray

John Hancock Center, Suite 3503, 875 N Michigan Avenue, at E Delaware Place (312 642 8877/www.richardgraygallery.com). CTA Chicago (Red). **Open** Sept-June 10am-5.30pm Tue-Sat; by appointment Mon. July, Aug 10am-5.30pm Tue-Fri; by appointment Mon. **Credit** details on request. **Map** p306 J9.

Chicago's pre-eminent gallery, with a sister operation in New York, specialising in modern masters from the august to the more adventurous.

moniquemeloche: all small letters but some capital contemporary art. *See p209.*

RS Johnson Fine Art
645 N Michigan Avenue, at E Erie Street (312 943 1661). CTA Chicago (Red). **Open** 9am-5.30pm Mon-Sat. **No credit cards. Map** p306 J10.
Paintings, drawings, prints and sculpture from artists of the calibre of Picasso, Rembrandt and Goya. According to owner, lecturer and publisher Johnson, almost 50 museums have bought here.

The Gold Coast

Coletti Collection
67 E Oak Street, at N Michigan Avenue (312 664 6767). CTA Chicago (Red)/36, 145, 146, 147, 151 bus. **Open** 10am-6pm Mon-Thur, Sat; 10am-7pm Fri; noon-5pm Sun. **Credit** AmEx, MC, V. **Map** p306 J9.

The **Flatiron Building.**
See p209.

Antique posters, ceramics and furniture from art nouveau through to art deco: look out for works by Mucha, Steinlen and Lautrec, among others.

Galleries Maurice Sternberg
140 E Walton Street, at N Michigan Avenue (312 642 1700/www.galleriesmauricesternberg.com). CTA Chicago (Red)/36, 145, 146, 147, 151 bus. **Open** 11am-6pm Mon-Sat; noon-5pm Sun. **Credit** AmEx, MC, V. **Map** p306 J9.
This established gallery in the Drake Hotel specialises in paintings and drawings by heavyweight European and American masters of the calibre of Cassatt, Chagall, Manel and Matisse.

Hart Gallery
64 E Walton Street, at N Michigan Avenue (312 932 9646/www.hartgallery.com). CTA Chicago (Red)/36, 145, 146, 147, 151 bus. **Open** 10am-6pm Mon-Sat; 11am-6pm Sun. **Credit** AmEx, MC, V. **Map** p306 J9.
Modern and contemporary European sculpture and paintings by Wunderlich, Bruni, Gass and others.

Old Town

Eastwick
245 W North Avenue, at N Park Avenue (312 440 2322). CTA Sedgwick (Brown, Purple). **Open** 11am-7pm Wed-Fri; 11am-6pm Sat; noon-5pm Sun. **Credit** AmEx, MC, V. **Map** p307 G7.
High-quality contemporary American paintings and photographs at an attractive corner gallery just north-west of Pipers Alley.

Lake View

Bell Studio
3428 N Southport Avenue, at W Roscoe Street (773 281 2172). CTA Southport (Brown). **Open** 11am-6pm Tue-Fri; 10am-3pm Sat, Sun. **Credit** AmEx, Disc, MC, V. **Map** p309 D2.
The exhibitions in a variety of media by Chicago-based artists change every six weeks. The gallery also offers framing and graphic design services.

Arts & Entertainment

Chicago calendar Art

Chicago in February can be a bleak place. Thank goodness, then, for **Around the Coyote** (773 342 6777/www.aroundthecoyote.org). This three-day multimedia festival in Wicker Park is held twice a year, its long-standing September date complemented by a February version. Art in all its mutations can be seen at galleries, studios and streetcorners around the junction of Damen, Milwaukee and North Avenue; anything tangible is usually for sale.

Around the Coyote couldn't differ more from Chicago's two biggest art fairs. May's **Art Chicago** (312 587 3300/www.artchicago.com) sees more than 200 galleries pour exhibits from upwards of 3,000 artists on to Navy Pier for a few days. During the fair, a shuttle bus transports visitors from Navy Pier to the gallery-heavy River North and West Town. In mid October, **SOFA** (the International Exposition of Sculpture, Objects and Functional Art; 312 654 9049/www.sofaexpo.com) fills Navy Pier for four days with dealers from the US and abroad.

Also look out for the several good-natured, street-based art fairs in Chicago during the summer months, where galleries and artists submit their works to the public in the hope of making a sale. Held in the first weekend in June, the **57th Street Art Fair** in Hyde Park (773 493 3247/www.57thstreetartfair.org) is the oldest and the best, and the crowds that mill around the junction of E 57th Street and S Kimbark Avenue are duly appreciative.

The following weekend, the **Wells Street Art Festival** (773 868 3010) offers work by 250 artists along Wells Street between Division and North Avenue, while half a mile away, near the junction of N Lincoln Park West and W Wisconsin Street (312 337 1938), the **Old Town Art Fair** caters more to the thirsty rover than the discriminating collector. And in August, artists flood the area around Erie and LaSalle, hoping to chip away at the local wealth at the **Gold Coast Art Fair** (312 744 2400/www.amdurproductions.com/goldcoast).

West Side

Aron Packer
118 N Peoria Street, at W Randolph Street (312 226 8984). Bus 8, 20. **Open** 10.30am-5.30pm Tue-Sat; also by appointment. **Credit** Disc, MC, V.
New visual artists and photographers, often with artist lectures alongside the exhibits.

Flatfile
118 N Peoria Street, at W Randolph Street (312 491 1190/www.flatfilefoto.com). Bus 8, 20. **Open** 11am-6pm Tue-Sat. **Credit** AmEx, MC, V.
Uup-and-coming and established photographic artists from the United States and around the world.

GR N'Namdi
110 N Peoria Street, at W Randolph Street (312 587 8262). Bus 8, 20. **Open** 11am-6pm Mon-Fri; 10am-5pm Sat. **Credit** MC, V. **Map** p306 G10.
Contemporary African-American and international artists using paint, photography and sculpture.

moniquemeloche
951 W Fulton Street, at N Morgan Street (312 455 0299/www.moniquemeloche.com). Bus 8, 20. **Credit** MC, V.
Contemporary international art in all media with a conceptual focus.

Peter Miller
118 N Peoria Street, at W Randolph Street (312 226 5291/www.petermillergallery.com). Bus 8, 20. **Open** 10am-5.30pm Tue-Sat. **No credit cards**.

A three-room gallery showing multimedia, paintings and sculpture by emerging US artists, including sound and video installations.

Thomas McCormick Gallery
835 W Washington Boulevard, at N Green Street (312 226 6800/www.thomasmccormick.com). Bus 8, 20. **Open** 10am-6pm Tue-Sat. **Credit** MC, V.
Paintings, drawings and sculpture from the 18th through 20th centuries by Tony Fitzpatrick, Richard Hunt, Robert McChesney and others.

Walsh Gallery
118 N Peoria Street, at W Randolph Street (312 829 3312/www.walshgallery.com). Bus 8, 20. **Open** 10.30am-5.30pm Tue-Sat. **Credit** AmEx, MC, V.
Owner Julie Walsh favours emerging Asian artists (primarily from China) in her installations.

Wicker Park & Bucktown

The **Flatiron Building**, at 1579 N Milwaukee Avenue, is home to many artists' studios.

Wood Street Gallery & Sculpture Garden
1239 N Wood Street, at W Division Street (773 227 3306/www.woodstreetgallery.com). CTA Division (Blue). **Open** 11am-5.30pm Tue-Fri; 10am-5pm Sat. **Credit** MC, V. **Map** p310 C8.
Located in a renovated school building and adjacent outdoor yard, located near the southern border of Wicker Park, this is an important showplace for new and established artists' painting and sculpture.

Arts & Entertainment

Gay & Lesbian

You'll have a gay old time: decadence is a way of life in Chicago's homo 'hoods.

In one episode of *Sex and the City*, the frisky foursome venture to a gay club, and find themselves flabbergasted by the vast sea of glistening Adonises. Are straight men this hot?, they wonder. The answer, of course, is no.

Most straight boys go to pot as they approach their 30s. They stop wanting to get laid as often as possible and begin to entertain thoughts of marriage, when they can spend their time watching football and cultivating a beer belly. If a straight guy picks up a men's magazine and sees a sculpted male model, he might think, 'I'd like to have his body'. A gay man, on the other hand, looks at the rippling abs and bulging biceps and thinks, 'I'd like to have his body. Naked, pressed against mine…'.

Yes, the überfag ideal still dominates the Chicago scene. More and more 'mos are reliving the youth they spent in repression, entering the adult world free of responsibilities and earning an income that's purely disposable. Gay men fall into the routine of mainstream conformity, and the local scene loses its diversity. The mantra here seems to be hit the gym, shave your body, get down to the tanning salon and try desperately to look like a porn star.

The best Gay stuff

For dancefloor scenery
Circuit on Saturdays. *See p214.*

For earning some cash
Spin's Shower Power Contest. *See p231.*

For a guaranteed shag
Steamworks on Thursday, when the youngsters arrive en masse. *See p216.*

For cocktails
The **Kit Kat Lounge & Supper Club**: try one of the fruitinis. *See p212.*

For peeing your pants
The ridiculously long lines for the bathrooms at **Rehab Lounge**. *See p213.*

For gawping at a porn star
One of the shows at **Man's Country**. *See p216.*

HOMO HAVENS
This mantra is most in evidence up in **Boystown**, the nickname given to the blocks around Halsted Street and Broadway north of Belmont Avenue in Lake View and Chicago's Gay Central. Broadway hustles and bustles during the day, as boys browse at bookshops, cruise cafés and pump iron at the gym, but Halsted is the main nightlife drag. There's something going on every evening here.

The other homo hotspot is **Andersonville**, centred around N Clark Street and W Foster Avenue and accessible via the Red line to Berwyn. The residents here are more easygoing than in Boystown, and fiercely opposed to the idea of their homo sweet home becoming yuppified, like its neighbours to the south.

DRUGS & CLUBS
With all the attention here on bodily perfection, it's interesting that so many gay men here do drugs. Ecstasy is popular, but don't consider trying to buy a roll. It's illegal and there's a surprisingly high chance that it'll be a dud. The most alarming trend is the increased use of GHB, a liquid drug nicknamed 'swirly' that, when mixed with alcohol, can turn fatal. Almost every weekend, you'll see an ambulance pull up to a Chicago club to whisk away some pathetic, twitching man who has overdosed. Indeed, it's not unheard of for compulsive party-goers to slip G into others' drinks, especially at after-hours parties: it's difficult to measure and is all but undetectable, but can be fatal when mixed with alcohol. A simple solution: avoid it at all costs.

Not every gay boy parties this much, though, and there are plenty of other options: mellower bars, strip shows, leather clubs. But the trend seems to be to emulate the fabulous lifestyles portrayed on the small screen: to live as much like *Sex and the City* as possible. Or, failing that, at least as *Queer as Folk…*

CRUISING
There are still areas in Chicago where men can go for clandestine sexual encounters with strangers, but the hustlers and drag queen hookers have left the Halsted and Broadway strips. It seems such exchanges are performed more discreetly now, via phone numbers listed in *Gay Chicago*'s Escort section or online. Bear in mind that prostitution is illegal and getting

Look out, Indigo Girls: you've got competition at **Girlbar**. *See p213*.

caught soliciting sex could carry a jail sentence. Sex in public is also a punishable offence. Montrose Harbor is a popular cruising ground, especially with those in cars: drive the circuitous route and you'll see solitary men sitting in their vehicles, tapping brake lights and flashing brights as a signal for sex.

LESBIAN NIGHTLIFE

Bad news, girls: **Star Gaze** (*see p214*) and **Girlbar** (*see p213*) are the only predominantly female drinking and dancing spots in the city, though lesbians can also always be found at **The Closet** (*see p213*). Your best bet is to take the Red line to Berwyn and head towards Clark Street in Andersonville.

In addition to these few, the nightclub **Berlin** (*see p231*) offers Women's Obsession most Wednesdays, though its Prince Sundays is similarly popular with the gals. The **Mountain Moving Coffee House** showcases female comics and singers in a monthly event that is strictly for women and children only. It's held at the Summerdale Community Church in Andersonville; call 312 409 0276 for details.

MEDIA

Perhaps the first thing you should do when you arrive in Chicago is head to Halsted Street or Broadway in the heart of Boystown, stop in at one of the many restaurants or shops and pick up one of the free gay and lesbian weeklies, which will give you the latest news on the scene.

Boi burst on to the scene in 2001, forcing its rival, the irreverent *Gab*, out of business. This glossy mini-mag contains listings, stylishly designed fluff pieces and the occasional article on drugs or workout routines. However, everyone picks it up for the photo pages.

News-wise, grab the **Chicago Free Press** or the inferior **Windy City Times**, now part of the Lamda group (www.outlineschicago.com). **Blacklines** and **En La Vida** are monthly publications pitched, respectively, at black and Spanish-speaking gay and lesbians.

For events listings with frivolous filler editorial – Filth, Billy Masters' gossip column, is one of the only things inside actually worth reading – flip through the ads in **Gay Chicago**. Don't miss Savage Love, the hilarious sex advice column at the end of Section 4 of the **Chicago Reader**. And turn that dial to WCKG 105.9 FM for the Windy City Radio show, which runs 10.30pm to midnight on Sundays.

Restaurants & cafés

Ann Sather

929 W Belmont Avenue, at N Sheffield Avenue, Lake View (773 348 2378/www.annsather.com). CTA Belmont (Brown, Purple, Red). **Open** 7am-9pm daily. **Main courses** $9-$12. **Credit** AmEx, DC, MC, V. **Map** p309 E2.

This gay-owned Swedish eaterie has been serving up hearty meals and cinnamon rolls for years, and still impresses. The owners are contributors to local

A right royal knees-up

As regulars at the Baton Lounge (*see p215*) and the Kit Kat Lounge & Supper Club (*see p212*) will all too readily vouch, drag queens are not yet a thing of the past, even though you see fewer and fewer around town these days. However, a decidedly 21st-century twist on the ancient art of gender-bending is beginning to erode the ubiquity and popularity of the cocks-in-frocks: the hot new trend in the Windy City is for girls to be boys. And, by golly, they do it so *well*.

Enter, stage left, the **Chicago Kings**, a troupe of performers that have created quite a buzz locally with their sporadic shows at various venues around town. At each event – details of which can be gleaned by calling 773 384 2437 or logging on to www.chicagokings.com – 30 or so drag kings take to the stage, lipsynching, camping, strutting and generally hamming it up. Past highlights have included a freaky one-armed Solid Gold dance to *Disco Inferno*,

a jab at the Boy Scouts, a sexy version of *Sweet Child O' Mine*, and a boy-band parody going under the name of *N*Stink*.

The girls adopt various personae as easily as they slip into their costumes. Every stereotype of masculinity and gay culture finds its way on to the stage. You'll see rockabilly bad-asses, fey poofters, sleazy pimps and leather daddies. Regular kings include Jeff Stroker, Maxx Hollywood, Mr Iggie Big and Andre Del Los Santos, who works the screaming crowd up into a frothing frenzy as easily as the Beatles did. Indeed, these rumple-haired chicks with drawn-on stubble have made many a gay boy swoon.

The shows are always raucously entertaining, the crowd filled with lesbian party gals, hipster homos and curious voyeurs. Be sure to bring a pocketful of dollar bills: you can show your appreciation by shoving money down a performer's pants. The queen is dead: long live the king...

---

gay charities, and are highly regarded in the community. For details of the various branches in town, check its website.
Branches: throughout the city.

Caribou Coffee
3300 N Broadway, at W Aldine Avenue, Lake View (773 477 3695/www.cariboucoffee.com). CTA Belmont (Brown, Purple, Red). **Open** 6am-11pm Mon-Thur, Sun; 6am-midnight Fri, Sat. **Credit** AmEx, MC, V. **Map** p309 F2.
Some gay men do temporarily give their livers a break, and this cosy coffeeshop is where they sip their mocha-skim-lattes-no-whipped-cream.

Deville
3335 N Halsted Street, at W Buckingham Place, Lake View (773 525 2505). CTA Belmont (Brown, Purple, Red). **Open** 6-11pm Mon, Wed-Sun. **Main courses** $14-$27. **Credit** AmEx, DC, Disc, MC, V. **Map** p309 F2.
This contemporary restaurant serves new American cuisine. Entrées run a bit pricey, but it's popular for dates and with groups. Tables are tightly packed, so take the opportunity to chat up your neighbours.

Kit Kat Lounge & Supper Club
3700 N Halsted Street, at W Waveland Avenue, Lake View: Wrigleyville (773 525 1111). CTA Addison (Red). **Open** 5.30pm-1am Tue-Sun. **Main courses** $13-$26. **Credit** AmEx, DC, Disc, MC, V. **Map** p309 F1.
A bright interior and white leather sofas feature in this hip hangout. The restaurant is narrow, but that's fine: it works as a runway for the drag queen

performers. The food is great, but many come here for the frou-frou martinis, including the Angel, garnished with a virginal cherry and a white feather.

Melrose
3233 N Broadway, at W Melrose Street, Lake View (773 327 2060). CTA Belmont (Brown, Purple, Red). **Open** 24hrs daily. **Main courses** $8-$17. **Credit** MC, V. **Map** p309 F2.
The place to see and be seen the morning after: after all, how else will you find out who went home with who and when? The diner fare has improved here, though Melrose draws many of its punters simply by dint of its all-hours opening.

Nookies Tree
3334 N Halsted Street, at W Buckingham Place, Lake View (773 248 9888). CTA Belmont (Brown, Purple, Red). **Open** 7am-midnight Mon-Thur, Sun; 24hrs Fri, Sat. **Main courses** $5-$12. **No credit cards**. **Map** p309 F2.
A cosy Lake View diner with a sidewalk café mural and pleasingly salubrious opening hours on the weekends. The attractive staff and surprisingly gourmet meals usually satisfy both the after-hours munchies and the morning-after brunch.

Bars

Big Chicks
5024 N Sheridan Road, at W Argyle Avenue, Andersonville (773 728 5511/www.bigchicks.com). CTA Argyle (Red). **Open** 4pm-2am Mon-Fri, Sun; 3pm-3am Sat. **No credit cards**.

Arts & Entertainment

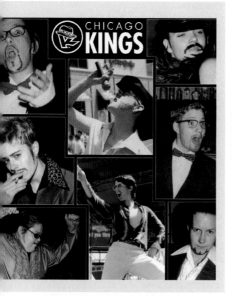

Lesbian-owned and operated, this tiny bar is a popular high-energy, late-night option, becoming packed with gay boys dancing to Britney and Madge once the other bars close.

Cocktail

3359 N Halsted Street, at W Roscoe Street, Lake View (773 477 1420). CTA Belmont (Brown, Purple, Red). **Open** 4pm-2am Mon-Fri; 2pm-3am Sat; 2pm-2am Sun. **Credit** AmEx, MC, V. **Map** p309 F2.
Small but swank, hip but unpretentious, this glammed-up bar is known for its cosmopolitans (think 'sissy Martinis') and its go-go boys, who gyrate at Spank, the Tuesday and Thursday staple. A great place to kick off the night's festivities.

Felt

3341 N Halsted Street, at W Roscoe Street, Lake View (773 404 8100). CTA Belmont (Brown, Purple, Red). **Open** 5pm-2am Mon-Fri, Sun; 5pm-3am Sat. **Credit** AmEx, MC, V. **Map** p309 F2.
A new-ish addition to the social fabric of Boystown, Felt offers cabaret acts some nights. At weekends, you'll be crushed like velvet the moment you walk in: the space is long and narrow, but oh-so-loungey and swank. Order one of the signature drinks at the bar, which glows a delightful shade of tangerine, and tumble into a cushy booth.

Girlbar

2625 N Halsted Street, at W Wrightwood Avenue, Lincoln Park (773 871 4210/www.girlbar.com). CTA Fullerton (Brown, Purple, Red). **Open** 7pm-2am Tue-Fri; 7pm-3am Sat; 7pm-2am Sun. **No credit cards. Map** p308 F4.
If you're a lesbian looking for some lovin', this is your best bet in the city. There's a small dancefloor, two patios and pool tables, and though it's mellow on most nights, weekends – when it'll cost you $5 to get in – can be jumping.

Rehab Lounge

3641 N Halsted Street, at W Addison Street, Lake View: Wrigleyville (773 325 2233/www.circuitclub.com). CTA Addison (Red). **Open** 4pm-2am Mon-Thur; 4pm-4am Fri, Sun; 4pm-5am Sat. **Credit** Disc, MC, V. **Map** p309 F1.
This small bar attached to Circuit (*see p214*) is best experienced early in the week. On Mondays at 9pm, it's Disco Bingo, an enjoyably twisted, drag queen-hosted version of the old church-hall favourite. Tuesdays, meanwhile, see the floor open up for the Rehab's karaoke night, which pleasingly welcomes wannabes and neverwillbes in equal measure.

Roscoe's

3354 N Halsted Street, at W Roscoe Street, Lake View (773 281 3355). CTA Addison (Red). **Open** 2pm-2am Mon-Thur; 1pm-2am Fri; noon-3am Sat; noon-2am Sun. **Credit** MC, V. **Map** p309 F2.
With pool rooms, bars, a dancefloor and a patio, this legendary, crowded guppie bar is frequented mostly by suburbanites and out-of-towners. Saturdays (when admission is $3) and Sundays are

This fun hangout is part-gallery, part-bar: owner Michelle Fire displays her eclectic collection of paintings and photographs. The predominantly male crowd enjoys the midnight special of free shots, but they also pile in for Fire's free barbecue on Sundays.

Cell Block

3702 N Halsted Street, at W Waveland Avenue, Lake View: Wrigleyville (773 665 8064/www.cellblock-chicago.com). CTA Addison (Red). **Open** 4pm-2am Mon-Fri; 2pm-3am Sat; 2pm-2am Sun. **No credit cards. Map** p309 F1.
The prison motif dominates this appropriately seedy bar. The leather dress code is strictly enforced for entry into the backroom, known as the Holding Cell. Venture into the Yard, with a chain web and a narrow cage, for S&M sexploits.

Chicago Eagle

5015 N Clark Street, at W Winnemac Avenue, Andersonville (773 728 0050). CTA Argyle (Red)/22 bus. **Open** 8pm-4am Mon-Fri, Sun; 8pm-5am Sat. **No credit cards.**
Entering through the back of a semi truck sets the rough-and-tumble mood at this leather bar. Get your boots spit-shined upstairs at the Eagle's cruisey bar, while in the Pit, there's a chain-link fence cage for holding 'prisoners' and plenty of dark corners.

The Closet

3325 N Broadway, at W Buckingham Place, Lake View (773 477 8533). CTA Belmont (Brown, Purple, Red). **Open** 2pm-4am Mon-Fri; noon-5am Sat; noon-4am Sun. **No credit cards. Map** p309 F2.

The star-spangled **Big Chicks**. *See p212.*

popular, but be sure to gawk at the guys in the Wet Boxers Contest on the last Thursday of the month. Monday's karaoke night is populated by singers who take themselves way too seriously.

Nightclubs

In addition to the clubs detailed below, **Berlin** (*see p231*) is big with queer clubbers. Weekends get packed and are a pansexual free-for-all: it's just as common to see two heteros mashing as electronica as it is to see two homos going at it. However, after 2am on Thursdays is when the gay boys really flock in, while Women's Obsession, held most Wednesdays with go-go gals galore, is big with the lesbian party crowd. On Sunday nights at **Crobar** (*see p230*), meanwhile, Circuit Mom lauds over seething masses of shirtless queer boys.

Charlie's

3726 N Broadway, at W Waveland Avenue, Lake View: Wrigleyville (773 871 8887). CTA Addison (Red). **Open** 3pm-2am Mon, Tue; 3pm-4am Wed-Fri, Sun; 3pm-5am Sat. **Admission** free-$3. **Credit** AmEx, DC, Disc, MC, V. **Map** p309 F1.
Yee-haw! The dancefloor is corralled off as gay men move in unison under the cowboy boot-shaped disco ball. If you don't know the steps, you won't be able to join until late, when the music shifts to pop dance. The bar is awash with Southern gents with aw-shucks attitudes that'll charm your pants off.

Circuit

3641 N Halsted Street, at W Addison Street, Lake View: Wrigleyville (773 325 2233/ www.circuitclub.com). CTA Addison (Red). **Open** 9pm-2am Wed, Thur; 9pm-4am Fri, Sun; 9pm-5am Sat. **Admission** $5-$12. **Credit** AmEx, Disc, MC, V. **Map** p309 F1.
Once the premier spot for Latino queers, this warehouse space has been taken over by pretty boys. Smooth, sculpted gays writhe about half-naked to pop-oriented house at the weekends, Saturday being *the* night to go. Two nights a week, the club returns to its roots: Wednesdays feature salsa DJs, while Thursdays offer Latino female impersonators.

Manhole

3458 N Halsted Street, at W Cornelia Avenue, Lake View: Wrigleyville (773 975 9244). CTA Addison (Red). **Open** 9pm-4am Mon-Fri, Sun; 9pm-5am Sat. **Admission** free-$8. **No credit cards. Map** p309 F2.
The sign above the entrance reading 'Stop moping and start groping' has gone, but this sewer-like stroke-and-poke is still going strong. Pornos play, and there's often an (un)dress code for the backroom dancefloor: you can't go in without taking off your shirt. Check for the Lights Out parties.

Sidetrack

3349 N Halsted Street, at W Roscoe Street, Lake View (773 477 9189). CTA Addison (Red). **Open** 3pm-2am Mon-Fri; 2pm-3am Sat; 2pm-2am Sun. **Credit** AmEx, DC, Disc, MC, V. **Map** p309 F2.
You can tell how people feel about this video bar by whether they call it Sidesnacks or Sidetrash. No matter how far it expands, the place is still jammed with cruising A&F-clad boys. Each night has its own theme: Sundays are showtunes, '80s music plays on Tuesdays, and Thursdays are a comedic yuckfest.

Star Gaze

5419 N Clark Street, at W Foster Avenue, Andersonville (773 561 7363). CTA Berwyn (Red). **Open** 6pm-2am Tue-Thur; 5pm-2am Fri; 11am-3am Sat; 3pm-3am Sun. **Credit** AmEx, Disc, MC, V.
This attitude-free lesbian hangout on the edge of Andersonville has the right stuff: a super-friendly bartender, pool tables and a dancefloor. It's a frisky place for the pussies to roam and show off their ping-pong talents.

The hole truth... **Manhole**.

Arts & Entertainment

Chicago calendar Gay & lesbian

Gays have never really needed a reason to celebrate: any old excuse will do. That said, there are a number of 'official' homo-themed events for which to be thankful; mark your calendars and time your visits accordingly...

One of two circuit parties held in Chicago, the **Fireball** is a Valentine's Day weekend event that draws party boys from around the world, even though it's in the middle of winter. Various activities take place all weekend, from club nights to classical concerts, with proceeds benefiting AIDS charities. Pick up one of the various free gay weeklies for listings, or check its website at www.thefireball.com.

Memorial Day weekend in May brings with it **International Mr Leather** (773 878 6360). Recently, the rather bizarre leather bazaar has been held at the venerable and venerated Palmer House Hotel, leaving shellshocked out-of-towners slack-jawed at the sight of the glitzy baroque lobby overrun with gleaming leather daddies.

On the last Sunday in June comes the fun-packed **Pride Parade** (773 348 8243), which runs along Halsted Street and Broadway in Boystown. Fill water bottles with celebratory Mimosas to kickstart the festivities, find a spot to cheer the floats as they cruise by, and head to Diversey Harbor for the rally that follows the parade. As a protest against the catcalls and boob-grabbing that have taken place at the Pride Parade, a hardcore local group called the Lesbian Avengers has started an alternative parade called the **Dyke March** (312 409 3705).

Mid August finds locals flocking to the largest of the city's summer street fairs, the weekend-long **Northalsted Market Days**. Mill about in the sunshine, browse the various booths, dehydrate yourself with alcohol and dance 'til you drop. The fair runs between Belmont and Grace, and you'll find yourself wandering back and forth all day. A month later, show your support for research by joining the **AIDS Walk** (312 422 8200), on the last Sunday in September.

The second circuit party hosted in Chicago is **Pumpkinhead**, held on Hallowe'en weekend and following a similarly full-on format as Fireball. Also around Hallowe'en is the **Night of 100 Drag Queens** at Sidetrack (see p214), with two stages filled with wannabes having their 15 minutes. It can be a bit overwhelming, but a good time is more or less guaranteed. The fabulous **Hallowe'en Parade and Costume Contest** along Halsted is usually entertaining, too: look for the man who dyes his pooch a different colour every year. And the following month, it's the **Chicago Lesbian & Gay International Film Festival** (see p200 **Chicago calendar: Film**).

Entertainment

About Face Theatre

3212 N Broadway, at W Belmont Avenue, Lake View (773 549 3290/www.aboutfacetheatre.com). CTA Belmont (Brown, Purple, Red). **Open** Box office times vary. **Tickets** $15-$25. **Credit** MC, V. **Map** p309 F2.
Consistency and quality rule the city's pre-eminent gay theatre troupe, whose productions are always of a high calibre. Sadly, 2002 may be the group's last year at its Broadway home: although it is looking for a new permanent base, it seems likely it will be itinerant for 2003 and possibly longer. Check its website for details.

Bailiwick Repertory

1229 W Belmont Avenue, at N Racine Avenue, Lake View (773 883 1090/www.bailiwick.org). CTA Belmont (Brown, Purple, Red). **Open** Box office 11am-showtime daily. **Tickets** $20-$35. **Credit** AmEx, Disc, MC, V. **Map** p309 E2.
Less serious than About Face, Bailiwick stages what can generously be described as progressive theatre: what the productions lack in engaging dialogue, they make up for in male nudity. It also hosts Pride Fest, a series of new and stylistically varied one-act plays, in July and August.

Baton Lounge

436 N Clark Street, at W Illinois Street, Near North (312 644 5269/www.thebatonshowlounge.com). CTA Grand (Red) or Merchandise Mart (Brown, Purple). **Open** Shows 8.30pm, 10.30pm, 12.30am Wed-Sun. **Admission** $8-$10. **Credit** AmEx, DC, Disc, MC, V. **Map** p306 H10.
Chicago's premier drag venue only allows pre-ops to perform, but these queens are so convincing that straight men have been known to fall for them. Look out for Mimi Marks, the Marilyn Monroe-esque belle of the ball who's worked the circuit for years, and October's Miss Continental Pageant. Chances are you'll be seated near a tittering bachelorette party.

Gentry

440 N State Street, at W Illinois Street, Near North (312 836 0933/www.gentryofchicago.com). CTA Grand (Red). **Open** 4pm-2am Mon-Fri, Sun; 4pm-3am Sat. **Admission** free. **Credit** AmEx, DC, Disc, MC, V. **Map** p306 H10.

Arts & Entertainment

Gentry: well, it's cheaper than a stage. *See p215.*

Gay professionals gather at this pair of splendid, mellow piano bars, with the Near North location the larger of the pair. Crooners sing cabaret-style, from *Showboat* to Stevie Nicks. Show 'em your stuff at the open-mic on Sundays downtown and on Tuesdays in Boystown.

If the singing at the Boystown branch hits all the wrong notes, head a block north to **Voltaire** (3441 N Halsted Street; 773 281 9320), a fine gay-friendly full-service restaurant and cabaret room. **Branch**: 3320 N Halsted Street, Lake View (773 348 1053).

Lucky Horseshoe Lounge
3169 N Halsted Street, at W Belmont Avenue, Lake View (773 404 3169). CTA Belmont (Brown, Purple, Red). **Open** 3pm-2am Mon-Fri; noon-3am Sat; noon-2am Sun. **Admission** free. **No credit cards. Map** p309 F3.
A seedy haunt frequented mostly by older gents who like to gawk at the low-rent strippers on the two platforms. Interesting, if a bit creepy.

Madrigal's
5316 N Clark Street, at W Berwyn Avenue, Andersonville (773 334 3033/www.madrigalsclub.com). CTA Berwyn (Red)/22 bus. **Open** 5pm-2am Mon-Fri, Sun; 5pm-3am Sat. **Admission** 2-drink minimum. **Credit** Disc, MC, V.
At weekends up at this Andersonville haunt, the hot male strippers do their best *Showgirls* moves on the pole on the stage. Less iffy than the 'Shoe, certainly.

Bathhouses & boothstores

Bijou Theatre
1349 N Wells Street, at W Evergreen Avenue, Old Town (312 943 5397/409 8100/www.bijouworld.com). CTA Clark/Division (Red) or Sedgwick (Brown, Purple). **Open** 24hrs daily. *Shows* 8.30pm, 10.30pm Mon, Thur; 2pm, 4pm, 8.30pm, 10.30pm Wed; 8pm, 10pm, midnight Fri, Sat. **Admission** *Shows* $19-$20. **No credit cards. Map** p307 H8.

Don't let the quaint Victorian townhouse exterior fool you: this theatre, at the southernmost tip of Old Town, fields hardcore flicks and exotic dancers.

Man's Country
5015 N Clark Street, at W Argyle Street, Andersonville (773 878 2069/www.manscountrychicago.com). CTA Argyle (Red). **Open** 24hrs daily. **Admission** $10-$40. **No credit cards**.
A bathhouse on the fringes of Andersonville, popular with thirtysomethings and featuring nude porn star dancers at weekends.

The Ram
3511 N Halsted Street, at W Cornelia Avenue, Lake View: Wrigleyville (773 525 9528). CTA Addison (Red). **Open** 24hrs daily. **Admission** prices vary. **Credit** AmEx, MC, V. **Map** p309 F2.
Porno movies and sexual devices are sold up front at this hangout up near Wrigley. Pay for entry to the back room, where men wander the narrow, labyrinthine hallway, head to booths or watch movies to get them in the mood.

Steamworks
3246 N Halsted Street, at W Belmont Avenue, Lake View (773 929 6081/www.steamworksonline.com). CTA Belmont (Brown, Purple, Red). **Open** 24hrs daily. **Admission** $6 membership; $7-$14 lockers; $20-$50 room rentals. **Credit** MC, V. **Map** p309 F2.
Choose a locker or a room, wrap in a towel and wander to your loins' content at the most pleasant of the city's bathhouses. You've got a better chance of scoring during the week: at weekends, the men can be full of attitude.

Shops

Barbara's Bookstore
1350 N Wells Street, at W Evergreen Avenue, Old Town (312 642 5044). CTA Clark/Division (Red). **Open** 9am-10pm Mon-Sat; 10am-9pm Sun. **Credit** AmEx, Disc, MC, V. **Map** p307 H8.

A cheery lesbian-owned store on the fringes of Old Town with a great array of titles, including children's books, fiction and biographies.

Batteries Not Included

3420 N Halsted Street, at W Roscoe Street, Lake View: Wrigleyville (773 935 9900/www.toysafterdark.com). CTA Belmont (Brown, Purple, Red). **Open** noon-midnight daily. **Credit** AmEx, MC, V. **Map** p309 F2.
Run out of lube in the middle of the night? Head to this sex shop, where the fun, queeny owner will let you test his favourite variety. Indulge your libido in the knowledge that half of the profits go to charity.

Beatnix

3400 N Halsted Street, at W Roscoe Street, Lake View: Wrigleyville (773 281 6933). CTA Addison (Red). **Open** noon-9pm Mon-Wed, Fri; noon-10pm Thur; 11am-midnight Sat; 11am-10pm Sun.
Credit MC, V. **Map** p309 F2.
You can't miss the glamorous window displays at this trendy boutique, which peddles new fashions and thrift-store duds. A good place to snazz up your wardrobe on a limited budget, it's also wig-and-dress central for the town's drag queens.

Gay Mart

3457 N Halsted Street, at W Cornelia Avenue, Lake View: Wrigleyville (773 929 4272). CTA Addison (Red). **Open** 11am-7pm Mon-Thur, Sun; 11am-8pm Fri, Sat. **Credit** AmEx, Disc, MC, V. **Map** p309 F2.
An expansive kitsch-fest jam-packed with Wonder Woman, Dr Seuss, Curious George and Star Wars memorabilia. Giggle over the anatomically gifted Billy dolls: they'd make Barbie and Ken blush.

Unabridged Bookstore

3251 N Broadway, at W Belmont Avenue, Lake View (773 883 9119). CTA Belmont (Brown, Purple, Red). **Open** 10am-10pm Mon-Fri; 10am-8pm Sat, Sun. **Credit** AmEx, Disc, MC, V. **Map** p309 F2.
The megastores haven't closed down this indie outfit, which stocks great selections of magazines and books. The staff stick cards with their recommendations along the shelves. Columnist Dan Savage once said this was the first place he shoplifted porn.

Universal Gear

3153 N Broadway, at W Belmont Avenue, Lake View (773 296 1090/www.universalgear.com). CTA Belmont (Brown, Purple, Red). **Open** 11am-10pm Mon-Thur, Sun; 11am-11pm Fri, Sat. **Credit** AmEx, Disc, MC, V. **Map** p309 F3.
Dubbed Universal Queer and selling contemporary Euro chic duds for men, this is where the fashionable gays shop 'til they drop.

We're Everywhere

3434 N Halsted Street, at W Newport Avenue, Lake View: Wrigleyville (773 404 0590). CTA Addison (Red). **Open** 11am-8pm Mon-Fri; 11am-7pm Sat, Sun. **Credit** AmEx, Disc, MC, V. **Map** p309 F2.
Where else would you buy your Boystown T-shirt? This gay gift shop is filled with homo-themed clothes and rainbow jewellery.

Need souvenirs? Try **Batteries Not Included**.

Women & Children First

5233 N Clark Street, at W Foster Avenue, Andersonville (773 769 9299/ www.womenandchildrenfirst.com). CTA Berwyn (Red). **Open** 11am-7pm Mon, Tue; 11am-9pm Wed-Fri; 10am-7pm Sat; 11am-6pm Sun.
Credit AmEx, Disc, MC, V.
Dykes and Tykes, as some call it, is a must for feminist and child-oriented literature, specialising in lesbian and gay titles, music, videos and magazines.

Arts & Entertainment

Music

It's sweet home Chicago, but don't go telling locals all they have is the blues.

Rock, Blues & Jazz

Chicago in the new millennium finds itself between music movements. During the 1940s and '50s, the city was the world centre for blues. Post-war African-Americans from the south flocked to Chicago; when they got here, they plugged in their guitars and invented the electric blues, the reverberations of which are still felt in the 21st century. But the heyday of Muddy Waters and Howlin' Wolf are long gone, and while the electric blues can still be heard in town, it's nowhere near as prevalent as it once was (and less popular with locals).

But as the blues fade away, the void is being filled. During the early 1990s, the Smashing Pumpkins led a vanguard of alternative rock bands; then, as alt rock gave way to indie rock, the city kept pace via labels such as Drag City and Thrill Jockey. Hand in hand with the indie rock scene, post-rock and all its intelligent greyness became a city force, led by Tortoise. And then came the insurgent country scene of the late '90s, with artists such as the Handsome Family finding an audience with a brand of country that had little in common with Shania.

The net result of all this? No one genre dominates Chicago's scene; the variety is huge. Regardless of the local flavour, Chicago is also a critical destination for any touring band worth its salt. Though bands seem

loath to hit Chicago during winter, the spring, summer and autumn months are near bursting with music.

The music scene remains relatively static in Chicago, with new venues rarely opening. We have Mayor Daley to thank for this: strict city regulations concerning loud music and liquor licences tend to stifle artistic hotbeds before they're even born. The venues listed here are the cornerstones of the scene.

TICKETS AND INFORMATION

For details on what's on, check *Newcity* and the *Chicago Reader*. *Newcity*, the smaller of the two, doesn't list every event in the city, but the listings are fairly extensive and its format makes for easy sifting. The *Chicago Reader* is murderously comprehensive. For advance planning, try www.chicagoreader.com or www.newcitychicago.com.

Tickets for most club shows are available only at the door, though even popular bands playing small clubs rarely sell out before the day of the show. Some record shops sell tickets, but inconsistently: you're best off going to the venue or **Ticketmaster** (312 902 1500/ www.ticketmaster.com). Blues and jazz clubs don't sell advance tickets unless the act is huge.

Weekday shows in smaller clubs (up to **Double Door** or even **House of Blues** size) usually start at about 9pm and finish at 1am. On Fridays and Saturdays, shows run 10pm to 2am. In giant venues such as the **Allstate Arena** and the **United Center**, shows start and finish earlier: usually 7.30pm to 10.30pm. And for the clubs and bars, anything not designated an all-ages show is only open to those over the age of 21. Carry a photo ID.

The best | Live music

Symphony Center
Where Dan's the man. *See p226.*

Hideout
Roots manoeuvres. *See p220.*

Grant Park
Summer in the city. *See p225*
Chicago calendar.

Green Mill
Jazz done right. *See p224.*

Checkerboard Lounge
Damn right, they got the blues. *See p222.*

General & rock clubs

Abbey Pub
3420 W Grace Avenue, at N Elston Avenue, Avondale (773 478 4408/www.abbeypub.com). CTA Addison (Blue). **Open** 11am-2am Mon-Fri; 9am-1am Sat, Sun. **Credit** AmEx, DC, Disc, MC, V.
The front is an Irish restaurant, and the back was – until recently – an underused space devoted to Irish music. But 2001 and 2002 saw the Abbey Pub come into its own. The Abbey combines a great space with good acoustics, and has become one of the city's premier venues. Its location, however, makes it difficult to get to by public transport; take a cab.

Abbey Pub: a religious experience. *See p218.*

Allstate Arena

6920 N Mannheim Road, at W Higgins Road, Rosemont (847 635 6601/www.allstatearena.com). CTA Rosemont (Blue). **Open** *Box office* 11am-7pm Mon-Fri; noon-5pm Sat; 3hrs before show Sun. **Credit** AmEx, Disc, MC, V.

Home to American Hockey League franchise the Chicago Wolves, this super-venue is reserved for bands too small for the United Center *(see p222)*. The arena has decent sound, but its northern location in Rosemont, closer to O'Hare than downtown) makes it more attractive to suburbanites than city dwellers.

Aragon Ballroom

1106 W Lawrence Avenue, at N Broadway, Uptown (773 561 9500/www.aragon.com). CTA Lawrence (Red). **Open** *Box office* from 5pm on day of show. **No credit cards.**

Built more than 70 years ago, the Aragon Ballroom (or 'Brawlroom', as it's unlovingly dubbed by local gig-goers) was constructed for ballroom dancing. These days, the 4,500-seater venue is the place to hear bands such as Primus and Gorillaz. Unfortunately, the stately surroundings make for terrible sound: unless you're one of the lucky ones up front, you'll just catch echoes.

Cubby Bear

1059 W Addison Street, at N Clark Street, Lake View: Wrigleyville (773 327 1662/www.cubbybear.com). CTA Addison (Red). **Open** *Cubs games* 10am-2am Mon-Fri, Sun; 10am-3am Sat. *Other times* 4pm-2am Mon-Fri; 11am-3am Sat; 11am-2am Sun. **Admission** free-$7. **Credit** AmEx, DC, Disc, MC, V. **Map** p309 E1.

A long-time venue that's changed names more often than the Cubs change managers, the Cubby Bear offers anything from Digital Underground to Lee 'Scratch' Perry or Grateful Dead cover bands. Its location means it's a favourite spot for post-Cubs games revelry, more's the pity. *See also p161.*

Double Door

1572 N Milwaukee Avenue, at N Damen Avenue, Wicker Park (773 489 3160/www.doubledoor.com). CTA Damen (Blue). **Open** 8pm-2am Mon-Fri, Sun; 8pm-3am Sat. **Admission** $3-$12. **Credit** (bar only) AmEx, Disc, MC, V. **Map** p310 B7.

The Metro's younger, smaller brother *(see p220)*, the Double Door is a decent-sized room close to the buzzing Damen-North-Milwaukee junction that fits 500 and hosts rock as well as hip hop and DJ events. Get away from the music downstairs, with pool tables, video games and a second full-service bar.

Elbo Room

2871 N Lincoln Avenue, at W George Street, Lake View (773 549 5549/www.elboroomchicago.com). CTA Diversey (Brown, Purple). **Open** 7pm-2am Mon-Fri; 7pm-3am Sat; 8pm-2am Sun. **Admission** free-$25. **Credit** AmEx, Disc, MC, V. **Map** p309 D3.

A two-floor venue in Lake View area, the artfully misspelt Elbo Room books an eclectic range of acts: everything from straight rock to acid jazz, hip hop to funk. The ground-floor room is a good but hardly enormous space; the dimly lit upstairs bar offers sanctuary from the sounds. *See also p159.*

Empty Bottle

1035 N Western Avenue, at W Cortez Street, Wicker Park (773 276 3600/www.emptybottle.com). CTA Damen (Blue). **Open** 3pm-2am Mon-Fri; noon-3am Sat; noon-2am Sun. **Admission** $3-$12. **No credit cards. Map** p310 A9.

One of the city's premier club-sized venues, the Empty Bottle hosts rock, punk, metal, jazz and pop shows. A slew of cheap beers and liquors ensures that it gets business from a loyal group of regulars. Owner Bruce Finkleman has a good ear for music: the place is usually jammed on Fridays and Saturdays. Tuesdays are held for Ken Vandermark; Wednesday is the night for jazz and improvised and experimental music.

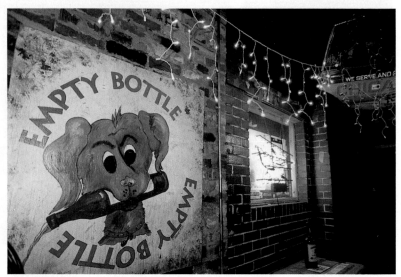

Empty Bottle: full of sounds. *See p219.*

Fireside Bowl

2646 W Fullerton Avenue, at N Talman Avenue,
Bucktown (773 486 2700). CTA California (Blue
(NW)). **No credit cards. Open** 6pm-2am daily.
The lanes and pins are still in residence at this 800-
capacity venue, but bowling comes second to the
punk and hardcore shows here. The Fireside's status as the city's only all-ages venue means it attracts
a young, up-for-it crowd, though it's rarely over
half full. During summer, the Fireside's lack of air-
conditioning or windows makes it feel like its name.

Hideout

1354 W Wabansia Avenue, at N Ada Street, Wicker
Park (773 227 4433/www.hideoutchicago.com).
CTA 9, 72 bus. **Open** 8pm-2am Mon; 4pm-2am
Tue-Fri; 7pm-3am Sat; occasional special events Sun.
No credit cards.
Hidden in an industrial corridor on the fringes of
Wicker Park, the Hideout is Chicago's most beloved
roots bar, and a hangout for those on the city's coun-
try scene. Tuesdays are reserved for Devil in a
Woodpile, a country blues act that often packs the
place on a night when few bars are occupied. Owner
Tim Tuten enthusiastically introduces every act.

HotHouse

31 E Balbo Drive, at S Wabash Avenue, South Loop
(312 362 9707/www.hothouse.net). CTA Harrison
(Red). **Open** 5pm-2am Mon-Fri, Sun; 5pm-3am
Sat. **Admission** $5-$30. **Credit** AmEx, MC, V.
Map p305 H13.
The HotHouse was a floating operation until a few
years ago, when it settled into this South Loop home
and became the city's premier world music venue.

It incorporates two spaces that fit around 200 people
each, though they're rarely in use simultaneously.
You might catch the Congo's Sam Mangwana on one
night, the Chicago Samba School the next and Native
American poetry readings the night after.

House of Blues

329 N Dearborn Street, at W Kinzie Street, Near
North (312 923 2000/www.hob.com). CTA Grand
(Red) or State (Brown, Green, Orange, Purple). **Open**
Restaurant 11.30am-10pm daily. *Music* hours vary.
Credit AmEx, DC, Disc, MC, V. **Map** p309 H11.
Chicago's branch of the HoB chain is worth visiting
if only to see the gaudy art, which places the ambience between juke joint and opera house. The venue
presents some of the best national and international
acts (rarely blues) on one of the city's best sound systems. Purists scorn the place, but its strength lies not
in the blues, but its eclecticism: any place that runs
the gamut from Common to Frankie Knuckles to
T-Model Ford must have something going for it.
There's a gospel brunch in the restaurant on Sunday.

Metro & Smart Bar

3730 N Clark Street, at N Racine Avenue, Lake View:
Wrigleyville (773 549 0203/www.metrochicago.com).
CTA Addison (Red). **Open** *Metro* hours vary.
Smart Bar 10pm-4am Mon-Fri, Sun; 10pm-5am Sat.
No credit cards. Map p309 E1.
The mid-sized Metro has a great reputation and
attracts national and international bands to its intimate space. The main floor is standing only; there
are tables and chairs on the balcony. The sound
is great and the sightlines better, and the Metro
remains one of the best venues in the city. Long-time

owner Joe Shanahan's attention has helped bring notoriety to local acts such as Smashing Pumpkins, though we shouldn't hold him entirely responsible.

Downstairs, the Smart Bar features DJs nightly, spinning anything from Chicago house to hip hop or punk; major touring DJs like Kid Koala also put in appearances here. The neighbourhood crowd is an interesting mix of club hoppers, alternative hipsters, gig-goers, goths and frat kids.

Old Town School of Folk Music

4544 N Lincoln Avenue, at W Montrose Avenue, Ravenswood (773 728 6000/www.oldtownschool.org). CTA Western (Brown). **Open** *Box office* 9.30am-10pm Mon-Thur; 9.30am-5pm Fri-Sun. **Admission** $5-$30. **Credit** AmEx, MC, V.

The 44-year-old Old Town School of Folk Music recently moved from its digs in, um, Old Town to this spacious facility on the edge of Ravenswood. The place is primarily a music school, but on most weekends, concerts by folk, bluegrass and country artists are held in its 420-seat theatre. *See also p195.*

Park West

322 W Armitage Avenue, at N Clark Street, Lincoln Park (773 929 5959/www.parkwestchicago.com). CTA Armitage (Brown, Purple). **Open** *Box office* 10.30am-4.30pm Mon-Fri; also 6-8pm on show nights. **Admission** $20-$30. **No credit cards**. **Map** p308 G6.

This upscale venue caters to an older audience. Acts ranging from jazz to light rock are the order of the day, with occasional visits from the Dark Star Orchestra, a pathetic Grateful Dead cover band who pull in legions of idiots. A semicircle of booths and chairs surrounds the stage (phone ahead to reserve), and it usually operates a no-smoking policy.

Riviera Theatre

4746 N Racine Avenue, at W Lawrence Avenue, Uptown (773 275 6800). CTA Lawrence (Brown). **Open** *Box office* 1-2hrs before show. **No credit cards**.

Part of the Uptown triumvirate (with the Aragon Ballroom, *see p219* and the Green Mill, *see p224*), the Riviera is larger than the Metro (*see p220*) but smaller than the Aragon. You're not likely to find anything above and beyond radio fare here on a bill that might range from the Offspring to Yes.

Schubas Tavern & Harmony Grill

3159 N Southport Avenue, at W Belmont Avenue, Lake View (773 525 2508/www.schubas.com). CTA Belmont (Brown, Purple, Red) or Southport (Brown). **Open** 11am-2am Mon-Fri; 8am-3am Sat; 9am-2am Sun. **Admission** free-$25. **Credit** AmEx, DC, Disc, MC, V. **Map** p309 D3.

The backroom of Schubas is a catch-all venue for every type of music you could hope to find or avoid. It put itself on the map as a venue for insurgent country in the late 1990s, but has since garnered a reputation as an indie-rock hub. While the front bar is an established – and yuppie-ish – hangout, the back attracts all sorts. The adjacent

Now playing Rock

Given the number of rock venues around town, it's a good job Chicago has so many decent bands to play them. Among the best? The **Dishes** offer simple, Detroit-style punk rock with catchy female vocals, while **Atombombpocketknife** are an insanely loud rock quartet on Southern Records that blend angular guitars with a sense of melody. **Califone** count former members of Red Red Meat among their number; the **Nerves** play edgy garage rock with snarling vocals and splashes of 1960s psychedelia. A couple of duos are worth looking out for: **Cash Audio**, who play hardcore, stripped-down blues rock with enough Elvis in the vocals to keep the old guys happy, and **Evil Beaver**, who play raunchy thrash metal.

Thanks to local label Bloodshot Records, Chicago's been setting the pace in alternative country for a while, and many acts play regularly in town. Mekons main man Jon Langford relocated from Leeds to Chicago (well, who wouldn't?) a few years back, and fronts beer-soaked reprobates the **Waco Brothers** and chaotic collective the **Pine Valley Cosmonauts**. The Cosmonauts backed up singer and sometime Hideout bartender **Kelly Hogan** on her fine *Beneath the Country Underdog* record; Hogan, meanwhile, sung back-up on **Neko Case**'s gutsy *Furnace Room Lullaby*. None of them have ever appeared on albums by **Devil in a Woodpile** (*pictured*; they play the Hideout every Tuesday), **Anna Fermin's Trigger Gospel** or the marvellous **Robbie Fulks**. But it's surely only a matter of time.

Checkerboard Lounge: blues standard.

Harmony Grill dishes up splendid gourmet sandwiches, and is an easy and cheap place in which to grab a meal before the show.

United Center

1901 W Madison Street, at N Damen Avenue, West Town (312 559 1212). CTA Ashland (Green) or Medical Center (Blue). **Open** *hours vary.* **Credit** AmEx, Disc, MC, V.

The United Center is a monstrous venue that's home to the Chicago Bulls, the Chicago Blackhawks and, from time to time, concerts by mammoth touring artists both national and international. It comes with all the cavernous acoustics and terrible sightlines that you'd expect from such a place, not to mention the prohibitively expensive concessions.

Wild Hare

3530 N Clark Street, at W Newport Avenue, Lake View: Wrigleyville (773 327 4273). CTA Addison (Red). **Open** *7pm-2am Mon-Fri, Sun; 7pm-3am Sat.* **No credit cards. Map** p309 E2.

The city's only reggae bar, the Wild Hare pulls international acts as well as those from the healthy local scene. There's reggae seven nights a week, with an occasional ska or Jamaican soul act thrown in. As close to a dancehall as you'll get here, though too often the music leans towards lovers' rock.

Blues clubs

Blue Chicago

736 N Clark Street, at W Superior Street, Near North (312 642 6261/www.bluechicago.com). CTA Chicago (Red). **Open** *8pm-2am Mon-Fri; 8pm-3am Sat.* **Admission** *$7.* **Credit** AmEx, MC, V. **Map** p306 H10.

This pair of clubs does a good job of recreating a juke joint feel, though both are filled with out-of-towners. Blue Chicago at Superior is the larger, with the Ohio location built in the long tavern style. Acts are local, and while aficionados will cringe at the first four notes of *Sweet Home Chicago*, the venues' penchant for catering to tourists ensures that you'll hear it, and every other tired standard, at least once a night. **Branch**: 536 N Clark Street, Near North (312 661 0100).

Buddy Guy's Legends

754 S Wabash Avenue, at E Balbo Drive, South Loop (312 427 0333/www.buddyguys.com). CTA Harrison (Red). **Open** *5pm-2am Mon-Thur; 4pm-2am Fri; 5pm-3am Sat; 6pm-2am Sun.* **Credit** AmEx, DC, Disc, MC, V. **Map** p305 H13.

Buddy Guy *is* Chicago blues, and his club, despite the heavy presence of tourists, is one of the city's most dynamic, offering a sampling of new and old blues artists (Guy plays a long run in January). Unlike the juke joints it attempts to recall, Buddy's is large; it offers live blues nightly, with a free acoustic show for the after-work crowd on Fridays. The barbecue would smoke the glitter off the House of Blues' walls. A tourist trap, but one with substance. The club will be moving a block north during 2003, to 635 S Wabash.

Checkerboard Lounge

423 E 43rd Street, at S Martin Luther King Drive, South Side (773 624 3240). Bus 4. **Open** *11am-2am Mon-Fri, Sun; 11am-3am Sat.* **Admission** *$3-$10.* **No credit cards.**

A one-time home-from-home for Buddy Guy and Junior Wells, the Checkerboard is one of the few blues clubs over 25 years old. A little run down and, thanks to King Drive renovations, in danger of closing, it's among the most authentic clubs in the city, its heritage all the more realistic due to its South Side location (take a cab). A great alternative to the plain-Jane downtown clubs, and a little seedy 'n' all.

Kingston Mines

2548 N Halsted Street, at W Wrightwood Avenue, Lincoln Park (773 477 4646/www.kingstonmines.com). CTA Fullerton (Brown, Purple, Red). **Open** *8pm-4am Mon-Fri, Sun; 8pm-5am Sat.* **Admission** *$10-$15.* **Credit** AmEx, DC, Disc, MC, V. **Map** p308 F4.

Another veteran of Chicago's blues scene, Kingston Mines has been bringing the city solid electric blues for more than 30 years. Its Lincoln Park location attracts a number of tourists but not to the extent of the downtown clubs, and its late licence brings in a huge after-hours crowd. With two stages in adjoining rooms, the venue boasts non-stop blues from 9.30pm until last call. There's a restaurant attached.

Lee's Unleaded Blues

7401 S Chicago Avenue, at 74th Street, South Side (773 493 3477). CTA 30 bus. **Open** noon-2am Mon-Fri, Sun; noon-3am Sat. **No credit cards**.

A gritty juke joint inhabited mainly by long-time regulars, Lee's has been one of the South Side's favourite clubs for over two decades. The acts here aren't big names, but the intimate confines encourage call-and-response interaction between performer and crowd.

Lilly's

2513 N Lincoln Avenue, at W Altgeld Street, Lincoln Park (773 525 2422). CTA Fullerton (Brown, Purple, Red). **Open** 4pm-2am Wed-Fri; 4pm-3am Sat. **Admission** free-$5. **No credit cards**. **Map** p308 F5.

A cosy two-floor blues spot that keeps things cheap. What sets it apart is the dizzying array of beers and the piano, an instrument few Chicago clubs bother with. Acts draw on the local talent pool, though an occasional touring bluesman stops in. It's a small club, but rarely gets too crowded.

Rosa's

3420 W Armitage Avenue, at N Kimball Avenue, Hermosa (773 342 0452/www.rosaslounge.com). CTA 73, 82 bus. **Open** 8pm-2am Tue-Fri; 8pm-3am Sat. **Admission** $5-$10. **Credit** AmEx, Disc, MC, V.

While not necessarily the most authentic blues club in the city, this West Side hangout is widely considered to be the best. Owners Tony and Rosa book 100% authentic blues – some from the Mississippi Delta, some Texas blues, some Chicago blues – and the crowd knows how to appreciate it.

Smoke Daddy

1804 W Division Street, at N Wood Street, Wicker Park (773 772 6656). CTA Division (Blue). **Open** 11am-1am Mon, Fri-Sun; 5pm-1am Tue-Thur. **Credit** AmEx, Disc, MC, V. **Map** p310 C8.

Attempting to mimic a vintage roadhouse/diner joint, Smoke Daddy serves up a fiery barbecue in the TexArkana style and features free music nightly. Jazz and rockabilly both find a home here, but the weekend slant is towards the blues. An excellent excuse to enjoy a beef brisket sandwich and explore this edge of Wicker Park's Division Street.

Jazz clubs

Green Dolphin Street

2200 N Ashland Avenue, at N Clybourn Avenue, Lincoln Park (773 395 0066/www.jazzitup.com). Bus 6, 70. **Open** *Dining room* 5.30-10pm Tue-Thur, Sun; 5.30-11pm Fri, Sat. *Jazz club* 8pm-1am Tue-Thur; 8.30pm-2am Fri, Sun; 8.30pm-3am Sat. **Admission** $5-$15. **Credit** AmEx, DC, MC, V. **Map** p308 D5.

A wannabe high-end restaurant/music venue aimed at and patronised by well-paid 30- to 50-year-olds. Light jazz is the general fare, though Tuesdays feature Latin and world jazz. Still, an evening here is less about the music than the fine food and the general ambience.

Now playing Jazz

Five-time Grammy nominee **Kurt Elling** (*pictured*) is kind of a Mark Murphy for the 21st century, a beatnik song stylist, improviser and master of vocalese. Check out *Live from Chicago* (Blue Note) for a great take on the rent party theme, or try *Flirting with Twilight* (Blue Note) for Elling at his best. If he's in town, he plays the Green Mill (*see p224*) on Wednesdays.

Pianist and singer **Patricia Barber** is a study in contrasts – intensely detached or seriously frivolous – but rarely off the mark. Her *Modern Cool* and *Nightclub* recordings (on Premonition) reflect Barber's years as the solo act at the now-vanished Gold Star Sardine Bar on Lake Shore Drive.

Plugged-in guitarist **Bobby Broom**, another Premonition act, debuted in 2001 with *Stand*, a masterful collection of 1960s tunes by the likes of the Beatles and Simon and Garfunkel. Broom plays at Martyrs (3855 N Lincoln Avenue, Lake View; 773 404 9494) on Sundays.

Other jazz acts worth catching include Pat Metheny Group drummer (and Northwestern University faculty member) **Paul Wertico**, Latin jazz mogul **Marshall Vente**, critically acclaimed trumpeter **Orbert Davis**, MacArthur 'genius' grant recipient and reedster **Ken Vandermark**, sultry vocalist **Bobbi Wilsyn** and acoustic guitar phenomenon **Fareed Haque**.

Arts & Entertainment

Rosa's: best blues in town? *See p223.*

Green Mill

4802 N Broadway, at W Lawrence Avenue,
Uptown (773 878 5552). CTA Lawrence (Brown).
Open noon-4am Mon-Fri; noon-5am Sat; 11am-4am
Sun. **Admission** $3-$8. **Credit** AmEx.
This venerable club dates back to the days of Al
Capone, who used to sit in the booth facing the door
so no one could get in without him seeing. It's small
and fills fast on the weekends: get there early if you
want to sit. Acts range from jump blues to experi-
mental jazz, with Sundays reserved for the Uptown
Poetry Slam (*see p242* **Made in Chicago**).

Jazz Showcase

59 W Grand Avenue, at N Clark Street, Near North
(312 670 2473). CTA Grand (Red). **Open**
8pm, 10pm Tue-Thur; 9pm, 11pm Fri, Sat; 4pm,
8pm, 10pm Sun. **Credit** MC, V. **Map** p306 H10.
Owner Joe Segal has been promoting shows for more
than 50 years, and sticks to what he knows best:
bebop, hard bop and just plain old bop. The music's
great, but the club is smoke-free and isn't the friendliest of places: it stops shy of a dress code, but you'll
feel the eyes if you show up in jeans and a T-shirt.

The Note

1565 N Milwaukee Avenue, at N Damen Avenue,
Wicker Park (773 489 0011). CTA Damen (Blue).
Open 8pm-4am Mon, Wed, Thur; 10pm-4am
Tue, Sun; 8pm-5am Sat. **Admission** $5-$10.
Credit AmEx, MC, V. **Map** p310 B7.
This hip Wicker Park joint – designated on the outside by a solitary, neon blue quaver – offers everything from salsa to R&B, but the emphasis is on jazz,
acid jazz and hip hop. Weekends here are a flurry of
jazz fans, intelligent punks and anyone else bored
with the consensus: an equal swathe of all ages, cul-
tures and colours, one of the friendliest crowds in
town. There's a pool table and bar out front, with
music going off in the long, table-filled back room.

Pops For Champagne

2934 N Sheffield Avenue, at W Wellington Avenue,
Lake View (773 472 1000/www.popschampagne.com).
CTA Wellington (Brown, Purple). **Open** 5pm-2am

Mon-Thur, Sun; 5pm-2am Fri; 8pm-3am Sat.
Admission $6 Mon-Thur; $10 Fri, Sat; free Sun.
Credit AmEx, DC, Disc, MC, V. **Map** p309 E3.
A bar with more than 100 kinds of champagne, Pops
features smooth piano jazz for an over-50s crowd
(yikes) and a high degree of sophistication: there's a
fireplace, minimal lighting and very professional
waiting and bar staff. The jazz isn't the most
dynamic. And neither's the venue. *See also p161.*

Velvet Lounge

2128 S Indiana Avenue, at E 21st Street, South
Side (312 791 9050/www.velvetlounge.net). CTA
Cermak/Chinatown (Red). **Open** 9.30pm-1.30am
Thur-Sat; 7-11.30pm Sun. **Admission** $7-$10.
No credit cards. Map p304 J16.
Just south of McCormick Place, the Velvet Lounge,
owned by jazz great Fred Anderson, is an insiders'
jazz venue, attracting members (both in the audience
and on stage) of the local avant-garde jazz scene. It's
a small room with good acoustics and a heart of bop.

Classical & Opera

Full orchestral and classical music are woefully
under-represented in Chicago. That's not to
say it doesn't exist, but outside the **Chicago
Symphony Orchestra** and the university
ensembles, few orchestras have their own
performance spaces, which doesn't make for a
very stable scene. There's also very little public
arts funding in Chicago. That's the bad news.
The good news is that Chicago boasts two of
the world's premier classical music groups in
the form of the CSO and the **Lyric Opera**.

Now in its 111th year, the CSO has cemented
its reputation among the planet's elite since
Daniel Barenboim took over as musical director
in the early 1990s. Barenboim's adventurous
spirit is given full flight, as classic works rub
shoulders with challenging new pieces in the
CSO's nine-month season, launched with a
free day of music on a Saturday in September.
The CSO also runs the only training orchestra
association in the US: the **Civic Orchestra
of Chicago**. Founded in 1920, it presents eight
to ten concerts a year, all of them free.

The Lyric Opera, meanwhile, is headed by
William Mason, who succeeded general director
Ardis Krainik in 1997, and who has worked for
the Lyric for most of his 30-year career. Though
Bruno Bartoletti retired as artistic director in
April 2000, Matthew Epstein has carried on the
good work. It's work that's much appreciated
by locals: most performances are sellouts.

Among the chamber groups worth looking
out for are the Chicago Chamber Musicians, the
Chicago Sinfonietta, the Concertante di Chicago,
the Pacifica String Quartet and the Music of
the Baroque. During summer, two main venues

open up for music: **Ravinia** and **Grant Park**, the latter of which doesn't charge for entry unless you want to sit in the really posh bit.

TICKETS

Tickets for the CSO, Lyric Opera and Ravinia are available through their respective offices, as well as through **Ticketmaster** (312 902 1500/ www.ticketmaster.com). Tickets are rarely sold in advance for small chamber concerts; in any case, many are free. Concerts in churches are also free, though the prices in other venues vary wildly: the Civic Opera charges up to $120, for example. For information on what's on when, pick up the *Chicago Reader*.

Leaving aside Symphony Center, the Lyric, Ravinia and Grant Park, performances are held in the city and suburbs with little consistency. Listed here are the venues used most frequently for classical events, though the companies that play each venue vary from year to year.

Venues

Anderson Chapel at North Park University

3225 W Foster Avenue, at N Sawyer Avenue, North Side (773 244 5743). Bus 92. **Open** hours vary. **No credit cards**.
Anderson Chapel is home to the Chamber Music at North Park series. Weekends also occasionally feature gospel, symphonic choirs and symphony orchestras. As you'd expect, it's church seating here, but it is surprisingly comfortable.

Chapel of St James Quigley Preparatory Seminary

831 N Rush Street, at E Pearson Street, Gold Coast (312 787 8625). CTA Chicago (Red). **Open** hours vary. **No credit cards. Map** p306 J9.
Built in 1919 and patterned after Paris's Sainte-Chapelle, this building, in the National Register of Historic Places, features mostly smaller-scale performers. Soloists in recital, choirs such as His Majestie's Clerkes and the Chicago Sinfonietta play, usually for free, on a regular basis. During the warmer months, concerts are held in the courtyard.

Civic Opera House

20 N Wacker Drive, at E Madison Street, the Loop (312 332 2244/www.lyricopera.com). CTA Washington (Brown, Orange, Purple). **Open** *Box office* noon-6pm Mon-Sat (open Sun mid Sept-late March). **Credit** AmEx, DC, Disc, MC, V. **Map** p305 G12.
A full-on art deco motif dominates this refurbished space, home to the Lyric Opera. The Lyric generally runs two productions in rotation, five evenings a week. Despite its size – the capacity here is more than 3,500 – the acoustics are the best in the city and sightlines allow the kids to watch the opera instead of the backs of heads.

DePaul University Concert Hall

800 W Belden Avenue, at N Halsted Street, Lincoln Park (773 325 7260). CTA Fullerton (Brown, Purple, Red). **Open** hours vary. **No credit cards. Map** p308 F5.
A former chapel with pew seating and vaulted ceilings, the DePaul University Concert Hall – also known as Belden Hall – hosts university-based

Chicago calendar Music

During summer, **Grant Park** becomes the focus of Chicago's music scene. The backbone of the summer is the **Grant Park Music Festival** (312 742 4763/ www.grantparkmusicfestival.com), a series of free evening orchestral concerts and the only free, publicly funded, outdoor classical music festival in the US. It's usually held at the Petrillo Music Shell in Grant Park, but it will finally move to a new pavilion in the long-delayed Millennium Park in 2003 or 2004.

The **Gospel Festival** (312 744 3315) draws gospel musicians to the park for three days of soulful jubilation in early June. The four-day **Chicago Blues Festival** (312 744 3315), the behemoth of Chicago's summer musical festival family, follows, before folk, bluegrass, Cajun and rockabilly take centre stage at the **Country Music Festival** (312 744 3315), spread over two days in early July.

In late August, the Latin-, Cuban- and salsa-themed **Viva! Chicago** (312 744 3370) gives way almost immediately to the **Chicago Jazz Festival** (312 744 3370), which brings some of the most acclaimed names on the jazz circuit to town alongside a splendid art fair. And rounding off the season, September's **Celtic Fest Chicago** (312 744 3315) celebrates Celtic heritage from around the world, with traditional music and dance.

Though the vast majority of music festivals in Chicago do take place in the park during summer, there are a few other decent events scattered throughout the rest of the year. The most worthwhile is the self-explanatory **World Music Fest** (312 742 1938/ www.ci.chi.il.us/WorldMusic), a grab-bag of musical events in various venues around the city over ten days in late September.

Lyric Opera on song. *See p225.*

recitals as well as smaller chamber acts such as the Chicago Chamber Musicians, the Vermeer Quartet and the Pacifica String Quartet.

Fourth Presbyterian Church
126 E Chestnut Street, at N Michigan Avenue, Gold Coast (312 787 4570). CTA Chicago (Red). **Open** *Performances* noon-1pm Mon-Fri. **Map** p306 J9.
The Gothic-styled Fourth Presbyterian Church has hosted the Noonday Music series for more than two years, providing a daily dose of solo recitals and chamber music away from the hustle and bustle of Mag Mile shopping. The church also occasionally hosts other classical and chamber music concerts.

Ganz Hall at Roosevelt University
430 S Michigan Avenue, at E Van Buren Street, the Loop (312 341 3780/www.roosevelt.edu). CTA Jackson (Red) or Library (Brown, Orange, Purple). **Open** hours vary. **No credit cards. Map** p305 J13.
Formerly part of the Sullivan Hotel, Ganz Hall is now part of the Roosevelt University's music school. In addition to various student recitals and soloists, the likes of the Chicago Chamber Musicians and the Contemporary Music Ensemble often play here.

Grant Park Petrillo Music Shell
235 S Columbus Drive, at E Jackson Drive, the Loop (312 742 4763/www.chicagoparkdistrict.com). CTA Adams (Brown, Green, Orange, Purple) or Jackson (Blue, Red). **Open** *Mid June-Aug* concerts, usually Wed-Sat. **No credit cards. Map** p305 J12.
This large bandstand hosts the free Grant Park Music Festival during summer (*see p225* **Chicago calendar**), where regular performers include the Chicago Symphony Orchestra, the Ravinia Festival Orchestra, the Civic Orchestra of Chicago and, most often, the Grant Park Festival Orchestra.

Mandel Hall at the University of Chicago
1131 E 57th Street, at S University Avenue, Hyde Park (773 702 8069). Metra 55th-57th Street. **Open** hours vary. **No credit cards. Map** p311 X17.
Home to many University of Chicago-sponsored events, the Hall is also the venue for the Howard Mayer Brown International Early Music Series and the University of Chicago Chamber Music Series.

Old St Patrick's Church
700 W Adams Street, at S Desplaines Street, West Side (312 648 1021). CTA Clinton (Blue). **Open** hours vary. **No credit cards.**
One of the few survivors of the Chicago Fire, the city's oldest church (it was built in 1856) features a stunning panorama of 12 stained-glass windows. Though the concert schedules are erratic, Old St Pat's has hosted concerts by the likes of the Metropolis Symphony and Music of the Baroque.

Preston-Bradley Hall
Chicago Cultural Center, 78 E Washington Boulevard, at N Michigan Avenue, the Loop (312 744 6630). CTA Randolph (Brown, Green, Orange, Purple) or Washington (Blue, Red). **Open** *Center* 10am-7pm Mon-Wed; 10am-9pm Thur; 10am-6pm Fri; 10am-5pm Sat; 11am-5pm Sun. *Performances* hours vary. **Map** p305 J12.
Part of the Chicago Cultural Center, Preston-Bradley Hall – the original site of Chicago's public library – hosts concerts under the world's largest Tiffany stained-glass dome. Any number of classical music events can be seen here, from small chamber performances to choral symphonies.

Ravinia Festival
Ravinia Park, Green Bay Road, Highland Park (847 266 5100/www.ravinia.com). Metra Ravinia Park. **Open** hours vary. **Credit** AmEx, DC, Disc, MC, V.
The Ravinia is a trio of music spaces. The Pavilion is a gigantic lawn space, open for concerts ranging from classical to folk to pop, while smaller jazz and classical ensembles play the Bennett-Gordon Hall or the Martin Theatre. During the warm months, there are concerts almost every day at the Pavilion.

Symphony Center
220 S Michigan Avenue, at E Adams Street, the Loop (312 294 3000/www.cso.org). CTA Adams (Brown, Green, Orange, Purple) or Jackson (Blue, Red). **Open** *Box office* 10am-6pm Mon-Sat; 11am-4pm Sun. **Credit** AmEx, DC, MC, V. **Map** p305 J12.
A multi-million-dollar renovation in 1997 turned the Symphony Center into a veritable music mall. In addition to functioning as the CSO's home, the Symphony Center houses the Civic Orchestra of Chicago, the Chicago Youth Symphony, a learning centre, a music-themed restaurant (Rhapsody) and the Chicago chapter of the National Academy of Recording Arts and Sciences. The Center runs a monthly jazz programme and hosts touring orchestras, chamber groups and choral ensembles. Children's concerts are held on Saturday mornings.

Nightclubs

Don't get caught in the velvet ropes: stay up for Chicago's high energy clubbing.

Chicago nightlife has an identity crisis. Many clubs continue to promote an absurd myth of luxury and exclusivity that tends to colour club experiences in the Windy City. The illusion of glamour that larger clubs insist on may prime you for disappointment. But clubbers willing to look the part and unload a mountain of cash can partake in the fantasy for a night.

It's fun for some, but frustrating for others. Doormen keep long lines waiting as they look for clubbers with the right gender, attitude or outfit to complement the party. Inside, upper-tier accoutrements pirated from Miami (VIP rooms, say, or reserved bottle service) for which dancefloor-oriented clubbers have little use are all the rage, but even at the proletariat bars at these superclubs, prices approach the larcenous.

But look past the chintz and you'll find plenty of intimate club nights. DJs, industry folk and city-dwellers are loyal to nights early in the week (such as Monday's Boom Boom Room at Red Dog), when suburban, collegiate and early-rising professional interlopers are tucked up in bed. There's a surplus of friendly parties around town, so you can afford to be picky. And no matter where you end up, getting an eyeful of the crowd can be just as entertaining as hitting the dancefloor.

If you're game for the big production club experience, keep in mind that many clubs have a dress code: 'smart dress', 'dress to impress' or 'creative casual' are just some of the ways managers and doormen put people off wearing jeans, T-shirts and sneakers. And be very wary of a club advertising a free cocktail reception: this usually means a few drinks tickets at a bar that's hours away from being happening.

The year 2001 may be remembered as the year that officials decided to try and stamp out 'club drugs'. Having cracked down on illegal warehouse raves and closed suburban teen spot Club X after ecstasy was found there, officials went after legit nights where drugs were suspected to be in use. The local crackdown is evidence of how pervasive the use of drugs in the Chicago area was: in early 2002, a local cop was found guilty of selling ecstasy on the job.

Club drugs are still widely available, especially at gay-oriented clubs and parties, while it is also rumoured that VIP rooms at some of the major clubs offer freebies to their VIPs. Security has increased, and it's harder to

track down ecstasy, ketamine and GHB than it once was. But judging from the madness on the dancefloors at some of the popular clubs here, there are plenty on the scene still dropping pills, and they must be getting them somewhere.

THE MUSIC

Chicago is a mecca to many international DJs. House music, after all, is named for the Warehouse, a 1980s Chicago club where Frankie Knuckles began stretching disco hits by looping their funky parts and mixing in a drum machine. Derrick Carter, Jesse de la Pena and Felix da Housecat all spin around town. It's not all four-to-the-floor, though: between them, promoters Pure, Bass by the Pound, Spectrum of Sound and Dust Traxx (see p229 **Bringing it all back home**) are drawing more cutting-edge DJs of every flavour to town – Richie Hawtin, Deep Dish, Timo Maas, Miss Kittin – on the weekends.

The proliferation of lounges means that even some corner bars now feature DJ nights, even if there's usually not much room for dancing. Some of the best parties in town – **Danny's Lounge** (see p162) mod-soul night, for one – have become so popular with hipsters that they usually take place unannounced, while other nights, such as Dubshack's D&B gig Brockout, have bounced around from venue

The best Nightclubs

For talking on your cellphone like a hip hop impressario
Transit. See p232.

For seeing an actual hip hop impressario
E2. See p232.

For showing off your rock-hard abs
Crobar. See p230.

For name-dropping European techno DJs
Rednofive. See p231.

For meeting a one-night stand
Bar Chicago. See p229.

Arts & Entertainment

Pray the music lives up to the extravagant decor at **Zentra**. *See p231*.

to venue, so keep an ear to the ground. In addition, some rock clubs run occasional dance nights, such as the **Empty Bottle**'s Big Up! and the **Metro**'s regular big name DJ gigs.

INFORMATION

Pick up either the *Reader* or *Newcity* for details on what's on when; club listings are the only reason to pick up monthly *UR*. Many clubs and promoters have websites and email lists to keep you in the loop; record stores and clothing shops – among them **Gramophone Records**, **Reckless Records** (for both, *see p183*), **Untitled** (*see p174*) and **Softcore** (*see p173*) – stock flyers for forthcoming DJ events.

Many clubs stay open until 4am usually, or 5am on Saturday nights, but others close as early as 2am. Over-21s policies are strictly enforced at Chicago's dance clubs, so make sure you have a valid ID in your best dancing pants.

Nightclubs

For information on gay nightclubs, *see 214*. For the **Smart Bar**, *see p220*.

Near North

Buzz

308 W Erie St, at N Franklin Street (312 475 9800/ www.3ppchicago.com). CTA Merchandise Mart (Brown, Purple). **Open** 4pm-4am Mon-Fri; 10pm-5am Sat; 6pm-2am Sun. **Admission** free-$25. **Credit** AmEx, MC, V. **Map** p306 G10.

This lively River North club with a loft look serves stiff drinks. Guys and gals dress in a casual yet classy style and loosen up on a packed floor to hip hop and disco. Wednesdays see free salsa lessons.

Club 720

720 N Wells Street, at W Superior Street (312 397 0600/www.club720.com). CTA Chicago (Brown, Purple). **Open** 7pm-4am Tue, Thur, Fri; 10pm-5am Sat. **Admission** $5-$20. **Credit** AmEx, Disc, MC, V. **Map** p310 H10.

Four storeys, three of which have dancefloors, await at this salsa/merengue hotspot. A lively crowd dirty dances in the ultra-posh setting, but be warned: groups of men may have to wait a while before being allowed in. Come early for salsa or tango lessons.

Mystique

157 W Ontario Street, at N LaSalle Street (312 642 2582). CTA Grand (Red). **Open** 9pm-2am Tue-Fri, Sun; 9pm-3am Sat. **Admission** $10. **Credit** AmEx, Disc, MC, V. **Map** p306 H10.

A smorgasbord of worn-out club themes and gimmicks: an Asian pillow-room, a plush Gothic look and a ladies-only lounge. Business travellers and suburban professionals whoop it up on weekends.

Q Nightlife

358 W Ontario Street, at N Orleans Street (312 944 3586/www.qnightlife.com). CTA Chicago (Brown, Purple). **Open** 5pm-2am Thur, Sun; 9pm-2am Fri; 9pm-3am Sat. **Admission** free. **Credit** AmEx, DC, Disc, MC, V. **Map** p306 G10.

This tropical-themed joint is modelled after a Miami club, and a stylish crowd comes here to salsa and merengue on its spacious dancefloor.

Bringing it all back home

It may be globally known as the home of house music, but Chicago has a notably lower profile on the international dance music scene right now. And that's putting it mildly: a quick survey of Chicago dance club DJs finds that more than a few believe the scene is all but dead. 'Except,' they add enthusiastically, 'for **Dust Traxx**.'

Since 1997, Dust Traxx has been working to bring original house music vibes back to the Windy City. It made a name for itself promoting some of the first US raves, and hosted international names such as Carl Cox and Daft Punk when they were virtually unknown here. Now, the multi-faceted record label/promo company/booking agency maintains an old school, underground bent in all its ventures. As the company's Laura Renaldo puts it, 'We offer the Windy City musical adventure into the roots of house music.'

The booking agency side of the operation harvests the city's talent, looking after notable Chicago DJs (including some vets of the '80s dance explosion). The label maintains more than 19 imprints – among them Clashbackk Recordings, STX and Kid Dynamite – that serve as outlets for the likes of Paul Johnson, Felix da Housecat and Joey Beltram.

The firm even runs a variety of club nights at venues around town, which tend to be more adventurous than most other events on the calendar. Sweat is an classic house gig, while Forte combines live jazz and disco with DJs. More details on these and other events, along with news on the label's releases, can be found online at www.dusttraxx.com.

Snack on tamales and tostadas if you need a breather from the action. Tuesday nights feature free dance lessons for those with two left feet.

Spy Bar

646 N Franklin Street, at W Erie Street (312 587 8779). CTA Chicago (Brown, Purple). **Open** 10pm-4am Tue-Fri, Sun; 10pm-5am Sat. **Admission** $5-$20. **Credit** AmEx, MC, V. **Map** p306 G10.
Yet another ultra-glam lounge, this one is at least underground and low on attitude. Sink into fluffy couches and admire the finer touches, such as the fur on the bathroom doors (it's faux). DJs spin funk, soul and progressive house.

Volasati

219 W Erie Street, at N Wells Street (312 915 5986). CTA Grand (Red) or Merchandise Mart (Brown, Purple). **Open** 10pm-4am Thur, Fri, Sun; 10pm-5am Sat. **Admission** $10-$25. **Credit** AmEx, MC, V. **Map** p306 H10.
A funky, late-night hip hop hangout in River North, Volasati has apparently hosted celebs such as Chris Rock and Jay-Z. Expect a combination of streetwise and flashy folks sipping champagne just like they do on MTV. The music is mostly popular R&B.

Voyeur

151½ W Ohio Street, at N LaSalle Street (312 832 1717). CTA Grand (Red). **Open** 10pm-4am Thur-Sat. **Admission** free-$10. **Credit** AmEx, MC, V. **Map** p306 H10.
Keep watch! Hidden cameras film club-goers at this gimmick-laden establishment, but the power lies with the women in the bathroom: they have the prime viewing spot. Curvy booths, four bars and a steel-plated dancefloor make up the decor; the music is generally hip hoppy or housey. No denim.

White Star Lounge

225 W Ontario Street, at N Wells Street (312 440 3223/www.whitestarlounge.com). CTA Grand (Red) or Merchandise Mart (Brown, Purple). **Open** 10pm-4am Fri; 10pm-5am Sat. **Admission** $10-$20. **Credit** AmEx, DC, MC, V. **Map** p306 H10.
Clubbers either love or hate this haughty River North club: no wonder it takes such pride in the absurdly long lines it maintains on weekends. Still, all the griping about the bouncers and the general snobbery doesn't change the fact that it remains a place to see and be seen for the beautiful people.

Gold Coast

Bar Chicago

9 W Division Street, at N State Street (312 654 1120). CTA Clark/Division (Red). **Open** 9pm-4am Wed-Fri; 9pm-5am Sat. **Admission** $5-$7. **Credit** AmEx, MC, V. **Map** p307 H8.
Right on Division, and dontcha just know it. The centre-floor DJ will never play anything you haven't heard a zillion times (*Baby Got Back, Come On Eileen*). Gung-ho staff encourage outrageous behaviour: a typical night will find half a dozen gals shaking it on the bar. There's no style or sophistication, but that's the way (uh-huh, uh-huh) they like it.

Le Passage

937 N Rush Street, at W Oak Street (312 255 0022/www.lepassage.tv). CTA Clark/Division (Red). **Open** 7pm-4am Wed-Fri; 7pm-5pm Sat. **Admission** free-$20. **Credit** AmEx, Disc, MC, V. **Map** p306 H9.
Go down an alley and a dark staircase to this upmarket lounge, which appeals largely to designer-clad Gold Coasters. Aspiring beautiful people construct the scene at this gilded cage, dining, dancing and sipping tropical drinks in the Yow bar.

Something from the bar? **Berlin**. *See p231.*

Lincoln Park

Bacchus
2242 N Lincoln Avenue, at W Belden Avenue (773 477 5238). CTA Fullerton (Brown, Purple, Red). **Open** 7pm-2am Tue-Fri; 7pm-3am Sat. **Admission** free-$5. **Credit** AmEx, MC, V. **Map** p308 F5.
Opened in 2001, Bacchus introduced sports bar-dominated Lincoln Park to the lounge. But the club is reserved, its loungers of the khaki-clad, Kate Spade bag-toting variety. DJs spin familiar tunes through a formidable system pumped into all three tiers.

Biology Bar
1520 N Fremont Street, at W North Avenue (312 266 1234). CTA North/Clybourn (Red). **Open** 9pm-4am Mon, Wed-Fri; 9pm-5am Sat. **Admission** $5-$20. **Credit** AmEx, MC, V.
A tornado light fixture welcomes club-goers, the bars are covered in papyrus, and everything is awash with bright neon blue-green. The owners claim the ionisation air filtration system removes the smell of smoke from your clothes as Latino pop blasts forth.

Circus
901 W Weed Street, at N Fremont Street (312 266 1200/www.circuschicago.com). CTA North/Clybourn (Red). **Open** 9pm-4am Wed-Fri; 9pm-5am Sat. **Admission** $15-$25. **Credit** AmEx, MC, V.
A three-room big-top spectacle in the clubby corridor found south of Lincoln Park and west of Old Town, beginning with a psychotic ringmaster leering from the ceiling in the funked-out, whimsical front lounge. Tightrope walkers and fire jugglers on stilts entertain the crowds on the spacious floor.

Crobar
1543 N Kingsbury Street, at W Weed Street (312 413 7000/www.crobarnightclub.com). CTA North/Clybourn (Red). **Open** 10pm-4am Fri, Sun; 10pm-5am Sat. **Admission** $5-$20. **Credit** AmEx, MC, V.

This legend, which has a similarly popular sister in the thick of the action on Miami Beach, is still a pure adrenaline rush. Go-go cages hang above the dancefloor, a stained-glass window sits at the back, a catwalk winds along near the DJ booth, and the mezzanine holds a chill-out space.

Dragon Room
809 W Evergreen Avenue, at N Halsted Street (312 751 2900). CTA North/Clybourn (Red). **Open** 10pm-4am Fri, Sun; 10pm-5am Sat. **Admission** $10-$15. **Credit** AmEx, MC, V. **Map** p307 F8.
Sip saké and nibble on sushi at this three-tiered nightclub in the middle of nowhere: to construct the decor, the owners must have ransacked Chinatown. Upstairs, DJs such as Detroit's Derrick May dominate, while downstairs mainstream hip hop rules.

Exit
1315 W North Avenue, at N Elston Avenue (773 395 2700/www.exitchicago.com). CTA Damen (Blue) or North/Clybourn (Red). **Open** 8pm-4am Mon-Fri, Sun; 8pm-5am Sat. **Admission** free-$5. **Credit** AmEx, Disc, MC, V.
Motorcycle men mix riotously with babes in black leather at this legendary punk club. The theme is S&M-inspired, and the dancefloor is essentially a cage in which a rowdy crowd can cavort to industrial music, dirty punk and other deafening treats.

Glow
1615 N Clybourn Street, at W North Avenue (312 587 8469). CTA North/Clybourn (Red). **Open** 10pm-4am Fri, Sun; 8pm-5am Sat. **Admission** free-$20. **Credit** AmEx, MC, V. **Map** p307 F7.
Contemptuous model-wannabes strut their stuff on the catwalk and nibble on exotic cuisine at this exclusive, la-di-da restaurant-club from the owners of Crobar (*see above*). Downtempo drum 'n' bass often pumps out, but house dominates on club nights.

Kustom

1997 N Clybourn Avenue, at W Armitage Avenue (773 528 3400/www.kustomnightclub.com). **CTA** *Armitage (Brown, Purple).* **Open** 9pm-2am Thur, Fri; 9pm-3am Sat. **Admission** $10-$20. **Credit** AmEx, DC, Disc, MC, V. **Map** p308 E6.
There's more attitude than is necessary at this place. Kustom claims it has the largest dancefloor in the city, and boasts several VIP rooms and an outdoor lounge. Chicago's glitzier, fashion-conscious clientele get down to poppy R&B and high-energy dance, but this place is about being seen, not cutting loose.

Liar's Club

1665 W Fullerton Street, at N Ashland Avenue (773 665 1110/www.liarsclub.com). **CTA** *Fullerton (Brown, Purple, Red).* **Open** 8pm-2am Mon-Fri, Sun; 8pm-3am Sat. **Admission** free-$5. **Credit** AmEx, DC, Disc, MC, V. **Map** p308 D5.
This basement hangout for the low-maintenance rock 'n' roll crowd has an impressive collection of Kiss memorabilia. Liar's hosts occasional drum 'n' bass nights but mostly pumps out classic rock and punk on to the small slanted dancefloor.

Zentra

923 W Weed Street, at N Sheffield Avenue (312 787 0400/www.zentranightclub.com). **CTA** *North/ Clybourn (Red).* **Open** 10pm-4am Wed-Fri, Sun; 10pm-5am Sat. **Admission** $10-$20. **Credit** AmEx, DC, Disc, MC, V.
Jumping on the eastern Zen trip bandwagon, Zentra comes with an opium den motif, including hookah girls offering flavoured tobacco. There are grass patches in the middle of the floor, a precarious too-dark stairwell and progressive dance music on the large dancefloor.

Lake View

Berlin

954 W Belmont Avenue, at N Sheffield Avenue (773 348 4975/www.berlinchicago.com). **CTA** *Belmont (Brown, Purple, Red).* **Open** 8pm-4am Mon; 5pm-4am Tue-Fri; 5pm-5am Sat; 8pm-4am Sun. **Admission** free-$5. **No credit cards.** **Map** p309 E2.
Anything goes at this libidinous free-for-all, which draws a healthy mix of gays and straights. Get caught up in the swirl: thrust yourself on to the crowded dancefloor, then at the cutie next to you. Music? House to big beat and all points in between.

Spin

800 W Belmont Avenue, at N Halsted Street (773 327 7711/www.spin-nightclub.com). **CTA** *Belmont (Brown, Purple, Red).* **Open** 4pm-2am Mon, Tue, Thur, Fri, Sun; 8pm-2am Wed; 4pm-3am Sat. **No credit cards.** **Map** p309 F2.
Up front, it's a video bar; out back, there's darkness and dancing, flashing lights and glowsticks. The crowd leans toward gay males and their straight female friends; leave your 'tude at the door. Friday's Shower Power sees contestants vie for prizes by getting drenched as seductively as possible.

West Side

Big Wig

1551 W Division Street, at N Ashland Avenue (773 235 9100/www.bigwignightclub.com). **CTA** *Division (Blue).* **Open** 8pm-2am Tue-Fri; 8am-3pm Sat; 8pm-2am Sun. **Admission** free-$12. **Credit** AmEx, MC, V.
This club shows only a few traces of what was once a kitschy beauty salon theme. Now it features a broad range of DJ nights featuring drum 'n' bass, deep house and even an occasional live Detroit electro performance and breakdancing competition.

Blonde

820 W Lake Street, at N Green Street (312 226 4500). **CTA** *Clinton (Green).* **Open** 9pm-2am Tue-Fri; 9pm-3am Sat. **Admission** free-$10. **Credit** AmEx, MC, V.
In a building previously home to Aqua and Mint, Blonde's gimmick is that its waitress vixens wear blonde wigs. Fuel your late-night boogie with food from the club's full-scale kitchen.

Club Nocturnal

1111 W Lake Street, at N Aberdeen Street (312 491 1931/www.clubnocturnal.com). **CTA** *Racine (Blue)/20 bus.* **Open** 9pm-2am Thur, Fri; 9pm-3am Sat. **Admission** $5-$20. **Credit** AmEx, DC, Disc, MC, V.
Chrome-decorated Nocturnal seems the least full of itself of the industrial spaces-turned-dance palaces out west. While the crowd isn't discerning about the music (run-of-the-mill house and trance), there's plenty of energy when the club swells on Saturdays.

Funky Buddha Lounge

728 W Grand Avenue, at N Halsted Street (312 666 1695). **CTA** *Chicago (Blue).* **Open** 9pm-2am Mon-Fri, Sun; 9pm-3am Sat. **Admission** $10-$20. **Credit** AmEx, MC, V. **Map** p306 F10.
A large metal replica of a Buddha greets patrons willing to spend so much they'll be forced to take a vow of abstinence after a night here. A chic crowd mingles as candles and chandeliers light the room, and funky house wafts through the air.

Rednofive/Fifth Floor

440 N Halsted Street, at W Hubbard Street (312 733 6699/www.rednofive.com). **CTA** *Chicago (Blue) or Clinton (Green).* **Open** 10pm-4am Thur, Fri; 10pm-5am Sat. **Admission** $10-$25. **Credit** AmEx, DC, Disc, MC, V. **Map** p306 F11.
Technically, the dark downstairs is Rednofive, and the loungier upstairs is Fifth Floor. Either way, you're in for a global clubbing experience where superstar DJs such as Basement Jaxx rule. In the basement, the clubbers come to dance, not pose; upstairs, scoping and sipping seem more apropos.

Rive Gauche

306 N Halsted Street, at W Fulton Street (312 738 9971/www.rivegauchenightclub.com). **CTA** *Clinton (Green) or Grand (Blue).* **Open** 10pm-4am Wed-Fri; 10pm-5am Sat. **Admission** $5-$10. **Credit** AmEx, Disc, MC, V.

Arts & Entertainment

A Chicago **Transit** authority of sorts.

This hotspot in Fulton Market has a Parisian theme – replicas of the Eiffel Tower, crystal chandeliers – that's seen it through the years. Weekend clubbers dress smartly here, but there's no dress code for Shattered Thursdays, featuring local DJs and performance art.

Slick's Lounge

1115 N Branch Street, at W Division Street (312 932 0006/www.slickslounge.com). CTA Chicago (Blue). **Open** 7pm-2am Tue-Thur; 7pm-4am Fri; 7pm-5am Sat, Sun. **Admission** free. **Credit** AmEx, Disc, MC, V.

Formerly known as Hell, this Caribbean restaurant and lounge attracts a racially mixed crowd for urban electronica, funk and occasional live jazz. Tuesday nights are usually industry-oriented and come highly recommended.

Transit

1491 W Lake Street, at N Ogden Avenue (312 491 8600/9729/www.transit-usa.com). CTA Ashland (Green). **Open** 9pm-2am Thur, Fri; 9pm-3am Sat. **Admission** $10-$20. **Credit** AmEx, MC, V.

This converted industrial space, the best of the clubs on Lake, has a clean futuristic look and a powerful sound system. A young set packs the place, posing, downing vodka-Red Bulls and listening to progressive techno sounds (on the mezzanine, it's R&B).

Wicker Park & Bucktown

Artful Dodger

1734 W Wabansia Avenue, at N Hermitage Avenue (773 227 6859). CTA Damen (Blue). **Open** 5pm-2am Mon-Fri; 8pm-3am Sat; 8pm-2am Sun. **Admission** usually free. **Credit** MC, V. **Map** p310 C7.

Once a full-on boho hangout, the Artful Dodger has stayed fairly shabby – early in the week, it's as much bar as club – but now offers an array of fancy drinks

for clientele from the fast-gentrifying neighbourhood. Move to an eclectic mix of hip hop, house and pop on the day-glo lined dancefloor.

Red Dog

1958 W North Avenue, at N Damen Avenue (773 278 1009/www.reddogclub.com). CTA Damen (Blue). **Open** 10pm-4am Mon, Fri; 10pm-5am Sat. **Admission** $5-$15. **Credit** MC, V. **Map** p310 B7.

This party starts as you walk in the door: one step posits you in the middle of a pulsating dancefloor often packed with a diverse crowd: straights and gays, blacks, Hispanics and whites, females and males. There's a mellow area up top, but anywhere else, you're forced to hit the dancefloor.

Square One

1561 N Milwaukee Avenue, at W North Avenue (773 227 7111/squareonecafe.com). CTA Damen (Blue). **Open** 11am-2am Mon-Thur; 11am-4am Fri, Sat; 11am-midnight Sun. **Admission** free. **Credit** AmEx, Disc, MC, V.

This shiny orangey-red juice bar and health food café features DJs during the day. There's a wide selection of magazines, video projections and you can bring your own booze. Get downstairs on weekend nights for dancing.

South Side

E2

2nd floor, 2347 S Michigan Avenue, at E 24th Street (312 326 2300). Bus 1. **Open** 10pm-4am Wed; 9pm-5am Sat. **Admission** $5-$15. **Credit** AmEx, DC, Disc, MC, V.

Upmarket hip hop club E2 might be aiming for an elite clientele, but anyone willing to pay the cover can get freaky on the floor. Look out for special events – a low-key Alicia Keys gig, say – and leave the jeans and gym shoes at home.

Sport & Fitness

You don't need to visit the zoo in Chicago to see some Bears, Cubs or Hawks.

Most big American cities love their sports. Chicago, though, obsesses over them. The hoop-shooting Bulls need no introduction, but neither do the rough-and-tumble Bears or the ever-inept Cubs. You can guarantee that one team or another will be the favourite topic of conversation at any tavern you happen to stumble across.

Many, too, choose to have a go themselves, at anything from fishing to sledding. As befits a city of its size, Chicago boasts some excellent sporting facilities, which visiting health nuts will doubtless devour with glee.

Spectator sports

American football

Chicago is a football town. One of the National Football League's oldest franchises, the tough, gritty play that distinguishes the **Chicago Bears** is beloved by locals. The Bears won the Super Bowl in 1986 under the guidance of Mike 'Da Coach' Ditka, an irascible loudmouth who still enjoys God-like status among Bears faithfuls despite having left the team in 1993.

The 1990s saw the team's fortunes fall, thanks to bad coaching, bad draft picks and bad players. But it all came back in 2001, when

second-year coach Dick Jauron led a crew of youngsters, such as rookie running back Anthony 'The A-Train' Thomas and awesome middle linebacker Brian Urlacher, to the top of the NFC Central. A loss in the playoffs put a halt to the storybook season, but the pieces seem to be in place for a stretch of domination.

Their home, the 66,944-capacity Soldier Field remains a Chicago institution. That's exactly what saved it from the wrecking ball: hours after the last game of 2001, the city began extensive work on the venerable stadium. When it reopens in 2003, it will boats an entirely new interior; only the mock-Greek façade will remain. For the 2002 season, the Bears will play at the University of Illinois' Memorial Stadium, three hours south in Urbana-Champaign: call **Amtrak** (1-800 872 7245) for details on train times and prices for game days.

Chicago Bears

2002 season: Memorial Stadium, University of Illinois at Urbana-Champaign (information 847 295 6600/tickets 312 559 1212/www.chicagobears.com). **Season** Aug-Jan. **Tickets** $40-$65. **Credit** AmEx, DC, Disc, MC, V.
From 2003: Soldier Field, 425 E McFetridge Place, at S Lake Shore Drive, Museum Campus. CTA Roosevelt/State (Red) or Roosevelt/Wabash (Green, Orange). **Map** p304 J15.

Baseball

Their record for futility is unparalleled: they haven't won a World Series since 1908. But everybody – well, everybody except White Sox fans – loves the **Chicago Cubs**. Why? Well, they have one of the game's most popular players in rightfielder Sammy Sosa, they have some of the game's more characterful (read: drunk) fans in the shape of the Bleacher Bums, and they play in the greatest baseball stadium on the planet: Wrigley Field (*see p104* **Made in Chicago**). What's more, the Cubs are finally putting together a great team: with the organisation stocked with hot prospects (none hotter than wunderkind pitcher Mark Prior), the team looks like it'll contend for years to come.

The **Chicago White Sox** have a similarly dismal record – their last World Series triumph was 1917 – though the last few years have seen the team be competitive. However, the South Side Sox have never garnered the sort of affection bestowed on the North Side Cubs, and

Arts & Entertainment

Chicago Cubs slugger Sammy Sosa gets ready to knock another one out of the park.

don't enjoy nearly the fan support of their rivals. It doesn't help that in Comiskey Park, they have one of the most soulless stadia in the majors. However, a decent seat is easy to come by, the Sox usually field a decent team, and those with things to do during the day will be pleased to note that, unlike the Cubs, the Sox play most games at night.

As a cheaper, more personable alternative, try one of the area's minor-league teams: among those within an hour's drive of the Loop are the **Cook County Cheetahs** of the Frontier League (708 489 2255/www.gocheetahs.com), the Northern League's **Schaumburg Flyers** (847 891 4545/www.flyersbaseball.com), and Florida Marlins farm team the **Kane County Cougars** (630 232 8811/www.kccougars.com).

Chicago Cubs
Wrigley Field, 1060 W Addison Street, at N Clark Street, Lake View: Wrigleyville (information 773 404 2827/tickets within Illinois 312 831 2827/tickets outside Illinois 1-800 347 2827/ www.cubs.com). CTA Addison (Red). **Season** Apr-Oct. **Tickets** $6-$30. **Credit** AmEx, DC, Disc, MC, V. **Map** p309 E1.

Chicago White Sox
Comiskey Park, 333 W 35th Street, at S Shields Avenue, South Side (information 312 674 1000/ tickets 312 831 1769/www.chisox.com). CTA Sox-35th Street (Red). **Season** Mar-Oct. **Tickets** $8-$30. **Credit** AmEx, DC, Disc, MC, V.

Basketball

The **Chicago Bulls** dominated the NBA in the 1990s. But when Michael Jordan quit in 1997, the team broke up; the Bulls have played atrocious ball in the seasons since. Tickets are harder to come by than you might think, but season-ticket holders who bought during the

good years and haven't given up hope often sell single-game tickets cheaply, either outside the arena or in *Tribune* and *Reader* classifieds.

Chicago Bulls
United Center Arena, 1901 W Madison Street, at N Damen Avenue, West Town (information 312 455 4000/tickets 312 559 1212/www.nba.com/bulls). CTA Ashland (Orange) or Medical Center (Blue). **Season** Nov-Apr. **Tickets** $10-$85. **Credit** AmEx, DC, Disc, MC, V.

Hockey

The **Chicago Blackhawks** missed the playoffs for five straight years (a difficult task in the NHL) before getting back to form in 2001-02, bringing in blue-collar coach Brian Sutter and getting big contributions from low-key free agents such as Alexander Karpovtsev and Phil Housley. Tickets aren't usually hard to come by during the first four months of the season – or at least until the Bears' season ends – with the exceptions of games against arch rivals the Detroit Red Wings, which usually sell out the United Center Arena (as much because of the rabid Wings' following), and against the Hawks' next closest rival, the St Louis Blues.

Chicago Blackhawks
United Center Arena, 1901 W Madison Street, at N Damen Avenue, West Town (information 312 455 7000/tickets 312 559 1212/ www.chicagoblackhawks.com). CTA Ashland (Orange) or Medical Center (Blue). **Season** Oct-Apr. **Admission** $15-$75. **Credit** AmEx, Disc, MC, V.

Soccer

The **Chicago Fire** is the one sports franchise in the city that can boast a growing fanbase: the team's appeal has spread beyond diehard soccer fans to include kids and sports nuts disenchanted with the other teams. The Fire will burn at North Central College's Cardinal Stadium in the suburb of Naperville during 2002, while Soldier Field is renovated.

Chicago Fire

2002-03 season: Cardinal Stadium at North Central College, 30 N Brainard Street, Naperville (tickets 312 705 7200/559 1212/www.chicago-fire.com). **Tickets** $15-$30. **Credit** AmEx, DC, Disc, MC, V.
From 2003-04: Soldier Field, 425 E McFetridge Place at Lake Shore Drive, Museum Campus (312 705 7200). CTA Roosevelt/State (Red) or Roosevelt/Wabash (Green, Orange).

Active sports & fitness

Sure, Chicago has four seasons like everywhere else. But forget spring, summer, autumn and winter for a moment. There are really only two different times of year here: when it's warm enough to leave the house and when it isn't.

That said, while Chicago's weather is notorious, recent years have seen a succession of mild winters, and the sight of people jogging by the water in February is not as unusual (or odd) as it once was. In summer, though, the **Lakefront Trail** (*see p237*) gets packed with skaters, cyclists and runners, all competing for the best views over the city: a jog on the trail is the finest sightseeing bargain in town.

Before you start donning your lycra tights or Sammy Sosa jersey, pick up the invaluable monthly **Windy City Sports** magazine (312 421 1551/www.windycitysports.com), which offers information on just about every amateur sport in the Chicago area. Look for it, gratis, in the vestibules of sporting goods stores, bookshops and health clubs.

Basketball

The Chicago Park District boasts more than 1,000 courts in the city. Many are in fine nick, some are in disrepair, but almost all of them

Play big

A bastardised version of baseball, softball – played by the same rules as baseball but using slower, underhand pitches and with an extra tenth fielder – takes its name from the ball. A regular softball measures 12 inches (30 centimetres) in circumference and is slightly softer than a baseball, a combination that makes it easier to hit but more difficult to hit *hard*.

However, Chicago plays a different brand of softball. The game here is played without gloves, which makes it unique in itself, but even stranger is the size of the ball: a mammoth 16 inches (41 centimetres) in circumference. Chicagoan 16-inch softball harks back to the days of 19th-century baseball, when players who used mitts were sissies and the ball had less pop than Salt Lake City.

Though 16-inch softball looks just like regular softball to the untrained eye, there are differences, albeit subtle ones. For starters, the ball is *very* soft, and hence extremely difficult to hit with power: outfielders generally play very close to the bat. With no gloves, serious players often use their chest or bodies to stop a ball once it's been hit. Do that in 12-inch softball, and you'll finish the game on the bench gasping for breath; do it in baseball, and you'll watch the rest of the game from the hospital.

To passers-by, very little happens fast. The ball seems to float to the batter, and even the burliest of men with the strongest of swings can't make the ball go any faster than a beach-ball. Throwing the ball often resembles a shot-put toss: it often feels like the only way to throw the thing. But it's these idiosyncrasies that make the game. And unlike baseball or softball, you don't need a glove, and so if there's a bat and a ball, everyone can play.

So popular is the game here that Chicago's Hawthorne Racetrack contains the office for the 16-Inch Softball Hall of Fame (www.chi16in-halloffame.com). The sport originated in 1887, and the Hall of Fame honours its pioneers. Many are from the 1930s and '40s, when the rules were set down and teams coalesced. Men like Harold 'Swede' Roos, who introduced the game to Portland, Oregon in the 1930s, share space with Harold 'Geetz' Gucwa, who played in a game televised by ABC's *Wide World of Sports* in 1962.

Though the onset of basketball has siphoned people from the game, 16-inch softball remains a Chicago pastime. And remember, anyone can play, so if you see a group of kids in the park having a go at it, don't hesitate to fill a spot – even if you've never played baseball.

are packed on a sunny day. Call the **Chicago Park District** on 312 742 7529 or see www.chicagoparkdistrict.com for details.

Hoops the Gym
1380 W Randolph Street, at N Racine Avenue, West Town (312 850 4667). CTA Ashland (Green). **Open** 24hrs daily, on reservation. **Rates** $110/hr. **Credit** MC, V.
If you're willing to pay to play, the two excellently maintained Hoops are where Jordan wannabes congregate to see who's got game (along with MJ himself, who prepared for his 2001 comeback here). The seemingly sizeable fee becomes reasonable if split between a big group.
Branch: 1001 W Washington Street, Greektown (312 850 9496).

Boating
Although it undoubtedly helps, you don't have to be Donald Trump to enjoy Lake Michigan up close and personal. Several groups offer sailing lessons, including the **Chicago Park District** (312 747 0737) and the **Chicago Sailing Club** (Belmont Avenue; 773 871 7245/ www.chicagosailingclub.com), which also offers rentals and charters.

Bowling

Diversey River Bowl
2211 W Diversey Parkway, at N Logan Boulevard, Bucktown (773 227 5800/www.drbowl.com). CTA Western (Blue (NW)). **Open** noon-2am Mon-Fri, Sun; 9am-3am Sat. **Rates** $19-$26/lane per hr. **Credit** AmEx, Disc, MC, V.
Saturday night's Rock 'n' Bowl is a rite of passage here. There are 36 lanes, and the music is loud.

Southport Lanes
3325 N Southport Avenue, at W Aldine Avenue, Lake View (773 472 6600/www.southportlanes.com). CTA Southport (Brown). **Open** 5pm-2am Mon-Thur; noon-3am Fri, Sat; noon-2am Sun. **Rates** $14-$16/lane per hr. **Credit** AmEx, DC, Disc, MC, V. **Map** p309 D2.
Pin boys reset the pins on four hard-to-book alleys, while a young, hip crowd packs the popular bar sipping the drink *du jour*. Tip pin boys for faster resets.

Waveland Bowl
3700 N Western Avenue, at W Waveland Avenue, Irving Park (773 472 5900/www.wavelandbowl.com). CTA Western (Brown). **Open** 24hrs daily. **Rates** $1-$6/game. **Credit** MC, V.
Insomniac bowlers have recourse to Waveland's 40 lanes every waking hour.

Go fish

If, in spring, you find yourself motoring along Lake Shore Drive in the wee small hours, you may notice winking lights along the water's edge. They are a sure sign that the smelt fishing season has arrived; they also signal the start of a uniquely Chicagoan party. Smelt fishing along the lakefront is as much about drinking as it is about fishing. In fact, the pastime has about as much in common with Izaak Walton as rap has with Rachmaninov.

Smelting is a rite of spring. Come early March, aficionados monitor the grapevine for the magical words, 'the smelt are running' (in Chicago argot, it's pronounced 'schmelt'). These worthies then equip themselves with nets, weights, buckets and lanterns, load up coolers with beers and snacks, and head for their own particular tailgate party.

Ostensibly, the object of the excitement is a finger-sized fish (related to salmon and trout) that heads towards shore to spawn. During the smelt run, these tiny iridescent fish may arrive in large schools, meaning the action can get hot and heavy, nets glinting with silvery fish ready to be scooped into buckets. Otherwise, there's always the beer, the schnapps, the munchies and the boomboxes pumping out

music (hardly ever Rachmaninov). Unlike the genteel, purist sport that is fly-fishing, excessive noise doesn't interfere with smelting. Smelt, driven by a primeval instinct to deposit their eggs on the gravel near the shore, are not fazed by punk or nu metal. Instead, they press onwards, with all the verve of landing craft on D-Day.

Most sporting goods stores can set you up for smelt fishing for around $50 (try the Park Bait Company at 600 W Montrose Avenue; 773 271 2838), and most veteran smelters will gladly give you pointers – particularly if you're generous with your brews. You'll need an Illinois fishing licence (*see p238*) and some kind of seine, gill or dip net. And, of course, you'll need buckets for your catch and a cooler for your beers. To join the party, pitch up around 1am and head for a likely stretch of the lake. A popular spot is Burnham Harbor.

If it turns out to be an unproductive night for fishing and you find yourself skunked, head for Boston Blackies (*see p153*). The popular sports bar not only serves some of the city's best hamburgers, but also offers crispy, deep-fried smelts as a standard.

Da Bears... *See p233.*

Cycling

Cycling in Chicago is a contact sport: wear a helmet, and be vigilant for erratic drivers. Be sure to always lock your bike with a U-lock. For more information, contact the **Chicago Bicycle Federation** (Suite 300, 650 S Clark Street, South Loop; 312 427 3325/www.biketraffic.org), which publishes an excellent seven-county map of bike trails ($6.95 for non-members) as well as riders' picks of the best city routes.

In 2002, Chicago introduced 30 miles of new bike lanes, including the leafy, six-mile Major Taylor Trail. However, the best route in town is one of the oldest: the 15-mile **Lakefront Trail**. Stretching south of the University of Chicago and north to Evanston, the path offers majestic views of the skyline, Navy Pier and Museum Campus. Keep your eye on the road if you don't want to spend part of your stay in one of Chicago's fine hospitals. Finding the path is as easy as riding a bike: head for the lake (east of wherever you are, unless you're swimming in it), and look for the yellow lines.

Bike Chicago

Navy Pier, at 600 E Grand Avenue, Near North (312 755 0488/www.bikechicago.com). CTA Grand (Red)/29, 65, 66 bus. **Open** *Apr, May, Oct, Nov* 9am-7pm daily. *June-Sept* 8am-10pm daily. *Tours* 11.30am daily. **Rates** $10-$30/day. **Credit** AmEx, Disc, MC, V. **Map** p306 K10.

Rates include locks, helmets and maps. Bike Chicago also arranges tours for all levels of ability.

Branch: North Avenue Beach, Lincoln Park (773 327 2706); 63rd Street Beach, 6300 S Lake Shore Drive, South Side (773 324 3400).

On the Route

3146 N Lincoln Avenue, at N Ashland Avenue, Lake View (773 477 5066/www.ontheroute.com). CTA Southport (Brown). **Open** *Mar-Sept* 11am-8pm Mon-Fri; 11am-6pm Sat, Sun. *Oct-Feb* noon-8pm Mon-Thur; noon-7pm Fri; noon-4pm Sat, Sun. **Rates** $35-$40/day. **Credit** AmEx, Disc, MC, V. **Map** p309 D3.

Fishing

The easiest fish to catch in Lake Michigan are alewives, which float to the shore in summer. Dead. A whiff of that 'dead alewive' aroma, and you'll know to leave 'em be. Thankfully, most of the alewives have now been eaten by the Pacific salmon, bizarrely imported in the 1960s, that have spawned a huge charter fishing industry. The lake also boasts many other live fish: perch are the most sought-after catch among pier anglers, while the smelt fishing season (*see p236* **Go fish**) is a sight to behold.

Arts & Entertainment

Dinner!

You'll need a licence to fish legally in Illinois; they're available to over-16s at bait stores (check the *Yellow Pages*), sporting goods stores, currency exchanges or the City Clerk's office. The **Illinois Department of Natural Resources** (312 814 2070/http://dnr.state.il.us) offers guides on where to fish. For starters, try Chicago's parks (details from the **Chicago Park District** on 312 742 7529); **Cook County Forest Preserve** (1-800 870 3666); and, of course, **Lake Michigan**: you can cast off the shore at **Belmont Harbor** (3200 North; 312 742 7673/0737), **Diversey Harbor** (2800 North; 312 742 7762), **Monroe Harbor** (100 South; 312 742 7643) and **Burnham Park Harbor** (2800 South; 312 742 7762).

Fitness clubs

If your hotel doesn't have a club on site or offer an 'in' at a nearby club – and many do – you'll still be able to stay in shape while you're here. Among the more popular clubs are **Bally Total Fitness** (820 N Orleans Street, Near North; 312 573 4300/www.ballyfitness.com), some of whose 12 branches allow daily visitors; the four Chicago **Lakeshore Athletic Clubs** (there's one at 441 N Wabash Avenue, Near North; 312 644 4880/www.lsac.com); and the lively **Lehman Sports Club** (2700 N Lehmann Court, Lincoln Park; 773 871 8300), where day membership is $15.

Golf

The Chicago Park District runs several courses; call 312 245 0909 for the nearest. Otherwise, call **Chicagoland Golf** (630 719 1000) for details.

Sydney R Marovitz Course

3600 N Recreation Drive, in Lincoln Park (312 742 7930). CTA Addison (Purple, Red). **Open** sunrise-sunset daily. **Rates** *Non-residents* $15-$16.50; $8.25-$9.25 concessions. **Credit** MC, V. **Map** p309 G1.
This nine-hole Lincoln Park course enjoys a fantastic setting. The course is good, too; book ahead.

Cog Hill Golf & Country Club

12294 Archer Avenue, Lemont (630 257 5872/www.coghillgolf.com). Metra Lemont. **Open** *Winter* 6am-5pm daily. *Summer* 6am-9pm daily. **Rates** $34-$125. **Credit** Disc, MC, V.
A series of four 18-hole courses; one, Dubsdread, is home to the Western Open each July.

Jackson Park

S Hayes Drive, at E 63rd Street, South Side (312 245 0909). Metra 63rd Street. **Open** sunrise-sunset daily. **Rates** *Non-residents* $20-$22; $12 concessions. **Credit** MC, V. **Map** p311 Z18.
The Chicago Park District's one 18-holer should challenge even low handicappers.

Family Golf Center

216 N Columbus Drive, at E Wacker Drive, the Loop (312 616 1234). CTA Lake or State. **Open** 6.30am-10pm daily. **Rates** $15/9 holes; $10/100 balls. **Credit** AmEx, DC, Disc, MC, V. **Map** p305 J11.
A strange but endearing little nine-hole course down by the river, north-east of The Loop. Be sure to book.

Horse riding

Noble Horse Equestrian Center

1410 N Orleans Street, at W North Avenue, Old Town (312 266 7878/www.noblehorsechicago.com). CTA Sedgwick (Brown, Purple). **Open** *Rides* 10am-9pm daily. *Shows* Wed-Sun. **Rates** *Rides* from $30/30mins; $60/hr. *Shows* $47; $32 under-12s. **Credit** MC, V. **Map** p307 G7.
Lessons, but also carriage rides downtown.

In-line skating

Chicago drivers tend not to notice skaters until one slams against the hood of their car. Still, the **Lakefront Trail** (*see p237*) is a pleasant way to while away an afternoon. Skates can be hired from the places listed below (prepare to pay a deposit), and **Bike Chicago** (*see p237*).

Londo Mondo

1100 N Dearborn Street, at W Maple Street, Gold Coast (312 751 2794/www.londomondo.com). CTA Clark/Division (Red). **Open** 10am-7pm Mon-Fri; 10am-6pm Sat; 11am-6pm Sun. **Rates** $7/hr; $20/day. **Credit** AmEx, Disc, MC, V. **Map** p306 H9.

Windward Sports
3317 N Clark Street, at W Belmont Avenue, Lake View (773 472 6868). CTA Belmont (Brown, Purple, Red). **Open** 11am-6pm Mon; 11am-8pm Wed, Thur; 11am-7pm Fri; 11am-5pm Sat, Sun. **Rates** $10-$30/day. **Credit** AmEx, Disc, MC, V. **Map** p309 F2.

Pool

In many Chicago bars, the tradition that the winner keeps the table stays in effect. However, you can rent a table by the hour at Chris's and others in the city. The **Ginger Man** bar (*see p161*) is another good spot to play.

Chris's Billiards
4637 N Milwaukee Avenue, at W Lawrence Avenue, Jefferson Park (773 286 4714). CTA Jefferson Park (Blue). **Open** 9.30am-2am daily. **Rates** $5.95-$7.25/hr. **No credit cards**.
Pool, billiards and snooker, with tournaments for the true hustler and lessons for the true hack. *The Color of Money* was filmed at this North Side joint.

Running

The **Chicago Area Runners Association** (203 N Wabash Avenue, the Loop; 312 666 9836/ www.cararuns.org) has information on upcoming races to ideal running routes, though the **Lakefront Trail** (*see p236*) is popular with locals. For the **Chicago Marathon** (312 904 9800/www.chicagomarathon.com), *see p191.*

Skating & sledding

Wintertime visitors can sled courtesy of the Chicago Park District, which runs a number of toboggan runs with wooden chutes (*see p197*). Also in winter, ice rinks are set up on State Street (**Skate on State**, in a vacant lot at the corner with Washington) and at **Navy Pier**.

Going nowhere: **Lehman Sports**. *See p238.*

Soccer

Given the city's large Latin American population, it's no surprise the beautiful game is popular here. Some of the liveliest action happens off the lake at Montrose Avenue. For details, contact the **Illinois Soccer Association** (773 283 2800) or the **National Soccer League of Chicago** (773 237 1270).

Swimming

In summer, thick-skinned aquanauts swim from Navy Pier north toward the Oak Street Beach, and buoys (theoretically) protect swimmers from boats. The lake is officially open for swimming from Memorial Day to Labor Day.
The Chicago Park District (312 747 7529/ www.chicagoparkdistrict.com) has numerous indoor pools that are both free and, generally, well maintained. Among the best is **Welles Park**, a full-size pool in a great Lincoln Square building (2333 W Sunnyside Avenue, at N Western Avenue; 312 742 7515).

Tennis

With over 600 courts around Chicago, it's easier to find a court than a partner. Fees vary wildly. If you prefer to play indoors, there are courts at health clubs such as the Lincoln Park branch of the **Lakeshore Athletic Club** (*see p238*). The best public courts are listed below; for details of others, call the Chicago Park District (312 742 7529/www.chicagoparkdistrict.com).

Daley Bicentennial Plaza
337 E Randolph Street, at N Columbus Drive, the Loop (312 742 7648). CTA Randolph (Brown, Green, Orange, Purple). **Open** 7am-10pm Mon-Fri; 9am-5pm Sat, Sun. **Rates** $7/hr. **Credit** MC, V. **Map** p305 J12.
Rally beneath the skyscrapers, but you'll have to pay a nominal fee.

Diversey
138 W Diversey Parkway, at N Lake Shore Drive, Lincoln Park (773 348 9533). CTA Diversey (Brown, Purple). **Open** 7am-10pm Mon-Fri; 9am-5pm Sat, Sun. **Rates** $5/hr. **No credit cards**. **Map** p308 G4.
If you like to think you've got a game similar to Pete Sampras, try out the only four clay courts in the city.

Volleyball

Along the lake, it's the same wherever you go: pickup games galore: try **Foster Beach** (at Foster Avenue), **Montrose Beach** (at Montrose Avenue) and the **North Avenue Beach** (at North Avenue), the Centre Court of Chicago beach volleyball. In bad weather, check with health clubs or the YMCA for a nearby court.

Theatre, Comedy & Dance

It may be famous for improv, but not everything in Chicago is played for laughs.

Theatre

With a diverse roster of over 200 indigenous theatre companies and a growing reputation as the try-out location of choice for pre-Broadway shows, Chicago has emerged in the last two decades as one of the most important theatre cities in the world. But with this increase in status has also come a tangible self-importance.

In the last decade, it dawned on bureaucrats that Chicago theatre had become a major draw for tourists. So, thanks in no small measure to theatre-loving mayoral spouse Maggie Daley, the city expended millions on an orgy of theatre renovations and building projects, many of them in the Loop (*see p241* **As good as new**). In recent years, no American city – and that includes New York – has spent more public money on new theatres than Chicago. Yet the heart of Chicago theatre still lies in the smaller neighbourhood spaces.

Much hyperbolic ink has been expended on trying to define what constitutes Chicago-style theatre, but most agree that it's more gutsy, blue-collar and in-your-face. Sure, Chicago has a number of big, famous companies – notably the Goodman, Court and Steppenwolf – and

once-native celebrities like Gary Sinise and John Malkovich command attention when they show up. But the best and most progressive Chicago theatre is often found in little storefronts, where the clattering of the El can be heard as the actors pause for breath.

With the exception of alums such as Sinise and Brian Dennehy, you won't find many film or TV stars treading the Chi-town boards. This is a city where an actor comes to get noticed, then leaves for bigger rewards. Instead, there are seemingly thousands of hungry actors, all swimming like hyper-kinetic sperm in the same underfunded, but constantly thrilling, pond.

TICKETS & INFORMATION

Strong coverage of Chicago theatre is found in the *Reader* (which has the most comprehensive listings) and in the *Tribune*'s Friday section (which carries most theatre ads). *Tribune* reviews of current shows can be found at www.metromix.com. The **League of Chicago Theatres** (www.chicagoplays.com) publishes a generally accurate quarterly guide that can be ordered over the phone or picked up for free in most hotels and tourist centres.

Though most companies and touring shows sell seats via the ubiquitous **Ticketmaster** (312 902 1500/www.ticketmaster.com), it's generally best to buy direct from box offices and avoid surcharges. Prices vary hugely, from $10-$15 at fringe venues up to over $50 at the likes of the Steppenwolf.

For half-price tickets on the day of performance, go to one of the League's three **Hot Tix** booths. The Loop branch (78 W Randolph Street) opens 8.30am-6pm Tue-Fri, 10am-6pm Sat and noon-5pm Fri, while the Water Works (163 E Pearson Street, Near North) and Skokie (at the North Shore Center for the Performing Arts) locations are open 10am-6pm Tue-Sat, noon-5pm Sun. Each morning, a list of the shows for which cheap seats are available is posted at www.hottix.org; information is also available at 1-900 225 2225.

Note that many Chicago theatres, especially the small ones, perform from Thursday to Sunday only. On Fridays and Saturdays, late-night shows typically begin around 11pm.

The best Theatre, etc

Goodman Theater
The biggest and the best. *See p242.*

Roadworks Productions
Out of the Loop, and proud of it. *See p244.*

Green Mill Poetry Slam
Comedy? Theatre? Poetry? All three and more. *See p242* **Made in Chicago**.

Hubbard Street Dance Chicago
Tap into the local dance scene. *See p247.*

Second City
The originals, and still funny. *See p246.*

Major companies

There are so many theatres in Chicago that what follows is a necessarily selective list. Since local actors and other creative types work all over the place, it's a smart idea to pick shows based on what's getting good reviews.

For **About Face Theatre** and the **Bailiwick Repertory**, *see p215*.

American Theater Company

1909 W Byron Street, at N Lincoln Avenue, Irving Park (773 929 1031/www.atcweb.org). CTA Irving Park (Blue). **Open** *Box office* noon-showtime Thur-Sun; hours vary Mon-Wed. **Tickets** $20-$30. **Credit** AmEx, MC, V.

An Irving Park theatre proud of its blue-collar origins and working class sensibility, ATC specialises in classic and contemporary fare performed with high energy and low budgets. The kind of theatre where the actors are happy to go drinking with you after the show. It often rents to other troupes.

Chicago Shakespeare Theater

800 E Grand Avenue, at Navy Pier, Near North (312 595 5600/www.chicagoshakes.com). CTA Grand (Red)/29, 65, 66 bus. **Open** *Box office* 10am-4pm Tue-Sat; extended hours on show days. **Tickets** $25-$52. **Credit** AmEx, Disc, MC, V. **Map** p306 K10.

This Old Bill-centred troupe moved to an opulent new Navy Pier home in 1999, modelled on the Swan Theatre in Stratford-upon-Avon. The theatre offers stunning views from its lobbies and is surrounded by numerous restaurants and bars in which to spend the rest of the night (or the second act). The diet is RSC redux, though edgier stuff appears in the studio theatre and there are also musicals and comedies aimed at tourists in summer.

Chicago Theatre Company

500 E 67th Street, at S Rhodes Avenue, South Side (773 493 0901). CTA 3 bus. **Open** *Box office* 6.30-9pm Fri, Sat; 1-5pm Sun. **Tickets** $25; $2 over-60s. **Credit** Disc, MC, V.

Of the several theatres whose work is aimed at African-American audiences, CTC upholds the highest standards. Offering a mix of original works and revivals, it's based in a tiny South Side basement where the audience feels part of the action. A proud part of a highly supportive community, work at the CTC invariably has something worthwhile to say.

Court Theatre

5535 S Ellis Avenue, at E 55th Street, Hyde Park (773 753 4472/www.courttheatre.org). CTA 55 bus. **Open** *Box office* noon-5pm Mon-Thur; noon-showtime on performance days. **Tickets** $24-$40. **Credit** AmEx, Disc, MC, V. **Map** p311 X17.

The upmarket Court specialises in revivals of classic plays: if your tastes run to Greek drama, the Spanish Golden Age or Molière, head here to see productions executed to a high standard by a troupe of resident and guest actors under the leadership of Charles Newell.

As good as new

The recent theatrical salvage operation in the Loop has resulted in a rebranding of an area centred around Randolph Street as the Theatre District. It'll never be Broadway, of course, but the handful of sumptuous venues here are growing in stature almost daily: Chicago even got Mel Brooks's The Producers first, for a tryout at the Cadillac Palace, before it moved to Broadway and broke all manner of box-office records.

Most of the venues in the Theatre District are former movie palaces and vaudeville houses that had fallen into various states of disrepair over the last half of the 20th century. However, during the last decade or so, vast mountains of city money were spent restoring them to their former glory; now, their interiors are so spectacular that some shows have a hard time competing.

Of the big five, musicals and other Broadway-style fare dominate at the over-the-top **Oriental Theatre** (24 W Randolph Street) and the more dignified **Cadillac Palace** (151 W Randolph Street); the **Chicago Theatre** (175 N State Street) offers concerts, dance, drama and the most iconic sign in the city (*pictured*); the huge **Auditorium Theatre** (50 E Congress Parkway) boasts 4,000 seats and a stunning Louis Sullivan interior; and the less overwhelming **Shubert Theatre** (22 W Monroe Street) is the best place in Chicago to see Broadway plays and smaller musicals.

Tickets for all venues listed above are available from **Ticketmaster** (*see p240*).

Goodman Theatre

170 N Dearborn Street, at W Randolph Street, the Loop (312 443 3800/3820/www.goodman-theatre.org). CTA Randolph (Brown, Green, Orange, Purple) or Washington (Blue, Red). **Open** *Box office* 10am-5pm Mon; 10am-8pm Tue-Sat; noon-8pm Sun. **Tickets** $30-$50. **Credit** AmEx, Disc, MC, V. **Map** p305 H11.

Now located in a splendiferous Theatre District home with two new state-of-the-art spaces, the Goodman continues to maintain its reputation as the most prestigious theatre in the city. Now over 75 years old, it's the high priest of the theatrical establishment, though the work on its two stages has been far from stuffy under the exemplary stewardship of artistic director Robert Falls. The season is a top-drawer mix of classical and contemporary (2002 saw the world premiere of Philip Glass's opera *Galileo Galilei* and a new play by Carol Burnett and her daughter Carrie Hamilton): many of its shows in recent seasons have transferred quickly to New York.

Lifeline Theatre

6912 N Glenwood Street, at W Farwell Avenue, North Side (773 761 4477/www.lifelinetheatre.com). CTA Morse (Red). **Open** *Box office* noon-6pm Tue-Thur, Sun; noon-8pm Fri, Sat. **Tickets** $16-$20. **Credit** Disc, MC, V.

Chicago has a growing tradition of supporting original adaptations of novels and poems, and the Lifeline is one of the best places in town in which to find drama that goes beyond the usual scripted cannon. With a commitment to shows suitable for families, Lifeline is an intimate but literate theatre.

Next Theatre

927 Noyes Street, at Ridge Avenue, Evanston (847 475 1875/www.nexttheatre.org). CTA Noyes (Purple). **Open** *Box office* noon-4pm Mon-Fri; noon-showtime on performance days. **Tickets** $22-$28. **Credit** AmEx, Disc, MC, V.

Located in the Noyes Cultural Arts Center (home to the Piven Theatre Workshop), this small but reliable company offers a progressive season of shows with an emphasis on the new. Next, which turned 20 years old in 2001, has more maturity than some of its scrappier competitors but has never settled for stodginess. There's a tradition of socially aware theatre here.

Steppenwolf Theatre Company

1650 N Halsted Street, at W North Avenue, Lincoln Park (312 335 1650/www.steppenwolf.org). CTA North/Clybourn (Red). **Open** *Box office* 11am-5pm daily, or 11am-7pm during performance runs. **Tickets** *Main stage* $35-$55. *Studio* $18-$27. *Garage* $10. **Credit** AmEx, DC, Disc, MC, V. **Map** p307 F7.

Made in Chicago Poetry slams

If you know of the Green Mill, it's probably for one of two reasons: Al Capone used to hang there, and the live jazz is usually terrific (*see p224*). But on Sunday nights, a select bunch head there for a different kind of groove: the rhythm, scat and swing of live poetry. The **Uptown Poetry Slam**, founded and now hosted by poet Marc Smith, has brought thousands of prose hopefuls to the Mill since 1986; indeed, loyal devotees claim that it's served as the model for all other poetry slams in the US.

The routine is the same each week. The event begins at 7pm with an open mic, with Smith alternately jeering and cheering on the participants. At 8pm, there's a performance by a featured poet. Then at 9pm, it's the slam itself, an out-and-out competition with five audience members judging the performances of the poets. The prize for the lucky winner? A whopping ten bucks.

A fierce competitive spirit and love of performing keep a core group of Green Mill habitués caught up in the wordplay week after week, but there are also plenty of first-timers – the 'virgin-virgins', as Smith calls them – who consider a slot here their big-break stage debut. On an average night, you can

expect to see a ragtag mix of bearded ex-professors, sprightly sorority types, angst-ridden adolescents and full-on thespians; not quite the best minds of their generation, but never mind. The material ranges from painstaking personal tales to pure camp.

And the audience? Animated isn't the half of it. Take a cue from Smith and follow the Slam rules. If a poet's rhyme is all too obvious, then go ahead and shout out the next word along with him ('then watch his face,' he adds). If things are getting boring, snap your fingers or stomp your feet. Keats and Yeats this ain't. Fun it certainly is.

Lookingglass Theatre Company. *See p244.*

Steppenwolf gained fame as the blue-collar brand leader in macho acting, typified by John Malkovich's famously insane performance in a 1982 production of Sam Shepard's *True West*. But thanks to the accomplishments of its star-laden ensemble – which also includes co-founder Gary Sinise, Martha Plimpton and Joan Allen – the rough and ready house style is now played out in a posh, high-tech house. Since attendance suggests street-cred among locals, tickets are perennially hard to snag. Don't expect to see the big names every week, but standards are reliably high and the work is rarely dull.

Strawdog Theatre Company

3829 N Broadway, at W Grace Street, Lake View (773 528 9696/www.strawdog.org). CTA Sheridan (Red). **Open** *Box office* 24hrs daily (answerphone). **Tickets** $15. **No credit cards**. **Map** p309 F1.
The surroundings are rough at this Lake View theatre, but Strawdog usually offers edgy, interesting work. Based on the desires of an ensemble of resident actors and directors, it's big on new work and cutting-edge American material. The theatre is so intimate that you can see the actors sweat. And on a hot summer night, you'll be perspiring yourself.

Trap Door Productions

1655 W Cortland Street, at N Paulina Street, Wicker Park/Bucktown (773 384 0494/ www.trapdoortheatre.com). CTA Damen (Blue)/ 73 bus. **Open** *Box office* times vary. **Tickets** $15. **No credit cards**. **Map** p310 C6.

Uninterested in money or conventional success, the Trap specialises in out-there productions of obscure works by maverick Europeans such as Ionesco and Witkiewicz. The space seats only about 50 in not much comfort, and if you venture out here, be aware that the quality of the work can be widely uneven. But if nihilism, neo-absurdism and wacky experimentation are your bag, you won't be bored.

Victory Gardens Theater

2257 N Lincoln Avenue, at W Webster Avenue, Lincoln Park (773 871 3000/www.victorygardens.org). CTA Fullerton (Brown, Purple, Red). **Open** *Box office* noon-8pm Tue-Sat; 10am-4pm Sun. **Tickets** $20-$33. **Credit** AmEx, Disc, MC, V. **Map** p308 F5.
The winner of the 2001 Tony Award for Excellence in Regional Theatre, this much-loved and defiantly informal Chicago citadel of new work offers an exclusive diet of premières, most penned by its team of affiliated writers: the playwright and his or her words always have the principal focus here. There are four stages in the complex, three of which are rented out to carefully picked tenants.

Itinerant companies

Defiant Theatre

312 409 0585/www.defianttheatre.org.
The boys and girls at Defiant like to think of themselves as 'Chicago's most dangerous theatre company', which generally means a mix of physical acting, profanity and sex. Luckily, they're a pretty

Arts & Entertainment

talented bunch, and most productions are full of invention. There's an interest here in puppetry, Kabuki and other non-realistic theatrical traditions.

Famous Door Theatre Company
773 404 8283/www.famousdoortheatre.org.
With an eclectic repertoire covering everything from Pinter to Sobol, Famous Door has become one of Chicago's most reliable medium-sized companies. Run by a group of regular folks who've scraped and saved for years to keep their dream going, Famous Door savvily hires the best directors in town. Its favoured venue is the Theatre Building (*see below*).

Lookingglass Theatre Company
773 477 9257/www.lookingglasstheatre.org.
Since founding member David Schwimmer encountered fame as one of the *Friends*, this troupe has taken on a slight Hollywood dimension. But it built its reputation on inventive adaptations of classical myths and contemporary novels, emphasising a physical style of acting. Ensemble member Mary Zimmerman found Broadway acclaim with *Metamorphoses*, a work of staggering invention and imagination that began here. The theatre will take up residence in the Water Tower on Michigan Avenue in 2003.

Roadworks Productions
312 492 7150/www.roadworks.org.
Roadworks' speciality is in articulating the angst of disenfranchised youth by focusing on British and American playwrights who capture the daily grit of life for those poor, misunderstood kids. A lively ensemble specialises in hyper-realistic work.

Teatro Vista
312 494 5767/www.teatrovista.org.
Given the size of Chicago's Latino population, it's a surprise the city doesn't support more companies dedicated to its community. But Teatro Vista ('the-atre with a point of view') does a nice job of bringing north work by playwrights from south of the border, as well as new plays that dramatise the concerns of all Chicagoans. Standards are reliably high and performances are almost always in English.

Other venues

For the Loop's Theatre District, *see p241* **As good as new**.

Briar Street Theatre
3133 N Halsted Street, at W Belmont Avenue, Lake View (773 348 4000/www.blueman.com). **CTA** Belmont (Brown, Purple, Red). **Open** Box office 9am-10pm Mon-Sat; noon-7pm Sun. **Tickets** $43-$53. **Credit** AmEx, Disc, MC, V. **Map** p309 F3.
This mid-sized rental house that was gutted in 1998 to make way for *Blue Man Group*, a hugely successful high-tech piece of performance art that was still going strong four years later. It attracts a young and decidedly hip crowd.

Chicago Center for the Performing Arts
777 N Green Street, at W Chicago Avenue, West Side (312 327 2000/www.theaterland.com). **CTA** Chicago (Blue). **Open** Box office 9am-6pm daily. **Tickets** $30-$60. **Credit** AmEx, MC, V.
A cosy venue located a mile west of the Mag Mile (take a cab), this loft-like theatre offers a mixed diet of mainstream fare. You take your chances on a show-by-show basis, but the exceptionally comfortable theatre does sport one of the city's nicest bars.

Mercury Theatre
3745 N Southport Street, at W Addison Street, Lake View/Wrigleyville (773 325 1700). **Open** Box office times vary. **Tickets** $20-$40. **Credit** AmEx, DC, Disc, MC, V. **Map** p309 D1.
Michael Cullen's top-notch little theatre specialises in long-running commercial shows, replete with a splattering of off-Broadway hits and pre-New York tryouts (Barry Manilow has worked here). It's an intimate and classy place in the middle of the Southport restaurant district, but Cullen's, the Irish bar next door, is what really pays the bills.

Royal George Theatre
1641 N Halsted Street, at W North Avenue, Old Town (312 988 9000). **CTA** North/Clybourn (Red). **Open** Box office 10am-7pm Mon-Sat; noon-6pm Sun. **Tickets** $20-$50. **Credit** AmEx, MC, V. **Map** p307 F7.
This commercial theatre on the fringes of Old Town generally hosts recent hits from the off-Broadway season, as well as productions transferring from Chicago's resident theatres. Located opposite the Steppenwolf (*see p243*), the Royal George's cabaret specialises in small musicals and popular shows.

Theatre Building Chicago
1225 W Belmont Avenue, at N Southport Avenue, Lake View (773 327 5252). **CTA** Belmont (Brown, Purple, Red) or Southport (Brown). **Open** Box office noon-6pm Wed; noon-showtime Thur-Sun. **Tickets** $15-$30. **Credit** AmEx, Disc, MC, V. **Map** p309 D3.
A pioneer of Chicago's off-Loop scene, TBC includes three black-box theatres located in a former industrial space. The quality and type of theatre vary, but there are usually several shows on offer in an arts centre that is the preferred home of several of Chicago's itinerant companies. TBC also sponsors a resident company that incubates new musicals.

Theatre on the Lake
2400 N Lake Shore Drive, at W Fullerton Avenue, Lincoln Park (312 742 7994). Bus 151. **Date** mid June-mid Aug. **Tickets** $10. **Credit** V. **Map** p308 H5.
Some of the best received off-Loop productions that premiered the previous year – from theatres such as Steppenwolf and Second City – are presented in a semi-outdoor theatre in Lincoln Park each summer. Restaged shows do not always match the quality of the original and when it's humid it's hellish, but this can be a charming way to spend a summer evening by the water. Tickets are a bargain at $10.

Comedy

Separating comedy from theatre in Chicago is tough. It's not that Chi-town lacks famous comedic names. *Au contraire*: Chris Farley, Andy Richter, Elaine May, Mike Nichols, John and James Belushi, Bill Murray, Shelley Long, George Wendt and many others all honed their craft in this city. It's just that the comedy scene in Chicago is not about guys getting up before microphones in smoky backrooms of bars. This is the improv capital of the world.

Ever since Paul Sills and Bernard Shamans founded **Second City** (*see p246*) in 1959, would-be comedy stars have come here to learn how to improvise for fun and funds. Almost all the masters of the form have Chicago roots. Viola Spoil invented her 'theatre games' here. Elaine May and Mike Nichols did funny stuff at the old Compass Players, which pre-dated even Second City. And each year, it seems like Chi improv spits out the next star of *Saturday Night Live*: Tina Fey and Rachel Dratch are just the most recent examples in a long, long line of notable alumni.

There are many definitions of improv, but all involve original, actor-created material, some relationship to current events and an aim of making people laugh. True improv involves performers making up material from audience suggestions on the spur of the comedic moment. In 'short form', that usually means a series of skits or sketches and the lighting guy hitting a blackout button.

In the more challenging 'long form', a single suggestion can provide the basis for a two-hour play. But Second City and its imitators do what Shamans termed 'sketch comedy'. A blend of scripted and spontaneous material, it vaguely resembles *Saturday Night Live* but goes to far deeper places.

Since the real money is on the coasts, improvisers come and go here with dizzying rapidity. And since a show can rock on one night and stink on the next, improv comes with no money-back guarantee. But there are some citadels of improv in this town that have seen it all, and you can't help but feel the weight of history. A trip to one of them is a vital part of a visit to Chicago.

TICKETS & INFORMATION

The *Chicago Reader* and *Newcity* offer listings for almost every venue in town. Tickets can be bought directly from box offices. Many improv troupes don't perform in a set location: check listings for details on their movements.

Venues

ComedySportz of Chicago

2851 N Halsted Street, at W Belmont Avenue, Lake View (773 549 8080/www.comedysportzchicago.com). CTA Belmont (Brown, Purple, Red). **Open** Box office 10am-6pm Mon-Wed, Sun; 10am-midnight Thur-Sat. *Shows* 8pm Thur; 8pm, 10.30pm, midnight Fri; 2pm, 8pm, 10.30pm, midnight Sat. **Tickets** $10-$17. **Credit** Disc, MC, V. **Map** p309 F2.

ComedySportz is the Starbucks of its field, though it's no surprise that Chicago hosts one of the stronger franchises (not saying much). Two teams battle each other at improv games, complete with a scoreboard. The performers are generally talented, but the place is aimed more at providing harmless fun for the masses than extending the boundaries of the art form. To the horror of purists, ComedySportz operates in a historic Chicago theatre where many of the works of David Mamet once premièred.

Free Associates

Royal George Theatre, 1641 N Halsted Street, at W North Avenue, Old Town (312 988 9000). CTA North/Clybourn (Red). **Open** Box office 10am-6pm Mon-Sat; noon-6pm Sun. *Shows* usually 7.30pm, 9.30pm Fri, Sat. **Tickets** $20. **Credit** AmEx, MC, V. **Map** p307 F7.

Chicago calendar Comedy

The once-small **Chicago Improv Festival** (773 862 5082/www.cif.com) is now a major week-long event on the international improv calendar. It's held in April mainly at the **Athenaeum Theatre** (*see p248*), and has featured such main stage acts as Upright Citizen's Brigade, the Improv Bandits from New Zealand, Tokyo's Yellow Man Group and various stars of *Saturday Night Live*. Workshops and other improv-related events complete the calendar.

The five-year-old **Chicago Comedy Festival** (www.comedytown.com), held in late May/ early June, attempts to encompass all that is funny: sketches, films, one-man shows and stand-up. Based at around a dozen venues in Old Town and Near North, the week-long event has grown quickly – if unevenly – and attracts attention in the comedy industry. And that means more big-name performers alongside unknowns waiting to be signed by HBO and network reps.

Arts & Entertainment

Improv-based parodies of movies, literature and TV are the niche this long-established group, which relocated to the George in 2002, has carved for itself. *Cast on a Hot Tin Roof* and *Blithering Heights* were both successes, while *BS*, a parody of TV show *ER*, was a huge hit. Audience members, often intoxicated, shout crass suggestions and the cast, with varying degrees of success, try to turn it all into intelligent parody.

ImprovOlympic

3541 N Clark Street, at W Addison Street, Lake View/ Wrigleyville (773 880 0199/www.improvolymp.com). CTA Addison (Red). **Open** *Shows* times vary. **Credit** Disc, MC, V. **Map** p309 E1.

The most respected Chicago venue for hardcore improv, ImprovOlympic counts Andy Richter and Mike Myers among its alums. The speciality of the house is a long-form improv style called the Harold. Created by Del Close, it features improvising teams creating fluid acts loosely revolving around one audience suggestion. But this is just one of numerous shows at a venue busy all nights of the week and all hours of the night.

The Noble Fool

16 W Randolph Street, at N State Street, the Loop. (312 726 1156/www.noblefool.com). CTA Lake (Red) or Randolph (Brown, Green, Orange, Purple). **Open** *Box office* 10am-7pm Tue-Thur; noon-10pm Fri, Sat; noon-3pm Sun. *Shows: Main stage* 7.30pm Wed-Fri; 4.30pm, 8pm Sat; 3pm Sun. *Studio* 7.30pm Thur; 7.30pm, 10pm Fri; 4pm, 7pm, 9.30pm Sat; 3pm Sun. *Cabaret* 9pm. **Tickets** *Main stage* $31-$36. *Studio* $29. *Cabaret* $10. **Credit** AmEx, Disc, MC, V. **Map** p305 H12.

Stand up and be counted at **Zanies**.

The wacky guys at Noble Fool hit the jackpot in April 2002. Bankrolled in part by the City of Chicago's desire to diversify its theatre district, it was effectively handed a prime piece of Loop real estate in 2002, with three brand new theatres for it to ply its trade of comedy theatre and original improv. It's an irreverent, youthful kind of place with good-spirited shows of varying quality and sophistication. Long-runners include *Flanagan's Wake*, a satirical treatment of an Irish funeral, and *The Baritones*, a *Sopranos* spoof, but Noble Fool plans to keep all its theatres busy with a diet of original material, seasonal attractions, and comedies from the past.

The Playground

3341 N Lincoln Avenue, at W Roscoe Street, Lake View (773 871 3793/www.the-playground.com). CTA Paulina (Brown). **Open** *Shows* 8pm Thur-Sat. **Tickets** $8. **Credit** Disc, MC, V.

Graduates of the Second City and ImprovOlympic programmes can find a place to perform here, a tiny 40-seat, BYOB shopfront space featuring plenty of nascent troupes. It even hosts something called the Improv Incubator, where lonely improvisers pay a small fee to meet each other. As entertainment, the result is hit and miss, but in a typical night, four troupes perform 30-minute long-form acts, one of which is bound to be funny. Tickets are cheap.

Second City

1616 N Wells Street, at W North Avenue, Old Town (312 337 3992/www.secondcity.com). CTA Sedgwick (Brown, Purple). **Open** *Box office* 10.30am-9pm Mon-Thur; 10.30am-11pm Fri, Sat; noon-9pm Sun. *Shows: Main stage* 8pm Mon; 8.30pm Tue-Thur; 8pm, 11pm Fri, Sat; 8pm Sun. *ETC stage* 8.30pm Thur; 8pm, 11pm Fri, Sat; 8pm Sun. **Tickets** $8-$17. **Credit** AmEx, DC, Disc, MC, V. **Map** p307 H7.

The granddaddy of all improv theatres and the most reliable bet for Chi-style comedy, Second City is the brand name for funny biz in Chicago. Now over 40 years old, it's a well-polished machine and a top tourist attraction, but deservedly so. The city's best comic actors perform here, waiting to be snatched away by *Saturday Night Live* or Mad TV, but the humour is still cutting edge. A different – and often gutsier – revue plays in the Second City ETC, the second stage, Thursday to Sunday. Get there early on weekends as most shows sell out.

Zanies

1548 N Wells Street, at W North Avenue, Old Town (312 337 4027). CTA Sedgwick (Brown, Purple). **Open** *Shows* 8.30pm Tue-Thur, Sun; 8.30pm, 10.30pm Fri; 7pm, 9pm, 11.15pm Sat. **Tickets** $16-$20. **Credit** MC, V. **Map** p307 H7.

Though it's the one major stand-up club in the city to survive the post-1980s bust doesn't create much of a buzz, it's a reliable place to see seasoned local comics you've never heard of, as well as the odd national act with a few TV spots under their belt. A typical night features an MC, an opening comic and a headliner. Audiences tend to be loud and boorish.

Second City, first rate. *See p246.*

Classes

As the likes of Bill Murray and Chris Farley have graduated from Chicago stage to national TV screen, a few souls have sat in the audience thinking, 'I can do that'. Most can't, of course. But some venues started offering courses that help the wannabes improve at improv.

Second City (*see p246*) offers numerous classes in its Old Town space, from beginners' lessons to the Conservatory Level, geared to those who are serious about taking the stage one day. Those more interested in long-form should try **ImprovOlympic** (*see p246*), which offers five tiers of classes, plus performance-level lessons for the talented and lucky students who get stage time in its Wrigleyville theatre.

Other companies have gotten in on the act. For *Whose Line Is It Anyway?*-style laughs, hit **ComedySportz of Chicago** (*see p245*). The Player's Workshop offers the fundamentals in its new digs at the **Chicago Center for the Performing Arts** (*see p244*); **Noble Fool** (*see p246*) also has a brand new location.

Classes start at $200 for an eight-week programme, though some theatres do offer unpaid internships in exchange for free classes.

Dance

In late 2003, the brand new, 1500-seat **Music & Dance Theater Chicago** in Millennium Park is expected to provide a shot in the legs to Chicago's dance community. The $56-million, multi-company venue will be the downtown home of many of the city's leading troupes (and some visiting companies). Today, the city supports two world-famous companies – one of which migrated here from New York – and a host of smaller troupes and independent choreographers who come and go. Due to the heritage of the city, the traditions of jazz and theatrical dance are especially well respected and represented here.

TICKETS & INFORMATION

The *Chicago Reader*, the *Chicago Tribune* and the *Chicago un-Times* have extensive dance listings and reviews. Some dance events are available at the half-price **Hot Tix** booths (*see p240*), depending on venues. **Ticketmaster** (312 902 1500/www.ticketmaster.com) also has details of most events.

Major dance companies

In addition to those listed in full below, other notable companies in Chicago not tied to any one theatre include the witty **DanceLoop Chicago** (630 552 8428); the largely youth-oriented **Ballet Chicago** (312 251 8838/www.balletchicago.org); **Hedwig Dances** (773 871 0872/www.hedwigdances.com); the **Chicago Moving Company** (773 880 5402/www.chicagomovingcompany.org), and Evanston's **Gus Giordano Jazz Dance** (847 866 9441/www.giordanojazzdance.com).

Hubbard Street Dance Chicago

1147 W Jackson Boulevard, at S Racine Avenue, West Town (312 850 9744/977 1700/www.hubbardstreetdance.com). CTA Racine (Blue). Founded in 1977 by choreographer Lou Conte (still artistic director), Chicago's premier dance company offers an eclectic mix of modern tap and classical with a repertoire that has frequently drawn on the work of Twyla Tharp and Bob Fosse. The spacious dance centre is the venue for classes and rehearsals but not shows. The troupe is often on tour, but performs annually at the Auditorium Theatre (*see p241* **As good as new**) and, each summer, at the Ravinia Festival (*see p226*).

Arts & Entertainment

The **Joffrey Ballet**, a local favourite for half a century.

Joffrey Ballet of Chicago

Auditorium Theatre, 50 E Congress Parkway, at S Michigan Avenue, the Loop (information 312 739 0120/tickets 312 902 1500). **Open** *Box office hours vary.* **Tickets** $34-$74. **Credit** MC, V. **Map** p305 J13.
One of the leading smaller American ballet companies, with a resume numbering more than 235 ballets by 85 choreographers in its 50 years. It moved here in 1995; though it remains a touring company, local engagements include an annual *Nutcracker* and dates at the Ravinia Festival (*see p226*).

Muntu Dance Theatre of Chicago

Kennedy King College, 6800 S Wentworth Avenue, at W 67th Street, South Side (773 602 1135/www.muntu.com). CTA 69th Street (Red). **Tickets** $12-$20. **Credit** AmEx, MC, V.
'Muntu' means 'the essence of humanity', and this troupe is continually exploring its roots through African and African-American dance and music. Much of its work features the synthesis of dance, rhythm and song, and audiences find it hard to stay in their seats. Outside the college, the group performs often at the Athenaeum Theatre (*see below*).

River North Dance Company

312 944 2888/www.rivernorthchicago.com.
Now over a decade old, this hip and lively touring troupe's trademark is a breezy style with an emphasis on accessibility; most of the choreography comes from Chicago-based artists. Co-artistic director Sherry Zunker Dow often describes River North as 'the dance company for the MTV generation'.

Major dance venues

Athenaeum Theatre

2936 N Southport Avenue, at N Lincoln Avenue, Lake View (773 935 6860/http://athenaeum. livedomain.com). CTA Wellington (Brown, Purple). **Open** *Box office* 3-8pm Mon-Fri; 2-3hrs before show Sat, Sun. **Tickets** $10-$30. **Credit** AmEx, MC, V. **Map** p309 D3.

The annual Next Dance Festival takes place over three winter weekends at this 900-seat theatre, showcasing small Chicago troupes and solo artists. The theatre presents other dance events during the year and is also an increasingly significant music and theatre venue.

Dance Center of Columbia College

1306 S Michigan Avenue, at E 13th Street, South Loop (312 344 8300/www.colum.edu/ undergraduate/dance). CTA Roosevelt/State (Red) or Roosevelt/Wabash (Green, Orange) **Open** *Box office times vary.* **Tickets** $16-$20. **Credit** AmEx, Disc, MC, V. **Map** p304 H15.
An offshoot of one of the area's best college dance programmes, Columbia College's Dance Center presents a combination of student, faculty and professional work in a spiffy black box that offers the chance to see high-quality contemporary dance in an intimate venue.

Museum of Contemporary Art

220 E Chicago Avenue, at N Mies van der Rohe Way, Near North (312 280 2660/ www.mcachicago.org). CTA Chicago (Red). **Open** 10am-8pm Tue; 10am-5pm Wed-Sun. **Tickets** $10; $6 over-65s, students; free under-12s. **Credit** AmEx, Disc, MC, V. **Map** p306 J10.
The multi-disciplinary MCA has emerged as one of Chicago's most important presenters of international dance companies, as well as performance artists and other non-commercial touring performers who need the support of a large museum. The basement theatre is a charming, intimate facility.

Ruth Page Center for the Arts

1016 N Dearborn Street, at W Oak Street, Gold Coast (312 337 6543/www.ruthpage.org). CTA Clark/Division (Red). **Open** 10am-9pm Mon-Thur; 10am-7.30pm Fri; 9am-4.30pm Sat. **Tickets** vary. **Credit** MC, V. **Map** p306 H9.
The spiritual heart of Chicago's dance community, the intimate and dance-oriented Ruth Page hosts a variety of classes and events throughout the year.

Trips Out of Town

Getting Started

Chicago is the jewel of the Midwest. But while you're here, try and take time to check out the states that surrounds it.

Diversity – of both the land and its people – is part of the lure of the Midwest. Flat prairies are juxtaposed with craggy, unglaciated regions of hills and valleys; and pockets of European cultural tradition – such as German, Swiss and Norwegian settlements – are dotted around Chicago's neighbouring states.

In a south-west region of Wisconsin, there are valleys so much like those in Switzerland that they drew a settlement of immigrants who, to this day, fervently maintain Swiss customs and traditions in towns such as **New Glarus**. In the same region are the tiny communities of **Mount Horeb** and **Little Norway**, settled by Norwegians; in **Milwaukee**, you'll find all manner of things Teutonic, with beer halls and German restaurants the predictable standouts for most visitors.

There's variety in the landscape. Within easy driving reach of the skyscrapers and concrete canyons of Chicago are the towering pines of pristine North Woods and the rolling sand dunes of Lake Michigan's shore. Poet Carl Sandburg, while impressed by Chicago's 'Big Shoulders', was also an admirer of those magnificent sand dunes, saying that they are to the Midwest what the Grand Canyon is to Arizona and Yosemite is to California.

Lake Michigan, also shared by Illinois, Indiana, Michigan and Wisconsin, is a great source of recreation. Sometimes wild and raging, often benevolently calm, this great inland sea provides beaches and yacht harbours, fishing and boating, diving and bird-watching. It is ideal, too, for simply watching and dreaming, as it changes colour with weather and season from sombre gun-metal grey to bright and lively aquamarine blue.

The lake, too, has a beneficial effect on flora and fauna around its shores. It produces a moderating effect that in springtime transforms **Berrien County**, Michigan (a little more than an hour's drive east of Chicago) into a spectacular garden of wildflowers, with close to 150 species. By buffering temperatures, Lake Michigan also helps produce conditions that are ideal for growing grapes that have spawned a rapidly expanding winemaking industry.

Another factor that makes Chicago an ideal centre for touring the Midwest is its geography. Drive east from downtown Chicago and within

half an hour you're in Indiana; in little more than an hour you're in Michigan. Wisconsin is only an hour's drive north (Milwaukee itself is a mere 90 minutes away), and you can get as far as the Mississippi River and neighbouring Iowa in less than three hours. Even St Louis, Missouri can be reached by road in about five hours. In fact, it is estimated that around 20 per cent of the nation's population lie within a reasonably comfortable one-day drive of the Windy City.

And drive you absolutely should. To enjoy most of the destinations in this chapter, you'll need to rent a car. Long-distance bus services from companies such as **Greyhound** (1-800 229 9424/www.greyhound.com) are spotty, and train services to many communities are non-existent (contact **Amtrak** at 1-800 872 7245/www.amtrak.com for details on trains). There are exceptions, of course, such as travelling from Chicago to **Springfield** or **Milwaukee** by train: both cities are connected to Chicago by a decent Amtrak service. But mostly, you're best off hiring a car and hitting the open road. For more on car hire firms in Chicago, *see p280*.

Nonetheless, wherever you go, however you get there, you'll usually receive a warm welcome. Folk in America's heartland are mostly genuinely friendly to strangers, and as interested to hear your stories as you will surely be to learn about their towns. So what are you waiting for? Hit the road.

The best Trips

Columbus, Indiana
Not had your fill of great architecture? Head to this charming yet dynamic town. *See p257.*

Milwaukee, Wisconsin
One of the finest zoos in the US, but more besides. *See p267.*

Springfield, Illinois
If it was good enough for Lincoln, it's good enough for us. *See p255.*

Illinois

... Or how Honest Abe met a herd of hogs on Route 66.

Galena

Driving the backroads east of Galena over the rolling terrain of one of the few hilly regions in prairie-flat Illinois, you may come across a bright red stagecoach pulled by a pair of brown Belgian drafthorses. An authentic reproduction of a 19th-century Concord stagecoach, it's similar to the vehicles that travelled these roads in the 1800s, taking mail and passengers on the five-day journey from Chicago to Galena. The vehicle runs year-round over old stagecoach routes, weather permitting, at one point fording a narrow stream. It's one of many living-history experiences that await in Galena.

Galena is the quintessential time-warp town. Established in the 1820s during a lead-mining boom, it's tucked away in Illinois's north-west corner, where Iowa, Wisconsin and Illinois converge near the Mississippi. More than 85 per cent of its buildings appear on the National Register of Historic Places; many are now occupied by the town's more than 100 shops.

Housed in an 1858 Italianate mansion, the **Galena/Joe Daviess County Historical Society & Museum** is a good spot to start. An hourly audio-visual presentation chronicles how the town became what it is today. You can take a peek into the original shaft of one of the lead mines to which Galena owes its existence. More history can be enjoyed at the **Ulysses S Grant Home**, a reminder of the day (18 August 1865) when, with a jubilant procession, speeches and fireworks, the proud local citizens welcomed home their returning Civil War hero.

Before going off to war, Grant had worked at a Galena store owned by his father and run by his kid brothers. Upon his return, townsfolk presented Grant with a handsome, two-storey brick mansion. The house has since been restored to the way it appeared in drawings published in a 1868 edition of Frank Leslie's *Illustrated Newspaper*, and also features memorabilia of the 18th president.

The Napa Valley this ain't, but the tasting room of **Galena Cellars Winery**, housed in a restored 1840s granary, does offer evidence that not all good American wines are made in California. The winery produces more than two dozen varieties of grape and fruit wines, including an award-winning Pinot Noir; the vineyards, planted with around four acres of grapes, lie a ten-minute drive from town through beautiful countryside along the historic Stagecoach Trail. Views from this region, which contains the highest point in what is otherwise a monotonously flat state, are spectacular.

Galena Cellars Winery
515 S Main Street, Galena (1-800 397 9463/815 777 3330/www.galenacellars.com). **Open** *Jan-May* 9am-5pm Mon-Thur; 9am-8pm Fri, Sat; 9am-6pm Sun. *Memorial Day-Dec* 9am-8pm Mon-Sat; 9am-6pm Sun. **Admission** free. **Credit** AmEx, DC, Disc, MC, V.

Galena/Joe Daviess County Historical Society & Museum
211 S Bench Street, Galena (815 777 9129/ www.galenahistorymuseum.org). **Open** 9am-4.30pm daily. **Admission** $4; $3 10-18s; free under-10s. **Credit** MC, V.

Stagecoach Trails Livery
203 Hickory Street, Apple River (815 594 2423). **Open** by reservation only. **Tickets** $75/carriage (up to 12). **No credit cards.**

Ulysses S Grant Home State Historic Site
500 Bouthillier Street, Galena (815 777 3310/ www.granthome.com). **Open** 9am-5pm daily. **Admission** *Suggested donation* $3. **No credit cards.**

Where to eat

Galena has more fine eateries than you'd expect in a town its size. Among the best of them is the **Perry Street Brasserie** (124 N Commerce Street, 815 777 3773/ www.perrystreetbrasserie.com, closed Mon, Sun in summer, closed Mon-Wed, Sun in winter, main courses $19-$28), a former dockside warehouse run by an expat Brit (Steve Dowe) who's cooked for royalty and big-name entertainers. Be sure to book ahead. Other fine choices include a couple of Italian restaurants: **Fried Green Tomatoes** (1301 N Irish Hollow Road, 815 777 3938/ www.friedgreen.com, main courses $16-$28), set in the rolling countryside just outside town in a historic brick farmstead, and **Vinny Vanucchi's** (201 S Main Street, 815 777 8100/ www.vinnyvanucchis.com, main courses $9-$15), where the decor is ordinary and generic but the food is well executed.

Where to stay

The 300 secluded homes at the **Eagle Ridge Inn and Resort** (444 Eagle Ridge Drive, 1-800 892 2269/www.eagleridge.com, rates $89-$259) are ideal for families or groups, though there's also also an 80-room inn on a wooded bluff overlooking Lake Galena.

The **Chestnut Mountain Resort** (8700 W Chestnut Road, 1-800 397 1320/ www.chestnutmtn.com, double $89-$139) offers 119 rooms, a pool, a restaurant and some splendid skiing. Also in the area are many serviceable motels and a few B&Bs.

Getting there

By car

Galena is approximately 165 miles (265km) north-west of Chicago. Take the I-90 (Northwest Tollway) to Rockford, then take US 20.

Tourist information

Galena/Jo Daviess County Convention & Visitors' Bureau

Old Train Depot, 101 Bouthillier Street, Galena (1-888 777 4099/www.galena.org). **Open** 9am-5pm Mon-Sat; 10am-5pm Sun.
There is also a visitors' centre at the **Old Market House**, 123 N Commerce Street (815 777 1448).

Rockford & the Rock River

There are few cultural chasms greater than that separating traditional Japanese gardens containing 16th-century sukiya-style architecture and the loud, high-powered world of the Harley-Davidson motorcycle. Yet both are well represented at Rockford, Illinois. The second largest city in Illinois is at once home of Anderson Gardens, rated No.2 among Japanese gardens around the world outside Japan, and the world's oldest Harley dealer.

Anderson Gardens, spread over eight acres, combines three essential elements of Japanese gardening: water, for its soothing qualities; rock, for its sense of permanence; and plants, for their textures. Paths wind around ponds containing Japanese koi, Chinese grass carp, crayfish and turtles, and past stone pagodas, four soothing waterfalls, and a teahouse, guesthouse and gazebo.

In between these two extremes, though, Rockford is a surprisingly zesty destination. Surprising, because 15 years ago, the town's reputation – well-deserved at that – was as a gritty industrial city with high unemployment. The turnaround isn't quite complete yet, but with excellent museums, galleries and cultural

venues and tangible evidence of more general city beautification projects, Rockford is dispelling the image that once prevailed.

One of its real gems, though, is some 75 years old, though an $18.5 million project has only just restored it to its old glories. The **Coronado Theatre** (314 N Main Street; 815 968 5222) is a grand, lavish beauty: part Spanish castle, part Italian villa, wildly opulent and superbly decadent. With a painted skyline of Moorish castles and a ceiling filled with twinkling star-lights, the effect is designed to resemble a Spanish courtyard on a summer's evening. Among the acts who've graced its stage are Bob Hope, the Marx Brothers, Louis Armstrong and Liberace; in 1941, Gypsy Rose Lee scandalised the community by performing her striptease routine on Easter Sunday.

Grouped together in Riverfront Museum Park are a trio of excellent, newer museums: the **Discovery Center Museum**, a hands-on children's museum with a planetarium and a science park; **Rockford Art Museum**, downstate Illinois's largest art museum, with a permanent collection of 19th- and 20th-century American art; and the splendid **Burpee Museum of Natural History**, with its subject-matter mix of dinosaurs and Native American history. The latter's signature exhibit is a coal forest with simulated thunderstorms, two-storey-high trees and an 85-foot (26-metre) mural that sets the stage for a full-size adult Tyrannosaurus rex skeletal cast.

Rockford's Swedish heritage dates back to a period in the 19th century when every sixth person in Sweden left for America. Many settled in Rockford, creating one of the largest Swedish settlements in the Midwest and establishing Rockford's pre-eminence in furniture making through their skilled craftsmanship. During its heyday, there were 93 furniture companies in Rockford. Many one-of-a-kind pieces made by Swedish craftsmen can be seen in a guided tour of the Victorian brick mansion owned by furniture magnate John Erlander and now run as the **Erlander Home Museum**.

The stretch of the Rock River between Rockford and **Dixon** is picturesque to a fault. Along one especially pretty two-mile stretch – just south of Castle Rock State Park – the road is canopied by leafy branches dappled with sunlight. Though scenic Route 2 parallels much of the river's course along its west bank, the river twists and turns so much that you find yourself crossing it. Follow the river south to learn the story of the 'Plow that won the West'. **Grand Detour** is as pretty now as it was when French explorers named it for the bend in the river. But Native Americans have the most lyrical description

Pump it up

Bill Shea is known as the 'King of the Road'. At least, he is to those who get their kicks cruising down Route 66. Shea pumped gas along the fabled highway in Springfield, Illinois, for almost four decades. Today, travellers visit his former gas station not for a fill-up, but rather for an animated rundown of his adventures working on ol' 66.

On most days, you'll find 80-year-old Shea chatting with visitors at the station, which doubles as a self-made **Route 66 Museum**. Shea's museum is packed with road trip relics and collectibles culled from his years in the gasoline business. You'll find vintage gas pumps, old cash registers and many quirky rarities, such as an 80-year-old peanut dispenser and a 15-cents-a-pack cigarette machine.

As you sift through the treasures that symbolise Shea's longstanding love affair with the road – don't pass up his original Texaco uniform – be sure to get him to weave a tale or two. But don't be surprised if Shea shoots back just as many questions in return: he's more than a little curious about other people's travels. His guest book, filled with hundreds of messages from visitors who have come from as far away as Australia, is proof. Sign it on your way out; you'll be joining the ranks of other intrepid travellers who never knew that going to the pump could be so fun.

Route 66 Museum
2075 Peoria Road, Springfield (217 522 0475). **Open** 7am-4pm Tue-Fri; 7am-noon Sat. **Admission** free.

for this sweeping oxbow bend: they say the river is so pretty that it doubles back to take another look at itself.

Grand Detour's most famous citizen was John Deere, a brawny blacksmith from Vermont who stepped off a riverboat to begin a new life. Deere discovered that the ploughs farmers had brought west were unsuitable for the gumbo-like rich black soil of the prairies: every few steps, the farmer would have to stop the team and clean the plough. The ingenious Deere found fortune by creating a steel plough with a highly polished surface that scoured itself clean, an achievement commemorated at the **John Deere Historic Site**. The original blacksmith shop has been

excavated and an archaeological exhibition building now covers the site. Tours include a demonstration by a working blacksmith.

Nearby **White Pines Forest State Park** is threaded with hiking trails that wind through the last stands of virgin white pines in Illinois. You can drive through a large section of the park, splashing through fords across a stream. The park lodge provides rustic lodging and home-cooked meals.

At the river town of Dixon is the family home of Ronald Reagan, who moved here with his parents in 1920, aged nine. The **Ronald Reagan Boyhood Home** is now a museum and visitors' centre chronicling the formative

Trips Out of Town

years of the 40th president. The house has been restored to the way it looked when the Reagans lived there, furnished with pieces typical of the period. Ronald and his older brother Neil shared one of three upstairs rooms; Mrs Reagan, who supplemented the family's income by taking in mending, used another as a sewing room.

Anderson Gardens
318 Spring Creek Road, Rockford (815 229 9390/ www.andersongardens.org). Open May-Oct 10am-5pm Mon-Fri; 10am-4pm Sat; noon-4pm Sun. **Admission** $5; $3-$4 concessions; free under-4s. **Credit** AmEx, Disc, MC, V.

Burpee Museum of Natural History
737 N Main Street, Rockford (815 965 3433/ www.burpee.org). Open 10am-5pm Mon-Sat; noon-5pm Sun. **Admission** $4; $3 concessions; free under-3s. **Credit** MC, V.

Discovery Center Museum
711 N Main Street, Rockford (815 963 6769/ www.discoverycentermuseum.org). Open Late May-early Sept 10am-5pm Mon-Sat; noon-5pm Sun. *Early Sept-late May* 10am-5pm Tue-Sat; noon-5pm Sun. **Admission** $4; $3 children; free under-2s. **Credit** Disc, MC, V.

Erlander Home Museum
404 S 3rd Street, Rockford (815 963 5559). **Open** 1-4pm Wed-Fri; 2-4pm Sun. **Admission** free. **No credit cards.**

John Deere Historic Site
8393 S Main Street, Grand Detour (815 652 4551/www.deere.com). Open Apr-Oct 9am-5pm daily. *Nov-Mar* group tours only (call in advance). **Admission** $3; free under-12s. **Credit** MC, V.

Rockford Art Museum
711 N Main Street, Rockford (815 968 2787/ www.rockfordartmuseum.org). Open 11am-5pm Tue-Fri; 10am-5pm Sat; noon-5pm Sun. **Admission** *Suggested donation* $2. **No credit cards.**

Ronald Reagan Boyhood Home
816 S Hennepin Avenue, Dixon (815 288 3404). Open Feb-Mar 10am-4pm Sat; 1-4pm Sun. *Apr-Sept* 10am-4pm Mon-Sat; 1-4pm Sun. **Admission** *Suggested donation* $1. **No credit cards.**

Where to eat

The handsome **White Pines Inn** (6712 W Pines Road, Mount Morris, 815 946 3817/ www.whitepinesinn.com, main courses $10-$20) was built by the Civilian Conservation Corps in the 1930s, and now dishes up hearty fare such as chicken pot pie and prime rib. Moving down a notch, the **Stockholm Inn** (2420 Charles Street, 815 397 3534, main courses $6-$10) is known for Swedish dishes such as thin pancakes and meatballs; try flaskpannkaka, a baked egg and pork breakfast dish. And for

Burpee Museum of Natural History.

something completely different, try **Kegel's Diner** (7125 Harrison Avenue, 815 332 7200, breakfast and lunch only, main courses $4-$7), a biker-themed '50s-style diner adjoining a huge Harley-Davidson dealership. Cruise up to the counter and straddle the leather saddle of a Hog.

Where to stay

A comfortable all-suites hotel along the Rock River, **Cliffbreakers Comfort Suites** (700 W Riverside Boulevard, 1-800 478 9395, suite $83-$500) has an indoor pool, a Swedish hot-rock sauna, a gym, a restaurant and river views from 87 of the 104 rooms. The aforementioned **White Pines Inn** (6712 W Pines Road, Mount Morris, 815 946 3817/www.whitepinesinn.com, double $77) goes with a rustic theme in its 25 one-room log cabins, all with full bathrooms. For the personal touch, try the 150-year-old **Colonial Rose Inn** (8230 S Green Street, Grand Detour, 815 652 4422/www.colonialroseinn.com, double $85): reminiscent of a New England hostelry, it has a mere five rooms. Lodgings include a full and hearty breakfast.

Getting there

By car
Rockford is about 85 miles (137km) north-west of Chicago. Take the I-90 (Northwest Tollway) to Rockford. Follow US 2 along the Rock River between Rockford and Dixon.

Tourist information

Blackhawk Waterways Convention & Visitors' Bureau

201 N Franklin Avenue, Polo (1-800 678 2108/ 815 946 2108/www.blackhawkwaterwayscvb.org). **Open** 8.30am-4.30pm Mon-Fri.

Rockford Area Convention & Visitors' Bureau

211 N Main Street, Rockford (1-800 521 0849/ 815 963 8111/www.gorockford.com). **Open** 8.30am-5pm Mon-Fri.

Springfield

Although Lincoln is not the only game in town for Springfield, Illinois, he certainly is the main attraction. The Illinois capital is affectionately known as 'Mr Lincoln's Home Town', and the presence of the 16th president is inescapable. In many instances, the careful restoration of some of the historic sites creates the impression that Honest Abe has only just left the building.

The **Lincoln's Home National Historic Site** is operated by the National Park Service, and offers guided tours given by park rangers. Lincoln occupied the modest, two-storey frame home, which he purchased for $1,200 in a still-attractive, leafy neighbourhood, for some 17 years; it's the only home he ever owned. Visit the parlour where Lincoln was asked to run for president. Hanging on a peg in the hall is a tall hat such as Lincoln wore, suggesting, perhaps, that the bootstrap lawyer has simply slipped out to tend the garden or play with the kids.

The **Old State Capitol** is a fine example of Greek revival architecture. Built in 1837, it's been painstakingly restored and its Hall of Representatives and Senate Chamber appear as if the legislators of the day had just left for a temporary adjournment. It was here in 1858 that Lincoln made his 'house divided' speech on slavery. A scant seven years later, the body of the slain president lay in state in the same building. Tours are offered year round.

Across from the Old State Capitol are the **Lincoln-Herndon Law Offices**, where Lincoln practised law. Cases were tried in the federal court below the law offices; sometimes, Lincoln would lie on the office floor and observe the proceedings in the courtroom below through a peephole in the floorboards. Another must-see is the **Lincoln Depot**, from where he delivered his famous farewell address – which some say ranks with the Gettysburg Address – on 11 February 1861 before departing to Washington, DC to assume the Presidency. Inside the restored depot are

waiting rooms, a ticket seller's cage and an audio-visual re-creation of Lincoln's 12-day journey to his inauguration.

Springfield's most moving site, though, is undoubtedly **Lincoln's Tomb**. Each Tuesday evening at 7pm between June and August, a retreat ceremony is held in front of the tomb with drill, musket firing and the haunting sound of the Retreat and Taps played by a bugler. Captured in an inscription on the north window are the poignant words spoken by Secretary of War Edwin M Stanton at Lincoln's death: 'Now he belongs to the ages.'

Although Lincoln is Springfield's most famous citizen, another of its native sons had an international reputation. **Vachel Lindsay** (1879-1931) was one of America's best-known poets during the early decades of the 20th century. His birthplace and home has been restored as a State Historic Site and opened to the public in 2001. Lindsay was the first American poet invited to recite at Oxford University and, according to the editor/publisher of *Poetry Magazine*, was 'perhaps the most gifted and original poet we've ever printed'.

Springfield also boasts two other interesting attractions. The **Dana-Thomas House State Historical Site** is considered to be one of the best preserved and most complete of Frank

Old State Capitol. Lincoln not pictured.

Lloyd Wright's early Prairie School houses. And then there's the new **Museum of Funereal Customs**. Well, if the undertaking business can work as the subject of a hit prime time television show (HBO's *Six Feet Under*), why not as the focus of a museum?

Dana-Thomas House State Historical Site

301 E Lawrence Avenue, Springfield (217 782 6776). **Open** 9am-4pm Wed-Sun. **Admission** *Suggested donation* $3; $1 children. **No credit cards.**

Lincoln's Home National Historic Site

S 8th Street, Springfield (217 492 4241/www.nps. gov/liho). **Open** *Apr-Sept* 8am-6pm daily. *Oct-Mar* 8.30am-5pm. **Admission** free. **No credit cards.**

Lincoln-Herndon Law Offices State Historic Site

6th Street, Springfield (217 785 7289). **Open** *Mar-Oct* 9am-5pm daily. *Nov-Feb* 9am-4pm daily. **Admission** *Suggested donation* $2; $1 children. **No credit cards.**

Museum of Funeral Customs

1440 Monument Avenue, Springfield (217 544 3480/ www.funeralmuseum.org). **Open** 10am-4pm Tue-Sat; 1-4pm Sun. **Admission** $3; $1.50-$2 concessions; free under-5s. **Credit** AmEx, Disc, MC, V.

Lincoln Tomb State Historical Site

1500 Monument Avenue, Springfield (217 782 2717). **Open** *Nov-Feb* 9am-4pm daily. *Mar-Oct* 9am-5pm daily. **Admission** free. **No credit cards.**

Old State Capitol State Historic Site

1 Old State Capitol Plaza, Springfield (217 785 7960). **Open** 8am-5pm daily. **Admission** *Suggested donation* $2. **No credit cards.**

Vachel Lindsay Home State Historic Site

603 S 5th Street, Springfield (217 524 0901). **Open** noon-4pm Tue-Sat. **Admission** *Suggested donation* $2. **No credit cards.**

Where to eat

Remy's (620 S 1st Street, 217 744 3333, main courses $16-$35), an upmarket steakhouse near the State Capitol, is popular with the pols. Beef is aged for 30 days and top choices include bone-in ribeye and Kansas City strip steak. Mid-range **Café Brio** (524 E Monroe Street, 217 544 0574/www.cafebrio.com, main courses $10-$18) serves such palate-tempters as pork tenderloin with Caribbean spices, filet mignon and Margaritas made from freshly squeezed juice. And for a snack, head to either the characterful **Cozy Dog Drive-In** (2935 S 6th Street, 217 525 1992/www.cozydogdrivein.com, main courses

Lloyd Wright's **Dana-Thomas House.**

$3-$7) for memorabilia, tall stories, doughnuts and dogs, or to the **Feed Store** (516 E Adams Street, 217 528 3355, main courses $3-$7) for terrific fresh soup in town: it's reputed to shift some 250 quarts a day.

Where to stay

The **Hilton Springfield** (700 Adams Street, 217 789 1530/www.hilton.com, double $89-$169) enjoys a nice downtown location within walking distance of the Lincoln Historic Sites, plus a pool and a good Cajun restaurant named Gumbo Ya Ya's. The smart **Crowne Plaza Hotel** (3000 S Dirksen Parkway, 217 529 7777/ www.crowneplazaspringfield.com, double $79-$139) is endowed with a concierge floor, an indoor pool, a fitness centre, a rooftop garden and a top-notch restaurant, the Rosewood. Neither hotel, though, are anywhere near as old as **The Inn at 835** (835 S 2nd Street, 1-888 217 4835/www.innat835.com, double $100-$195). Built in 1909 as Springfield's first modern apartment house, this ten-room inn is listed on the National Register of Historic Places.

Getting there

By car

Springfield is around 200 miles (322km) south-west of Chicago. Take I-55 from Chicago to Springfield, exit 98-B (Clearlake).

By train

Amtrak provides a Chicago–Springfield service with three trains daily in each direction. Travel time is about 3½ hours.

Tourist information

Springfield Illinois Convention & Visitors' Bureau

109 N 7th Street, Springfield (1-800 545 7300/ 217 789 2360/fax 544 8711/www.visit- springfieldillinois.com). **Open** 8am-5pm Mon-Fri.

Indiana

One designer city and lots of country style.

Columbus

Everyone loves an underdog, and tiny Columbus, Indiana, with a population of only 39,000, is a veritable David among architectural Goliaths. In 1957, the Cummins Engine Company, a Fortune 500 company that is the town's major employer, offered to pay the architectural fees for sorely needed new schools, stipulating that distinguished national architects be asked to design them. Now this Hoosier town, surrounded by stubby cornfields, has more distinguished architecture than cities 50 times its size, with nearly 60 buildings designed by world-renowned architects including IM Pei, Richard Meier and Robert Venturi. When an up-and-coming architect is invited to design a building in Columbus, they know that they've arrived.

To get the most out of Columbus's architectural gems, stop first at the **Columbus Area Visitors' Center** built in 1864 and

Indianapolis Museum of Art in Columbus.

expanded and redesigned by Kevin Roche. It is a showcase for the *Yellow Neon Chandelier and Persian Window*, an installation by glass artist Dale Chihuly, and also offers one- and two-hour bus tours from **Columbus Architectural Tours**, maps and self-guided tours.

One of the highlights of the tour is the **First Christian Church**, a geometric building of bluff brick and limestone designed by Eliel Saarinen and dedicated in 1941. Its bold simplicity influenced the subsequent design of contemporary churches in America. Among many other delights are: Eero Saarinen's (son and partner of Eliel Saarinen) North Christian Church, irreverently dubbed the 'Oil Can Church' because of its cone-shaped roof and 192-foot (58.5-metre) spire, and Fire Station No.1, a seamless 1990s addition to a 1941 building that is an eclectic blend of art nouveau and art deco. The bank, post office and numerous schools are all tour stops, as is the steel, glass and concrete Cummins Engine Company corporate headquarters. There's also the two-block long Commons Mall, a skylighted shopping centre with exhibition halls and a play area dominated by Chaos I, a 30-foot (nine-metre), seven-ton moving sculpture by Jean Tinguely of Switzerland.

Columbus is the antithesis of dull and provincial. Innovative and culturally rich, invitingly clean and well-scrubbed, 'It is,' observed architectural writer Blair Kamen, 'a textbook case of what a small town should be.' But it is not just the architecture. It is the spirit, too: grade-school kids take architecture classes; factories have fountains and landscaped gardens where workers take their lunch; there are outdoor symphony concerts; and the public art includes sculptures by Henry Moore, J Seward Johnson Jr, Jean Tinguely and Dale Chihuly. There are two symphony orchestras, a city band, a dance company, theatrical groups, two universities, an exemplary school system, 15 public parks, an enclosed ice rink and the only branch of the **Indianapolis Museum of Art**. The annual **Popfest**, held in June, attracts 7,000 people with lawn chairs, blankets and coolers to the public library plaza to listen to music in the shadow of a Henry Moore.

Columbus's **Otter Creek Golf Course**, designed by Robert Trent Jones, was rated at four and a half stars (Pebble Beach got five)

Life's a beach at the **Indiana Dunes National Lakeshore**. *See p259.*

by *Golf Digest*, and even the shopping around here packs a punch: **Prime Outlets** is a large factory-outlet mall located just north of town, next door to 'Exit 76 Antique Mall', with a mix of more than 400 booths and showcases. Credit cards are mandatory.

Visit **Wheatfields** to discover whimsical ways to use ordinary objects to enhance indoor and outdoor spaces. This hands-on learning centre for natural arts occupies a sixth-generation farm.

Then travel about ten miles north-west to learn all you ever wanted to know about popcorn. **Not Just Popcorn** offers tours and makes the nibbly stuff in 115 flavours (and also offers chocolates and toffee). What more could you ask from a town?

Columbus Architectural Tour

1-800 468 6564/812 378 2622/www.Columbus.in.us. **Tours** 10am Mon-Fri; 10am, 2pm Sat. *Mar-Nov* also 11am Sun. **Rates** $7-$9.50; $1.50-$9 concessions; free under-3s. **Credit** MC, V.

Indianapolis Museum of Art – Columbus Gallery

390 The Commons (812 376 2597/www.imac.org). **Open** 10am-5pm Tue-Sat; noon-4pm Sun. **Admission** free.

Not Just Popcorn

114 E Main Street, Edinburgh (812 526 8256/ www.notjustpopcorn.com). **Open** 10am-6pm Mon-Sat; noon-5pm most Suns. **Credit** AmEx, Disc, MC, V.

Wheatfields

4290 E 800 North (812 587 0046/www.wheatfields. org). **Open** *Apr-Oct* noon-6pm Tue-Fri; 7am-noon Sat; noon-5pm Sun. **Admission** free.

Where to eat

Zaharako's Confectionery (329 Washington Street, 812 379 9329, closed Sun) is a fab turn-of-the-century soda fountain, confectioner's and purveyor of good down-home cooking.

Where to stay

Best of the chains are the **Holiday Inn & Conference Center** (2480 Jonathan Moore Pike, 812 372 1541/1-800 465 4329, double $80-$100), with a pool, bakery, games room and exercise centre, and the **Ramada Inn** (2485 Jonathan Moore Pike, 812 376 3051, double $65-$95), whose above-average exercise facilities include tennis courts.

Trips Out of Town

The **Columbus Inn** (445 5th Street, 812 378 4289/www.thecolumbusinn.com, double $139) has stacks more character, though. It's the former city hall, built in 1895 and listed on the National Register of Historic Places.

Getting there

By car

Columbus is about 225 miles (362km) south-east of Chicago, off I-65, Indiana's major north–south artery that begins at Gary, east of Chicago.

Tourist information

Columbus Area Visitors' Center

506 5th Street, Columbus (1-800 468 6564/ www.Columbus.in.us). **Open** 9am-5pm Mon-Sat. *Mar-Nov* also 10am-4pm Sun.
Information, tours, an architecture exhibition and a well-stocked gift shop.

Lake & Porter Counties

Chicago's neighbouring counties to the east offer great quantities of the great outdoors: famous beaches and rolling dunes, excellent charter fishing for trout and salmon, pristine nature trails, a trio of wineries, top-rate restaurants and some pretty good spectator sports, albeit of the minor league variety.
In Lake County, the Gary Steelheads shoot baskets in the CBA and the Gary South Shore Railcats play baseball in the Independent Northern League. In 2003, they move to a state-of-the-art, 6,000-seat stadium.

When it comes to gambling, you'll find a clutch of riverboat casinos, including Hammond's **Horseshoe Casino**, the closest casino to Chicago. You can't miss its massive Vegas-style sign that burns 6,288 25-watt bulbs and is visible from the Chicago Skyway. It also houses a good eatery, Jack Binion's Steak House. **Harrahs East Chicago Casino** boasts a new luxury hotel.

Natural beauty, however, remains a large part of the charm of Lake and Porter counties. The sloping white expanses of the **Indiana Dunes National Lakeshore**, which covers 13,000 acres, encompass a state park and a state nature preserve where you can camp, swim, hike, bicycle and look for orchids, irises and prickly-pear cacti.

Though flames still leap into the sky from the steel mills and urban blight is still in evidence, Indiana's north-western corner has some bright new offerings to attract visitors. Just as Easterners cherish a trip to 'the shore', thousands of Chicagoans grew up looking forward to visiting 'the dunes'. This beach

playground offers swimming, bodysurfing and the exhilaration of a careering romp down steep sandy slopes after a leg-wearing climb to the summit. On a clear day, the Chicago skyline is visible, shimmering on the horizon of sparkling Lake Michigan.

A picturesque retreat lies just a few miles from the cookie-cutter commercialism of Merrillville, Indiana, where every chain that ever sold a franchise appears to be represented. At **Deep River County Park** is a working gristmill built in 1876, where visitors can watch a miller grind corn, wheat and rye and visit a shop, museum and art gallery. Early May is peak bloom time for about 5,000 tulips planted alongside a gazebo near the photogenic mill.

The surrounding 1,000-acre preserve offers canoeing, hiking trails and unique events such as after-dark 'owl walks'. In a meadow, the Deep River Grinders, a baseball team who play according to 1858 rules, take on teams from around the Midwest. The park also incorporates the **Deep River Water Park**, an aquatic theme park with slides and a lazy river.

Though its past as a gas station is still apparent, the **Lake Michigan Winery** at Whiting has had a makeover. Grease pits have been filled in and the concrete floors now bear a vintage Wurlitzer jukebox, a turn-of-the-19th-century barrel piano and café tables where cheese and sausage trays are served. The events here include a Father's Day tasting of more than 100 wines from across the state (Indiana now boasts more than a score of wineries).

The Lake County seat at **Crown Point** was once a marriage mill where Rudolph Valentino and his new bride circled the courthouse in a touring car, and where Ronald Reagan and Muhammad Ali were wed (not to each other). It was here that John Dillinger bluffed his way out of jail with a fake gun. Today, the imposing 1878 redbrick courthouse houses shops, boutiques and a historical museum.

Deep River County Park & Woods Historic Gristmill

9410 Old Lincoln Highway, Hobart (219 947 1958/ www.lakecountyparks.com). **Open** *May-Oct* 10am-5pm daily. **Closed** Nov-Apr. **Admission** free.

Deep River Water Park

US 30, east of I-65, Hobart (219 947 7850). **Open** *late May-early Sept* 10am-6pm daily. Closed 2wks Aug; early Sept-late May 10am-6pm Sat, Sun. **Admission** $14; concessions $6.50-$7. **Credit** Disc, MC, V.

Historic Lake County Courthouse

Courthouse Square, Crown Point (219 663 0660). **Open** *Summer* 10am-5pm Mon-Thur; 10am-6pm Fri; 10am-5pm Sat. *Winter* 8am-1pm Mon-Sat.

Trips Out of Town

Horseshoe Casino
*777 Casino Center Drive, Hammond (866 711 7463/
219 473 7000/www.horseshoe.com).* **Open** 24hrs daily.

Indiana Dunes National Lakeshore
off Highway 12, Chesterton (219 926 7561).
Open usually 6am-sunset daily but call ahead.

Indiana Dunes State Park
*End of SR 49, Chesterton (219 926 1952/
www.state.in.uk/dnr).* **Open** 7am-11pm daily.
Admission $5 per car. **No credit cards.**

Lake Michigan Winery
*816 119th Street, at Calumet Avenue, Whiting (219
659 9463).* **Open** 1-7pm daily. **Credit** AmEx, DC,
Disc, MC, V.

Where to eat

In the Horseshoe Casino, **Jack Binion's
Steak House** (866 711 7463, main courses
$16-$49) is a good dining spot even if you don't
gamble, with lovely Lake Michigan views.
In Hammond itself, **Phil Smidt's** (1205 N
Calumet Avenue, 1-800 376 4534/219 659 0025,
closed dinner Sun, main courses $12-$43) is
a favourite stop for buttery pan-fried perch
and sautéd frog's legs. For something more
contemporary, try **Miller Bakery Café** (555
S Lake Street, Miller Beach, 219 938 2229,
closed Mon, main courses $13-$25), a stylish
restaurant in a former bakery. At **Louis's
Bon Appetit** (302 S Main Street, Crown Point,
219 663 6363, closed Mon, Sun, main courses
$14-$26), an 1897 Romanesque mansion, the
speciality is cuisine from the Armagnac region
of France. Bastille Day celebrations in July
attract 3,000 revellers. A humbler Crown
Point alternative is **Valentino's Café & Ice
Cream Parlor** (Old Courthouse Square, 219
663 4812, closed Sun and dinner daily), where
the menu features salads, sandwiches, soups
and sundaes and the decor a collection of movie
stills of Rudolph Valentino, whose marriage
licence is displayed by the cash register.

Where to stay

The new property at **Harrahs East Chicago
Casino** (777 Harrah's Boulevard, 1-800 427
7247/877 496 1777/www.harrahs.com, double
$89-$129) adds a badly needed luxury hotel
to the region, though Merrillville has the
Radisson at Star Plaza (I-65 at US 30,
219 769 6311/www.radisson.com, double
$109-$159). At the other end of the spectrum,
Porter's Spring House Inn (303 N Mineral
Springs Road, 1-800 366 4661/219 929 4600/
www.springhouseinn.com, double $69-$139)
is nestled alongside wildflower-carpeted
woodlands on the banks of the Little Calumet.

Getting there

By car
Take the Chicago Skyway and I-80-90-94.

By train
The Chicago South Shore & South Bend Railroad
follows the curve of the Lake Michigan shoreline into
Indiana and makes several stops in Lake and Porter
counties. Trains leave from **Randolph Street RTA**
station on Randolph Street, at Michigan Avenue (312
836 7000).

Tourist information

Lake County Convention &
Visitors' Bureau
*I-80/I-94, at Kennedy Avenue, Hammond (1-800
255 5253).* **Open** *Summer* 8am-8pm Mon-Fri;
9am-6pm Sat, Sun. Closed autumn-spring.
In addition to picking up maps and brochures, you
can watch videos about local attractions and visit
the John Dillinger Museum.

Parke & Montgomery Counties

These two west-central Indiana counties do
a good job of exemplifying rusticity. Here's
where you'll find banjo pickers and chicken
dumpling dinners, folk crafts and crossroads
general stores, twisting blacktop roads, dusty
lanes and meandering streams. You'll also find
photogenic covered bridges. Lots of them.
    Early in the 19th century, it was found
that roofed bridges, with their protected
superstructures, long outlasted open-trestle
wooden bridges. In Parke County, no fewer
than 32 remain: creaking, rustic structures that
attract tourists, artists and photographers, and
that are the focus of a festival every autumn.
    Rockville is a good spot to begin a tour.
Wander the square, with its beautifully
restored historic brick buildings sporting
immaculate tuckpointing. Across from the
gingerbread 1879 courthouse are a number
of quaint shops and restaurants.
    As you follow covered-bridge trails, you'll
see a Clydesdale farm at Tangier, a one-room
schoolhouse at Mecca and the bed of the
famed Wabash and Erie Canal at Montezuma.
Mansfield and Bridgeton are mill towns, with
double-span bridges, rushing waters and
working gristmills.
    Billie Creek Village is a recreated
turn-of-the-19th-century settlement with a
tree-lined creek and three covered bridges.
Included among 30 buildings are two churches,
a schoolhouse and one of the Midwest's largest
handmade crafts consignment shops. Designed

Your money or your life

Like consumers of *Playboy* who claim an unusually strong interest in fiction, gamblers going to Las Vegas can plausibly argue that cheap buffets, fake volcanos and dodgy lion tamers are the real reason they're going to the desert. Right. But the riverboat casinos that ring Chicago refuse to participate in such gimmickry. The only reason to visit them, you poor sucker, is if you just cannot stand another day without a turn of a card, a roll of a dice or the clatter of a slot. As a public service to the addicted gambler, these Midwest casinos offer as few other pleasures as possible.

Forget the live entertainment. Forget the free booze. Forget the cavernous gambling floor with the lovely fresh oxygen. Forget the beautiful Bond girls. Say hello to vistas of closed steel factories, boats that go nowhere, omnipresent smoke and a truly obsessed and whacked-out clientele that sucks down video poker like it was a filterless cigarette. And yes, that beer is still $3.50 even if you just unwisely doubled down and lost five hundred bucks.

There are seven casinos within an easy hour's drive of Chicago. The closest four are just across the state line in Indiana, but the state's gaming laws mean you can board for only 30 minutes within every two-hour 'cruise'. (Most of the time, the boats don't leave the dock. No one notices.)

The **Horseshoe Casino** in Hammond (*see p259*), which boards on even hours (8-8.30pm, then 10-10.30pm, for example) is only about a 20-minute drive from the Loop. An extra ten minutes of industrial wasteland and you'll be at **Harrah's East Chicago Casino** (*see p260*), odd hours, while a further five minutes away are the **Majestic Star Casino** (even hours) and the **Trump Casino** (odd hours). These last two emporia share a pavilion, so you can shift from one to the other to change your luck.

Of this quartet, the Horseshoe is the most crowded and mean; Harrah's has the nicest staff; the chilled-out Majestic affects a down-home atmosphere as it takes your cash; and The Donald offers by far the best slots and blackjack, insurance and all. All are free and have food and drink, while Harrah's and Trump have passable hotels attached. If you spend up, beg for a room. They may take pity. They can afford it.

The Hollywood Casino in Aurora, Harrahs and the Emerald Casino in Joliet and the Grand Victoria in Elgin are all about an hour from Chicago. Civilised Illinois laws let you board any time (that may come to Indiana soon) and the casinos are larger and nicer.

At the time of writing, there was wrangling over a possible new casino in Rosemont, close to O'Hare airport. It has been stymied by the alleged involvement of unsavoury, Mob-linked characters. Hard to believe.

to be a working village, this crossroads hamlet features costumed artisans working their trades at a newspaper handpress, the blacksmith's anvil, the foot-powered loom and the potter's wheel. Get around it by horse-covered wagon.

Watch for bald eagles along the **Wabash River** and **Sugar Creek**, a spectacularly scenic river that runs though deep gorges and towering sandstone bluffs, flowing under two covered bridges. Popular with canoeists, it offers exciting but manageable rapids and quieter stretches ideal for swimming and fishing. It runs through **Turkey Run State Park**, which has rock canyons to explore, 14 miles (22.5 kilometres) of hiking trails and stands of virgin wood, with sycamore, tulip poplar and huge black walnut trees. Home cooking is served at a comfortable inn.

Clements Canoes, near Crawfordsville, offers a number of trips, ranging from a 30-mile (48-kilometre) journey through Sugar Creek

(with overnight camping) to a mini-trip with stops for picnicking and swimming, plus a four-to-six-hour whitewater trip.

Diversions in **Crawfordsville** include the **Ben-Hur Museum**, housed in a handsome building that served as General Lew Wallace's studio. Wallace somehow found time in his distinguished military, political and diplomatic career to write *Ben-Hur*, published in 1880. The book was the best-selling novel of the 19th century, outsold only by the Bible. Wallace, a true Renaissance man, even designed the building that now houses the museum and personally supervised its construction.

Another Crawfordsville museum, the **Old Jail Museum**, houses one of only seven known rotary jails and is the last in fully working order. Built in 1882, the rotary cell block consists of a two-tiered turntable divided into pie-shaped wedges. The design was intended to control prisoners with few guards and without personal contact between prisoners and jailer.

Trips Out of Town

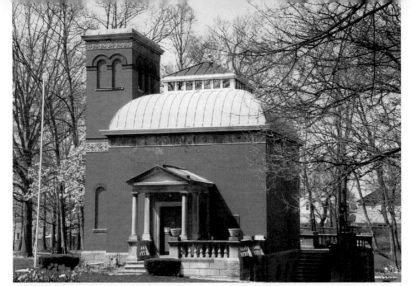

The Lew Wallace-designed **Ben-Hur Museum** in Crawfordsville.

Ben-Hur Museum

501 W Pike Street, at Wallace Avenue,
Crawfordsville (765 362 5769/www.ben-hur.com).
Open 1-4.30pm Tue-Sun; extended hours June-Aug.
Admission $3; $1 concessions. **No credit cards.**

Billie Creek Village

US 36, 1 mile east of Rockville (765 569 3430).
Open 9am-4pm daily. **Admission** *Summer only*
$3.50. **Credit** AmEx, Disc, MC, V.

Clements Canoes

613 Lafayette Avenue, Crawfordsville (765 362
2781/www.clementscanoes.com). **Open** *Apr-Sept*
8am-5pm daily. Closed Oct-Mar. **Rental** $23-$54/
2-person canoe. **Credit** MC, V.

Old Jail Museum

225 N Washington Street, Crawfordsville (765 362
5222). **Open** *June-Aug* 1-4.30pm Tue, Sun; 10am-
4.30pm Wed-Sat. *Apr, May, Sept, Oct* 1-4.30pm
Wed-Sun. Closed Nov, Dec. **Admission** free.

Turkey Run State Park

State Road 47, Marshall (765 597 2635).
Open dawn-11pm daily. **Admission** $5/vehicle.
No credit cards.

Where to eat

In Coxville, the **Long Horn Tavern &**
Restaurant (Rural Route 1, 765 548 9282,
closed dinner Sun, main courses $7-$17), a
former grocery store, gas station and tavern
built in 1923, is a good spot for steaks and
excellent fried chicken (but it's wise to avoid
the fatty ribs). **Weber's Family Restaurant**
in Rockville (105 S Jefferson Street, 765 569
6153, closed dinner Sun, main courses $7-$9) is
a popular eaterie with all-you-can-eat evening

specials. Steaks, catfish and shrimp are reliably
good choices, as are the fruit cobblers and pies
if you still have room afterwards.

Where to stay

It's the country, so stay in an inn. Staff at the
Billie Creek Inn (Rural Route 2, Box 27,
Rockville, 765 569 3430, doubles $49-$79) wear
19th-century garb, but amenities are modern.
Carbon's **Old Maple Inn** (Rural Route 1, 765
548 0228, doubles $65-$125) is a century-old
farmhouse offering comfortable quarters, home
cooking, friendly hosts and a take-home gift.
During your stay, walk to the picturesque 1907
covered bridge over Conley's Ford.

Getting there

By car

Crawfordsville is approximately 150 miles (241km)
south of Chicago. Take I-80-90-94 east to I-65 south.
About ten miles (16km) south of Lafayette, take
IN 158 west, then US 231 south into Crawfordsville.

Tourist information

Montgomery County Visitors'
& Convention Bureau

218 E Pike Street, Crawfordsville (765 362 5200/
www.crawfordsville.org). **Open** *Dec-Mar* 8am-4.30pm
Mon-Fri. *Apr-Nov* also 10am-4pm Sat.

Parke County Tourist Center

Highway 36, 3 blocks east of Rockville Square,
Rockville (765 569 5226/www.coveredbridges.com).
Open 8am-4pm Mon-Fri. *Late May-Sept* also 8am-
4pm Sat, Sun.

Trips Out of Town

Michigan

Barely an hour from Chicago lies the Midwest's own little wine country.

Berrien County

The rolling hills and fertile valleys of Berrien County, in south-western-most Michigan, are only a small distance west of the shore-tracing Red Arrow Highway and not much more than an hour's drive from downtown Chicago. The buffering effect of Lake Michigan produces a moderate microclimate that makes the region ideal for wine-making. And they're getting pretty good at it around here, too: Michigan is now the fourth largest grape-growing state in the US. Tucked away in this verdant, hilly woodland is a trio of wineries all within just a short car ride of each other. While all offer tempting wine tastings and educative tours, each is quite distinct in the experience it offers to its visitors.

Tabor Hill Winery tends to attract couples in search of fine dining and romantic sunsets over gentle hillsides. Windows look out onto vineyards; on the horizon are the dark, brooding humps of the dune ridges along Lake Michigan. Tabor Hill offers almost a score of wines, with its Grand Mark sparkling wine a consistent gold-medal winner.

Rick Moersch was winemaker at Tabor Hill for 14 years before he opened his own winery, **Heart of the Vineyard**, in 1992. Tastings of more than two dozen wines – including many award-winners – are conducted in an 1881 post-and-beam barn. But the winery's most distinctive building is the round Amish barn, discovered in northern Indiana, dismantled, transported 90 miles (144 kilometres) to the winery and rebuilt by Amish craftsmen. A crescent-shaped copper bar has matching wall sconces decorated with alchemy symbols from the Middle Ages.

The third of the trio, the family-owned and family-oriented **Lemon Fruit Farm & Winery**, is a vast working farm with a fruit stand, pick-your-own orchards, tractor rides for kids and abundant wildlife, including deer, foxes, hawks and owls, plus waterfowl that settle on a five-acre pond. The vineyards produce five white wines, ranging from dry Chardonnay to sweet Vidal Blanc, three reds (including an award-winning Cabernet Sauvignon), grape and raspberry sparkling wines, and three delicious, non-alcoholic sparkling juices (grape, raspberry and peach).

If the inner reaches of Berrien County overwhelm you with their rurality, there are more urban communities along the lakeshore. **New Buffalo** is a stylish weekend resort, with millions of dollars' worth of yachts bobbing at anchor in a harbour lined with upscale condominiums and elegant summer homes. Also on Lake Michigan's shore is **St Joseph**, the Berrien County seat. Once known as the 'Atlantic City of the Midwest', with a vast amusement park, wide boardwalk, and elegant hotels that lured famous big bands, St Joseph is now a quiet, rather genteel resort.

A wide boulevard flanked by parkland sits atop high bluffs that offer splendid views of Lake Michigan. It houses the **Curious Kids Museum**, the **Krasl Art Center**, the comfy **Boulevard Inn**, a restaurant or two, and a breezy bandstand where Sunday concerts are held. At the foot of the bluffs are wide expanses of sandy beach that draw swimmers and sun worshippers. A pier poking its finger out into Lake Michigan has at its tip a pink lighthouse, made famous as the subject of a postage stamp.

An excellent way to explore St Jo is to pick up a brochure for the self-guided 'SculpTour', featuring almost two dozen points of interest. St Joseph is well endowed with public art old and new, and showcases it effectively with this tour that covers about two miles around town.

Curious Kids Museum

415 Lake Boulevard, St Joseph (616 983 2543/ www.curiouskidsmuseum.org). **Open** *June-Aug* 10am-5pm Mon-Sat; noon-5pm Sun. *Sept-May* 10am-5pm Wed-Sat; noon-5pm Sun. **Admission** $4-$5. **Credit** MC, V.

Heart of the Vineyard Winery

10981 Hills Road, Baroda (1-800 716 9463/ www.heartofthevineyard.com). **Open** 10am-6pm Mon-Sat; noon-6pm Sun. **Admission** free. **Credit** AmEx, DC, MC, V.

Krasl Art Center

707 Lake Boulevard, St Joseph (616 983 0271/ www.krasl.org). **Open** *Sept-May* 10am-4pm Mon-Thur, Sat; 10am-1pm Fri; 1-4pm Sun. *June-Aug* 10am-4pm Mon-Sat; 1-4pm Sun. **Admission** free. **No credit cards.**

Lemon Creek Fruit Farm & Winery

533 East Lemon Creek Road, Berrien Springs (616 471 1321). **Open** noon-5pm Fri-Sun. **Admission** free. **Credit** call for details.

Push the boat out at the **Michigan Maritime Museum** in Springfield. *See p265.*

Tabor Hill Winery

185 Mount Tabor Road, Buchanan (1-800 283 3363/ www.taborhill.com). **Open** *Tours: May-Nov* noon-4.30pm Mon-Sun; *Dec-Apr* by appointment Mon-Fri; noon-4.30pm Sat, Sun. *Tastings: summer* 10am-5pm Mon, Tue; 10am-10pm Wed-Sat; noon-9pm Sun; *winter* 10am-5pm Mon-Thur; noon-9pm Fri, Sat; noon-5pm Sun. **Admission** free. **Credit** AmEx, DC, Disc, MC, V.

Where to eat

At the **Tabor Hill Restaurant** (185 Mount Tabor Road, Buchanan, 1-800 283 3363/ www.taborhill.com, closed Mon-Tue May-Nov, closed Mon-Thur Dec-Apr, main courses $16-$25), sample terrific pheasant breast Wellington. Housed in a century-old mansion, **Hannah's** (115 South Whittaker Street, New Buffalo, 616 469 1440/www.hannahsrestaurant.com, main courses $16-$25) counts roast pork loin, crisp roast duck and old-fashioned pot roast as its specialities. And at Frank Lloyd Wright-influenced **Schuler's Restaurant** (5000 Red Arrow Highway, Stevensville, 616 429 3273/www.schulersrest.com, main courses $8-$24), try classic prime rib or contemporary fare such as steamed mussels with bruschetta.

Where to stay

The rooms at the **Harbor Grand Hotel & Suites** (111 W Water Street, New Buffalo, 616 469 7700/www.harborgrand.com, double $139-$329) are comfortably furnished; bonuses include an indoor pool and complimentary bicycles. The smart **Boulevard Inn** (521 Lake Boulevard, St Joseph, 616 983 6600/www.theboulevardinn.com,

suite $135-$205) contains a stylish French restaurant, Bistro on the Boulevard, whose deck affords stunning views of Lake Michigan.

Getting there

By car

St Joseph is approximately 95 miles (153km) north-east of Chicago. Take I-94 east to the Stevensville exit. The winery exits are posted along I-94.

By train

Amtrak passenger trains provide a service from Chicago to St Joseph.

Tourist information

Southwestern Michigan Tourist Council

2300 Pipestone Road, Benton Harbor (616 925 6301/www.swmichigan.org). **Open** *Nov-May* 8.30am-5pm Mon-Fri. *June-Oct* 8.30am-5pm Mon-Sat.

South Haven

Chicago-area residents have a long history of vacation getaways to South Haven, which lies across the lake in Van Buren County in south-west Michigan. Early last century, 'resorting' in South Haven was such a major pastime that, in 1925, 250,000 visitors descended upon the town by steamship. Even earlier, schooners were used to ship lumber, fruit and passengers from South Haven to Chicago and other lake cities.

Although most Chicagoans arrive by car these days, this stylish port city remains closely tied to the rhythms of Lake Michigan. Charter fishing for trout and salmon is a major attraction, as are the 'party boats' that go in search of schools of perch, the canoe trips on the Black River and, of course, the fine beaches. For all manner of maritime lore and history surrounding the Great Lakes, head for the **Michigan Maritime Museum**, where the collections include historic watercraft, a wide range of ship models, tools and equipment from fishhooks to fathometers, and a collection of personal possessions reflecting the customs and lifestyles of people around the Great Lakes.

Those without watery inclinations tend to head straight for the **GingerMan Raceway**, a two-mile (3.2-kilometre), 36-foot (11-metre) wide road course with 13 turns. The annual calendar here includes events for the Sports Car Club America (for production, GT and formula racecars), super-speedway racing karts, vintage sports-racing cars, historic sports cars and super-speedway motorcycles.

Close to South Haven is a trailhead of the **Kal-Haven Trail** that stretches eastward to Kalamazoo. On bright, sunny days, traffic can be brisk along the 33 miles (53 kilometres) of trail, with people of all ages hiking, pedalling bicycles, or gliding effortlessly on inline skates. Originally a railroad, completed in 1870, the railbed has been converted to a trail with a limestone/slag surface for hikers, cyclists, equestrians, cross-country skiers and – when there is a four-inch snow base – snowmobilers. Scenery varies from sleepy countryside, farm fields and orchards to sections that nudge the busy Interstate.

Mostly, though, the Kal-Haven Trail is a quiet rural route that connects lazy villages with cheerful coffee shops. In autumn, farm stands are piled high with shiny apples and colourful Indian corn, pumpkins and gourds. Travellers are transfixed by a hilly area full of wildflowers that attract colourful butterflies, wetlands with blue irises, and the community of **Mentha**, once the world's largest producer of mint. At **Bloomingdale**, a restored depot and caboose now serves as a museum; near Mattawan is the **Michigan Fisheries Interpretive Center**, site of a fish hatchery.

Because South Haven is located on the eastern shore of Lake Michigan, it enjoys dramatic sunsets. One of the most enjoyable ways to witness these pretty pink spectacles is from the decks of the **White Rose**, a 50-foot (15-metre) excursion boat that also offers moonlight cruises and a dinner cruise on the Black River and Lake Michigan.

GingerMan Raceway
61414 Phoenix Road, South Haven (616 253 4445/ www.gingermanraceway.com). **Open** 9am-5.30pm Mon-Fri; 9am-6pm Sat, Sun. **Admission** $5-$10; free under-12s. **Credit** AmEx, Disc, MC, V.

Michigan Maritime Museum
260 Dyckman Avenue, South Haven (616 637 8078/www.michiganmaritimemuseum.org). **Open** 10am-5pm Tue-Sat; noon-5pm Sun. **Admission** $2.50; $1.50 concessions. **Credit** Disc, MC, V.

South Haven Center for the Arts
602 Phoenix Street, South Haven (616 637 1041). **Open** 10am-5pm Tue-Thur; 10am-4pm Fri; 1-4pm Sat, Sun.

White Rose
815 E Wells Street, South Haven (1-888 828 7673/616 639 8404/www.whiterosecruises.com). **Cruises** May-Sept dinner cruise 5-7pm Thur-Sat; sunset cruise sunset Tue-Sun; afternoon cruise 1.30pm Fri, Sat. **Rates** $10-$37.50. **Credit** MC, V.

Where to eat

Clementine's (500 Phoenix Street, 616 637 4755/www.ohmydarling.com, main courses $9-$14) is a popular downtown eaterie that incorporates the 1897 Citizens Bank Building, original tin ceilings and all. Favourites include honey mustard chicken salad. Upscale roadhouse **Tello's Trattoria** (7379 North Shore Drive, 616 639 9898/www.tellostrattoria.com, main courses $6-$19) also has a tempting menu: try crab cakes or grilled pork tenderloin with tomato fritters.

Where to stay

Situated on the banks of the Black River, the 37-room **Old Harbor Inn** (515 Williams Street, 616 637 8480/www.oldharborinn.com, double $75-$190) is part of a charming complex of shops and boutiques designed to resemble a New England fishing village. The smaller and smarter **Yelton Manor** (140 North Shore Drive, 616 637 5220/www.yeltonmanor.com, double $90-$280) occupies a pair of Victorian mansions, incorporating a traditional B&B and a more private guesthouse.

Getting there

By car
South Haven is approximately 120 miles (193km) north-east of Chicago. Take I-94 east to Benton Harbor, then I-196 north.

Tourist information

South Haven/Van Buren County Lakeshore Convention & Visitors' Bureau
415 Phoenix Street, South Haven (616 637 5252/ www.southhaven.org). **Open** *Summer* 9am-5pm Mon-Sat. *Winter* 9am-5pm Mon-Fri.

Trips Out of Town

Wisconsin

An All-American state, in a Germanic, Swiss and Norwegian kind of way.

Madison

Come Saturday morning in Madison, the term 'Wake up and smell the coffee' takes on a more literal meaning. This is when locals and tourists, some 18,000 each week, converge on the **Dane County Farmers' Market**, held on Saturdays between 6am and 2pm from May to October in the square around Wisconsin's Capitol, a neo-classical building dating from 1917 with the only granite dome in the US.

However, it's neither history nor architecture but more sensual pleasures that draw the crowds. The aroma of freshly brewed coffee and the sweet scent of basil. The taste of fresh bakery and handmade cheeses. And the prospect of shopping for farm-fresh produce: free-range eggs, pungent onions, spicy sausages, and home-made bread, jam and honey. When you're ready for a break (or a snack), rest on the lawn or on the Capitol steps where there is usually a concert going on.

Even aside from this delightful Saturday morning ritual, it's easy to see why Madison is not only a fun place to visit but also on many shortlists for best, healthiest and safest place to live. It keeps getting better. A 14-storey Hilton popped up in 2001 to connect with the Monona Terrace Community & Convention Center (more of that soon). And in the summer of 2002, the new Thai Pavilion opened at Olbrich Botanical Gardens. Crafted without nails or screws, the centrepiece features gold-leaf etchings, a lacquer finish and intricate decorations.

Madison is built on an isthmus bordered by Lake Monona and Lake Mendota: with five lakes in the area, 13 public beaches and more than 200 parks, outdoor recreation focuses on biking, hiking, fishing and canoeing. Culturally, Madison offers a resident orchestra, opera, theatre and a full performing arts schedule at the University of Wisconsin. Downtown's 'Museum Mile' includes the **Wisconsin Historical Museum**, the **Madison Children's Museum**, **Madison Art Center** (renamed the **Madison Museum of Contemporary Art** in autumn 2002), the university's **Elvehjem Museum of Art** and the **Wisconsin Veteran's Museum**, which uses dioramas to chronicle American military activities from the Civil War through to the

Persian Gulf conflict. And then there's the aforementioned **Monona Terrace Community & Convention Center**. Conceived by Frank Lloyd Wright more than 60 years ago, it opened in 1997 after decades of architectural and civic controversy. There are tours of the building every day.

Elsewhere, the clusters of boutiques and speciality shops on **Monroe Street** and the used and antiquarian bookstores around State Street draw collectors from Chicago and further afield in search of rare first editions. One don't-miss stop is the Canterbury Booksellers Café Inn, a bookstore that's also a great place to stay.

Elvehjem Museum of Art
800 University Avenue, Madison (608 263 2246/ www.lvm.wisc.edu). **Open** 9am-5pm Tue-Fri; 11am-5pm Sat, Sun. **Admission** free. **Credit** *Shop* MC, V.

Madison Art Center
211 State Street, Madison (608 257 0158/ www.madisonartcenter.org). **Open** 11am-5pm Tue-Thur; 11am-9pm Fri; 10am-9pm Sat; 1-5pm Sun. **Admission** free. **Credit** *Shop* AmEx, Disc, MC, V.

Madison Children's Museum
100 State Street, Madison (608 256 6445/ www.kidskiosk.org). **Open** *Sept-May* 9am-4pm Tue-Sat; noon-4pm Sun. *June-Aug* 9am-4pm Mon-Sat; noon-4pm Sun. **Admission** $4; under-1s free. **Credit** AmEx, MC, V.

Monona Terrace Community & Convention Center
1 John Nolen Drive, Madison (608 261 4000/ www.mononaterrace.com). **Open** 8am-5pm daily. *Tours* 1pm daily. **Admission** free. *Tours* $3.

Wisconsin Historical Museum
30 N Carroll Street, Madison (608 264 6565/ www.wisconsinhistory.org). **Open** 9am-4pm Tue-Sat. **Admission** *Suggested donation* $3; $2 children. **Credit** MC, V.

Wisconsin Veteran's Museum
30 W Mifflin Street, Madison (608 267 1799/ http://museum.dva.state.wi.us). **Open** 9am-4.30pm Mon-Sat. **Admission** free. **Credit** *Shop* AmEx, MC, V.

Where to eat
At the **Admiralty Room** at the Edgewater (666 Wisconsin Avenue, 1-800 922 5512/608 256 9071 x120/www.theedgewater.com, main courses $22-$32), staff perpetuate the dying art

Monona Terrace: perfectly Frank. *See p266.*

of tableside cooking with the likes of steak Diane. Try and get there to coincide with one of the spectacular sunsets.

The flavourful steaks at the **Mariner's Inn** (5339 Lighthouse Bay Drive, 608 246 3120/ www.nautigal.com/mariners, main courses $14-$40) match those of many big-city steakhouses, but at modest prices. The lawn sweeps down to the water's edge; boaters pull up for drinks.

Moving downscale: for terrific barbecue, head to **Big Mama & Uncle Fats** (6824 Odana Road, in the Trading Post Center, 608 829 2683, closed Sun, Mon, main courses $10-$16), and for some remarkable ice-cream, visit the **UW student union** (800 Langdon Street) or **UW Babcock Hall** (1605 Lindon Street), produced by the UW School of Agriculture since the early 1900s and sinfully creamy.

Where to stay

Since it was built in 1948, the 111-room **Edgewater** (666 Wisconsin Avenue, 1-800 922 5512/www.theedgewater.com, double $169-$399) has hosted all manner of luminaries. A gallery in the Cove Lounge draws guests into a game of 'who was who': when you get stuck, ask for a booklet identifying the celebs.

Conventioneers' favourite the **Madison Concourse Hotel** (1 W Dayton Street, 1-800 356 8293/608 257 6000/www.concoursehotel.com, double $99-$229) offers 390 rooms, an indoor pool, a fitness centre and restaurants, while the **Hilton Madison Monona Terrace** (9 E Wilson Street, 1-800 445 8667/608 255 5100/

www.hilton.com, double $129-$199) features an all-weather skywalk that links to Monona Terrace Convention Center.

Inn-cum-bookstore **Canterbury Booksellers Inn** (315 W Gorham Street, 608 258 8899/www.madisoncanterbury.com, double $130-$200) lives up to its name: rooms are identified by Chaucerian characters, and whimsical murals depicting scenes from *The Canterbury Tales* cover each door.

Getting there

By car
Madison is 145 miles (233km) north-west of Chicago. Take I-90 to Beltline Highway (US 12/18); follow signs to downtown (look for the Capitol dome symbol).

Tourist information

Greater Madison Convention & Visitors' Bureau
615 E Washington Avenue, Madison (1-800 373 6376/608 255 2537/www.visitmadison.com). **Open** 8am-5pm Mon-Fri.

Milwaukee

Chicago it ain't. Provincial it may be. And sometimes it may seem as though Milwaukee rolls up the sidewalks at night. Nonetheless, it's easy to find reasons for a getaway to Chicago's neighbour to the north (even if it is Packer country, home of the cheeseheads).

Enigmatic Milwaukee is as traditional as an oompah band, as contemporary as its experimental theatre. It has big-city assets – museums, galleries, a symphony orchestra, opera and ballet companies, varied dining and entertainment, parkland and pro sports. Yet it is compact enough to be eminently explorable. Visitors delight in practicalities such as convenient parking meters and clear roads; that locals take them for granted is indicative of the city's easygoing qualities.

Like Chicago, Milwaukee was settled by the Native American Potawatomie tribe, before being overrun by white speculators in the 1830s. Milwaukee, though, comes with more Native American heritage than even its Illinois neighbour: aside from the Potawatomies, at least half a dozen other Native American tribes were resident in the area known as Millocki before most were evacuated in 1838.

It was around this time that the Germans arrived in force, an influx that was to have a huge effect on both the character and the economy of the city. For with the Germans came beer, and the economic foundations on which Milwaukee would be built. Pabst, Schlitz and – most famously – Miller all started in Milwaukee from German families, and all went on to find huge economic success.

The beer remains. Although **Miller** is the only surviving megabrewery in Milwaukee, it's complemented nicely by several microbreweries that have started up over the last decade. And though the post-war period hasn't always been a tale of unbridled economic joy, the city is back on the rise. Swathes of the admittedly small downtown area have been redeveloped to pleasing effect – most notably the Historic Third Ward – and new businesses seem to be springing up all over.

Much of this prosperity is mirrored in a new downtown development – especially on the River Walk along the Milwaukee River – that the city hopes will bring more visitors. Perhaps influenced by the economic rewards reaped by Chicago from McCormick Place, Milwaukee built its own model: the Midwest Express Center, a vast convention venue boasting 28 meeting rooms and a 189,000-square-foot (17,577-square-metre) exhibition space.

A major reason for visiting the town is the $100-million expansion of the **Milwaukee Art Museum** completed in 2001. Designed by world-renowned architect Santiago Calatrava, it was inspired by the museum's lakefront location: check out the cabled pedestrian bridge with a mast suggested by the form of a sailboat, a curving single-storey galleria reminiscent of a wave, and, most strikingly, the moving steel louvres inspired by the wings of a bird. It's a credit to the collection held by the museum – 20,000 works, including a large selection by Milwaukee native Georgia O'Keefe – that the art itself is not overshadowed.

Then, of course, there's the lake. You don't need to be shanghaied to become part of the crew of the 133-foot (40.5-metre), three-masted **SV Dennis Sullivan**, a recreated 19th-century Great Lakes schooner that sails on three-hour excursions on Lake Michigan from its port in downtown Milwaukee. Passengers can participate as much or as little as they want – striking a sail, hauling a line, taking a turn at the helm or simply going along for the ride.

Golden brew and stinky poo

One of the more enjoyable pastimes at Monroe, Wisconsin, just north of the Illinois stateline, is visiting Baumgartner's Tavern. Visitors invariably enjoy quaffing the locally brewed Huber beer. Regulars, though, get just as much of a kick from watching visitors try the Limburger cheese.

The family-owned Joseph Huber Brewing Company, established in 1845, is the second-oldest continuously operated brewery in the United States. It opened a hospitality centre in 2001 where you can watch a ten-minute video and sample products (along with the local cheese). Many award-winning beers are brewed under the Berghoff label, but Huber also makes Blumer's Old Fashioned Root Beer in bottles and in kegs.

While there, you may meet brewmaster Hans Kestler, who learned that fame does, indeed, have its price. Kestler, born in a Bavarian brewery but resident in the US for 25 years, has a delightful accent that makes him sound like a stage German. The image-spinners thought it comical; Kestler was recruited for a series of commercials and gained fame as the voice of Huber's Augsburger beer. Soon after, Kestler was forced to get an unlisted phone number because curious imbibers would call his home just to hear his voice and see if he was for real.

Tour the brewery and you'll learn that Berghoff is brewed European-style with a storage time of about five weeks (versus the 14 days of most domestic lager). You'll also discover that its time-honoured recipe uses ten per cent more malt and 50 per cent more hops than most mainstream brands. But Kestler admits that the brewery is small. 'Anheuser Busch probably spills in one week what we produce in one year,' he quips.

As for Limburger, made exclusively by the nearby Chalet Cheese Co-operative, consider the reaction of a teenage visitor to the factory. 'It smells worse than those old sneakers my Mom always complains about,' he said, pulling his T-shirt up over his nose. The comparison probably wasn't far off the mark. Long-aged Limburger emits a strong ammonia odour that has decidedly barnyard aromas. When it's only two or three months old, it's soft like Brie and has a tangy taste. Aficionados recommend eating Limburger on dark rye with a slice of raw onion and mustard.

Joseph Huber Brewing Co
1208 14th Avenue, Monroe (608 325 3191/ www.berghoffbeer.com). **Open** *Tours* 11am, 1pm, 3pm Thur-Sat. *Gift shop* 8am-4pm Mon-Sat. **Admission** $2; free under-14s. **Credit** MC, V.

Calatrava's extension to the **Milwaukee Art Museum**. See p268.

Families on vacation here love the **Milwaukee Public Museum**. This three-floor natural history museum, which holds a stock of some six million exhibits, is terrifically enjoyable. On the first floor, there's a cute little evocation of the old streets of Milwaukee, while across the hall are exhibits detailing dinosaur life (including the world's largest dinosaur skull). The best stuff, though, is on the second floor: the North American Indians exhibit, compiled with the help of Wisconsin tribes, is a particular winner.

Opened in 2000, the Puelicher Butterfly Wing is a two-storey addition with a spacious tropical butterfly garden and butterflies from around the world. It provides a permanent home to hundreds of tropical and domestic butterflies in a rainforest environment, complete with foliage, blooming plants, tranquil music and a cascading waterfall. The gallery's centrepiece is a working laboratory, where visitors study butterflies and moths through interactive stations. Children roam a super-sized butterfly garden habitat and even transform themselves into 'caterpillars' and 'butterflies'.

The area around Milwaukee Public Museum is home to a couple of the city's other main attractions and is known informally as Museum Centre. There's **Discovery World: the James Lovell Museum of Science, Economics & Technology**, full of interactive exhibits. And there's the **Humphrey IMAX Dome Theater**, which boasts a six-storey-high screen and a 12,000-watt sound system.

However, if you're only in town briefly and if the weather isn't too horrific, you should make **Milwaukee County Zoo** your first port of call. One of the largest zoos in the country –

3,000 animals, 200 acres, 250 staff – it's also one of the best. Founded in 1892 as a tiny display in Washington Park, the zoo moved to its present site in 1958. Since then, the zoo has grown, and is now an extremely impressive attraction.

Every conceivable animal is included, and presented – if that's the right word – sympathetically and informatively in a peaceful setting that's a delight just to walk around on a sunny summer's day. It'll take you upward of three hours to do it justice, but it's well worth it for the colourful aviary, the flamingos, the petting mandrills, the mischievous golden lion tamarin, the gazelle-like bongo, the emus, the bats and – our favourite – the springhaas, which look like rabbits and jump like kangaroos but which are actually rodents. Many of the displays emphasise the role of the zoo in conservation and breeding programmes, and the zoo is a member of the Special Survival Plan.

While slightly less culturally educative, the **Miller Brewing Co** does at least offer free (if self-aggrandising) tours. Learn how Frederic Miller started at a tiny Plank Street property (a replica of which sits outside the main plant); how the brewery churns out six gazillion bottles of Miller Lite a minute; and that Miller has five of the top ten selling beers in the US, one of which – Milwaukee's Best – isn't cheap, merely 'popularly priced'. This last piece of alcoholic revisionism was, at least, relayed with a knowing smile by the chatty guide, while gratis beers are a fitting end to the brisk tour.

Outside of the Art Museum's extension, the other big construction project in recent years bears the name of the beer company: **Miller Park**, the new home of local baseball team the Milwaukee Brewers. A vast, high-tech field, it's

Trips Out of Town

International Clown Hall of Fame.

a dramatic improvement on County Stadium, the team's previous home. Shame, then, that the Brewers stink worse than year-old cheese.

Back in central Milwaukee, you'll find several other smallish museums. The **Betty Brinn Children's Museum** is an interactive place designed for under-tens and parents, while **America's Black Holocaust Museum** is the only museum of its type in the US and is highly educative. Down by the charming River Walk is the **Milwaukee County Historical Society**, another interesting museum set in a lovely old building. And, perhaps most bizarrely, there's the **International Clown Hall of Fame**. Here you can learn about how Lou Jacobs 'started in showbiz as the rear end of a stunt alligator', and that Hall of Famer Mark Anthony is 'perhaps the foremost sculptor of foam props in the world'. Fans of comically gargantuan shoes will find much to admire.

While you'll find no Picassos or Van Goghs in one of Milwaukee's newest and most fascinating museums, you may see a collection of 'Guinness is good for you' posters or the Burma Shave signs that once lined America's highways. At the **William F Eisner Museum of Advertising & Design**, you'll find out how advertising impacts on our culture, and that the average person sees 20,000 television commercials in a year. An interactive

radio booth allows visitors to practise and then record and playback commercials that involve selling Ivory soap on a 1940s radio show, singing a jingle and delivering a rap message; elsewhere, settle into comfortable leather seats in a TV gallery and watch commercials aired before the 1971 ban on cigarette advertising.

It's not all museums in Milwaukee, of course. Shoppers will be charmed by the **Historic Third Ward**, and specifically by stores such as **Artasia** (159 N Broadway; 414 220 4292), a would-be boho shop chock-full of eastern and Asian artefacts, and **Broadway Paper** (181 N Broadway; 414 277 7699), a store dedicated to the art of giftwrapping. Elsewhere, the Shops of Grand Avenue Mall on the main Wisconsin Street drag should fulfil most people's chain-shopping needs, while bookworms will find solace poring over a tome in the fabulously musty **Renaissance Book Shop** (834 N Plankinton Street; 414 271 6850).

Culturally, too, Milwaukee's on the up. Aside from the festivals – the biggest of which is the musical **Summerfest**, held late June to early July (1-800 273 3378/www.summerfest.com) – there's the **Milwaukee Symphony Orchestra** and a bounty of theatre groups. Incidentally, make sure you don't get the **Marcus Center for the Performing Arts** (929 N Water Street; 414 273 7121), downtown's main entertainment venue, confused with **Art's Performing Center**, a superbly named strip joint a few blocks away.

Side-trip destinations from Milwaukee include **Racine** and **Kenosha**, for a bounty of Frank Lloyd Wright architecture, prime outlet shopping, and a chance to sample the kringle, the traditional coffee cake brought over by Danish immigrants. At historic **Cedarburg** stroll across a covered bridge dating back to 1876, stay at an old stagecoach inn, and visit a winery and a clutch of one-of-a-kind shops in a former woollen mill dating back to 1864.

America's Black Holocaust Museum

2233 N 4th Street, Milwaukee (414 264 2500/ www.blackholocaustmuseum.com). **Open** 9am-5pm Mon, Tue, Thur, Fri; noon-5pm Sun. **Admission** $5; $3-$4 concessions. **Credit** AmEx, Disc, MC, V.

Betty Brinn Children's Museum

929 E Wisconsin Avenue, Milwaukee (414 390 5437/www.bbcmkids.org). **Open** 9am-5pm Tue-Sat; noon-5pm Sun. *June-Aug* also 9am-5pm Mon. **Admission** $4; free under-1s. **Credit** Disc, MC, V.

Discovery World

815 N James Lovell Street, Milwaukee (414 765 9966/www.discoveryworld.org). **Open** 9am-5pm daily. **Admission** $5.50; $4-$4.50 concessions. **Credit** Disc, MC, V.

Humphrey IMAX Dome Theater

800 W Wells Street, Milwaukee (414 319 4629/ www.humphreyimax.com). **Tickets** $6.50; $5-$5.75 concessions. **Credit** AmEx, Disc, MC, V.

International Clown Hall of Fame

Suite LL700, Grand Avenue Mall, 161 W Wisconsin Avenue, Milwaukee (414 319 0848/ www.clownmuseum.org). **Open** 10am-4pm Mon-Fri. **Admission** $2; free under-6s. **Credit** MC, V.

Milwaukee Art Museum

700 N Art Museum Drive, Milwaukee (414 224 3200/www.mam.org). **Open** 10am-5pm Tue, Wed, Fri-Sun; noon-8pm Thur. **Admission** $6; $4 concessions; free under-12s. **Credit** AmEx, MC, V.

Milwaukee County Historical Society Library & Museum

910 N Old World 3rd Street, Milwaukee (414 273 8288/www.milwaukeecountyhistsoc.org). **Open** *Museum* 9.30am-5pm Mon-Fri; 10am-5pm Sat; 1-5pm Sun. **Admission** *Suggested donation* $2. **No credit cards.**

Milwaukee County Zoo

10001 W Bluemound Road, Milwaukee (414 771 3040/www.milwaukeezoo.org). **Open** *Oct-Mar* 9am-4.30pm daily. *May-Sept* 9am-5pm Mon-Sat; 9am-6pm Sun. **Admission** $9; $6-$8 concessions. **Credit** MC, V.

Milwaukee Public Museum

800 W Wells Street, Milwaukee (414 278 2702/ www.mpm.edu). **Open** 9am-5pm daily. **Admission** $6.50; $4-$5 concessions. **Credit** AmEx, Disc, MC, V.

William F Eisner Museum of Advertising & Design

208 N Water Street, Milwaukee (414 847 3290/ www.eisnermuseum.org). **Open** 11am-5pm Tue-Sat. **Admission** $4.50; free-$2.50 concessions. **Credit** AmEx, MC, V.

Where to eat & drink

Eating options in Milwaukee are quite varied. **Barolotta's Lake Park Bistro** (3133 E Newberry Boulevard, 414 962 6300, main courses

$8-$29) occupies the upstairs of a park-district pavilion built into a high bluff, and serves French bistro cuisine. About as German as you could hope to find – and about as touristy, too – **Mader's** (1037 N Old World 3rd Street, 414 271 3377/www.maders.com, main courses $16-$32) offers sturdy Teutonic fare in a traditional setting. And don't miss the **African Hut** (1107 N Old World 3rd Street, 414 765 1110, main courses $8-$18), which offers delectable dishes from assorted African countries.

There are a fair few bars and eateries in the Third Ward, among them pleasingly airy gay bar the **M&M Club** (124 N Water Street, 414 347 1962) and the **Milwaukee Ale House** (233 N Water Street, 414 226 2337/www.ale-house.com), a microbrewery that's been spinning a twist on beertown since the late 1990s. Decent watering holes can also be found around Walker's Point to the south of downtown, among them **Steny's Tavern** (800 S 2nd Street, 414 672 7139) and **Fritz's on 2nd** (814 S 2nd Street, 414 383 3211).

However, most of Milwaukee's nightlife is centred around Water Street. Be sure to stop by the excellent **Water Street Brewery** (1101 N Water Street, 414 272 1195), a microbrewery whose bar food is a cut above. There is also a rash of fine bars and eateries further north-east on Brady Street, including the **Nomad World Pub** (1401 E Brady Street, 414 224 8111).

The **Safe House** (779 N Front Street, 414 271 2007) is a James Bond-themed bar-restaurant that's been wheeling out its cheeky line in spy schtick for years. It's looking a little tired now, but there's still fun to be had in its multi-roomed layout. It takes its theme to the front door, innocently labelled 'International Exports, Ltd' in true Ian Fleming fashion. And no, we're not telling you the password.

Where to stay

The characterful, century-old **Pfister Hotel** (424 E Wisconsin Avenue, 1-800 558 8222/www.thepfisterhotel.com, double $264-$1,050) is perhaps *the* hotel in which to stay when in town. Mid-range options include the **Astor Hotel** (924 E Juneau Avenue, 1-800 558 0200/www.theastorhotel.com, double $69-$119), close to Lake Michigan. The **Hotel Wisconsin**, meanwhile, is a fine budget choice in a central location (720 N Old World 3rd Street, 414 271 4900/www.wia.com, double $79-$89). Several chains have branches in Milwaukee, including the **Holiday Inn** (611 W Wisconsin Avenue, 414 273 2950), the **Hyatt Regency** (333 W Kilbourn Avenue, 414 276 1234) and the **Hilton** (509 W Wisconsin Avenue, 414 271 7250).

Getting there

By car
Milwaukee is approximately 90 miles (145km) north of Chicago on the I-94.

By rail
Milwaukee is a 90-minute train ride from Chicago's Union Station; services are frequent.

Tourist information

Greater Milwaukee Convention & Visitors' Bureau
Midwest Express Centre, 400 W Wisconsin Avenue, Milwaukee (1-800 231 0903/414 273 7222/www.officialmilwaukee.com). **Open** 8am-5pm Mon-Fri.

Mount Horeb

In Norway, the gnome-like creatures known as trolls are said to inhabit deep, dark forests and rugged mountains. In Mount Horeb, Wisconsin, settled by Norwegians in the 1870s, you can find them downtown. In fact, Main Street in this scrubbed-clean little town (population 5,860) is known as 'the Trollway' and is decorated with wooden trolls carved by local artist Michael Feeney. Should you decide to take a 'troll stroll', you'll not only encounter these delightful creatures but also find lots of shops offering Scandinavian imports, freshly baked Norwegian pastries, rye bread and the like.

Mount Horeb lies within the unglaciated area of south-western Wisconsin that slipped through the icy fingers of the great glaciers that covered much of the region during the Ice Age. As a result, the land retained its rugged, craggy topography of high ridges and steep-sided valleys. This is picture-book country, perfect for hiking, cycling and just plain exploring, where soaring, wooded hillsides etched with intricate rocky outcrops overlook sparkling brooks, and prize dairy herds graze in ridiculously green pastures. The area drew early Norwegian settlers because of its similarity to their homeland, and the quaint town of Mount Horeb reflects their culture.

Nordic heritage is preserved in even greater detail at **Little Norway**, located three miles (five kilometres) west of Mount Horeb, where insights into pioneer history are provided by costumed guides. The property portrays life on an 1856 Norwegian pioneer farmstead and is furnished with one of the largest privately owned collections of Norwegian antiques in the United States. When Norway's King Harald (then crown prince) visited Little Norway in 1965, he remarked how much the settlement resembled its namesake.

New Glarus. See p274.

The first settler here, though, was Osten Olson Haugen from Tinn Telemarken, Norway. In 1856 he bought 40 acres of land and made the area his home, building a farm in which his family worked until 1920. For the next five years, although the fields were rented and the hillsides pastured, the buildings themselves remained unoccupied. When Isak Dahle purchased the property in 1927, he named it Nissedahle, after Nissedal, Norway, where his grandparents had been born. The name translates to 'Valley of the Elves'.

Since Dahle's great-phew Scott Winner took over Little Norway in 1982 – his family homesteaded the area in the 1840s – he has spent countless hours personally doing the carpentry to restore and maintain the historic settlement. It is a labour of love that becomes apparent when Scott dons native Norwegian costume to conduct a tour and whistle a few bars of Grieg's *Peer Gynt*.

One of the tour highlights is a visit to a replica of a 12th-century *stavekirke*, or stave church, built in Norway for the Norwegian government and used as its pavilion at the World's Columbian Exposition of 1893 in Chicago. After the Exposition, the building was moved to Lake Geneva, Wisconsin, and was later sold to the prominent Wrigley family, who moved it to grace their summer estate. In 1936 the *stavekirke* found a home at Little Norway, which is where it still stands.

The ornate building is made of hewn pine and has a high-peaked roof and gingerbread decorations. Dragons breathing flame from the gables watch in vigilance against evil spirits, and the faces of pagan Norwegian kings and queens peer down from beam-ends. Before World War II there were more than 900 such churches in Norway, dating back to the 11th and 12th centuries. Today, fewer than 30 remain.

The former Exposition pavilion is now once again home to Norwegian crafts and culture. There are dozens of beautiful chests and finely embroidered wall hangings, and exquisite pieces of furniture include a large spice cabinet with secret compartments, fireside benches with intricately carved dragonheads, handsome sideboards, looms, cabinets and cupboards.

Back in town, don't miss a stop at the bizarre **Mount Horeb Mustard Museum**. Nearby, the **Cave of the Mounds** is a significant underground cavern filled with stalactites, stalagmites and other formations, first discovered in 1939.

Cave of the Mounds

2975 Cave of the Mounds Road, Brigham Farm, Blue Mounds (608 437 3038/www.caveofthemounds.com). **Open** *15 Mar-Memorial Day, Oct-15 Nov* 10am-4pm Mon-Fri; 9am-5pm Sat, Sun. *June-Labor Day* 9am-7pm daily. *15 Nov-14 Mar* 10am-4pm Mon-Fri; by appointment Sat, Sun. **Admission** $10; $5 5-12s. **Credit** Disc, MC, V.

Little Norway

3576 County Highway JG, Blue Mounds (608 437 8211/www.littlenorway.com). **Open** *May, June, Sept, Oct* 9am-5pm daily. *July, Aug* 9am-7pm daily. **Admission** $8; $3-$7 concessions. **Credit** AmEx, MC, V.

Trips Out of Town

Magician **Rick Wilcox** entertains in the Wisconsin Dells. *See p275.*

Mount Horeb Mustard Museum

100 West Main Street, Mount Horeb (1-800 438 6878/www.mustardweb.com). **Open** 10am-5pm daily. **Admission** free. **No credit cards**.

Where to eat

The **Grumpy Troll** (105 S 2nd Street, 608 437 2739/www.grumpytroll.com) is a typical brewpub with that Wisconsin staple, the all-you-can-eat Friday night fish fry. At the **Main Street Pub & Grill** (120 E Main Street, 608 437 5733, sample home-made soups and good burgers and sandwiches (with lots of condiments from the Mustard Museum).

Getting there

By car

Mount Horeb is about 165 miles (265km) north-west of Chicago. Follow I-90 to Madison, then travel west on Highway 18 for 20 miles (32km).

Tourist information

Mount Horeb Area Chamber of Commerce

Office *100 S 1st Street, Mount Horeb (608 437 5914/www.trollway.com).* **Information hut** *in front of 214 E Main Street, Mount Horeb.* **Open** *Office* 9am-3pm Mon-Fri. *Information hut (late May-late Sept)* 9am-6pm daily.
The Chamber of Commerce can provide information about Mount Horeb and the surrounding region. Stroll by the information hut during summer.

New Glarus

In 1845, 108 inhabitants of the Swiss canton (state) of Glarus travelled to America, hoping to escape poverty. The journey involved a trip to Holland by canal and Rhine riverboat, a 49-day voyage to Baltimore and a trek by rail, canal and riverboat to Galena, Pittsburgh and St Louis. The immigrants walked the last 60 or so miles to their new Wisconsin home and settled on 1,280 acres of land, purchased at $1.25 an acre. This became New Glarus, a village still as Swiss as an unnumbered bank account

The Swiss immigrants sought a landscape resembling the one they had left behind, and found it cradled in the Little Sugar River valley of Green County. Cresting a hill and sighting the valley where the pretty village is snuggled, it would not be startling to hear a yodel echo across the valley. In fact, on the first Sunday in August, yodellers, alphornists and folk dancers meet and celebrate **Swiss Independence Day**.

The village resembles a Swiss mountain town. Chalet-style buildings feature carved balconies decorated by colourful coats of arms, Swiss flags and banners and window boxes spilling with bright red geraniums. The clank of cowbells welcomes you to shops selling lace, embroidery, cheese, baked goods (including rich, dense stollen) and a variety of *wurst*, including *landjäger*, a dried sausage favoured by Swiss hunters that makes a great munchie.

The **Swiss Historical Village Museum** is a replica pioneer village with log cabins, a log church and a one-room schoolhouse. Operated by the local historical society, it tells the story of Swiss immigration as well as early colonial life in the town. Meanwhile, the **Chalet of the Golden Fleece Museum** is a copy of a Swiss-Bernese mountain chalet, characterised by a white plaster foundation and brown-stained wood walls. The museum houses a collection of more than 3,000 Swiss items from dolls to kitchenware.

A new winery, the **New Glarus Primrose Winery**, makes table wines and dessert wines primarily from Wisconsin-grown grapes and fruit. It occupies a former funeral parlour and, yes, they have heard all the jokes about 'a cold one' and wine with 'body'. You'll find handcrafted beers at the **New Glarus Brewing Co**, among them lager, pilsner, bock and seasonal specialities such as *weiss* (wheat beer).

Over the Labor Day weekend, the **Wilhelm Tell Festival** celebrates Switzerland's most endearing folk hero with a performance of Friedrich Schiller's *Wilhelm Tell*. Staged in a wooded glen, it has a cast of more than 200 area residents, many on horseback, in authentic 13th-century costume. The festival also includes musical events and a candlelit parade.

The countryside surrounding New Glarus is ideal for cycling and hiking: in particular, the 23-mile (37-kilometre) **Sugar River Trail**, which runs from New Glarus to Brodhead. Tracing an abandoned railroad right-of-way, the trail passes through rolling hills and state wildlife refuges, past dairy farms, across old planked trestle bridges and under a covered bridge.

Chalet of the Golden Fleece Museum
618 2nd Street, New Glarus (608 527 2614). **Open** *late May-Oct* 10am-4pm daily. **Admission** $5; $2 concessions. **No credit cards.**

New Glarus Brewing Co
County Track W & Highway 69, New Glarus (608 527 5850/www.newglarusbrewing.com). **Open** *Self-guided tours* 10.30am-4pm Mon-Fri; noon-5pm Sat (June-Sept only). *Guided tours June-Sept* noon-5pm Sat. **Admission** *Self-guided tours* free (tasting $2.50). *Guided tours* $3.50 (incl tasting). **Credit** MC, V.

New Glarus Primrose Winery
226 2nd Street, New Glarus (608 527 5053). **Open** *Jan-Apr* noon-5pm Mon, Thur, Fri, Sun; 10am-5pm Sat. *May-Dec* 10am-6pm Mon-Sat; noon-6pm Sun. **Admission** free. **Credit** Disc, MC, V.

Swiss Historical Village
612 7th Avenue, New Glarus (608 527 2317/ www.swisshistoricalvillage.com). **Open** *May-Oct* 10am-4pm daily. **Admission** $6; $2 6-13s. **No credit cards.**

Volksfest
New Glarus (1-800 527 6838/608 527 2095/ www.swisstown.com/Volksfest/volksfest.html). **Date** 1st Sun in Aug.

Wilhelm Tell Festival
New Glarus (1-800 527 6838/608 527 2095/ www.swisstown.com/Wilhelm/wilhelm.html). **Date** Labor Day weekend.

Where to eat

Hans Lenzlinger, who learned to cook during a stint in the Swiss Army, offers many traditional favourites at the **New Glarus Hotel** (100 6th Avenue, 608 527 5244/www.newglarushotel.com, closed Tue Nov-Apr, main courses $10-$18), whose enclosed balcony has picture windows looking out on Main Street and over rooftops to the green hills that surround the village.

Where to stay

New Glarus is small, so options are limited. Aside from the Swiss-style **Chalet Landhaus Inn** (801 Highway 69, 1-800 944 1716/608 527 5234/www.chaletlandhaus.com, double $80-$100), the **New Glarus Hotel** (*see above*) has a number of rooms and the hotels of **Madison** (*see p266*) are within easy reach.

Getting there

By car
New Glarus is 150 miles (241km) north-west of Chicago. Take the I-90 to Rockford, then US 20 west to Freeport, where Highway 26 will take you across the stateline to Highway 69. It's then only 30 miles (48km) to New Glarus via Monroe.

Tourist information

New Glarus Tourism & Chamber of Commerce
16 5th Avenue, New Glarus (1-800 527 6838/608 527 2095/www.swisstown.com). **Open** *Late May-late Oct* 9am-4pm Mon-Fri; 10am-4pm Sat, Sun; otherwise 9am-4pm Mon-Fri.

Wisconsin Dells

It's brash, it's noisy, and it's one of the greatest kid-pleasers in America's heartland, with adventure parks and video arcades. It's where you ride in helicopters, go-karts and Hydrojet boats, take a bungee plunge and play a round of mini-golf. It's a spot to munch hot dogs, fudge and frozen custard, to buy moccasins and tacky T-shirts. It's a place to take in timeless attractions such as the **Famous Tommy Bartlett Thrill Show** and the entertaining concert offered by magician **Rick Wilcox**. The Wisconsin Dells is where you go when the kids tire of countryside and want something to *do*.

The Dells is forever reinventing itself, adding new attractions every season. None, though, has had the same impact of the indoor waterparks that have popped up all over town, such as the **Wilderness Hotel & Golf Resort**, the

Mid-Continent Railway. *See p275.*

Great Wolf Lodge and the Kalhari Resort
& Convention Center. They have helped
transform the Dells from a strictly seasonal
resort into a year-round destination.

Despite its relentless hoopla, the Dells
somehow remain the scenic destination they
were when 19th-century photographer Henry
Hamilton Bennett first set out to capture them
and catapulted them to popularity among
vacationers. The towering sandstone cliffs and
cool, fern-filled gullies remain unspoiled, and a
tour of the upper and lower rivers by boat or
aboard an amphibious duck – a World War II
landing craft – are enjoyable outings. To see
the Dells as Bennett saw them, visit the **HH
Bennett Studio and History Center**.

Also off the whizz-bang circuit is the 80-acre
reserve **International Crane Foundation**
reserve at Baraboo. There are 15 species of
cranes throughout the world, 11 of which are
considered endangered. Baraboo is the only
place in the world that's home to all 15, including
the whooping crane, the tallest bird in North
America; the adult stands up to five feet (1.5
metres) high. Its name was inspired by its loud,
distinctive call, audible up to two miles away.

Nearby, you can ride a steam train through
the Baraboo Hills from the **Mid-Continent
Railway Museum** at North Freedom. It
operates steam trains such as the 1907 Chicago
& North Western No.1385. The one-hour
excursions pass through the ghost town of
LaRue, a former iron-mining community.
Exhibits of railroading memorabilia, including
a steam-powered rotary snowplough, are housed
in an 1894 depot and in train and coach sheds.

HH Bennett Studio & History Center

*215 Broadway, Wisconsin Dells (608 253 3523/
www.shsw.wisc.edu/sites/bennett).* **Open** *May-Sept*
10am-5pm daily. *Oct-Apr* 10am-5pm Sat, Sun.
Admission $5; $2.50-$4.50 concessions. **Credit** MC, V.

International Crane Foundation

*E11376 Shady Lane Road, Baraboo (608 356 9462/
www.savingcranes.org).* **Open** *Mid Apr-late Oct* 9am-
5pm daily. *Guided tours: Apr, May, Sept, Oct* 10am,
1pm, 3pm Sat, Sun. *June-Aug* 10am, 1pm, 3pm daily.
Admission $7; $3.50-$6 concessions. **Credit** MC, V.

Mid-Continent Railway & Museum

*W Walnut Street, North Freedom (608 522 4261/
www.mcrwy.com).* **Open** *Museum grounds: late
May-early Sept* 9.30am-5pm daily. *Trains: late May-
early Sept* 10.30am, 12.30pm, 2pm, 3.30pm daily.
Admission $11; $6-$10 concessions; free under-3s.
Credit AmEx, Disc, MC, V.

Original Wisconsin Ducks

*1890 Wisconsin Dells Parkway, Wisconsin Dells
(608 254 8751/www.wisconsinducktours.com).*
Open call for details. **Admission** $16.75; $9
concessions; free under-5s. **Credit** Disc, MC, V.

Rick Wilcox Theater

*1666 Wisconsin Dells Parkway, Wisconsin Dells
(608 254 5511/www.rickwilcox.com).* **Open** varies.
Admission $19-$23; $14-$18 5-12s. **Credit** MC, V.

Tommy Bartlett Thrill Shows

*560 Wisconsin Dells Parkway, Wisconsin Dells (608
254 2525/www.tommybartlett.com).* **Shows** *late May-
early Sept* 1pm, 4.30pm, 8.30pm. **Admission** $11-$18;
$9-$16 concessions. **Credit** Disc, MC, V.

Where to eat

Housed in a handsome wood-and-brick building,
the **Cheese Factory** (521 Wisconsin Dells
Parkway South, Lake Delton, 608 253 6065/
www.cookingvegetarian.com, closed Tue
summer, closed Mon-Wed winter, main courses
$8-$13) is a fun vegetarian restaurant. At
Marley's (1470 Wisconsin Dells Parkway, 608
254 1800/www.marleysclub.com, main courses
$11-$25), diners chow down on a variety of
fine jerk dishes that include chicken, pork
and grouper. And try to save room for dessert
at **Culver's**, (12 Broadway, 608 253 9080/
www.culvers.com, main courses $6-$7), where
you'll find the best frozen custard in town.

Where to stay

At the 309-room **Great Wolf Lodge** (I-90/94
& Highway 12, at exit 92, 608 253 2222/
www.greatwolflodge.com, double $139),
youngsters delight at a stuffed buffalo head
that moves and talks on command, and the
large indoor waterpark. The **Kalahari Resort**
(I-90/94 & Highway 12, at exit 92, 1-877 253
5466/www.kalahariresort.com, four-person
room $99-$259) is one of the more elegant of
the area's waterparks, while the **Wilderness
Hotel** (511 E Adams Street, 1-800 867
9453/www.wildernessresort.com, double
$90-$235) boasts an 18-hole golf course to
complement its indoor and outdoor waterparks.

Getting there

By car

Wisconsin Dells is 188 miles (303km) north-west of
Chicago. Follow I-90 from Chicago to Dells exits 92,
89, 87, 85 (the best for downtown is exit 87).

Tourist information

Wisconsin Dells Visitor &
Convention Bureau

*701 Superior Street, Wisconsin Dells (1-800 223
3557/www.wisdells.com).* **Open** 8am-5pm daily
Summer closing times vary; call for details.
Stop by to make your lodging reservations and to
pick up maps, brochures and other information.

Directory

Features

Directory

Getting Around

Arriving & leaving

By air

Chicago is served by two airports: **O'Hare International** (ORD) and **Chicago Midway** (MID).

Chicago O'Hare International Airport

I-190 West (773 686 2200/ www.ohare.com/ohare/home.asp).
O'Hare is one of the largest and busiest airports in the world, and thus a little daunting. All domestic flights and international departures by domestic airlines use Terminals 1, 2 and 3; non-US international airlines use Terminal 5 (except for Lufthansa departures, which go from Terminal 1). The terminals are linked by a shuttle that runs 24 hours daily.

The CTA provides a 24-hour El service on its Blue line between O'Hare and downtown Chicago. The journey takes around 45 minutes, at least once you've found the station. At the airport, follow signs marked 'Trains to the city': pedestrian passageways link the airport's CTA station (deep under a vast car park) with the terminals. If you're still confused, pick up a map of the airport from one of the many information stands. Like all CTA fares (for more, *see below*), it'll cost $1.50.

The next cheapest option for getting into town is the **bus**. Airport Express (1-800 654 7871/312 454 7799/www.airportexpress.com), which has a booth in the baggage reclaim area, charges $20 single or $36 return for the journey downtown.

There's a **taxi** rank outside the baggage reclaim area of each terminal. The fare to downtown Chicago should come to about $30-$35 plus tip, though the traffic on I-90 can extend the usual 30-minute travel time – and the fare – at busy times. Money can be saved by partaking in the Shared Ride scheme: up to four passengers can share a cab from O'Hare to downtown Chicago (designated by the authorities to be as far north as Fullerton Avenue and as far south as McCormick Place) for a flat fee of $15 per person, though you may have to wait a little longer.

Chicago Midway Airport

5700 S Cicero Avenue (773 838 0600/ www.ohare.com/midway/home.asp).
Midway Airport is considerably smaller than O'Hare, though it is slightly closer to town. It is used mostly by lower-cost airlines.

Travelling to and from town on the El is straightforward, with the Orange line linking downtown Chicago and Midway Airport. The journey time is around 35 minutes, and the fare is the standard $1.50.

Bus-wise, Airport Express (1-800 654 7871/312 454 7799/ www.airportexpress.com) charges $15 single or $27 return for the journey downtown. Its booth is located in the baggage reclaim area.

The **taxi** ride to downtown Chicago from Midway should cost around $20-$25 plus tip and take 20-25 minutes. The Shared Ride scheme (detailed under Midway Airport) allows for a flat fee of $10 per person.

By bus

Greyhound buses (1-800 229 9424/www.greyhound.com) runs routes to Chicago from innumerable towns and cities. Services arrive at the **main bus station**, located in the West Loop at 630 W Harrison Street (at S Desplaines Street; 312 408 5980).

By rail

Amtrak trains (1-800 872 7245/www.amtrak.com) serve the gloriously grand **Union Station** (210 S Canal Street, at E Adams Street; 312 558 1075) in the West Loop.

Public transport

Information

Chicago's **Regional Transportation Authority (RTA)** oversees transport in the metropolitan area. The service is divided between the **Chicago Transit Authority (CTA)**, which operates buses and the elevated/subway train system (widely known as the 'El') in Chicago and 38 of its suburbs; the **Metra** suburban rail system; and **Pace**, a suburban bus system.

For a map of the El system *see p315*; for an El and bus map for downtown, *see p314*.

Chicago Transit Authority

CTA Customer Assistance, 7th floor, Merchandise Mart, at N Wells Street & E Kinzie Street, Near North (1-888 968 7282/ www.transitchicago.com). **Open** 7am-8pm Mon-Fri. **Map** p306 G11.

RTA Travel Center

11 S Wells Street, at W Madison Street, the Loop (312 836 7000/ www.rtachicago.com). **Open** 5am-1am daily. **Map** p305 H12.
The RTA Travel Center provides information on Chicago's buses and trains. Maps and timetables can also be ordered on the above number.

CTA fares & tickets

CTA buses and the El operate a simple flat-rate fare across the network. A single fare is $1.50, or 75¢ for children aged seven to 11. Senior citizens and disabled travellers can apply for reduced fares by phone (312 836 7000). Children under seven go free if accompanied by a fare-paying adult. A transfer, allowing you an onward journey (or quick return) by bus or El within two hours, is an extra 30¢.

Ticketing is done mostly with **Transit Cards**, which can be purchased from machines at CTA stations for as little as $1.50 and as much as $100: the customer decides how much they want to spend.

When the card runs out or drops below the minimum fare threshold, you can recharge it at any ticket machine.

It's a good idea to pay more than the minimum $1.50 when you buy your ticket, for two reasons. Firstly, you get an extra transfer free on your first journey. And secondly, for every $10 you spend at one time, you get an extra dollar's worth of travel for free.

The fare for each journey is deducted automatically as you pass your card through the turnstile or fare box. Transfers are recognised automatically. The card can be shared by up to seven people at once as long as it is inserted the correct number of times.

The main alternative to a Transit Card is a CTA **Visitor Pass**, which allows unlimited travel on CTA buses. The one-day pass is known, rather quaintly, as a **Fun Pass**, and costs $5. Other Visitor Passes are available for two ($9), three ($12) and five ($18) days. They are available from Visitors' Centres, Union Station, O'Hare and Midway Airports, some CTA stations, Hot Tix booths and some museums, but can also be booked in advance by phone (312 836 7000) or on www.transitchicago.com. CTA Visitor Passes entitle the bearer to discounts at selected museums and theatres.

CTA trains

The CTA's elevated/subway train system – or the 'El', as it is known to just about everyone in the city – consists of seven colour-coded lines (Blue, Brown, Green, Orange, Purple, Red and Yellow) that serve vast swathes of the Chicago area. The service is, in the main, both fast and reliable, if a little creaky in parts.

Most lines run every five to 15 minutes until late at night, with both the Red and Blue lines running around the clock

(between 1.30am and 4.30am, Red line trains are scheduled every 15 minutes, Blue line trains once an hour). Care should be taken late at night. Train routes and destinations are shown on the platform and on the front and side of trains.

Confusingly, several stations on the El share the same name: Chicago, for example, is the name of a station on the Red line (at Chicago Avenue and State Street), on the Brown and Purple lines (at Chicago Avenue and Franklin Street in River North) and on the Blue line (at Chicago Avenue and Milwaukee Avenue, in the middle of nowhere). For clarity, we list the line(s) referred to after the station name.

There are plenty of El stations in the Loop: in the area bounded by Wells, Wacker, Michigan and Van Buren – six blocks east to west, eight blocks north to south – there are no fewer than 16 stops. We've listed the nearest one or two to each place listed in this book, but if you're travelling within the Loop, it'll be almost as quick to walk.

CTA buses

CTA bus stops are marked by white and blue signs listing the names and numbers of the routes they serve followed by the destination. Most routes run every ten to 15 minutes from dawn until at least 10.30pm daily (routes 10, 130 and 157 are not daily). Night buses, known as 'Night Owls', run every 30 minutes on routes marked by a picture of an owl. If you don't have a Transit Card, you can pay for your fare and any transfer by handing over the correct change.

Below are some of the more popular and/or useful routes:

22: Clark
Southbound, the 22 runs on Clark Street between the far North Side and Polk Street in the Loop.

The northbound route runs up Dearborn Street from Polk Street to Washington Square, where it joins Clark Street and continues north.

29: State
The 29 runs up State Street from the far South Side to Illinois Street just north of the Chicago River, where it turns east and heads to Navy Pier. The return journey follows the same route, but leaves Navy Pier along Grand Avenue until State Street before heading south.

36: Broadway
Southbound, the 36 runs from the far North Side down Broadway to Diversey Parkway, then heads south on Clark Street before joining State Street at Division Street and continuing south to Polk Street in the Loop. The northbound service begins at Polk Street, heading up Dearborn Street as far as Illinois Street where it joins State Street. At Division Street, it joins Clark Street, and at Diversey Parkway, it joins Broadway and continues to the far North Side.

66: Chicago
Runs east along Chicago Avenue between the far West Side and Fairbanks Court in Streeterville, then heads south on Fairbanks to Illinois Street and then east to Navy Pier. The westbound route is identical but for the fact it leaves Navy Pier along Grand Avenue instead of Fairbanks.

72: North
Runs along North Avenue between Lincoln Park and the far West Side.

151: Sheridan
Runs in a slightly circuitous fashion around parts of the Loop, taking in Union Station and then heading along Jackson Boulevard, turning north on State Street, then east on Washington Boulevard and north again on Michigan Avenue. It then joins Lake Shore Drive at Oak Street, passing directly through Lincoln Park (stopping by the Zoo) and eventually picking up Sheridan Road at Diversey Parkway. After turning left on Byron Street, it rejoins Sheridan Road north of Wrigley Field and continues to the far North Side.

Metra rail

The Metra is a 12-line commuter rail system that serves 245 stations in north-east Illinois, as well as parts of Indiana. The Metra's Chicago termini are **LaSalle Street Station** (414 S LaSalle Street, at E Congress Parkway, the

Loop); **Randolph Street Station** (E Randolph Street, at N Michigan Avenue, the Loop); the **Richard B Ogilvie Transportation Center** (500 W Madison Street, at S Canal Street); and **Union Station** (*see p278*). Metra offers a variety of fares, from simple single-route fares to ten-route tickets – saving 15 per cent – and a $5 pass for unlimited weekend travel.

Metra

Metra Passenger Services, 547 W Jackson Boulevard, at S Clinton Street, the Loop (312 322 6777/ www.metrarail.com). **Open** 8am-5pm daily. **Map** p305 G12.

Pace

Pace buses serve Chicago's outlying suburbs. **Single fare** prices vary according to the route from $1.25 (local fare) to $1.50 (regular fare) to $3 (premium fare). Reduced-price tickets are available for children under 12, and others on application to the RTA. The CTA Transit Card (*see p278*) is valid on Pace routes. Pace also offers a number of reduced rate passes including the **10-ride ticket**, which offers 11 rides for the price of ten and can be shared by multiple travellers.

Pace

Pace Passenger Services (847 364 7223/www.pacebus.com). **Open** 8am-5pm Mon-Fri.

Taxis

Taxis are prevalent in the Loop and surrounding areas and can be hailed on the street. Further out, you'd be better off booking a taxi by calling one of the major cab companies on the numbers below.

Meters start at $1.90, then increase $1.60 for every mile, or 20¢ for every 45 seconds of waiting time. Extra passengers aged between 12 and 65 are charged 50¢. There is no charge for baggage. Tipping is optional, but usually expected.

For longer journeys, drivers may agree in advance to a flat fee. The Shared Ride scheme (*see p278*) offers flat rates per person to and from the airports and from McCormick Place.

Registered taxis are usually safe and reliable. If you have a complaint, however, contact the **Department of Consumer Services** (312 744 9400).

Checker Cabs *312 243 2537.*
Flash Cabs *773 561 1444.*
King Drive Cab Company *773 487 9000.*
Yellow Cabs *312 829 4222.*

Driving

As in most major cities, driving in Chicago is not recommended, and shouldn't be undertaken by the faint-hearted. The city's grid system makes it relatively easy to negotiate and cars can prove useful if you're planning on spending time out in the suburbs. Otherwise, it's not really worth the hassle of hiring a car. If you're arriving in the city in your own car, you're best off leaving it at your hotel (though parking charges may be steep) and using the CTA or cabs.

Breakdown services

American Automobile Association

Suite 213, 100 W Randolph Street, at N Clark Street IL 60601 (1-800 222 4357/www.autoclubgroup.com/ chicago). **Open** 24hrs daily.
Not just a breakdown service: also a source of maps, guidebooks and hotel discounts, free to affiliated organisations such as the British AA.

Parking

Parking in Chicago is prohibitively expensive. Car parks charge upwards of $15 per day and hotel garages can cost even more. Street parking is limited and most of it is controlled by meters. Be careful not to park in a towing area, otherwise you could end up paying not only a fine, but also the cost of retrieving your car from the pound. If you do get towed for illegal parking, call the **Chicago Police Department** (312 744 6000).

Vehicle hire

In most cases, you'll need to be 25 or over to rent a car – some firms, though, will rent to over-21s – and a credit card is essential. Rental rates should include unlimited mileage but will be subject to a special and not inconsiderable city and state tax of 18 per cent.

If you're renting a car, you'll be offered a basic liability insurance and a collision-damage waiver. If your home policy doesn't cover you, we recommend you take both. It's expensive, but not as expensive as the bill you'll face should the worst come to the worst.

The best time to rent is at the weekends when there are fewer business travellers in the city. All the major companies have outlets at O'Hare and, in most cases, in the city itself and at Midway.

Rental companies

Alamo *1-800 327 9633/ www.alamo.com.*
Avis *1-800 831 2847/ www.avis.com.*
Budget *1-800 686 6800/ http://budget.com.*
Dollar *1-800 800 4000/ http://dollar.com.*
Hertz *1-800 654 3131/ www.hertz.com.*
National *1-800 227 7368/ www.nationalcar.com.*
Thrifty *1-800 367 2277/ http://thrifty.com.*

Cycling

The CTA allows bicycles on trains on Saturdays and Sundays during the summer from Memorial Day Weekend (late May) until Labor Day (first Mon in Sept). Under 18s must be accompanied by an adult. For bike hire, *see p236.*

Water transport

For sightseeing cruises on the Chicago River and Lake Michigan, *see p66.*

Shoreline Water Taxi

Information 312 222 9328/ www.shorelinesightseeing.com. CTA Grand (Red). **Open** *Memorial Day-Labor Day* 10am-6pm daily. **Tickets** *Single* $6; $3-$5 concessions. *All-day pass* $12; $6-$10 concessions. **Map** p306 K10. Fast and frequent connections between Navy Pier and the Shedd Aquarium or Sears Tower.

Resources A-Z

Addresses

Chicago is a terrifically easy place to get around. The city works, like many American cities, on a grid system, with street numbers corresponding to a fairly simple pattern.

Ground zero from a street-numbering point of view is in the Loop, at the corner of State Street, which runs north to south, and Madison Street, which runs east to west. All north–south streets north of Madison are prefixed 'N', with those south of Madison prefixed 'S'; east–west streets east of State are prefixed 'E', with the rest prefixed 'W'.

The numbering of the streets works outwards from these points, with each 800 measuring one mile. Thus, 800 N Clark Street is a mile north of Madison, 1600 S Michigan Avenue is two miles south of Madison, 200 E Wacker Drive is a quarter of a mile east of State and so on.

Throughout this guide, we have given the full street addresses with the nearest cross-street. The maps at the back of the book are also marked with many points of interest and block-numberings every half-mile (for example, 'N Halsted Street 800W' and 'W Belmont Avenue 3200N').

Age restrictions

The legal drinking age in Chicago is 21, though you'll be carded regularly if there's even the remotest possibility that you're under 21. Always carry a photo ID that gives your age and, preferably, your date of birth (though the UK date-before-month system may confuse). Smokers must be 18 to buy cigarettes, while only those over the age of 16 can legally drive. The age of consent in Illinois is 17.

Attitude & etiquette

Chicago is a casual, friendly city, something that will be apparent from the moment you touch down at O'Hare. While it's a buzzing modern metropolis, tolerant of alternative lifestyles, it's also in the heart of the Midwest, and comes with all the relaxed, unpretentious good manners that characterise its location. Some high-end restaurants will insist on jacket or jacket and tie (call to check), while a few nightclubs operate a dress code (albeit often nothing more than whether the doorman thinks you're cool enough to come in). But mostly, while it might be an exaggeration to suggest that anything goes in Chicago, pretty much everything is tolerated.

Business

Back in the bad old days, before it attracted so many tourists, Chicago found itself a niche. That niche, of course, was conventions. And what started off as a relatively humble enterprise has spiralled into a behemoth: Chicago now hosts an astonishing four million-plus conventioneers each year.

The bulk of convention action (if those two words are not mutually exclusive) occurs at the vast **McCormick Place**: 2.2 million square feet of exhibition space, a further 170,000 square feet of banquet, ballroom and meeting room space, all spread over three separate buildings (named North, South and East) that cover a total of 27 acres. So large is the site that you need to factor journey time into your appointments – and once you've got where you're

supposed to be, don't expect to find your way out in a hurry. However, the facilities are dazzlingly modern, though be warned that there is absolutely nothing to do within several blocks of the centre.

The other main convention centre in Chicago is a relatively new operation on Navy Pier. There are a mere 170,000 square feet of exhibition space in **Festival Hall**, but the facilities are just as modern as McCormick's and Navy Pier offers plenty of attractions and eateries for light relief.

Further out – close to O'Hare International Airport, which explains the plethora of business-oriented hotels in the area – is yet another monster meeting place. The **Rosemont Convention Center** benefits from its location in terms of space – there are 600,000 square feet – but also suffers for it: while McCormick is slightly set apart from the downtown action, Rosemont is a long way away from it.

The **Chicago Hilton & Towers** (see p50), the **Chicago Marriott** (see p51) and the **Hyatt Regency** (see p45; there's also a Hyatt Regency at McCormick Place itself) are particularly geared towards business travellers, and the majority of hotels in downtown Chicago offer some form of business facilities.

Conventions & conferences

McCormick Place Convention Complex
2301 S Lake Shore Drive, at E 23rd Street, South Side (312 791 7000/ www.mccormickplace.com). Metra 23rd Street.

Festival Hall
Navy Pier, 600 E Grand Avenue, at Lake Michigan, Near North (312 595 5300). CTA Grand (Red)/29, 65, 66 bus. Map p306 K10.

Rosemont Convention Center

5555 N River Road (near O'Hare Airport, off I-190), Rosemont (847 692 2220).

Couriers & shippers

Apex Courier

448 N Halsted Street, at W Grand Avenue, West Side (312 666 4400). CTA Clinton (Green). **Open** 24hrs daily. **Credit** AmEx, MC, V.

Arrow Messenger Service

1322 W Walton Street, at N Milwaukee Avenue, West Side (773 489 6688). CTA Chicago (Blue). **Open** 24hrs daily. **No credit cards**.

Federal Express

233 S Wacker Drive, at W Adams Street, the Loop (1-800 463 3339). CTA Quincy (Brown, Orange, Purple). **Open** 9am-7pm Mon-Fri. **Credit** AmEx, Disc, MC, V. **Map** p395 G12.

United Parcel Service

1500 S Jefferson Street, at W 15th Street, West Side (1-800 742 5877/www.ups.com). CTA Roosevelt/State (Red) or Roosevelt/Wabash (Green, Orange). **Open** 8am-6pm Mon-Fri. **Credit** AmEx, MC, V. **Map** p304 G15.

Office hire & business services

Acme

218 S Wabash Avenue, at E Adams Street, the Loop (312 922 1155). CTA Adams (Brown, Green, Orange, Purple) or Jackson (Red). **Open** 8am-5pm Mon-Fri. **Credit** MC, V. **Map** p305 H12.
Digital printing, layout and DTP, laminating, photo reproductions, mounting and drafting supplies.

Alphagraphics

645 N Michigan Avenue, at E Erie Street, Near North (312 266 9266). CTA Chicago (Red). **Open** 8am-9pm Mon-Thur; 8am-6pm Fri; 9am-2pm Sat. **Credit** AmEx, DC, Disc, MC, V. **Map** p306 J10.
Copying central, basically.
Branch: 208 S LaSalle Street, at E Adams Street, the Loop (312 368 4507).

Kinko's

55 E Monroe Street, at S Dearborn Street, the Loop (312 701 0730). CTA Monroe (Blue, Red). **Open** 6am-10pm Mon-Fri. **Rates** *Computer hire* $12/hr (PC); $24/hr (Mac). **Credit** AmEx, DC, Disc, MC, V. **Map** p305 H12.
All the usual Kinko's services, morning, noon and night.
Branches: 1201 N Dearborn Street, Gold Coast (312 640 6100); 444 N Wells Street, Near North (312 670 4460); and throughout the city.

Secretarial services

HQ Global Workplaces

225 W Washington Boulevard, at N Franklin Street, the Loop (312 419 7150/www.hq.com). CTA Washington (Brown, Orange, Purple). **Open** 8.30am-5pm Mon-Fri. **Credit** AmEx, DC, V. **Map** p305 G12.
Full office support services.
Branch: 203 N LaSalle Street, at W Lake Street, the Loop (312 346 2030).

Translators & interpreters

Lingua

200 W Madison Street, at N Wells Street, the Loop (312 641 0488). CTA Washington (Brown, Orange, Purple). **Open** 8am-7.30pm Mon-Fri. **Credit** AmEx, Disc, MC, V. **Map** p305 H12.

TransPerfect Translations

150 N Michigan Avenue, at E Randolph Street, the Loop (312 444 2044). CTA Washington (Brown, Orange, Purple). **Open** 9am-6pm Mon-Fri. **Credit** AmEx, MC, V. **Map** p305 G11.

Useful organisations

Harold Washington Public Library

400 S State Street, at W Van Buren Street, the Loop (312 747 4300/www.chipublib.org). CTA Library (Brown, Orange, Purple). **Open** 9am-7pm Mon-Thur; 9am-5pm Fri, Sat; 1-5pm Sun. **Map** p305 H13.

Loyola Graduate Business School

6th floor, 25 E Pearson Street, at N State Street, Gold Coast (312 915 6625). CTA Chicago (Red). **Open** 8am-10pm Mon-Thur; 8am-6pm Fri; 10am-6pm Sat; noon-6pm Sun. **Map** p306 H9.
Non-Loyola students can't check anything out from this library, but can browse at will.

Consumer

City of Chicago Department of Consumer Services

Room 808, 121 N LaSalle Street, at W Washington Street, the Loop (312 744 4006/www.ci.chi.il.us/ ConsumerServices). CTA Washington (Brown, Orange, Purple). **Open** 8.30am-4.30pm Mon-Fri. **Map** p305 H12.
Deals with consumer complaints about shops and cabs, among others.

Customs & immigration

During your flight, along with an immigration form, you will be handed a white customs declaration form to be presented after you've cleared Immigration. US regulations allow visitors to import the following, duty-free: 200 cigarettes or 50 cigars (not Cuban; over-18s only) or two kilograms of smoking tobacco; one litre (1.05 US quart) of wine or spirits (over-21s only); and up to $100 in gifts ($400 for returning Americans). The import of previously exported US-made cigarettes and other tobacco products is banned. You can take up to $10,000 in cash, travellers' cheques or endorsed bank drafts in or out of the country tax-free. You may need to declare foodstuffs (some of which are prohibited), plants, plant products, fruits and vegetables, and canned or processed items are restricted. The US Customs Service (202 927 6724; www.customs.gov/ travel/travel.htm) can advise.

UK Customs & Excise allows returning travellers to bring in £145 worth of gifts and goods and and any sum of money you can prove is yours.

Disabled

While Chicago is reasonably accessible to disabled visitors (a lot of the buses are fitted with lifts, there are lifts on elevated CTA platforms and the sidewalks have ramps), it is always wise to call ahead to check accessibility.

Accessible Journeys
1-800 846 4537/
www.disabilitytravel.com.
An organisation dedicated to providing safe and accessible travel opportunities for disabled people. It has offices around the world and publishes an electronic newsletter.

Mayor's Office for People with Disabilities
312 744 7050/hearing impaired 312 744 4964. **Open** 8.30am-4.30pm Mon-Fri.
Good source of general information about all aspects of disabled and handicapped access in the city. Best to call before you come to town.

Getting around

RTA Travel Center
Ground floor, 11 S Wells Street, at W Madison Street, the Loop (312 836 7000/hearing impaired 312 836 4949/www.rtachicago.com). **Open** 5am-1am daily. **Map** p305 H12.
The RTA can provide information on which public train platforms and buses are wheelchair accessible.

Special Services
7th floor, Merchandise Mart, at N Wells Street & E Kinzie Street, Near North (312 432 7025/hearing impaired 432 7140/fax 312 432 7116). CTA Merchandise Mart (Brown, Purple). **Open** 7am-6pm Mon-Fri. **Map** p306 J11.
A programme run by the city and the CTA that arranges to pick up disabled people from the airport in a vehicle with disabled access. Contact the centre at least two weeks before arriving and note that certificates of disability must be provided.

Drugs

You only have to walk into any bar to realise how strict the Chicago authorities are about drugs – if they're going to be that strict about serving alcohol to under-21s, then drugs too must be heavily policed. They are, too; foreigners caught in possession of anything illegal (ie anything from grass upwards) should expect to be treated harshly.

Electricity

Rather than the 220-240V, 50-cycle AC used in Europe, Chicago (and the US as a whole) uses a 110-120V, 60-cycle AC voltage. Except for dual-voltage, flat-pin plug shavers, foreign visitors will need to run small appliances via an adaptor, available at airport shops.

Bear in mind, too, that most US videos and TVs have their own frequency: you will not be able to play back your camcorder footage. But you can buy and use blank tapes.

Embassies & consulates

All foreign embassies are located in Washington, DC, although many countries also have a consulate in Chicago; **www.ci.chi.il.us** has a complete list.

Canadian Consulate General
Suite 2400, 2 Prudential Plaza, 180 N Stetson Avenue, at E Lake Street, the Loop (312 616 1860/ www.can-am.gc.ca/menu-e.asp? mid=6). CTA Lake (Red) or State (Brown, Green, Orange, Purple). **Open** 8.30am-4.30pm Mon-Fri. **Map** p305 J11.

Republic of Ireland Consulate
Suite 911, Wrigley Building, 400 N Michigan Avenue, at E Hubbard Street, Near North (312 337 1868). CTA Grand (Red). **Open** 10am-noon, 2-4pm Mon-Fri. **Map** p306 J11.

United Kingdom Consulate General
Suite 1300, Wrigley Building, 400 N Michigan Avenue, at E Hubbard Street, Near North (312 970 3800/fax 312 970 3852). CTA Grand (Red). **Open** 8.30am-5pm Mon-Fri. **Map** p306 J11.

Emergencies

If it's an emergency, call **911** (ambulance, police or fire): the number is free from any telephone. However, anything

less than absolutely critical should rather be directed to **311** or the following numbers:
Chicago Police Department *312 746 6000.*
Chicago Fire Department *312 744 6666.*
FBI *312 431 1333.*
Illinois State Police:
Chicago District *847 294 4400.*
Illinois Poison Control *1-800 942 5969/TDD 312 942 2214.*

For **helplines** and **hospitals**, *see p284*, and for **local police stations**, *see p287*.

Gay & lesbian

Chicago Area Gay & Lesbian Chamber of Commerce
3356 N Halsted Street, at W Buckingham Place, Lake View (773 871 4190/ www.glchamber.org). **Open** 9.30am-6pm Mon-Fri. **Map** p309 F2.
A great place to start a homosexual exploration in Chicago.

Gerber-Hart Library
1127 W Granville Avenue, at N Broadway, North Side (773 381 8030/www.gerberhart.org). CTA Granville (Red). **Open** 6-9pm Wed, Thur; noon-4pm Fri-Sun. **Admission** free. *Annual membership* $35. **Credit** AmEx, MC, V.
The Midwest's largest lesbigay library, archive and resource centre. Membership is required to check out books, but anyone can browse.

Horizons Community Services
961 W Montana Street, at N Sheffield Avenue, Lake View (773 929 4357). CTA Fullerton (Brown, Purple, Red). **Open** 6-10pm Mon-Fri. **Map** p305 E5.
Education and support groups in a wonderful environment. A great spot for gay youths to hang out and feel accepted.

Health

Accident & emergency

There is no national health care system in the United States, so if you are treated in a healthcare facility you will be required either to show proof of insurance or to pay in full. If possible, get hold of your insurance company first and it will let you

Directory

know which hospital you should go to. Make sure that you have ID and insurance details on you at all times, so that in case of an emergency, you have them at the ready. Waits in the emergency room tend to be long and prices are exceedingly high, so don't take a trip there unnecessarily.

Contraception & abortion

Planned Parenthood

6th floor, 14 S Michigan Avenue, at E Madison Street, the Loop (312 427 2270/www.plannedparenthood.org). CTA Jackson (Blue, Red). **Open** 9.30am-6pm Mon; 9am-2pm Tue, Sat; 10am-6.30pm Wed, Thur; 11am-6pm Fri. **Map** p305 H13.
A non-profit organisation that can supply contraception, treat STDs and perform abortions.
Branches: throughout the city.

Dentists

Chicago Dental

1-800 577 7322.
Dental referrals.

Hospitals

Chicago is home to several world-class hospitals (though they're not quite as exciting as they look on *ER* or *Chicago Hope*). For general information call **Advocate Health** (1-800 323 8622), a central phone number that can connect you to eight hospitals in the metropolitan area. Emergency rooms at the following hospitals are open 24 hours daily.

Children's Memorial Hospital

700 W Fullerton Avenue, at N Lincoln Avenue, Lincoln Park (773 880 4000/www.childrens memorial.org). CTA Fullerton (Brown, Purple, Red). **Map** p308 F5.
A full range of pediatric services.

Cook County Hospital

1835 W Harrison Street, at S Wood Street, West Side (312 633 6000). CTA Medical Center (Blue).

Northwestern Memorial Hospital

250 E Superior Street, at N Fairbanks Court, Near North (312 908 2000/www.nmh.org). CTA Chicago (Red). **Map** p306 J10.
A new, state-of-the-art facility, with luxury hotel-like furniture, soaring atriums and food so good that non-sick locals have been known to stop in for a bite.

Rush-Presbyterian-St Luke's Medical Center

1653 W Congress Parkway, at S Ashland Avenue, West Side (312 942 5000/www.rush.edu). CTA Medical Center (Blue)/ 7, 26 bus.
Probably the most technologically advanced hospital in the city and one of the most renowned in the world.

University of Chicago Hospital

5841 S Maryland Avenue, at E 58th Street, Hyde Park (773 702 1000/www.uchospitals.edu). Metra 59th Street.

Opticians

For details of opticians in Chicago, *see p183.*

Pharmacies

Many pharmacies in the city are open until late at night (10pm, say), but the branch of **Osco Drug** at 3101 N Clark Street in Lake View (773 477 1967) and the 757 N Michigan Avenue outpost of **Walgreens** (312 664 8686) are two that stay open 24 hours daily. For details of other round-the-clock opening Osco Drugs, call 1-888 443 5701; for information on other 24-hour Walgreens, call 1-800 925 4733. For more on pharmacies, *see p184.*

STDs, HIV & AIDS

Howard Brown Health Center

4025 N Sheridan Road, at W Irving Park Road, Lake View (773 388 1600/www.howardbrown.org). CTA Sheridan (Red). **Open** 9am-7.30pm Mon-Thur; 9am-5pm Fri.
The centre provides comprehensive health services for the gay community, including primary care, anonymous HIV testing, support groups and research, as well as supplies of free condoms.

Helplines

Alcoholics Anonymous

312 346 1475.

Illinois AIDS/ HIV & STD Hotline

1-800 243 2437.

Narcotics Anonymous

708 848 4884.

ID

If you're planning on drinking in Chicago, then carry photo ID that contains your date of birth (a driving licence or a passport, say): you'll almost certainly be carded if there's even a 1,000-1 chance that you're under 21. Note that you need to show two 'government-issued IDs' at airport ticket counters.

Insurance

Non-nationals should arrange baggage, trip-cancellation and medical insurance before they leave home. Medical centres will ask for details of your insurance company and your policy number if you require treatment; always keep this information with you.

Internet

Aside from the cybercafés below, several other locations offer net access. **Afterwords** (*see p167*) has a few terminals, and many branches of the **Chicago Public Library** offer all-comers free access. Head to **www.chipublib.org** for a complete list of locations.

BEANnet

10 S LaSalle Street, at W Madison Avenue, the Loop (312 332 7531/ www.beannet.com). CTA Washington (Brown, Orange, Purple). **Open** 8am-6pm Mon-Fri. **Rates** $1/20min. **Credit** AmEx, DC, Disc, MC, V. **Map** p305 H12.
Branches: throughout the city.

Off The Wall

1909 W North Avenue, at N Wolcott Avenue, Wicker Park (773 782 0000/ www.offthewallwireless.com). CTA Damen (Blue). **Open** 7am-10pm Mon-Thur; 7am-9pm Fri; 8am-9pm Sat; 9am-9pm Sun. **Rates** 15¢/min. **Credit** AmEx, DC, Disc, MC, V. **Map** p310 C7.

Screenz

2717 N Clark Street, at W Diversey Parkway, Lincoln Park (773 348 9300/www.screenz.com). CTA Diversey (Brown). **Open** 8am-midnight Mon-Thur, Sun; 9am-1am Fri, Sat. **Rates** $8.40/hr. **Credit** AmEx, Disc, MC, V. **Map** p308 F4.

Directory

Left luggage

Airports

Neither O'Hare nor Midway offers any left luggage facilities.

Rail stations

Union Station has both lockers and a baggage check desk ($1.50 per piece per day).

Legal help

Your first call in any serious legal embroilment should either be to your insurance company (depending on your policy) or your consulate (*see p283*).

Libraries

In addition to the **Harold Washington Library Center** in the Loop, branches of the Chicago Public Library include the **Lincoln Park Library** (1150 W Fullerton Avenue, at N Racine Avenue, Lincoln Park; 312 744 1926); **Near North Library** (310 W Division Street, at N Wells Street, Gold Coast; 312 744 0992) and the **John Merlo Library** (644 W Belmont Avenue, at Broadway, Lake View; 312 744 1139). All are open from 9am to 9pm Monday to Thursday and from 9am to 5pm on Friday and Saturday.

Harold Washington Library Center

400 S State Street, at W Congress Parkway, the Loop (312 747 4999/www.chipublib.org). CTA Library (Brown, Orange, Purple). **Open** 9am-7pm Mon-Thur; 9am-5pm Fri, Sat; 1-5pm Sun. **Map** p305 H13. Located in a state-of-the-art building on the southern edge of the Loop, the main branch of the Chicago Public Library is the second largest in the world. It houses two million volumes, plus an auditorium theatre, the Chicago Blues Archives and the Jazz, Blues and Gospel Hall of Fame. There are also 30 terminals available for free public Internet access, though you'll often have to wait in line to use one and the 30-minute time limit is strictly enforced.

Lost property

If you lose something on a bus or train, call the CTA's lost and found department. It's divided into numerous different regions, depending on the train or bus line you were using when you lost the item.

Airports

Lost property at O'Hare Airport is dealt with by each individual airline at their respective Lost & Found offices in the baggage retrieval area. Call 773 694 9111 for more details. At Midway, meanwhile, there's a police department near Concourse C in the old terminal building, and a security booth on the upper level of the new terminal. Phone 773 838 3003 for more details.

Public transport

For items left on a bus, call 312 664 7200 or 312 744 2900 during business hours and ask for 'lost and found'.

If you leave something on the El, call the relevant phone number from the list below (open 8am to 6pm, Monday to Friday).

Blue *773 686 0785.*
Brown *773 539 3434.*
Green *708 366 0083.*
Orange *773 581 9281.*
Purple/Red/Yellow *773 262 4163.*

Taxi

If you lose something in a cab, call the taxi company direct.

Media

Home to the country's third-largest media market and with a newspaper heritage to rival that of New York, Chicago is taken seriously as one of the US's media big-hitters.

Daily newspapers

Founded in 1847, the **Chicago Tribune** is the reigning daily newspaper. It's also one of the most powerful papers in Illinois, if not the US. Among its strengths: regional sports and arts coverage; foreign news; and the entertainment-led 'Friday' supplement. However, nationally, the *Trib* is still considered a second-tier paper, so those looking for the best paper in town will want to pick up the special Midwest edition of the *New York Times*.

The **Chicago Sun-Times** is the tabloid competitor to the *Tribune*, and has been in sharp decline of late. Though it offers the occasional slice of gritty reporting on city politics and good coverage of Chicago sports, arts coverage is weak (with the notable exceptions of the output of acerbic music scribe Jim DeRogatis and legendary movie hack Roger Ebert), and most news stories are squeezed into a few paragraphs. At 35¢, though, it is still cheaper than the *Trib* by a whopping 15¢.

The **Daily Herald** and the **Daily Southtown** round out Chicago's dailies, but neither attempts to compete with the *Trib* or *Sun-Times* inside the city. The *Herald* publishes zoned suburban editions, while the *Southtown* concerns itself only with the southernmost area of the city.

Magazines & weekly papers

The **Chicago Reader** is the dominant free weekly, and is a must-have for both locals and visitors. For that reason, it's often difficult to track down a copy after the paper is published on Thursday: if you can't find one in the yellow newspaper boxes around town, check inside the doorway of the nearest local business for a stack of copies.

The *Reader* offers excellent coverage of music, movies, theatre and art, and has the most comprehensive events listings. The news section specialises in lengthy human interest pieces that some find tedious. But it does offer a from-the-ground-up view of many neighbourhoods and a welcome alternative view of the community.

Newcity is Chicago's other alternative weekly freesheet, and is available in many bars and shops, and from orange boxes on street corners. While it doesn't compete with the *Reader* in terms of quality or quantity, it's not without its merits. It offers a variety of annual specials on stuff like eating out and movies and the occasional off-the-beaten-track newsy gem. It, too, features cultural listings.

The **Onion** is certain to startle anyone who isn't already familiar with its immensely popular website (www.theonion.com). In addition to the satire for which it's best known, it provides excellent coverage of music and movies, deadly accurate reviews, and a 'Savage Love' sex advice column. It's available free every week in most bars and convenience stores downtown.

Directory

Made in Chicago This American Life

Ira Glass doesn't consider himself a celebrity. He can walk down the street unaccosted. He isn't chased for photos and autographs. He's not in the spotlight. But in Chicago, he's found his own quiet form of fame.

Glass's radio show *This American Life* has become something of a phenomenon since it first hit the airwaves in 1995. Broadcast live from Navy Pier, it has gone from a narrow-market programme to a nationwide hit, now aired on over 400 stations across the country.

The show's success rests on its original format. Packaged as a series of vignettes and/or real-life stories, *This American Life* is not made up of the standard back-and-forth banter usually heard on talk radio. The tales in the one-hour show, told through narrative and interviews, revolve around specific themes, anything from funerals to nudist camps, by turns humorous and heart-rending.

It help that Glass has an ear for new talent. He is credited with springboarding the career of essayist David Sedaris by putting his *Santaland Diaries* piece on the air in his former role as producer of National Public Radio's *Morning Edition*. Since then, a new, hip lit crowd has joined *This American Life*'s ranks, with writers Sarah Vowell, David Rakoff and Sandra Tsing Loh all featured to wide acclaim. But Glass is the glue that holds the show together. And though he's still not getting stared at in restaurants or trailed on the street, an awful lot of Americans now recognise his voice.

This American Life is broadcast on Chicago's WBEZ 91.5 FM on Fridays at 7pm, Saturdays at 1pm and Sundays at 5pm. See www.thislife.org for a schedule in other US markets, and for a Real Audio archive of previous shows.

The rest of the street-corner boxes are filled with a variety of other weekly, fortnightly and monthly freesheets. A few are specific to the neighbourhood in which they're found, while others – such as gay weeklies the **Windy City Times** and the **Chicago Free Press** – are targeted at specific communities. Among the others are **Chicago Social**, a vehicle for advertisers and society photographers; **Chicago Women**, self-explanatory and yawnsome; and **UR Chicago**, a scrappy entertainment rag that pales next to the *Reader* and *Newcity*. Local paid-for magazines include the monthly **Chicago** magazine, an upscale, surprisingly cultured read, and **Where Chicago**, tilted at the tourist market and likely to be found on the coffee table in your hotel room (assuming your hotel room has a coffee table, of course).

Radio

Radio in Chicago isn't great. The major FM rock stations are bland and practically indistinguishable, with **WXRT** (93.1 FM), **WKQX** (101.1 FM) and **WTMX** (101.9 FM) the main offenders. Oldies may care to tune to **WUBT** (103.5 FM) or **WJMK** (104.3 FM), while fans of classic and '80s rock can take their pick between **WXXY** (103.1 FM), **WXCD** (94.7 FM), **WLUP** (97.9 FM) and **WCKG** (105.9 FM), the Chicago outlet for Howard Stern's morning rantings. Adult contemporary

sounds can be found all over the dials: the major stations are **WIND** (560 AM), **WMAQ** (670 AM), **WLIT** (93.9 FM) and **WNUA** (95.5 FM).

The more interesting sounds often emanate from the college stations: Northwestern University's **WNUR** (89.3 FM); Columbia College's **WCRX** (88.1 FM); **WDCB** (90.9 FM) from the College of DuPage; Loyola University's **WLUW** (88.7 FM); the University of Chicago's **WHPK** (88.5 FM); St Xavier University's **WXAV** (88.3 FM); and **WUIC** (89.5 FM) from the University of Illinois at Chicago. But the pick of the pack is **WBEZ** (91.5 FM), Chicago's public radio station. In addition to National Public Radio shows, it regularly features famous Chicago author and activist Studs Terkel on *Eight Forty-Eight*, broadcast from 9.30am to 11am, Monday to Friday.

Television

As the country's third-largest media market, Chicago is home to numerous TV stations. In addition to the local affiliates of the four major broadcast networks, namely – **WLS-Channel 7** (ABC), **WMAQ-Channel 5** (NBC), **WBBM-Channel 2** (CBS) and **WFLD-Channel 32** (Fox) – Chicago is home to both a local cable station (**CLTV-Channel 11**) and a national one (**WGN-9**).

But for all its size and importance, TV here offers little bang for its large advertising buck. News shows are virtually indistinguishable and tend

toward sensational coverage, and sports coverage is lacklustre. Only Chicago's talk shows – Oprah, Springer and Jenny Jones film here – seem to be thriving. The best local programming can be found on public television (**WTTW-Channel 11**).

Money

Each dollar ($) is divided into 100 cents (¢). Coins range from copper pennies (1¢) to silver nickels (5¢), dimes (10¢) and quarters (25¢), plus rarer half-dollar (50¢) and one dollar coins. A new 'golden' $1 coin was launched in early 2000.

Currency notes (bills) come in six denominations: $1, $5, $10, $20, $50 and $100, although the $100 is not accepted by all businesses.

ATMs

Automated Teller Machines (ATMs) or cashpoints are easy to find. Most will accept Mastercard and Visa credit cards (note that you'll be charged interest), selected debit cards including American Express and cash cards bearing the symbols of internationally recognised networks such as Cirrus or Plus. Use your usual PIN. Domestic users pay a stipulated charge; this is waived for international users, though their bank will add a fee that's worth finding out in advance since it often leaps up at certain thresholds.

If you want to find out the location of the nearest ATM, phone **Plus ATM Location Service** (1-800 843 7587) or **Cirrus** (1-800 424 7787).

Banks

American National Bank

120 S LaSalle Street, at W Monroe Street, the Loop (312 661 5000). CTA Quincy (Brown, Orange, Purple) or Monroe (Blue). **Open** 8.30am-4pm Mon-Fri. **Map** p305 H12. **Branches**: throughout the city.

Bank of America

231 S LaSalle Street, at W Adams Street, the Loop (312 828 2345). CTA Quincy (Brown, Orange, Purple). **Open** 8.30am-4pm Mon-Fri. **Map** p305 H12.

Bank One

35 W Wacker Drive, at N Dearborn Street, the Loop (312 732 1000). CTA Clark (Blue, Brown, Green, Orange, Purple). **Open** 8am-5pm Mon-Fri. **Map** p305 H11.

Citibank

100 S Michigan, at Monroe, the Loop (312 419 9002/automated teller 312 263 6660). **Open** *Counter service* 8am-4.30pm Mon-Fri. *Telephone enquiries* 24hrs daily. **Map** p305 H12.

Bureaux de change

A word of warning: stores that bill themselves as currency exchanges in Chicago will not help you exchange your currency. Currency exchanges in Chicago are basically cheque-cashing services and don't accept or change foreign currency. To exchange your foreign currency for US dollars, try one of the banks (*see above*) or the following genuine bureaux de change.

American Express

605 N Michigan Avenue, entrance E Ohio Street, Near North (312 435 2570). CTA Chicago (Red). **Open** 8.30am-6pm Mon-Fri; 9am-5pm Sat. **Map** p306 J10. **Branch**: 122 S Michigan Avenue, at E Adams Street, the Loop (312 435 2595).

Thomas Cook

19 S LaSalle Street, at W Madison Street, the Loop (312 807 4940). CTA Monroe (Blue). **Open** 9am-5.30pm Mon-Fri. **Map** p305 H12.

Credit cards

Most establishments in Chicago, whether they be restaurants, shops or theatres, will take at least one and usually more credit cards. The most widely accepted cards, in order, are Visa, Mastercard, American Express, Discover and Diners Club. If you lose your credit cards and/or travellers' cheques, call:

American Express *1-800 528 4800.*
AmEx travellers' cheques *1-800 221 7282.*
Diners Club *1-800 234 6377.*
Discover *1-800 347 2683.*
Mastercard *1-800 307 7309.*
Thomas Cook travellers' cheques *1-800 223 7373.*
Visa *1-800 336 8472.*

Tax

In Chicago, sales tax on the vast majority of goods is 8.75 per cent, not included in the price marked. The main exceptions are newspapers (tax-free) and central restaurants (9.75 per cent). For hotel rooms and services, though, tax rises to a nasty 14.9 per cent, while car rental is billed at a tax rate of 18 per cent.

Travellers' cheques

The majority of establishments in Chicago accept dollar travellers' cheques, including restaurants, bars, shops and hotels.

Opening hours

Listed below are some general guidelines on opening hours. However, the key word here is 'guidelines': hours are extremely variable in all cases.
Banks 8.30am-4pm Mon-Fri.
Bars 11am-2am daily.
Businesses 9am-5pm Mon-Fri.
Convenience stores 9am-11pm daily; many stores open 24hrs.
Post offices 8am-5pm Mon-Fri, plus Sat morning.
Shops 10am-6pm Mon-Sat; some stores open shorter hours Sun.

Police stations

You don't have to report non-emergency crimes in person: phone them in on **311** (or, from out of town, 312 746 6000). The details will be taken and any paperwork can be sent to you at home.

Chicago PD – First Precinct

1718 S State Street, at E 17th Street, Near South Side. Metra 18th Street. **Map** p304 H16. Chicago's most central police station. For details of local offices, call 312 744 4000.

Postal services

Post office opening hours in Chicago are usually 8am to 5pm Monday to Friday, with many branches also open on Saturday mornings. The main office is open 24 hours daily.

Stamps for standard letters weighing up to 1oz cost 33¢ within the US, 55¢ to Canada and $1 to all other countries. Postcards cost 22¢ (domestic) or 55¢ (international). US mailboxes are red, white and blue with the bald eagle logo on the front and side. For security reasons, mailings over a certain weight must be taken to a post office counter. There is usually a schedule of pick-ups and a list of restrictions inside the lid. Make sure you don't put mail into FedEx or other couriers' boxes.

For more information on the **US Postal Service**, head to www.usps.com.

Post offices

Main Post Office

433 W Harrison Street, at S Canal Street, Chicago, IL 60607 (1-800 275 8777). CTA Clinton (Blue). **Open** 24hrs daily. **Map** p305 G13.

Fort Dearborn

540 N Dearborn Street, at W Grand Avenue, Near North (1-800 275 8777). CTA Grand (Red). **Open** 7.30am-5pm daily. **Map** p307 H10.

Loop Station

211 S Clark Street, at W Adams Street, the Loop (1-800 275 8777). CTA Jackson (Blue). **Open** 7am-6pm Mon-Fri. **Map** p305 H12.

Ontario

227 E Ontario Street, at N St Clair Street, Near North (1-800 275 8777). CTA Grand (Red). **Open** 8am-6pm Mon-Fri. **Map** p306 J10.

Directory

Poste restante

If you have no fixed address while travelling and want to receive post when you are away, you can have it sent poste restante 'c/o General Delivery' to any post office with a zip code. You will need proof of identity (passport) in order to collect it.

Religion

Devout travellers are in luck in Chicago. There are places of worship for almost every denomination you can imagine (and a few you can't).

Baptist

Unity Fellowship Baptist Church
211 N Cicero Avenue, at W Maypole Avenue, West Side (773 287 0267). CTA Cicero (Green). **Services** 8.15am, 11.15am, 5pm Sun.

Catholic

Holy Name Cathedral
735 N State Street, at E Superior Street, Near North (312 787 8040). CTA Chicago (Red). **Services** 6am, 7am, 8am, 12.10pm, 5.15pm Mon-Fri; 8am, 12.10pm, 5.15pm, 7.30pm Sat; 7am, 8.15am, 9.30am, 11am, 12.30pm, 5.15pm Sun. **Map** p306 H10.

Old St Mary's Church
23 E Van Buren Street, at S State Street, the Loop (312 922 3444). CTA Library (Brown, Orange, Purple). **Services** 7.15am, 12.10pm Mon-Fri; noon, 5pm Sat; 8am, 10.30am, noon Sun. **Map** p305 H13.

Eastern Orthodox

St George Orthodox Cathedral
917 N Wood Street, at W Iowa Street, West Side (312 666 5179). CTA Chicago (Blue). **Services** Vespers 5pm Sat. *Service* 9.30am Sun.

Episcopal

Grace Episcopal Church
637 S Dearborn Street, at W Harrison Street, South Loop (312

922 1426). CTA Harrison (Red). **Services** 12.15pm Wed; 8am, 10am Sun. **Map** p305 H13.

Episcopal Church St James Cathedral
65 E Huron Street, at N Wabash Avenue, Near North (312 787 7360). CTA Chicago (Red). **Services** 12.10pm Mon, Tue, Thur, Fri; 12.10pm, 5.30pm Wed; 9am Sat; 8am, 9am, 11am Sun. **Map** p306 H10.

Jewish

Chicago Loop Synagogue
16 S Clark Street, at W Madison Street, the Loop (312 346 7370). CTA Monroe (Blue, Red). **Services** 8.05am, 1.05pm, 4.45pm Mon-Fri; 9am, 4.30pm Sat, Sun. **Map** p305 H12.

Chicago Sinai Congregation (Reform)
15 W Delaware Place, at N State Street, Gold Coast (312 867 7000). CTA Chicago (Red). **Services** 6.15pm Fri (year-round); 11am Sun (Sept-May). **Map** p306 H9.

Lutheran

First St Paul's Evangelical Lutheran Church
1301 N LaSalle Street, at W Goethe Street, Gold Coast (312 642 7172). CTA Clark/Division (Red). **Services** 7am, 7pm Wed; 8.30am, 11am Sun. **Map** p307 H8.

Methodist

Chicago Temple First United Methodist Church
77 W Washington Boulevard, at N Clark Street, the Loop (312 236 4548). CTA Washington (Brown, Orange, Purple). **Services** 5pm Sat; 8.30am, 11am Sun. **Map** p305 H12.

Muslim

Downtown Islamic Center
218 S Wabash Avenue, at E Jackson Boulevard, the Loop (312 939 9095). CTA Adams (Brown, Green, Orange, Purple) or Jackson (Red). **Open** 10.30am-5.30pm Mon-Fri. **Services** 1.30pm, 5.20pm Mon-Thur; noon Fri. **Map** p305 H12.

Presbyterian

Fourth Presbyterian Church
126 E Chestnut Street, at N Michigan Avenue, Near North (312 787 4570). CTA Chicago (Red). **Services** 8am, 9.30am, 11am, 6.30pm Sun. **Map** p306 J9.

Quaker

Fellowship of Friends
515 W Oak Street, at N Mohawk Street, Near North (312 944 4493). CTA Chicago (Brown, Purple). **Services** 11am Sun. **Map** p306 G9.

Safety & security

Safety in Chicago is pretty much a matter of common sense. Follow the same precautions as you would in any urban area and you should be alright. Among the dos and don'ts are:

● Don't draw attention to yourself by unfolding a huge map and looking lost.

● Don't leave your purse, pocketbook or wallet in a place where you could easily be pickpocketed (for example, in your back pocket, or in an undone bag).

● Do beware of hustlers: while one person is disturbing you from the front, another could already be half a block away with your cash and credit cards.

● Do leave valuables in a hotel safe if at all possible.

● Don't carry too much cash at any one time, and if you have multiple credit cards, leave one or more at the hotel in case of emergencies.

● Do avoid deserted areas late at night: the West Loop, for example.

In addition, there are some parts of town that are no-go areas for tourists. Among them are the Cabrini-Green housing complex (south of Division Street and west of Orleans); some parts of the West Side, especially around Little Italy; and parts of the South Side.

Study

It's probably only a matter of time before some marketing genius in the mayor's office comes up with a slogan like 'City of Big Learners'. The prevalence of educational establishments in Chicago is of obvious benefit to the city: not least because there are a lot of students who want a lot of places in which to drink, which boosts the local economy. Though there are plenty of bars downtown, students tend to hang out close to their schools.

Among the other colleges in Chicago not detailed below are the **School of the Art Institute**, **Columbia College**, **Wheaton College**, **North Park College** and **Illinois Benedictine University**.

Language schools

Berlitz Language Center
2 N LaSalle Street, at E Madison Street, the Loop (312 943 4262). CTA Washington (Brown, Orange, Purple). **Credit** AmEx, Disc, MC, V. **Map** p305 H12.

International Language Communication School
333 N Michigan Avenue, at the Chicago River, Near North (773 549 6441). CTA Grand (Red). **Credit** MC, V. **Map** p306 J11.

Universities & students' unions

DePaul University
1 E Jackson Boulevard, at N State Street, the Loop (773 325 7000/www.depaul.edu). Map p305 H13.
Students' union *2250 N Sheffield Street, at W Belden Avenue, Lincoln Park (773 325 7400).* **Map** p308 E5.
While not the most prestigious school in the city, DePaul University has it made when it comes to nightlife thanks to the Lincoln Park location of its oldest campus. There are clubs, bars and storefront theatres just littering the place. The natives – frat boys, many of them – can get restless at times, but there's

usually another, quieter spot just around the corner. The **John Barleycorn Memorial Pub** (*see p157*) and the **Red Lion Pub** (*see p158*) are both classic DePaul watering holes.

Loyola University Chicago
6525 N Sheridan Road, at W Devon Avenue, Far North (773 274 3000/www.luc.edu). CTA Loyola (Red, Purple).
Students' union *1125 W Loyola Avenue, at N Sheridan Road (773 508 8880). CTA Loyola (Red, Purple).*
The Chicago branch of Loyola University has about 14,000 students on its two campuses. The Water Tower campus is near the Gold Coast, but there's not much student housing down there and so very little campus life (though law students tend to throng across the street to **Flapjaws Saloon**, 22 E Pearson Street, at N State Street; 312 642 4848). The main campus is on the North Side lakeshore in Rogers Park. It's a diverse neighbourhood with a good selection of unpretentious bars such as **Hamilton's Pub** (6341 N Broadway, at W Rosemont Avenue; 773 764 8133).

Northwestern University
633 N Clark Street, at W Ohio Street, Near North (847 491 3741/www.northwestern.edu). CTA Foster (Purple).
Students' union *1999 S Campus Road (847 491 2301/ www.hereandnow.nwu.edu). CTA Foster (Purple).*
Like Loyola, Northwestern University is split between a north lakeshore and a downtown campus. Most of the almost 18,000 students, live on or near the school's Edenic, tree-lined main campus in Evanston. The most common complaint of students is the lack of serious nightlife up there, though **Pete Miller's Steakhouse** (1557 Sherman Avenue; 847 328 0399) is a great, though expensive, place for a Martini, a steak and some live jazz. Northwestern's Magnificent Mile campus has some lakeshore housing, and students there (mostly business and medical) tend to head up to the nearby Rush and Division bars.

University of Chicago
5801 S Ellis Avenue, at E 58th Street, Hyde Park (773 702 1234/ www.uchicago.edu). Metra 59th Street. **Map** p311 X17.
Students' union *Reynolds Club, 5706 S University Avenue, at E 57th Street, Hyde Park (773 702 9554).* **Map** p311 X17.

One of the most renowned educational institutions in the world, the University of Chicago is set in beautiful Hyde Park, known more for its museums and bookstores than its nightlife, though the **Woodlawn Tap** (1172 E 55th Street, at S Woodlawn Avenue; 773 643 5516) is one of the few notable bars here, not least because it keeps an encyclopedia and a compete Shakespeare on hand with which to settle disputes.

University of Illinois-Chicago
1200 W Harrison Street, at S Halsted Street, West Side (312 996 7000/www.uic.edu). CTA UIC-Halsted (Blue).
Students' union *Chicago Circle Center, 750 S Halsted Street, at W Polk Street, West Side (312 996 5000. CTA UIC-Halsted (Blue).*
The University of Illinois-Chicago was built a little to the west of the Loop in 1965 by Mayor Daley. Boasting some 25,000 students, it's now the largest school in the city. Unfortunately, Daley bulldozed a formerly vibrant community to make way for the school, and it's taken it a while to recover. A few blocks north is the West Loop neighbourhood with a thriving bar and restaurant scene.

Telephones

Dialling & codes

There are five area codes in the Chicago metropolitan area. Area code 312 covers downtown Chicago (roughly as far north, west and south as 1600 on the street grid); 773 covers the rest of the city; the northern suburbs are 847; the southern and western suburbs are 708; and the areas to the far west are 630.

Making a call

If you are calling within an area code, you don't need to dial it. Otherwise, you should dial 1, followed by the appropriate area code and a seven-digit number (this applies to all US and Canada numbers).

When calling Chicago from abroad, dial the international access code of the country from which you are calling (00 from the UK), followed by the US country code (1), followed by the area code and number (as before). Numbers prefaced by 1-800, 1-888 and 1-877 are toll-free internally. Numbers prefaced with 1-900 are charged at a premium rate.

If you encounter voicemail, note that the 'pound' key is the one marked # and the 'star' key *.

Directory

On automated answering systems, 0 may get you straight to an operator.

To call abroad from Chicago (or anywhere else in the States), dial the international access code (011), followed by the country code (44 for the UK; 64 New Zealand; 61 Australia; 49 Germany; 81 Japan – see the phone book for others) and then the area code and number.

If you want to make a collect (reverse charge) call, dial 0 for the operator before dialling the number you are trying to reach.

Operator services

Information numbers depend on the phone company, but 411 is always good for local numbers and usually for national numbers, too (or the correct information number). The operator can be reached on 0, while the international operator is on 00.

Public phones

To use a public phone, pick up the receiver, listen for a dialling tone and feed it change (35¢ for a local call); some phones ask you to dial first, and then assess the cost. Operator, directory and emergency calls are free. It is not advisable to use a payphone for long-distance or international calls, as a quarter (25¢) is the highest denomination a payphone will accept. A recorded voice will tell you how much you need to put in to complete the call.

It's worth remembering that in Chicago, calling a number that's only several blocks away can sometimes mean using an entirely different area code, which can cost at least $1. You may be better off using a phone card.

European-style prepaid phone cards that you insert directly into public phones are not available in the States. However, several phone companies provide charge cards, available from supermarkets, drugstores and convenience stores in various denominations.

Shop around for the longest talk-time for the lowest price. Don't just look at the price per minute to the area you think you'll be calling most: also check connection charges.

A phone card can also save you money if you're staying in a hotel. Many high-end hotels – and more than a few low-end ones – charge absurd rates for calls made from guestrooms, with charges getting more ludicrous the further away you're calling (international calls, for example, are impossibly dear). Sadly, they often charge a buck or so for the 1-800 calls you'll need to make to access your phone card (tip: not the case in a payphone or lobby phone).

Mobile phones

Pretty much everywhere in the Chicago metropolitan area is well covered for cellular phone service. If you're leaving town, you might experience some service difficulties in downstate Illinois or central Wisconsin. Foreign visitors should also note that Chicago's cellular phone network is not GSM-compatible, though their phone service provider may have options.

If you want to get cellular service while you're in town, check the *Yellow Pages* for dealers, or try these:

AT&T Wireless Service

235 W Monroe Street, at N Franklin Street, the Loop (312 920 0414/ technical support & customer service 1-800 888 7600). CTA Quincy *(Brown, Orange, Purple).* **Open** 8am-6pm Mon-Fri. **Map** p305 G12.

Cellular One

170 W Ontario Street, at N LaSalle Street, Near North (312 642 7800). CTA Grand (Red). **Open** 9am-6pm Mon-Fri; 10am-5pm Sat. **Map** p306 H10.

Time

Chicago operates under US Central Standard Time (CST), six hours behind Greenwich Mean Time (GMT) and one hour behind Eastern Standard Time (EST). The border between Eastern and Central Standard Times is just to the east: Michigan and most of Indiana are in on EST. From the first Sunday in April until the last Sunday in October 'Daylight Saving Time' puts the clocks forward an hour.

Tipping

First rule of tipping: don't be a tightwad. Waiters, bartenders, bellhops and the like are often paid a menial wage and many depend on tips to get by.

In general, tip bartenders and waiters 15 per cent or thereabouts. Cab drivers should also get around 15 per cent. Hotel staff also expect – and deserve – tipping. Bellhops should be given a buck a bag, while doormen, parking valets and chambermaids merit a

dollar or two (for the latter, leave it on the pillow each morning as you leave).

Toilets

Public toilets are few and far between in Chicago. Head instead to a shopping mall, a department store, a shop with a café attached (such as Borders) or a fast food outlet. Bars and restaurants can be a little sniffy unless you buy something while you're there.

Tourist information

Chicago Convention & Tourism Bureau

McCormick Place, 2301 S Lake Shore Drive, at Lake Michigan, South Side (312 567 8500/fax 312 567 8533/ www.chicago.il.org). Metra 23rd Street. **Open** 8am-5pm Mon-Fri. Information on conventions and, to a lesser extent, tourism in the city.

Chicago Cultural Center Visitors' Information Center

77 E Randolph Street, at N Michigan Avenue, the Loop (312 744 6630). CTA Randolph (Brown, Green, Orange, Purple) or Washington (Blue). **Open** 10am-7pm Mon-Wed; 10am-9pm Thur; 10am-6pm Fri; 10am-5pm Sat; 11am-5pm Sun. **Map** p305 J12. An essential stop for all visitors, the Cultural Center was built as the city's first public library in 1897. Pick up tourist information, free leaflets and maps or join one of several tours of the city. Art exhibitions and live shows are also often held here.

Chicago Office of Tourism

Chicago Cultural Center, 78 E Washington Boulevard, at N Michigan Avenue, the Loop (312 744 2400/1-877 244 2246/fax 312 744 2359/www.877Chicago.com). CTA Randolph (Brown, Green, Orange, Purple) or Washington (Blue). **Open** 10am-5pm Mon-Fri; noon-5pm Sat, Sun. **Map** p305 J12. Contact the Office of Tourism for a free visitor information pack on Chicago's events and attractions.

Chicago Water Works Visitors' Center

163 E Pearson Street, at N Michigan Avenue, Near North. CTA Chicago (Red). **Open** *Information* 7.30am-7pm daily. *Hot Tix* 10am-6pm Tue-Sat; 11am-5pm Sun. **Map** p306 J9.

Average temperatures

Month	High (°F/°C)	Low (°F/°C)
January	32/0	18/-8
February	34/1	20/-7
March	43/6	29/-2
April	55/13	40/4
May	65/18	50/10
June	75/24	60/16
July	81/27	66/19
August	79/26	65/18
September	73/23	58/14
October	61/16	47/8
November	47/8	34/1
December	36/2	23/-5

Located in a 19th-century pumping station, the recently renovated visitors' centre includes a tourist information booth; the City of Chicago Store, which sells souvenirs and collectibles; Hot Tix, which offers half-price tickets for over 125 theatres in the Chicago area (*see p240* **Theatre, Dance & Comedy**), and a restaurant.

Illinois Bureau of Tourism

Suite 3400, James R Thompson Center, 100 W Randolph Street, at N LaSalle Street, the Loop (1-800 226 6632/312 814 4732/www. enjoy illinois.com). CTA Washington (Brown, Orange, Purple). **Open** *1-800 number 24hrs daily; office & 312 number 8.30am-5pm Mon-Fri.* **Map** p305 H11.
Details on tourism and attractions in the state of Illinois.

Visas & immigration

Under the Visa Waiver Programme, citizens of the UK, Japan, Australia, New Zealand and all west European countries (except for Portugal, Greece and the Vatican City) do not need a visa for stays in the US of less than 90 days – business or pleasure – if they have a passport valid for the full 90-day period (six months is safer) and a return ticket.

Canadians and Mexicans do not need visas but must have legal proof of residency. All other travellers need visas.

Note that any country can change its immigration regulation at any time. Before you commit to a trip, check visa requirements with your nearest US embassy or consulate – find it on www.embassyworld.com.

If you do need a visa, send in your application at least three weeks before you plan to travel. Visas required more urgently should be applied for via the travel agent booking your ticket.

US Embassy Visa Information (UK only)

Recorded information 0891 200 290 (50p per minute)/advice & appointments 0991 500 590 (£1.50 per minute)/fax 020 7495 5012.

Weights & measures

The US uses the imperial system. Here are a few basic metric equivalents.

1 foot = 0.3048 metre
1 mile = 1.6093 kilometre
1 square yard = 0.836 square metre
1 pound = 0.4536 kilogramme
1 pint (16fl oz) = 0.4732 litre

When to go

Climate

Weather in Chicago is, to put it mildly, changeable. For average temperatures see the box on the left, but also factor in that summer can be uncomfortably humid, winter brings close to 40 inches of snow and, year round, there's the wind to contend with. Whatever the season, prepare for anything.

Public holidays

New Year's Day (1 Jan); **Martin Luther King, Jr Day** (3rd Mon in Jan); **Presidents' Day** (3rd Mon in Feb); **Memorial Day** (last Mon in May); **Independence Day** (4 July); **Labor Day** (1st Mon in Sept); **Columbus Day** (2nd Mon in Oct); **Veterans' Day** (11 Nov); **Thanksgiving** (4th Thur in Nov); **Christmas Day** (25 Dec).

Women

In so far as Chicago is a safe city, it's a safe city for women (*see p288* **Safety**). However, when walking the streets at night – especially alone, which is not ideal – you'd do well to take as much care as you'd take in any big city: avoid unlit and deserted streets and be alert for people trailing you. When travelling on trains late at night, choose a busy carriage.

Chicago Rape Crisis Hotline

1-888 293 2080. **Open** 24hrs daily.
Rape crisis counselling, and referrals to other organisations.

National Organization for Women (NOW)

Suite 400, 200 N Michigan Avenue, at E Lake Street, the Loop (hotline 312 578 9351/www.chicagonow.org). CTA Adams (Brown, Green, Orange, Purple). **Open** *Hotline 24hrs daily.* **Map** p305.
A group devoted to furthering feminist issues and causes.

Working in the US

Foreigners seeking work in the US must enlist a US company to sponsor them for an H-1 visa, which permits the holder to work in the US for five years. It will also have to convince the Immigration department that no American could do the job. Contact your American embassy for details.

Further Reference

Books

Fiction

Nelson Algren
The Neon Wilderness (1947)
This collection of short stories made Algren's name when it emerged, and set the scene for novels such as *The Man with the Golden Arm* (1949).
Saul Bellow *The Adventures of Augie March* (1953)
A coming-of-age tale of sorts, and one of several Chicago novels by Bellow; check out, too, the magisterial *Humboldt's Gift* (1975).
Theodore Dreiser
Sister Carrie (1900)
Perhaps the first great Chicago novel, a tale of the corruption of a young woman in the big bad city.
James T Farrell
Studs Lonigan (1935)
Farrell's three Lonigan books, collected in one University of Illinois-published paperback, tell of the coming of age of an Irish-American in Chicago in the early 20th century.
Eugene Izzi *The Criminalist* (1996)
Izzi was found hanging outside the window of his Loop office in 1996, a situation that would, were he still alive, have made a great premise for one of his gritty city crime novels.
Sara Paretsky
Indemnity Only (1982)
The first outing for Paretsky's 'tec creation VI Warshawski, who also crops up in the more recent *Total Recall* (2001) and short-story set *Windy City Blues* (1995).
Scott Turow
The Laws of Our Fathers (1996)
One of many blockbusting page-turners from the Chicago lawyer turned author; others include *Presumed Innocent* (1987) and *Personal Injuries* (1999).
Richard Wright *Native Son* (1940)
A prescient tale of murder and racial issues in Chicago.

Non-fiction

Jane Addams
20 Years at Hull-House (1910)
An autobiography of sorts from the pioneering social reformer.
Eliot Asinof
Eight Men Out (1963)
The story of how the Chicago White Sox threw the 1919 World Series, ably told.
Simone de Beauvoir
Beloved Chicago Man (1997)
The French writer's letters to one-time beau Nelson Algren make for fascinating reading.

Gwendolyn Brooks
Selected Poems (1963)
An excellent collection of poetry from the first African-American winner of the Pulitzer Prize.
Sandra Cisneros
Loose Woman (1994)
Poems by the author of the fine *A House on Mango Street*.
Adam Cohen, Elizabeth Taylor
American Pharaoh (2000)
A real missed opportunity, but despite its many faults (it's lazily written and fairly incomplete), this biography of Daley has enough in it to keep the reader interested.
Nadine Cohodas
Spinning Blues into Gold (2000)
The story of Chess Records has been waiting to be told for years; Cohodas has done a fine job telling it.
Robert Cromie
The Great Chicago Fire (1958)
How the city lost its innocence. And most of its buildings too.
Peter Golenbock *Wrigleyville* (1996)
Golenbock's history of the Chicago Cubs is a highly entertaining read.
Ben Hecht and Charles MacArthur *The Front Page* (1928)
A classic stage work co-authored by a notable local hack.
LeAlan Jones and Lloyd Newman *Our America* (1997)
Subtitled 'Life and Death on Chicago's South Side', *Our America* tells of life in Chicago's ghettos as seen through the eyes of two teenaged residents.
Richard Lindberg
To Serve and Collect (1991)
A splendidly titled survey of police corruption in Chicago between 1855 and 1960.
David Garrard Lowe
Lost Chicago (rev.2000)
A wonderful book detailing and illustrating, with judicious use of old and rare photographs, some marvellous Chicago buildings that didn't survive the wrecking ball.
David Mamet *Mamet Plays 1* (1994)
A selection of stage works, including *Sexual Perversity in Chicago* (1977) and *American Buffalo* (1976).
Donald L Miller
City of the Century (1996)
'The epic of Chicago', reads the wonderfully appropriate subtitle for this, the definitive history of the city.
Mike Royko *One More Time* (1999)
A collection of articles by the grand old man of Chicago journalism. Also worth a look is his exhilarating biography of former mayor Richard J Daley, *Boss* (1971).
Carl Sandburg
Selected Poems (1996)
This collection includes the classic *Chicago Poems* (1916).

Eric Schlosser
Fast Food Nation (2001)
Schlosser's classic tract is kind of 21st-century update of sorts to Sinclair's *The Jungle*, and includes a fascinating section on Chicago's meatpacking industry.
Richard Schneirov et al (eds)
The Pullman Strike and the Crisis of the 1890s (1999)
One of the city's defining moments gets the essay treatment in this surprisingly engrossing book.
Upton Sinclair *The Jungle* (1906)
Sinclair's masterpiece, which caused a major sensation when it was published, is set in the Chicago stockyards at the turn of the century.
Alice Sinkevitch (ed)
AIA Guide to Chicago (1993)
'AIA' stands for the American Institute of Architects, which, with the Chicago Architecture Foundation, is behind this excellent survey of the city's notable buildings. As architectural companions go, this one is among the best.
Bob Skilnik *The History of Beer and Brewing in Chicago 1833-1978* (1999)
A somewhat slight but largely engrossing history of suds in this most boozy of cities.
David Starkey, Richard Guzman (eds)
Smokestacks and Skyscrapers (1999)
Chicago Writing 101, with extracts from works by over 70 Chicago writers. Useful.
Studs Terkel
Division Street: America (1967)
One of many worthwhile books from the country's premier social historian, and a local legend: others include *Coming of Age* (1995) and *Working* (1974).
Bill Veeck with Ed Linn
Veeck As In Wreck (1962)
The autobiography of the legendary one-legged baseball executive who planted the ivy at Wrigley Field before later buying the White Sox. One of the most entertaining sports books ever.
Lynne Warren et al (ed)
Art in Chicago 1945-1995 (1996)
Exactly what you'd expect: a survey of over 100 artists who worked in Chicago during the 50 years following World War II.

Films

About Last Night...
dir. *Edward Zwick* (1986)
The singles scene on Division Street forms the basis for this lame 1980s flick based on David Mamet's play *Sexual Perversity in Chicago*.

Directory

Backdraft *dir. Ron Howard* (1991)
Fire in Chicago, albeit 120 years after
the biggest fire of them all.
The Blues Brothers
dir. John Landis (1980)
Feeble sketch extended to breaking
point or riotously funny musical
romp? Either way, Chicago should
get a starring credit alongside John
Belushi and Dan Aykroyd.
The Color of Money
dir. John Hughes (1986)
Paul Newman and Tom Cruise shoot
some stick in an assortment of North
Side pool halls in this follow-up to
The Hustler.
Eight Men Out
dir. John Sayles (1988)
Sayles' retelling of the Black Sox tale
succeeds despite its treacle-thick
sympathies for 'Shoeless' Joe Jackson.
Ferris Bueller's Day Off
dir. John Hughes (1986)
Matthew Broderick bunks off school
to hit the Art Institute, Wrigley Field
and countless other local landmarks.
'Bueller…? Bueller…? Bueller…?'.
The Fugitive
dir. Andrew Davis (1993)
Harrison Ford on the run.
Go Fish *dir. Rose Troche* (1994)
A winning Chicago-set romantic
comedy with a twist: it's set on the
lesbian scene.
Hardball *dir. Brian Robbins* (2001)
Keanu Reeves stars as a bum who
takes over a Little League team from
the projects of Cabrini-Green. Daniel
Coyle's book was better.
Hellcab *dir. Mary Cybulski
& John Tintori* (1998)
A nice concept, this – 14 hours in the
life of a Chicago cab driver, with the
action dependent on the stories his
passengers have to tell – but one that
doesn't quite come off.
**Henry: Portrait of a Serial
Killer** *dir. John McNaughton* (1986)
A truly hideous no-budget vérité
chiller. If you see anyone on Lower
Wacker Drive claiming their car has
broken down, just keep driving.
High Fidelity
dir. Stephen Frears (2000)
Needless but surprisingly successful
translation of Nick Hornby's London-
set novel to Chicago.
Hoop Dreams
dir. Steve James (1994)
Enthralling documentary following
two young Michael Jordan wannabes
in Chicago.
My Best Friend's Wedding
dir. PJ Hogan (1997)
Julia Roberts and Cameron Diaz find
love (well, kinda) in the Windy City.
Ordinary People
dir. Robert Redford (1980)
Redford's directorial debut is a little
overcooked, but the actors – Donald
Sutherland and Mary Tyler Moore
chief among them – carry it through.
Risky Business
dir. Paul Brickman (1983)

A ludicrous plot – Tom Cruise plays
a teenager on the make, Rebecca de
Mornay his hooker acquaintance –
is saved by sharp scripting and
judicious use of Chicago locations.
Running Scared
dir. Peter Hyams (1986)
Billy Crystal, now officially The
Nicest Man in Hollywood, stars with
Gregory Hines in this comic cop flick.
The Untouchables
dir. Brian de Palma (1987)
Competent, Costner-starring retelling
of the Capone-Ness battles of the '20s.

Music

Big Black
Songs About Fucking (1987)
Grim and grubby, fierce and
fearsome. Leader Steve Albini has
gone on to produce a staggering
number of indie notables.
Chicago Transit Authority
Chicago Transit Authority (1969)
After a name change, they carved out
a career as purveyors of hideous soft-
rock ballads. But Chicago's debut –
nearest touchstone Blood, Sweat &
Tears – is a cracker.
Felix Da Housecat
Kittenz and Thee Glitz (2001)
As a teenager, Felix Stallings, Jr was
a protégé of the legendary DJ Pierre.
As an adult, he's making some of the
most thrilling dance records around.
Robbie Fulks
Country Love Songs (1996)
As his live show illustrates, Fulks
defies categorisation, but this first
record is an alt.country landmark.
The Handsome Family
In The Air (2000)
The most consistent record from
husband-and-wife duo Brett and
Rennie Sparks, country with more
twists than Chubby Checker.
Curtis Mayfield *Superfly* (1972)
A revelatory piece of movie scoring,
and a Blaxploitation classic. His
debut *Curtis*, made two years earlier,
is a masterpiece of politico-soul.
Liz Phair *Exile In Guyville* (1993)
A startling rethink of the Stones'
Exile On Main Street, an alt.rock
classic of sorts. She's not come close
to matching it since.
Tortoise *Standards* (2001)
The most accessible album from the
post-rock doyennes. The earlier *TNT*
makes a fine companion piece.
Wilco *Yankee Hotel Foxtrot* (2002)
The record that saw Jeff Tweedy, a
founder member of Belleville, Illinois
combo Uncle Tupelo, finally shed the
alt.country tag. The cover is a picture
of the Marina City towers.
Various *Chicago 2018…*
It's Gonna Change (2000)
A fine survey of the city's alternative
scene, with contributions from
Tortoise, Jim O'Rourke and Ken
Vandermark, among others.

Various *Chicago House* (1996)
Marshall Jefferson, Phuture and a
raft of others appear on this 3-CD set,
a perfect summary of the scene that
revolutionised dance in the 1980s.
Various *The Chess Story
1947-1975* (1999)
Deep breath… 15 CDs, 335 tracks…
Everything you ever wanted to know
about Chess Records but were afraid
to ask. Essential.

Websites

http://chi.yahoo.com
A directory of Chicago information
and links, including links to the
online *Yellow Pages* and *Mapquest*'s
terrifically useful online city maps.
www.chicagoreader.com
Locally, the *Reader*'s website is
used mainly for apartment-hunting.
However, also good is the Restaurant
Finder, which allows you to search for
eateries by neighbourhood, cuisine,
price and distance from more than 200
theatres, clubs, cinemas and the like.
www.chicagotribune.com
The city's flagship newspaper site
boasts its best news website. Most of
the regular paper's content is posted
online, along with up-to-the-minute
news and sports.
www.ci.chi.il.us
The city's homepage is helpful and
easy to navigate, and includes a
seasonal guide to Chicago festivals,
a city map, links to O'Hare and
Midway airports and a list of special
events in town.
**www.geocities.com/Hollywood/
Lot/8254/shitcago.html**
Aka '101 Reasons Why Chicago
Sucks'. Among them: 'The city shuts
down at, like, 7pm'; 'Sports-related
riots every time one of the sucky
teams wins a game'; and 'Smashing
Pumpkins'. Ho hum.
www.metromix.com
The *Chicago Tribune*'s web-based
entertainment guide, and the best
Chicago resource on the internet.
What really makes the site valuable
is its full use of the internet's
potential. Dependable reviews of
practically every nightclub, bar and
restaurant in the city are easy to find,
while concert and museum listings
are available and ticket bookings can
be handled online. A must-visit.
www.newcitychicago.com
An online version of the weekly
freesheet, with plenty of sparky
comment and listings content to get
your teeth into. There's also a free
web-based email service on the site.
www.transitchicago.com
Everything you ever wanted to know
about the Chicago Transit Authority,
including downloadable system
maps (in PDF format), details of fares
and passes and information on
timetables for trains and buses.

Directory

Index

Note: page numbers in **bold** indicate section(s) giving key information on topic; *italics* indicate illustrations.

abortion 284
accommodation *see* hostels; hotels
Addams, Jane **11**, 94, 97, **111**
Adler, Dankmar **25**, 100
Adler Planetarium 16, *81*, **81-82**
African American history **14**,121, 122-123, 192
  race riots 13-14, 17-18, *18*
Agam, Yaacov
  Communication X9 74
age policies 228, **281**
AIDS advice & care 284
AIDS Walk 215
air show 191
air trips, children's 195
airports 278
  lost property 285
Alcoholics Anonymous 284
Algren, Nelson **33-34**, 117, 163
Allstate Arena 219
Alta Vista Terrace 29
ambulance 283
American Automobile Association 280
American football 233
American Girl Place 186, **196**
American Theater Company 241
amusement parks 108, 259, 275-276
Andersonville **106**, 144, 210, 211
  Midsommerfest 189
antiques 164-165
  markets 183
Aon Center **30**, 74
aquarium **84**, 194
Aragon Ballroom 219
Archbishop's Residence 96
architecture **24-32**, 85, 86, 89, 90
  art deco **29**, 97, 116
  Astor Street **96-97**, *98*
  Beaux Arts 26
  bookshop 167
  Chicago Plan 26
  Chicago School 25-26
  Chicago Window 26
  Columbus, Indiana 257, 258
  contemporary 31-32
  International Style 29-31
  Old Town Triangle 100
  Prairie Style **26**, 119, 120, 123, 255-256
  shop 181
  ten tallest buildings 30
  tours 32, **66**, 86
  see also Wright, Frank Lloyd
Armour, Philip **7**, 10
Armstrong, Louis 14, *14*
Around the Coyote 209
Arrigo Park 112
art
  apprentice work for sale 181
  festivals & fairs 209
  galleries 124, **204-209**
    the best 205
  tours 205
  murals 113
  public 74-75

supplies 165
  see also under museums
Art Institute of Chicago 26, 78, **79-80**
  children's activities 79-80, 194
  Lions (by Kemey) 75
  shop 181
Astor Street **96-97**, *98*
AT&T Center 30
Athenaeum Theatre 245, **248**
ATMs 286-287
audio equipment 171
Auditorium Building & Theatre 25, 77, **241**

b

babysitters 193
bags 177-178
bakeries 112, **178-179**
Bank One Plaza 30
banks 287
bars & pubs 95, 100, 103, 105, 109, 116, 117, 141, **150-163**
  the best 150
  champagne bar (Pops) 224
  gay & lesbian 212-214
  Goose Island 160
  hotel bars 57
  piano bars 154-155
  sports bars 150, 153, 157, 158, 161
  wine bar (Webster's) 159
  see also p299 bars index
baseball **233-234**, 259, 269-270
basketball **234**, 259
  courts 235-236
Batcolumn 70, **70**
Baum, L Frank 36, 77, 103, 195
beaches 94, 98, 259, 263, 265
  volleyball 239
beauty products & services 182
Bed & Breakfast Chicago 44
beer 180
breweries 268, 269, 274, 275
Bellow, Saul 34
Beman, Solon Spencer 11, 25
Ben-Hur 261, 262
Berghoff 73, **150**, *151*
  Oktoberfest 191
Berrien County 250, **263-264**
bicycle hire 101, **237**
billiards 37, 161, **239**
Billie Creek Village, Indiana 260-261, 262
Biograph Theatre 103
Black History Month 192
Black Panthers 18
Bloomingdale's 168
Blue Chicago 42, **222**
blues 39-42
  archives/Hall of Fame 80
  festival 225
  Maxwell Street 110
  museum 85-86
  record shops 183
  venues 42, **222-223**
Blues Brothers, The 19, 37, **38**, *198*
Blues Heaven Foundation 42, **85-86**
boat trips & cruises 66, **68**, 94, 265, 268

boating **236**, 261, 265
  events 190, 192
book fairs 98, 189
bookshops 34, 100, 124, **165-167**, 181
  gay & lesbian 216-217
  used & antiquarian 80, **167**
bowling 161, **236**
Boystown 104, 210
Briar Street Theatre 244
Bronzeville 14
Brookfield Zoo *119*, **119**
Brooks, Gwendolyn 35
Bucktown 114
  bars 162-163
  clubs 232
  restaurants 146-149
  shops (index) 185
Bud Billiken Day Parade & Picnic 190
Buddhist Temple, Midwest **99**, *99*
Buddhist Temple of Chicago festival 189
bureaux de change 287
Burnham, Daniel 12, 16, 25, 26
Burroughs, Edgar Rice 119
buses 278-279
  Greyhound 250, **278**
  Pace 280
  tours 68
business services 281-282
buttons 171
Byrne, Jane 19, 38

c

Cabrini-Green housing development 23, 38, **99**
Cadillac Palace 241
Café Brauer 101
Calder, Alexander
  Flamingo 75
  Universe 69
candles 182
canoeing 261, 262, 265
Capone, Al 13, 14, 15, 103, 105, 224
car hire 280
Carbide & Carbon Building 29, 73
carriage rides 91, 238
cars & driving 280
  Auto Show 192
  out of town routes
  Illinois 252, 254, 256
  Indiana 259, 260, 262
  Michigan 264, 265
  Wisconsin 267, 272, 274, 275, 276
Carson Pirie Scott 168
  architecture 26, 73, 168
casinos 259, 260, **261**
cathedrals
  Holy Name 88, 288
  Holy Trinity Orthodox 115
  St George Orthodox 288
  St James 88
  St Nicholas Ukrainian Catholic 115
  St Volodymyr's Orthodox 115,115
Cedarburg, Wisconsin 270
Celtic Fest Chicago 225
Cermak, Anton 'Tony' 15-16

Chagall, Marc *74*, **75**
Chaplin, Charlie 36
Checkerboard Lounge 42, **222**
Chess Records **40-42**, 85
Chicago Academy of Sciences 101-103
Chicago Air & Water Show 191
Chicago Architecture Foundation & Center **26**, 75
  shop 181
  tours 32, **66**
Chicago Auto Show 192
Chicago Bears **233**, *237*
Chicago Blackhawks 234
Chicago Blues Festival 225
Chicago Board of Trade 29, **71**
  Options Exchange 71
Chicago Boat, RV & Outdoors Show 192
Chicago Botanic Garden 108
Chicago Bulls 234
Chicago Carifete 190
Chicago Center for the Performing Arts **244**, 247
Chicago Children's Museum 94, *194*, **194**
Chicago Convention & Tourism Bureau 291
Chicago Cubs 104-106, 153, **233**, *234*, **234**
Chicago Cultural Center 26, 74, *77*, **77**, **201**
  Preston-Bradley Hall 226
  Visitors' Center 290
Chicago Daily News Building 29
'Chicago Eight' trial 18
Chicago Fire (soccer team) 235
Chicago Garden & Flower Show 188
Chicago Genealogical Society 98
Chicago Green City Market 180
Chicago Greeter programme 22-23, **68**
Chicago Historical Society 100
Chicago Jazz Festival 225
Chicago Kings 212-213
Chicago Mercantile Exchange 69-70
Chicago Office of Tourism 188, **290**
  tours 68
Chicago Playworks for Families & Young Audiences 197
Chicago Shakespeare Theater 94, **241**
Chicago Sun-Times 202, **285**
  building 90
Chicago Symphony Orchestra 224
  shop 182
Chicago Theater 26, 73, **241**
Chicago Theatre Company 241
Chicago Theological Seminary 124
  bookshop 166
Chicago Transit Authority 13, **278-279**
Chicago Tribune 202, **285**
Chicago Water Works 90-91
  Visitors' Centre 290
Chicago White Sox 233-234
childcare 193
children's attractions 193-197
  admittance to cinemas 199
  amusement parks 108, 259, 275-276
  Art Institute 79-80, 194

Advertisers' Index

Pleas refer to the relevant pages for addresses
and telephone numbers.

Place of interest and/or entertainment	☐
Railway stations	☐
Parks	☐
Hospitals/universities	☐
Neighbourhood	LOOP
Metra Station	Ⓜ
CTA Station . . . . Clark	≡
(Colour designates line)	

Maps

Chicago Overview

PETERSON AVE - 6000N

N LINCOLN AVE

N BROADWAY ST

N RIDGE ST

W FOSTER AVE - 5200N

N ASHLAND AVE

North Branch Chicago River

W LAWRENCE AVE - 4800N

W MONTROSE AVE - 4400N

N PULASKI RD

N KEDZIE AVE

N LINCOLN AVE

N SHERIDAN RD

N CLARENDON AVE

Lake

See Pages 308-9

W IRVING PARK RD - 4000N

W ADDISON ST - 3600N

N KIMBALL AVE

N ELSTON AVE

N WESTERN AVE

N DAMEN AVE

N BROADWAY ST

Michigan

Belmont Harbor

W BELMONT AVE - 3200N

N CLARK ST

N MILWAUKEE AVE

W DIVERSEY AVE

W DIVERSEY PKWY - 2800N

90

94

Lincoln Park

W FOLLERTON AVE - 2400N

N CALIFORNIA AVE

N KEDZIE BLVD

N LINCOLN AVE

See Pages 306-7

W ARMITAGE AVE - 2000N

N CLYBOURN AVE

N PULASKI RD

W NORTH AVE - 1600N

Humboldt Park

N HALSTED ST

N STATE PKWY

W DIVISION ST - 1200N

See Page 310

W CHICAGO AVE - 800N

See Pages 304-5

W LAKE ST

Garfield Park

N HOMAN AVE

SACRAMENTO BLVD

W WASHINGTON BLVD

W WARREN BLVD

W MADISON ST - 1N

N CALIFORNIA AVE

N MICHIGAN AVE

Grant Park

290

S OGDEN AVE W

S MORGAN AVE

S RACINE AVE

W ROOSEVELT RD - 1200S

Douglas Park

S WESTERN AVE

S BLUE ISLAND AVE

W 15TH PL

S STATE ST

W 16TH ST - 1600W

W 18TH ST

W OGDEN AVE

✈ *Merrill C Meigs*

W CERMAK RD - 2200S

W 26TH ST

S CALIFORNIA AVE

S DAMEN AVE

W 31ST ST

E 31ST CHI

W 31ST ST

55

W 35TH ST

E 35TH ST

S COTTAGE GROVE AVE

S PULASKI RD

S ARCHER AVE

W PERSHING RD

90

S KING DR

94

S MICHIGAN AVE

E 43RD ST

W 43RD ST

S ASHLAND AVE

S HALSTED ST

S LAKE PARK AVE

W 47TH ST

S WESTERN BLVD

S DAMEN AVE

W 47TH ST

E 47TH ST

See Page 311

W 51ST ST

S STATE ST

E 51ST ST

E HYDE PARK BLVD

S KEDZIE AVE

S CALIFORNIA AVE

Washington Park

S WOODLAWN AVE

S COTTAGE GROVE AVE

E 55TH ST

Jackson Park

W 55TH ST

W GARFIELD BLVD

W 59TH ST

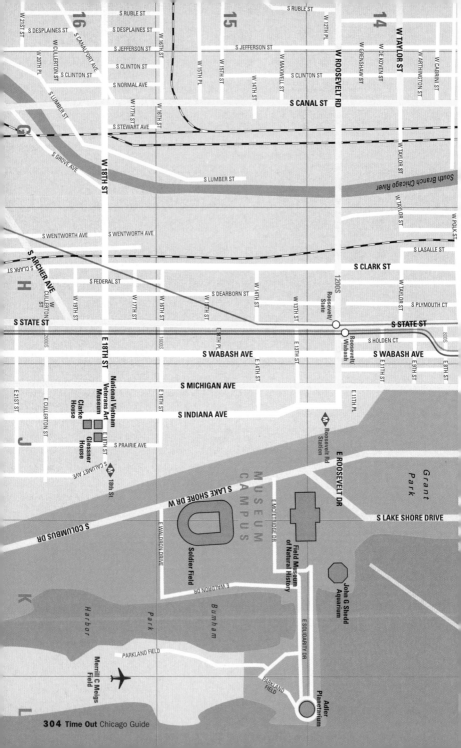

S RUBLE ST
S RUBLE ST
W 12TH PL
14
W TAYLOR ST
W TAYLOR ST

S DESPLAINES ST
S DESPLAINES ST

16
S DESPLAINES ST
S JEFFERSON ST
S JEFFERSON ST
W GRENSHAW ST
W DE KOVEN ST
W ARTHINGTON ST
W CABRINI ST

S CANALPORT AVE
W CULLERTON ST
S CLINTON ST
S CLINTON ST
W 15TH PL
W 15TH ST
W 15TH ST
W MAXWELL ST
W ROOSEVELT RD
S CLINTON ST

W 20TH PL
S NORMAL AVE
W 14TH ST
S CANAL ST

S LUMBER ST
W 17TH AVE
W 16TH ST
W 14TH ST

C
W STEWART AVE
S GROVE AVE

W 18TH ST
S LUMBER ST
S Branch Chicago River

W TAYLOR ST

S WENTWORTH AVE
S WENTWORTH AVE
W TAYLOR ST
W POLK ST

S ARCHER AVE
S CLARK ST
S CLARK ST
S LASALLE ST
S PLYMOUTH CT

S CLARK ST
W CULLERTON ST
S FEDERAL ST
W 19TH ST
S DEARBORN ST
W 14TH ST
W 13TH ST
W TAYLOR ST
S HOLDEN CT

H
1200 S
Roosevelt/
State

S STATE ST
S STATE ST

2000 S
W 17TH ST
W 16TH ST
W 15TH ST
E 14TH PL
E 13TH ST
Roosevelt/
Wabash

E 18TH ST
1600 S
S WABASH AVE
E 14TH ST
S WABASH AVE
E 11TH ST
E 9TH ST
E 8TH ST

E 21ST ST
E CULLERTON ST
S MICHIGAN AVE
E 16TH ST

J
National Vietnam Veterans Art Museum
Clarke House
S INDIANA AVE
E 11TH PL

Glessner House
E 18TH ST
S PRAIRIE AVE
S CALUMET AVE
18th St
M Roosevelt Rd Station
E ROOSEVELT DR

S LAKE SHORE DR W
Grant Park

S COLUMBUS DR
MUSEUM CAMPUS
E MCFETRIDGE DR
E ROOSEVELT DR

E WALDRON DRIVE
S LAKE SHORE DRIVE

K
Harbor
Park
Burnham
Soldier Field
E WALDRON DR
Field Museum of Natural History
John G Shedd Aquarium

PARKLAND FIELD

Merrill C Meigs Field
PARKLAND FIELD
E SOLIDARITY DR
Adler Planetarium

L

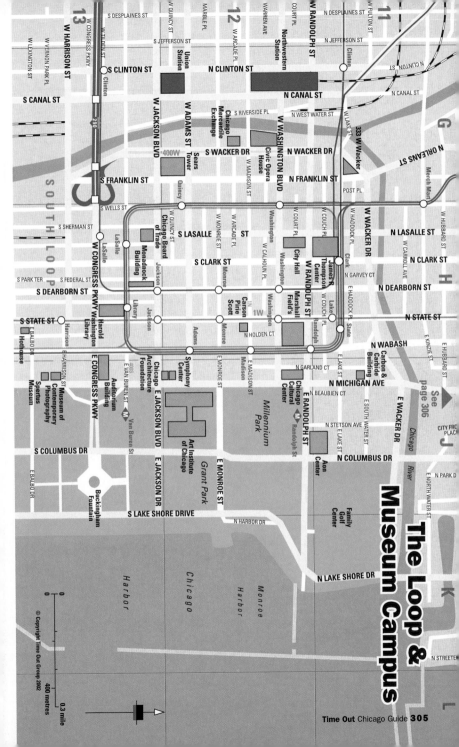

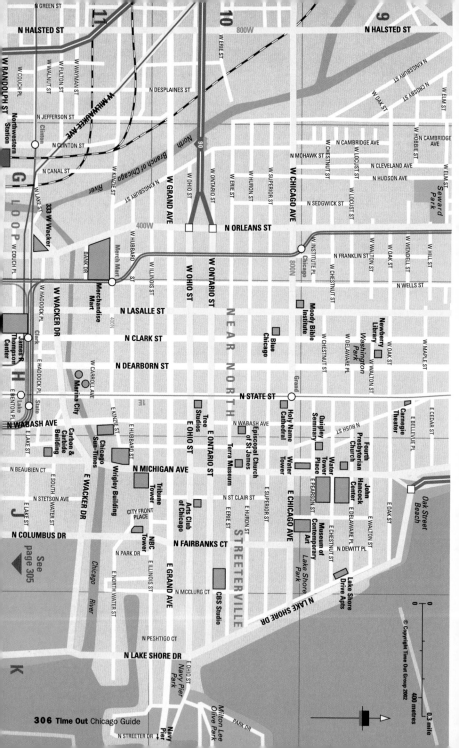

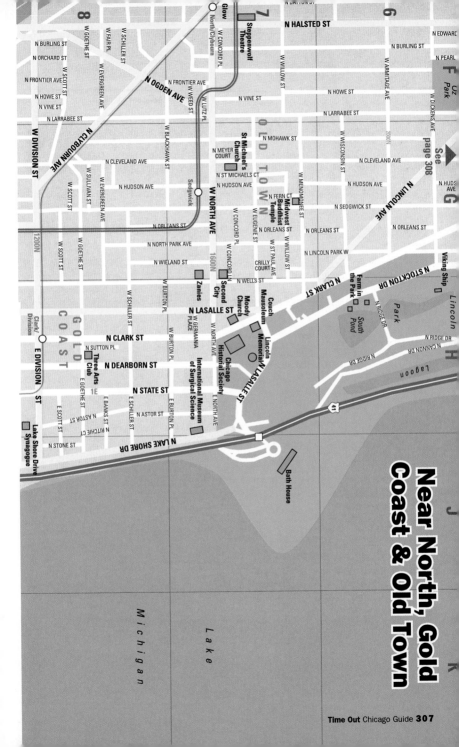

Near North, Gold Coast & Old Town

N HALSTED ST

N BURLING ST

N ORCHARD ST

N FRONTIER AVE

N HOWE ST

N VINE ST

N LARRABEE ST

W DIVISION ST

W SCOTT ST

W SCOTT ST

N CLYBOURN AVE

N OGDEN AVE

W GOETHE ST
W SCHILLER ST
W FAIR PL
W EVERGREEN AVE
W GOETHE ST
W SULLIVAN ST
W EVERGREEN AVE
W SCOTT ST

Glow
North/Clybourn

Steppenwolf Theatre

W CONCORD PL
N CONCORD PL
W WEED ST
W LUTZ PL

N BLACKHAWK ST
N CLEVELAND AVE
N HUDSON AVE

N ORLEANS ST

N NORTH PARK AVE
N WIELAND ST

Sedgwick

W NORTH AVE

1600N

1200N

Clark/
Division

E DIVISION ST

GOLD COAST

W SCHILLER ST
W BURTON PL

N SUTTON PL
Three Arts
Club

N CLARK ST

N DEARBORN ST

N STATE ST

1E

N GOETHE ST
E GOETHE ST
E BANKS ST
E SCHILLER ST
E SCOTT ST
E BURTON PL

N RITCHIE CT
N ASTOR ST
N STONE ST

Lake Shore Drive
Synagogue

N WILLOW ST

N HOWE ST

N LARRABEE ST

O L D   T O W N

N MOHAWK ST

St Michael's
Church

N MEYER
COURT
N ST MICHAELS CT
N HUDSON AVE

W CONCORD PL
W EUGENIE ST

N NORTH PARK AVE

Midwest
Buddhist
Temple

N FERN CT
W MENOMONEE ST

W EUGENIE ST
W WILLOW ST
W ST PAUL AVE
CRILLY
COURT

N ORLEANS ST

N WELLS ST

Zanies

Second
City

N LASALLE ST

W GERMANIA
PLACE

W NORTH AVE

N CLARK ST

Moody
Church

Couch
Mausoleum

Lincoln
Memorial

Chicago
Historical Society

International Museum
of Surgical Science

N LASALLE ST

E NORTH AVE

N LAKE SHORE DR

Bath House

N DARTON ST

N EDWARD

N BURLING ST

N PEARL

F
Uz
Park

W DICKENS AVE

N ARMITAGE AVE

W WILLOW ST

N HOWE ST

N LARRABEE ST

2500N

N WISCONSIN ST

N CLEVELAND AVE

N HUDSON AVE

N SEDGWICK ST

N ORLEANS ST

N LINCOLN PARK W

N CLARK ST

See
page 308

G

N LINCOLN AVE

N HUDS
AVE

Farm in
the Park

Viking Ship

N STOCKTON DR

N RIDGE DR

South
Pond

Park

N RIDGE DR
N CANNON DR
N RIDGE DR

H

Lincoln

Lagoon

J

K

L a k e

M i c h i g a n

N ASHLAND AVE

N BOSWORTH AVE
N MONTANA ST
W ALTGELD ST
Wrightwood Park
N BOSWORTH AVE

N GREENVIEW AVE

N JANSSEN AVE
W LILL AVE
W DRUMMOND PL
N JANSSEN AVE
W DIVERSEY PKWY
W WOLFRAM ST

N SOUTHPORT AVE

N WAYNE AVE
N WAYNE AVE

N LAKEWOOD AVE
N LAKEWOOD AVE

N SURREY CT
N MAGNOLIA AVE
W DRAPER ST
W LILL AVE
N MAGNOLIA AVE

W FULLERTON AVE
N RACINE AVE
W WRIGHTWOOD PL
W SCHUBERT AVE
W DIVERSEY SCHOOL CT
W DIVERSEY PKWY
W WOLFRAM ST

N CLIFTON AVE
W MONTANA ST
W DRUMMOND PL
N LINCOLN AVE

N SEMINARY AVE
N POE ST
N KENMORE AVE
N KENMORE AVE
W LILL AVE
N KENMORE AVE CT

N MAUD AVE
Armitage
N SHEFFIELD AVE
Fullerton
N WILTON AVE
W SCHUBERT AVE
Diversey

N BISSELL ST
W WISCONSIN ST
N FREMONT ST
W WEBSTER AVE
W BELDEN AVE
LINCOLN PARK
Lilly's
Kingston Mines
N DAYTON ST
W MILDRED AVE

N DAYTON ST
Biograph Theatre
N HALSTED ST

N EDWARD CT
N BURLING ST
N BURLING ST
N ORCHARD ST
N ORCHARD ST
W SCHUBERT AVE
2800N

See page 307
N ARMITAGE AVE
N PEARL CT
Oz Park
Victory Gardens Theatre
W KEMPER PL
W ARLINGTON PL
W DRUMMOND PL

N HOWE ST
N GENEVA TER
W LEHMANN CT
N HAMPDEN CT
N CAMBRIDGE AVE

W MOHAWK ST
W WISCONSIN ST
N LINCOLN AVE
2000N
N DICKENS AVE
N CAMBRIDGE AVE
2400N
W DEMING PL
W SAINT JAMES PL
W WRIGHTWOOD AVE
W GRANT PL

N HUDSON AVE
N HUDSON AVE
W DEMING PL
W ROSLYN PL
N PINE GROVE AVE

N SEDGWICK ST
W FULLERTON PKWY
W LAKEVIEW AVE
W ARLINGTON PL

N ORLEANS ST
Cultural Arts Center
N COMMONWEALTH AVE
North Pond

Academy of Sciences
Viking Ship
N LINCOLN PARK W
N LAKE SHORE DR
W DIVERSEY PKWY

Farm in the Park
N RIDGE DR
Park
N STOCKTON DR
Lincoln Park Conservatory
Peggy Notebaert Museum
Diversey Harbor
W DIVERSEY PKY

South Pond
Lincoln
Lincoln Park Zoological Grdn
N RIDGE DR

N RIDGE DR

© Copyright Time Out Group 2002

0 400 metres
0 0.3 mile

3 2 1

1600W N ASHLAND AVE

D

W OAKDALE AVE
W NELSON ST
W BARRY AVE

W BELMONT AVE
W MELROSE ST
W HENDERSON ST
W ROSCOE ST
W CORNELIA AVE

N BOSWORTH AVE
N GREENVIEW AVE
N JANSSEN AVE
N SOUTHPORT AVE

Sheil Park

Music Box Theatre
N JANSSEN AVE

Schubas Tavern
Southport Lanes
N WAYNE AVE
W GRACE ST

Athenaeum Theatre

W NELSON ST
W FLETCHER ST
Southport
1200W

N LAKEWOOD AVE
N MAGNOLIA AVE

Bailiwick Repertory/ Theatre Building

N RACINE AVE

W PATTERSON AVE
W WAVELAND AVE
N CLIFTON AVE

Metro
Annoyance Theatre
N CLARK ST

E

Elbo Room
W GEORGE ST
W WELLINGTON AVE

N CLIFTON AVE
N SEMINARY AVE
N KENMORE AVE

W ADDISON ST
W EDDY ST

Wild Hare

Wrigley Field
N SEMINARY AVE
N ALTA VISTA TER

Pops for Champagne
Wellington
W OAKDALE AVE

W BELMONT AVE
Vic Theatre
Berlin
N SHEFFIELD AVE

WRIGLEYVILLE

Improv Olympic

N KENMORE AVE

Belmont
N WILTON AVE
N WILTON AVE
W NEWPORT AVE
W CORNELIA AVE

Addison
3600N
N WILTON AVE

N MILDRED AVE
W NELSON ST
W FLETCHER ST

Briar Street Theatre
Spin
W DAYTON ST
W ALDINE AVE
W BUCKINGHAM PL

N FREMONT ST
N RETA AVE
W BRADLEY PL

Gill Park
Strawdog Theatre

F

Ivanhoe Theatre
N CLARK ST
N BURLING ST
W OAKDALE AVE
W SURF ST

W BARRY AVE
W CALIFORNIA TER
N ORCHARD ST
N WATERLOO CT
3200N

Comedy Sportz
W ELAINE PL

800W
N HALSTED ST

N BROADWAY ST
W BROMPTON AVE
W PATTERSON AVE
W ADDISON ST
W BROMPTON AVE
N PINE GROVE AVE
N LAKE SHORE DR

W SURF ST
N PINE GROVE AVE
W BARRY AVE
W BRIAR PL
N PINE GROVE AVE
N HUDSON AVE
N CAMBRIDGE AVE
W MELROSE AVE
W ALDINE AVE
W ROSCOE ST
W HAWTHORNE PL
W STRATFORD PL
W BROMPTON AVE

47

N SHERIDAN RD
N COMMONWEALTH AVE
N LAKE SHORE DR

G

Belmont Harbor

Lake Michigan

Lincoln Park & Lake View

H

Wicker Park & Bucktown

A   **B**   **C**

N ROCKWELL ST
N MAPLEWOOD AVE
N CAMPBELL AVE
N ARTESIAN AVE
N MONTANA ST
N AVONDALE AVE
N LEAVITT ST
N CLYBOURN AVE

W MONTANA ST

5

W FULLERTON AVE

W MEDILL AVE

W BELDEN AVE

N WESTERN AVE

Holstein Park

W LYNDALE ST

W LYNDALE ST

W PALMER ST

N OAKLEY DR
N OAKLEY AVE
N BELL AVE

N SEELEY AVE
N LISTER AVE
N ELSTON AVE
N WOOD ST

W PALMER ST

W SHAKESPEARE AVE

W CHARLESTON ST

N MILWAUKEE AVE

W WEBSTER AVE

W WEBSTER AVE

W SHAKESPEARE AVE

N AVONDALE AVE

W CHARLESTON ST

BUCKTOWN

N BINGHAM ST
N STAVE ST

W MCLEAN AVE

W DICKENS AVE

W MCLEAN AVE

N DAMEN AVE

W DICKENS AVE

N AVONDALE AVE

N HOLLY AVE

6

Western

W ARMITAGE AVE

W HOMER ST

N WILMOT AVE

N OAKLEY AVE

2000N

W HOMER ST

W CORTLAND ST

N WINCHESTER AVE
N WOLCOTT AVE
N HONORE ST
N WOOD ST
N HERMITAGE AVE

W MOFFAT ST

W MOFFAT ST

W CHURCHILL ST

W MOFFAT ST

N WINNEBAGO AVE

W BLOOMINGDALE AVE

N MARSHFIELD AVE
N PAULINA ST

W BLOOMINGDALE AVE

W BLOOMINGDALE AVE

2400W

W ST PAUL AVE

N WILMOT AVE

W WILLOW ST

2000W

W ST PAUL AVE

W WABANSIA AVE

W WABANSIA AVE

N CLAREMONT AVE

W WABANSIA AVE

7

N MAPLEWOOD AVE
N ARTESIAN AVE

Pedro Albizu
Campos Museum

W CATON ST

W CONCORD PL

W CONCORD PL

W NORTH AVE

1600N

Damen

Padrewski House

The Note

W NORTH AVE

N OAKLEY AVE

W PIERCE AVE

Gingerbread
House

Double
Door

N ELK GROVE AVE

W PIERCE AVE

W LE MOYNE ST

N BELL AVE

W LE MOYNE ST

W LE MOYNE ST

W JULIAN ST

N ROCKWELL ST

**WICKER
PARK**

W SCHILLER ST

N WICKER PARK AVE

W BEACH AVE

N DEAN ST

W HIRSCH ST

*Wicker
Park*

N CAMPBELL AVE

W EVERGREEN AVE

N MILWAUKEE AVE

8

W POTOMAC AVE

N WESTERN AVE

W CRYSTAL ST

W ELLEN ST

N MOORMAN ST

N HONORE CT
N MARION CT

W DIVISION ST

1200N

N DAMEN AVE

W DIVISION ST

N PAULINA ST
N MARSHFIELD AVE

W HADDON AVE

W HADDON AVE

N HERMITAGE AVE
N HONORE ST
N WOLCOTT AVE
N WOOD ST

W THOMAS ST

Holy Trinity
Orthodox Cathedral

N OAKLEY BLVD

W CORTEZ ST

Empty Bottle

St Volodymyr
Ukranian Orthodox
Cathedral

N WINCHESTER AVE

W CORTEZ ST

9   **310** Time Out Chicago Guide

N LEAVITT ST
N HOYNE AVE

W AUGUSTA BLVD

W WALTON ST

0   0.3 mile

0   400 metres

© Copyright Time Out Group 2002

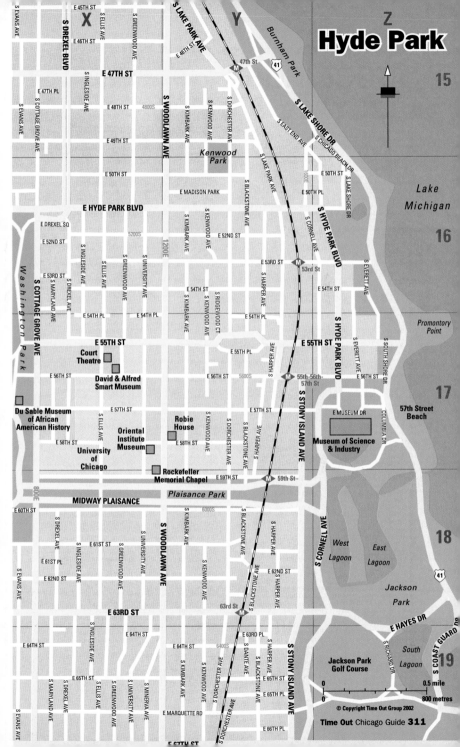

Street Index

Downtown Travel

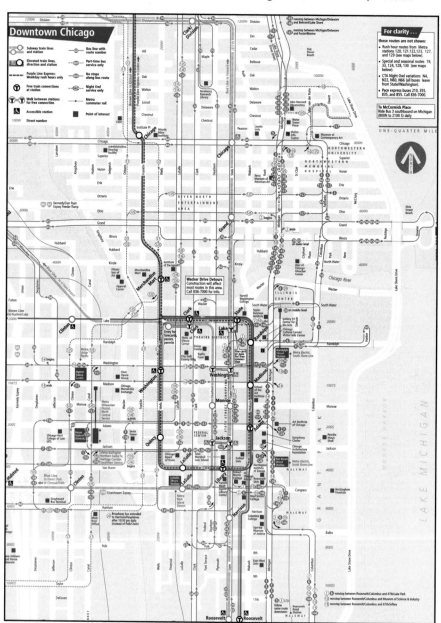

CTA Rail System

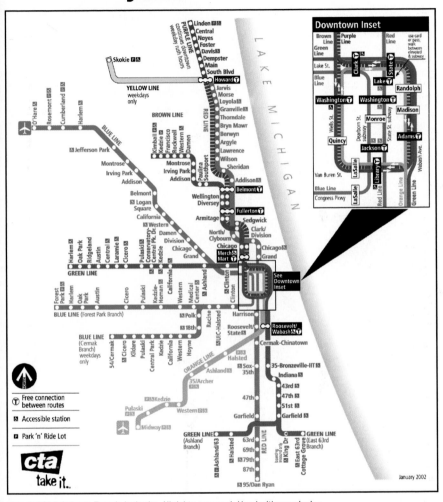

Trips Out of Town

© Copyright Time Out Group 2002

0 ——— 150 km
0 ——— 100 miles

WISCONSIN

Stevens Point

Green Bay

Appleton

Oshkosh

Wisconsin Dells

Baraboo

Madison

Mount Horeb

Waukesha

Milwaukee

New Glarus

Galena

Rockford

Arlington Heights

Aurora

Moline

ILLINOIS

Peoria

Bloomington

Champaign

Decatur

Springfield

Mackinac Island
Lake Huron

Mackinaw City

Beaver Island

Washington Island

Traverse City

Lake Michigan

Green Bay

Cadillac

MICHIGAN

Grand Rapids

Lansing

Holland

South Haven

Kalamazoo

CHICAGO
See Overview Map

Gary

Hobart

South Bend

Fort Wayne

INDIANA

Kokomo

Anderson

Crawfordsville

Rockville

Indianapolis

Terre Haute

Columbus

Time Out Chicago Please let us know what you think

About this guide...

1. How useful did you find the following sections?

	Very	Fairly	Not very
In Context	☐	☐	☐
Accommodation	☐	☐	☐
Sightseeing	☐	☐	☐
Eat, Drink, Shop	☐	☐	☐
Arts & Entertainment	☐	☐	☐
Trips Out of Town	☐	☐	☐
Directory	☐	☐	☐
Maps	☐	☐	☐

2. Did you travel to Chicago...?

Alone ☐ With children ☐
As part of a group ☐ On vacation ☐
On business ☐ To study ☐
With a partner ☐ I live here ☐

3. How long was your trip to Chicago?
(write in) _____ days

4. Where did you book your trip?

Time Out Classifieds ☐
On the Internet ☐
With a travel agent ☐
Other (write in) ☐
_____

5. Where did you first hear about this guide?

Advertising in *Time Out* magazine ☐
On the Internet ☐
From a travel agent ☐
Other (write in) ☐

6. Is there anything you'd like us to cover in greater depth?

_____
_____

7. Are there any places that should/ should not* be included in the guide?
(*delete as necessary)

_____
_____
_____

8. How many other people have used this guide?

none ☐ 1 ☐ 2 ☐ 3 ☐ 4 ☐ 5+ ☐

9. What city or country would you like to visit next? (write in)

_____

About other Time Out publications...

10. Have you ever bought/used *Time Out* magazine?

Yes ☐ No ☐

11. Have you ever bought/used any other Time Out City Guides?

Yes ☐ No ☐

If yes, which ones?
_____
_____

12. Have you ever bought/used other Time Out publications?

Yes ☐ No ☐

If yes, which ones?
_____
_____

About you...

13. Title (Mr, Ms etc): _____

First name: _____
Surname: _____
Address: _____

P/code: _____

Email: _____
Nationality: _____

14. Date of birth: ☐☐/☐☐/☐☐

15. Sex: male ☐ female ☐

16. Are you...?
Single ☐
Married/Living with partner ☐

17. What is your occupation?

_____

18. At the moment do you earn...?

under £15,000 ☐
over £15,000 and up to £19,999 ☐
over £20,000 and up to £24,999 ☐
over £25,000 and up to £39,999 ☐
over £40,000 and up to £49,999 ☐
over £50,000 ☐

☐ Please tick here if you do not wish to receive information about other Time Out products.
☐ Please tick here if you do not wish to receive mailings from third parties.

Time Out Guides

FREEPOST 20 (WC3187)
LONDON
W1E 0DQ